A DESCRIPTIVE CATALOG OF W.B. YEATS'S LIBRARY

GARLAND REFERENCE LIBRARY
OF THE HUMANITIES
(Vol. 470)

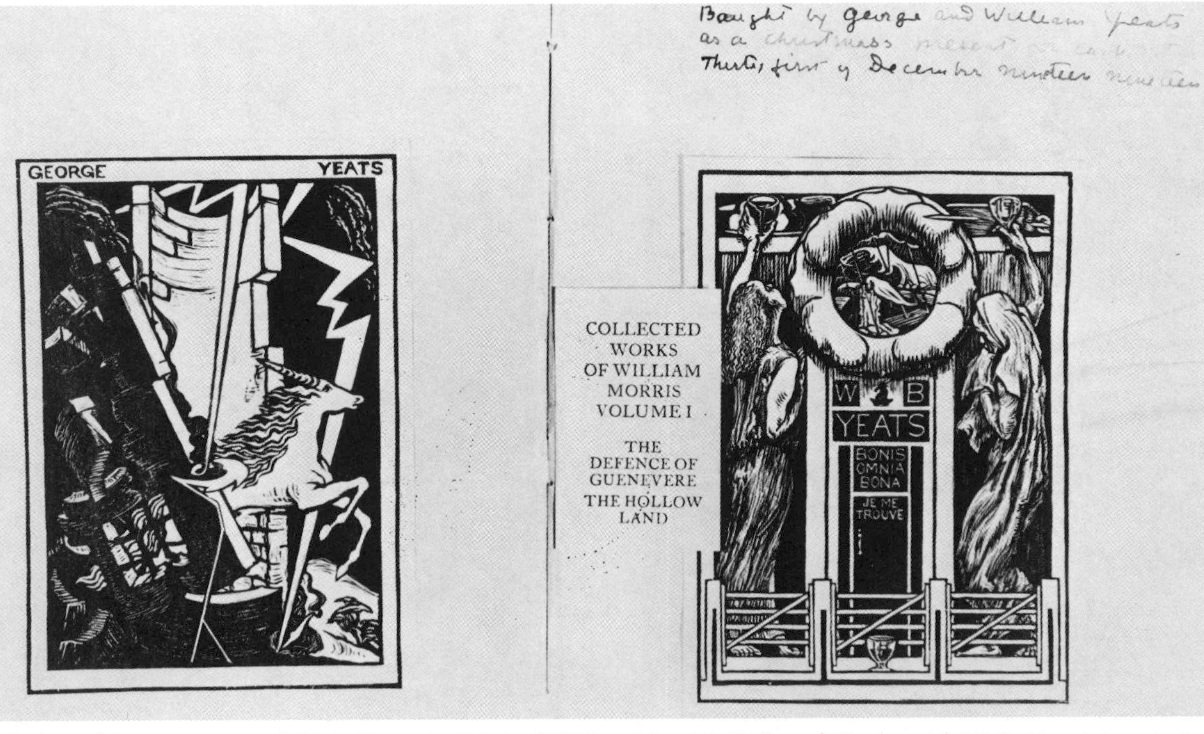

Bookplate of George Yeats and W. B. Yeats, in Vol. 1 of William Morris's *Collected Works*, with W. B. Yeats's inscription indicating that this was a mutual Christmas present.

A DESCRIPTIVE CATALOG OF W.B. YEATS'S LIBRARY

Edward O'Shea

GARLAND PUBLISHING, INC. • NEW YORK & LONDON
1985

Library of Congress Cataloging in Publication Data

O'Shea, Edward
A descriptive catalog of W. B. Yeats's library.

(Garland reference library of the humanities ; v. 470)
Includes index.
1. Yeats, W. B. (William Butler), 1865–1939—Library—Catalogs. 2. Yeats, W. B. (William Butler), 1865–1939—Books and reading. I. Title. II. Series.
Z997.Y39074 1985 017'.2'09418'3 83-49314
ISBN 0-8240-8997-9

Printed on acid-free, 250-year-life paper
Manufactured in the United States of America

FOR ANNE YEATS

CONTENTS

PREFACE

This catalog provides at a minimum a basic bibliographical entry for each item in W.B. Yeats's private library as it is maintained by his daughter Anne Yeats in Dalkey, Ireland. Excluded are items that were not available to Yeats during his lifetime because they were published or added to the library after January 1939, but intentionally included are items belonging to other family members that might have been accessible to him, for, from the evidence of inscriptions and annotations, books were circulated freely in the Yeats family and among his friends. An asterisk (*) before an item number indicates that it appears in an anonymously compiled catalog of Yeats's books done sometime in the early 1920s. For reasons of space, that entire listing (which recorded only basic bibliographical information) is not included here, but there are some 500 items in that catalog which are not found in the library today, and their location is unknown.

Ephemeral items like newspaper reviews and theater programs which are often pasted or tucked into books in the library are given a separate catalog number (when they can be identified) and are cross-referenced with the associated item. My general policy has been to give multi-volume works separate catalog numbers when the individual volumes have different publication dates or when, as in a few cases, heavy annotation makes a separate treatment desirable. Separate editions are given a basic item number with an upper case designation, as 402A. I have followed the practice used in Allan Wade's bibliography of assigning separate numbers for the English and American editions. Additional copies of an item or subsequent printings are given a lower case designation, as 755a.

Catalog entries are by author, when available, or by title when not, with a few necessary exceptions: because of the nature of the material, there are subject entries for maps, prints (under "Irish Scenes"), and government documents (as "Ireland," "Irish Free

State," "Great Britain"). Discrete serial articles or reviews are entered by author; lacking this information, they are found under the serial title, such as *Irish Times*. Separate and bound complete numbers of newspapers and journals are entered under the serial title. While W.B. Yeats apparently organized his library by *subject* (see Introduction), I have decided that the present arrangement would be more helpful to users of this catalog. In any case, a comprehensive subject index is included as well as a separate index of autographs. In the entry format for each item, the limitation number, when there is one, follows the collation (as 6/50), then owner's bookplate and signature in abbreviated form as, for example, Bp: WBY. Sig.: WBY.

Following the preliminary entry, I have recorded, at a minimum, the extent to which Yeats used an item. In most cases, I have transcribed verbatim Yeats's annotations keyed into the relevant sections or passages. The entries following a colon (:) are judged to be W.B. Yeats's annotations unless otherwise noted or unless the context clearly suggests otherwise. Annotations by other hands are noted but are generally *not* included. Variations in Yeats's hand over the years or multiple annotators sometimes make identification very difficult. When it has seemed desirable for comprehension, I have silently emended annotations for punctuation and spelling, but transcriptions of poem drafts, etc., are presented diplomatically. In a small number of cases, as with the facsimile of *The Marriage of Heaven and Hell* or the astrological ephemera where annotations are extremely complex or heavy, I have been content with a description of their nature and extent. In reporting the status of Yeats's revisions in his own work, my references to "*Variorum*," whether to poems or plays, can be determined from the context. References to "*Variorum* (of the Poems) main text" are to the two-volume "definitive edition" of 1949.

With the exceptions noted, the reader will find that the transcriptions of annotations are, in almost all cases, inclusive rather than selective. This entails including minutiae that some may judge trivial or unimportant. But from my own experience, and from the inquiries I receive about the library, one person's irrelevance may be the object of another's Grail quest, and I leave it to the readers of this catalog to sift for the useful. I have been content with recording and presenting Yeats's annotations, not generally with interpreting their meaning or importance (though I have attempted some of this elsewhere, and with Yeats's revisions of his own work I have tried at least to determine the import of these revisions for the transmission of his texts). Similarly, I have not tried to record systematically the uses that have already been made of the library, i.e., books and articles based on materials in the library, but I do occasionally report such items when they make my own job of presenting books in the library easier.

State University of New York–Oswego E.O'S.
19 September 1984

ACKNOWLEDGMENTS

My foremost debt for the present catalog is to Glenn O'Malley, late of Arizona State University, Tempe, who began this project in the summer of 1971. Within the space of some three difficult months, he compiled, heroically, a basic file of entries for all items in the library, excluding Yeats's own editions (those which appear under "W.B. Yeats" in this catalog). His entries included a bibliographical citation and, in many cases, some indication of use, and my own work has been completed on his solid foundation. Unfortunately, ill health, which eventually ended in his death, prevented Glenn O'Malley from finishing the catalog, and it was at this point that the project passed on to me on the recommendation of Donald Torchiana of Northwestern University, a man and teacher to whom I owe my own enthusiasm for, and slighter knowledge of, the work of W.B. Yeats. My contribution has been to add to the basic catalog entries transcriptions of Yeats's annotations and to make entries for Yeats's copies of his own work, which include presentations of his own revisions and some indication of where items fit into the history of Yeats's publishing.

This catalog has depended from its inception on the constant support and encouragement of Anne Yeats. She not only provided, ungrudgingly, access to her father's library for three extended visits, but when energy flagged she served up innumerable cups of tea and entertaining anecdotes about her poet-father and her own experiences at Thoor Ballylee—stories that have somehow still eluded Yeats's biographers.

Others have made indispensable contributions as well. Mary Jo O'Shea transcribed annotations, typed file cards, photographed materials in the library, read preliminaries, and in one instance, with a cadre of neighborhood children, filed alphabetically hundreds of xeroxed slips to make a trans-Atlantic trip lighter. Her encouragement and patience for a project that always seemed to need a few more months were very welcome. Christina Hunt Mahony took time out from her own research in Dublin to help transcribe and verify annotations and to provide information from her own substantial knowledge of Irish letters and culture, and the catalog is much stronger for her help.

My thanks also to Linda Mjolsnes for tracking down material at the Lily Library, Indiana University, to Tsuyoshi Hasegawa for providing transliterations of Japanese items, to Donald Masterson for his expertise on William Blake and for reading preliminaries, and to Lewis Turco for lending his Collier edition of Spenser. David Erdman and Richard Ellmann helped with crucial identifications and Narayan Hegde of SUNY–Stonybrook with some timely photocopies. William H. O'Donnell relayed information about Cuala Press books in the possession of Michael Yeats. Roger Nyle Parisious provided information about Yeats's occult and theosophical interests. The staffs of the following institutions assisted with information: Penfield Library, SUNY–Oswego; Olin Library, Cornell; Syracuse University Library; Lily Library, Indiana University; University of Chicago Library; Newberry Library, Chicago; and The New York Public Library.

I am also grateful to the National Endowment for the Humanities and to the Research Foundation of the State University of New York for providing summer grants that made possible the completion of this catalog.

Previously unpublished annotations, drafts, and inscriptions by W.B. Yeats and members of the Yeats family which appear in the catalog are used with the permission of Michael Yeats and Anne Yeats and Macmillan London Ltd.

For previously unpublished letters to W.B. Yeats, I would like to acknowledge permission from the following: the Society of Authors as the literary representative of the Estate of John Masefield; Miss Riette Sturge Moore and D.C. Sturge Moore for T. Sturge Moore; Maxwell Sturm for F.P. Sturm; P.C. Gupta for Rabindranath Tagore; the Estates of A.H. Bullen and Augustus John.

INTRODUCTION

W.B. Yeats's surviving library in Dalkey contains something more than 2500 items, depending on how one regards multiple copies and ephemera. We know from an anonymously compiled catalog from the 1920s that there were at least another 500 items that in one way or another were dispersed from the library. But even a listing of what survives in the library documents in a very vivid way how much Yeats as one individual opened up his own mind and therefore English literature to multiple and even heterodox influences: to the oriental, the occult, theosophy, magic, myth, the antiquarian, anthropology, philosophy, archaeology, the visual arts, and the list could obviously be extended. Of course, we knew something of this from reading his poems, plays, letters, essays, and works such as *A Vision*, but the catalog will affirm what we already surmised from this other work: that Yeats was a most active reader and that his tastes were for the exotic, as well as for the primary texts of Western—and Eastern—civilization. Of course, he had his blind spots—fiction (though he knew Balzac and Flaubert), American literature (excepting Whitman, Thoreau, and Emerson), and contemporary poetry, especially after Eliot (though his editing of *The Oxford Book of Modern Verse* [1936] helped him remedy that oversight somewhat). His reading was then not simply that of a "man of letters." If anything, he slighted the strictly literary in favor of more general reading, and who would deny that his work is stronger for it? He was a poet, yet the reading that most engaged his mind, from the evidence of the library, was, with some obvious exceptions, more abstract and diagrammatic than sensuous and specific.

This descriptive catalog does not attempt to duplicate the unique organization of Yeats's library as Anne Yeats remembers it was arranged in his lifetime and as it has been reconstituted by Glenn O'Malley according to broad subject categories: poetry; drama;

religion and myth; history; classical literatures; fiction; philosophy; theosophy, magic, astrology; Irish materials; and art (including Blake). Each category has its own interest, but within these areas there are certain centers which provide some distinct focuses for the collection. Yeats acquired many of the volumes of English poetry while selecting materials for *The Oxford Book of Modern Verse*, and many of these books contain lists of initial choices which were inevitably refined as he moved towards his final selections. His typical practice was to tear out pages for a selection to have them turned into typescript, and many volumes show evidence of this kind of mutilation. A number of mostly younger poets sent Yeats their work while he was making *The Oxford Book of Modern Verse*, hoping for a place in that anthology, and some books contain obsequious inscriptions, but uncut pages make their own silent judgment. Even at that, we should be careful of making too much of *cut* pages, for Anne Yeats tells of her mother routinely cutting pages of new books of verse as they arrived. But weighed against over-blown inscriptions are testimonials from often established writers testifying to Yeats's impact on their work, authors such as Ezra Pound (item 1629), John Masefield (item 1257) and Sean O'Casey (item 1472). These project more conviction. Yeats's library could be a dead letter office for the hopes of aspiring writers and for other expectations as well. Many books on loan or sent in the hope of an inscription never found their way out of the library again. An otherwise unmarked copy of Yeats's *The Winding Stair* (item 2448b) contains this note by the poet:

> Never send a book to an author to be autographed (1) because he has (no) sealing wax (2) because he has no string (3) because he does not know how to tie up a parcel (4) because you will probably not get the book back. Thomas Hardy once showed me a corner cupboard full of such books. He gave them to his friends on their birthdays.

Yeats's library does not contain cupboards of such books, but there are more than a few.

Another of Yeats's editing projects that provides a focus for the books in the library is the 1893 *The Works of William Blake*, a collaboration with Edwin Ellis. The library contains many editions of Blake, including a rare facsimile of *The Marriage of Heaven and Hell*, thoroughly annotated by Yeats and Ellis, as well as a number of theosophical works that have special associations with the Blake edition. In making their Blake, Yeats and Ellis worked from the known to the unknown. Both men were steeped in the esoteric tradition deriving from the Cabala, from Swedenborg, and from Boehme, and they used this knowledge to elucidate unknown corners of Blake's work, especially the prophetic works. While later Blake critics often judged this application wrongheaded, it allowed Yeats and Ellis to place Blake in a recognizable tradition, and it helped them past some of the obscurities and difficulties they encountered—well before generations of Blake scholars made his work less forbidding. The most important theosophical works in the library in this connection are the first volume of Swedenborg's *Arcana Coelestia* (item 2037), the first three volumes of his *Spiritual Diary* (items 2040, 2040A, 2040B) and Franz Hartmann's compendium of Boehme, *The Life and Doctrines of Jacob Boehme* (item 853), a book that both Yeats and Ellis annotated thoroughly.

Yeats gave much importance to what he saw as the direct connection between Blake's emphasis on the primary, creative qualities of the human imagination and its roots in Boehme's thought and in the tradition elaborated from him. Annotations in diverse works echo each other as he reminds himself in a note to John Muirhead's *Coleridge as Philosopher* (item 1398) that he had carefully copied out an 18th-century definition of the "sovereign imagination" in his own edition of Blake (item 209), a definition half-consciously recollected in a further annotation to Denis Saurat's *Blake and Modern Thought* (see item 1846 on page 238). Saurat's *Blake* elicited from Yeats some of the fullest annotations in the library, almost as if they were meant for eyes other than his own, very unlike the typical cramped, cryptic, often ungrammatical notes Yeats intended only for himself. Yeats is often impatient with Saurat, as in one memorable instance when Saurat glosses a passage in *Jerusalem* as an example of "a strange mystic imperialism" that Blake shares with other Anglo-Saxons. Yeats then glosses Saurat: "Oh Saurat! When England 'awakes' she becomes the whole world because 'the flood of time and space' has disappeared—you cannot localize or imperialize eternity."

Some of the richest annotations in Yeats's books are in philosophy and in those which can be broadly grouped under the term "gnostic": theosophy, spiritualism, the occult, magic, hermeticism, and related topics. One of the tasks of future research on Yeats will be to investigate further his reading in these areas, their interconnections, and the way he applied esoteric categories to academic philosophy as he does in his annotations to Croce's *Logic as the Science of the Pure Concept* (item 444). Most important is the impact of Yeats's esoteric and philosophical reading on his own work, most vividly documented in a draft like that of "A Needle's Eye" at the end of one of the volumes of Swedenborg's *Principia* (item 2039A). This draft gives us the rare chance to ground the beginnings of a poem in a specific act of reading, but lacking this kind of connection, we should still be able to determine in a more general way the relationship between Yeats's esoteric and philosophical reading and his creative work from examining the library.

Yeats read much of the esoteric materials and philosophy while revising *A Vision* (1925) to make the second edition of 1937. Yeats tells us in the Introduction to the later work that his informants had forbidden him to read philosophy while he was at work on the first version of his system. In fact, there is evidence that he likely was reading philosophy before that time (see, for example, item 445), but after the spring of 1925 the library books attest that he immersed himself in philosophical reading in an attempt to confirm the features of his system, especially in the writing of contemporary philosophers. He found the work of Bergson, Croce, Whitehead, and McTaggart especially congenial, and a book like McTaggart's *The Nature of Existence* (item 1202) documents a close interchange between Yeats's reading in philosophy and his work on *A Vision.* Yeats found Bertrand Russell less to his liking, and his comments in Russell's *An Outline of Philosophy* (item 1798) constitute a continuing refutation of what he labels Russell's "materialism." Against it he marshals the philosophy of Berkeley and that of his modern descendants of the Idealist school, writers like Croce and Gentile and other anti-mechanists like Bergson and Whitehead. Yeats's annotations to his philosophy books will show that at times he misunderstood or read tendentiously, always with one eye on his own system, but they also show that Yeats, to use Harold Bloom's term, was a "powerful misreader," and he could turn misunderstanding into a productive creative strategy.

The large "centers" in the library, Blake, theosophy, philosophy, compel our attention in an obvious way. But there are other vistas that suddenly open out on the unexpected. How, for example, did Sacheverell Sitwell's *Canons of Giant Art* (item 1936) supply the mental nudge that was the beginning of "Beautiful Lofty Things"? Or how much of *Purgatory* is derived from Tyrrell's *Science and Psychical Phenomena* (item 2178) or how much of *The Resurrection* from Cecily Phillimore's *Paul: The Christian* (item 1564)? And, on a smaller scale, is Henry More's 1662 collection of "philosophical" writings (item 1377) a more likely source of "Golden-thighed Pythagoras" in "Among School Children" than Thomas Taylor?

A draft of a poem at the end of a book that Yeats was reading is dramatic evidence of the importance of his reading for his own work. Another is lists of topics for writing done concurrently with his reading or for future writing. One example is the list of titles or topics at the end of Bergson's *Matter and Memory* (item 157) which seems to point to poems in the volume called *The Tower*: "Byzantium / Tower / The man's love / The woman's love / Convent School / Christ / Sermon on Mount." Lady Gregory's *Gods and Fighting Men* (item 795) and *Poets and Dreamers* (item 807) are especially rich in notes apparently for future prose writings, and they document Lady Gregory's pervasive presence in the library—either through the books she presented to Yeats or lent him from the Coole library, such as the Collier edition of Spenser (item 1978).

George Yeats, as the autograph index will show, owned a large number of books in the library. These books are of two kinds, personal volumes, some of which were acquired before her marriage, and her copies of her husband's work. Each category has its own special interest. The latter attests to George Yeats's considerable role as bibliographer and editor of W.B. Yeats's work. Richard Finneran's new edition of *The Poems of W.B. Yeats* (1983) and his *Editing Yeats's Poems* (1983) call into question George Yeats's role as editor, and while the debate over her role in establishing Yeats's text is likely to continue for some time, the catalog provides some of the documentation that can make possible an intelligent discussion of the issue.

But it is a consideration of George Yeats's books in the first category, her own reading, that may turn out ultimately to be more fruitful. We know much and we are learning more about George's role as facilitator of her husband's work, but what of her own intellectual life? We share with WBY some ignorance here. In a passage in the 1937 *A Vision*, Yeats writes, "When the automatic script began, neither I nor my wife knew, or knew that we knew, that any man had tried to explain history philosophically." In one of the copies in the library, George has written at this passage: "Untrue. GY had read Hegel's philosophy of history." Given George's crucial role in the formation of *A Vision*, we need to know more about what she read to determine precisely how much of Yeats's system was in fact her own. Some large patterns in George Yeats's reading are obvious from even a superficial examination of the library: a wide interest in occult subjects, especially astrology which pre-dates her association with WBY; a considerable knowledge of Italian literature and culture, especially Dante; an active interest in contemporary poetry and drama—both English and Irish—that may have surpassed her husband's.

George Yeats, in her role as bibliographer, has entered long lists of dates, places, and circumstances of composition in a number of Yeats's own books (see especially items 2315a, 2323, and 2381). I have included these lists even though many entries duplicate information provided in Richard Ellmann's *The Identity of Yeats* because there are some amplifications in George Yeats's lists and because it seemed useful to provide a primary source for these identifications. For the same reasons, I have included Lily Yeats's annotations to her copy of *Reveries Over Childhood and Youth* (item 2414). Though some of her identifications are familiar enough by now, many are not, and some provide interesting corrections or refinements of her brother's memory, as when WBY calls a woman who had taught him spelling "an old gentlewoman" and Lily objects: "Miss Armstrong had been bridesmaid to Mama so she can't have been old."

The copies of Yeats's own books in the library in many cases contain his revisions for subsequent editions. The status of these revisions obviously varies considerably. In some cases where neat holograph or typed revisions are pasted over the printed text (items 2325 and 2334 are examples), or where printers' notations are inserted (item 2401), the revised versions clearly constitute copy text. In others, where revisions seem more haphazard and cumulative (item 2338) or contain unique variants, we probably have a working text rather than, strictly speaking, copy text. Whatever their status, Yeats's revised editions provide essential information for tracing the evolution of his texts, especially his plays.

In the context of Yeats's revisions of his texts, the absence of Dun Emer and Cuala Press books from the library is a puzzle. Since these editions in many cases constituted the first printed versions of Yeats's works, we would expect the process of revision for subsequent editions to begin in them. But because they were limited editions and a source of his sisters' livelihood, Yeats may have spared these beautifully printed editions (though even the rare Kelmscott Chaucer in the library has some pencil stroking, presumably by WBY). In any case, Michael Yeats reports that a collection of Cuala Press books in his possession came from his aunts rather than his father, and while some Cuala books with inscriptions by W.B. Yeats have been sold, none were revision copies.

Considering the variety and richness of what remains in W.B. Yeats's library, we should probably be content, but there will always be interest in fugitive items, and I invite information about books that have left the library so that at some future date this listing may be made more complete.

ABBREVIATIONS

Persons

GHL	George Hyde-Lees
GY	George Yeats
JBY	John Butler Yeats
LY	Lily Yeats
WBY	W.B. Yeats

Works by W.B. Yeats

BIV	*A Book of Irish Verse* (1895; rev. 1900)
E&I	*Essays and Introductions* (1961)
FFT	*Fairy and Folk Tales of the Irish Peasantry* (1888)
IFT	*Irish Fairy Tales* (1892)
Letters	*The Letters of W.B. Yeats* (1954)
OBMV	*The Oxford Book of Modern Verse* (1936)
RIT	*Representative Irish Tales* (1891)
Var.	*The Variorum Edition of the Poems of W.B. Yeats* (1957)
Var.	*The Variorum Edition of the Plays of W.B. Yeats* (1966)

Terms from A Vision

BF	Body of Fate
CB	Celestial Body
CM	Creative Mind
PB	Passionate Body

Miscellaneous Terms

BMC	British Museum Catalogue of Printed Books
NUC	National Union Catalog
WADE	Allan Wade. *A Bibliography of the Writings of W.B. Yeats*. 3rd ed., revised and edited by Russell K. Alspach. London, 1968.
Bp	Bookplate
Sig.	Signature

Alphabetical List
by Author
of Items in W.B. Yeats's Library

1. A., OE. THE HAZEL WAND. London: Grant Richards, 1925. 46 pp. Poems.

2. THE ABBEY ROW NOT EDITED BY W.B. YEATS. Dublin: Maunsel, 1907. 12 pp.

A parody of the controversy over Synge's PLAYBOY.

3. [Abbey Theatre program], 23 February 1907. Lady Gregory's THE WHITE COCKADE and THE JACKDAW.

Inserted in 58.

3a-d. Four more copies inserted in 58a-d.

4. [Abbey Theatre program], 27 December 1925. Twenty-first birthday anniversary performance.

Cover: George Yeats. 1925.
Final p.: Frank J. Fay/ 27 Dec. 1925
Program included Yeats's THE HOUR GLASS.

4a-g. Seven more copies.

5. [Abbey Theatre program], 17 November 1930. First production of Yeats's THE WORDS UPON THE WINDOW PANE.

Folded in at end of 2407.

6. [Abbey Theatre program], 25 June 1931. Special performance in honor of the bi-centenary of the Royal Dublin Society.

6a-g. Seven more copies.

7. [Abbey Theatre program], 10 August 1938. First production of Yeats's PURGATORY.

8. [Abbey Theatre Dramatic Festival Souvenir], 6-20 August 1938. 36 pp.

Includes Lennox Robinson's "The Irish National Theatre" and F.R. Higgins's lecture "W.B. Yeats."

9. Abdul-Ali, Sijil. "An Interpretation of Alchemy in Relation to Modern Scientific Thought." Offprint from THE JOURNAL OF THE ALCHEMICAL SOCIETY 1 (March 1913): 34-48.

Pp. 42-3 uncut.

*10. Abercrombie, Lascelles. MARY AND THE BRAMBLE. Much Marcle, Herefordshire: Published by the Author, 1910. [12 pp.]

Crayon, paper cover: WBY from O. Elton

11. ———. THE POEMS OF LASCELLES ABERCROMBIE. London: Oxford Univ. Press, 1930. x,550 pp.

Pp. 7-10, 15-17, 275-80 excised to make Abercrombie's selection for OBMV. Poems taken are "Hope and Despair," "The Fear," "The Stream's Song" and "Mary and the "Bramble."

12. Abercrombie, Patrick, Sydney Kelly, and Arthur Kelly. DUBLIN OF THE FUTURE. London: Hodder and Stoughton, [1923]. xvi,58 pp.

Back cover, pencil: Miss Long/ 9 Ely Place/ Tel 4344 [probably WBY]

13. THE ACORN. An illustrated quarterly magazine devoted to literature and art. London: Caradoc Press, 1905. 152 pp. Bp: GY

Includes Yeats's "Do Not Love Too Long"

14. Acton, Lord [John Emerich Edward Dalberg]. THE CAMBRIDGE MODERN HISTORY. Planned by the late Lord Acton. Edited by A.W. Ward, etc. 13 vols. Cambridge: The Univ. Press, 1902-11.

Vol. 2, section on Reformation cut.
Vol. 4, section on The Thirty Years War cut.
Otherwise, many pp. uncut in all vols.

15. Adam, C.G.M. FRESH SIDELIGHTS ON ASTROLOGY. London: Modern Astrology Office, 1916. 100 pp. Bp: WBY

16. Adams, Henry. THE DEGRADATION OF THE DEMOCRATIC DOGMA. New York: Macmillan, 1920. xv,817 pp. Bp: WBY

17. ———. THE EDUCATION OF HENRY ADAMS. Boston: Houghton Mifflin, 1918. x,519 pp. Bp: WBY

Inserted, newspaper review of THE DECLINE OF THE WEST, see 675.

18. ———. THE EDUCATION OF HENRY ADAMS. London: Constable, 1928. x,517 pp.

19. ———. MONT-SAINT-MICHEL AND CHARTRES. Boston: Houghton Mifflin, 1913. xiv,401 pp. Bp: WBY

*20. Adams, Morley. IN THE FOOTSTEPS OF BORROW & FITZGERALD. London: Jarrold, [1914]. 262 pp. Bp: WBY

Some pp. uncut.

ADDISON, Joseph. See 1968.

AE, A.E., See Russell, George William.

21. Aeschylus. THE AGAMEMNON OF AESCHYLUS. Translated by Louis MacNeice. London: Faber and Faber. 1936. 71 pp.

Inside back cover, a draft of a poem, ink, WBY:

Yang & Yin

A bird sighs for the air
Thought for I know not where
For the womb seed sighs
But sink a like rest
On intellect [one word canceled] on nest
On the straining thighs?
[See VAR., 574.]

22. Aeschylus. THE HOUSE OF ATREUS, being the Agamemnon, Libation-bearers and Furies. Translated by E.D.A. Morshead. London: Macmillan, 1901. xxxiv,185 pp.

23. Agnelli, Guiseppe. FERRARA E POMPOSA. Con 137 illustrazioni e 1 tavola. Bergamo: Instituto Italiano d'Arti Grafiche, 1906. 124 pp.

Inserted, three blank postcards of Ferrara.

24. Agrippa von Nettesheim, Heinrich Cornelius. OPERA, in duos tomos concinne digesta.... Lugduni: Per Beringos Fratres, n.d. xxii,668 pp. [The imprint is fictitious; the Harvard College Library catalog lists Eberhard Zetner of Strasbourg publisher and the date 1620 or 1630; one volume only.]

Flyleaf: April 15, 1780 [covers and spine are missing]
Marginal notes, strokes, underscorings, symbols; some, in pencil, may be contemporary with Yeats but doubtfully his.
Pasted in between pp. 174 & 5 is an elaborate, carefully-executed diagram in watercolor on modern graph paper with the heading: The Thirty Two Parts of the Sepher Yetzivah.
Another watercolor between pp. 262 & 3 is headed: The Tree of Life. The outward and visible Sign of an inward and Spiritual grace.
Another insert between pp. 306 & 7 is headed: (1) The 22 Tarot Trumps (2) The 32 Paths of Wisdom [but the list gives only the first]

*25. Aksakoff, Alexandre. ANIMISME ET SPRITISME. Essai d'un examen critique des phénomènes mediumniques. Translated from the Russian edition by Berthold Sandow. 5th ed. Paris: Librairie des sciences psychiques, 1906. xxxii, 635 pp. Sig., paper cover: WBY

Marginal strokes: 395, 396, 404, 410, 412, 417, 474, 536, 537, 627.

26. Aksakoff, Serghei. A RUSSIAN GENTLEMAN. Translated from the Russian by J.D. Duff. Oxford: Oxford Univ. Press, 1934. x,283pp.

27. ———. A RUSSIAN SCHOOLBOY. Translated from the Russian by J.D. Duff. Oxford: Oxford Univ. Press, 1924. ix,288 pp.

28. Aldington, Richard. IMAGES, 1910-1915. London: The Poetry Bookshop, [1915]. 31 pp.

Inside frt. cover: To W.B. Yeats from/ R.A.

29. ———, trans. MEDALLIONS, from Anyte of Tegea, Meleager of Gadara, the Anacreontea, Latin Poets of the Renaissance. London: Chatto & Windus, 1930. 116 pp.

30. [Alfieri, Dino and Luigi Freddi]. EXHIBITION OF THE FASCIST REVOLUTION [MOSTRA DELLA RIVOLUZIONE FASCISTA]. First Decennial of the March on Rome. Rome: National Fascist Party, 1933. 258,[3] pp.

31. Aliotta, Prof. Antonio. THE IDEALISTIC REACTION AGAINST SCIENCE. Translated by Agnes McCaskill. London: Macmillan, 1914. xxii,483 pp.

*32. Allingham, Hugh. CAPTAIN CUELLAR'S ADVENTURES IN CONNACHT AND ULSTER, A.D. 1588. London: Elliot Stock, 1897. 72 pp.

*33. Allingham, William. EVIL MAY-DAY. London: Longmans, [1883]. 100 pp.

*34. ———. FLOWER PIECES. London: Longmans, Green, 1893. x,194 pp.

*35. ———. LIFE AND PHANTASY. London: Reeves and Turner, 1889. vii,161 pp.

Many pp. uncut.

*36. ———. THOUGHT AND WORD AND ASHBY MANOR, A PLAY. London: Reeves and Turner, 1890. viii,184 pp.

Uncut.

37. [Alt, Phyllis Innocent]. RAPALLO PAST AND PRESENT. With map and illustrations. 6th ed. Milan: Modernissima, 1926. xix,219 pp.

38. [Altdorfer, Albrecht]. ALBRECHT ALTDORFER. A book of 71 woodcuts. Introduction by T. Sturge Moore. London: At the Sign of the Unicorn, 1902. [10]pp., 30 plates.

39. Anderson, Maxwell. WINTERSET. Washington: Anderson House, 1935. xi,134 pp.

Flyleaf: With best wishes to Lennox Robinson. Kenneth Thorpe Rowe

40. ANNALS OF PSYCHICAL SCIENCE, THE. 2 (July-December 1905).

Bound volume; marks, brief notes, pp. 32n., 33, 39, 51, 194.
P. 32, note: psychic fluid melts in water. Hence a ghost cannot pass water.

41. ———. 3 (January-June 1906).

Bound volume.

42. ———. 4 (July-December 1906).

Bound volume.

43. ———. 5 (January-June 1907).

Bound volume; marginal strokes, pp. 156-210; brief summarizing notes, pp. 40, 43, 141, 184; e.g., p. 141, pars. 2 & 3: dream symbolic of a union of being.

44. ———. 6 (July-December 1907).

Title p.: Wrong title page - should come in middle of book [but title page is correct]

45. ———. 7 (January-December 1908).

Contains "A Master of Art: Blake the Visionary" by François Benoit, pp. 3-23, illus.
Marginal strokes, pp. 71, 79; marks, pp. 10, 13, 14.

46. ———. 8 (January-March 1909).

47. Apuleius. THE GOLDEN ASSE OF LUCIUS APULEIUS. Translated by William Adlington. 1566. Reprint. London: Simpkin, Marshall, Hamilton, Kent, [1925]. 234 pp.

ARABIAN NIGHTS. See 251, 676.

*48. Archer, William, gen. ed. EMINENT ACTORS. 3 vols. in 1. London: Kegan Paul, Trench, Trubner, 1890-1. Vol. 1: WILLIAM CHARLES MACREADY, by William Archer; Vol. 2: THOMAS BETTERTON, by Robert W. Lowe; Vol. 3: CHARLES MACKLIN, by Edward Abbott Parry.

49. Ardill, Rev. John Roche. ST. PATRICK. London: John Murray; Dublin: Hodges, Figgis, [1931]. ix,221 pp.

Flyleaf: WB Yeats/ 'cursed be he who steals this book'.

ARISTAENETUS. See 1648.

50. Aristophanes. LYSISTRATA. Translated by Jack Lindsay. Illustrations by Norman Lindsay. London: Fanfrolico Press, 1926. xii,51 pp.

Limitation p.: No. 397 [of 725]/ from Jack Lindsay/ to W.B. Yeats

*51. Armitage, Ella S[ophia]. THE EARLY NORMAN CASTLES OF THE BRITISH ISLES. With plans by D.H. Montgomerie. London: John Murray, 1912. xvi,408 pp. Bp: WBY.

52. Arnold, Matthew. LETTERS OF MATTHEW ARNOLD, 1848-1888. Edited by George W.E. Russell. 2 vols. London: Macmillan, 1895.

53. ———. ON TRANSLATING HOMER. London: Longman, Green, Longman, and Roberts, 1862. 69 pp.

Half title p.: J.H. Webb, Jan 27th '86/ from W.B (parting) [not WBY's]
Title p.: H.T. Tucker. 1897.
Text, pp. 28, 29, 32, a few marginal comments translating Latin, French, and German words in Arnold's quotations, unlikely WBY's.

54. ———. POETICAL WORKS. London: Macmillan, 1892. xii, 510 pp. Sig.: WBY

55. ———. THE STUDY OF CELTIC LITERATURE. London: Smith, Elder, 1891. xix,152 pp.

Marginal marks, underscoring, pp. 127, 130, 134, 135, 140-1.

56. ARROW, THE. Edited by W.B. Yeats. No. 1 (20 October 1906).

57. ———. No. 2 (24 November 1906).

57a. Another copy.

58. ———. No. 3 (23 February 1907).

Inserted, Abbey Theatre Program. See 3.

58a-f. Six other copies

Inserted in 4 copies, Abbey Theatre Program. See 3a-d.

59. ———. No. 5 (25 August 1909).

60. ARTS, THE (Brooklyn, N.Y.). Edited by Hamilton Easter Field. (May 1921).

Frt. cover: Lily Yeats June 11th 1921/ See pages 16 to 23. J.Q. [refers to a group of paintings John Quinn lent to an exhibition at the Metropolitan Museum. Includes reproductions of work by Redon, Derain, Picasso, Gauguin]

61. Ashton, Leigh. AN INTRODUCTION TO THE STUDY OF CHINESE SCULPTURE. London: Ernest Benn, 1924. xviii,113 pp., 63 plates. Bp: WBY

62. [ATHENAEUM]. Review of A BOOK OF IRISH VERSE (1895) ed. by WBY, ATHENAEUM, [6 Apr. 1895, pp. 434-5.]

Title is "Four Irish Books."
Inserted in 2441a.

*63. ATLAS OF ANCIENT AND CLASSICAL GEOGRAPHY. London: J.M. Dent, 1910. 27 maps, 93 pp.

Flyleaf: G[eorgie] H[yde] L[ees]

64. Auden, W[ystan] H[ugh]. LOOK, STRANGER! London: Faber & Faber, 1936. 68 pp.

Back of dust jacket: s d,d,r/ d t r / s t/ t [in pencil, canceled through; exactly as above].

65. ———. THE ORATORS. London: Faber & Faber, 1932. 116 pp.

P. 65, ink stroke and check mark at the beginning of the ballad "Beethameer, Beethameer, bully of Britain." Pp. 14-15 uncut.

66. ———. Poems. 2nd ed. London: Faber & Faber, 1933. 89 pp.

Pp. 51-4 are excised, also 67-70 for the poems "It's no use raising a shout," "This lunar beauty," "Before this loved one," "The silly fool, the silly fool," and "The strings' excitement."

67. ——— and Christopher Isherwood. THE DOG BENEATH THE SKIN. London: Faber & Faber, 1935. 180 pp. Sig.: WBY.

Pp. 10-14 torn out (the first Chorus)
P. 160, the first journalist's speech beginning "Standing outside" is marked by an "X"

*68. Augustine, Saint. THE CONFESSIONS. Edited by Arthur Symons. London: Walter Scott, [1898], xx,297 pp.

69. Austen, Jane. THE NOVELS OF JANE AUSTEN. 2nd ed. Edited by R.W. Chapman. Vol. 2: PRIDE AND PREJUDICE. Oxford: Clarendon Press, 1926. xiii,415 pp.

70. AUTHOR'S AND WRITER'S WHO'S WHO. Edited by Edward Martell. London: Shaw Publishing, 1934. 894 pp.

Includes entries for WBY and Jack Yeats

AVALON, Arthur. See 943.

71. Aventinus, Johannes. DES HOCHGELERTEN WEIT BERÜHMBTEN BEYERISCHEN GESCHICHTSCHREIBERS CHRONIK [Bavarian Chronicle]. Frankfurt am Mann; Ben Georg Raben, [etc.]. 1566. [46],532,[50] pp. Bp: GY

Title p.: Wilhelm Keeg. 1890.

72. Baedeker, Karl. ITALY FROM THE ALPS TO NAPLES. With 93 maps and plans. 3d ed. rev. Leipzig: Karl Baedeker, 1928. xl,488 pp.

Back flyleaf, pencil: Demeter's headdress

73. ———. SOUTHERN ITALY AND SICILY. With excursions to Sardinia, Malta, and Corfu. With 30 maps and 34 plans. 16th ed. rev. Leipzig: Karl Baedeker, 1912. lvi,508 pp., map.

Marks and underscoring, in section on Naples, pp. 51 (Cappella Reale), 54 (Santa Chiara), 55 (San Domenico Maggiore & Cappella del Crocifisso), 61 (The Cathedral), 159 (Pompey--the House of Marcus Obellius Firmus), 322 (Museo Nazionale, Palermo--colossal Atalantes or Telamones from the temple of Zeus at Girgenti), 324 (Etruscan sculptures), 325 (Sala Araba), 403 (Taormina--Hotel Naumachi is underlined).

74. Ball, F[rancis] Elrington. SWIFT'S VERSE. London: John Murray, 1929. xv,402 pp.

75. Ballantyne, R[obert] M[ichael]. MAN ON THE OCEAN. A Book about Boats and Ships. A Book for Boys. London: T. Nelson and Sons, 1874. vi,368 pp.

Bookplate of Jack B. Yeats painted in.
Flyleaf: From Grandmama/ to Willie/ Christmas 1876
Also, on a bp. pasted in: Jack B. Yeats's Book

76. Balzac, Honoré de. COMÉDIE HUMAINE. Temple ed. Edited by George Saintsbury. 40 vols. New York: Macmillan, 1901. Vol. 1: ABOUT CATHERINE DE' MEDICI, translated by Clara Bell. xii,350 pp. Bp:WBY

Inside frt. cover: 40. last volume/ of this edition/ There should be 4/ more volumes/ "Physiologie of Mariage"/ "Petites Miseres of Une/ vie conjugale/ "Contes Drolatiques" 2 vols. [throughout this series, WBY takes exception to the ordering of the stories and renumbers each volume to establish his own order. While there are eds. listed in the NUC that approximate Yeats's ordering, there is none that follows it exactly.]
Inside back cover: 4797

77. Vol. 2: AT THE SIGN OF THE CAT AND RACKET, translated by Clara Bell. xii,277 pp.

Inside frt. cover: 1 [WBY's renumbering of the vols.]

78. Vol. 3: THE ATHEIST'S MASS, translated by Clara Bell. xvi,292 pp. Bp: WBY

Inside frt. cover: [vol.] 8 [below this, under heading "Proper order" WBY lists nine stories from this and other vols.]: 1. Colonel Chabert 2. Honorine 3. The Commission in Lunacy 4. A Daughter of Eve 5. Savarus 6. A start in Life 7. Madame Firmiani 8. The Member [?] 9. The Atheist's Mass

79. Vol. 4: A BACHELOR'S ESTABLISHMENT, translated by Clara Bell. xii,324 pp. Bp: WBY

Inside frt. cover: [vol.] 13

80. Vol. 5: BEATRIX, translated by James Waring. xii,364 pp. Bp: WBY

Inside frt. cover: [vol.] 6

81. Vol. 6: THE CHOUANS, translated by Ellen Marriage. xv,370 pp. Bp: WBY

Inside frt. cover: [vol.] 31/ should contain/ second story "Une Passion dans le Désert"
P. 151 in "II. A Notion of Fouché's," marking, underscoring in a passage referring to the suppression of a young woman's real name
Back flyleaf, recto, a list of characters and identifications, under the heading: Other royalists not in the/ dispute [and] Other parties.
Back flyleaf, verso, a list of characters and identifications under the heading: Those who alone ask nothing.
Back cover, a list of characters and identifications under the heading: Royalists who/ make no demands for themselves.

82. Vol. 8 [7 missing]: THE COUNTRY PARSON, translated by Ellen Marriage. xii,299 pp. Bp: WBY

Inside frt. cover: [vol.] 33

83. Vol. 9: COUSIN BETTY, translated by James Waring. xii, 484 pp. Bp: WBY

Inside frt. cover: [vol.] 25

84. Vol. 10: COUSIN PONS, translated by Ellen Marriage. x,345 pp. Bp: WBY

Inside frt. cover: [vol.] 26

85. Vol. 11: A DAUGHTER OF EVE AND LETTERS OF TWO BRIDES, translated by R.S. Scott. xiv,398 pp. Bp: WBY

Inside frt. cover: [vol.] 7 - see note in vol. 8 [item 78]

86. Vol. 12: A DISTINGUISHED PROVINCIAL AT PARIS, translated by Ellen Marriage. xii,368 pp. Bp: WBY

Inside frt. cover: [vol.] 18./ This should have/ come after 'The Two Poets'/ in the middle of/ 'Lost Illusions' (vol 17) ["Lost Illusions" has two parts, "Two Poets," "Eve and David"]

87. Vol. 13: EUGENIE GRANDET, translated by Ellen Marriage. xii,229 pp. Bp: WBY

Inside frt. cover: [vol.] 11

88. Vol. 14: A FATHER'S CURSE, translated by James Waring. xii,342 pp. Bp: WBY

Inside frt. cover: [vol.] 39

89. Vol. 15: A GONDREVILLE MYSTERY, translated by Ellen Marriage. viii,260 pp. Bp:WBY

Inside frt. cover: [vol.] 28
Back cover, under the heading "Gondreville Mystery," a list of ten characters with identifications such as "mayor," "spies," "gendarme."

90. Vols. 17, 18 (16 is missing): A HARLOT'S PROGRESS, translated by James Waring. xvi,322; xii,280 pp. Bps: WBY

Inside frt. covers: [vol.] 19 [vol.] 20

91. Vol. 19: THE JEALOUSIES OF A COUNTRY TOWN, translated by Ellen Marriage. xii,330 pp. Bp: WBY

Inside frt. cover: [vol.] 15
Flyleaf: page 89 'revenge'/ is equated with revolt exactly/ as in Nietzsche
Title p.: W B Yeats/ 18 Woburn Buildings/ London
P. 89, passage lightly underlined dealing with the character Athanase as one of: those at the bottom of the wheel for whom revolt means revenge.
P. 281, "the Abbé Du Croisier" corrected to: the Abbe Couturier

92. Vol. 20: THE LILY OF THE VALLEY, translated by James Waring. xii,312 pp. Bp: WBY

Inside frt. cover: [vol.] 16

93. Vol. 21: LOST ILLUSIONS, translated by Ellen Marriage. xiv,385 pp. Bp: WBY

Inside frt. cover: [vol.] 17

94. Vol. 22: A MARRIAGE SETTLEMENT, translated by Clara Bell. xiv,419 pp. Bp: WBY

Inside frt. cover: [vol.] 4 "Gobseck" which is in vol. 3 should follow this. See note in vol 8 [item 78; vol. 3, Yeats's numbering, is missing]

95. Vol. 23: THE MEMBER FOR ARCIS, translated by Clara Bell. xii,515 pp. Bp: WBY

Inside frt. cover: [vol.] 30

96. Vol. 24: THE MIDDLE CLASSES, translated by Clara Bell. viii,537 pp. Bp: WBY

Inside frt. cover: [vol.] 27

97. Vol. 25: MODESTE MIGNON, translated by Clara Bell. xii,293 pp. Bp: WBY

Inside frt. cover: [vol.] 5

98. Vol. 26: OLD GORIOT, translated by Ellen Marriage. xii,308 pp. Bp: WBY

Inside frt. cover: [vol.] 9

99. Vol. 27: PARISIANS IN THE COUNTRY, translated by James Waring. xii,246 pp. Bp: WBY

Inside frt. cover: [vol.] 14

100. Vol. 28: THE PEASANTRY, translated by Ellen Marriage. xii,382 pp. Bp: WBY

Inside frt. cover: [vol.] 34 [below this, upside down]: S L Robinson/ 9:15 PM/ Oct. 4/ 86./ Cork
[Lennox Robinson's date and place of birth; for a horoscope?]

101. Vol. 29: PIERRETTE AND THE ABBE BIROTTEAU, translated by Clara Bell. x,238 pp. Bp: WBY

Inside frt. cover: [vol.] 12

102. Vol. 30: A PRINCESS'S SECRETS, translated by Ellen Marriage. xii,332 pp. Bp: WBY

103. Vol. 31: THE QUEST OF THE ABSOLUTE, translated by Ellen Marriage. x,226 pp. Bp: WBY

Inside frt. cover: [vol.] 36

104. Vol. 32: THE RISE AND FALL OF CESAR BIROTTEAU, translated by Ellen Marriage. xii,348 pp. Bp: WBY

Inside frt. cover: [vol.] 22

105. Vol. 33: THE SEAMY SIDE OF HISTORY, translated by Clara Bell. xiv,264 pp. Bp: WBY

Inside frt. cover: [vol.] 29

106. Vol. 34: SERAPHITA, translated by Clara Bell. xii, 316 pp. Bp: WBY

Inside frt. cover: [vol.] 37/ Order of stories in vol 37/ & 38 not Balzac's but all/ belong to "Etudes Philosophiques." [This vol. includes "Louis Lambert."]

107. Vol. 35: THE THIRTEEN, translated by Ellen Marriage. xiv,308 pp. Bp: WBY

Inside frt. cover: [vol.] 21/ This book should contain "La Fille aux Yeux d'or" but publisher or Saintsbury too prudish.

108. Vol. 36: THE UNCONSCIOUS MUMMERS, translated by Ellen Marriage. xvi, 248 pp. Bp: WBY

Inside frt. cover: [vol.] 23./ (The stories in 24 are in/ some cases put by Balzac/ before some of those in/ this volume)
Back cover, ink: turn to [but no page number given]

109. Vol. 37: THE UNKNOWN MASTERPIECE, translated by Ellen Marriage. xiv,362 pp. Bp: WBY

Inside frt. cover: [vol.] 38
Markings, pp. 6, 7, 8, 11, 12, 15

110. Vol. 38: URSULE MIROUËT, translated by Clara Bell. xiv,259 pp. Bp: WBY

Inside frt. cover: [vol.] 10

111. Vol. 39: THE WILD ASS'S SKIN, translated by Ellen Marriage. liv,288 pp. Bp: WBY

Inside frt. cover: [vol.] 35
P. li, at "Tomes 23-25": not in this edition
[also an illegible comment on SCENES DE LA VIE PARISIENNE]
P. lii, referring to UNE PASSION DANS LE DESERT: not in this edition [vol. 40, original numbering, is missing]

112. ———. DROLL STORIES, collected from the Abbeys of Touraine. Translated by [George R. Sims]. Illustrated by Gustave Dore. London: Camden Hotten, [1874]. xxxii,650 pp., illus.

113. Baring-Gould, S[abine]. THE LIFE OF NAPOLEON BONAPARTE. London: Methuen, 1897. xxxi,624 pp.

Frontispiece: John Butler Yeats/ Bedford Park/ London/ 1898/ [below this]: Now this belongs to J.B.Y.'s/ grandson Michael B. Yeats/ Feb. 3d 1939/ Dundrum/ Dublin
Pp. 5, 15, 255, sketches of cats
Markings, pp. 503 (Napoleon after abdication), 504.
P. 624: page 459 [at this page a par. stroked commenting on Napoleon's ungentlemanliness; both unlikely WBY's].
Back flyleaf, a sketch by JBY with caption: Mrs. Jack B. Yeats/ as Napoleon

114. Barker, Ernest. GREEK POLITICAL THEORY. London: Methuen, 1918. xiv,404 pp.

115. Barker, George. CALAMITERROR. London: Faber and Faber, 1937. 53 pp.

Inserted is a typed letter of presentation from the author dated 8 April 1937, Plush, Piddletrenthide, Dorset suggesting that his selection in Yeats's OBMV did not reflect his latest concerns (as does the present poem) for the social conditions of men.

116. ———. POEMS. London: Faber and Faber, 1935. 64 pp.

Checked in Contents the titles "The Wraith-Friend," "Venerable All Hills," "Fistral Bay," "The Leaping Laughers," "The Crystal," "Elegy Anticipating Death," "He Comes Among," and "The Poppy Trembling"; the texts of these poems have been excised, apparently to make

Yeats's selection for the OBMV. But only "The Wraith-Friend," "The Leaping Laughers," and "The Crystal" finally appear there.

117. ———. THIRTY PRELIMINARY POEMS. London: David Archer, The Parton Press, 1933. 37 pp.

118. Barnes, Major J[ames] S[trachey]. FASCISM. Home University Library. London: Thornton Butterworth, 1931. 251,[1] pp.

119. Barrett, Sir William F. ON THE THRESHOLD OF THE UNSEEN. An examination of the phenomena of spiritualism and of the evidence for survival after death. London: Kegan Paul, Trench, Trubner, 1917. xx,336 pp. Bp: WBY

120. Barrington, Sir Jonah. RECOLLECTIONS OF JONAH BARRINGTON. Dublin: The Talbot Press; London: T. Fisher Unwin, [1918]. xx,485 pp. Sig.: GY

*121. Bartholomew, J[ohn] G[eorge]. A LITERARY AND HISTORICAL ATLAS OF AMERICA. London: J.M. Dent, [1911]. xiv,231 pp., maps.

122. ———, ed. THE TIMES SURVEY ATLAS OF THE WORLD. London: The Times, 1922. 112 plates. [the general index is missing]

*123. Barton, Sir D[unbar] Plunket, Bart. LINKS BETWEEN IRELAND AND SHAKESPEARE. Dublin and London: Maunsel, 1919. xii,271 pp.

Flyleaf: To/ Mr. W.B. Yeats/ with the/ Author's compliments./ May, 1919
Inserted, a slip of paper at p. 219.

*124. Basilius Valentinus. [THE LAST WILL AND TESTAMENT OF BASIL VALENTINE] with his treatise concerning the microcosme ... man's body ... with two treatises, the first ... his manual operations.... The second discovereth things natural and supernatural.... London: Edward Brewster, 1670. [8],534 pp. Bp: WBY

The first title p. is missing.
The table of matter has been augmented in ink in a very old hand.

*125. ———. THE TRIUMPHAL CHARIOT OF ANTIMONY. With the commentary of Theodore Kerckringius. Being the Latin version published at Amsterdam in the year 1685 translated into English with a biographical preface [by Authur E. Waite]. London: James Elliott, 1893. xxxiii,204 pp.

126. Basnage, Mr. [Jacques]. THE HISTORY OF THE JEWS. Being a supplement and continuation of the history of Josephus.

Translated from the French by Thomas Taylor. London: J. Beaver and B. Lintot, 1708. x,[6],759,[1] pp.
Bp: WBY

127. Bastide, Charles. THE ANGLO-FRENCH ENTENTE IN THE SEVENTEENTH CENTURY. London: John Lane, 1914. xiii,238 pp.

*128. Bate, Percy H. THE ENGLISH PRE-RAPHAELITE PAINTERS. London: George Bell, 1899. xvi,126 pp., illus.

129. Baudelaire, Charles. LES FLEURS DU MAL. Bibliotheca Mundi. Leipzig: Insel-Verlag, n.d. 293,[1] pp. French text.

*130. ———. POEMS IN PROSE. Translated by Arthur Symons. London: Elkin Mathews, 1905. 61 pp.

Some pp. uncut.

131. Baudouin, Charles. SUGGESTION AND AUTOSUGGESTION. A psychological and pedagogical study based upon the investigations made by the new Nancy school. Translated from the French by Eden and Cedar Paul. London: George Allen & Unwin, 1922. 288 pp.

*132. Bayley, Harold. A NEW LIGHT ON THE RENAISSANCE, DISPLAYED IN CONTEMPORARY EMBLEMS. London: J.M. Dent, 1909. viii,270 pp., illus.

133. Beardsley, Aubrey. UNDER THE HILL AND OTHER ESSAYS IN PROSE AND VERSE. London and New York: John Lane, 1904. xi,[5],70 pp., plates.

Half title p.: To W.BY,/ from J[ohn] Q[uinn]

134. Beauclerk, Helen. THE GREEN LACQUER PAVILION. Adorned with nine cuts and a portrait of the author by Edmund Dulac. London: W. Collins Sons, 1926. 319 pp.
A novel.

Flyleaf: To/ W.B. Yeats/ from/ Helen Beauclerk/ &/ Edmund Dulac/ 1926

*135. Beaumont, Francis and John Fletcher. THE WORKS OF FRANCIS BEAUMONT AND JOHN FLETCHER. 10 vols. Cambridge: The Univ. Press, 1905-1912. Vol. 1: THE MAID'S TRAGEDY and other plays, edited by Arnold Glover.

*136. Vol. 2: THE ELDER BROTHER and other plays, edited by Arnold Glover and A.R. Waller.

Flyleaf: For Court/ see page 50
P. 50 (THE ELDER BROTHER, V, i., speech of Eustace), passage stroked and underlined in part, "you make the Court, that is the abstract of all Academies, to teach and practise noble undertakings...."

*137. Vol. 3: THE MAD LOVER and other plays, edited by A.R. Waller.

[no more vols. in library]

138. Beaumont, John. AN HISTORICAL, PHYSIOLOGICAL AND THEOLOGICAL TREATISE OF SPIRITS, APPARITIONS, WITCHCRAFTS, AND OTHER MAGICAL PRACTICES, with refutation of Dr. Bekker's World Bewitch'd.... London: Printed for D. Browne, J. Taylor, R. Smith, F. Coggan, T. Browne, 1705. [16],400 pp. Bp: WBY

Embossed and stamped several times at beginning of book: Fraser Institute Montreal

This vol. has been annotated and marked in possibly four hands, two in ink, two pencil; one in ink is likely WBY's, as pp. 82 & 91; one in pencil is possibly WBY's, as on pp. 288, 289, 334; one in ink is an older hand as on title p. and pp. 3 & 16.
Pencil markings, pp. 71, 104, 129, 136, 137, 155, 170, 189, 191, 216, 228, 231, 235, 245, 247, 248, 265, 267, 271, 283, 284, 290, 294, 296, 297, heavy on 313, 314, 315, 316, etc.
Back flyleaf, recto: 378 Syllogisms in German by a madman [illegible hand; may be WBY's]
Back flyleaf, verso: Cudworth/ Harris/ Hosley [below this in the same hand]: 352 pages of the Devil's Philosophy/ a good idea for a play? [Not WBY's].
Inside back cover: 306 [336?] The Order[?] of the Viper [same hand as on preceding flyleaf]
Also, a list of p. numbers, likely Ezra Pound's: 235, 247, 267, 283, 284, 290, 297 spirit, 320, 321, 342, 348, 376, 381, 385, 386, 389, 395.
Inserted, a sheet of paper folded quarto, watermark of the "Sussex Society" with headings and p. numbers; same hand as inside back cover, i.e. Ezra Pound's: Beaumont/ P. 9 Images/ P. 10 [?] [3 words illegible] existence/ 381/ 71, 81, 91, 104, 136, 189, 191, 205 - tenebrosus luminosus, 216, 221, (228 angels & images), 235 Images & Vibrations

[on facing page]: Amyraldus on Dreams (in French) 1678.

247, 265, 267, 271, 283, 284, 290, 294, 297, 320, 324, 326, 328, 336/ BEAUMONT

*139. Beckford, William. THE EPISODES OF VATHEK. Translated by Sir Frank T. Marzials. London: Stephen Swift, 1912. xxxi,207,127 pp. Bp: WBY

Title p., stamped: Presentation copy
Includes French text, separately paginated.

*140. ———. THE HISTORY OF THE CALIPH VATHEK. London: Ward, Lock, 1891. xxviii,549 pp. Bp: WBY

Almost wholly uncut.

141. Beedham, R. John. WOOD ENGRAVING. With introduction and appendix by Eric Gill. 4th ed. Hassocks, Sussex: Pepler & Sewell, 1935. vii,39 pp.

142. Beerbohm, Max. THE HAPPY HYPOCRITE. New York: John Lane, 1906. 53 pp.

Flyleaf: With best wishes from H.T.T. [H.T. Tucker?]

*143. ———. THE POET'S CORNER. London: William Heineman, 1904. [2] pp., plates.

Contains the cartoon "Mr. W.B. Yeats, presenting Mr. George Moore to the Queen of the Fairies."

*144. [Bellini, Giovanni]. GIOVANNI BELLINI. Introduction by Everard Meynell. London: George Newnes, [1906]. xx pp., plates.

145. Belloc, Hilaire. THE CHANTY OF THE NONA. No. 9 of The Ariel Poems. London: Faber & Gwyer, [1928]. 3 pp.

146. BELTAINE. [Edited by W.B. Yeats.] No. 1 (May 1899). Sig.: Lily Yeats

Pages uncut.

WADE 226

146a. Another copy.

Frt. cover: Lily Yeats from E C Yeats/ May 1899
Inserted at end, the program for the first performance of the Irish Literary Theatre, see 973.

146b. Another copy.

147. ———. No. 2 (February 1900).

Front cover: Lily Yeats/ Not to be lent/ by order./ Lily

147a. Another copy.

Pages uncut.

148. ———. Bound vol., 1899-1900.

Containing Nos. 1-3. With a title p. listing Yeats as editor and with a new title p. for No. 1. See WADE 226.

149. Benavente, Jacinto. PLAYS. Second Series. Translated by John Garrett Underhill. New York: Charles Scribners, 1923. xviii,309 pp.

150. Benda, Julien. THE GREAT BETRAYAL [La Trahison des Clercs]. Translated by Richard Aldington. London: George Routledge, 1928. x,188 pp.

151. Benson, E[dward] F[rederic]. CHARLOTTE BRONTE. London: Longmans, Green, 1932. xiii,313 pp. Sig.: WBY

152. Benson, Stella. KWAN-YIN. San Francisco: Edwin Grabhorn, 1922. [12] pp.

A verse play.

153. Berdyaev, Nicholas. THE BOURGEOIS MIND AND OTHER ESSAYS. Translated by Countess Bennigsen and Donald Attwater. London: Sheed & Ward, 1934. 130 pp.

154. ———. THE END OF OUR TIME, together with an essay on the general line of Soviet philosophy. Translated by Donald Atwater [sic]. London: Sheed & Ward, 1933. 258 pp.

*155. Berger, P[ierre]. WILLIAM BLAKE, POET AND MYSTIC. Translated by Daniel H. Conner. London: Chapman & Hall, 1914. xii,420 pp. Bp: WBY

Some pp. uncut.

156. Bergson, Henri. CREATIVE EVOLUTION. Translated by Arthur Mitchell. London: Macmillan, 1922. xvi, [1] 425 pp.

Marks, underscorings, brief notes through p. 157; thereafter none.

P. 20, corner turned down.

Pp. 29-36, fairly heavy marginal stroking and underlining in text ("Biology, Physics & Chemistry").

P. 41, next to "Finalism thus understood is only inverted mechanism": Yes, but there is prevision/ one has to add Spinoza

Pp. 41-47, marginal stroking, fairly heavy.

P. 52, next to passage "And we shall probably be aided in this by the fringe of vague intuition.... [to] It is there accordingly....": In life the disreputable [?] movements

P. 53-4, at passage "the higher we ascend the stream of life the more do diverse tendencies appear complementary to each other.": the 'complimentary dream' perhaps

P. 83, next to passage "If (as seems probable to us) a habit contracted by the individual were transmitted to its descendants.... [to] Let us say, then, how the problem seems to us to present itself....": Mcdougal experiments with rats in tank

P. 90, next to passage "We cannot help believing that these differences are the development of an impulsion which passes from germ to germ across the individuals. ...": exfoliation through germs

P. 94, next to passage "Life does not proceed by the association and addition of elements, but by dissociation and division.": Primary Impulse

P. 100, next to passage, "it may indeed be said that the whole of the effect is explained by the whole of the cause [emphasis added by WBY]": Kant
Next to passage, "The greater the effort of the hand, the farther it will go into the filings. But at whatever point it stops, instantaneously....": eye limits vision
Next to passage, "So with vision and its organ.": complexity is resistance [?]
P. 101, next to passage "It could not be partial, because, once again, the real process which gives rise to it has no parts,": in Kant because timeless
P. 152, next to passage "Where consciousness appears, it does not so much light up the instinct itself as the thwartings to which instinct is subject....": Mind & B.F./ also C.M.
P. 153, next to passage "Essentially, consciousness only emphasizes the starting-point of instinct....": C.M. & choice

157. ———. MATTER AND MEMORY. Translated by Nancy Margaret Paul and W. Scott Palmer. London: Allen & Unwin, 1919. xx,339 pp.

Flyleaf: The future is - perception without memory - the present unites it to memory. The future is perceptible, but we do not know that we perceive it.
The text of this book has been very heavily marked and annotated in pencil by WBY.
P. ix, next to a passage on Berkeley: B. denies that he does this. It is "in" mind but not in only [?] mind.
P. 1, next to passage "Yet there is one of them that is distinct": Image

affection
(hate) [?]

P. 14, at first 5 lines:
P. 29, lengthwise in margin at passage "suppose [to] by our freedom": Leibnitz would perhaps say this meaning "perception without memory" "dreamless sleep"
P. 39, lengthwise in margin at passage "such an image [to] parcel with representation": In "Vision" the senses limit perception. A cup dipped into a sea of light that we may drink.
P. 40, next to passage "That matter should be [to] because such perception would be of no use.": 'perceived here means linked to memory'
P. 69, next to passage "perception is indeed [to] does not take":

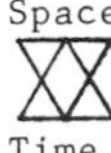

P. 72, midpage, next to phrase "pure perception": when I try to recall (say) Ballylee, I find that the less abstract the forms, all the more have they an hallucinatory element of form in colour – this hallucination must be Bergson's perception.

P. 73, bottom margin, four names? very illegible: Mathers [?], Frazer [?], [?], St. Charles Martyr [?].

P. 74, at passage "pure perception is our dawning action": P.B. receives the C.B. from solitude.

P. 75, top margin: Perception plus memory (Leibnitz) = Perception plus "nascent act" (Bergson)

P. 75, bottom margin: In Bergson creation is by diminution [?] of the marble till it is a statue; in (say) Croce by adding, as with the clay model.

P. 77, top margin: why 'vibration'?

P. 79, bottom margin: There is continuity of pure perception. Insofar therefore as perception mingles with act we share this continuity of life. It has everything of immortality but the knowledge that it has. That comes from memory. Yet it may be happening.

P. 80, at "The truth is ... ": Berkeley

P. 82, at passage beginning "matter is here as elsewhere": Hence insistence of spiritual fact that we only create and have a present.

P. 87, at "in the form of motor contrivances": automatic [?]/ "no concrete image is from the memory" (Vision) [canceled]/

P. 88, left of first 7 lines, two diagrams:

P. 92, at "the first records": The Record/ Perhaps [?] C.B. is pure [?]

P. 99, bottom margin: ?Habit memory = Husk/ B.F. images bound to us by habit memory

P. 114, top margin: Motor memory/ "acquired knowledge"/ husk.

Chapter II, "Realization of Memories," is only lightly marked at beginning.

P. 180, at "That which I call my present ... ": D. identifies images with the past ideas (?pain [?] perhaps) with the future.

P. 181, bottom margin: When he says "consciousness" he means consciousness plus memory. i.e. self-consciousness. Perception must be conscious but need not have memory.

P. 182, at "office of consciousness": consciousness of the inconcrete [?]

P. 194, next to phrase "We remain seated": Fucci stung by serpent.

P. 195, at "two memories": "abstract memory" basis of habits.

P. 195, at "Habit rather than memory": ?Husk

P. 201, at first 4 lines: (1) "Record"/ concrete different

P. 201, at "conscious automation": (2) habit/ abstract resemblance.
P. 201, bottom margin: Dreaming Back is the elimination of [?].
P. 202, end of first par.: (1) + (2)/ general idea
P. 206, at "That which interests us": Image & Mask & [one word illegible] definition
P. 206, bottom margin: Imagination serves "need" not as in Croce/ reveals the particular. Intellect dissolves it into particular and universal in contrast.
P. 208, at "Sensation is unstable" [to] "to be confined": "automatic" faculty "in Vision"/ "Controls" [one word illegible] "Unity of Being."
P. 209, a passage heavily canceled at top and illegible.

P. 210, last third of page: image

[one word illegible]

P. 211, bottom margin: He identifies dreams with memory yet dreams do not recall remembered images. There is always a difference perhaps because the habit [?] mechanism is always changing and is [?] forming different connections.
P. 215, top margin: Daimon = that which compels unity of being.
P. 215, bottom margin: "?undivided memory = record"
P. 216, top margin: Bergson does not consider an expansion not of memory, not of perception (clairvoyance etc.) of living world past and future.

P. 217, at "at the point s":

P. 218, at "action ... part of this": Recovery of past lives between lives. Action of body a narcotic.

P. 220, at "the other upon rotation upon itself":

P. 226, top: past = matter/ personality = form
P. 226, referring to word "encasing" in line 4: actions not so "encased" but realized by the mind are perhaps the arts. They require ideal circumstances.
P. 226, at "it must touch present reality on some side": Pirandello's dreams which just touch reality. Forms of the mask.
P. 227, at "the body is only a place of meeting and transfer, where stimulations received result in movements accomplished": railway junction. "Spirits" need its help to meet. Case of "Ellen Ellis" [?]
P. 262, at "our needs are": masks/ images
P. 265, at "thus each atom occupies": see Whitehead
P. 269, bottom margin: memory "contracts" into habits and general ideas and movements into colours.

P. 275, right margin: "covens" may have such consciousness.
P. 276, top: The perception is a "correspondence" not a representation.
P. 279, at "If there are actions" [to] "long intervals": critical moments
P. 279, bottom margin: Is a general idea a forecast or a memory? If I say "goodness" say I mean the good that is not [one word], that which I hope. The uneaten dinner.
P. 280, at "diagrammatic design" [to] "Homogeneous space":

P. 287, at "deus ex machina": thoughts of God
P. 294, at "It is distinct from matter in that it is, even then, <u>memory</u>": spirit [two words] is distinct from Monad.
P. 294, at "the distinction between body and mind must be established in terms not of space but of time": antithetical and primary.
P. 297, at "If matter does not remember the past, it is because it repeats the past unceasingly": Contra Leibnitz's Monads which are free [?]
P. 297, at "But a being which evolves more or less freely creates something new every moment": compare Dionestes [?] on importance of incarnation.
P. 298, a diagram followed by a long note:

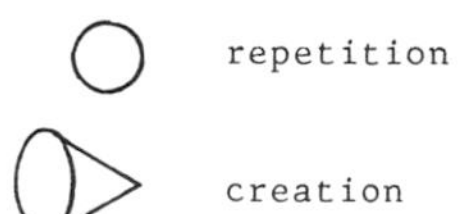

A state of existence which all confines. This nature would be free and without change. There would be no code and no change, no limit and so no compulsion. Bergson confines freedom to constancy of creation--to partial freedom. That is, he sees "the intelligible" not as Liebnitz, a free monad, but as world of "pure perception" where all is bound to all. This "pure perception" is a consciousness which neutralises itself. This I do not understand. He does not explain "neutralise" in this book. We are in the present "pure perception," also in past and future. May it not be that we forget?
P. 305, at "outrun perception": There are spirits and monads.
P. 331, top: ?our perception contraction of a greater will/ its own memory.
Back flyleaf: Bible authors on infallibility of church. Is the endeavor of a historical church to preserve the position established by another after the experience

on which it was founded has disappeared. It preserves that which Greek philosophy established about "the authentic existence" etc. in an age which began all reasoning with individual psychology. A new age with experience like that of the early Greeks might yet preserve our science.
Inside back cover: Byzantium/ Tower/ The man's love/ The woman's love/ Convent School/ Christ/ Sermon on Mount

158. Beritens, Germán. ABERRACIONES DEL GRECO. Científicamente Consideradas. Nueva Teoría que explica las anomalías de las obras de este artista. Madrid: Librería de Fernando Fé, 1913. 56 pp.

159. Berkeley, George. BERKELEY'S COMMONPLACE BOOK. Edited by G.A. Johnston. London: Faber & Faber, 1930. xxiv, 158 pp.

159a. Another copy.

160. ———. THE WORKS OF GEORGE BERKELEY. 2 vols. Dublin: John Exshaw, 1784. Bp, both vols.: WBY

Title p. missing from vol. 1.
A few marginal strokes and symbols in vol. 1, first 60 pp., not WBY's.
P. 68, a note, pencil, not WBY's.

161. Bevan, Edwyn. STOICS AND SKEPTICS. Four lectures delivered in Oxford during Hilary term 1913 for the Common University fund. Oxford: Clarendon Press, 1913. 152 pp. Sig.: WBY

*162. Bhattâchâryya, Shiva Chandra Vidyârnava. PRINCIPLES OF TANTRA. Edited by Arthur Avalon. 2 vols. London: Luzac, 1914-16.

Vol. 1 mostly uncut.
Vol. 2 cut through Preface and Introduction by Shrîyukta Baradâ Kanta Majumdâr; after this almost wholly uncut.

*163. BIBELOT, THE (Portland, Maine). A reprint of poetry and prose for book lovers, chosen in part from scarce editions and sources not generally known. Edited by Thomas B. Mosher. 1 (September 1895). "Hand and Soul" by Dante Gabriel Rossetti.

Mostly uncut.

*164. ———. 4 (January 1898). "St. Agnes of Intercession" by Dante Gabriel Rossetti.

Uncut after p. 11.

*165. ———. 5 (July 1899). "Translations from the French of Villon" by Algernon Charles Swinburne.

*166. ———. 8 (March 1902). "The Story of the Unknown Church and Lindenborg Pool" by William Morris.

*167. ———. 9 (February 1903). "Chrysanthema (concluded) and a Little Cycle of Greek Lyrics."

Uncut.

*168. ———. 9 (March 1903). "Stéphane Mallarmé" by Arthur Symons.

*169. ———. 9 (April 1903). "Lyrics" by Arthur Symons.

Mostly uncut.

*170. ———. 9 (May 1903). "The Madness of King Goll" by W.B. Yeats.

*171. ———. 9 (October 1903). "Lyrics" by W.E. Henley.

Uncut.

*172. ———. 9 (June 1903). "The Land of Heart's Desire" by W.B. Yeats.

On frt. cover: Corrected
WBY's moderate pencil revisions in text first followed in WADE 14, 1909 New York ed. of the play.
Inserted, a sheet folded quarto with a draft of possibly six fragmentary lines, heavily revised; for this play?

*172a-e. Five more copies; some pp. uncut.

*172f. Another copy. Bound in greyish-blue boards; no advertising at end.

*173. ———. 10 (March 1904). "Poems" by Lionel Johnson.

Uncut.

*174. ———. 10 (May 1904). "Lyrics" by Rosamund Marriott Watson.

2 pp. uncut.

*175. ———. 10 (June 1904). "Poems in Prose" by Oscar Wilde.

*176. Another copy.

Uncut.

*177. ———. 10 (October 1904). "Ballades" by William Ernest Henley.

*178. ———. 11 (March 1905). "For Those Who Love Music and Raffaella" by Axel Munthe.

Uncut.

*179. ———. 11 (July 1905). "Lecture on the English Renaissance and Rose Leaf and Apple Leaf: L'Envoi" by Oscar Wilde.

Uncut.

*180. ———. 11 (October 1905). "Death's Disguises and Other Sonnets" by Frank T. Marzials.

Uncut.

*181. ———. 11 (November 1905). "Vision and Memory by Edward McCurdy.

Uncut.

*182. ———. 12 (March 1906). "Lyrics" by Margaret L. Woods.

Uncut.

*183. ———. 12 (April 1906). "Two Songs of the Springtides: I. Thalassius. II. On the Cliffs" by Algernon Charles Swinburne.

Uncut.
Inserted, the calling card of WBY.

*184. ———. 12 (June 1906). "Poems" by Thomas William Parsons.

Uncut.

*185. ———. 12 (July 1906). "Charles Lamb: An Appreciation" by Walter Pater.

Uncut.

*186. ———. 12 (October 1906). "Giordano Bruno" by Walter Pater. "Four Sonnets on Bruno" by Algernon Charles Swinburne.

Uncut.

187. ———. 19 (July 1913). "Riders to the Sea" by John M. Synge.

Only the intro. which refers to Yeats is cut.

188. ———. 19 (August 1913). "In the Shadow of the Glen" by John M. Synge.

Almost wholly uncut.

189. Bickley, Francis. J.M. SYNGE AND THE IRISH DRAMATIC MOVEMENT. London: Constable, 1912. 95 pp.

Flyleaf: W. B. Yeats esquire/ with the author's thanks/ & compliments./ 1 Oct. 1912

*190. Billson, Charles J. THE POPULAR POETRY OF THE FINNS. Popular Studies in Mythology, Romance, and Folklore, no. 5. London: David Nutt, 1900. 37 pp.

191. Binyon, Laurence. THE COURT PAINTERS OF THE GRAND MOGULS. London: Oxford Univ. Press, 1921. 86 pp.

192. ———. THE DRAWINGS AND ENGRAVINGS OF WILLIAM BLAKE. Edited by Geoffrey Holme. London: The Studio, 1922. ix,29 pp., plates. 87/200

193. ———. "Mogul and Rajput Schools / Rock Temples of Ajanta," THE TIMES, 17 Nov. 1921, p. xiv.

Inserted in Item 859.

*194. ———. PAINTING IN THE FAR EAST. An introduction to the history of pictorial art in Asia, especially China and Japan. 2nd ed. London: Edward Arnold, 1913. xviii, 295 pp. Bp: WBY

Some pp. uncut.
Inside back cover, pencil: Hiroshige (first of that name)/ Snow scene at Kamudo/ Toto Musko Seru [pencil] [not apparently a specific reference to this book]

*195. Bisson, Juliette Alexandre. LES PHENOMENES DITS DE MATERIALISATION. Etude expérimentale. Paris: Librairie Felix Alcan, 1914. xx,311 pp., plates.

P. vi, marginal stroke.

196. Bithell, Jethro. W. B. YEATS. Translated [into French] by Franz Hellens. Paris: Editions du masque, [1913?]. 49 pp.

Flyleaf: A W. B. Yaets [sic],/ Avec ma grande et sincère admiration| Franz Hellens.
P. 26, a note in pencil, at bottom of p., probably G.Y.'s, providing an alternative or corrected translation of Hellens's rendition of "Stars grown old in dancing silver sandalled on the sea" ("Des étoiles vieillies dans de l'argent dansant glissaient sur la mer"): Des étoiles vieillies en dansant/ sur la mer dans des souliers (sandales) d'argent

*197. Bjørnson, Björnstjerne. PASTOR SANG (Over AEvne). Translated by William Wilson. Frontispiece by Aubrey Beardsley. London: Longmans, Green, 1893. 109 pp.

BLACAM, Aodh De. See De Blácam.

198. Blake, William. THE BOOK OF AHANIA. Lambeth: William Blake, 1795; facsimile ed. London: Quaritch, [1892]. [5] pp.

This is the lithographic facsimile by William Griggs. Five pp., cut down from originals, pasted to 5 sheets. Inserted in Item 220a.

199. ———. [FACSIMILE OF THE ORIGINAL OUTLINES BEFORE COLOURING OF THE SONGS OF INNOCENCE AND OF EXPERIENCE, EXECUTED

BY WILLIAM BLAKE. Edited by Edwin Ellis (and W.B. Yeats?). London: B. Quaritch, 1893. xxi pp., 54 plates.]

Outlines in red ink, uncolored; 53 plates on 53 leaves; plate 26 missing; no prefatory material; loose leaves in a binder.

200. ———. ILLUSTRATIONS OF THE BOOK OF JOB. London: William Blake, 1825. 22 plates on 22 leaves.

Nos. 1-21 marked "proof."
Title p. contained in box, imprinted in spine: Book of Job/ Blake/ 1825 [page is hinged on left].
Nos. 1-21 framed.

201. ———. ILLUSTRATIONS OF THE BOOK OF JOB. London: William Blake and John Linnell, 1826; facsimile ed., London: J.M. Dent, 1902; New York: J.P. Putnam's, 1902. 21 plates. Bp: WBY

202. ———. ILLUSTRATIONS TO THE DIVINE COMEDY OF DANTE. London: The National Art-Collections Fund, 1922. 102 plates.

Plate 83, Canto XIII of PURGATORIO, "The Souls of the Envious" is missing.

*203. ———. THE LETTERS OF WILLIAM BLAKE, together with a life by Frederick Tatham. Edited by Archibald G.B. Russell. London: Methuen, 1906. xlvii,237 pp. illus.

Flyleaf: W.B. Yeats/ gratefully/ from/ Archie Russell/ 24 October 1906

204. ———. THE MARRIAGE OF HEAVEN AND HELL. London: William Blake, [c. 1790-3]; facsimile ed., London: J.C. Hotten, 1868. 27 plates, hand-colored.

This facsimile was very heavily annotated by Edwin J. Ellis and W.B. Yeats while they prepared their jointly edited THE WORKS OF WILLIAM BLAKE (1893).

Flyleaf, full-face pencil drawing of a male figure, probably by Ellis; upper right hand corner, a rendering of a dog and the date 1872 (1870?).
Plate 4, marginal pencil drawings of male heads and a figure, probably Ellis's.
Back flyleaf, a pencil sketch of a male torso.
Annotations in pencil and ink, some very heavy, appear on verso of title p., plates 2, 3, 4, 4 verso, 5, 6, 7, 8, 9, 10, 11, 12, 13, 14, 15, 16, 17, 25, 26, 27 (the last three in "A Song of Liberty"). The handwriting, difficult to differentiate, is apparently predominantly Ellis's, though occasional annotations are WBY's and "W.B.Y." appears prominently in the upper left margin on plate 6.

205. ———. THE MARRIAGE OF HEAVEN AND HELL [and] THE BOOK OF LOS. Offprints bound in one vol. from CENTURY GUILD HOBBY HORSE 2 (1887): 137-57 and 5 (1890): 82-9. Includes an introductory note to THE BOOK OF LOS by F. York Powell.

Inside frt. cover: W B Yeats./ These reprints of "Book of Los" & of "Heaven & Hell"/ were published in the "Hobby Horse" and were/ bound into this book in November 1891.

P. 148, "A Memorable Fancy" (beginning "I was in a Printing house in Hell"), at the passage "In the fifth chamber were Unnam'd forms, which cast the metals into the expanse": Compare the [followed by four or five Hebrew letters, undecipherable]

The Nameless ones of the/ Kabala. They are called/ sometimes "The nameless/ terrors" & are the/ symbols of the void. [And the elemental symbols for "earth," "water," "air," and "fire" respectively are entered after the preceding four pars.]

206. ———. MILTON, A Poem in 2 Books. Facsimilied ... by William Muir, J.D. Watts, H.T. Muir, and E. Druitt. London: Bernard Quaritch, 1886. [10] pp., 45 plates.

Stamped on paper cover: Copy No. 29

Sheets are loose from binding.

On most plates lines have been numbered in pencil by fives; throughout are pencil notes, queries, and corrections of printing errors in Blake; the annotations are sometimes very heavy, though many have been erased and are now illegible; the legible annotations do not appear to be WBY's and are likely Edwin Ellis's. From the erasures and the numbering of lines, it appears that these pages were used to make the photographic reproductions for the Yeats-Ellis ed. of Blake (1893).

Plate 9 (numbered 7 in this copy), at passage "upon the clouds of Jehovah": what? clouds = sexes woven by Urizen = literal scripture [not WBY's]

Plate 25, ("Loud shout the Sons of Luvah"), top margin: When seed is sown on earth words fall into the ear-/ Below the bottoms of the graves (whose caverns are the places of that seed)/ silence is the place where contraries are equally true./ The grapes are human thought crushed in War by the iron hand of power [not WBY's]

Last 4 lines: Rome/Babylon/Tyre/ 7 mountains of Rome/ Satanic for 7 eyes. [not WBY's]

Inserted, an unidentified facsimile of a letter by Blake to William Hayley, 16 March 1804; unidentified clipping, a notice of publication of John Milton's COMUS: A MASK. With eight illustrations by William Blake. Edited by Darrell Figgis. London: Ernest Benn, 1926.

*207. ———. THE POEMS OF WILLIAM BLAKE. Comprising Songs of Innocence and Experience together with Poetical Sketches and some copyright poems not in any other collection. New ed. [Edited by R.H. Shepherd.] London: Pickering and Chatto, 1887. xx,165 pp.

Flyleaf: Miss Katherine Tynan,/ from/ R.W.C.
Flyleaf, verso: Richd. W. Colles,/ 30/12/87.
Pp. 146-9, lightly marked in pencil.
P. 146, in "Auguries of Innocence," the passage "The Wild Deer" to "Speaks the unbeliever's hurt" is canceled in pencil.

*208. ———. THE POEMS OF WILLIAM BLAKE. The Muses' Library. Edited by W.B. Yeats. London: Lawrence & Bullen, 1893. liv,252 pp. WADE 219

Flyleaf: "For wisdom is a butterfly/ And not a gloomy bird of prey"/ W B Yeats/ May 5 1925

209. ———. THE POEMS OF WILLIAM BLAKE. Large paper edition. Edited by W.B. Yeats. London: Lawrence & Bullen, 1893. liv,252 pp. 39/200. WADE 220

P. xxii, "cathedral" corrected to: Abbey [see Yeats's note on Westminster Abbey in Wade]
P. xxvi, a query in margin next to "51, Leicester Fields": ? Green St.
P. xlvii, "Florentine" corrected to: Venetian
P. 182, "x" in margin next to passages "Where she gets poison" [and] "and the winged eagle why he loves the sun."
Back flyleaf, a long note in ink: Imagination as understood by Boehme. The following definitions are given in the appendix to 'The Way to Christ' Bath M.DCC.LXXV. [i.e., THE WAY TO CHRIST DISCOVERED. Bath: S. Hazard, 1775] They are compiled from Boehme and Law's interpretations of his 'A Word Image meaneth not only a Creaturely Resemblance; in which sense Man is said to be the Image of God.' But it signifieth also a Spiritual Substance, Birth or Effect of a Will, wrought in and by a Spiritual Being or Power. And Imagination which we are apt erroneously to consider only an airy, idle and impotent faculty of the human mind, dealing in Fiction, and roving in Fancy or Idea without producing any powerful or permanent effects is this Magia or Power of raising and forming such Images or Substances. Now this Magia, or Imaginative Property, which hath desire for its root or mother is the greatest Power in Nature; its works cannot be hindered because it creates and substantiates as it goes and all things are possible to it. xxxx It is the eternal ground, scene, and subject of both good and evil and is therefore the Key of both Heaven and Hell. And the Reason it is thus powerful and important is because it is an Out-birth of this Divine Magia or Imagination. xxxx These (our desires) communicate with eternity and kindle a life

which always reaches either Heaven or Hell ... and here lies the ground of the great efficacy of Prayer, which when it is the Prayer of the Heart, the prayer of faith, has a kindling and creating Power and forms or transforms the soul into everything that its desires reach after. Page 418. [Yeats's transcription differs somewhat in phrasing from the version in the New York Public Library copy of the 1775 ed. of THE WAY TO CHRIST DISCOVERED where it is found on pp. 425-6.]

210. ———. POEMS OF WILLIAM BLAKE. Edited by W.B. Yeats. Books that Marked Epochs, no. 2. London: George Routledge, 1910. 1,280 pp. WADE 221

*211. ———. THE POETICAL WORKS OF WILLIAM BLAKE. Edited and annotated by Edwin J. Ellis. 2 vols. London: Chatto & Windus, 1906.

Vol. 1, some pp. uncut, usually in notes.
Vol. 2, many pp. uncut.

212. ———. THE POETICAL WORKS OF WILLIAM BLAKE, LYRICAL AND MISCELLANEOUS. Edited by William Michael Rossetti. The Aldine Ed. of the English Poets. London: George Bell, 1890. cxxxiii,231 pp.

Frt. cover: W B Yeats/ October,/ 1890
Inside, frt. cover: W B Yeats,/ October/ 1890
Flyleaf, verso, ink, a biographical outline of Blake from 1757 to 1804, giving Blake's age at various dates with events in Blake's life and publications, e.g.: born 1757 at 28 Broad St. Golden Square [also] 47. 1804. Milton, Jerusalem [last entry].
Eighteen entries of this kind.
There are notes and marks throughout this copy.
In Contents, pp. iv, v, vi, 16 titles are checked, others categorized as "childhood" (as for SONGS OF INNOCENCE, "The Little Boy Found), "love" ("The Garden of Love"), and one other undecipherable label.
There is little correlation between the marked poems and the selections in Yeats's 1893 ed. of Blake's poems. Throughout the volume, poems are checked, stroked, queried (?), and numbered in stanzas and lines, apparently to make an ed. of Blake's poems.
In Preface, p. xxxiii, at "Fuseli": see "verse" page 130 "what Fuseli gave"
P. xxxvi, at "lines": He had also some knowledge of Greek
P. xciv, in poem, at "break, bereave": symbolic
Pp. c-ciii, titles of some paintings are underlined and some numbered
P. 21, passage in "King Edward III" underlined, from "Beat slow" to "all forlorn."
P. 37, "The Divine Image" is checked at a note beneath: This is a contrast to "the human abstract" and

represents that human form but as one whereas the other is the human form abstract with many. [pencil]

P. 95, after "The Voice of the Ancient Bard," "Folly is an endless maze": Satan's labyrinth

Pp. 96-97, beginning of "Songs of Experience," a diagram running along the top margin from 96-97:

[96]

<u>Tears</u>

Bard = Milton. - Blake = Palamabron

<u>Joy</u>

Druids = Newton. - Balahek spectre [?] Rintrah Condemned

Druid kills joy [?]

Bard cures tears

[97]

night - Angels of sin [sense?]	Moon	<u>God</u>	England & Britain [?]
day - Apollo.	Sun	Satan	Albion

Pp. 96-110, poems "Xed" are "The Clod and the Pebble," "The LIttle Girl Lost," "The Chimney Sweeper," "The Angel," "The Tiger," "The Garden of Love," and "The Little Vagabond."

P. 111, poem checked, "The Human Abstract" and note, pencil: In the Kabala the tree of good & evil represents the human form divided. See Kabala Unveiled

P. 112, at "ruddy" in "The Human Abstract": My clairvoyance saw in air [?] with black flowers and covered with black lizards

P. 112, a note leading from last line of "The Human Abstract": a clairvoyant subject of mine found it in the air [2 words?] the [one word?] corresponding to the lower intellect. He saw the trunk [3 words?]

Pp. 113-4, poems "Xed" are "Christian Forbearance" and "A Little Boy Lost."

P. 121, "Lafayette" checked and a note, ink: The whole poem is allegoric and deals not with historic matter so much as with the spectre & vegetater imination [sic]. Hayley is used in the same allegoric fashion on page xciv of Introduction.

Pp. 123-7, poems checked are "The Gates of Paradise," "Epilogue," and "To Mr. Butts" [in the last, lines are numbered in text]

P. 127, lines 61-4, from "my fold" to "of the deep": go [pencil]

P. 127, line 67, "of the lion and wolf": or ⋀⋀↗ [ink]

P. 131, "And Butts shall give what Fuseli gave": compare letter on page 173 of <u>Life</u> [and a fuller note at bottom of p., ink] Compare the letter on p. 173 of <u>Life</u> in which he writes "Behind the sere of time & Space roars and follows swiftly" & generally discusses the matters in this poem.

P. 144, lines numbered in text of "The Everlasting Gospel."
P. 146, line 64: Mary Magdalen
P. 158, stanza three: loins
P. 158, stanza four, first 2 lines: Heart
P. 158, stanza four, last 2 lines: Head
P. 163, "The Golden Net," line 6, "Fire": △ Head
line 7, "wire": 🜁 Heart
line 8, "sighs": ▽ loins
line 10, "golden twine": love
P. 163, "The Golden Net," last 5 lines: night = the net; hence he longs for morning
P. 223, at "His five daughters ran": five senses
P. 223, at "Hela, my youngest daughter": sight
P. 224, at "Thirty of Tiriel's sons": 30 cities

*213. ———. THE POETICAL WORKS OF WILLIAM BLAKE. Edited by John Sampson. London: Oxford Univ. Press, 1914. lvi, 453 pp.

Inserted at end, a brown sheet of paper with an unidentified plan.

*214. ———. THE PROPHETIC BOOKS OF WILLIAM BLAKE. JERUSALEM. Edited by E.R.D. Maclagan and A.G.B. Russell. London: A.H. Bullen, 1904. xxii,127 pp.

Flyleaf: To W.B. Yeats/ from the Editors - / Eric R. D. Maclagan,/ Archibald G.B. Russell./ March, 1904.

215. ———. THE PROPHETIC BOOKS OF WILLIAM BLAKE, MILTON. Edited by E.R.D. Maclagan and A.G.B. Russell. London: A.H. Bullen, 1907. xix,57 pp.

Flyleaf: To W. B. Yeats/ from the editors/ Eric R.D. Maclagan,/ Archibald G.B. Russell./ Nov. 30 1907.
Introduction cut; some pp. of poem uncut.

216. ———. THE PROPHETIC WRITINGS OF WILLIAM BLAKE. 2 vols. Edited by D.J. Sloss and J.P.R. Wallis. Oxford: The Clarendon Press, 1926.

Vol. 1, most pp. uncut.
Vol. 2, General Intro. and Index of Symbols cut.

217. ———. SELECTIONS FROM THE WRITINGS OF WILLIAM BLAKE. With an introductory essay by Laurence Housman. London: Kegan Paul, Trench, Trubner, 1893. xxxi,259 pp. Sig.: W B Y

218. ———. WILLIAM BLAKE, Being all his woodcuts photographically reproduced in facsimile with an Introduction by Laurence Binyon. Little Engravings, Classical & Contemporary, no. 2. Edited by T. Sturge Moore. London: At the Sign of the Unicorn, 1902. Unpag.

Plates are numbered in pencil by WBY.

219. ———. WILLIAM BLAKE'S DESIGNS FOR GRAY'S POEMS, reproduced full size in monochrome or colour from the unique copy belonging to his grace the duke of Hamilton. London: Oxford Univ. Press, 1922. 21 pp., plates. 24/650

220. ———. THE WORKS OF WILLIAM BLAKE. 3 vols. Edited by Edwin Ellis and W.B. Yeats. London: Bernard Quaritch, 1893.

Large paper ed. Yeats's own vellum bound copy described in WADE 218.

VOL. 1, flyleaf, the long note about the making of this edition quoted in Wade, "The Writing of this book" etc. (dated 1900).
VOL. 1, p. 2 in "Memoir," "Irish extraction" underlined in text and a note below: my authority for Blake's Irish extraction was Dr. Carter Blake who claims to be descended from a branch of the family that settled at Malaga and entered the arms [?] trade there. WBY. [this note and the following in the same black ink as the long note on the flyleaf dated 1900]
P. 3, underlined in text "political enthusiasm of his grandfather" and a note, ink, in margin: This is rather too definite. I gathered this from Carter Blake's words, but he for some reason or other was keeping something back I thought. WBY.
P. 3, underlined in text, "worldly imprudence" with a note in margin canceled: This is Ellis' deduction from some matter
P. 36, "Book of Hell" corrected to: Book of Thel
Pp. 138, 139, 143, 144, 145, marginal strokes and underscoring, sometimes heavy.
P. 146, marginal comment, pencil, at passage beginning "The oddest thing he said": Does this allude to the unfinished 'Milton'?
P. 147, pencil, beside passage "The 'above' mention of Blake is not printed by Mr. Robinson": quote if printed
P. 148, underlining in passage on Dante and Christ.
P. 235, in "The Necessity of Symbolism," "Rosicrucian student" is underlined and a comment in margin: 'The Hermetic students of the G[olden] D[awn]'
P. 260, in the table "The five atmospheres and their symbols and correspondences," an asterisk at "Alulro is" and a note, pencil, bottom: 'The western gate' were it not closed would open upon 'Ideas' [?]. See description of Golgonooza in book 1 of Jerusalem (P 17). There however the Eastern gate is impurely (?) that tower 'ulro.'
P. 265, ink, in margin beside passage "Tharmas ... never travels from the West": authority HPB [H.B. Blavatsky], a doubtful authority - I would never quote her now
P. 312, ink, next to "occultists who have made the symbolism of sun-worship their special study": Boodie

Innis, a member of this order told me of this symbolism. WBY

P. 312, ink, next to "It is the universal custom of mystics to make white": rather white light than white. WBY

P. 312, 313, corrections, including "totoms" to: tatwas

P. 314, at bottom, after table of color symbolism: I am now convinced that Blake's colour scheme is found on Boehme's colour scheme. March 1902. WBY

P. 336, a suggestion for a revision or correction of the original passage: Mr. Johnston has found the name Hyle in the Greek hymns translated by Taylor the Platonist

P. 420, ink, bottom: 186

VOL. 2, p. 250, pencil beside par. beginning "The reference to the Spectre probably coincides": confused

P. 251, in second par. "Gihon," "Pison" and "Hiddekel" underlined and in margin:

Gehon = [symbol for water] in Kabala

Pison = [symbol for fire] in Kabala

Hiddekel = [symbol for air]

P. 266, "inner speech" corrected to: gentle speech

P. 267, "The mind, Los, has to choose" corrected to: has to cease

P. 267, "Imaginative well" corrected to: Imaginative will

P. 268, "Thullius, the female Leviathan" is underlined and a query in margin: ?

Pp. 319 ff., in "Marginal Notes to the Discourses of Sir Joshua Reynolds" as earlier there are many corrections passim as if a new edition was contemplated.

P. 325, at passage beginning "Blake: Mechanical Excellence is the only Vehicle of Genius": not use of vehicle. Compare Los vehicle of Urthona

P. 325, next to passage "The Lives of Painters say that Rafael died of Dissipation": Los is this exertion

P. 327, next to passage "This is most false" to "Nonsense": Copying

P. 333, pencil, after "Blake: Vulgarity and not Elegance": not using word 'Vulgar'

P. 345, IV, the heading "Our Illustrations" revised to: Illustrations in this Book

P. 349, passage canceled, "The wild scratches on the last page show the hand of a man whose whole artistic power is wrecked by the unnerving effect of anger, apprehension, agitation, and disturbance of mind. Poetry can flourish in this atmosphere, but we have Michel Angelo's own word for it that art cannot" and a comment, pencil, in margin: unconvincing and fanciful

P. 363-4, underlining and marginal stroking.

P. 377, at last par., a query in margin: ? Felpham period [pencil]

"Blake the Artist" is underlined passim.

VOL. 3, plate 91 in facsimile of Jerusalem, lines 33-50, a comment in margin: quote apropos of Dante/ Leviathan war of [?] See combine[d] RA drawing
Lines 47-52 stroked in margin and in pencil: quote
P. 24, line 186 of Night II of Vala: The altar of incense.
P. 24, line 190: altar or burnt offerings
P. 61, top, in Night VI: Urizen gives from South and East etc. The reverse of his nature's way, which is the torch [?] of the sun. Is this all his Fall? ["falling" is underlined in line 155].
P. 62, lines 176-78 in Night VI: vortex= science=wheel= void
P. 63, line 194 in Night VI: When he labours all is upward/ When he rests all is downcast.

220a. ———. A black and white facsimile of Blake's JERUSALEM bound as a volume, lettered on spine THE SONG OF JERUSALEM. No prefatory matter. The size of the facsimile reproduction is the same as for JERUSALEM in Vol. 3 of the Ellis-Yeats WORKS. It seems then that sheets from Vol. 3 were simply bound separately to make this volume.

Inserted, a sheet of stationery headed "18. Woburn Buildings,/ W. C." and folded quarto. On p. 1, a list in pencil: "Jerusalem/ Page 6/ Page 39/ Page 46/ Page 78."
Inserted, 198, facsimile of BOOK OF AHANIA

221. ———. THE WRITINGS OF WILLIAM BLAKE. 3 vols. Edited by Geoffrey Keynes. London: The Nonesuch press, 1925.

Vol. 1, some pp. uncut passim.
Vol. 2, mostly cut; "Vala" wholly cut; pp. 32, 283 marked by paper slips.
Vol. 3, mostly cut except for "Jerusalem"; pp. 92, 112, 119, 160 marked by paper slips.

222. Blum, Etta. POEMS. New York: Golden Eagle Editions, 1937. 62 pp.

Inside frt. cover: For William Butler Yeats/ Etta Blum/ 7/14/38

223. Blunden, Edmund. THE AUGUSTAN BOOKS OF MODERN POETRY, EDMUND BLUNDEN. London: Ernest Benn, [1925]. vii,30 pp.

224. ———. THE POEMS OF EDMUND BLUNDEN, 1914-30. London: Cobden-Sanderson, 1930. xvii,336 pp.

Flyleaf: In Festubert 9/ Forefathers 67/ Almswomen 60/ The Mole Catcher 82/ The Survival 291
Pages from these poems all excised; also "Report on Experience," p. 284. These poems appear in OBMV.

225. ———. THE WAGGONER AND OTHER POEMS. London: Sidgwick & Jackson, 1920. vi,70 pp.

A few pp. uncut.

226. ———. WINTER NIGHTS, A REMINISCENCE. The Ariel poems, no. 17. London: Faber & Gwyer, [1928]. 5 pp.

*227. Blunt, Wilfrid Scawen. THE BRIDE OF THE NILE. A Political Extravaganza in Three Acts of Rhymed Verse. Privately printed, 1907. 43 pp.

228. ———. FAND OF THE FAIR CHEEK. A Three-Act Tragedy in Rhymed Verse. Written for the Irish National Theatre Society. Privately printed, 1904. 50 pp.

P. 5, top, opening of play: All songs to be cut down
P. 23: This act not to be played at all

228a. Another copy. Sig.: WBY

228b-e. Four other copies.

229. [Blunt, Wilfrid Scawen]. "Proteus." SONNETS AND SONGS. London: John Murray, 1875. vii,112 pp.

Flyleaf: Wilfrid Blunt left me this book/ in his will. it was sent me/ after his death by Dorothy/ Carleton/ W B Y. March 9, 1922

230. Boas, George. THE ADVENTURES OF HUMAN THOUGHT. The Major traditions of European philosophy. New York and London: Harper, 1929. x,498 pp.

*231. Boccaccio, [Giovanni]. THE DECAMERON OF GIOVANNI BOCCACCIO. Translated by J.M. Rigg with illustrations by Louis Chalon. 2 vols. London: A.H. Bullen, 1903.

*231a. ———. DECAMERON. A folder containing eight illustrations to the DECAMERON by Chalon.
Published with 231.

Included is a loose title p., "Additional Plates to the Decameron."
Also included, a small loose flyleaf with "Blake's Illustrations & Thornton's Virgil, no. 2 & 3/ no. 5/ no. 6/ no. 7 & 8/ no. 10."

232. ———. LIFE OF DANTE. Translated by Philip Henry Wicksteed. San Francisco: Printed by John Henry Nash for his friends, 1922. [6],53 pp. 193/250

233. Bodkin, Thomas. HUGH LANE AND HIS PICTURES. Verona: The Pegasus Press for the Government of the Irish Free State, 1932. xiv,81 pp., 49 plates.

Includes John Butler Yeats's portrait of Hugh Lane.

*234. Boehme, Jacob. THE AURORA. Edited by C.J. B[arker] and D.S. H[ehner]. Translated by John Sparrow. London: John M. Watkins, 1914. xlviii,724 pp. Bp: WBY

Many pp. uncut.

Marginal stroking, pp. 474, 417, 412, 410, 404, 395, 396, 536, 537, 627; p. 435 marked by slip of paper.

*235. ———. CONCERNING THE THREE PRINCIPLES OF THE DIVINE ESSENCE. Translated by John Sparrow. London: John M. Watkins, 1910. lxiv,809 pp. Bp: WBY

Many pp. uncut.

*236. ———. THE FORTY QUESTIONS OF THE SOUL AND THE CLAVIS. Translated by John Sparrow. Emendated by D.S. Hehner. London: John Watkins, 1911. liii,[1],310,[2]; vi,[1], 54 pp. Bp: WBY

Marginal stroking or corners turned back, pp. 85, 96, 97, 238, 258, 259, 260.

*237. ———. THE HIGH AND DEEP SEARCHING OUT OF THE THREEFOLD LIFE OF MAN THROUGH, OR ACCORDING TO, THE THREE PRINCIPLES. Translated by John Sparrow. London: 1650; reprint ed. by C.J. B[arker], London: John M. Watkins, 1909. xlvii,[1],628 pp. Bp: WBY

P. 95, margin, for No. 17:

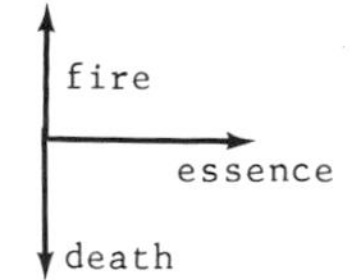

P. 274, top: ☉ { ☿ ɯ ♀ = △̶ feminine; ♂ △ masculine ——— tincture

P. 275, margin: ♀ ▽ V love

P. 276, at "The six planets run round about the sun": strange - before Galileo

P. 277, last 3 lines: Tincture = △/△̶ = ▽

P. 278, top: ♄ ♃ ♂ } △life ♀ ☿ ♄ } air government [?]

P. 279, bottom: ♃ = upper matrix

Inside back cover, a note discussing color symbolism, quoting from p. 185: colour page 185/ blue - substantiality/ red - glance of fire/ yellow - light and majesty of God the Son/ dusky brown (or purple) - other kingdom of darkness in the fire.

238. ———. MYSTERIUM MAGNUM OR AN EXPOSITION OF THE FIRST BOOK OF MOSES CALLED GENESIS. Edited by C.J. B[arker].

Translated by John Sparrow. 2 vols. London: John M. Watkins, 1924.

Both vols. almost wholly uncut.

*239. ———. THE WORKS OF JACOB BEHMEN THE TEUTONIC THEOSOPHER. CONTAINING I. THE THREEFOLD LIFE OF MAN. II. THE ANSWERS TO FORTY QUESTIONS CONCERNING THE SOUL. III. THE TREATISE OF THE INCARNATION. IV. THE CLAVIS. With Figures, illustrating his Principles, left by the Rev. William Law. London: Joseph Richardson, 1763. 230, 120, 160, 58 pp.

II, p. 56, the Eighth Question, pars. 3-17, corner of page folded back.
The flyleaf indicates the book was purchased in Philadelphia in 1785 and bought by Joseph Jewell of London in 1791.

240. Bolton, L[yndon]. AN INTRODUCTION TO THE THEORY OF RELATIVITY. With 38 diagrams. London: Methuen, 1921. xii,180 pp.

Corners turned back, pp. 28, 146, 160.

241. Bond, C[harles] J[ohn]. SOME CAUSES OF RACIAL DECAY. An Inquiry into the Distribution of Natural Capacity in the Population. The Galton Lecture, Feb. 16, 1928. London: The Eugenics Society, [1928]. 20 pp.

Inserted in 353.

242. THE BOOKMAN. An illustrated monthly journal. 5 (Oct. 1893).

Includes "The Reader./ W.B. Yeats" by Katharine Tynan, pp. 13-14. With photo of WBY.
Yeats's "Old Gaelic Love Songs," a review of Hyde's LOVE SONGS OF CONNACHT, appears on pp. 19-20.

243. ———. 5 (Feb. 1894).

Contains Yeats's review of Edwin Ellis's SEEN IN THREE DAYS.

244. ———. 6 (June 1894).

Contains Yeats's reviews of William Larminie's WEST IRISH FOLK TALES. Inserted in this copy, an unsigned review of Yeats's A BOOK OF IRISH VERSE and a review of the same anthology by Dora Sigerson; newspaper sources not identifiable.

245. ———. 6 (Aug. 1894).

Contains Yeats's review of George Russell's HOMEWARD: SONGS BY THE WAY.

246. ———. 11 (March 1897).

247. ———. 12 (Sept. 1897)

Contains "The Reader. Living Poets. Mr. W.B. Yeats" by Richard Ashe King; also Yeats's review of Maeterlinck's AGLAVAINE AND SELYSETTE.

248. ———. 27 (Jan. 1905).

Contains two photographs of WBY.

248a. Another copy.

249. THE BOOK OF COMMON PRAYER. Oxford: The Univ. Press, [1935?]. 696 pp.

250. THE BOOK OF THE RHYMERS CLUB. London: Elkin Mathews, 1892. xvi,94 pp.

P. iv, facing half-title: W B Yeats./ Feb. 1892
P. 9, line 45 in "A Man Who Dreamed of Fairyland," "dances" corrected to: dancer

251. THE BOOK OF THE THOUSAND NIGHTS AND ONE NIGHT. Rendered from the literal and complete version of Dr. J.C. Mardrus and collated with other sources by E. Powys Mathers. 4 vols. London: The Casanova Society, 1923. 1795/2250

Vol. I, sig.: WBY

252. Borthwick, Norma, ed. IRISH READING LESSONS. With illustrations by Jack B. Yeats. Book 2. Dublin: The Irish Book Co., 1914. 28 pp.

253. ———. IRISH READING LESSONS. With illustrations by Jack B. Yeats. Book 3. Dublin: The Irish Book Co., [191?]. 40 pp.

254. Bosanquet, Bernard. THE MEETING OF EXTREMES IN CONTEMPORARY PHILOSOPHY. London: Macmillan, 1924. xxviii,220 pp.

Marginal strokes, underscorings, comments, pp. 7, 8, 13, 30, 48, 51, 63, 65, 66, 76, 128, 129, 130, 131, 132, 134, 137, 138, 139, 144, 145, 146, 148, 149.
P. 8, midpage: spiritual memory
P. 30, at "If a man were to dream ...": Masefield had this experience in America as a boy.
P. 51, at "though not what transcends experience": man's experience, but note Berkeley's phrase "some spirit"
P. 128, a comment canceled in margin, midpage.
P. 129, bottom: critical reaction is Berkelean so far as all the seen is concerned, but believes in an unseen peg or prop - Mills "permanent possibility of experience"
P. 131, at par. 2: compare "spiritual" only because of analogy.
P. 139, top: Daemon is "conscious"

Back flyleaf, verso: The spirit, or C.M., where it discovers or constructs unity does so by means of logical forms from "spiritual memory" which is "memory of forms in the minds of others - according to the script. Hence that the universe is an arbitrary construction [?], conditioned by the past and present of associated minds - outside [one word illegible] all that can be imagined.

255. Bosis, Lauro de. THE STORY OF MY DEATH. With the original text in French and a biographical note. Translated by Ruth Draper. London: Faber & Faber, 1933. 31,[1] pp.

*256. Boswell, James. BOSWELL'S LIFE OF JOHNSON. Edited by Augustine Birrell. 6 vols. London: The Times Book Club, 1912.

Inserted in vol. 1, an otherwise blank postcard, printed on one side: From W.B. Yeats/ 42 Fitzwilliam Square/ Dublin/ Phone 61831.

BOSWELL-STONE, see Stone, W.G.B.

*257. Bottomley, Gordon. CHAMBERS OF IMAGERY. Second Series. London: Elkin Mathews, 1912. 41 pp.

Half-title p.: With Gordon Bottomley's remembrances/ Cartmel, May 11th 1912.

*258. ———. THE GATE OF SMARAGDUS. London: At the Sign of the Unicorn, 1904. lxvi pp.

Flyleaf: With Gordon Bottomley's/ obeisances/ June 27th. 1904.

259. ———. GRUACH AND BRITAIN'S DAUGHTER. Two Plays. London: Constable, 1921. 130 pp.

Flyleaf: To W.B. Yeats,/ the renewer of poetic drama;/ with Gordon Bottomley's/ unchanging admiration./ Silverdale. 22nd. December, 1921.
Inserted, a letter of presentation from Bottomley, same date, remembering their experiences in common with Ricketts and Shannon.

*260. ———. KING LEAR'S WIFE, THE CRIER BY NIGHT, THE RIDING TO LITHEND, MIDSUMMER EVE, LAODICE AND DANAE. London: Constable, 1920. vii,223 pp.

Flyleaf: To W.B. Yeats/ from his ancient admirer/ Gordon Bottomley./ Sept. 11th, 1920/ The Sheiling, Silverdale.

260a. Another copy.

Presented to the Dublin Drama League Library by GY.

261. ———. LYRIC PLAYS. London: Constable, 1932. xi,166 pp.

Flyleaf: To W.B. Yeats/ with forty years of delight/ in his work still vivid and new;/ from Gordon Bottomley./

The Sheiling: Silverdale: Carnforth, Lancashire/ 1st. November 1932.
Inked under dedicatory poem "To W.B. Yeats": Out of long admiration and regard.

*262. ———. MIDSUMMER EVE. With drawings by James Guthrie. Harting, Petersfield, Hampshire: Pear Tree Press, 1905. 34, [2] pp.

Uncut.

263. ———. SCENES AND PLAYS. London: Constable, 1929. 122, [1] pp.

Flyleaf: To W.B. Yeats, with Gordon Bottomley's admiration./ Silverdale: 18th June 1929.

264. Boucicault, Dion. THE COLLEEN BAWN OR, THE BRIDES OF GARRY OWEN. London: Samuel French, [1860?]. 56 pp.

*265. Boyd, Ernest A[ugustus]. THE CONTEMPORARY DRAMA OF IRELAND. Boston: Little, Brown, 1917. 225 pp.

*266. Boyle, William. THE MINERAL WORKERS. A Play in Four Acts. Dublin: M.H. Gill, 1910. 109 pp.

267. Brabazon, Elizabeth Jane. OUTLINES OF THE HISTORY OF IRELAND FOR SCHOOLS AND FAMILIES. Dublin: Printed by J.S. Folds, 1844. 379 pp.

Copy lacks title p. and spine.
Inside frt. cover: Revd. W. B. Yeats
P. i, beginning of Preface: J. Yeats/ From his/ Dear Papa
Back flyleaf: W.B. Yeats/ 4 Athol Academy [?]/ [one word illegible]/ Isle of Man. [Rev. W. B. Yeats's]
Inside back cover: John/ Yeats/ to [?] France [WBY's]
Inside frt. cover and on p. 1, a childish hand has imitated the inscription in pencil.

268. Bradby, G[odfrey] F[ox]. SHORT STUDIES IN SHAKESPEARE. London: John Murray, 1929. viii,195 pp.

269. Bradley, F[rancis] H[erbert]. APPEARANCE AND REALITY. A Metaphysical Essay. London: George Allen & Unwin, 1925. xxiv,628 pp.

Some pp. uncut passim.

*270. Bradley, John W[illiam]. ILLUMINATED MANUSCRIPTS. Little Books on Art. London: Methuen, 1905. xiv,290 pp.

271. Brereton, Austin. HENRY IRVING. A Biographical Sketch. New York: Scribner and Welford, 1884. ix,136 pp.

*272. Breton, Nicholas. PASTORAL POEMS. George Wither. SELECTED POETRY. William Browne of Tavistock. PASTORAL POETRY. The Pembroke Booklets, First Series, No. 3. Hull: J.R. Tutin, 1906. 64 pp.

*273. Brewer, R[obert] F[rederick]. ORTHOMETRY. The Art of Versification and the Technicalities of Poetry. With a new and complete rhyming dictionary. Edinburgh: John Grant, 1912. xv,376 pp.

BRIDGES, Elizabeth. See Daryush, Elizabeth

*274. Bridges, Robert. ACHILLES IN SCYROS. London: George Bell, 1892. 68 pp.

*275. ———. EIGHT PLAYS. Vol. 4: THE CHRISTIAN CAPTIVES. London: Edward Bumpus, 1890.

PP. uncut, except 124-6.

*276. ———. EROS AND PSYCHE. London: George Bell, 1894. 170 pp.

277. ———. NEW VERSE, written in 1921, with the other poems written in that year and a few earlier pieces. Oxford: Clarendon Press, 1925. viii,89 pp.

Card inserted: With the Compliments of the Delegates of the Clarendon Press, Oxford.

278. ———. ODE, FOR THE BICENTARY COMMEMORATION OF HENRY PURCELL. London: Elkin Mathews, 1896. 44 pp.

*279. ———. POEMS WRITTEN IN THE YEAR MCMIII. Chelsea: Printed by St. John Hornby at the Ashendene Press, 1914. 20 pp.

One of an edition of ninety-one copies.

*280. ———. THE SHORTER POEMS. London: George Bell, 1890. 91 pp.

Flyleaf: W B Yeats/ 1890/ November 1st
P. 36, at poem "Spring. Ode II. Reply," a crude sketch of what appears to be a personification of Spring.
Pp. 44 and 80, slight verbal corrections, possibly WBY's.

281. ———. THE TESTAMENT OF BEAUTY. Oxford: Clarendon Press, 1929. 191 pp.

Half title p.: ὰγαηητῶ / William Butler Yeats/ from/ Robert Bridges.

Uncut.

282. ———, ed. THE CHILSWELL BOOK OF ENGLISH POETRY. London: Longmans, Green, 1924. xiii,272 pp.

Includes two poems by WBY, "A Faery Song" and "The Lake Isle of Innisfree."

*283. ———, ed. THE SPIRIT OF MAN, AN ANTHOLOGY. London: Longmans, Green, 1916. Unpag.

*284. British Museum. Dept. of Egyptian and Assyrian Antiquities. A GUIDE TO THE FIRST AND SECOND EGYPTIAN ROOMS. Predynastic Antiquities, Mummies, Mummy-cases, and other objects connected with the funeral rites of the ancient Egyptians. [By E.A. Wallis Budge]. 2nd ed. London: By order of the trustees, 1904. vii,156 pp.

*285. ———. Dept. of Manuscripts. REPRODUCTIONS FROM ILLUMINATED MANUSCRIPTS. Second Series. London: Longmans, 1907. Unpag.

286. [Brodie-Innes, J.W.]. Sub Spe., Th. A. M., Former Imperator of Amen Ra. CONCERNING THE REVISAL OF THE CONSTITUTION AND RULES OF THE ORDER R.R. & A.C. [1901]. 12 pp.

Pp. 2, 3, 10, 11 uncut.
See George Mills Harper, ed. YEATS'S GOLDEN DAWN, Chapt. 6, pp. 90-1 and Appendix M.

287. Brodzky, Horace. HENRI GAUDIER-BRZESKA. 1891-1915. London: Faber & Faber, 1933. 182 pp.

Includes printed letters from John Quinn.

*288. Brooke, Rupert. POEMS. London: Sidgwick & Jackson, 1911. viii,88 pp. Bp: WBY

Flyleaf: W B Yeats/ from/ Rupert Brooke

*289. Browne, Sir Thomas. RELIGIO MEDICI, AND URN-BURIAL. [Edited by Israel Gollancz]. The Temple Classics. London: J.M. Dent, 1896. vi,196 pp.

Flyleaf: W B Yeats./ June, 1897.

290. ———. RELIGIO MEDICI, URN BURIAL, CHRISTIAN MORALS, AND OTHER ESSAYS. Edited with an intro. by John Addington Symonds. London: Walter Scott, 1886. xxxii,262 pp.

Inside frt. cover: J.E. Masefield
Many marginal strokes, symbols, and some notes passim; apparently John Masefield's.

291. Another ed. Edited by C.J. Holmes, Decorated by C.S. Ricketts. London: The Ballantyne Press, 1902. cxcix pp. Bp: WBY

Flyleaf: To W. B. Yeats/ 13.6.1905/ from/ E. Maclagan.

BROWNE, William, of Tavistock. See 272.

*292. Brownell, W[illiam] C[rary]. FRENCH ART. CLASSIC AND CONTEMPORARY. PAINTING AND SCULPTURE. Westminster: Archibald Constable, 1902. 228 pp.

293. Browning, Elizabeth Barrett. POEMS. 3 vols. 5th ed. London: Chapman & Hall, 1862.

VOL. 1, Bp: LY
Flyleaf: To Susan M. Pollexfen/ from J.B.Y./ Given to Anne Butler Yeats/ granddaughter of the above/ Susan Pollexfen & John/ Butler Yeats by her Aunt/ Susan M. Yeats (Lily Yeats)/ Xmas 1941 -- Dublin/ S.M.P. & J.B.Y. became engaged/ in 1862 & were married at/ St John's Sligo Sept 10th 1863./ L.Y.
A number of marginal strokes and underscorings in "A Vision of Poets," pp. 201ff. Some marginal strokes and underscorings in "Isobel's Child," pp. 293ff.
Inside back cover, a crude sketch of a woman.

VOL. 2, Bp: LY
Verso of last page, a sketch of a woman, possibly by JBY.

VOL. 3, Bp: LY
Flyleaf, verso, a very slight sketch of a long-robed man ringing a bell.
Back flyleaves, sketches of heads and a female nude.

*294. ———. PROMETHEUS BOUND and other poems. London: Ward, Lock & Bowden, 1896. xix,330 pp.

Some pp. uncut.

*295. ———. A SELECTION FROM THE POETRY. Leipzig: Bernhard Tauchnitz, 1872. 318 pp.

Almost wholly uncut.
On paper cover: 26 less T [?] pages in Unwin [?] book/ 34 T [?] pages in this.

*296. Browning, Robert. THE POETICAL WORKS. 4th ed. Vol. 2: TRAGEDIES AND OTHER PLAYS. London: Chapman and Hall, 1865. 605 pp.

Flyleaf: J B Yeats/ 23 Fitzroy Road/ Regents Park/ 1868
The sketches and very likely the other markings in this vol. are by JBY.
Back flyleaves, a pencil sketch of a man; three sketches of heads of women or girls; pencil sketch of a male bust.
Numerous marginal strokes and underscorings in "Pippa Passes." A faint sketch, possibly of a woman on p. 67, the last of "Pippa Passes."
P. 75, in "King Victor and King Charles," a sketch of a grotesque male head.
P. 355, in "Colombe's Birthday," a slight sketch of a head.
Some marginal strokes and underscorings in "Strafford."

*297. Vol. 3: PARACELSUS, CHRISTMAS-EVE AND EASTER-DAY, SORDELLO. London: Chapman and Hall, 1865. 465 pp.

Flyleaf, pencil, at top: J.B. Yeats/ 23 Fitzroy Road/ Regents Park [and below this, the name and address repeated]
Facing flyleaf, a sketch of a cat.
Opposite title p., two sketches of cats.

Contents p., verso, sketch of a girl's head.
In "Paracelsus" and in the "Note" that follows, numerous marginal strokes and underscorings.
P. 255, in "Sordello," two sketches of heads in margin, evidently to illustrate the texts "not a face/ But wrath made livid" and "men grave and grey/ Stood, with shut eyelids."
P. 258, bottom: Guelf = Adelardi/ Ghibelline = Salinguerra [the latter a major character in "Sordello"].
Back flyleaves, various sketches of cats and women.
All the sketches above are by JBY.

298. ———. THE POETICAL WORKS OF ROBERT BROWNING. [Edited by Augustine Birrell and Sir Frederic G. Kenyon]. 2 vols. London: John Murray, 1919. Bps: WBY

299. Bruck, Arthur Moeller van den. GERMANY'S THIRD EMPIRE. Condensed by E.O. Lorimer. London: George Allen & Unwin, 1934. 268 pp.

BRUNO, Giordano. See 186.

300. BRYAN'S DICTIONARY OF PAINTERS AND ENGRAVERS. New ed., rev. and enlarged under the supervision of George C. Williamson. 5 vols. London: G. Bell, 1919-21.

Vol. 3, p. 363 marked by paper slip, probably for "Gustave Moreau."

301. Bunting, Basil. REDIMICULUM MATELLARUM. Milan: Grafica Moderna, 1930. 32 pp.

Poems.
Inside frt. cover, on a pasted sheet in hand not WBY's, possible etymologies for title.

301 a-d. Four more copies.

302. Bunyan, John. THE PILGRIM'S PROGRESS. London: The Religious Tract Society, [1820?]. 378 pp.

Inside frt. cover: John Butler Yeats./ The Gift of his Papa,/ W B Yeats/ Decr. 25th 1850.

*303. Burdy, Samuel. THE LIFE OF PHILIP SKELTON. Dublin: William Jones, 1792; reprint ed., Oxford: Clarendon Press, 1914. xxvii,255 pp. Bp: WBY

Mostly uncut.

*304. Burghclere, Lady (Winifred Gardner). THE LIFE OF JAMES FIRST DUKE OF ORMONDE, 1610-1688. 2 vols. London: John Murray, 1912. Bps: WBY

Many pp. uncut.

305. Burke, Edmund. SELECTIONS. With essays by Hazlitt, Arnold & Others. Oxford: Clarendon Press, 1928. xvi,192 pp.

306. ———. THE WORKS OF THE RIGHT HONOURABLE EDMUND BURKE. 8 vols. Bohn's Standard Library. London: George Bell, 1877-83.

VOL. 1, most of "The Sublime and the Beautiful" is uncut; corners turned back, pp. 310, 375, 492; marginal marks and underscoring, pp. 311, 312, 379, 406, 407, 424, 428.

VOL. 2, some pp. uncut; corners turned back, pp. 195, 324.

VOL. 3, corners turned back, pp. 37, 41, 107, 340; markings, pp. 141, 142, 384, 528.
Back flyleaf: Ireland never was an independent nation under one nationality. When a stone in the legal edifice of the constitution appears rather dangerous to the whole we take it out but replace it with one as exactly like what [was] cast aside [the rest illegible; not WBY's]

VOL. 4, first 50 pp. or so of "Against Warren Hastings" cut; otherwise mostly uncut.

VOL. 5, "A Letter to a Noble Lord" cut; otherwise mostly uncut; stroking, pp. 120, 147, 148.

VOL. 6, mostly uncut.
Back flyleaf: "Nation - not only the people living at one time 146" [Burke, in "Reform of representation in the house of Commons," discusses this, pp. 146-147; <u>not</u> WBY's hand]
Also back flyleaf: Peers 170 [not WBY's; same hand as above and in VOL. 3]

VOL. 7 (separately numbered as Vol. 1 of BURKE'S SPEECHES, but in fact a continuation of the set); mostly uncut.

VOL. 8 (Vol. 2 of BURKE'S SPEECHES); almost wholly uncut.

307. Burkitt, F[rancis] C[rawford]. Offprint. Review of ST. PATRICK--A.D. 180 by the Rev. John Roche Ardill. THE JOURNAL OF THEOLOGICAL STUDIES 33 [July 1932].

On cover, ink: "W.B. Yates [sic] D. Litt./ with best wishes from/ F.C. Burkitt."
Below inscription: S. Patrick's Date/ J.T. St. xxxiii.
Inserted, a letter from Burkitt, at Cambridge, 8 June 1933 to "Dear Mr. Yates" presenting the review and going into detail about astrological hours and signs in connection with Christ's birth, crucifixion, burial, and resurrection, especially the latter.

308. Burnet, John. EARLY GREEK PHILOSOPHY. London and Edinburgh: Adam and Charles Black, 1892. vii,[1],378 pp. Bp: WBY

Title p.: Aberdeen/ May 19. 1923 [WBY's?]
Title p. verso, pasted in, a newspaper clipping, anonymous article of two pars. under headlines "Mathematics

of B.C./ Ancient Egyptian Papyrus Deciphered"; inked between the headlines by W.B.Y.: "Observer, Sept. 23, 1928." [and next to date] "See pages/ 17.18.19."
As reported in the newspaper article, a Russian savant, Struve, argues that Egyptian mathematics were as advanced as European mathematics of the Middle Ages. This would confute Burnet, pp. 17-19.
Marginal strokes, pp. 63, 66, 70, 88, 91, 135, 136, 137, 138, 139, 140, 141, 186, 201, 221, 222, 223, 224, 294, 296, 298, 299.
P. 86, at "Processes of sowing, growing, reaping, threshing": Eleusinian/Productive
P. 86, at "purification": orphic/purgative
P. 187, lines 95-100: Time as illusion
P. 226, a marginal stroke along sections 170-85 of "remains of Empedokles"; also:

P. 293, at "The truth probably is that Anaxagoras substituted Nous, still conceived as a body, for the Love and Strife of Empedokles ...": Change to Primary conception.
P. 293, bottom: Anaxagoras physiological prepares for p[hase] 22
Swedenbourg physiological prepares for p[hase] 22 or return gyre
P. 363, at "he is careful to attribute to air": mind

309. [Burney, Fanny]. CAMILLA: OR, A PICTURE OF YOUTH. 3 vols. Dublin: Printed by William Porter, 1796.

Vol. 3, title p., among persons for whom the book has been printed, the name W. Corbet is underlined in ink with a note: great friend Father/ L.Y.
Vol. 3, Bp: Elizabeth Corbet Yeats
Sig. all 3 vols.: Hugh Pollock/ 2 Feb. 1878

*310. Burns, Robert. THE POETRY OF ROBERT BURNS. Edited by William Ernest Henley and Thomas F. Henderson. 4 vols. The Centenary Burns. London: T.C. & E.C. Jack, [1896-7].

Many pp. uncut.

*311. Burton, Robert. THE ANATOMY OF MELANCHOLY. Edited by Rev. A.R. Shilleto. 3 vols. Bohn's Libraries. London: G. Bell, 1912. Bps: WBY

VOL. 1, pp. cut, 152-249; 206-11, 213-15; 218-19; 226-28; marginal strokes on pp. with headings "Nature of Devils," "Nature of Spirits," "Digression of Spirits," "Causes of Melancholy."

VOL. 2, pp. 40-83 cut.

VOL. 3, pp. 48-57 cut; also 96-107; 400-09.
P. 52, a marginal stroke against the passage "learned Magician in those days ... accordingly did it" and a line leading from this passage to WBY's comment at the

top of the p.: "Cross-roads" ["crossway" occurs in the passage].

312. Bury, J[ohn] B[agnell], S.A. Cook, and F.A. Adcock, eds. THE CAMBRIDGE ANCIENT HISTORY. 13 vols. Cambridge: The Univ. Press, 1923-1936.

Vols. 1-11 only.
Some pp. uncut in all vols.
VOL. 2, entire Trojan and Homer section cut, pp. 432-552.
VOL. 4, section on Greek lyric poetry, the Mysteries, and cult of Orphism cut, pp. 480-578.

313. ———. THE CAMBRIDGE ANCIENT HISTORY. VOLUME OF PLATES I (-V). Prepared by C.T. Seltman. Cambridge: The Univ. Press, 1927+.

Vols. 1-4 only.

314. ———. THE CAMBRIDGE MEDIEVAL HISTORY. Edited by H.M. Gwatkin and J.P. Whitney. 8 vols. Cambridge: The Univ. Press, 1911-1936.

Vols. 6 & 7 missing.
All vols. precut.

315. Busch, Julius Herrmann Moritz. BISMARCK, SOME SECRET PAGES OF HIS HISTORY. Being a diary kept by Dr. Moritz Busch during 25 years' official and private intercourse with the great chancellor. Condensed ed. London: Macmillan, 1899. ix,576 pp.

316. Bushell, Stephen W[ooton]. CHINESE ART. 2 vols. London: Victoria and Albert Museum, 1921.

Vol. 2 missing.

317. Butler, Samuel. THE POETICAL WORKS. With Life etc. by Rev. George Gilfillan. 2 vols. Edinburgh: James Nichol, 1854.

318. Butt, Isaac. THE HISTORY OF ITALY, from the abdication of Napoleon I. 2 vols. London: Chapman and Hall, 1860.

VOL. 1, p. ix, a crude sketch of a man.
VOL. 2 missing.

*319. BUTTERFLY QUARTERLY, THE. (Philadelphia). No. 5 (Winter 1908-9). 281/300

*320. ———. No. 6 (Spring 1909). -/300

Contains "Yeats and Synge, a Celtic Contrast" by Louis Untermeyer, pp. 11-13.

*321. Butterworth, Adeline M. WILLIAM BLAKE, MYSTIC, A STUDY. Together with Young's Night Thoughts: Nights I & II. With illus. by William Blake and frontispiece Death's

Door, from Blair's 'The Grave.' Liverpool: The Liverpool Booksellers, 1911. 42 pp. Bp: WBY

322. Bynner, Witter. THE NEW WORLD. San Francisco: John Henry Nash, 1919. 14 pp. -/350

323. Byron, George Gordon, Lord. THE LETTERS AND JOURNALS OF LORD BYRON, SELECTED. Camelot Classics. London: Walter Scott, 1886. xvi,346 pp.

Flyleaf: W B Yeats/ 1887/ Dublin
Back flyleaf, sketch of a girl's head by JBY.

324. ———. LORD BYRON'S CORRESPONDENCE, chiefly with Lady Melbourne, Mr. Hobhouse, The Hon. Douglas Kinnaird, and P.B. Shelley. Edited by John Murray. 2 vols. London: John Murray, 1922.

325. ———. POETICAL WORKS OF GEORGE LORD BYRON. London: T. Noble, 1853. vii,666 [42].

Frt. cover, Bp: LY. With inked note: This must have belonged to our great grandmother Middleton.
Half title p., sig.: Elizabeth Middleton

*326. ———. THE POETICAL WORKS OF LORD BYRON. Reprinted from the original editions. With explanatory notes etc. London: Frederick Warne, [1889]. x,668 pp.

Pp. 667-8, marginal strokes in "On This Day I Complete My 36th Birthday."

327. Byron, Robert and David Talbot Rice. THE BIRTH OF WESTERN PAINTING. A History of Colour, Form, and Iconography, illustrated from the Paintings of Mistra and Mount Athos of Giotto and Fuccio, and of El Greco. London: George Routledge, 1930. xviii,236 pp., 94 plates. Bp: WBY

328. C., A.L.O. MY NEIGHBOUR'S SHOES; or FEELING FOR OTHERS. London: T. Nelson, 1875. 108 pp.

Flyleaf: To Lolly from her/ Aunt Gracie Xmas 75.

329. C., S.A. (Mrs. Sophia Anne Cotton?). ANCIENT DEVOTIONS FOR HOLY COMMUNION FROM EASTERN AND WESTERN LITURGICAL SOURCES, compiled by S.A.C. London: Burns Oates & Washbourne, 1923. xiv,207 pp.

Inserted, a letter to George Yeats from Eve (?), Sept. 6, from Spider's Bay, Clonbur (?), Co. Galway. Refers to the gift of a book to George: I know you will like the reproduction anyway, one of my favourite windows in Chartres. [This seems to refer to a book mark, also inserted, which reproduces "Notre Dame de la Belle Verrière" in Chartres Cathedral. Letter concludes:] Wonder did you hear anything satisfactory from Omar Pound?

330. Cabell, James Branch. BALLADES FROM THE HIDDEN WAY. New York: Crosby Gaige, 1928. 41 pp. -/831

331. Cafferata, Canon Henry Taylor. THE CATECHISM SIMPLY EXPLAINED. New rev. and enlarged ed. London: Burns Oates & Washbourne, [1932]. viii,180 pp.

Marginal strokes, underscoring on about 8 pp.
P. 80, corner turned back.
Inside back cover a note, possibly GBY's: A Map of Life by F.J. Sheed (Sheed & Ward).

332. Caffin, Charles H[enry]. AMERICAN MASTERS OF PAINTING. Being Brief Appreciations of Some American Painters. New York: Doubleday, Page, 1903. x,195 pp.

Flyleaf: To Mr. John B. Yeats from Julia E. Ford in memory of pleasant days in the studio.

333. Calvert, Edward. TEN SPIRITUAL DESIGNS. Enlarged from proofs of the originals on copper, wood and stone, MDCCCXXVII - MDCCCXXXI. Portland, Maine: Thomas Bird Mosher, 1913. ix,15 pp., 10 plates. Bp: WBY

On frt. of case: Large Paper Copy [in ink]
Inserted, a color reproduction of the Blessed Virgin and the Christ child astride a sheep.

334. Calvert, Samuel. A MEMOIR OF EDWARD CALVERT, ARTIST. By his third son. Illustrated with reproductions from his own paintings and sketches. London: Sampson Low, Marston, 1893. xix,236 pp. 26/350. Sig: Samuel Calvert

Inserted, 4 color reproductions, "Innocence" by Sir Joshua Reynolds, "Evening" by T.F. Wainewright, another signed "L. Haghe/ 1861," another with no attribution showing boaters on a lake among mountains.

CAMBRIDGE ANCIENT HISTORY, see 312, 313.

CAMBRIDGE MEDIEVAL HISTORY, see 314, 1221.

CAMBRIDGE MODERN HISTORY, see 14.

*335. Campbell, John Gregorson. THE FIONS: OR, STORIES, POEMS, & TRADITIONS OF FIONN AND HIS WARRIOR BAND. Collected entirely from oral sources. With intro. and notes by Alfred Nutt. Waifs and Strays of Celtic Tradition. Argyllshire Series, No. 4. London: David Nutt, 1891. xxxviii,292 pp.

*336. ———. SUPERSTITIONS OF THE HIGHLANDS & ISLANDS OF SCOTLAND. Collected entirely from oral sources. Glasgow: James MacLehose, 1900. xx,318 pp.

Flyleaf: Alexander Carmichael [?]/ Fayannillt [?]/ 1900.
Slight marginal strokes and checks on about 6 pp., for discussions of Gaelic terms.

CAMPBELL, Joseph, see Mac Cathmhaoil, Seosamh.

337. Campbell, Roy. ADAMASTOR. Poems. London: Faber & Faber, 1932. 108 pp.

Flyleaf: Song for the people 42/ The Serf 45/ The Zulu Girl 46/ Autumn 91/ The sisters 76. [all of these poems appear in the OBMV and all are excised from this vol.]

338. ———. THE FLAMING TERRAPIN. Poems. London: Jonathan Cape, 1924. 94 pp.

Some pp. uncut.

339. Canfield, Curtis, ed. PLAYS OF CHANGING IRELAND. New York: Macmillan, 1936. xv,481 pp.

Flyleaf: To W.B. and George Yeats/ With all my gratitude and best wishes --/ Curtis Canfield/ Amherst, Massachusetts/ 1936.
Includes THE WORDS UPON THE WINDOW PANE.

340. Čapek, Karel. THE MACROPULOS SECRET. A Comedy. Translated by Paul Selver. London: Robert Holden, 1927. 211 pp.

Inside frt. cover: Lennox Robinson/ 1927

341. ———. R.U.R. (Rossum's Universal Robots). Translated by P. Selver and adapted for the English stage by Nigel Playfair. London: Oxford Univ. Press, 1923. 102 pp.

342. Caran d'Ache (Emmanuel Poiré). ALBUM (ALBUM TROISIÈME). Paris: E. Plon, Nourrit, n.d. 54 pp. Sig.: Lolly Yeats

Humorous drawings, with captions.

343. Carleton, William. ART MAGUIRE, OR THE BROKEN PLEDGE. Dublin: James Duffy, [188?]. viii,254 pp.

On paper cover, sig.: WBY

344. ———. THE BLACK PROPHET. A Tale of Irish Famine. Illus. by J.B. Yeats. London: Lawrence & Bullen, 1899. xvi,408 pp.

Frontispiece: "Yeats" [not WBY's]

345. ———. REDMOND COUNT O'HANLON. The Irish Rapparee. Dublin: James Duffy, 1886. 200 pp.

On paper cover, sig.: WBY

346. ———. RODY THE ROVER, OR THE RIBBONMAN. Dublin: James Duffy, [188?]. 239 pp.

On paper cover, sig.: WBY

*347. ———. TRAITS AND STORIES OF THE IRISH PEASANTRY. Edited by D.J. O'Donoghue. 4 vols. London: J.M. Dent, 1896.

Some pp. uncut in vols. 2 & 4.

348. Carr, H[erbert] Wildon. THE PHILOSOPHY OF BENEDETTO CROCE. The problem of Art and History. London: Macmillan, 1917. x,213 [2] pp.

Half title p.: Read in 1926.
Marginal strokes, underscorings, brief notes and comments, almost all between pp. 50-66 and applying the terminology of A VISION to Croce.
P. 50, in margin at last 6 lines: C.M. + B.F.
P. 50, bottom: C.M. forming ideas of the external changes image into fact
P. 52, margin, mid-page: C.M. - creative when influenced by mask
P. 61, margin, par. 2, lines 2-4: Not wholly, they interest in themselves
P. 61, margin, mid-page: the primary intuition must have "reality"
P. 63, margin, lines 4-5: Note insistence of "documents" upon abstraction in bodily life. "Mere matter" is product of Will + B.F. or of Will, C.M. + B.F.
P. 63, margin, at "What is brutal and impulsive": will
P. 64, margin, lines 5-6: Feeling is identified by him with "will" or "act."
P. 64, lines 21-22: Developed by Gentile
P. 64, bottom of p.: This reconciles the abstract nature of B.F. with its association with "fact"; That which is fated.
P. 177, marginal strokes in section on Art & Religion.

349. Carrà, Carlo. ANDRÉ DERAIN. Avec 32 reproductions. Rome: Valori Plastici, 1921. 22 pp., 32 plates.

350. Carroll, Lewis. THROUGH THE LOOKING-GLASS and what Alice found there. Illus. by John Tenniel. London: Macmillan, 1872. [12],224 pp.

351. Castiglione, Baldassare. THE BOOK OF THE COURTIER. Translated by Sir Thomas Hoby. The Tudor Translations. London: David Nutt, 1900. lxxxvii,377 pp. Bp: WBY

*352. CATALOGUE OF THE CELEBRATED COLLECTION OF GREEK, ROMAN, AND EGYPTIAN SCULPTURE AND ANCIENT GREEK VASES. Being a portion of the Hope Heirlooms ... which will be sold by Auction ... on Monday, July 23, 1917 ... by Messrs. Christie, Manson, and Woods. London: Printed by William Clowes, 1917. 47 pp.

353. Cattell, Raymond B[ernard]. THE FIGHT FOR OUR NATIONAL INTELLIGENCE. London: P.S. King, 1937. xx,166 pp.

Inserted, a pamphlet, 241.

354. Caulfield, James, ed. THE HISTORY OF THE GUN-POWDER PLOT. London: Vernor and Hood, 1804. 94 pp.

355. Cavalcanti, Guido. RIME, con introduzione e appendice bibliografica di E[milio] C[ecchi]. Lanciano: R. Carabba, 1910. 166 pp.

On paper cover: Georgie Hyde Lees/ Rome, May 1913.

356. ———. SONNETS AND BALLATE OF GUIDO CAVALCANTI. Translated by Ezra Pound. London: Stephen Swift, 1912. viii,135 pp.

Some pp. uncut after 51.

356a. Another copy.

P. 1, a stamped seal: Presentation Copy
Flyleaf: Georgie Hyde Lees./ June 28, 1912
P. 30, an ink stroke along "Sonetto VIII'
Inserted, two sheets, on each a handwritten copy of a poem in Italian with an English translation, "Epigramma di Giovanbattista Strozzi sopra la statua della" and "Resposta di Michelagnolo in persona della Notte." Hand unknown.

357. Cecil, David. THE STRICKEN DEER OR THE LIFE OF COWPER. London: Constable, 1930. xi,303 pp. Sig.: GY

358. Cellini, Benvenuto. THE LIFE OF BENVENUTO CELLINI. Translated by John Addington Symonds. London: Macmillan, 1923. liv,464 pp.

Some pp. uncut.

359. A CELTIC CHRISTMAS. Christmas Number of THE IRISH HOMESTEAD, Dec. 1902.

Includes Yeats's "She Dwelt Among the Sycamores."

360. ———. Dec. 1903.

Includes illustrations by Jack Yeats and Mrs. Jack Yeats.

361. ———. Dec. 1904.

Includes illustrations by Jack Yeats.

361a. Another copy.

362. ———. Dec. 1905.

Includes illustration by Jack Yeats.

*363. Cerfberr, Anatole and Jules Christophe. RÉPERTOIRE DE LA COMÉDIE HUMAINE DE H. DE BALZAC. Paris: Callman Lévy, 1893. xiii,563 pp. Bp: WBY

364. Chadwick, Hugh Brailsford. SAFETY GREEN. Selected poems and verses. Poole: The Wessex Press, 1935. 49 pp.

Flyleaf: To W.B. Yeats [there follows a dedicatory poem to Yeats]

365. CHAMBERS'S BIOGRAPHICAL DICTIONARY. Edited by David Patrick and Francis Hindes Groome. London: W. & R. Chambers, 1911. 1006 pp.

P. 990, an entry for WBY.

*366. CHAMBERS'S CYCLOPAEDIA OF ENGLISH LITERATURE. New edition by David Patrick. 3 vols. London: W. & R. Chambers, 1903.

VOL. 1 only, through Restoration literature.

*367. CHAMBERS'S ENGLISH DICTIONARY. Pronouncing, explanatory, etymological etc. Edited by Thomas Davidson. London: W. & R. Chambers, [1914]. 1294 pp.

368. Chapman, George. THE COMEDIES AND TRAGEDIES OF GEORGE CHAPMAN. 3 vols. London: John Pearson, 1873.

VOL. 1, ALL FOOLES is wholly cut.
VOL. 2, BUSSY D'AMBOIS cut; first half of MAY-DAY cut.
VOL. 3, uncut.

*369. ———. THE WORKS OF GEORGE CHAPMAN. Vol. 1: PLAYS, edited by Richard Herne Shepherd. New ed. London: Chatto & Windus, 1889. v,550 pp.

Plays cut in this vol. are THE BLIND BEGGAR OF ALEXANDRIA, BUSSY D'AMBOIS, THE REVENGE OF BUSSY D'AMBOIS, BYRON'S CONSPIRACY, THE TRAGEDY OF PHILIP CHABOT, ADMIRAL OF FRANCE.
P. 144: court
P. 149: idea of a king
P. 198, lengthwise in margin, a long comment, largely undecipherable, comparing violence in Bussy D'Ambois's day to present violence. (This at very end of Act III of THE REVENGE OF BUSSY D'AMBOIS.)
P. 199, bottom margin, a comment, completely canceled.
P. 203, a comment lengthwise in margin, partially undecipherable at passage beginning "To love nothing outward/ Or not within our own powers to command" in REVENGE OF BUSSY D'AMBOIS.
P. 217, in BYRON'S CONSPIRACY at line 5ff.: Man as machine [pencil; not WBY's].
End of vol., what would be p. 552 if paginated (just before advertisements), a long comment, only partially decipherable, attributing the popularity of the Byron tragedies to their: intense subjectivity.... Did not this subjectivity, by catching the attention with logic and feeling create ability? [The modern suppression of subjectivity, Yeats comments, has disrupted this old theatrical audience as well as the audience for oratory. The comment concludes:] They were quicker in thoughts as well as higher.

*370. ———. THE WORKS OF GEORGE CHAPMAN. Vol. 2: POEMS AND MINOR TRANSLATIONS. With an intro. by Algernon Charles Swinburne. New ed. London: Chatto & Windus, 1904. lxxv,435 pp.

Many pp. uncut.
Cut, Swinburne's "Essay on the Poetical and Dramatic Works of George Chapman," "Ovid's Banquet of Sense," "A Coronet for his Mistress Philosophy," the "Second Sestyad" of "Hero and Leander," THE SECOND MAIDEN'S TRAGEDY through Act 11, scene 2.

371. Charpentier, John. COLERIDGE, THE SUBLIME SOMNAMBULIST. Translated by M.V. Nugent. London: Constable, 1929. x,332 pp.

Flyleaf: list of topics, pencil, with p. refs:
Wittstengein [not WBY's; canceled; ink]
Coleridge meets a sage at Reading/ page 59
Read Plato, Plotinus, Berkeley/ page 84
Probably met Wordsworth in 1795/ page 118
Has influence on Wordsworth/ page 121/ 274 [?] (Words [?] 27)
When writing "Ancient Mariner," "Cristabel" etc. was reading Berkeley/ page 132
Ancient Mariner, first part of Cristabel & Kubla Khan was written [the following canceled] between spring of 1797 and [?] of 1798.
Marginal strokes on pp. 116, 118, 119, 120, 121, 131, 132, 133, 134, 135, 195, 205.
P. 56, line 9: Boethius
P. 59, line 12: "illuminate"
P. 84, at second par.: Plato, Plotinus, Berkeley
P. 110, lines 3-5: Thomas Taylor
P. 172, at "where Schiller resides": so far knew nothing of German philosophy
P. 172, at "in his notebooks": Boehme
P. 206, lines 1-5: light as sensation
A slip of paper inserted at P. 226 and annotations stop there.

372. Charubel (pseud.). THE DEGREES OF THE ZODIAC SYMBOLISED. To which is added THE THEORETICAL VALUE OF THE DEGREES OF THE ZODIAC by H.S. Green. London: Nichols, 1898. viii,121 pp. Bp:GY

P. iii gives a photograph of Charubel and the birth date of 9 Nov. 1826.

*373. Chatelain, Heli, ed. FOLK-TALES OF ANGOLA. Fifty Tales, with Ki-Mbundu text, literal English etc. Boston and New York: Published for the American Folk-lore Society by Houghton, Mifflin, 1894. xii,315 pp.

P. 51, bottom: Cinderella
P. 59, third par.: Cinderella again
P. 71, top, at "Thou ... divide so that we be equal":

Note ending is moral
P. 71, lengthwise in margin: note various tales of animals befriended. Cf. Georgian Tales about supper for lions[?].
P. 87, at pars. 2, 3, 4: Compare Georgian tales of children who [three words undecipherable].
P. 141, end of Tale XIII: compare Mermaid tales of girls [who] married men from heaven.
P. 247, end of Tale XLVIII: unusual moral
P. 252, blank page before Notes, a three line note, difficult to decipher, apparently listing topics from the Notes that follow.

374. Chatterton, Thomas. THE ROWLEY POEMS. Edited by Robert Steele. Decorated by Charles Ricketts. 2 vols. London: Hacon & Ricketts, 1898. -/210. BPS: WBY

375. Chattopadhyaya, Harindranath. CROSS-ROADS. Poems. Madras: Shama's Publishing House, 1934. 43 pp.

Flyleaf: W.B. Yeats,/ with the Author's Compliments/ c/o Sri Aurobindo/ Assam, [?]/ Pondicherry,/ S. India

*376. Chaucer, Geoffrey. THE POETICAL WORKS, from the text of Prof. Skeat. 3 vols. The World's Classics. London: Grant Richards, [1903]. Vol. 3: London: Oxford Univ. Press, [1906].

377. ———. THE WORKS OF GEOFFREY CHAUCER. Edited by F.S. Ellis; ornamented by Sir Edward Burne-Jones; printed by William Morris. Hammersmith: The Kelmscott Press, 1896. ii,554 pp.

Inside back cover: To W B Yeats/ For June 13, 1905 from/ [in column form] S C Cockerell, Edmund Gosse, A.H. Bullen, Wilfred Scawen Blunt, A.E. Horniman, Will Rothenstein, Augusta Gregory, Robert Gregory, E. Montgomery, Maurice Baring, Elkin Mathews, Castletown, John Masefield, Arthur Symons, Charles Ricketts, C.H. Shannon, Gilbert Murray, C.E. Lawrence, Una Birch, Hugh P. Lane, William Orpen, John Quinn, A. Sullivan, R.C. Trevelyan, Millicent Sutherland, John Shaw-Taylor.

*378. ———. THE WORKS OF GEOFFREY CHAUCER. Edited by Alfred W. Pollard etc. The Globe Edition. London: Macmillan, 1908. lv,772 pp.

Flyleaf: W B Yeats. Dec 9. 1910.
First 3 books of TROILUS cut; most of LEGENDE OF GOOD WOMEN cut; Glossary cut; otherwise mostly uncut.

379. Chekhov, Anton. THE CHERRY ORCHARD and other plays. Translated by Constance Garnett. London: Chatto & Windus, 1925. 273 pp.

Includes UNCLE VANYA, THE SEA-GULL, THE BEAR, THE PROPOSAL.

*380. ———. THE SEAGULL. Translated by Julius West. London: Hendersons, 1915. 74 pp.

381. Cheney, Sheldon. THE NEW MOVEMENT IN THE THEATRE. New York: Mitchell Kennerley, 1914. 303 pp.

Flyleaf: To/ W. B. Yeats/ with the kind/ regards of his/ Friend/ John Quinn/ New York/ April 8. 1915
Includes a reference to the Abbey Theatre.

CHESSON, Nora. See Hopper, Nora.

382. Chettur, Govinda Krishna. SOUNDS AND IMAGES. London: Erskine Macdonald, [1922]. 55 pp.

Flyleaf: With the Author's/ Compliments/ 17.xii.21
Dedicated to WBY.

383. Choiseul-Meuse, Félicité, Comtesse de. THE RETURN OF THE FAIRIES. Dublin: John Cummings, [1824]. vii,275 pp.

Flyleaf, an inscription from a Mrs. Baxter to Noah Watts, January 1845.
Inside frt. cover, a set of initials and the date: 1834. Also, a note [pencil, WBY]: [one word?] front titles/ [following this, a set of page numbers] 44 ["The King of Cocagne"]; 123 ["The Black Cat"]; 145 ["The Marvelous Voyage"]; 169 ["The Woodcutter's Daughter"].
P. 54, in "King of Cocagne" is cancelled.
None of these selections appear in Yeats's editions of fairy or folk tales.

384. Church, Richard. THE GLANCE BACKWARD. New Poems. London: J.M. Dent, 1930. xi,90 pp. -/750

Flyleaf: G.Y./ First Cuckoo/ p. 45
"On Hearing the First Cuckoo" is excised and appears in the OBMV.

385. ———. TWELVE NOON. Poems. London: J.M. Dent, 1936. viii,66 pp.

Inserted, a printed card presenting the book "With the author's compliments."
Also inserted, an envelope with a note from Church to Yeats, dated "7:ii. 36." Church would like Yeats to consider the poems in this vol. for the OBMV.

*386. [Cibot, Pierre Martial]. LETTRE SUR LES CARACTERES CHINOIS par Le Reverend Pere **** [Cibot], De la Compagnie de Jesus. [Bound with this]: LETTRE DE PÉKIN, SUR LE GÉNIE DE LA LANGUE CHINOISE, ET LA NATURE DE LEUR ÉCRITURE SYMBOLIQUE, COMPARÉE AVEC CELLE DES ANCIENS ÉGYPTIENS ETC. Bruxelles: J.L. De Boubers, 1773. 46 [49], plates, xxxviii pp.

Title p., the name "Kirker" is written in ink to the right of the asterisks for the author's name, but this is a mistaken attribution.

387. Cicero, Marcus Tullius and Pythagoras. SOMNIUM SCIPIONIS. Translated with an essay "The Vision of Scipio" considered as a fragment of the Mysteries" by L.O. THE GOLDEN VERSES OF PYTHAGORAS [translated with notes] by A.E.A. THE SYMBOLS OF PYTHAGORAS [translated with notes] by S[apere] A[ude]. COLLECTANEA HERMETICA. Edited by W. Wynn Westcott. Vol. 5. London: Theosophical Publishing Society, 1894. 72 pp.

Stamped on flyleaf: G.T. Pollexfen,/ Sligo
Title p., verso, a long note by WBY, very difficult to decipher, discussing classical sources for the "Great Year," especially the 8th, 9th, and 10th ages; sources mentioned are Servius (?), Plutarch, Sulla, and Censorinus (DE DIE NATALI, 17)
P. 3., stamped: G[eorge] T. Pollexfen/ Sligo.
P. 12, marginal markings, notes for section dealing with "Great Year."
Top margin: Macrobeas [Macrobius] - 15,000
Margin, at "original configuration": map
P. 13, notes dealing with the length of the "Great Year"
Top margin: length of Great Year - / 12,994 [but revised to 12,954] - Hortensius. p. 26 / (quoted) Tacitus - developed on [?], 28,816. chap. 16
Bottom margin: from death of Romulus to [one word] date of dreams 573 multiples of 20 = 11460
Pp. 16-30, marginal markings, underscorings for "Vision of Scipio."
P. 72: Dollinger Gentile & Jew/ p. 394
Back flyleaf:

Great Year

Plato
Polit. 269c
Tim[aeus] 39.D.F+
Rep[ublic] 545 C&F
Cic[ero] Timaeus 34 ff [canceled]

[James] Adam, Republic
ii.p.264 ff [Cambridge, 1897 & 1902]
Tim[aeus] 38 D.

Cic[ero] Timaeus 33; [one word] Som[nium] Scipionis, ii.2.29; Stobaeus, Eclogues (vol 1, p. 107, hence).
Seneca, Naturales Quaestiones, iii.29 th.ff.
Four Eclogues
Harvard [?] Studies. xiv. 19ff etc.
Warde Fowler.

388. THE CITIZEN'S MANUAL, being a simple guide through the new [Irish] constitution. By a member of the Bar. Dublin: James Duffy, 1938. 47 pp.

389. Clarke, Austin. PILGRIMAGE and other poems. London: George Allen & Unwin, 1929. 45 pp. -/500

*390. ———. THE VENGEANCE OF FIONN. Dublin & London: Maunsel, 1917. 60 pp.

Flyleaf: To W.B. Yeats,/ Poet./ In respect,/ Austin Clarke.

391. Clark, Barrett H[arper]. THE BLUSH OF SHAME. A few considerations on verbal obscenity in the theater. New York: Gotham Book Mart, 1932. 16 pp.

Title p.: For Wm. Butler Yeats/ with respect and/ admiration/ Barrett H. Clark/ 21 March 1932.

392. ———. THE BRITISH AND AMERICAN DRAMA OF TO-DAY. New York: Henry Holt, 1915. xiii,315 pp.

Flyleaf: To William Butler Yeats/ In memory of one of the/ most interesting and/ pleasant evenings I ever spent./ With the gratitude and best wishes of/ Barrett H. Clark/ New York 1915.

393. Claudel, Paul. L'ANNONCE FAITE À MARIE. Mystère en quatre actes. Paris: Nouvelle Revue Française, 1913. 210 pp.

394. ———. CORONA BENIGNITATIS ANNI DEI. 4th ed. Paris: Nouvelle Revue Française, 1915. 241 pp.

Poems.

395. Clifton, Harry. DIELMA and other poems. London: Duckworth, 1932. 88 pp.

Flyleaf: As Homage to the greatest Poet/ of Our Age/ Yeats/ "Much did I rage when young/ Being by the world oppres't..../ from the young poet Harry Clifton."
Some textual corrections and additions by the author.

396. ———. FLIGHT. Poems. London: Duckworth, 1934. 52 pp.

Flyleaf: Upon the Wheel/ To sage or fool/ It is thus and I try/ to follow the revolution/ of that starry wheel Yeats/ Harry Clifton/ As spirit to spirit/ not friend to friend.
Some textual corrections by author.

397. Clodd, Edward. MEMORIES. London: Watts, 1926. xi,288 pp.

Reminiscences include Edward Fitzgerald, F. York Powell, and Samuel Butler.

398. Cocteau, Jean. ORPHÉE. Tragedie en un acte. Paris: Librairie Stock, 1927. 131 pp. Sig.: GY

*399. Coleridge, Mary E[lizabeth]. POEMS. London: Elkin Mathews, 1909. xxi,214 pp.

400. Coleridge, Samuel Taylor. BIOGRAPHIA EPISTOLARIS, being the biographical supplement of Coleridge's Biographia

Literaria, with additional letters etc. by A. Turnbull. 2 vols. London: G. Bell, 1911.

401. ———. BIOGRAPHIA LITERARIA ... and two lay sermons "The Statesman's Manual" and "Blessed are ye that sow beside all waters." New ed. London: George Bell, 1876. v,440 pp.

Inside frt. cover, on paper label: From Coventry Patmore's Library
On 1st Contents p.: man & state - 360/ "notion of time" & space 61 [WBY's].
Pp. 61, 353, 354, 360, marginal strokes.
At pp. 56-7, a piece of paper inserted with: plating behind a looking-glass [WBY's; refers to passage on p. 57, "It is the mere quicksilver plating behind a looking glass ..."].

402. ———. THE FRIEND: a series of essays. London: George Bell, 1875. [6],389 pp.

On label inside frt. cover: From Coventry Patmore's Library.

402A. Another edition. Bohn's Standard Library. London: George Bell, 1906. [6],415 pp.

P. 102, marginal strokes and at top of p.: reason spirit/ understanding - G.M.
P. 104, a note referring to last two pars.: reasoning = spirit/ ideas = Celestial Body
P. 118, margin, mid-page: understanding
pure reason
P. 138, midpage: principle
Section I, marginal stroking passim.

*403. ———. POEMS. Selected and arranged with an intro. and notes by Arthur Symons. London: Methuen, 1905. 223 pp.

404. ———. THE POETICAL WORKS OF SAMUEL TAYLOR COLERIDGE. Edited by James Dykes Campbell. London: Macmillan, 1925. xcciv,667 pp. Sig.: GY

P. 149, page corner turned back for "Ode to Georgiana, Duchess of Devonshire."

405. ———. SELECT POETRY AND PROSE. Edited by Stephen Potter. London: Nonesuch Press, 1933. xxx,821 pp. Sig.: WBY

Inside back cover, WBY's signature, upside down.

406. ———. TABLE TALK, AND THE RIME OF THE ANCIENT MARINER, CHRISTABEL ETC. London: George Routledge, [1884]. xxvii,298 pp.

407. Coleridge, Sara. MEMOIR AND LETTERS OF SARA COLERIDGE. Edited by Edith Coleridge. 4th ed., abridged. London: Henry S. King, 1875. xxiv,439 pp.

*408. Collins, Clifton W[ilbraham]. SOPHOCLES. Ancient Classics for English Readers. Edinburgh and London: William Blackwood, 1897. 181 pp.

Back flyleaf, a list of titles of Greek plays by Sophocles, Aeschylus, and Euripides: Prometheus (A)[eschylus]/ Oedipus the King/ Oedipus at Colonus/ Seven against Thebes (A)[eschylus]/ Antigone/ Alcestis (E)[uripides]/ The Women of Trachis/ The Death of Ajax/ Philoctetes/ Agamemnon (A)[eschylus]/ Choephoroe (A)[eschylus] Electra (E)[uripides]/ Eumenides

409. COLLINS FOREIGN DICTIONARIES. ITALIAN. Italian-English, English-Italian. London and Glasgow: Collins, n.d. 448 pp.

410. Colum, Padraic. CREATURES. New York: Macmillan, 1927. 58 pp.

411. ———. POEMS. London: Macmillan, 1932. viii,223 pp.

On Contents p., a check beside "A Drover," p. 86, "Old Soldier," p. 104, "No Child," p. 115, "The Poor Girl's Meditation," p. 118, "Crane," p. 172. All except the last are excised in the text and appear in the OBMV. Checked in the text are "A Mountaineer," p. 106, and "An Old Woman of the Roads," p. 92.

412. ———. WILD EARTH. A Book of Verse. Dublin: Maunsel, 1907. 39 pp.

Flyleaf: to W.B. Yeats/ from/ Padraic Colum
Flyleaf, verso: A drover [there is also a stroke beside this title in Contents]
Corrections, not WBY's, inked in text, pp. 5, 8, 22, 38.
A few pp. uncut.

*412A. Another ed. Dublin: Maunsel, 1916. vi,73 pp.

Inserted, a small slip of paper with notes by WBY: Copy the Drover, pages 5 & 6. The sea bird on the wave, page 44.

413. THE COLUMBAN (Dublin) [a school journal]. 59 (April 1938).

The College of St. Columba.

*414. Colvin, Sidney. LANDOR. English Men of Letters. London: Macmillan, 1902. viii,229 pp. Bp: WBY

P. 27, passage on style and language in GEBIR stroked.

415. COMMON CONDITIONS. Edited by Tucker Brooke. Elizabethan Club Reprints, no. 1. New Haven: Yale Univ. Press, 1915. xv,90 pp.

An ed. of an anonymous Elizabethan play, A PLEASANT COMEDY, called COMMON CONDITIONS (1576).

Flyleaf: To Mrs. Yeats with the sincere/ regards of/ The Elizabethan/ Club/ Yale 18 Feb. 1920.
Uncut.

*416. CONCORDANCE TO THE CANONICAL BOOKS OF THE OLD AND NEW TESTAMENTS, to which are added a Concordance to the Books called Apocrypha and a Concordance to the Psalter. London: Society for Promoting Christian Knowledge, [1859]. iv,1168,75 pp.

*417. Congreve, William. THE COMEDIES. Edited by William E. Henley. 2 vols. English Classics. London: Methuen, 1895.

Pp. uncut in both vols.

418. Connolly, James B[rendan]. HEAD WINDS. Charles Scribners, 1916.

Comprises only the chapter titled "Mother Machree" which has been excised from the book (pp. 125-7); included is a cover sheet, but the rest of the book is missing.

419. ———. OUT OF GLOUCESTER. Charles Scribners, 1902.

Comprises only the chapter titled "A Fisherman of Costla" which has been excised from the book (pp. 93-129); included is a cover sheet, but the rest of the book is missing.

420. Conrad, Joseph. THE SISTERS. New York: Crosby Gaige, 1928. 70 pp.

Some pp. uncut.

421. ———. WELL DONE! London: Privately printed by Clement Shorter, 1918. 20 pp.

Opposite title p.: This little book contains three papers by Joseph Conrad first contributed to THE DAILY CHRONICLE of August 22nd, 23rd and 24th, 1918. They are issued here in an edition of twenty-five copies by kind permission of the author for private distribution among my friends. [in ink]: XI Clement Shorter.
About one-third uncut.

*422. Copleston, Reginald S[tephen]. AESCHYLUS. Ancient Classics for English Readers. Edinburgh and London: William Blackwood, 1870. [8],196 pp. Sig.: WBY

422A. Another edition, 1897.

423. Coppard, A[lfred] E[dgar]. THE COLLECTED POEMS. London: Jonathan Cape, 1928. 109 pp.

Flyleaf: The Apostate 74/ Mendacity 86/ ?Epitaph 93 [excised from text; they appear in OBMV].
Other poems with checks or queries (?), "Truant," 13;

"The Way to Tipperary," 15; "Autumn Song," 76; "Christmas Apple," 77; "Betty Perrin," 84; "The Troubadour," 95-96 (in the text, a pencil stroke canceling fifth stanza).

424. Cornford, Frances. DIFFERENT DAYS. Poems. London: The Hogarth Press, 1928. 47 pp.

Flyleaf: The Unbeseechable p 14/ A Glimpse p 24 ["A Glimpse" appears in OBMV].
Pp. 13-16, 23-4 excised.

425. ———. MOUNTAINS AND MOLEHILLS. Poems. Cambridge: The Univ. Press, 1935. viii,64 pp.

Flyleaf: Near an old Prison, p. 35; London Despair, p. 37; Soliloquy, p. 50; The Lake and the Instant, p. 51 [all excised from text except "Soliloquy"].
Checked in text, "After the Eumenides," "Night Nursery Thoughts," "Soliloquy."

*426. Coryate, Thomas. CORYAT'S CRUDITIES. London: 1611; reprint ed., 2 vols. Glasgow: James MacLehose, 1905. -/1000. Bp: GY

427. Cotterill, H[enry] B[ernard]. A HISTORY OF ART. 2 vols. London: George G. Harrap, 1922-4.

COUCH, Sir A.T.Q., see Quiller-Couch.

428. THE COURIER. (London) [newspaper], 18 January 1815.

P. 1, bracketed in ink, an advertisement announcing the foundation of a new "Galway School" erected by the Governors of Erasmus Smith's Schools.
P. 2, an "X" against an article entitled "Court Martial on Sir Jonh [sic] Murray, held at Winchester."
P. 3, an "X" against an unheadlined piece which begins "A Gentleman just returned from Ireland has sent us the following observations on the riots in the Dublin Theatre, and we give them in his own words."

429. Cousens, Henry. THE ARCHITECTURAL ANTIQUITIES OF WESTERN INDIA. London: The India Society, 1926. xi,86 pp., 57 plates.

*430. Cousins, James H[enry]. STRAIGHT AND CROOKED. Poems. London: Grant Richards, 1915. 64 pp.

Card inserted: To W.B. Yeats,/ Master,/ from/ pupil. James H. Cousins./ Garston,/ Spring 1915.
Some pp. uncut.

431. Cousturier, Lucie. SEURAT. Éditions des "Cahiers D'Aujourd'hui." Paris: Georges Crès, 1921. 35 pp., 41 plates. 160/1100

432. Craig, Edward Gordon. BOOKS AND THEATRES. London & Toronto: J.M. Dent, 1925. viii,163 pp.

433. ———. Review of DIDEROT'S WRITINGS ON THE THEATRE edited by F.C. Green and AN ACTOR PREPARES by Constantin Stanislavsky. THE SUNDAY TIMES, 20 June 1937, p. [9].

Inserted in 1218.
Across the top: Here it is. W.B.Y.

*434. ———. TOWARDS A NEW THEATRE. Forty Designs for Stage Scenes with Critical Notes by the Inventor. London: J.M. Dent, 1913. xvi,89 pp.

435. [Crane, Walter]. WALTER CRANE'S TOY BOOKS. [Eight short children's books bound in one volume--The Frog Prince, Goody Two Shoes, Beauty and the Beast, The Alphabet of Old Friends, The Yellow Dwarf, Aladdin or The Wonderful Lamp, The Hind in the Wood, Princess Belle Etoile]. London & New York: George Routledge, [1874?].

The bound vol. is introduced by a typed list of Contents.

436. Crespi, Angelo. CONTEMPORARY THOUGHT OF ITALY. London: Williams and Norgate, 1926. ix,249 pp.

P. 160, bottom: I (let us say) negate Swinburne, as part of an historical movement. But as transcendental ego I recreate his world. The transcendental ego may not be dialectical, but only empirical. [WBY]
P. 161-3, marked.

437. THE CRITERION (London). 2 (July 1924).

Includes THE CAT AND THE MOON (uncut).

438. ———. 14 (July 1935).

Includes Yeats's MANDOOKYA UPANISHAD; title has been changed by WBY (ink) to: Introduction to Mandookya Upanishad.
The translations have been canceled; looks like printer's copy.

439. ———. Index. 14 (Oct. 1934-July 1935).

Index includes items by or about Yeats.

440. Croce, Benedetto. AESTHETIC AS SCIENCE OF EXPRESSION AND GENERAL LINGUISTIC. Translated by Douglas Ainslie. 2nd ed. London: Macmillan, 1922. xxx,503 pp.

Marginal strokes, underscorings in first 189 pp.
P. 6, at "abstraction is mechanism": B.F.
P. 6, at "It is the matter ... is changeable": See description of the luring [?] of the subjective in Carr. See "A Vision."
P. 60, last par. is stroked and a comment below:

Aesthetic knows nature = ? P.B. (Beauty)
economical wills nature = Husk (use)
Intellect knows universals = ? Spirit (brute [?])
Moral nature wills universal = C.B. (good [?])

P. 122, at "confound expression with impression": medicine [?] = impression

P. 146, comment at "so in the case of language": B. Russell does this because Realist [?]

Markings are heaviest from pp. 122-150.

441. ———. ARIOSTO, SHAKESPEARE AND CORNEILLE. Translated by Douglas Ainslie. London: George Allen & Unwin, [1921]. viii,440 pp.

442. ———. AN AUTOBIOGRAPHY. Translated by R.G. Collingwood. Oxford: The Clarendon Press, 1927. 116 pp. Bp: WBY

443. ———. HISTORICAL MATERIALISM AND THE ECONOMICS OF KARL MARX. Translated by C.M. Meredith. London: George Allen & Unwin, 1922. xxiv,188 pp.

A few marginal strokes to p. 90.
After p. 121, many pp. uncut.
Inserted, a newspaper clipping, 996.

444. ———. LOGIC AS THE SCIENCE OF THE PURE CONCEPT. Translated by Douglas Ainslie. London: Macmillan, 1917. xxxiii,[1],606 pp.

Many marginal strokes, underscorings, and brief notes and comments, especially in first half of book.

P. 35, at phrase "of acquired knowledge": See System in 'Vision.'

P. 42, lines 11-15 stroked in margin and comment at bottom: What he calls definition of group Berkeley calls by a name. Much of this book is Berkeley clarified.

P. 56, at phrase "That is to say ... the spirit": Pure Thought

P. 57, bottom margin: ? Concrete = CB
Universal = spirit

P. 58, at "facts ... as effective forces": Bert. Russell

P. 73, a comment referring to lines 17-20: does 'distinction' imply space - it would to a pre-Socratic, space or air, and does 'clearness' imply Time. Only a moment of perception?

P. 81, in top margin, referring to lines 6-11: "Unity of Being"

P. 85, referring to lines 23-7: great wheel

P. 88, at phrase "a certain number of concepts":

P. 88, at phrase "hence we are compelled":

p. 95, at bottom, referring to line 8: x p[hase] 3 and p[hase] 17 are certainly two positives to our contemplation but certainly "sin" being "out of phase", is not from "the opposite" but made up as his other values [last four words ??].

P. 97, top margin, referring to lines 9-12: Blake distinguishes between opposite and negations

P. 97, bottom margin: P[hase] 17 affirms its 'intensity' against the "dispersal" of p[hase] 3 which in its turn is physically [?] radiant as against the concentration of p[hase] 17. Each affirms the other.

P. 107, bottom margin, referring to lines 3-5: He does not account for the ancient pairs of opposites, △ & ▽ 🜃 & 🜁 & their spiritual equivalent for which the Four Moments descend. If they are not opposites, what is the experience which makes us so name them? It is true that if △ sees himself as △ the ▽ will be his mere negation, and if he desire to become B (his beloved) he may see her as ▽ & his △ as negation, but to C, A is △ & B is ▽ .

P. 157, at lines 6-10: see Plotinus/ also (alone) the one/ - the good.

P. 159, top margin, an arrow drawn from first par. of p. 158 to:

obscure sensibility	= "will"	Alone creative
clear intuition	= 'mask'	
Thought of universe	= "C.M."	reflex
knowledge of event	= "B.F."	

P. 172, referring to par. 2: sense - data reaction

P. 177, bottom margin, referring to end of first par.:

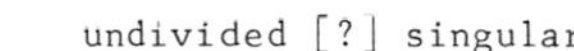

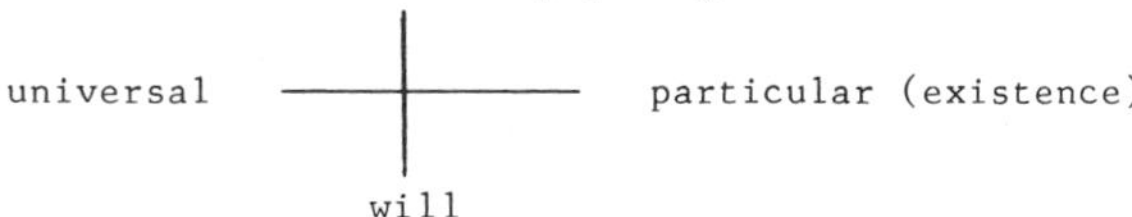

P. 208, at lines 9-10: Diomedes [?]

P. 227, at last 10 lines: Platonic
Christian

P. 228, lines 1-3: materialist

P. 228, lines 13-5: Blake's use of mystery

P. 230, at phrase "continuous operation of the a priori": ? Daimon

P. 239, top margin, referring to phrase "all the predicates that exhaust ... ": Daimon = Reality itself or creation as ordered in all lives by its individual

P. 239, bottom margin: God is all reality. Therefore we always think him. He is the negation of mystery.

P. 259, bottom margin: Should I count memory which is broken and conditioned by pseudo concepts an abstraction? The "Record" is not abstraction.

P. 263, at lines 4-8: ? Daimon

P. 285, at "predicate": apparition

P. 304, bottom margin, continued on 305: in dream "no concrete image from the memory" = no isolated image recalled by an empirical concept. Dream is pure representation of (mask only) yet we never affirm anything as real, all that comes [?] is as nothing

P. 304, top, a continuation of the above: memory abstract. Therefore can have no part in the Divine Vision.
P. 310, bottom margin referring to lines 12-3: implies Spengler if not 'Dove or Swan'
P. 313, bottom margin continued on top of p. 314 referring to lines 15-19 and first two on 314: in 'Dove or Swan' all is history but not if philosophical problems of art and emotional life in general are creative, this reflex (practical) [???]
P. 316, bottom margin: ? "experience" which "consumes itself away" not being antithetical. The representative ephemeral in event is immortal being a wish. It confers its immortality on what enters it. Revelation because it meets desire [?] is not consumed away - desire [?] of life not of proof.
P. 320, at lines 12-16: Spengler seems to but truth does not mean this
P. 329, at lines 15-19: P [?] affirms by the concept what is. X in all its change
P. 344, at lines 12-22: Berkeley "non existence of matter"
P. 394, at lines 5-6: ? Daimon
P. 394, at lines 8-10: to man
P. 394, at lines 18-20: non-being
P. 442-529 not marked.
P. 530, comment referring to last 3 lines: early Berkeley. Is this time [?]
P. 540 to end, no marks.

445. ———. THE PHILOSOPHY OF GIAMBATTISTA VICO. Translated by R.G. Collingwood. London: Howard Latimer, 1913. xii,317 pp.

Flyleaf: W.B. Yeats. August 1924/ from George Yeats
Marginal strokes, underscorings, a few brief notes.
P. 103, top: state of nature = savage/ Practical certitude = heroic or barbaric/ Practical truth = civilised
P. 163: Stephens or the Veda, is the way to interpret early Ireland.
P. 209, at "when in a popular republic": Dr. Swift

446. ———. PHILOSOPHY OF THE PRACTICAL. ECONOMIC AND ETHIC. Translated by Douglas Ainslie. London: Macmillan, 1913. xxxix,[1],591 pp.

Flyleaf: W B Yeats/ April 1926
Many marginal strokes, underscorings, and brief notes and comments throughout.
P. 45, top margin, referring to lines 7 and 8: will comes before judgment
P. 75, top margin, referring to lines 2-4: becoming in Gentile
P. 79, top margin, referring to lines 2-4: BF is CM of other
P. 80, referring to lines 20-3: only true of the "empiric ego"/ There is prevision

P. 86, referring to line 7: Unity of Being
P. 90, top, referring to line 7: art
P. 90, top, referring to line 8: primary
P. 92, referring to lines 17-19: History
P. 93, first par.: argument again final. Heaven & Hell
P. 171, at lines 11-15: inward = theoretical/ outward = practical
P. 173, at lines 7-9: See page 45
P. 205, top: will & Aesthetic = particular = man/ Intellect & Ethic = general = daimon [one word?]
P. 205, at lines 11-17: Husk not in daimon
P. 205, bottom: Daimon = good & truth
Man = Beauty; pleasure & pain
P. 206, top: In daimon pleasure (say) exists as in the subject matter of a picture where all is beauty.
P. 342, at lines 20-3: will is amoral (but see p. 513)
P. 342, at bottom: aesthetic is amoral
P. 347, bottom: morality implicit in will/ Philosophy implicit in aesthetic
P. 351, bottom: after death the good (C.B.) prevails but the [one word?]/ This in truth (spirit)
P. 355, at line 9: C.B.
P. 355, at line 12: Spirit
P. 358, top: Will = all activities dominated exclusively by conceptions of pleasure and pain.
P. 363, at line 23: Will
P. 363, at line 24: B.F.
P. 410: passions = will/ Hence mask and will are particulars.
P. 443, top: economic = volition of individual (will)
ethic = volition of universal (B.F.)
P. 458, top, referring to first 4 lines: consider in relation to Shelley's "liberty"
P. 484, referring to "platinum ... degrees": not volitional
P. 508, at lines 12-13: "apples" is a pseudo-concept. They are like each other, not cliched.
P. 513, at lines 21-7: Blake note to Swedenborg/ 'no good will' but see p. 355, line 16 and what is said elsewhere (p. 342) of innocence that is also "will."
P. 529, at lines 2-4: Morality and interpretation of of souls each is other's B.F. & Mask
P. 540, at line 9: Modern Italy
P. 546, at lines 16-21: 17th century & natural rights
Inside back cover:

Japanese
ritual & masks
- art of the few
b[?] of art studies
studio
= moon
Cuchulain - Bales [sic] Strand
Four Plays
Hawk Woman

447. ———. THE POETRY OF DANTE. Translated by Douglas Ainslie. London: George Allen & Unwin, 1922. vi,313 pp.

A few pp. uncut.

448. ———. WHAT IS LIVING AND WHAT IS DEAD OF THE PHILOSOPHY OF HEGEL. Translated by Douglas Ainslie. London: Macmillan, 1915. xviii,217 pp. Sig.: WBY

449. Crookes, William. RESEARCHES IN THE PHENOMENA OF SPIRITUALISM. Reprint from THE QUARTERLY JOURNAL OF SCIENCE. London: J. Burns, [1874]. 112 pp. Bp: Annie M. Cooke

450. Cuala Industries. MEMORANDUM AND ARTICLES OF ASSOCIATION OF CUALA INDUSTRIES, LIMITED. Incorporated 6 Oct. 1938. 16 pp.

Inserted, a holograph letter to "The Registrar of Companies, Dublin Castle": Dear Sir/ The Cuala Industries Ltd., having no assets or liabilities wish to be struck off the Register./ Yours faithfully/ Bertha Georgie Yeats/ director [no date].

451. Cuala Press. COMPLETE LIST OF BOOKS PRINTED AND PUBLISHED BY CUALA PRESS, FORMERLY NAMED DUN EMER PRESS, 1903-1926, n.d. 6 pp.

"x's" inked beside a number of titles.
P. 6, WBY's,: 37 in all [37 titles that is] [one or two illegible words] W B Yeats/ 1926.

452. ———. LIST OF BOOKS. CUALA PRESS. Churchtown, [1914]. 4 pp.

P. 1, (John Quinn's hand?): Fred Hanna Bookseller 29 Nassau St./ has some of the out of print books.
P. 2-3, marks and notes. Listed as "In preparation" is "Memory Harbour: A Revery On My Childhood and Youth by W.B." "Memory Harbour" has been canceled.
Inserted, a 4 pp. leaflet, an advertisement for The Dun Emer Press. Listed as in preparation is A.E.'s THE NUTS OF KNOWLEDGE (1903).

*453. Cudworth, R[alph]. THE TRUE INTELLECTUAL SYSTEM OF THE UNIVERSE. The first part; wherein, all the reason and philosophy of atheism is confuted.... London: Richard Royston, 1678. [20],889,[84] pp. Pagination is erratic.

Flyleaf: to William Butler Yeats/ from Emery Walker/ March 26, 1917.
Paper slips inserted at pp. 238-9 (Hesiod's THEOGONIA); 334-5 (Egyptians belief in a first and supreme god); 470 [should be 365] (Euripides and other Greek poets as asserters of a divine monarchy; also quotes Euripides on "everlasting gyres").
A few pencil strokes in the unpaginated Preface.

454. Another edition. 3 vols. London: Thomas Tegg, 1845. Bps : WBY

Some pp. uncut.

455. Cumont, Franz. ASTROLOGY AND RELIGION AMONG THE GREEKS AND ROMANS. New York and London: G.P. Putnam's, 1912. xxvii,208 pp. Bp: GY

Marginal strokes, underscorings, and brief notes passim.
P. 11, bottom: Sophocles dies 406/ Plato dies 348
P. 135, lines 10-12: see Blake
P. 137, line 14: not to Plutarch
P. 165, line 12: check Plautus [one word?]

456. Ćurcin, M[ilan]. IVAN MESTROVIĆ. A Monograph. London: Williams and Norgate, 1919. xiv,94 pp., 68 plates.

Plate XV, "The Slave," and "A Portal Figure" is marked by an envelope addressed to WBY at Riversdale, Rathfarnham and dated 3 Aug. 1933. No insertion.

*457. Curry, S[amuel] S[ilas]. IMAGINATION AND DRAMATIC INSTINCT. Some practical steps for their development. Boston: The Expression Co., 1896. [4],369 pp.

*458. ———. THE PROVINCE OF EXPRESSION. A Search for Principles underlying adequate methods of developing Dramatic and Oratoric Delivery. Boston: School of Expression, 1891. xv,[4],461 pp.

*459. Curtin, Jeremiah, ed. HERO-TALES OF IRELAND. London: Macmillan, 1894. lii,558 pp.

Stamped on title p.: Presentation Copy
Marks and underscoring pp. 101, 135, 161, 162, 163, 170, 179, 180, 181.
P. 104, a note: They say wild cats have hooks in the tail.
Inside back cover: 11 [?] change to a dark witch

*460. Däath, Henrich. MEDICAL ASTROLOGY. Astrological manuals, no. 9. London: Sold by L.N. Fowler, n.d. xi,[1],108 pp.

Flyleaf, upside down: Norreys [?] Connell - probably Eve 29. April. 1874.

461. Dalton, O[rmonde] M[addock]. BYZANTINE ART AND ARCHAEOLOGY. Oxford: Clarendon Press, 1911. xix,727 pp. Bp: WBY

Flyleaf: W B Yeats. August 1924.
Pp. 212 & 213 marked by paper slip. Subject is carving in ivory. Two plates here, "Translation of relics" and "An empress."
Pp. 404 & 405 marked by paper slip. Subject is mosaics

in Christian East. Plate of mosaics in the Martorana, Palermo.

462. Daly, James. THE GUILTY SUN. [Pittsburgh]: Folio Press, 1926. 43 pp.

Poems.
Flyleaf: August, 1927/ Humbly to/ W.B. Yeats/ from/ James Daly

463. Damon, S[amuel] Foster. WILLIAM BLAKE, HIS PHILOSOPHY AND SYMBOLS. London: Constable, 1924. xv,487 pp.

Some pp. uncut.

*464. Dampier, Captain William. DAMPIER'S VOYAGES. Edited by John Masefield. 2 vols. London: Grant Richards, 1906.

Flyleaf: W B Yeats/ from John Masefield/ Dec 31, 1906
Many pp. uncut.

465. Dan, Professor Inō, ed. THE YEAR BOOK OF JAPANESE ART 1927. Toyko: National committee on intellectual co-operation of the League of Nations, 1928. xiii,[1],162 pp., 120 plates.

Includes plates of work by Puvis de Chavannes and El Greco.

*466. Dante Alighieri. IL CONVITO. THE BANQUET OF DANTE ALIGHIERI. Translated by Elizabeth Price Sayer. London: George Routledge, 1887. 286 pp. Sig.: A. Senier

Pp. 81-5 cut; otherwise uncut.

467. ———. THE CONVIVIO OF DANTE ALIGHIERI. [Translated by Philip H. Wicksteed.] The Temple Classics. London: J. M. Dent, 1909. ii,446 pp. Bp: GY. Sig.: Georgie Hyde Lees

Marginal pencil strokes passim.

468. ———. DANTE'S INFERNO. Translated by Laurence Binyon. London: Macmillan, 1933. ix,401 pp. Bp: WBY

469. ———. DANTE'S PURGATORIO. Translated by Laurence Binyon. London: Macmillan, 1938. vii,395 pp.

*470. ———. THE INFERNO OF DANTE ALIGHIERI. Translated by John Aitken Carlyle. Temple Classics. London: J.M. Dent, 1912. 402 pp.

Flyleaf: Georgie Hyde Lees/ January, 1911
Marginal strokes, suggestions for correction of the translation in the early cantos (through Canto vii), likely GY's.

471. ———. THE PARADISO OF DANTE ALIGHIERI. Translated by P.H. Wicksteed. Temple Classics. London: J.M. Dent,

1910. 418,[2] pp.

Flyleaf: Georgie Hyde Lees./ November, 1910
A number of quotations written in by G.Y.

*472. ———. THE PURGATORIO OF DANTE ALIGHIERI. Translated by T[homas] O[key]. Temple Classics. London: J.M. Dent, 1906. 442 pp.

Flyleaf: Georgie Hyde Lees/ January 1911

473. ———. THE PURGATORY OF DANTE ALIGHIERI. I-XXVII. Translated by Charles Lancelot Shadwell. Introduction by Walter Pater. London: Macmillan, 1892. xxviii,411 pp. Bp: WBY

Inserted, a printed slip: With the Translator's Compliments [and stamped:] Presentation Copy

474. ———. THE PURGATORY OF DANTE ALIGHIERI. PART II. THE EARTHLY PARADISE (CANTOS XXVIII - XXXIII). Translated by Charles Lancelot Shadwell. London: Macmillan, 1899. Bp: WBY

Introduction uncut; uncut after Canto XXX.

475. ———. A TRANSLATION OF THE LATIN WORKS OF DANTE ALIGHIERI. Translated by A.G. Ferrers Howell and Philip H. Wicksteed. Temple Classics. London: J.M. Dent, 1904. viii,428 pp.

Flyleaf: Georgie Hyde Lees/ Xmas, 1912.
Back flyleaf, GBY's, penciled notes on Quakers, intellectualism, Aquinas, Scotus, Pragmatism, and God.

476. ———. THE VISION: OR HELL, PURGATORY, AND PARADISE OF DANTE ALIGHIERI. Translated by H.F. Cary. The Chandos Classics. London and New York: Frederick Warne, 1890. 434 pp.

Title p.: W B Yeats. October 1891.
Mostly uncut after "Hell," Canto 13.
"Paradise," Cantos 29 to end mostly cut.

*477. ———. THE VITA NUOVA OF DANTE. Edited by Ralph Radcliffe-Whitehead. London: The Chiswick Press, 1892. 194 pp.

Flyleaf: Georgie Hyde Lees/ December, 1911
Back flyleaf, appreciations of Dante's work, in Italian, copied by GHL.

*478. D'Annunzio, Gabriele. FRANCESCA DA RIMINI. Translated by Arthur Symons. London: William Heinemann, 1902. xiv, 223 pp. Sig.: WBY

P. 67 which gives stage directions for Act II has slight pencil sketches as for the set.

479. D'Arcy, Charles F[rederick]. THE CHRISTIAN OUTLOOK IN THE MODERN WORLD. London: Hodder and Stoughton, [1929]. 256 pp.

Flyleaf: "Xmas 1929" [not WBY]
Inside frt. cover, pasted in, an unidentified newspaper review of this book.

*480. [Daryush, Elizabeth (Elizabeth Bridges)]. ΧΑΡΙΤΕΣΣΙ (CHARITESSI). Poems. Cambridge: Bowes and Bowes, 1912. 35 pp. Bp: WBY

Flyleaf, pencil: VII/ XV/ XVI [refers to poems in this vol.]

480a. Another copy.

481. ———. THE LAST MAN AND OTHER VERSES. London: Oxford Univ. Press, 1936. 62 pp.

Card inserted: With the author's compliments.
About half the pp. are uncut.

482. ———. SONNETS FROM HAFEZ AND OTHER VERSES. London: Oxford Univ. Press, 1921. 48 pp.

*483. ———. VERSES. Oxford: B.H. Blackwell, 1916. 30 pp.

484. ———. VERSES. London: Oxford Univ. Press, 1930. 43,[1] pp.

Flyleaf: XVI/ XX/ XXIII [refers to poems in this vol.]

485. ———. VERSES, SECOND BOOK. London: Oxford Univ. Press, 1932. 71,[1] pp.

Flyleaf: XLVII/ LIX/ LXI [refers to poems in this vol.]

486. David, Villiers. POEMS. London: The Unicorn Press, 1936. 44 pp.

Flyleaf: To W.B. Yeats/ from his humble admirer/ Villiers David
A letter of presentation from David to Yeats inserted mentioning that David met WBY at Emilie Grigsby's where Yeats gave him a ms. of one of his poems.

*487. Davidson, John. IN A MUSIC-HALL AND OTHER POEMS. London: Ward and Downey, 1891. vii,120 pp.

Half title p.: W.B. Yeats/ from J.D./ 13.1.92
In Contents, an "x" is placed against the titles "Selene Eden," "Epilogue," "The Gleeman," "The Triumph of Love," "Is Love Worth Learning," "For Lovers."

488. Davies, Rev. James. HESIOD AND THEOGNIS. Ancient Classics for English Readers. Edinburgh and London: William Blackwood, 1873. vii,166 pp. Sig.: Arthur Graves [?].

Back flyleaf, a few comments, not WBY's.

*489. Davies, Oliver. BETWEEN-TIME POEMS. London: John Lane, 1909. ix,106 pp. Sig.: Oliver Davies

Some pp. uncut.
Inserted, a 2 page letter from James Guthrie (Flansham, Bagnor, Sussex, 9 Oct. 1909) to WBY discussing the poetry of Oliver Davies and WBY's work on Blake.

490. Davies, W[illiam] H[enry]. AMBITION AND OTHER POEMS. London: Jonathan Cape, 1929. 32 pp.

Slip inserted in Contents (not WBY): Davies W.H. Ambition/ Page 12 For Sale/ Page 20 Moss and Feather/ 29-- Born of Tears/ 31-- In Winter [titles do not correspond to Davies's selection in OBMV]

*491. ———. COLLECTED POEMS. London: A.C. Fifield, 1916. vii,160 pp.

Corners turned back for a number of poems.
P. 83, "Money" marked by a ribbon and checked.

492. ———. LOVE POEMS. London: Jonathan Cape, 1935. 60 pp.

A few pp. uncut.

493. ———. MOSS AND FEATHER. The Ariel Poems, no. 10. London: Faber & Gwyer, 1928. 3 pp.

*494. ———. NATURE POEMS AND OTHERS. London: A.C. Fifield, 1908. 62 pp.

Flyleaf: To W.B. Yeats from James Guthrie

495. ———. THE POEMS OF W.H. DAVIES. London: Jonathan Cape, 1934. 475 pp.

Flyleaf, a list of poems which appear in the OBMV, sometimes with page number, sometimes poem number. "Schools Out," "Joy and Pleasure," "Truly Great," "Money," "The Sluggard," "Leisure." Pages for these poems excised. Also listed, "The Moth," p. 82, "In the Country," p. 203 and "The Best Friend," 153. Of these, only the last two are excised.

496. Davis, B[ernard] E[ustace] C[uthbert]. EDMUND SPENSER, A CRITICAL STUDY. Cambridge: The Univ. Press, 1933. vii, 266 pp.

497. Davis, Thomas. ESSAYS LITERARY AND HISTORICAL. With preface by D.J. O'Donoghue and an essay by John Mitchel. Dundalk: Dundalgan Press, 1914. xxiii,[3],456 pp.

*498. ———. PROSE WRITINGS. Edited by T.W. Rolleston. The Camelot Series. London: Walter Scott, [1890]. xiv, [2],285 pp. Sig.: WBY

Some pp. uncut.

498a. Another copy.

Pp. uncut.

499. [Day, John (attributed to)]. THE RETURN FROM PARNASSUS. Or the scourge of simony. Edited by Oliphant Smeaton. London: J.M. Dent, 1905. xxxii,135 pp.

500. De Blacam, Aodh. OLD WINE. Verses from the Irish, Spanish, and Latin done chiefly in Irish metres. Dublin: At the sign of the three candles, [1936?]. 35 pp.

501. Dee, Dr. John. A TRUE & FAITHFUL RELATION OF WHAT PASSED FOR MANY YEERS [sic] BETWEEN DR. JOHN DEE ... AND SOME SPIRITS .... Out of the original copy, ... kept in the library of Thomas Cotton. Edited with a preface by Meric Casaubon. London: T. Garthwait, 1659. [70], table,488,45,[15] pp. Bp: WBY

In Preface some passages marked by drawing of a hand with pointing finger. Not WBY's.

502. Dekker, Thomas. THE GULL'S HORNBOOK. Edited by R.B. McKerrow. London: The De La More Press, 1904. viii, 107 pp.

A few pp. uncut.

*503. ———. THOMAS DEKKER. The Mermaid Series. Edited by Ernest Rhys. London: T. Fisher Unwin, [1894]. xlv, [1],473 pp.

Includes THE SHOEMAKER'S HOLIDAY, THE HONEST WHORE, OLD FORTUNATUS, and THE WITCH OF EDMONTON.

504. De la Mare, Walter. ALONE. The Ariel Poems, no. 4. London: Faber & Gwyer, [1927]. 3 pp.

505. ———. AT FIRST SIGHT. A novel. New York: Crosby Gaige, 1928. 142 pp. Sig.: Walter de la Mare

Some pp. uncut.

506. ———. DING DONG BELL. London: Selwyn & Blount, 1924. ix,76 pp.

*507. ———. THE LISTENERS AND OTHER POEMS. London: Constable, 1916. ix,92 pp.

*508. ———. PEACOCK PIE, A BOOK OF RHYMES. London: Constable, 1913. viii,122 pp.

509. ———. POEMS, 1901 to 1918. 2 vols. London: Constable, 1932.

VOL. 1, flyleaf, a list of poems and p. numbers. All except "An Epitaph" are excised and appear in OBMV: Echo 88, Winter 128, What is that 142 [correct title is "All that's past"], An Epitaph, 178, The Listeners, 163.

VOL. 2, flyleaf, list of poems and p. numbers: Silver Penny vol. 2, 17, Off the ground 153, The Song of

Soldiers ["Silver Penny" appears in OBMV and is excised; the other two do not, though "Off the ground" is excised.]
Not listed, but excised and used in OBMV is "The Scribe," Vol. 1, p. 248.

510. ———. SELF TO SELF. The Ariel Poems, no. 11. London: Faber & Gwyer, [1928]. 3 pp.

511. ———. A SNOWDROP. The Ariel Poems, no. 20. London: Faber & Faber, [1929]. 3 pp.

512. ———. THE VEIL AND OTHER POEMS. London: Constable, 1928. xi,92 pp.

Uncut.

*513. Delanne, Gabriel. LES APPARITIONS MATÉRIALISÉES DES VIVANTS & DES MORTS. Tome II [only vol. here]. Paris: Librairie Spirite, 1911. iv,841 pp.

Includes photographs; many pp uncut.
P. 680, marginal stroke at passage referring to Katie King and Miss Cook.
P. 681, a reference to a book by Farmer, TWIXT TWO WORLDS, is underscored.
P. 689, a passage on a spirit who could not show himself to a woman because he was naked is marked and in margin: are ghosts naked?

514. Dempsey, Rev. T[homas]. THE DELPHIC ORACLE. Its early history, influence and fall. Oxford: B.H. Blackwell, 1918. xxiii,199,[1] pp.

Page corners turned back, 56 (women as mediums and oracles), 80 (chapter on D.O. and politics), 112 (D.O. and religion).

515. Dennis, J[onas]. SUBVERSION OF MATERIALISM, BY CREDIBLE ATTESTATION OF SUPERNATURAL OCCURRENCES. Bath: Upham, Collings, & Binns, 1826. xviii,159 pp.

516. De Quincey, Thomas. CONFESSIONS OF AN ENGLISH OPIUM-EATER. With intro. by William Sharp. London: Walter Scott, 1886. xxviii,275 pp. Sig.: WBY. 1887

Includes "Levana," "The Rosicrucians and Freemasons," "Notes from the Pocket-Book of the Late Opium-Eater" etc.

517. De Selincourt, Basil. Review of THE OXFORD BOOK OF MODERN VERSE edited by WBY. THE OBSERVER, 22 Nov. 1936, p. 5. Inserted in 1972.

518. Deussen, Paul. OUTLINE OF THE VEDANTA SYSTEM OF PHILOSOPHY ACCORDING TO SHANKARA. Translated by J.H. Woods and C.B. Runkle. 2nd ed. Cambridge: Harvard Univ. Press, 1927. x,45 pp.

P. 6, a slight correction in the text.

*519. De Vere, Sir Aubrey. JULIAN THE APOSTATE AND THE DUKE OF MERCIA. Historical Dramas. London: Basil Pickering, 1858. xx,[2],343 pp.

Half title p.: W.B. Yeats Esq/ from Aubrey de Vere

*520. Devine, Rev. Arthur. A MANUAL OF MYSTICAL THEOLOGY. London: R. & T. Washbourne, 1903. xvi,664 pp.

Marginal strokes, underscoring pp. 29-33, 41, 42, 204-6, 216, 378, 381, 399. P. 242 turned back.

521. Day, Sri Mukul Chandra. MY PILGRIMAGES TO AJANTA & BAGH. Intro. by Laurence Binyon. London: Thornton Butterworth, 1925. Plates, 245 pp.

522. THE DIAL. 76 (March 1924).

Includes illustrations by Jack Yeats, pp. 264-5.

*523. Diogenes Läertius. THE LIVES AND OPINIONS OF EMINENT PHILOSOPHERS. Translated by C.D. Yonge. Bohn's Classical Library. London: George Bell, 1909. viii,488 pp.

Flyleaf: Images. P. 441 [appears to be Ezra Pound's hand. On p. 441 an extended bracket in the right margin marks off two pars. in "Epicurus" from "It is useful, also, to retain this principle" to "these images are only light substances destitute of depth."]

524. Dobell, Sydney. THE POEMS OF SYDNEY DOBELL. London: Walter Scott, 1887. xxviii,316 pp.

525. Dodgson, Campbell. A CATALOGUE OF ETCHINGS BY AUGUSTUS JOHN, 1901-1914. London: Charles Chenil, 1920. xi,[1], 151 pp. 21/325. Bp: Bethel and Gertrude Solomons

526. THE DOME (London), no. 3. (Michaelmas Day, 1897).

P. 93, one of "Four Notes" reports a reader's disapproval of Yeats's "The Desire of Man and Woman" which had appeared in the previous number of THE DOME (no. 2).

*527. ———. n.s., 5 (Nov. 1899-Jan. 1900).

Contains "Aodh to Dectora. A Song." "The Irish Literary Theatre, 1900. A Note by W.B. Yeats."

*528. ———. n.s., 6 (Feb.-April 1900).

Contains "Symbolism in Modern Poetry. A Note by W.B. Yeats." Some pp. uncut.

529. Donaghy, John Lyle. PRIMORDIA CAECA. Dublin: Eason, 1927. 33 pp.

Poems.

Flyleaf: W B Yeats/ from J.L. Donaghy/ October 1927. Mostly uncut.

530. Donne, John. COMPLETE POETRY AND SELECTED PROSE. Edited by John Hayward. New York: The Nonesuch Press, 1929. xxiii,793 pp. 103/675. Bp: WBY

Flyleaf: WBY./ from George/ 1930

*531. ———. THE POEMS OF JOHN DONNE. Edited by Herbert J.C. Grierson. 2 vols. Oxford: Clarendon Press, 1912.

VOL. 1, many pages uncut; wholly or largely cut are "Songs and Sonets," "Elegies," "Satyres," "The Progress of the Soule," pp. 295-316.

VOL. 2, cut are Grierson's Introduction and the commentaries to the poetry listed under vol. 1; also cut the commentary on "Letters to Severall Personages."

*532. Donne, William Bodham. EURIPIDES. Ancient Classics for English Readers. Edinburgh and London: William Blackwood, 1872. vi,204 pp.

532a. Another printing, 1898.

533. Donnelly, John J. SUBJECTIVE CONCEPTS OF HUMANS. Source of Spiritistic Manifestations. New York: The International Press, 1922. xvi,555 pp.

Flyleaf: To Mr. W.B. Yeats/ With the compliments of the Author,/ John J. Donnelly/ Feby 4th, 1924.
Marginal strokes, pp. 12, 13, 27, 149.
P. 543, bottom: Yet each shares the whole mind if its prototype. Then dies - only this relation to one another.
Inside back cover and on back flyleaf are criticisms of the inadequacies of this book, very difficult to read:

Three states

(1) he is unaware of images

See Table — (2) aware but controlls each image/ thinks [?] these images own image of him [?]. He speaks to the primary image through this secondary image. John Doe controlls Peter Roe because controlls image of John Doe in Peter Doe's [sic] mind.

See Life [?] Table — (3) He loses control of the secondary image and the primary image he never controlls [-] gets an independent life.
Weakness of book is that it is confusing all phenomenon and the images, subordinate and primary, of persons perceived when alive. He thinks of the way that a secondary image cannot speak and the perception of primary images. Hence complexity [?] of insisting that St. Paul did not see Christ's

image [?] but that of some follower of his.

[The criticism continues for 14 lines on the facing page, very difficult to decipher; refers to William of Norgate and Swedenborg].

534. [Doolittle, Hilda]. H.D. HYMEN. Poems. London: The Egoist Press, 1921. 47 pp.

*535. ———. SEA GARDEN. Poems. London: Constable, 1916. v,47 pp.

Flyleaf: To/ William Butler Yeats/ from/ H.D.
Some pp. uncut.
Inserted, a holograph note: 44 Mecklenburgh Square/ W.C./ Dear Mr. Yeats: -- Richard has written me asking if I sent you my book -- he wanted to send it to you himself -- Do not concern yourself with comment upon the poems. I send it only as a slight mark of appreciation of your own beautiful work. With best wishes -- H. Aldington.

536. Doro, Edward. ALMS FOR OBLIVION. Poems. Paris: Casa Editorial Franco-Ibero-Americana, 1932. 38 pp.

*537. Doughty, Charles M[ontagu]. ADAM CAST FORTH. Sacred drama in five songs. London: Duckworth, 1908. 124 pp.

Many pp. uncut.

538. ———. TRAVELS IN ARABIA DESERTA. 2 vols. London: Jonathan Cape and the Medici Society, 1923. BPS: WBY

*539. ———. WANDERINGS IN ARABIA. Being an Abridgement of TRAVELS IN ARABIA DESERTA. Edited by Edward Garnett. 2 vols. London: Duckworth, 1908. BPS: WBY

540. Douglas, Norman. IN THE BEGINNING. London: Chatto and Windus, 1929. 272 pp.

Novel.

541. Dowden, John. THE SAINTS IN THE CALENDAR AND THE IRISH SYNOD. A sermon preached in St. Stephen's, Dublin, on Sunday, June 22, 1873. Dublin: Edward Ponsonby, 1873. 28 pp.

John Dowden was the elder brother of Edward Dowden.

*542. Dowson, Ernest. DECORATIONS: IN VERSE AND PROSE. London: Leonard Smithers, 1899. viii,50 pp.

*543. ———. THE POEMS OF ERNEST DOWSON. With a memoir by Arthur Symons and four illustrations by Aubrey Beardsley and a portrait by William Rothenstein. London: John Lane, 1909. xxxviii,166 pp. Bp: WBY

In Contents poems checked are "Non sum qualis eram...," "O Mors! quam amara est...," "Villanelle of the Poet's Road," "Dregs," "A Last Word." (All appear in OBMV.)

544. ———. THE POETICAL WORKS. Edited by Desmond Flower. London: Cassell, 1934. xxxvi,297 pp.

Flyleaf, a list of poems: To one in Bedlam 10, Flos Lunae 21, Non sum qualis etc. 22, O Mors 27, Vesperal 42, Extreme Unction 47, Villanelle of the poet's road 74, Dregs 87, Exchanges 93 [all appear in OBMV and all are excised].

*545. ———. VERSES. London: Leonard Smithers, 1896. xii, 57 pp. 93/300

Flyleaf: W B Yeats/ 1896
Flyleaf, verso: "Non sum qualis etc 17" "O Mors etc. 23"

546. Drayton, Michael. NIMPHIDIA, THE COURT OF FAYRIE. Stratford-upon-Avon: The Shakespeare Head Press, 1921. 30 pp. 510/283

547. THE DREAM OF RAVAN. A Mystery. Reprinted from THE DUBLIN UNIVERSITY MAGAZINE. London: The Theosophical Publishing Society, 1895. iv,248 pp.

Flyleaf: From James Stephens/ to W.B. Yeats/ Christmas 1933.

*548. Drinkwater, John. COPHETUA. A play in one act. London: David Nutt, 1911. [16] pp.

*549. ———. LYRICAL AND OTHER POEMS. Cranleigh: The Samurai Press, 1908. 56 pp.

Opposite title p.: To/ W.B. Yeats/ from/ John Drinkwater/ 1908/ One who has/ "come from among/ the runners and read" -- not quickly, but/ lovingly -- a little/ as a stranger, perhaps,/ but -- lovingly.

550. ———. PERSEPHONE. New York: William Edwin Rudge, 1926. 16 pp. Sig.: John Drinkwater

Mostly uncut.

*551. ———. POEMS OF LOVE AND EARTH. London: David Nutt, 1912. vi,63 pp.

Opposite title p.: W.B. Yeats/ from/ John Drinkwater/ July 1912.

*552. ———. POEMS OF MEN AND HOURS. London: David Nutt, 1911. viii,54 pp.

Opposite title p.: To/ W.B. Yeats/ from/ John Drinkwater/ July 1911.

*553. ———. REBELLION. A Play in Three Acts. London: David Nutt, 1914. 58 pp.

554. ———. RUPERT BROOKE. An essay. London: Printed for the author at the Chiswick Press, 1916. 22 pp. 114/115

Opposite title p.: To/ W.B. Yeats/ from/ John Drinkwater/ 1916.

*555. ———. THE STORM. A play in one act. [Birmingham]: Published by the author at the Birmingham Repertory Theatre, 1915. 19 pp.

Opposite title p.: To/ W.B. Yeats/ from/ John Drinkwater/ May 1915.

556. ———. SUMMER HARVEST, POEMS 1924-1933. London: Sidgwick & Jackson, 1933. xii,175 pp.

Flyleaf: W.B. Yeats,/ not asking him to read them,/ but in grateful thanks for an/ ever memorable first evening/ in Dublin, from/ John Drinkwater./ January 1937.

556a. Another copy with presentation from Drinkwater to Yeats, dated November 1933.

*557. Drummond, Sir William. THE OEDIPUS JUDAICUS. London: Reeves and Turner, 1866. 266 pp.

Mostly uncut.

*558. Drummond of Hawthornden, William. A CYPRESS GROVE. Stratford-on-Avon: The Shakespeare Head Press, 1907. [2],48 pp.

*559. Dryden, John. JOHN DRYDEN. Plays. Edited by George Saintsbury. 2 vols. The Mermaid Series. London: T. Fisher Unwin, [1904].

Includes ALL FOR LOVE, THE SPANISH FRIAR, ALBION AND ALBANIUS, DON SEBASTIAN, ALMANZOR AND ALMAHIDE, MARRIAGE A LA MODE, AURENG-ZEBE.

*559a. Another copy, vol. 2 only. Sig.: GY

*560. ———. THE POETICAL WORKS. Edited by W.D. Christie. London: Macmillan, 1908. lxxxviii,662 pp.

Cut are Contents p., a few songs, and "The Secular Masque."

561. DUBLIN FIGARO. The Topical Journal of Ireland, n.s., 1 (18 June 1892).

Includes "Sketch, literary and literal, of W.B. Yeats," pp. 278-9; sketch of Maude Gonne, p. 279. Drawings and literary gossip.

562. THE DUBLIN MAGAZINE. 2 (January 1924).

Includes "John Butler Yeats, R.H.A.," by Thomas Bodkin; with reproduced portraits of Lily Yeats and Mrs. Tynan Hinkson by JBY.

563. ———. 6 (Oct.-Dec. 1931).

Includes "THE WORDS UPON THE WINDOW PANE: A Commentary."

564. ———. 7 (Jan.-March 1932).

Includes "THE WORDS UPON THE WINDOW PANE: A Commentary. Part 2."

565. ———. 7 (Apr.-June 1932).

Includes "Introduction to FIGHTING THE WAVES."

566. ———. 8 (Oct.-Dec. 1933).

567. ———. 9 (Apr.-June 1934).

Includes Padraic Fallon's review of THE WINDING STAIR AND OTHER POEMS.

568. ———. 11 (Apr.-June 1936).

Includes Padraic Colum's "A Poet's Progress in the Theatre" (on Yeats's COLLECTED PLAYS) and an anonymous review of DRAMATIS PERSONAE.

569. ———. 13 (Apr.-June 1938).

Mostly uncut.

570. [DUBLIN] MUNICIPAL GALLERY OF MODERN ART. Illustrated Catalogue, with biographical and critical notes. Dublin: Dollard, 1908. [7],ix,[1],63,[iii] pp., plates.

On paper cover in blue pencil: Yeats [Ezra Pound's hand] Includes reproductions of JBY's portrait of Standish O'Grady and portraits of WBY, Dr. Douglas Hyde, Mrs. Katharine Tynan Hinkson, and Sir Horace Plunkett.

571. [DUBLIN] MUNICIPAL GALLERY OF MODERN ART AND CIVIC MUSEUM. [Book of plates of items in collections]. Dublin: Browne and Nolan, 1933. Unpaginated.

Flyleaf: To W.B. Yeats, Esq./ With Compts./ for John J. Reynolds/ Curator/ 30 Decr. 1933

571a. Another copy.

Flyleaf: To W.B. Yeats, Esq./ with compliments/ John J. Reynolds/ Curator/ 1 July 1933

572. [DUBLIN UNIVERSITY MAGAZINE]. Review of MEMOIRS OF JOSEPH HOLT edited by T. Crofton Croker. [DUBLIN UNIVERSITY MAGAZINE] 12 (July 1838): 72-4.

Inserted in 904.

572A. DUBLIN UNIVERSITY REVIEW. 1 (March 1885).

Includes Yeats's "Song of the Faeries," "Voices."

573. ———. 1 (April 1885).

Includes Yeats's "Island of Statues."

574. ———. 1 (May 1885).

Yeats's "Island of Statues" cont.

575. ———. 1 (Aug.-Dec. 1885). Bound vol.

Flyleaf: W B Yeats/ 58 Eardley Crescent/ South Kensington
Includes Yeats's "The Seeker" and "An Epilogue. To 'The Island of Statues' and 'The Seeker.'"

576. ———. 1 (Sept. 1885).

Includes "The Seeker."

576a. Another copy.

On cover: Yeats [not WBY's]
Some lines in "The Seeker" numbered in text

577. ———. 1 (Oct. 1885).

On cover: Yeats [not WBY's]
Includes "An Epilogue. To 'The Island of Statues' and 'The Seeker.'"
Lines numbered in text of "An Epilogue."

577a. Another copy.

Missing covers; on the back a sketch of three men by JBY.

578. ———. 2 (Feb. 1886).

On front cover: W.B. Yeats 151 [unlikely WBY's]
Includes Yeats's "Life."

579. ———. 2 (March 1886).

Front cover: Yeats [not WBY's]
Includes "The Two Titans, A Political Poem."

579a-b. Two other copies.

580. ———. 2 (April 1886).

Includes "On Mr. Nettleship's Picture at the Royal Hibernian Academy."
P. 281, two sketches of a woman, probably JBY's.
At back, a slight sketch and a recipe for minced beef.

581. ———. 2 (Oct. 1886).

Front cover: Yeats [not WBY's]
Includes "Miserrimus" and "From the Book of Kauri the Indian - Section V. on the Nature of God."

582. ———. 2 (Nov. 1886).

Includes "The Poetry of Sir Samuel Ferguson."

583. ———. 2 (Dec. 1886).

Front cover: (976) [refers to p. number of Yeats's "An Indian Song" included].
Also contains a printed letter critical of WBY's essay on Ferguson.

*584. Du Chaillu, Paul B[elloni]. THE VIKING AGE: THE EARLY HISTORY, MANNERS, AND CUSTOMS OF THE ANCESTORS OF THE ENGLISH-SPEAKING NATIONS. 2 vols. London: John Murray, 1889.

Vol. 1 only.

585. Duffy, The Honorable Charles Gavan, ed. THE BALLAD POETRY OF IRELAND 40TH ED. and THE NATIONAL AND HISTORICAL BALLADS, SONGS AND POEMS OF THOMAS DAVIS. Dublin: James Duffy, 1874. 244,x,254 pp.

Two vols. bound as one.
Marginal strokes in first 80 pp. of BALLAD POETRY.
Also marked in Contents "Soggarth Aroon," p. 57; "The Emigrant Mother," p. 78; "The Fair Hills of Ireland, p. 194" [possibly for Yeats's selection for A BOOK OF IRISH VERSE].

*586. ———. SHORT LIFE OF THOMAS DAVIS, 1840-1846. [sic] London: T. Fisher Unwin, 1895. [6],250 pp.

*587. ———. YOUNG IRELAND. A fragment of Irish history, 1840-5. London: T. Fisher Unwin, 1896. xvi,[2],196, xi,[3],240 pp.

Two vols. bound as one.

588. Dunne, J[ohn] W[illiam]. AN EXPERIMENT WITH TIME. London: A. & C. Black, 1929. viii,213 pp.

Inside frt. cover: Yeats [not WBY's]

589. Dunsany, Lord [Edward John Moreton]. THE OLD FOLK OF THE CENTURIES. A Play. London: Elkin Mathews & Marrot, 1930. [4],66 pp. 352/900

*590. ———. THE SWORD OF WELLERAN. And other stories. London: George Allen, 1908. xi,[1],243 pp. Bp: Anne Butler Yeats/ 1934

Flyleaf: W.B. Yeats/ from/ Dunsany

591. ———. THE TRAVEL TALES OF MR. JOSEPH JORKENS. London & New York: G.P. Putnam's, 1931. vii,[1],304,[1] pp.

*592. Düntzer, Heinrich. LIFE OF GOETHE. Translated by Thomas W. Lyster. 2 vols. London: Macmillan, 1883. xxii,462 pp.

Flyleaf: J.B. Yeats/ from T.W. Lyster/ October 27, 1883
P. 12, a slight comment on the text, not WBY's.
P. 27, JBY's marginal sketch of the boy Goethe "listening over the top of his book" to an Italian lesson being given by his father to his sister Cornelia.
P. 47, a marginal stroke against a reference to discrimination against Jews.

*592A. Popular edition. London: T. Fisher Unwin, 1908. xiv, 796 pp.

593. Du Prel, Carl. THE PHILOSOPHY OF MYSTICISM. Translated by C.C. Massey. 2 vols. London: George Redway, 1889. Bps: WBY.

Vol. 2, a few pp. uncut.

594. Durer, Albert. THE LITTLE PASSION OF ALBERT DURER. London: George Bell, 1894. 17 pp., 37 illus.

Plates with Latin poems on facing pages.
Flyleaf: George:/ from Lennox./ Oct. 16th 1925

*595. Dutt, Romesh Chunder. THE LITERATURE OF BENGAL. A biographical and critical history from the earliest times closing with a review of intellectual progress under the British rule in India. Calcutta: Thacker Spink, 1895. v,[1],250 pp.

Many pp. uncut.
Bottom of Contents p.: Vidyapati said to be chief [?] poet [ink, WBY]

596. Dutt, Toru. LIFE AND LETTERS OF TORU DUTT. [Edited by] Harihar Das. London: Oxford Univ. Press, 1921. xiv, [2],364 pp. Bp: WBY

Flyleaf: With love and best wishes/ From A. & M. T[ucker?]/ Christmas 1921.

597. Easdale, Joan Adeney. CLEMENCE AND CLARE. Hogarth Living Poets, no. 19. London: The Hogarth Press, 1932. 48 pp.

598. ———. A COLLECTION OF POEMS. London: The Hogarth Press, 1931. 88 pp.

599. THE EASTERN BUDDHIST. (Otani University Library, Kyoto, Japan). 1 (July 1921). Uncut.

599a-l. Twelve more consecutive numbers, from Vol. 1 (Aug. 1921) to Vol. 4 (July-Aug.-Sept. 1927).

Almost wholly uncut except 3 (Apr.-May-June 1924) which is mostly cut.

*600. Eastlake, Allan. THE ONEIDA COMMUNITY. A Record of an attempt to carry out the principles of Christian unselfishness and scientific race-improvement. London: George Redway, 1900. viii,158 pp. Stamped on half-title p.: Sent for review.

Many pp. uncut.

*601. Eckartshausen, The Councillor Von [Karl von]. THE CLOUD UPON THE SANCTUARY. Translated by Isabel de Steiger. Intro. by Arthur Edward Waite. London: Philip Wellby, 1903. xvi,116 pp.

602. Edel, Fritz. GERMAN LABOUR SERVICE. Terramare Publications, no. 6. Berlin: Terramare Office, 1937. 31 pp.

603. Eglinton, John [William K. Magee]. BARDS AND SAINTS. The Tower Press Booklets, no. 5. Dublin: Maunsel, 1906. 55 pp.

Mostly uncut.

604. ———. IRISH LITERARY PORTRAITS. London: Macmillan, 1935. [6],157,[1] pp.

Includes "Yeats and His Story," pp. 17-35.

605. ———. TWO ESSAYS ON THE REMNANT. Dublin: Whaley, 1894. [bound with] PEBBLES FROM A BROOK. Kilkenny: Standish O'Grady, 1901. xiii,[1],49,[1],115 pp.

In PEBBLES, some marginal strokes.
Also, p. 19, 81, 115, notes, mostly erased, from WBY to himself reminding him to quote material for the Dun Emer ed.
Pp. 26-7, deletion marks in "Heroic Literature."

606. ———, W.B. Yeats, A.E., and W[illiam] Larminie. LITERARY IDEALS IN IRELAND. London: T. Fisher Unwin, 1899; Dublin: Daily Express Office, 1899. xx,88 pp.

Yeats contributed "A Note on National Drama," "John Eglinton and Spiritual Art," and "Autumn of the Flesh." Some pencil corrections to advertisements at end.

606a. Another copy.

Sig.: J E Archer/ Sept. 12 1899
In brown paper jacket with title pasted on spine.

607. Einstein, Albert. THE MEANING OF RELATIVITY. Four lectures delivered at Princeton University, May, 1921. Translated by Edwin Plimpton Adams. London: Methuen, 1922. vi,124 pp.

608. THE ELECTION. A Comedy of Three Acts. London: no publisher, 1749 and James Thomson [after Shakespeare etc.]. CORIOLANUS. A Tragedy. Dublin: G. and A. Ewing,

J. Hoey, A. Bradley, J. Exshaw, W. Brien, and J. Esdall, 1749 [bound with] Thomas Otway [after Moliere] THE CHEATS OF SCAPIN. A Farce. Dublin: James Hoey, 1733 and P[aul] H[iffernan], M.D. THE SELF-ENAMOUR'D OR THE LADIES DOCTOR. A Comedy. Dublin: Augustus Long, 1750. 66[4],ii,57,[3],[1],vi,68 pp.

Four plays bound in one vol.

609. Eliot, John. THE PARLEMENT OF PRATLERS. A series of Elizabethan dialogues and monologues illustrating daily life and the conduct of a gentleman on the grand tour extracted from ORTHO-EPIA GALLICA etc. Edited by Jack Lindsay. London: The Fanfrolico Press, 1928. 119 pp. Sigs.: Hall Collins [illustrator] and Jack Lindsay.

75 copies; in place of the limitation no. is written: William Butler Yeats [not WBY's]

610. Eliot, T[homas] S[tearns]. AFTER STRANGE GODS. A Primer of Modern Heresy. London: Faber & Faber, 1934. 68 pp.

611. ———. COLLECTED POEMS, 1909-1935. London: Faber & Faber, 1936. 191 pp.

Flyleaf: to/William Butler Yeats/ with the author's homage/ T.S. Eliot/ 1936
P. 100, in ASH WEDNESDAY, section 5, line 8, "Against the World" corrected to: Against the Word [Eliot's]

612. ———. DANTE. London: Faber & Faber, 1929. 69 pp.

*613. ———. EZRA POUND, HIS METRIC AND POETRY. New York: Alfred A. Knopf, 1917. 31 pp.

Flyleaf: To W.B. Yeats/ With the kind regards/ of John Quinn/ January 18/ 18.

614. ———. HOMAGE TO JOHN DRYDEN. Three essays on the poetry of the seventeenth century. London: The Hogarth Press, 1924. 46 pp. Sig.: WBY

On dedication p.: W.B. Yeats from/ Lily Yeats/ Xmas 1924.

615. ———. JOURNEY OF THE MAGI. The Ariel Poems, no. 8. London: Faber & Gwyer, [1927]. [3] pp.

P. 3, bottom: for W.B. Yeats./ in admiration./ T.S. Eliot/ 17.8.27.

616. ———. MURDER IN THE CATHEDRAL. London: Faber & Faber, 1935. 87 pp.

Flyleaf: to/ William Butler Yeats/ from/ T.S. Eliot/ 5.11 [?].35
P. 11, three lines of the opening chorus have stress marks penciled in.

P. 18, the Chorus is bracketed.
P. 20, an "X" before "O Thomas our Lord ..."
P. 21, the second Priest's speech, to bottom of p., is bracketed.
P. 69, an ink stroke before the Chorus.
P. 70, an ink stroke before "Dead upon the tree ..."
P. 75, Chorus is bracketed to "Falling blood"
[These selections may have been intended for the OBMV, but they do not appear there.]

617. ———. POEMS, 1909-1925. London: Faber & Faber, 1932. 128 pp. Sig.: GY

617a. Another printing, 1933.

Contents, p. 7, WBY has written numbers beside 5 poem titles apparently to indicate space allotments in the OBMV; on the bottom of p. 8 he writes: about 13 pages. The numbers do not add up to 13, but Eliot's selection in the OBMV, with two additions, does total almost 13 pages:
Preludes 28: 3½
The Hippopotamus 67: 2½
Whispers of Immortality 72: 2
Sweeney among the Nightingales 78: 2-3/4
The Hollow Men 123: 6
Excised are pp. 27-32, 67-74, 77-80, 123-128.

*618. ———. PRUFROCK AND OTHER OBSERVATIONS. London: The Egoist, 1917. 40 pp.

619. Another copy.

Inserted, printed press notices of A PORTRAIT OF THE ARTIST.

620. ———. THE ROCK. A Pageant. London: Faber & Faber, 1934. 86 pp. Sig.: GY

621. ———. THE SACRED WOOD. Essays on Poetry and Criticism. London: Methuen, 1920. xviii,155 pp. Sig.: GY

Flyleaf: OM/ 1920 [not WBY's]
Back flyleaf, in pencil, unknown hand: T.S. Eliot/ 9. Clarence Gate Gardens/ NW./ Paddington 3331

622. ———. A SONG FOR SIMEON. The Ariel Poems, no. 16. London: Faber & Gwyer, [1928]. 3 pp.

623. ———. SWEENEY AGONISTES. London: Faber & Faber, 1932. 31 pp.

Pp. 25-6, short ink strokes are placed to mark off the beginning and the end of "Song by Wauchope and Horsfall/ Swarts as Tambo. Snow as Bones."

624. ———. THE USE OF POETRY AND THE USE OF CRITICISM. London: Faber & Faber, 1937. 156 pp. Sig.: GY

625. ———. THE WASTE LAND. London: The Hogarth Press, 1923. 35 pp.

Flyleaf: For William Butler Yeats Esqre/ in admiration of/ his work./ T.S. Eliot/ 26.4.23
Almost wholly uncut; with Eliot's inked corrections in the text, some on uncut pp.
P. 7, "under" to: over [in "A crowd flowed under London Bridge"]
P. 9, "Coloured" to: carvèn [sic] [in "In which sad light a coloured dolphin"]
P. 29, in Notes, "Macmillan" to: Cambridge [in "From Ritual to Romance (Macmillan)"]

625a. Another copy.

Bp: Lily Yeats

*626. Ellis, Edwin J[ohn]. SANCAN THE BARD. London: Ward and Downey, 1895. 55 pp.

A play.

*627. ———. SEEN IN THREE DAYS. Written, drawn, and tinted by Edwin J. Ellis. London: Bernard Quaritch, 1893. 59 pp.

A long poem, illustrated in the manner of Blake. Inserted, two reproductions of drawings by William T. Horton; one is entitled in pencil "The Beloved." Inserted, a sheet folded quarto on which Ellis has copied Blake's annotations to Lavater's "Aphorisms on Man," Nos. 44, 59, 60, 61, 62, 63, 66, 67, 68, 69, 70, 71, 73, 78, 80, 81, 82, 83, 86, 92, 93, 94, 96, 97, 98, 99, 107, 114, 115, 121, 124, 141, 150, 151, 157.

*628. Ellis, F[rederick] S[tartridge]. A LEXICAL CONCORDANCE TO THE POETICAL WORKS OF PERCY BYSSHE SHELLEY. London: Bernard Quaritch, 1892. xi,[1],818 pp.

EMERY, Florence. See Farr, Florence.

629. THE ENCYCLOPAEDIA BRITTANICA, 11th ed. 29 vols. New York, 1910.

630. ———. The New Volumes, constituting, in combination with the twenty-nine vols. of the eleventh ed., the Twelfth Ed. 3 vols. London, 1922.

Vol. 32, section on Philosophy, pp. 94, 95, 97, 98, 99, marks, underscorings, and notes.

P. 95, a note: Russell thinks we know "physical objects" by "description," as we know other minds by "description." There is no analogy, for we sense other minds because the "description" describes also our own minds. Other minds are merely "exciting causes."

P. 95 again in article signed by A[lfred] E[dward] T[aylor] a passage underlined, "Presentations, i.e. mental

'contents,' which psychologists have usually regarded as immediate objects of cognition from which we may go on to infer propositions about the extra-mental things which are their exciting causes, are then dismissed as unnecessary fictions."
P. 97, margin of 1st column: Berkeley & Whitehead
P. 99, margin of 1st column, a check against passage dealing with influence of Berkeley and Hume on J.T. Mertz and: Berkeley.

631. THE ENEMY. (London). A Review of Art and Literature. Edited by Wyndham Lewis. 1 (Jan. 1927).

632. ———. 1 (Sept. 1927).

633. ———. 1 (First Quarter, 1929).

No more published.

634. THE ENGLISH PRAYER BOOK. Together with the Psalter or Psalms of David. London: Society of SS. Peter and Paul, 1915. vii,[1],142 pp.

635. THE ENGLISH REVIEW, no. 117 (Aug. 1918).

Contains "In Memory of Robert Gregory," p. 82.
P. 82, slight corrections in text, "The tower set by the stream's edge" to: on the stream's edge. [first appears thus in THE LITTLE REVIEW, Sept. 1918]. "And Eserkely plains" to: Or Eserkelly plain [LITTLE REV.]
Underlined, "All the combustible world."

*636. Ennemosier, Joseph. THE HISTORY OF MAGIC. To which is added an appendix of the most remarkable and best authenticated stories of apparitions, dreams, second sight, somnambulism, predictions, divination, witchcraft, vampires, fairies, table-turning, and spirit-rapping. Translated by William Howitt. Edited by Mary Howitt. 2 vols. London: H.G. Bohn, 1854. Bp: George R. Alexander.

Vol. 1 only.
Markings, pp. 3, 8, 10, 11, 14.
Inserted at p. 17, the calling card of Mrs. Charlotte H. Berbine. On back: Judge & Mrs. LeFevre/ Hotel de Londres/ Rue Castiglione [not WBY's]

637. THE ERASMIAN. (Magazine of the High School, Dublin), n.s., 28 (Apr. 1937).

Contains "What Then?"
On cover: Dr. Yeats [not WBY's]

637a. Another copy.

638. Erdmann, Johann Eduard. A HISTORY OF PHILOSOPHY. English translation edited by Williston S. Hough. Vol. 2.

MODERN PHILOSOPHY. London: Allen & Unwin, 1924.

Inside front cover: (On Development of Berkeley's thought/ Herman Cohen) [possibly WBY's]
Back flyleaf: Sound and meaning in English poetry/ K.M. Wilson/ Cape [not WBY's]
Inside back cover, Yeats makes three drafts of his "Spilt Milk." The final draft first appears in WADE 168.

[I, ink] We that had such settled things
Such duties fixed and known
Are poured and thinned, and dribbled out
Like milk on a flat stone

[II, ink] We that had such thought
That
~~And~~ such great deeds had done,
Must ramble on
~~But Ramble now~~ - thinned out
Like milk on a flat stone

Nov 1930

[this draft canceled in pencil]

[III, pencil] - exactly as in WADE 168.

Stroking and underscoring, pp. 182-4, 188, 246, 374-97 (Kant).

*639. Ernst, Otto. MASTER FLACHSMANN (Flachsmann als Erzieher). A comedy. Translated by H.M. Beatty. London: T. Fisher Unwin, 1909. 155 pp.

640. Esson, Luis. DEAD TIMBER AND OTHER PLAYS. London: Hendersons, 1920. 60 pp.

641. Estens, John Locke. THE PARACLETE AND MAHDI. Or the exact testimony of science to revelation and exposition of the most ancient mysteries and cults [etc.]. Sydney: John Sands, 1912. xvi,498,xxv pp. Bp: GY

Title p. loose and mutilated.
Marginal strokes, underscorings, and brief notes passim.

642. [Eugen, Prins]. PRINS EUGEN [monograph on the Swedish artist]. Sma Konstböcker, no. 15. Lund: Gleerupska Universitets-Bokhandeln, [1912?]. 64 pp.

643. THE EUGENICS REVIEW (London). 28 (Oct. 1936).

Includes Raymond Cattell's "Is National Intelligence Declining," pp. 181-203.

644. Euripides. THE ALCESTIS. The Oxford text with English verse translation by Sixth form boys of Bradfield College, 1904. Oxford: James Parker, 1904. 77 pp.

*645. ———. THE ELECTRA. Translated by Gilbert Murray. London: George Allen, 1906. ix,99 pp.

645a. Another copy, paper covers.

*646. ———. THE HIPPOLYTUS. Translated by Gilbert Murray. London: George Allen, 1904. 86 pp.

Brief notes, directions entered for the chorus, i.e. "All," "all one side," "all the other side," "all softly" etc. [possibly WBY's]

*647. ———. THE IPHIGENIA IN TAURIS. Translated by Gilbert Murray. London: George Allen, 1912. xi,105 pp.

*648. ———. THE PLAYS OF EURIPIDES IN ENGLISH. 2 vols. Translated by Shelley, Dean Milman, Potter and Woodhull. Everyman's Library. London: J.M. Dent, [1906].

Vol. 1 only.
Includes THE CYCLOPS, HECUBA, THE TROJAN DAMES, HELEN, ELECTRA, ORESTES, ANDROMACHE, IPHIGENIA IN AULIS, IPHIGENIA IN TAURIS.

*649. EVERYMAN. With other Interludes, including eight miracle plays. London: J.M. Dent, 1910; New York: E.P. Dutton, 1910. xxi, 208 pp. Sig.: GY

650. THE EVENING WORLD (New York), 6 Sept. 1917, pp. 1-2.

Contains a photo of John Quinn speaking at the Lafayette monument. See 1660.

651. Ewing, Juliana Horatia. A FLAT IRON FOR A FARTHING. London: George Bell, 1899. 116 pp. Sig.: GHL

A children's book.

652. THE EXILE, no. 1 (Spring 1927). Edited by Ezra Pound.

Some pp. uncut.

652a. Another copy.

653. ———, no. 4 (Autumn 1928).

654. EXPOSITION D'ART IRLANDAIS. [Paris]: Galéries Barbazages, 109 Rue Du Faubourg-Saint-Honoré, 109. Ouverte du 28 Janvier au 25 Février 1922. 30 pp.

Included in the exposition were works of Jack Yeats, Elizabeth Yeats, and Lily Yeats.

654a. Another copy.

655. EXPOSITION OF THE MALTA QUESTION. With documents. February 1929 - June 1930. Vatican: Vatican Polyglot Press, 1930. 159 pp.

P. 87, corner turned back; deals with Lord Strickland, Prime Minister of Malta.

656. Eyre, Thomas S[tephen]. OUR DAYS AND HOURS. WHAT THEY TELL. A Method of Astro-Philosophy. Hull: The St. Stephen Press, 1907. 35 pp.

Some pp. uncut.

*657. Fairfax, Edward. DAEMONOLOGIA: A DISCOURSE ON WITCHCRAFT AS IT WAS ACTED IN THE FAMILY OF MR. EDWARD FAIRFAX, of Fuyston, in the county of York, in the year 1621; along with the only Two Eclogues of the same author known to be in existence. With a biographical intro. [etc.] by William Grainge. Harrogate: R. Ackrill, 1882. vii,191 pp.

Corners turned back, pp. 34, 52, 84.

658. Faraday, L[ucy] Winifred. THE EDDA: THE DIVINE MYTHOLOGY OF THE NORTH. Popular studies in mythology, romance and folklore, no. 12. London: David Nutt, 1902. 51 pp.

Some pp. uncut; no. 13, the second vol. of this study, not here.

659. Farnell, Lewis Richard. GREEK HERO CULTS AND IDEAS OF IMMORTALITY. The Gifford Lectures, delivered in the University of St. Andrews in the year 1920. Oxford: Clarendon Press, 1921. xv,434 pp.

*660. Farquhar, George. GEORGE FARQUHAR. Edited by William Archer. The Mermaid Series. London: T. Fisher Unwin, [1906]. 455 pp.

Contains THE CONSTANT COUPLE, THE TWIN-RIVALS, THE RECRUITING OFFICER, and THE BEAUX' STRATAGEM.

661. [Farr, Florence]. Advertisement for CHANTING AND SPEAKING TO THE MUSIC OF THE PSALTERY by Miss Florence Farr. [2] pp.

Inserted in 663.

662. ———. Advertisement for THE CHORUS OF CLASSICAL PLAYS TO THE MUSIC OF THE PSALTERY by Florence Farr. [2] pp.

Inserted in 663.

662a-c. Three more copies; inserted in 663.

662A. ——— (S.S.D.D. [Sapientia Sapienti Dono Data]). EGYPTIAN MAGIC. Collectanea Hermetica, vol. 8. London: Theosophical Publishing Society, 1896. vii,88 pp.

In Contents, all p. numbers have been corrected in pencil, likely WBY's.

*663. ——— and Olivia Shakespear. THE BELOVED OF HATHOR and THE SHRINE OF THE GOLDEN HAWK. All copyrights and acting rights reserved by the authors. No publishing info. Unpag.

Inserted, 661, 662, 662a-c.

664. Faure, Elie. HISTORY OF ART. Translated by Walter Pach. 4 vols. London: John Lane, 1921-24; New York: Harper, 1921-24.

Vols. on Ancient Art, Medieval Art, Renaissance Art, Modern Art.

665. Fechner, Theodor. ON LIFE AFTER DEATH. Translated by Hugo Wernekke. 3rd ed. Chicago and London: Open Court Publishing, 1914. ii,134 pp.

Marginal strokes, underscoring, brief notes, pp. 36-41, 43, 47, 48, 49, 53, 54, 56, 64, 67, 68-70, 75, 76, 77, 78-80, 82, 85, 87, 89, 91, 97.
P. 36, margin, mid-page: dreaming back and return
P. 40, top: one has to consider the individual is created in transmission[?]. Our Christ is more the historical Christ. Yet the dead do not create it seems.
P. 43, margin, mid-page: Dreaming back
P. 48, margin, mid-page: so did Sister Mary Ellen seek Mother Aloyisius. Free will is choice between spirits.
P. 53, margin, mid-page: covens
P. 54, top: if two spirits of the dead meet (on earth) their nations also meet
P. 56, margin, mid-page: spirits are fate
P. 64, first par.: Egyptian tombs
P. 67, par. two: Vision of the blood kindred
P. 69, par. three: cones/ in question/ cones
P. 69, par. four: Cabalistic Vedenic/ tree-buds in branches etc.
P. 77, first par.: But the dead possess our memories even while we live.
P. 77, end of first par.: "pure memory"
P. 82, first par.: Compare Adonais of Shelley
P. 82, end of first par.: Why the organs? To combine spirits, each of which would otherwise be enclosed in its ruling love, according to the degree of its separation.

666. Ferguson, Sir Samuel. HIBERNIAN NIGHTS' ENTERTAINMENTS. First series. Dublin: Sealy, Bryers & Walker, 1887. xii,146 pp.

Flyleaf: W B Yeats/ August/ 1887

667. ———. HIBERNIAN NIGHTS' ENTERTAINMENT. The Rebellion of Silken Thomas. Third series. Dublin: Sealy, Bryers & Walker, 1887. [4],278 pp.

Flyleaf: W B Yeats/ Dec 1,/ 1887

*668. ———. LAYS OF THE RED BRANCH. London: T. Fisher Unwin, 1897. xxviii,161 pp.

Flyleaf: W B Yeats./ Nov. 1897.
P. 38, a correction in the text, possibly WBY's.

*669. FESTIVE SONGS FOR CHRISTMAS. The Shakespeare Head Press Booklets, no. 2. Stratford: The Shakespeare Head Press, 1906. 30 pp.

670. Field, Michael. A SELECTION FROM THE POEMS. Preface by T. Sturge Moore. London: The Poetry Bookshop, 1923. 142 pp.

The following poems have been excised from this vol. to make Michael Field's selection for the OBMV, "The Tragic Mary Queen of Scots. I," p. 26; "The Tragic Mary Queen of Scots. II," p. 27; "Bury her at Even," p. 32; "And on my Eyes Dark Sleep by Night," p. 25; "Gold is the Son of Zeus: Neither Moth nor Worm may gnaw it," p. 23; "Sweeter Far than the Harp, More Gold than Gold," p. 35; "If They Honoured Me, Giving Me Their Gifts," p. 36; "To the Lord Love," p. 42; "Aridity," p. 137. [the order is that of the OBMV].

671. ———. WILD HONEY, FROM VARIOUS THYME. London: T. Fisher Unwin, 1908. xiii,194 pp.

*672. Fielding, Henry. THE WORKS OF HENRY FIELDING, ESQ. Edited by James P. Browne. 11 vols. London: Bickers, 1902. Bps., all vols.: WBY

Some pp. uncut passim.

673. Figgis, Darrell. THE PAINTINGS OF WILLIAM BLAKE. London: Ernest Benn, 1925. xv,[1],117 pp., 100 plates.

674. Fischer, E[duard] W[ilhelm]. ÉTUDES SUR FLAUBERT INÉDIT. Leipzig: Julius Zeitler, 1908. viii,140 pp.

Half-title p.: T. Sturge Moore/ 40 Well Walk/ London N.W. 3
Pp. 23 & 80, Sturge Moore's corrections of the French text.

675. Fisher, Right Hon. H[erbert] A[lbert] L[aurens]. Review of THE DECLINE OF THE WEST, by Oswald Spengler. THE OBSERVER, 27 January 1929.

Inserted in 17.

676. FIVE FAVOURITE TALES FROM THE ARABIAN NIGHTS IN WORDS OF ONE SYLLABLE. Edited by A. & A.E. Warner. London: H.K. Lewis, 1871. iv,66 pp. Bps: Elizabeth Corbet Yeats

Flyleaf: To Willy from/ his Papa 1872

677. Flambart, Paul. ÉTUDE NOUVELLE SUR L'HÉRÉDITÉ. Accompagnée d'un recueil de nombreux exemples avec dessins

de l'auteur. Paris: Bibliothèque Chacornac, 1903. [8], 127 pp.

Astrology.

678. Flammarion, Camille. DEATH AND ITS MYSTERY BEFORE DEATH. Proofs of the Existence of the Soul. Translated by E.S. Brooks [vol. 1] and Latrobe Carroll [vols. 2-3]. 3 vols. London: T. Fisher Unwin, 1921-23.

Some pp. uncut in all 3 vols.

679. Flaubert, Gustave. BOUVARD AND PECUCHET. Translated by D.F. Hannigan. London: H.S. Nichols, 1896. xvi,458 pp.

680. ———. THE FIRST TEMPTATION OF SAINT ANTHONY. Translated by Rene Francis from the 1849-1856 manuscripts edited by Louis Bertrand. London: Duckworth, 1910. viii,272 pp.

Inserted, apparently a leaf from a book, headed "Taf. I." and showing on one side two heads of William Blake with the printed legend, apparently in Blake's hand, "Portraits of Willm Blake." Verso blank.

681. ———. SENTIMENTAL EDUCATION. A Young Man's History. Translated by D.F. Hannigan. 2 vols. London: H.S. Nichols, 1898. Sig.: WBY

Vol. 2, inserted, a shopping list, possibly for theatre properties [not WBY's].

682. ———. THE TEMPTATION OF SAINT ANTONY. Translated by D.F. Hannigan. London: H.S. Nichols, 1895. xii,360 pp.

*683. Flecker, James Elroy. THE COLLECTED POEMS. Edited by J.C. Squire. London: Martin Secker, 1916. xxxi,249 pp.

Flyleaf: "The Golden Journey to Samarkand 144" [Prologue only] "Santorin 173" [both appear in the OBMV and are excised; also excised to make Flecker's selection, "The Old Ships," p.216].

684. Fletcher, Phineas. VENUS & ANCHISES (BRITTAIN'S IDA). And other poems. Edited by Ethel Seaton. London: Oxford Univ. Press, 1926. li,125 pp.

Almost entirely uncut.

*685. Flint, F[rank] S[tewart]. CADENCES. London: The Poetry Bookshop, [1915]. 31 pp.

Inside cover: To William Butler Yeats,/ homage of/ F.S. Flint.

*686. FLORILEGIO DI CANTI TOSCANI: FOLK SONGS OF THE TUSCAN HILLS. Translated by Grace Warrack. London: Alexander Moring, the de la More Press, 1914. lxxxii,305 pp.

Some pp. uncut.

Inserted, a note of presentation by the translator; no recipient given; dated Edinburgh, 4th Aug. 1914.

687. FORM. A QUARTERLY OF THE ARTS (London). 1 (April 1916). Edited by Austin O. Spare and Francis Marsden.

Includes "Eight Poems by W B Yeats," pp. 35-9; "The Dawn," "On Woman," "The Fisherman," "The Hawk," "Memory," "The Thorn Tree," "The Phoenix," "There is a Queen in China."

688. FORMES (Paris). An international review of plastic art, appearing ten times a year in two editions, French and English, no. 9 (Nov. 1930). English ed.

689. Forster, E[dward] M[organ]. WHAT I BELIEVE. London: The Hogarth Press, 1939. 22 pp.

*690. Forster, John. WALTER SAVAGE LANDOR, A BIOGRAPHY. 2 vols. London: Chapman & Hall, 1869. Bps: WBY

Vol. 1, back flyleaf: 461/467 [p. 461 quotes Landor on "the Roman Catholic superstition"; p. 467 refers to Dr. Parr's defence of the queen in 1820].
Vol. 2, pencil strokes on pp. 344, 348, 376, 379, 380, 381, 382, 386.

691. Fortescue, [Winifred] Lady. SUNSET HOUSE, MORE PERFUME FROM PROVENCE [Reminiscences of Provence]. Edinburgh and London: Blackwood, 1937. vii,312 pp.

692. Foster, Myles B[irket]. A DAY IN A CHILD'S LIFE. Illustrated by Kate Greenaway. London: George Routledge, [1882?]. 29 pp.

Music by Foster, words by various authors.
Back flyleaf: Anne [child's hand; presumably Anne Yeats's]

*693. Foucher, A[lfred]. THE BEGINNINGS OF BUDDHIST ART and other essays in Indian and Central Asian Archaeology. Revised by the author and translated by L.A. Thomas and F. W. Thomas. Issued to members of the India Society, 1917. London: Humphrey Milford, 1917. xvi,316 pp.

Most pp. uncut; loose from binding.

694. Franklin, Benjamin. AUTOBIOGRAPHY. Everyman's Library. London: J.M. Dent, 1937. xx,314 pp.

695. Frazer, J[ames] G[eorge]. THE BELIEF IN IMMORTALITY AND THE WORSHIP OF THE DEAD. The Gifford Lectures, St. Andrews, 1911-12. London: Macmillan, 1913. xxi,495 pp.

Mostly uncut.

696. ———. FOLK-LORE IN THE OLD TESTAMENT. Studies in Comparative Religion, Legend and Law. Abridged ed. London: Macmillan, 1923. xxx,476 pp.

Mostly uncut; cut, pp. 49-65 (dealing with Hebrew and Babylonian stories of a great flood; pp. 136-45 (dealing with the origin of flood stories).

697. ———. THE GOLDEN BOUGH. 3rd ed. A Study in Magic and Religion. Vols. 1 & 2: THE MAGIC ART AND THE EVOLUTION OF KINGS. London: Macmillan, 1911. BPS: WBY

Bookplates, both vols., stroked through, in ink, "From the Library of Ethel M. Coomaraswamy, Norman Chapel, Broad Campden."
Vol. 2, many pp. uncut.

698. ———. Vol. 3: TABOO AND THE PERILS OF THE SOUL. London: Macmillan, 1911. Bp: WBY

Mostly uncut after p. 89.

699. ———. Vol. 4: THE DYING GOD. London: Macmillan, 1911. Bp: WBY

Many pp. uncut.

700. ———. Vol. 5: ADONIS, ATTIS, OSIRIS. 2nd ed., rev. and enlarged. London: Macmillan, 1907. xix,452 pp. Bp: WBY

Bookplate of Ananda K. Coomaraswamy, canceled.
P. 377, margin, mid-page: "suggestion & concentration."
[The BMC lists 2 vols. under this title; this is the separately listed one vol. ed. added apparently to make the set more complete.]

701. ———. Vols. 6 & 7: SPIRITS OF THE CORN AND OF THE WILD. London: Macmillan, 1912. Bps: WBY

Many pp. uncut, both vols.
[Vol. 8, THE SCAPEGOAT, is missing]

702. ———. Vols. 9 & 10: BALDER THE BEAUTIFUL. THE FIRE-FESTIVALS OF EUROPE AND THE DOCTRINE OF THE EXTERNAL SOUL. London: Macmillan, 1913. Bps: WBY

Many pp. uncut.
Vol. 1, Chapter IV, most of pp. 106-209 cut, "The Lenten Fires," "The Easter Fires," "The Beltane Fires," part of "The Midsummer Fires."
Vol. 1 cut, pp. 184-249, "The external soul in plants," "The external soul in animals," "The ritual of death and resurrection."

703. ———. Vol. 12: BIBLIOGRAPHY AND GENERAL INDEX. London: Macmillan, 1915. Bp: WBY

Mostly uncut.

704. THE FREEMAN (New York). 3 (24 Aug. 1921).

Includes John Butler Yeats's "A Dialogue in Heaven," pp. 560-61.

704a. Another copy of JBY's essay only; in envelope labeled: Articles in "Freeman" U.S.A./ by JBY.

705. ———. 4 (4 Jan. 1922).

Includes John Butler Yeats's "A Painter of Pictures," pp. 401-2. On John Sloan.

705a. Another copy of JBY's essay only; in envelope as above.

706. ———. 4 (15 Feb. 1922).

Includes JBY's "The Soul of Dublin," p. 541.

706a. Another copy of JBY's essay only; in envelope as above.

707. ———. 4 (22 Feb. 1922).

Contains an obituary notice of JBY by E.A. Boyd, pp. 567-8.

707a. Another copy of the notice only; in envelope as above.

708. ———. 4 (1 March 1922).

"A Reviewer's Notebook," a remembrance of JBY, pp. 598-9.

708a-c. Three more copies.

Another copy of the remembrance only. At top: Van Wyck [Brooks] [in envelope as above].

709. [THE FREEMAN'S JOURNAL]. Review of the Irish Literary Theatre's first performance of Hyde's THE TWISTING OF THE ROPE and Yeats's and Moore's DIARMUID AND GRAINNE, THE FREEMAN'S JOURNAL, [22 Oct. 1901]. Inserted in 2389.

710. THE FREE STATE (Dublin). (19 Aug. 1922). War Special.

Includes report of the death of Arthur Griffith with eulogy by Gogarty.

711. ———. (30 Aug. 1922). Michael Collins Memorial Number.

With a memorial poem by O[liver] G[ogarty.?].

712. French, Cecil. BETWEEN SUN AND MOON. Poems and woodcuts. London: The Favil Press, 1922. x,47 pp.

P. iii, "This edition is limited to 350 copies, of which only those issued to original subscribers contain hand-printed proofs of the wood blocks signed by the artist. This is No. 1." Sig.: Cecil French. Dedicated to WBY. Inserted, two letters of presentation from the author to WBY, one to accompany this vol., another for 713. Both express French's debt to the "Woburn Nights."

713. ———. WITH THE YEARS. Poems. London: The Richards Press, 1927. 58 pp. 26/500. Sig.: Cecil French

Some pp. uncut.

714. Frercks, Rudolf. GERMAN POPULATION POLICY. Berlin: Terramare Office, 1937. 32 pp.

On paper cover: Uncorrected proof [not WBY'S].
Addresses the problem of the falling birth rate among "families hereditarily endowed with the highest qualities" and the rising rate among "families with a large number of socially unadaptable elements."

715. Frobenius, Leo. PAIDEUMA. Umrisse einer Kulturund Seelenlehre. Munchen: C.Y. Beck'sche Verlasbuchhandlung, 1921. vi,125 pp. Sig.: D. Yard

Flyleaf: Bard/ care/ E. Pound [Pound's]
P. 81, first par.: Jews on Third plane!/ History L. in America! [Pound's blue pencil]
Elsewhere, a few notes and comments in English, neither WBY's nor Pound's, by two separate annotators, one ink, one pencil.
Back flyleaf: 73, 78, 80, 85, 87 [unidentified hand]

716. FROM THE UPANISHADS. [Translated by] Charles Johnston. Portland, Me.: Thomas B. Mosher, 1913. xxii,[2],68,[1] pp.

Dedicated to George Russell.

717. IL FRONTESPIZIO (Florence), no. 6 (Giugno 1938).

Many pp. uncut.
In Contents, two ink strokes in left margin against Grattan Freyer's "Note sulla poesia religiosa in Inghilterra," pp. 397; inked to the right of this is: Margot Ruddock: THE LEMON TREE. [not WBY's].
Inserted at the article on English religious poetry, an anonymous newspaper review in THE IRISH TIMES of THE LEMON TREE. See 1005.

718. Fry, Roger. VISION AND DESIGN. The Phoenix Library. London: Chatto and Windus, 1928. 302 pp.

719. Fukui, Kikusaburo. JAPANESE CERAMIC ART AND NATIONAL CHARACTERISTICS. [Tokyo: K. Ohashi, 1927]. xv,[1] pp., 21 pl., 63,[1] pp., 62 plates.

Text in English and Japanese.

720. Fuller, Capt. J[ohn] F[rederick] C[harles]. THE STAR IN THE WEST. A critical essay upon the works of Aleister Crowley. London: Walter Scott, 1907. vi,327 pp.

Mostly uncut.
Cut, "The Virgin," pp. 51-108; "The Harlot," pp. 111-121.

721. THE GAEL (New York). 21 (Dec. 1902).

Includes "A Pen Picture of Dr. Douglas Hyde and Mr. Yeats," pp. 378-9 and portraits of Hyde, Yeats, and Lady Gregory, the last from a drawing by JBY; also includes A LOSING GAME, a play in one act by Lady Gregory.

722. ———, n.s., 22 (Feb. 1903).

Includes "Adam's Curse."
P. 33, a sketch, probably by JBY.

723. THE GAELIC AMERICAN (New York). 5 March 1904.

Pp. 1 & 5 contain "Emmet the Apostle of Irish Liberty. W.B. Yeats Delivers a Great Speech on the Patriot and his Legacy." Includes text of speech and portrait of Yeats from a photograph.

724. Gaiety Theatre (Dublin). PERFORMANCES BY THE ROYAL CARL ROSA OPERA COMPANY. 24 Oct. 1921 - 4 Nov. 1921. 8 pp.

Tosca performed on 4 Nov.; inserted in 1837.

725. Galassi, Giuseppe. ROMA O BISANZIO. I Mosaici Di Ravenna E Le Origini Dell'Arte Italiana. Roma: La Libreria Dello Stato, 1930. 310/750. xv,[1],336 pp., 147 plates.

Flyleaf: George Yeats/ Rome/ "volta congress" [?]/ 1934. Marked by many slips of paper, but the envelope from which they are torn is dated 1954.

726. Gardner, Arthur, ed. FRENCH SCULPTURE OF THE THIRTEENTH CENTURY. Seventy-eight examples of masterpieces of Medieval Art illustrating the works at Rheims [etc.]. With an Introduction and Notes by Arthur Gardner. The Medici Portfolios, no. 1. London: Philip Lee Warner, 1915. 22,[2] pp., 50 plates.

Unbound, in envelope; some pp. uncut in notes.

*727. Gardner, Charles WILLIAM BLAKE, THE MAN. London: J.M. Dent, 1919. 202 pp. Bp: WBY

*728. Gardner, Edmund G[arratt]. DUKES & POETS IN FERRARA. A study in the poetry, religion and politics of the fifteenth and early sixteenth centuries. London: Archibald Constable, 1904. xv,578 pp.

Inserted, an empty envelope, Palace Hotel, Florence stationery, addressed to Miss Horniman, London; never posted [WBY's?].

*729. ———. THE KING OF THE COURT POETS. A study of the work, life and times of Lodovico Ariosto. London: Archibald Constable, 1906. 3,xix,395 pp.

A few pp. uncut.
Inserted, unused post card showing "Casa di Lodovico Ariosto."

*730. Gardner, F[rederick] Leigh. A CATALOGUE RAISONNÉ OF WORKS ON THE OCCULT SCIENCES. Vol. 1: ROSICRUCIAN BOOKS. With an intro. by Dr. William Wynn Westcott. London: Privately printed, 1903. xvi,82 pp. 213/300. Sig.: F. Leigh Gardner

Half-title p.: To W B Yeats Esq/ With the Author's/ kind regards/ 29/9/03.
Some pp. uncut.
Inserted, a brief letter from author to WBY dated 29/9/03 encouraging Yeats to learn about the Golden Dawn through careful reading.

*731. Garnett, Lucy M[ary] J[ane]. GREEK FOLK POESY: Annotated translations, from the whole cycle of Romaic and folk-verse and folk-prose. Edited with essays [etc.] by J.S. Stuart-Glennie. New Folklore Researches, vol. 2. London: David Nutt, 1896. viii,541 pp.

Many pp. uncut.
Marginal strokes, underscorings, brief notes, pp. 486, 487, 497, 514, 519, 520.
P. 487, WBY's note next to printed note, bottom, very illegible; the subject is witchcraft.
P. 514, a query (?) before line 5 and a note above: the author of spiritual being obeys an intellectual necessity but still a necessity. A being who does not will [?] but is alone is above necessity.
P. 514, "Material, Spiritual Beings" underlined and a note: What was material to a people who believe that all was alive? [ink]

732. Garnett, Richard, trans. A CHAPLET FROM THE GREEK ANTHOLOGY. Cameo series. London: T. Fisher Unwin, 1892. 82 pp. Sig.: WBY

SEE ALSO Trent, A.G. (pseud.).

733. ——— and Edmund Gosse. ENGLISH LITERATURE. An illustrated record. 4 vols. London: William Heinemann, 1903.

Vol. 1, some pp. uncut.

*734. Gascoigne, George [and Francis Kinwelmersh]. SUPPOSES AND JOCASTA. Two plays translated from the Italian, the first by Geo. Gascoigne, the second by Geo. Gascoigne and F. Kinwelmersh. Edited by John W. Cunliffe. Boston and London: D.C. Heath, 1906. xxx,441 pp.

"SUPPOSES: a comedie written in the Italian tongue by Ariosto. Englished by George Gascoigne [etc.]."

"JOCASTA: a tragedie written in Greeke by Euripides translated and digested into acts by George Gascoigne and Francis Kinwelmersh [etc.]."

735. Gasparri, Peter Cardinal. THE CATHOLIC CATECHISM. Translated by the Dominican Fathers. London: Sheed and Ward, 1934. xxvi,482 pp.

736. Gaunt, W[illiam]. BANDITS IN A LANDSCAPE. A study of Romantic Painting from Caravaggio to Delacroix. London: The Studio Limited, 1937. viii,192 pp.

*737. Gayley, Charles Mills. PLAYS OF OUR FOREFATHERS, and some of the traditions upon which the plays were founded. London: Chatto & Windus, 1908. xi,349 pp.

Drama criticism.

738. THE GEETA. The Gospel of the Lord Shri Krishna. Translated by Shri Purohit Swāmi. London: Faber & Faber, 1935. 110 pp. 3/750. Sig.: Shri Purohit Swāmi

Flyleaf: My dear Yeats,/ I cannot thank you for/ your service, for your service/ is beyond thanks./ Yours affectionately/ Purohit Swami
P. 9, a printed dedicatory letter to WBY.
Some pp. uncut.

738a. Another copy. 4/750

Flyleaf: My dear Mrs. Yeats. Thank you for your kindness and god bless you. Purohit Swami.

738b-d. Three more copies. Nos. 29, 155, 156/ 750.

The last wholly cut.

739. Geley, Gustave. FROM THE UNCONSCIOUS TO THE CONSCIOUS. Translated by Stanley de Brath. London: William Collins, 1921. xxviii,328 pp., 12 plates.

P. 164, marginal stroke.
P. 165, gyres drawn next to the passage "From this point of view Spirit and Matter do not appear as opposed entities -- the statical terms of a fixed antithesis -- but rather as movement in inverse directions...." (quoted from Le Roy, UNE PHILOSOPHIE NOUVELLE).
Corners turned back, pp. 122, 130, 314, 40.

740. Gentile, Giovanni. LA NUOVA SCUOLA MEDIA. Firenze: Vallecchi Editore, 1925. 404 pp.

Uncut.

741. ———. THE REFORM OF EDUCATION. Translated by Dino Bigongiari. With an intro. by Benedetto Croce. London: Macmillan, 1922. xxviii,280 pp.

742. ———. THE THEORY OF MIND AS PURE ACT. Translated from the third ed. by H. Wildon Carr. London: Macmillan, 1922. xxviii,280 pp.

Flyleaf: 1928 [?]

Light underscorings, markings pp. 41, 59, 106, 107, 109, 110, 126 [brown pencil], 201, 241-4.
P. 126 at "Kant said" to "if we represent," the symbols for water and fire entered.
P. 201, at "'I' is an unconditioned absolute, free, and therefore a condition of everything.": True
P. 201, at "the object alone cut off from the subject": False

GEORGIAN POETRY, 1913 - 1915, see 1237.

*743. GESTA ROMANORUM. Translated by the Rev. Charles Swan. Revised and corrected by Wynnard Hooper. London: George Bell, 1905. lxxvi,425 pp.

*744. Ghose, Manmohan. LOVE-SONGS AND ELEGIES. London: Elkin Mathews, 1898. 40 pp.

Half-title p.: With the Author's/ compliments

*745. Gibbon, Edward. THE AUTOBIOGRAPHIES OF EDWARD GIBBON. Edited by John Murray. London: John Murray, 1896. xiv,435 pp.

Some pp. uncut.

*746. ———. THE HISTORY OF THE DECLINE AND FALL OF THE ROMAN EMPIRE. Edited by J.B. Bury. 7 vols. London: Methuen, 1909-14.

Some pp. uncut in all vols., except Vol. 3

Vol. 1, paper slips inserted at pp. 130-31 (Siege of Byzantium) and pp. 188-9.

Vol. 2, slip inserted at pp. 140-41; p. 161, corner of page turned back (edifices of Byzantium).

Vol. 3, a card inserted at pp. 24-5.

747. Gibbon, Monk. THE BRANCH OF HAWTHORN TREE. Poems. London: The Grayhound Press, 1927. 85 pp. 323/460. Bp: Lily Yeats

748. Gide, André. BACK FROM THE U.S.S.R. Translated by Dorothy Bussy. London: Martin Secker and Warburg, 1937. 120 pp. Sig.: WBY

749. Gill, Eric. AN ESSAY ON TYPOGRAPHY. London: Sheed & Ward, 1936. [4],133 pp.

*750. Glanvil, Joseph. SADDUCISMUS TRIUMPHATUS: Or, a full and plain Evidence, concerning Witches and Apparitions. In two parts. The First Treating of their Possibility. The Second of their Real Existence.... Translated with additions by Dr. Horneck. 4th ed. London: Printed for A. Bettesworth and J. Batley...; W. Mears, and J. Hooke, 1726. Pagination very erratic. Bp: WBY

Flyleaf, a presentation canceled and difficult to read, dated July, 1911, apparently with no connection to WBY.
Marginal strokes, pp. 9, 10-12, 294, 316, 326, 332, 334, 358, 398, 488, 489.
P. 14: They [evil spirits] see from our eyes. [pencil]
P. 306, at "The Devil ... leaving an ill smell behind him": materialization. [ink]
P. 143, corner turned back.
P. 225, a bus ticket inserted at section on witchcraft.
Inside back cover, pencil: 279, 294, 316, 326, 358, 398, 488, 492 [marginal pencil strokes appear on most of these pages]

751. Goblet d'Alviella, Eugène Félicien Albert, Compte. THE MIGRATION OF SYMBOLS. [Translated by ?] Sir George Birdwood. Westminster: Archibald Constable, 1894. xxviii,277 pp.

752. Goddard, E. H. and P[hilip] A[rnold]. CIVILISATION OR CIVILISATIONS. An essay in the Spenglerian Philosophy of History. London: Constable, 1926. xvi,35,230,[1] pp.

753. Goethe, Johann Wolfgag Von. THE FIRST PART OF THE TRAGEDY OF FAUST. Translated by Thomas E. Webb. New ed. with the Death of Faust, from the second part. London: Longmans, Green, 1898. 295 pp.

754. Gogarty, Oliver St. John. AS I WAS GOING DOWN SACKVILLE ST. A Phantasy in Fact. London: Rich & Cowan, 1937. [10],330 pp.

755. ———. AN OFFERING OF SWANS AND OTHER POEMS. London: Eyre & Spottiswoode, [1924]. 60 pp. WADE 274

Includes Preface by WBY.
Includes Gogarty's inked revisions of a number of poems, "Sunt apud inferos," p. 28; "To Ethne," p. 29; "Seven Concerning Hermione," p. 31; "III Excommunication," p. 32; "Off Sicily," p. 35; "To a Trout," p. 36. The revisions of all but "The Conquest" (one of "Seven Concerning Hermione") are followed in the OBMV. The poems "The Oak Wood" and "The Exorcism" have been "Xed" in the text but not by WBY.

755a. Another copy.

"Per iter tenebricosum" and "The Conquest" excised, apparently to make G.'s selection for the OBMV.

755b. Another copy.

756. ———. SELECTED POEMS. New York: Macmillan, 1933. xxxvi,177 pp.

Flyleaf: "To W.B./ the onlie begetter/ from Oliver St. J. Gogarty."

P. 36, pencil correction, Gogarty's, in title only, from "Sunt apud inferos tot milia formosarum" to: Sunt apud infernos tot milia formosarum.
P. 37, paper inserted and corner turned back for "Ringsend."
P. 166, Gogarty's revision in pencil of the second quatrain of "To Shadu 'L-Mulk (Delight of the Kingdom) from the Persian of Khalil Shah."

757. Goldsmith, Oliver. THE VICAR OF WAKEFIELD. London: Walker & Edwards, 1817. viii,196 pp.

758. Gore-Booth, Eva. POEMS. Complete edition ... with biographical introduction by Esther Roper. London: Longmans, Green, 1929. xx,653 pp. Bp: WBY

*759. Gosse, Edmund. ON VIOL AND FLUTE. Poems. London: William Heinemann, 1896. xi,213 pp.

Some pp. uncut.

760. [Gowans, Adam Luke, ed.]. SOME MOTHS AND BUTTERFLIES AND THEIR EGGS. Sixty photographs from nature by A.E. Tonge. Gowans's Nature Books, no. 15. London: Gowans & Gray, 1907. 71 pp.

*761. Gower, John. CONFESSIO AMANTIS. Edited by Dr. Reinhold Pauli. 3 vols. London: Bell and Daldy, 1857. Bps: WBY

Many pp. uncut in Vol. 2.

762. Grant, Sir Francis J[ames], ed. THE MANUAL OF HERALDRY. A concise description of the several terms used, and containing a dictionary of every designation in the science. New and rev. ed. Edinburgh: John Grant, 1937. viii,142 pp.

Inserted, p. 140, two photographs of Cork City, probably early 1940's. Anne Yeats thinks this may have been her book since the photos are hers.

763. Granville-Barker, Harley. ON POETRY AND DRAMA. The Romanes Lecture. Delivered in the Taylor Institution. 4 June 1937. London: Sidgwick & Jackson, 1937. 42 pp.

On paper cover: W. B. Yeats from H. Granville-Barker/ p. 11 et seq. [there a discussion of Yeats and Maeterlinck].

764. Grattan, Henry. THE SELECT SPEECHES OF THE RIGHT HON. HENRY GRATTAN; to which is added His Letter on the Union, with a commentary on his career and character. By Daniel Owen Madden. Dublin: James Duffy, 1845. liii,[1],471 pp.

Flyleaf: J D Noonan/ 17.9.1912

*765. ———. SPEECHES OF THE RIGHT HONORABLE HENRY GRATTAN. Vol. 1. Dublin: H. Fitzpatrick, 1811. xcvi,415,[1],x pp. Bp: George Pollexfen?

Flyleaf: The only volume published. [not WBY's]

766. Graves, Robert. THE AUGUSTAN BOOKS OF MODERN POETRY: ROBERT GRAVES. London: Ernest Benn, [1933?]. iv,31 pp.

Apparently the second impression.

767. ———. POEMS 1914-26. London: William Heinemann, 1928. xii,217 pp.

A few pp. uncut.
In Contents, a check placed against "Hemlock. 124."
In text of "Hemlock," p. 125, a stroke against the lines "He [Socrates] weeps glad tears of sacred scent/ When we prevail in argument/ Against some un-Greek jack-in-the-box...."
P. 102, corner turned back. Poems are "A Fight to the Death" and the beginning of "In Procession."

768. ———. POEMS, 1926-1930. London: William Heinemann, 1931. 89 pp.

769. ———. POEMS, 1930-1933. London: Arthur Barker, 1933. 38 pp.

P. 3, corner turned back for "Ulysses"
P. 17, corner turned back for "The Legs."

*770. Gray, John. SPIRITUAL POEMS. Frontispiece and border designed by Charles Ricketts. London: Hacon & Ricketts, 1896. cxiii pp.

771. [Great Britain]. Laws, Statutes etc. AN ACT FOR INCORPORATING A COMPANY FOR THE IMPROVEMENT OF WASTE LANDS IN IRELAND, 4th July 1836. 6 & 7 William 4, ch. 97.

772. ———. AN ACT FOR REGULATING AND IMPROVING THE TOWN OF GALWAY IN THE COUNTY OF THE SAME TOWN, 4th JULY 1836. 6 & & William 4, ch. 117.

773. ———. PATENTS, DESIGNS, COPYRIGHT AND TRADE MARKS EMERGENCY ACT, 1939. 2 & 3 Geo. 6, ch. 107.

774. Green, H.S. DIRECTIONS AND DIRECTING. With a foreword by Alan Leo. Astrological Manuals, no. 5. London: "Modern Astrology," 1905. viii,74 pp. Bp: GY

*775. Green, Joseph Henry. SPIRITUAL PHILOSOPHY: FOUNDED ON THE TEACHING OF THE LATE SAMUEL TAYLOR COLERIDGE. Edited with a memoir by John Simon. 2 vols. London and Cambridge: Macmillan, 1865. Bps: WBY

Vol. 1, flyleaf, verso: M B Wilkin/ from her Aunt Mrs. J H Green. [above this in pencil:] "& following/

Page 14 - 21 - 30
Vol. 1, marginal strokes, pp. 4, 5, 20, 21, 37, 51.
Vol. 1, p. 25, corner turned back.
Vol. 1, p. 295 (last of book): 20 / 4 / 37 / 51
Vol. 1, back flyleaf, pencil: "Space & Time = Objectivity & Subjectivity - Page 20"/ "Abstraction - page 21. Worth quoting in/ 'A Vision'".

*776. Greene, George A[rthur]. SONGS OF THE OPEN AIR. London: Elkin Mathews, 1912. viii,116 pp.

Flyleaf: To My Friend/ W.B. Yeats/ from the Author.

*777. THE GREEN SHEAF (London), no. 1 (1903). Edited by Pamela Colman Smith.

Includes "The Hill of Heart's Desire," translated from the Irish of Raftery.
Inserted, a reproduction of Crivelli's "The Annunciation" in the London National Gallery.

777a. Another copy.

*778. ———, no. 2 (1903).

*779. ———, no. 3 (1903).

Includes A.E.'s poem "Reconcilement."
Inserted, a reproduction of a drawing of Mrs. Stirling by D.G. Rossetti.

779a. Another copy. Insertion as above.

*780. ———, no. 4 (1903).

*781. ———, no. 5 (1903).

Includes "Cael and Credhe" translated from the Irish by Lady Gregory.

781a. Another copy.

*782. ———, no. 6 (1903).

Includes "A Deep Sea Yarn," a story by John Masefield.

782a. Another copy.

783. ———, no. 7 (1903).

Includes a poem by Masefield, "Blind Man's Vigil."
Inserted as a Supplement is A.E.'s DEIRDRE, A PLAY IN THREE ACTS; also inserted a folder with two colored illustrations for the play by Cecil French.

784. ———, no. 8 (1903).

785. ———, no. 9 (1904).

Inserted as a Supplement is John Todhunter's story, "A Dream."

786. ———, no. 11 (1904).

787. ———, no. 12 (1904)

788. ———, no. 13 (1904).

Included as a supplement is an account by F. York-Powell "A Horror of the House of Dreams."
Inserted as a loose sheet is a reproduction of a drawing of York Powell by J.B. Yeats.

789. Greenwood, Alice Drayton. HORACE WALPOLE'S WORLD. A Sketch of Whig Society under George III. London: G. Bell, 1913. xi,257 pp.

*790. Gregory, Isabella Augusta, Lady. A BOOK OF SAINTS AND WONDERS. London: John Murray, 1907. ix,[1],211,[1] pp. Bp: WBY

Flyleaf: To W B Yeats/ from Augusta Gregory Oct 1907.
Pp. 66-7, a paper book mark inserted.

791. ———. CASE FOR THE RETURN OF SIR HUGH LANE'S PICTURES TO DUBLIN. Dublin: The Talbot Press, 1926. 48 pp.

On paper cover: "advanced copy" [WBY's]

791a. Another copy.

*792. ———. CUCHULAIN OF MUIRTHEMNE: The Story of the Men of the Red Branch of Ulster. Arranged and translated by Lady Gregory. With a Preface by W.B. Yeats. 3rd ed. London: John Murray, 1907. xx,364 pp. Bp: WBY. Sig.: WBY. WADE 256.

Preface, pp. x-xv, WBY's revisions, pencil, to provide copytext for WADE 102, section II of "Thoughts on Lady Gregory's Translations," in CUTTING OF AN AGATE, New York, 1912. Some slight revisions are not followed in AGATE.
P. xvii, new version of title: Thoughts on Lady Gregory's translations of Irish heroic poetry [last 4 words canceled]
P. 344, bottom, a note: Copy from here [a marginal stroke runs down the whole of p. 345 and down the first five lines of 346, to "that is better than Ochone!"]
P. 346, a note: then skip to mark on page 349.
Pp. 349-50, a stroke against the passage "O Conall, what way are they" to "the music of the Sidhe."

*793. ———. THE FULL MOON. A Comedy in One Act. [Dublin]: Published by the author at the Abbey Theatre, 1911. 49 pp.

Half-title p.: W B Yeats/ from A Gregory

794. ———. THE GAOL GATE. Dublin: The Talbot Press, [1918]. 20 pp.

*795. ———. GODS AND FIGHTING MEN: The Story of the Tuatha de Danaan and of the Fianna of Ireland. Arranged and translated by Lady Gregory. With a preface by W.B. Yeats. London: John Murray, 1904. xxviii,476 pp. Bp: WBY. WADE 258

Flyleaf: Mrs. S. Muir [?]/ 5 Chester Street
Half-title p.: WB Yeats/ from Augusta Gregory.
Flyleaf, upside down, ink, apparently a list of subjects: Old house & her/ Folk art./ change - written art/ It[s] difficulty/ art of few/ tramp-scarecrow etc. [break] Arran [sic] & Galway Inn/ Arran sons/ Mary Hynes/ Ideal woman/ [break] English destroys these [break] Gaelic/ play [break] English/ Folk art - applied arts [break] Psaltery/ Dance/ Drama [break] Loss of personal utterance In Marion [?] [break] strength of personality/ Man & Woman
Preface is revised in pencil, mostly for changes in phrasing to provide copytext for WADE 102, "Thoughts on Lady Gregory's Translations," in CUTTING OF AN AGATE, New York, 1912.
Preface, p. xiv, the passage "I have wished to end" to the end of the page has been canceled.
Preface, p. xxiv, section X has been renumbered III and the beginning revised to: I praise but in brief words the noble writing of these books for words that praise a book ... [a draft of this passage, much the same, appears above Contents on next page; pencil].
Preface, end, "WB. Yeats" is canceled and the date "1902" inserted. [But WADE 102 has "1903."]
P. 382, inserted, a sheet with penciled instructions by WBY: "'Sleep a little' on p. 382 to 'between the streams' on p. 383. Leave out what I have crossed out in book." [On p. 383 WBY has crossed out "Diarmuid, hero of the bright lake of Carman" and the passage beginning "though he is in the woods" through "Ready for good swimming."]
P. 423, the passage beginning "And when Goll knew Finn to be watching" to the end of the page is bracketed.
P. 424, first 9 lines bracketed.
P. 428, pars. 2, 4, 5 bracketed.
P. 429, almost entire page stroked in margin.
P. 436, last par. in Book Ten is stroked in margin.
P. 457, passage beginning "I saw the household of Finn [to] I have seen the household of Finn" canceled, but in margin, pencil: start here.
Pp. 458, 460, marginal strokes.
Back flyleaf, recto: Importance of legends./ Arthur/ courtesy // Macpherson/ Irish legend/ bad translation/ good translation // Two cycles/ pastoral }dates [added later] / agriculture/ hunting/ Aryan - pure Aryan/ witch doctor // Finn or Ossian cycle/ describe/ Usheen & Patrick/ Last Pagan cycle // Cuchulain's

feeling [?] for art/ Heroic beauty - romantic love/ describe/ Emer/ men women desire
Verso, back flyleaf, the list seems to continue: men - the heroic qualities/ Ossian on Finn } quote Usher [?] on Finn // What happens/ Oscar // Goll & Wife [one undecipherable word] // Stories among people - seer / Supernatural life/ grey man in Lateran [?] chapel
Inside back cover: 3.30 Fensal [?] Hall/ Cor[ner] 23 and Maryland Ave. [not WBY's]
Inside back cover, lengthwise: water may come in a very little // fire & air [pencil]

*796. ———. HUGH LANE'S LIFE AND ACHIEVEMENT, with some account of the Dublin galleries. London: John Murray, 1921. xv,[1],290 pp.

P. 120, corner turned back for "Yeats on the Controversy."

797. ———. THE IMAGE AND OTHER PLAYS. London: G.P. Putnam's, 1922. iii,253 pp.

Flyleaf: W.B. Yeats/ from A Gregory/ Oct 29, 1922

*798. ———. IRISH FOLK-HISTORY PLAYS. First Series. The tragedies: GRANIA - KINCORA - DERVORGILLA. New York and London: G.P. Putnam's, 1912. v,[1],207 pp. Sig.: GY

798a. Another copy.

*799. ———. IRISH FOLK-HISTORY PLAYS. Second Series. The Tragic-Comedies: THE CANAVANS, THE WHITE COCKADE, THE DELIVERER. New York and London: G.P. Putnam's, 1912. v,[1],198 pp.

799a. Another copy.

*800. ———. THE KILTARTAN HISTORY BOOK. Illustrated by Robert Gregory. Dublin: Maunsel, 1909. viii,52 pp.

Half-title p.: W B Yeats/ from A Gregory/ Nov 26, '09.

801. ———. Another edition. London: T. Fisher Unwin, 1926. viii,155,[1] pp.

Half-title p.: W B Yeats/ from A Gregory/ April 21, '26.
Some pp. uncut.

802. ———. THE KILTARTAN WONDER BOOK. Illustrated by Margaret Gregory. Dublin: Maunsel, [1910]. [10],103,[2] pp.

Half-title p.: WBY/ from AG/ Xmas 1910
Some pp. uncut.

*803. ———. KINCORA. A Play in Three Acts. Abbey Theatre Series, vol. 2. Dublin: The Abbey Theatre, 1905. 70, [1] pp.

Title p.: W B Yeats/ from A Gregory
Mostly uncut.

804. ———. MIRANDOLINA: A Comedy translated and adapted from La Locandiera of Goldoni. London & New York: G.P. Putnam's, 1924. 77 pp.

Flyleaf: W B Yeats/ from A Gregory./ April, 1924.

805. ———. MY FIRST PLAY. London: Elkin Mathews & Marrot, 1930. 28 pp. 257/530. Sig.: A Gregory

*806. ———. OUR IRISH THEATRE. A Chapter of Autobiography. New York and London: G.P. Putnam's, 1913. v,[1],319 pp. Bp: WBY

*807. ———. POETS AND DREAMERS: Studies and Translations from the Irish. Dublin: Hodges, Figgis, 1903. [8],254 pp.

On sheet pasted on title p., notes that closely resemble those in 795, ink: I do not under rate now [?] or over rate Ireland. // Old word: cultured populace/ Ariosto/ Shakespeare/ Spoken not written/ Printed work aristocratic/ The Tramp // Galway inn/ Arran/ grief of a girl's heart/ Mary Hynes/ Maeve/ alone through the wilderness // Gaelic league/ to keep old arts alive // applied arts of design/ applied arts of literature/ Players, Reciter, singer/ Tradition to help us.
Markings on pp. 49, 50, 51, 64, 65, 83, 85.
P. 77, on a piece of paper pasted in, ink: The folk arts -/ - that of this [one word illegible] of the lyric or the play
P. 153, on a sheet of paper pasted in, ink: Where people are interested [?] they will be still [?]/ [one word?] eyebrows./ Plays on west legends/ Speech & Music & style/ young men from ships // Reciter not an actor/ Work of Miss Farr./ Similarity of speech/ Personality - a living[?] man/ Constructions // When literature goes all goes/ Lion Cub/ Old brings new
Back flyleaf, ink: old art & new/ The great Table [?]/ spoken and not written/ Tramp
Gaelic poetry/ Galway inn/ Arran. grief of a girl's Heart
nobility of speaking/ Mary Hynes/ Maeve/ Ideal Woman
Inside back cover, continuing the above: all this goes with Irish gaelic movement [one word illegible]. Folk arts. applied arts/ degradation of literature part of/ general degradation // drama & song. // speak with music [canceled] // love [canceled] Recitation - measure for // Love of listening to/ Love of poems/ Construction/ personality. abstract Power/ need [?] for literature/ Lions cub

808. ———. THE STORY BROUGHT BY BRIGIT: A Passion Play in Three Acts. London and New York: G.P. Putnam's, 1924. vi,97 pp.

Flyleaf: W B Yeats/ from A Gregory/ Oct 14, 1924

809. ———. THREE LAST PLAYS. London & New York: G.P. Putnam's, 1928. 220 pp.

Flyleaf: W.B. Yeats/ from A Gregory/ May 12, 1928.

810. ———. THREE WONDER PLAYS. London & New York: G.P. Putnam's, [1923]. 222 pp.

Inside frt. cover: Anne Yeats from her father/ W B Yeats. My dear Anne, I give you three "Wonder/ Plays" by my greatest friend. You will be able to/ act some scenes out of them./ W B Yeats.
Removed to Anne Yeats's personal library.

*811. ———. VISIONS AND BELIEFS IN THE WEST OF IRELAND. Collected and arranged by Lady Gregory. With two essays and notes by W.B. Yeats. 2 vols. New York and London: G.P. Putnam's, 1920.

Vol. 1 only.
P. 265, the title "Note 1" is canceled.
P. 272, the segment of Note 1 on this p. is canceled.
P. 293, Notes 40-44 canceled.
P. 247, inserted, a scrap of paper with a note, pencil, WBY's: Witches and Wizards and Irish Folklore/ 247-62.

*812. ———, ed. MR. GREGORY'S LETTER-BOX, 1813-1830. London: Smith, Elder, 1898. [8],352 pp.

Flyleaf: W. B. Yeats/ from the editor,/ March 6, 1898.

813. ———, ed. SIR WILLIAM GREGORY, K.C.M.G. Formerly Member of Parliament and Sometime Governor of Ceylon. London: John Murray, 1894. viii,[1],407 pp.

SEE ALSO 1330.

814. Greville, Charles C[avendish] F[ulke]. A JOURNAL OF THE REIGNS OF KING GEORGE IV. AND KING WILLIAM IV. Edited by Henry Reeve. The Greville Memoirs. 3rd ed. 3 vols. London: Longmans, Green, 1875.

815. Grierson, Francis. MODERN MYSTICISM AND OTHER ESSAYS. London: George Allen, 1899. viii,144 pp.

Some pp. uncut.

816. Grierson, Herbert J[ohn] C[lifford]. METAPHYSICAL LYRICS AND POEMS OF THE SEVENTEENTH CENTURY. Donne to Butler. Oxford: Clarendon Press, 1921. lviii,[2],244 pp.

Flyleaf: W. B. Yeats/ from his friend, the Editor/ 9.11.22.
Some pp. uncut.

GRIEVE, Christopher Murray. See M'Diarmid, Hugh

817. Griffith, Arthur. THE RESURRECTION OF HUNGARY: A Parallel for Ireland. With appendices on Pitt's policy and Sinn Fein. 3rd ed. Dublin: Whelan, 1918. xxxii,[2],170 pp.

818. Grose, S[idney] W[illiam]. CATALOGUE OF THE McCLEAN COLLECTION OF GREEK COINS. 2 vols. Cambridge: Univ. Press, 1923 & 1926. Sig.: WBY

819. Gubernatis, Angelo de. ZOOLOGICAL MYTHOLOGY or the legends of animals. 2 vols. London: Trübner, 1872.

820. Guedala, Philip. BONNET AND SHAWL, AN ALBUM. [Essays on 19th century women.] New York: Crosby Gaige, 1928. 200 pp. 18/571. Sig.: Philip Guedala

Many pp. uncut.

GUEST, Lady Charlotte. See 1166.

*821. Guiney, Louise Imogen. ROBERT EMMET. A Survey of His Rebellion and of His Romance. London: David Nutt, 1904. viii,102 pp.

Mostly uncut.

822. Gwynn, Stephen. IRISH LITERATURE AND DRAMA IN THE ENGLISH LANGUAGE: A SHORT HISTORY. London: Thomas Nelson, 1936. ix,[1],240 pp.

823. ———. THE LIFE AND FRIENDSHIPS OF DEAN SWIFT. London: Thornton Butterworth, 1933. 319,[1] pp.

P. 106, a marginal stroke against the passage "It was a theory of his, referred to in one of his TATLERS (No. 66), that 'a certain insensibility in the countenance recommends a sentence of humour and jest.'"

*824. THE GYPSY (London). 1 (May 1915).

Contains work of Arthur Symons, Edmund Gosse, Richard Le Gallienne, Katharine Tynan, Walter de la Mare, Arthur Machen.

825. Hackett, Francis. Review of POEMS AND TRANSLATIONS by John M. Synge. THE CHICAGO EVENING POST, FRIDAY LITERARY SUPPLEMENT, 2 July 1909, p. 1.

With a reproduction of Jack Yeats's "The Tinker" from THE SHANACHIE.

826. Hâfiz, Shīrāzī. SELECTIONS FROM THE RUBAIYAT & ODES OF HAFIZ. Translated by a member of the Persia Society of London. With an account of Sûfi Mysticism. London: John M. Watkins, 1920. 147 pp.

Preface and Glossary cut; otherwise mostly uncut.

827. Haldane, [Richard Burdon], Viscount. HUMAN EXPERIENCE. A Study of its Structure. London: John Murray, 1926. xxiv,230 pp.

Title p.: W.B. Yeats/ from/ The Writer

*828. Halévy, Daniel. THE LIFE OF FRIEDRICH NIETZSCHE. Translated by J.M. Hone. London: T. Fisher Unwin, 1911. 368 pp.

P. 213, marginal strokes for passage beginning "Et in Arcadia ego [to] My watch registered half-past five."
P. 243, corner turned back.

*829. Hall, H[arry] R[eginald]. AEGEAN ARCHAEOLOGY. London: Philip Lee Warner, 1915. xxi,[1],270 pp.

P. 83, corner turned back and this note at passage "The association of the cat with the snake...:" "All cats were once serpents" Irish belief - WBY.
P. 240, corner turned back, description of golden spiral coils.

*830. Hallam, Arthur Henry. THE POEMS OF ARTHUR HENRY HALLAM, together with his essay on the Lyrical Poems of Alfred Tennyson. Edited by Richard Le Gallienne. London: Elkin Mathews, 1893. xxxix,139 pp.

831. Hamer, John. SELECTIONS OF AMERICAN HUMOUR IN PROSE AND VERSE. London: Cassell, [1883?]. 318 pp.

Flyleaf: To Willy/ from his Grandmama/ Christmas 1886. [Also a sketch of a horse and jockey, by Jack Yeats?]
Missing binding.

*832. Hammer [-Purgstall], Joseph, trans. ANCIENT ALPHABETS AND HIEROGLYPHIC CHARACTERS EXPLAINED; with an account of the Egyptian priests, their classes, initiation, and sacrifices, in the Arabic language by Ahmad Bin Abubekr Bin Wahshih and in English by Joseph Hammer. London: G. and W. Nicholl, 1806. xxi,54,136 pp.

833. Hannay, James Ballantyne. THE RISE, DECLINE & FALL OF THE ROMAN RELIGION. London: Privately printed for the Religious Evolution Research Society, 1925. xiv,257 pp.

HARDENBERG, Friedrick Leopold. See Novalis.

*834. Hardy, Thomas. THE DYNASTS, An Epic-Drama of the war with Napoleon. London: Macmillan, 1910. xv,525 pp.

Flyleaf: to W.B. Yeats/ from/ Thomas Hardy/ June: 1912.
Almost entirely uncut.
Inserted, a program and a list of characters for a performance. See 1066.

835. ———. LATE LYRICS AND EARLIER, with many other verses. London: Macmillan, 1922. xxiv,288 pp.

836. ———. THE WESSEX NOVELS. Macmillan's Pocket Hardy. 18 vols. London: Macmillan, 1906- . Vol. 2 [Vol. 1 missing]: FAR FROM THE MADDING CROWD, 1906. Sig.: Georgie Hyde-Lees./ Jan. 1909

837. ———. Vol. 3: THE LIFE AND DEATH OF THE MAYOR OF CASTERBRIDGE, 1916.

838. ———. Vol. 4: JUDE THE OBSCURE, 1910.

839. ———. Vol. 5: THE RETURN OF THE NATIVE, 1907. Sig.: Georgie Hyde-Lees/ October, 1909

840. ———. Vol. 6: A PAIR OF BLUE EYES, 1906. Sig.: Georgie Hyde-Lees/ Oct. 16, 1908

841. ———. Vol. 7: TWO ON A TOWER, 1906. Sig.: Georgie Hyde-Lees,/ Xmas 1907

842. ———. Vol. 8: THE WOODLANDERS, 1906. Sig.: Georgie Hyde-Lees./ Xmas 1907

843. ———. Vol. 9: THE TRUMPET-MAJOR AND ROBERT HIS BROTHER. Sig.: Georgie Hyde-Lees/ October 1907

844. ———. Vol. 10: THE HAND OF ETHELBERTA, 1907. Sig.: Georgie Hyde-Lees/ February 1909

(Vol. 11 missing.)

845. ———. Vol. 12: DESPERATE REMEDIES, 1907. Sig.: Georgie Hyde-Lees,/ February, 1909

846. ———. Vol. 13: WESSEX TALES, 1907. Sig.: Georgie Hyde-Lees/ Jan., 1909

847. ———. Vol. 14: LIFE'S LITTLE IRONIES [etc.], 1907. Sig.: Georgie Hyde-Lees

(Vol. 15 missing.)

848. ———. Vol. 16: UNDER THE GREENWOOD TREE, 1907. Sig.: Georgie Hyde Lees/ Xmas 1907

849. ———. Vol. 17: THE WELL-BELOVED, 1907.

(Vol. 18 missing.)

850. Harrison, Henry. PARNELL VINDICATED. The Lifting of the Veil. London: Constable, 1931. viii,447 pp.

Title p.: W. B. Yeats/ from/ The Author/ 23.7.36.

*851. Hartland, Edwin Sidney, ed. ENGLISH FAIRY AND OTHER FOLK TALES. London: Walter Scott, [1890]. xxviii,282 pp. Sig.: W B Yeats/ June, 1890

852. ———. MYTHOLOGY AND FOLKTALES: THEIR RELATIONS AND INTERPRETATION. Popular Studies in Mythology, Romance & Folklore, no. 7. London: David Nutt, 1900. 53 pp.

Back flyleaf: Earlier life [?] - heroic literature [?]/ The coming to foreign lands/ 12-13 cent. [one word illegible]/ The fisher king/ sick king/ [one line undecipherable]/ -Tarot-/ Its history is European/ from North/ the globe/ Myths are powerful/ not from ancient living [two words illegible]/ recreate our myth

853. Hartmann, Franz. THE LIFE AND DOCTRINES OF JACOB BOEHME, THE GOD-TAUGHT PHILOSOPHER. An introduction to the study of his works. London: Kegan Paul, Trench, Trubner, 1891. xii,338 pp. Sig.: WBY

Markings and notes very heavy throughout. Two annotators, WBY and Edwin Ellis. Yeats's notes are in black and blue pencil and pen, Ellis's in purple pencil with a few in black pencil. Many notes refer to Blake, and this work was obviously used to prepare their joint ed. of THE WORKS OF WILLIAM BLAKE (1893). Except where noted, the annotations are judged to be WBY's (in pencil).

P. 7, at "The whole Christian religion": compare Vala [purple, Ellis]

P. 9, at "Look at the flowers": but they do [purple, Ellis]

P. 21, at "A third translation": no, it was only edited by Law. The translation was spurious [ink].

P. 26, last par., at "When": When? "Before Abraham was, I am" [purple, Ellis].

P. 30, at "mountain": mountain [purple, Ellis]

P. 62, at "Sense the mind of a man": asleep?

P. 69, at "so as to become revealed": out into what? If there is an out unity is dead.

P. 73, pars. 1 & 2: where were the six before generating the seventh?

P. 73, par. 5: What a figure of speech.

P. 74, par. 4: The word "become's" fatal to thought.

P. 76, top of p.: All this in Urizen.

P. 76, par. 1: produce!

P. 76, par. 3: thin-heavy

P. 77, par. 5: Los/anguish

P. 100, par. 2: separation/ quality of will/Urizen [purple, Ellis].

P. 103, par. 2: myths [purple, Ellis]

P. 105 (misprinted as 150), par. 5: fire [purple, Ellis]

P. 108, par. 2: sound [purple, Ellis]

P. 112, par. 3: Phantastry/ Phantastry opposed to imagination. See "Book of Urizen" Chapter 1.

P. 113, par. 2: Satan/ opacity [purple, Ellis]

P. 113, par. 4: compare Urizen called King

P. 116, par. 1: murder/ Orc [?] &/ Truth armour [purple, Ellis]

P. 117, par. 1: Urizen repelled/ by the Eternals
P. 117, par. 3: Urizen/ separation [purple, Ellis]
P. 121, par. 1: Thistle and nettle [purple, Ellis]
P. 128, par. 1: Compare Book of Los, Chapt. 2 & the differentiation [?] of the "element." [pencil, WBY]/ Compare Blake's Dark Hermaphrodite [purple, Ellis]
P. 131, par. 4: King & Councilors (Urizen) [purple, Ellis]
P. 132, par. 1: Stars from sun [purple, Ellis]
P. 133, par. 4: Orc
P. 134, par. 6: Compare 8th chapter of Urizen
P. 135, par. 6: "Female Will" in Blake
P. 136, par. 5: Quote in Blake book
P. 137, note: Will is Feminine. See last page but two [?]
P. 138, at "The expression that God": Compare Book of Thel/ Chapt. 3
P. 139, top: "mighty was the draught of voidness to draw creation in" [purple, Ellis]/ Blake [WBY]
P. 141, par. 2: "all gods exist within the human breasts"
P. 141, par. 5, bottom: spiritual intelligence food - see "Vala" [purple, Ellis]
P. 142, par. 2: "Trans-lucence"
P. 142, par. 4: external is sulphuric [purple, Ellis]
P. 142, par. 6: Los, iron forge growing [purple, Ellis]
P. 143, par. 2: Time [purple, Ellis]
P. 143, par. 3: mild fire (Vala) [purple, Ellis]
P. 145, pars. 6 & 7: Compare description in Jerusalem of universal man
P. 152, par. 3: "two wills they had & two intellects that as in time of old" [purple, Ellis]
P. 152, par. 4: Three Zoas each attempt to enslave man [purple, Ellis]
P. 154, par. 2: The Tree of mystery grown in the human brain [purple, Ellis]
P. 155, top: Moses = wisdom [purple, Ellis]
P. 155, par. 3: Tree [purple, Ellis]
P. 156, pars. 1-4; Compare sleep of Los in III Chapt. Book of Los
P. 160, par. 4: The vast form of nature like a serpent [purple, Ellis]
P. 160, par. 5: serpent/ Trees [purple, Ellis]
P. 161, par. 4: serpent/ Tree [purple, Ellis]
P. 171, par. 3: compare Book of Los/ Chapt. 1
P. 173, par. 3: why earth turns [purple, Ellis]
P. 174, passim: elements are states/ fire Urizen/ air Kanva/ water Manas [?]/ earth [one word?]/ elements/ Zoas war [purple, Ellis]
P. 175, par. 1: quote
P. 175, pars. 6 & 7: gold/ precious stones [purple, Ellis]
P. 176, pars. 5 & 6: animals & elements/ monkeys [purple, Ellis]
P. 177, at "Behold a tree": quote apropos of tree of knowledge
P. 178, par. beginning "Where a desire exists": Orc

P. 178, par. beginning "The tincture produces all colours": Quote apropos of The Rainbow.
P. 178, at "the oil therein is a light or a life...": quote apropos of Thel page 5 line 1
P. 179, last par.: quote apropos of correspondence
P. 191, par. 1: quote apropos of Adam
Pp. 206, 207, faint pencil notes, illegible.
P. 208, par. 1: quote apropos of Cain & Abel
P. 209, top: Cain - evil/ Abel - good/ seek the equilibrium/ Pallas or Hermetics [?]
P. 209, pars. 4 & 5: in Blake Cain who represents the corporal life is to be spared the vengeance seeking restriction sacrifice for sin - of this spiritual life
P. 210, top: Cain corporal fashioning mind
P. 214, bottom: "Religion of Priam"
P. 218, at note: Hence Blake's talk of "sacrifices for sin." The law robs man of infinity by catching from him his freedom [likely Ellis's].
P. 220, at note: compare Blake's animal symbols
P. 222, 1st par.: consummation [purple, Ellis]
P. 222, 2nd par.: will [purple, Ellis]
P. 224, after intro.: From the Smaragdine Table of Hermes [likely Ellis's]
P. 226, 2nd par.: Head, Heart, Loins [WBY's?]
P. 226, mid-page: planets [purple, Ellis]
P. 226, bottom: sun, moon, & stars/ in man [purple, Ellis]
P. 227, par. 4: Compare Blake on the Virgin "she should a harlot have been"
P. 228, top, referring to "eternal God" in line 2: Why not? If God is in man he must pass to man's son unless the son is born dead; then he is not a son but the empty case which might have contained a son [purple, Ellis]
P. 228, referring to last 4 lines of par. 1: all is based on the error that son of Man means, of vegetated man only. [purple, Ellis]
P. 228, par. 3: Contrast again (see last page). See Jerusalem page _____ [blank] for nature of this Virgin
P. 228, par. 4: this is out of keeping with 1st paragraph of this page [purple, Ellis]
P. 229, par. 2: not quite Blakean. The reason of this difference is that imagination and not purity is held by him as the great need.
P. 230, par. 3: Jerusalem enters Vala
P. 231, par. 4 at "extinguished": has this to do with the sun plunged into the water (Book of Los, Chapt. III) in any remote sense?
P. 235, par. 5: In Blake he was born magically (see drawing of this nativity)
P. 238, top, referring to "red-hot iron": a simile used I think more than once by Boehme and also I think by Swedenborg. Has it to do with the Blacksmith's work of Los in Blake? [likely Ellis's]

P. 238, par. 4: Jerusalem [Ellis's?]
P. 239, par. 2: The Universal Man [Ellis's?]
P. 241, bottom: These last three pages are fine and picturesque [Ellis's?]
P. 247, last par.: the fiery sword/ broken - quote [Ellis]
P. 251, top: Did not Blake say to someone that Christ was wrong to let them crucify him? [Ellis's?]
P. 243, at "regenerate that image": re-generation is a second giving off or producing of the divine image extinguished, not an improvement of corporeal character morally [purple, Ellis]
P. 244, end of 1st par.: serpent [purple, Ellis]
P. 244, par. 3, at "four elements": combination of the Zoas [purple, Ellis]
Markings break off after p. 255.

*854. ———. THE LIFE OF PHILIPPUS THEOPHRASTUS BOMBAST OF HOHENHEIM KNOWN BY THE NAME OF PARACELSUS [etc.]. 2nd ed. London: Kegan Paul, Trench, Trubner, [1896.]. xvi,311 pp. Bp: WBY

Many pp. uncut.
Chapt. 4, sections on Anthropology, Death cut, pp. 97-102.
Chapt. 5, Pneumatology, pp. 103-127, cut.

855. Hastings, James, and John A[lexander] Selbie et al., ENCYCLOPAEDIA OF RELIGION AND ETHICS. 12 vols. Edinburgh: T. & C. Clark, 1908-21.

VOL. 1, p. 184, marginal strokes and astrological symbols illustrating passages, pars. 1, 2, 3 ("The rulers of the zodiac are the sun, the moon, and Venus"), 6, 7 in "Ages of the World (Babylonian)."
P. 185, astrological symbols illustrating material in "2. The historic period" and column 2, par. beginning "In the region of further Asia" in "Ages of the World (Babylonian)."
P. 187, pars. 1 in column 1, 1 in column 2, 5 in column 2 are stroked and a note at bottom of p. referring to par. 5, column 2: Istar in Hades = all [?] lives before flood/ Noah the deliverer/ In reversed order of precursors [?] the entrance of Noah into Ark would be like an entrance into the womb./ Phase before 15./ In direct order it is the birth from womb into [one word].

VOL. 11, p. 753, 2nd column, marginal stroke at passage "The mind of a man is seen, on occasion, in the form of some animal...."
P. 791, top, 2nd column, marginal stroke for 20 lines at discussion of Holy Spirit.

VOL. 12, pp. 130, 135, 146, 151, 156, small ink spots as if a pen dripped or was sprayed on these pp.

856. Hauptmann, Gerhart. THE DRAMATIC WORKS. Edited by Ludwig Lewisohn. 7 vols. London: Martin Secker, 1912-14. Vol. 3: DOMESTIC DRAMAS, 1914.

Vol. 3 only.

857. ———. THE SUNKEN BELL. A fairy play in five acts. Translated by Charles Henry Meltzer. New York: R.H. Russell, 1899. 125 pp.

Flyleaf: W.B. Yeats Esq./ with compliments of/ Charles Henry Meltzer.

858. ———. THE WEAVERS. A drama of the forties. Translated by Mary Morison. New York: B.W. Huebsch, 1911. viii, 148 pp.

Title p.: Lennox Robinson/ Chicago. Feb. 1912.

859. Havell, E[rnest] B[infield]. A HANDBOOK OF INDIAN ART. London: John Murray, 1920. xvi,222 pp.

Inserted at p. 121, items 193 and 1006.

860. Hayes, Edward, ed. THE BALLADS OF IRELAND. 2 vols. London, Edinburgh, and Dublin: A Fullarton, 1855.

Title pp., both vols., stamped: Alexr G. Richey/ 27. Up Pembroke St/ Dublin.
Inserted in Vol. 1, the title p. and dedication p. of another copy of this book, Vol. 1, 4th ed.

861. Hazlemere, Robert. STARRY EARTH. A Book of Poems and Lyrics. Toronto: McClelland & Stewart, 1929. 80 pp.

P. 75, an "X" against the poem "One Artist to Another" which refers to WBY.

862. Head, Barclay V[incent]. SYNOPSIS OF THE CONTENTS OF THE BRITISH MUSEUM, DEPARTMENT OF COINS AND MEDALS. A Guide to the Principal Gold and Silver Coins of the Ancients. 2nd ed. London: Longmans, 1881. viii,128 pp., 70 plates. Bp: The Right Hon. W.H. Gregory. K.C.M.G./ Coole Park,/ Gort,/ Ireland

Many pp. loose from binding.

863. Heard, Gerald. THE ASCENT OF HUMANITY. An essay on the evolution of civilization from group consciousness through individuality to super-consciousness. London: Jonathan Cape, 1929. xiv,332 pp.

864. Heath, Lionel, ed. EXAMPLES OF INDIAN ART AT THE BRITISH EMPIRE EXHIBITION, 1924. With an introductory and critical note by Lionel Heath. London: The India Society, 1925. 31 pp.

865. Heath, Thomas. THE TWENTIETH CENTURY ATLAS OF POPULAR ASTRONOMY. Comprising in sixteen plates a series of

illustrations of the heavenly bodies. 3rd ed. Edinburgh: W. & A.K. Johnston, [1922?]. [8],134 pp., 16 plates.

Inside frt. cover: W B Yeats/ 82 Merrion Square

866. Heathcote, Sir Henry. TREATISE ON STAY-SAILS, for the purpose of intercepting wind between the square-sails of ships and other square-rigged vessels [etc.]. London: Baldwin, Cradock, and Joy, 1824. 77,[19] pp.

867. Hedin, Sven. TRANS-HIMALAYA. Discoveries and Adventures in Tibet. 3 vols. London: Macmillan, 1910-13. Bps: GY

Clipped to back flyleaf, Vol. 3, a review of Hedin's MOUNT EVEREST. See 2148.

868. Hegel, G[eorg] W]ilhelm] F[riedrich]. HEGEL'S LOGIC OF WORLD AND IDEA. A Translation of the second and third parts of the subjective logic. [Translated by] Henry S. Macran. Oxford: The Clarendon Press, 1929. 215 pp. Sig.: WBY

Inserted, an unidentified review of this book apparently in the IRISH TIMES.

869. ———. THE LOGIC OF HEGEL, translated from THE ENCYCLOPAEDIA OF THE PHILOSOPHICAL SCIENCES. Translated by William Wallace. 2nd ed. Oxford: The Clarendon Press, 1892. xxvi,[2],439 pp. Sig.: WBY

Marginal strokes, underscorings, brief notes pp. 36, 37, 50, 51, 52, 225, 226, 227, 228, 229, 259, 415, 416, 418.
Corners turned back, pp. 5, 68, 116, 313.
P. 37, lines 3-5: ?C.B.
P. 37, lines 9-10: B.F.
P. 259, at "equally recognise to be the only truth": compare Guido on love with Plato. Church view of marriage is Aristotelian.
P. 415, last 4 lines of final par.: Daimon/ Principle/ Faculties // Daimon/ and/ Time and Space

870. Heitland, W[illiam] E[merton]. THE ROMAN FATE. An Essay in Interpretation. Cambridge: The Univ. Press, 1922. 80 pp.

*871. Henderson, T[homas] F[inlayson]. SCOTTISH VERNACULAR LITERATURE. A Succinct History. 3rd ed. Edinburgh: John Grant, 1910. xiv,462 pp. Bp: WBY

Mostly uncut.

*872. Henley, W[illiam] E[rnest]. BURNS, LIFE, GENIUS, ACHIEVEMENT. Reprinted from The Centenary Burns. Edinburgh: T.C. and E.C. Jack, 1898. 233-348 pp.

A few pp. uncut.

*873. ———. ESSAYS. London: Macmillan, 1920. x,432 pp.

Cut exclusively for the essays "Byron's World," pp. 230-350, and for "'Pippin,'" "Balzac as He Was," and "The Two Hugos."

*874. ———. POEMS. London: Macmillan, 1921. xxiii,290 pp.

"Ballade of Dead Actors," p. 59 and "Since those we love and those we hate," p. 180 are excised to make half of Henley's selection for the OBMV.

*875. ———. VIEWS AND REVIEWS. Essays in Appreciation. London: Macmillan, 1921. xii,373 pp.

Cut are essays on Dickens, Thackeray, Victor Hugo, Rabelais, Landor, Boswell, Fielding and "A Note on Romanticism" [in art].

*876. ———, ed. LYRA HEROICA. A Book of Verse for Boys. London: Macmillan, 1921. xx,370 pp.

Many pp. uncut.

SEE ALSO 171.

*877. ——— and Robert Louis Stevenson. PLAYS. London: Macmillan, 1921. 295 pp.

Cut only for the first play, DEACON BRODIE.

*878. Herbert, Edward. THE AUTOBIOGRAPHY OF EDWARD, LORD HERBERT OF CHERBURY. With intro. [etc.] by Sidney Lee. 2nd ed. London: George Routledge, [1906]. xli,214 pp. Bp: WBY

Back flyleaf: 88/ 107/ 143
P. 143, two horizontal strokes against reference to Herbert applying himself to historical investigations, following example of More and Bacon.

879. Herbert, George. THE ENGLISH POEMS. Together with his collection of proverbs entitled Jacula Prudentum. London: Longmans, Green, 1902. xi,260 pp.

Back flyleaf: 28 Fitzwilliam Place [doubtfully WBY's]

*880. ———. THE WORKS OF GEORGE HERBERT. The Chandos Classics. London & New York: Frederick Warne, [1885?]. xiv,[2], 488 pp.

Some pp. uncut, especially in prose.

881. Hermes Trismegistus. HERMETICA. The Ancient Greek and Latin writings which contain religious or philosophic teachings ascribed to Hermes Trismegistus. Edited with translation and notes by Walter Scott. 3 vols. Oxford: The Clarendon Press, 1924.

VOL. 1, many marginal strokes, underscorings, astrological symbols, and notes.
P. 121, last par.: sphere [pencil]

P. 129, astrological symbols at key words in text:
[works] ♄ , [zone] ☿ , [lust] ♀ , [domineering] ☉,
[audacity] ♂, [seventh] ♃.[symbol]

P. 143, top:

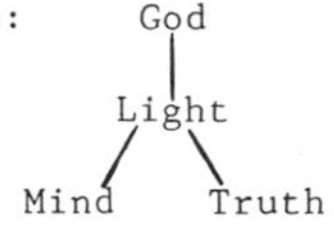

P. 177, lines 4-7: Cave & sphere
P. 199, lines 5-9: soul & spirit
P. 325, at 1st full par.: God/ life
P. 325, at 2nd par.: stars/ forms
P. 325, at 3rd par.: planets/ growth/ destiny [all the above bracketed and labeled with symbol "fire"]
P. 325, at 4th par.: instrument [and symbol for "air"]
P. 325, at 6th par.: Food [and the symbols for "water" and "earth"]
P. 327, bottom: Matter invisible apart from mind
P. 329, at "if they originate...": individual differs not from starry influence but because moments differ. Stars are but the clock.
P. 335, mid-page: union of opposites
P. 353, line 1, referring to "in motion": "daimon not phasal"
P. 355, last par.: Memory human alone
P. 357, par. 2, "Kosmos": cosmic mind needs no memory
P. 399, line 3: force = husk
P. 401, last par., "pain and enjoyment: Dreaming Back
P. 413, a diagram:

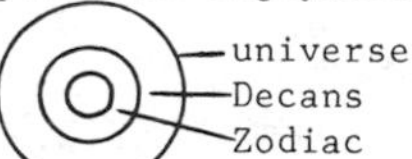

Inside back cover: Evolution - Libellus X/ Matter - 327 - 17b/ Memory - 355/ Destiny & Necessity 363, 365, 421, 437, 441, 541/ Necessity 433 (46) 435.

VOL. 2, many pp. uncut.

VOL. 3, mostly uncut.

882. ——— (Ermete Trimegisto). IL PIMANDRO OSSIA L'INTELLIGENZA SUPREMA CHE SI RIVELA E PARLA ED ALTRI SCRITTI ERMETICI. Translated into Italian by Dr. Giovanni Bonanni. Todi: "Atanòr," 1913. 180 pp.

Back flyleaf, a list, GBY's, of hermetic works and verso a list of waiters, porters etc. and how much they are to be tipped.
Inserted, a page of stationery from Hotel Elysee, Rome, with GBY's discussion of astrology in Hindu beliefs.

883. ———. THE PYMANDER OF HERMES. Edited with preface by W. Wynn Westcott, Supreme Magus of the Rosicrucian Society. Collectanea Hermetica, vol. 2. London:

Theosophical Publishing Society, 1894. vi,117 pp. Sig.: Jas Stephens

Some notes passim, James Stephens's.
Marginal strokes, "x's," pp. 16, 17, 19, 20-3, 25-30, 34-45, 47, 48, 50-60, 62, 63, 65, 66, 68, 69, 72-4, 76-84, 86-9, 91, 92-4, 97-99, 101, 103, 104, 107-110, 112, 115-17.
Inside back cover, a bookseller's notation.

*884. ——— (Hermès Trismégiste). TRADUCTION COMPLETE, précédée d'une étude sur l'origine des livres hermétiques par Louis Ménard. 2nd ed. Paris: Didier, 1867. cxii,302 pp.

*885. Herodotus. HERODOTUS. Translated by the Rev. Henry Cary. Bohn's Classical Library. London: G. Bell, 1912. vi, 613 pp. Bp: WBY

Flyleaf: 16/ 22, 42, 44/ The Notes, Markings etc. are all/ by Ezra Pound [WBY's hand]
In text, a few notes by Pound; also marginal stroking and symbols entered passim.
Back flyleaf and inside back cover, Pound's list of p. nos. and references: 375, 379, 381, 393, 414, 417 dream, 418-9, 422, 435, 453 Herald, 512, 539 foreign tongue, 584 afford [?], 591 fish [this list on flyleaf]
Inside back cover: 79, 104, 116, 121, 143, 202, 218, 243 Artist [canceled], 248 hyperborean virgins, 250 circum Africa, 262, 264, 272, 296 noh nishikigi, 299, 300, 328, 331, 341, 344 burnt garments, 346, 361.

*886. Herrick, Robert. THE COMPLETE POEMS. Edited by Alexander B. Grosart. 3 vols. London: Chatto and Windus, 1876.

Vol. 1, flyleaf: To W.B. Yeats/ from/ W[illiam] E[rnest] H[enley]./ 21.9.95
Vol. 3 is missing.

887. ———. DELIGHTED EARTH, a selection from Herrick's "Hesperides." Edited by Peter Meadows. Illustrated by Lionel Ellis. London: The Fanfrolico Press, [1927]. 171 pp. -/550

Flyleaf: William Butler Yeats's Copy/ from/ Lionel Ellis.

*888. ———. THE POEMS OF ROBERT HERRICK. Edited by John Masefield. London: E. Grant Richards, 1906. xxxiv,313 pp.

Flyleaf: W. B. Yeats/ from/ John Masefield/ Dec. 20, 1906.
Some pp. uncut.

*889. ———. POEMS SELECTED FROM THE HESPERIDES. With initial letters and decorations cut on wood from designs by H.M. O'Kane. New Rochelle, New York: Printed and sold by Clarke Conwell at the Elston Press, 1903. 154[1] pp.

Some pp. uncut.

890. Hessen, Prof. B[oris]. THE SOCIAL AND ECONOMIC ROOTS OF NEWTON'S 'PRINCIPIA.' Papers read to the Second International Congress of the History of Science and Technology, by the delegates of the U.S.S.R. London: June 29th to July 3rd, 1931. London: Kniga, 1931. ii, 62 pp.

*891. Hettinger, Franz. DANTE'S DIVINA COMMEDIA: ITS SCOPE AND VALUE. Edited [and translated?] by Henry Sebastian Bowden. 2nd ed. London: Burns & Oates, 1894. xxxvi, 425 pp.

Corners of pages 115 and 240 turned back; paper slip inserted at pp. 280-1.

*892. [Heywood, Thomas]. THOMAS HEYWOOD [Five Plays]. Edited by A. Wilson Verity. Introduction by J. Addington Symonds. The Mermaid Series. London: T. Fisher Unwin, [1903]. xxxiv,427 pp.

Includes A WOMAN KILLED WITH KINDNESS, THE FAIR MAID OF THE WEST, THE ENGLISH TRAVELLER, THE WIDE WOMAN OF HOGSDON, THE RAPE OF LUCRECE.

892a. Another copy.

H[IFFERNAN], P[aul] M.D. See 608.

893. Higgins, F[rederick] R[obert]. THE DARK BREED. A Book of Poems. London: Macmillan, 1927. viii,69 pp.

Checked in Contents, two poems that appear in the OBMV, "The Little Clan," and "The Ballad of O'Bruadir." Also a query beside "An Old Air."
Pp. 11-12, WBY has revised "The Ballad of O'Bruadir"; the version in the OBMV follows these revisions with some additional changes.
Inserted, a leaf torn, it appears, from a magazine; on one side a poem by Higgins, "The Little Field"; title is canceled in ink and revised to "The Song of a Fool." Last line, "seek" revised to: have [not WBY's]

894. ———. ISLAND BLOOD. With a foreword by A.E. London: John Lane, 1925. xii,[2],74 pp.

Flyleaf: To W.B. Yeats, Esq./ in deep admiration/ F R Higgins/ April '25.

894a. Another copy.

895. ———. SALT AIR. Poems. Decorated by W. Victor Brown. Dublin: Irish Bookshop, 1923. [6] pp.

895a. Another copy.

896. THE HIGH HISTORY OF THE HOLY GRAAL. Translated from the old French by Sebastian Evans. London: J.M. Dent, [1910]. xxii,379 pp.

897. THE HISTORY OF THE THEATRE ROYAL, DUBLIN. From its foundation in 1821 to the present time. Reprinted with additions from Saunders' News-letter. Dublin: Edward Ponsonby, 1870. 204 pp.

*898. Hofmannsthal, Hugo von. ELECTRA. A Tragedy in One Act. Translated by Arthur Symons. New York: Brentano's, 1908. 83 pp. Bp: WBY. Bp: Beatrice Stella Campbell

Parts of speeches canceled in pencil, pp. 32, 33, 37, 41, 42 [probably WBY's].
Inside back cover, the numbers I to VI; also a diagram, possibly a stage and the phrase: Have sent her [WBY's].

899. Hogg, Thomas Jefferson et al. THE LIFE OF PERCY BYSSHE SHELLEY AS COMPRISED IN THE LIFE OF SHELLEY: THE RECOLLECTIONS OF SHELLEY & BYRON by Edward John Trelawny; MEMOIRS OF SHELLEY by Thomas Love Peacock. [Edited] with an intro. by Humbert Wolfe. 2 vols. London & Toronto: J.M. Dent, 1933.

900. [Hokusai, Katsushika]. OWARI TOHEKIDO 20 HANGAFUSHO TEHON MOKUROKA [a vol. of a catalog of comic pictures by Hokusai]. Copied by Sirakuya Toshiro. No pub. info.

On slip pasted on cover: Sketches by <u>Hokusai</u> (about 1760-1850. [not WBY's]
Above two of the sketches, labels affixed identifying them as "A Ghost" and "The Ghost of the Sea" (not WBY's).

901. Holberg, Ludvig. THREE COMEDIES. Translated from the Danish by Lieut. Colonel H.W.L. Hime. London: Longmans, Green, 1912. [2],xi,207 pp.

902. Holmes, Edmond. THE SILENCE OF LOVE. Poems. London and New York: John Lane, 1899. [61] pp.

Flyleaf: from the author/ (a native of the Bog of Allen)/ 1899.

903. Holmes, William Gordon. THE AGE OF JUSTINIAN AND THEODORA. A History of the Sixth Century A.D. 2nd ed. 2 Vols. London: G. Bell, 1912.

Vol. 1 only.
Pp. 42-119, "Constantinople in the Sixth Century," many markings and marginal notes; most notes simply repeat a key word from the text.
P. 47: pillars and [?]
P. 48, near top: column
P. 49, near bottom: image of Christ
P. 51: Daphne statue
P. 57, mid-page: Public [?] and statues
P. 57, lower margin: Homer
P. 58, first full par.: bazaar/ silks etc.
P. 59, near top: silver statues
P. 59, near bottom: Golden column or milestone

P. 60, near top: arch/ equestrian statue
P. 63, near top: obelisk
P. 63, near bottom: column/ pillar
P. 64: statues/ archway
P. 65, near top: copies on [?]
P. 66: gilded horse/ eagle & viper
P. 67: Helen/ animals etc.
P. 68: elephant
P. 69: Sun god
P. 70: Fortune of City/ statues
P. 71: statues & fecundity
P. 72: columns/ arch
P. 73: brazen insects/ guest house
P. 74: storks
P. 75: Venus
P. 76: weather cocks/ Sons of Constantine
P. 77: measure between severed hands // Sun god/ Hercules/ dragon/ ox
P. 78: column
P. 80: column
P. 110, at "semantron": gong
Stroking and notes stop completely after p. 119.
Inside back cover: Burnt stump on Acropolis p. 11? [reference is apparently to the printed note on p. 11, "The tops of the various hills can now be distinguished by the presence of the following well known buildings .... 2. Burnt pillar."].

904. Holt, Joseph. MEMOIRS OF JOSEPH HOLT, General of the Irish Rebels, in 1798. Edited by T. Crofton Croker. 2 vols. London: Henry Colburn, 1838.

Vol. 1, pasted in, a review of this book; See 572.

905. Homer. THE ILIAD. Translated with notes by Theodore Alois Buckley. London: Bell and Daldy, 1870. [8],466 pp.

906. Another ed. Translated by Andrew Lang, Walter Leaf, and Ernest Myers. Rev. ed. London: Macmillan, 1930. vi, [2],454 pp. Sig.: WBY

*907. ———. THE ODYSSEYS OF HOMER. Translated by George Chapman. London: J.M. Dent, 1906. 2 vols. Sig., Vol. 2: Georgie Hyde Lees/ 1914

Some pp. uncut.

908. Hone, J[oseph] M[aunsell]. IRELAND SINCE 1922. Criterion Miscellany, no. 39. London: Faber & Faber, 1932. 32 pp.

908a. Another copy.

909. ———. THE LIFE OF GEORGE MOORE. London: Victor Gollancz, 1936. 515 pp. Sig.: GY

Many refs. to WBY; none marked.

*910. ———. WILLIAM BUTLER YEATS. The Poet in Contemporary Ireland. Irishmen of To-day. Dublin and London: Maunsel, [1915]. 8,134 pp. Bp: WBY

A few identifications passim, not WBY's.

911. ——— and M[ario] M[anlio] Rossi. BISHOP BERKELEY. His life, writings, and philosophy. With an intro. by W.B. Yeats. London: Faber & Faber, 1931. xxix,286 pp. Bp: WBY. WADE 280

WBY's light revisions of his Introduction, pp. xv, xxi n., xxii n., xxiii, xxv, xxix (ink and pencil).
P. xv, title of Introduction crossed out and the revision: Hone and Rossi's Bishop Berkeley
P. xxi, the note "His Infinite Observer is not infinite" is canceled and a line to a new note to be inserted: Because he believes in space, as something independent of the human mind his 'infinite' observer is entangled in what Hegel called 'The False Infinite.' [not followed in ESSAYS AND INTRODUCTIONS]

911a. Another copy.

912. Hone, Nathaniel and John Butler Yeats. A LOAN COLLECTION OF PICTURES BY NATHANIEL HONE, R.H.A. AND JOHN BUTLER YEATS, R.H.A. On view at 6 St. Stephen's Green [Royal Society of Antiquaries], October 21st [1901] to November 3rd [1901].

Includes F. York Powell's "John Butler Yeats: An Appreciation," pp. 8-11.
An independent exhibit organized by Sarah Purser.
See PRODIGAL FATHER, pp. 225-6.

*913. Hopkins, Gerard Manley. POEMS. Edited with notes by Robert Bridges. London: Humphrey Milford, 1918. 4,124 pp.

Flyleaf: To W.B.Y./ from/ J[ohn] Q[uinn]/ Jan. 28, 1920.

914. ———. POEMS OF GERARD MANLEY HOPKINS. Edited with notes by Robert Bridges. With additional poems [etc.] by Charles Williams. 2nd ed. London: Oxford Univ. Press, 1930. xvi,159 pp. 14/250.

Contents, a slight stroke under the page number (54) of "The Leaden Echo."

915. Hopper [Chesson], Nora. UNDER QUICKEN BOUGHS. Poems. London: John Lane, 1896. [8],151,[1] pp.

Flyleaf: W.B. Yeats/ with the/ Author's kind regards./ Oct. 7, 1896
Corners turned back, pp. 43, 45, 52, 149.

*915a. Another copy. Bp: W.H. Smith & Son's Subscription Library. Sig.: Nora Hopper/ 1899

In Contents, strokes against "The Dark Man," p. 65, (anthologized in Yeats's A BOOK OF IRISH VERSE); also "Phyllis and Damon," p. 149.
Includes author's corrections.

*916. Horne, Herbert P[ercy]. DIVERSI COLORES. Poems. London: Published by the Author at the Chiswick Press, 1891, 47 pp.

Flyleaf: W.B. Yeats,/ from The Writer.

*917. Horrwitz, E[rnest] P[hilip]. THE INDIAN THEATRE. A Brief Survey of the Sanskrit Drama. London: Blackie, 1912. xi,215 pp. Sig.: WBY

*918. Horton, W[illiam] T[homas]. A BOOK OF IMAGES. Drawn by W.T. Horton. Introduction by W.B. Yeats. London: The Unicorn Press, 1898. 61 pp. WADE 255

*919. ———. THE GRIG'S BOOK [a children's book]. London: Moffatt and Paige, 1900. Unpaginated.

Inside frt. cover: W.T. Horton/ to/ W.B. Yeats

*920. ———. THE WAY OF THE SOUL. A legend in line and verse. London: William Rider, [1910]. 207 pp.

Flyleaf: To W.B. Yeats/ from/ William Horton/ 1912/ With best wishes.

921. Housman, A[lfred] E[dward]. LAST POEMS. London: The Richards Press, 1934. xii,[61] pp.

Inside front cover, a list of poems and p. numbers: Grenadier p. 7/ Soldier from the War Returning p. 12/ How No More of Winter's Bitter [does WBY intend "The Chestnut Casts his Flambeau"?] p. 13/ Could Man be Drunk Forever p. 16/ The Deserter p. 18
In Contents, some poem titles and poem numbers are underlined - #'s v, vii, ix, x, xiii.
Four of these poems appear in Housman's selection in the OBMV.
Excised, pp. 7-20 and 59 to end of book.

922. ———. R.L.S. [a single sheet folded quarto]. An uncollected poem. Reprinted from THE ACADEMY of 22 December, 1894 in a limited edition of fifty copies, for the friends of Vincent Starrett and Edwin B. Hill.

*923. ———. A SHROPSHIRE LAD. London: Grant Richards, 1903. vii,96 pp. Sig.: Olivia Shakespear

Marked in Contents and excised in text are poem #'s xix, xxvi, liv.
Pp. excised in whole or part, 25-29, 37-41, 45, 83-4; none of the poems excised are anthologized in the OBMV.

924. Howell, John Cyril, ed. THE PRIEST'S ENGLISH RITUAL FOR PRIVATE MINISTRATIONS IN THE PROVINCES OF CANTERBURY AND YORK. 2nd ed. London: The Society of SS. Peter & Paul, 1920. [6],111,[1] pp.

925. Hsiung, S[hih] I. MENCIUS WAS A BAD BOY. A play. London: Privately Printed, [1934]. 23,[1] pp. 57/100

Flyleaf: With admiration to W.B. Yeats/ Sincerely yours, S.I. Hsiung.

926. Hubbell, Jay B[roadus] and John O[wen] Beaty. AN INTRODUCTION TO DRAMA. New York: Macmillan, 1927. xi,838 pp.

927. Huc, R[évérend] P[ère] [Évariste Régis]. SOUVENIRS D'UN VOYAGE DANS LA TARTARIE LE THIBET ET LA CHINE. Paris: Plon Nourrit, 1926. xiii,318 pp.

Mostly uncut.

927a. Another copy.

Uncut.

*928. Hueffer [Ford], Ford Madox. SONGS FROM LONDON. London: Elkin Mathews, 1910. xxxi pp.

Flyleaf: With the Compliments of the Season from/ Ford Madox Hueffer/ Xmas 1909./ Mr. W.B. Yeats. [only F.M.H.'s name appears to be in his own hand]
Dates are correct.
Corners turned back, pp. x, xviii,xxii.

929. Hügel, Baron Friedrich von. THE MYSTICAL ELEMENT OF RELIGION AS STUDIED IN SAINT CATHERINE OF GENOA AND HER FRIENDS. 2 vols. London: J.M. Dent, 1927. Bps: WBY

930. Hughes, Richard. CONFESSIO JUVENIS. Collected poems. London: Chatto & Windus, 1926. 95 pp. -/50

930A. Another ed. The Phoenix Library. London: Chatto & Windus, 1934. 92,[1] pp.

Flyleaf, a list of poems and p. nos.: The sermon p. 55/ Felo de se p. 67/ Old cat care p. 52/ Glaucopis p. 53/ Poets, Painters, Puddings p. 12/ Isaac Ball p. 47 [canceled]/ Winter p. 36/ The Ruin p. 27.
All of the above except "Poets, Painters, Puddings" and "Isaac Ball" are anthologized in the OBMV and the pp. for them excised; also excised, "The Walking Road," p. 30; "The Image," p. 35.

*931. Hughes, Rev. S[amuel] C[arlyle]. THE PRE-VICTORIAN DRAMA IN DUBLIN. Dublin: Hodges, Figgis, 1904. [4],viii,[2], 179 pp.

931a. Another copy.

*932. Hugo, Victor. DRAMAS. 2 vols. [4 vols in 2]. The Sterling Ed. Boston and New York: Univ. Press, [189?]. Sig.: Coraleen M. Paige/ 1894.

Vol. 1 includes HERNANI, THE TWIN BROTHERS, ANGELO, AMY ROBSART.
Vol. 2 includes CROMWELL and THE BURGRAVES.

933. ———. LE ROI S'AMUSE [and] LUCRECE BORGIA. Paris: Nelson, Editeurs, [1912?]. 369 pp. Sig.: Lennox Robinson

934. ———. TRANSLATIONS FROM THE POEMS OF VICTOR HUGO. Translated by Henry Carrington. London: Walter Scott, 1885. 325 pp.

Inside frt. cover: W B Yeats/ 10 Ashfield Terrace/ Harolds Cross.
Back flyleaf, a pencil sketch of a woman by JBY.
In Contents, many titles are marked.

935. Hulme, T[homas] E[rnest]. SPECULATIONS. Essays on Humanism and the Philosophy of Art. Edited by Herbert Read. London: Kegan Paul, Trench, Trubner, 1924. xvi,272 pp.

936. Hume, David. ESSAYS AND TREATISES ON SEVERAL SUBJECTS. 2 vols. New ed. Edinburgh: Bell & Bradfute and William Blackwood; and T. Cadell & W. Davies, 1809. Vol. 2 [only one here]: AN INQUIRY CONCERNING HUMAN UNDERSTANDING; A DISSERTATION ON THE PASSIONS; AN INQUIRY CONCERNING THE PRINCIPLES OF MORALS; AND THE NATURAL HISTORY OF RELIGION. Bp: Robert Corbet

937. Husserl, Edmund. IDEAS: GENERAL INTRODUCTION TO PURE PHENOMENOLOGY. Translated by W.R. Boyce Gibson. London: George Allen & Unwin, 1931. 467 pp.

*938. Hutchinson, Francis D.D. AN HISTORICAL ESSAY CONCERNING WITCHCRAFT [etc.]. With two sermons, one in proof of the Christian religion, the other concerning Good and Evil Angels. 2nd ed. with additions. London: R. Knaplock ... and D. Midwinter, 1720. xxxii,338 pp. Bp: WBY

939. Hüttemann, Gerta. WESEN DER DICHTUNG UND AUFGABE DES DICHTERS BEI WILLIAM BUTLER YEATS. Inaugural-Dissertation, Friedrich-Wilhelms-Universitat, Bonn, 1929. 88 pp.

Title p.: To Mr. and Mrs. Yeats/ in gratitude/ from G.H./ Aug. 24th 1929.
A few pp. uncut.

940. Huxley, Aldous. POINT COUNTER POINT. London: Chatto and Windus, 1930. 601 pp.

*941. Hyde, Douglas. A LITERARY HISTORY OF IRELAND. London: T. Fisher Unwin, 1899. xviii,654 pp.

942. ———, ed. [Gaelic title], or THE LAD OF THE FERULE; [Gaelic title], or ADVENTURES OF THE CHILDREN OF THE KING OF NORWAY. With translations, notes, and glossary. Irish Texts Society, vol. 1. London: The Irish Texts Society, 1899. xx,208,[12] pp.

Some pp. uncut.

943. HYMNS TO THE GODDESS. Translated from the Sanskrit by Arthur and Ellen Avalon. London: Luzac, 1913. xii, 179 pp.

Preface and Intro. cut only.

944. Hyslop, James H[ervey]. LIFE AFTER DEATH. Problems of the future life and its nature. New York: E.P. Dutton, 1919. x,346 pp.

*945. Iamblichus. IAMBLICHUS ON THE MYSTERIES OF THE EGYPTIANS, CHALDEANS, AND ASSYRIANS. Translated by Thomas Taylor. 2nd ed. London: Theosophical Publishing Society, 1895. xxvi,365 pp.

946. Ibsen, Henrik. GHOSTS AND TWO OTHER PLAYS. Translated by R. Farquharson Sharp. Everyman's Library. London: J.M. Dent, 1914. x,247 pp.

Includes THE WARRIORS AT HELGELAND and AN ENEMY OF THE PEOPLE

947. ———. LADY INGER OF OSTRAT; THE VIKINGS AT HELGELAND; THE PRETENDERS. Edited by William Archer. Translated by Charles and William Archer. London: Walter Scott, [1890]. xvii,379 pp.

948. ———. LADY INGER OF OSTRAAT; LOVE'S COMEDY; and THE LEAGUE OF YOUTH. Translated by R. Farquharson Sharp. Everyman's Library. London and Toronto: J.M. Dent, [1917?]. xi,286 pp.

949. ———. PEER GYNT. Translated by William and Charles Archer. London: Walter Scott, [1892?]. xxii,287 pp. Sig.: Bryan Cooper

Some bracketing in red pencil, not apparently WBY's.

950. ———. THE PILLARS OF SOCIETY. And other plays. Edited by Havelock Ellis. London: Walter Scott, 1888. xxx,315 pp.

Inside frt. cover: W B Yeats/ September 5/ 1888. Includes GHOSTS and AN ENEMY OF SOCIETY.

951. Elin, M. [Il'ya Yakovlevich Marshak]. MOSCOW HAS A PLAN. A Soviet Primer. Translated by G.S. Counts and N.P. Lodge. London: Jonathan Cape, 1931. 218 pp. Sig.: GY [erased]

952. L'ILLUSTRATION (Paris). No. 4579. 6 Décembre 1930.

On cover, printed under title: Noël 1930 [not WBY's]
Includes an illustrated article on book cover design.

953. Inchbald, Elizabeth, ed. THE BRITISH THEATRE. A collection of plays which are acted at the Theatres Royal, Drury Lane, Covent Garden, and Haymarket. 25 vols. London: Longman, Hurst, Rees, and Orme, 1800-17. Vol. 22: THE CASTLE OF ANDALUSIA by John O'Keefe, FONTAINBLEAU by John O'Keefe, WILD Oats by John O'Keefe, THE HEIRESS by General Burgoyne, THE EARL OF ESSEX by Henry Jones.

*954. Inge, William Ralph. THE PHILOSOPHY OF PLOTINUS. The Gifford Lectures at St. Andrews, 1917-18. 2 vols. London: Longmans, Green, 1918. Sig., both vols.: George Yeats/ February 1919

Vol. 1, p. 67, corner turned back.
Pp. 128-9, marking and underscoring.
P. 131, note by WBY at "A thing is matter": Matter = the Other, or B.F. of the Other

955. ———. THE PLATONIC TRADITION IN ENGLISH RELIGIOUS THOUGHT. The Hulsean Lectures at Cambridge, 1925-6. New York: Longmans, Green, 1926. vii,117 pp.

956. Ingoldsby, Thomas [Richard Harris Barham]. THE JACKDAW OF RHEIMS. Illustrated by Ernest M. Jessop. London: Eyre and Spottiswoode, [1889?]. xviii,[1] pp.

957. IRELAND TO-DAY (Dublin). 2 (January 1937).

Includes a review of the OBMV by J.J. Hogan; also "The Abbey Theatre Attacked I" by John Dowling and "The Abbey Theatre Attacked II" by Mervyn Wall.

958. Ireland (-1922). National Museum of Science and Art. GENERAL GUIDE TO THE ART COLLECTIONS. PART IX - GLASS. CHAPTER II - IRISH GLASS, by M.S.D. Westropp. Dublin: His Majesty's Stationery Office, 1913. 80 pp., 20 plates.

959. ———. GENERAL GUIDE TO THE NATURAL HISTORY COLLECTION. A LIST OF IRISH BIRDS, showing the species contained in the National Collection, by Richard Ussher. Dublin: His Majesty's Stationery Office, 1908. 54 pp.

960. ———. GUIDE TO THE COLLECTION OF IRISH ANTIQUITIES. PART V - IRISH ETHNOGRAPHICAL COLLECTION, by Thomas J. Westropp. Dublin: His Majesty's Stationery Office, 1911. 45 pp.

961. ———. SHORT GUIDE TO THE COLLECTIONS. 52nd ed. Dublin: Dept. of Agriculture and Technical Instruction for Ireland, 1916. 11 pp.

962. ———. DESCRIPTION OF THE RAISED MAP OF IRELAND. SHOWING THE RELATION BETWEEN THE GEOLOGICAL STRUCTURE AND THE SURFACE FEATURES OF THE COUNTRY, by Grenville A.J. Cole. Dublin: His Majesty's Stationery Office, 1909. 15,[1] pp., 10 plates.

963. Irish Free State (1922-49). COINAGE OF SAORSTÁT ÉIREANN 1928. Dublin: The Stationery Office, 1928. (10),65 pp. WADE 317

Yeats, as chairman of the committee, contributed "What We Did or Tried to Do." WBY has revised the title of his contribution to: Coinage of Saorstat Eireann [also section VIII is canceled as well as Yeats's name]

963a. Another copy. Two words entirely canceled on flyleaf.

963b. Another copy.

964. ———. Coimisiún na Gaeltachta. MAP NO. 1. A GENERAL MAP OF IRELAND, showing in respect of the 1911 census percentage of Irish speakers in each electoral division, 1926.

964a. ———. MAP NO. 2, showing in respect of the 1925 special enumeration for the counties of Donegal, Mayo etc., percentage of Irish speakers in district electoral division, 1926.

The maps are enclosed in a single folder devised to hold them in two parts.

965. ———. Laws, Statutes etc. CENSORSHIP OF PUBLICATIONS ACT. Number 21 of 1929. 31 pp.

966. ———. INDUSTRIAL AND COMMERCIAL PROPERTY (PROTECTION) ACT. Number 16 of 1927. 231 pp.

966a. Another copy.

967. ———. National Gallery of Ireland. CATALOGUE OF OIL PICTURES IN THE GENERAL COLLECTION. Dublin: The Stationery Office, 1932. x,(2),143 pp.

968. ———. CATALOGUE OF PICTURES and other works of art in the National Gallery of Ireland and the National Portrait Gallery. Dublin: Stationery Office, 1928. xix,(1),422 pp.

969. ———. OFFICIAL HANDBOOK OF SAORSTÁT ÉIREANN. ORDNANCE SURVEY MAP. Dublin: Ordnance Survey Office, 1931.

970. ———. Seanad Eireann. PARLIAMENTARY DEBATES: OFFICIAL REPORT, vols. 1-8 (11 December 1922 - 20 May 1927).

971. ———. STANDING ORDERS. VOL. 1: PUBLIC BUSINESS (1923). Sig.: WBY

IRISH HOMESTEAD, See CELTIC CHRISTMAS.

972. Irish Industries. ILLUSTRATED SOUVENIR OF THE IRISH INDUSTRIES PAGEANT held in Dublin St. Patrick's Eve 1909. Dublin: Maunsel, 1909. 63 pp.

973. [Irish Literary Theatre program]. First performances of THE COUNTESS CATHLEEN and THE HEATHER FIELD, Dublin, 8-9 May 1899.

Inserted in 146a.

974. IRISH PLEASANTRY AND FUN. A selection of the best humorous tales by Carleton, Lover, Lever and other popular writers. With 16 coloured illustrations by J.F. O'Hea. New Ed. Dublin: M.H. Gill, 1885. (6),380 pp.

In Contents, 24 titles are marked or underscored; at least twelve selections have been excised in the text apparently to get copy for Yeats's eds. of REPRESENTATIVE IRISH TALES (1891) and IRISH FAIRY TALES (1892). The selections marked in Contents and excised which also appear in IFT are "The Devil's Mill" and "The Little Weaver of Duleek Gate." Those marked and excised which appear in RIT are "Condy Cullen and the Gauger," "Barny O'Reirdon, the Navigator," "Paddy the Piper," "Trinity College" (Lever), and "Darby Doyle's Visit to Quebec."

975. THE IRISH REVIEW (Dublin). 2 (December 1912).

Includes Yeats's "At the Abbey Theatre."

976. [Irish scenes. Print]. ANTIQUITIES IN IRELAND. Four illustrations: Round tower at Kildare; Ruins of a convent at Kildare; A tumulus near Tipperary; An ancient brass sword. From LONDON MAGAZINE (September 1778).

977. ———. CASHEL CATHEDRAL, TIPPERARY, engraved by J. Walker from an original drawing by G. Holmes. London: J. Walker, 1800.

978. ———. CASTLE CONNELL IN THE COUNTY OF LIMERICK, by Eastgate. London: Alexander Hogg, n.d.

979. ———. GALWAY (FROM THE CLADDAGH), engraved by C. Cousen after W. H. Bartlett. London: George Virtus, n.d.

980. ———. GLENMORE CASTLE, the seat of Francis Synge, Esq., by J. Carr. London: R. Phillips, 1806.

981. ———. LOWER LAKE OF KILLARNEY, ROSS CASTLE AND ISLAND, by W. Westall. Engraved by E. Francis. No publishing info.

982. ———. THE SALMON LEAP, AT BALLYSHANNON, IN IRELAND. No other info.

983. ———. STREET IN GALWAY, by W.H. Bartlett. Engraved by T. Higham. No publishing info.

984. THE IRISH STATESMAN. 1 (23 August 1919).
Includes Yeats's "If I Were Four-and-Twenty"

985. ———. 1 (30 August 1919).
Includes part 2 of "If I Were Four-and-Twenty."

986. ———. 1 (8 November 1919).
Includes Yeats's "A Prayer For My Daughter."

986a-b. Two more copies.

987. ———. 1 (10 January 1920).
Includes J.B. Yeats's "The Independence of the Artist."

988. ———. 2 (31 January 1920).
Includes J.B. Yeats's "The Heart of the Belief."

988a. Another copy.

989. ———. 2 (21 February 1920).
Includes J.B. Yeats's "Self-indulgence and Self-refusal."

990. ———. 2 (3 April 1920).
Includes J.B. Yeats's "The Poet's Solitude."

991. ———. 2 (17 April 1920).
Includes J.B. Yeats's "Art and Imitation."

992. ———. 2 (24 April 1920).
Includes J.B. Yeats's "English Self-Complacency."

993. ———. 2 (1 May 1920).
Includes J.B. Yeats's "English Self-Complacency -- II."

*994. ———. 2 (January - June 1920).
Bound volume.

995. ———. 3 (8 November 1924).
Includes Yeats's "An Old Poem Re-Written."

996. ———. "The Dublin of Berkeley (1703-1710)," 7 Sept. 1929.
Clipping inserted in 443.

*997. THE IRISH THEOSOPHIST (Dublin). 3 (15 August 1895).
Includes A.E.'s "Yes, and Hope."

* 997a-b. Two more copies.

* 998. ———. 3 (15 September 1895).

Includes A.E.'s "The Robing of the King."

* 999. ———. 4 (15 October 1895).

Includes A.E.'s "Our Lost Others."

*1000. ———. 4 (15 November 1895).

Includes A.E.'s "The Free" with a slight correction of the text of the poem, not WBY's.

*1000a. Another copy.

*1001. ———. 4 (15 December 1895).

Includes verses by A.E.

*1002. ———. 4 (15 January 1896).

Verses by A.E. and a prose piece "III. The Slumber of Cuchullain, and the Message of Angus."

*1003. ———. 4 (15 September 1896).

Includes A.E.'s "The Places of the Sidhe."

*1004. ———. 5 (15 September 1897).

Includes A.E.'s "The Fountains of Youth."

1005. THE IRISH TIMES (Dublin). Review of THE LEMON TREE by Margot Ruddock, edited by WBY, [14 June 1937, p. 5].

Inserted in 717.

SEE ALSO 1923 and 2279.

1006. Jacob, Sir Lionel. "Architecture/ Hindu and Mogul/ Combining East and West," THE TIMES, 17 Nov. 1921, p. xiv.

Inserted in 859.

1007. James [I], King of Scotland. THE KINGIS QUAIR. Edited by Robert Steele. Designed by Charles Ricketts. London: The Vale Press, 1903. lv pp. -/260

Cover: File Copy/ not to be taken away. [WBY's?]

*1008. James, William. HUMAN IMMORTALITY. 2nd ed. Boston: Houghton, Mifflin, 1899. ix,[1],70 pp.

*1009. Another, 4th ed. Westminster: Archibald Constable, 1899. 126 pp. Sig.: WBY

Almost wholly uncut.

*1010. ———. PRAGMATISM. London: Longmans, Green, 1910. xiv, 310 pp.

Flyleaf: G. Hyde Lees/ from Harry Tucker/ 1911.

1011. Jammes, Francis. CLAIRIÈRES DANS LE CIEL, 1902-1906. Paris: Mercure de France, 1916. 225 pp.

Mostly uncut.

1012. ———. LE DEUIL DES PRIMEVERÈS, 1898-1900. Paris: Mercure de France, 1917. 213 pp.

1013. ———. LE ROMAN DU LIÈVRE. Paris: Mercure de France, 1918. 368 pp.

Mostly uncut after P. 211.

1014. ———. LE TRIOMPHE DE LA VIE, 1900-1901. Paris: Mercure de France, [1902?]. 249 pp.

1015. JAPANESE DRAMA AND THE SHŌCHIKU DRAMATIC COMPANY. Tokyo: Tokyo Printing, n.d. 30 pp.

Inserted in 1637.

1016. John, Ivor B[ertram]. THE MABINOGION. Popular Studies in Mythology, Romance, and Folklore, no. 11. London: David Nutt, 1901. 55 pp.

1017. John of the Cross, Saint. THE DARK NIGHT OF THE SOUL. 4th rev. ed. London: Thomas Baker, 1916. xxiv,210 pp.

1018. Johnson, Lionel. THE ART OF THOMAS HARDY. With a bibliography by John Lane. London: Elkin Mathews and John Lane, 1894. ix,276,lxiii,[1] pp. Bp: WBY

Flyleaf: To/ W.B. Yeats/ From/ Lionel Johnson

*1019. ———. IRELAND, with other poems. London: Elkin Mathews, 1897. xi,[1],127,[1] pp.

Flyleaf, stamped: With the Publisher's Compliments
In Contents WBY has dated each poem by consulting the dates after each poem in the text.
Checked in Contents, "An Ideal" and "Te Martyrum Candidatus." The latter appears in the BIV and OBMV.

*1020. ———. POEMS. London: Elkin Mathews, 1895. ix,[1], 115,[1] pp.

In Contents, check marks against "The Dark Angel," "Lucretius," "The Church of a Dream," "The Age of a Dream." All except "Lucretius" appear in the OBMV. Faint question marks appear against "Celtic Speech" on p. 47 and "Ways of War," p. 48; both appear in BIV.

*1021. ———. POETICAL WORKS. London: Elkin Mathews, 1915. xix,[5],320 pp.

Flyleaf: W B Yeats,/ from/ O[livia] S[hakespear]/ Decr. 1915.

Inside frt. cover: Te Martyrum Candidatus 252/ The Age of a Dream 98/ The Church of a Dream 97 To Morfydd 6 [All appear in OBMV].

1022. ———. POST LIMINIUM: Essays and Critical Papers. Edited by Thomas Whittemore. London: Elkin Mathews, 1911. xiv,307 pp. Bp: WBY

1023. ———. THREE POEMS. [Edited by Vincent Starrett]. Ysleta, Texas: Edwin B. Hill, 1928. [5] pp.

SEE ALSO 173.

1024. Johnston, Edward. WRITING AND ILLUMINATING, AND LETTERING. London: John Hogg, 1915. xxxii,500 pp.

Flyleaf: Dorothy Travers Smith/ 26th March 1917.

1025. Johnston, G[eorge] A[lexander]. THE DEVELOPMENT OF BERKELEY'S PHILOSOPHY. London: Macmillan, 1923. viii,400 pp. Bp: WBY

Marginal strokes, underscoring, pp. 163, 292, 293, 299, 301, 302-6, 309, 317; corners turned back, pp. 228, 298.

1026. Jones, Ernest. ESSAYS IN APPLIED PSYCHO-ANALYSIS. London: The International Psycho-analytical Press, 1923. [7],454 pp.

Flyleaf: J.O. Wisdom/ 10th July 1936/ 6 Sussex Gardens W.2.
Moderate markings, a few notes, not WBY's.
Contains "The Island of Ireland" and a ref. to "Cathleen ni Houlihan."

1027. Jones, W[illiam] Tudor. CONTEMPORARY THOUGHT OF GERMANY. 2 vols. London: Williams and Norgate, 1930. viii, 278 pp. Sig.: WBY

Vol. 1 only.
Some pp. uncut; markings in Chapter VI "Phenomenology" for discussions of Adolf Trendelenburg, Franz Brentano, Julius Bergmann, and Johannes Rehmke.
P. 225, at "Contents of Perception": Berkeley
P. 227, at "of the same nature as itself": ◇
Marginal strokes, pp. 218, 221, 222, 225, 226, 244, 245.
Uncut, pp. 234-5; 262-3; 266-7.

1028. Jonson, Ben. BEN JONSON. Edited by Brinsley Nicholson. 3 vols. The Mermaid Series. London: T. Fisher Unwin, [1893-5].

Vol. 3 only; includes VOLPONE, EPICOENE, THE ALCHEMIST.

1029. ———. BEN JONSON. Edited by C.H. Herford and Percy Simpson. 5 vols. Oxford: Clarendon Press, 1925-37. Bp: WBY

VOL. 1, "Life" uncut after p.77; cut almost wholly, "Conversations with Drummond"; pp. 178-227; "Books in Jonson's Library"; 275 to end of vol.

VOL. 2, many pp. uncut.

VOL. 3, many pp. uncut, but mostly cut, EVERY MAN IN HIS HUMOUR, the Quarto of 1601.
Inserted, a slip, unlikely WBY's listing characters and contemporary actors of VOLPONE and THE ALCHEMIST.

VOL. 4, almost wholly cut are CYNTHIAS REVELLS and EASTWARD HOE.

VOL. 5, mostly uncut.

*1030. ———. EVERY MAN IN HIS HUMOUR. Edited by W. Macneile Dixon. The Temple Dramatists. London: J.M. Dent, 1903. xvi,143 pp.

1031. Another ed. Edited by Percy Simpson. Oxford: Clarendon Press, 1919. lxiv,175 pp.

The editor has copied out Herrick's "Prayer to Ben Jonson" and put his signature below.

*1032. ———. MASQUES AND ENTERTAINMENTS. Edited by Henry Morley. London: George Routledge, 1890. xxxii,439 pp.

*1033. ———. THE WORKS OF BEN JONSON. Edited by Lt. Col. Francis Cunningham. 3 vols. London: Chatto and Windus, [1910-12]. Sig.: GHL

Vol. 3, some pp. uncut; TIMBER entirely cut.

1034. Joseph, H[orace] W[illiam] B[rindley]. THE LABOUR THEORY OF VALUE IN KARL MARX. London: Oxford Univ. Press, 1923. 176 pp.

1035. [Josephson, Ernst]. ERNST JOSEPHSON [monograph on the Swedish artist]. Sma Konstböcker, no. 14. Lund: Gleerupska Universitets-Bokhandeln, [1910?]. 64 pp.

1036. THE JOURNAL OF THE ALCHEMICAL SOCIETY (London). 1 (May 1913).

1037. ———. 2 (October 1913).

1038. ———. 2 (April 1914).

Contains "Some Reflections on 'Basil Valentine'" by Philip Sinclair Wellby.

1039. Jouve, P[ierre] J[ean]. PRÉSENCES (Poèmes). Première Série. Paris: George Crès, 1912. 127 pp. 124|500

Half title p., an inscription from the author to WBY, partially illegible, dated 11.10.12.

1040. Joyce, James. ANNA LIVIA PLURABELLE. New York: Crosby Gaige, 1928. xviii,[2],60,[1] pp.

*1041. ———. DUBLINERS. London: Grant Richards, 1914. 278 pp.

Back cover, a label: The Bargain Floor Library at Harrods Ltd., London, S.W. [stamped beside this:] 2 July 1914.

1041a. Another copy.

*1042. ———. EXILES. London: Grant Richards, 1918. [6], 158 pp.

1043. ———. POMES PENYEACH. Paris: Shakespeare and Company, 1927. [22] pp.

Inserted: With the compliments of Shakespeare and Company.

1043a. Another copy.

"A Flower Given to My Daughter," "Tutto è Sciolto," and "On the Beach at Fontana" are excised presumably to make Joyce's selection in the OBMV.

*1044. ———. A PORTRAIT OF THE ARTIST AS A YOUNG MAN. London: The Egoist, 1916. [4],299 pp. Bp: WBY

1045. ———. TWO TALES OF SHEM AND SHAUN. London: Faber and Faber, 1932. 45 pp.

Flyleaf: Lolly from George/ Xmas 1937.

1046. ———. ULYSSES. Paris: Shakespeare and Company, 1922. 732 pp. 939/1000

Flyleaf and second flyleaf: W B Yeats [George Yeats's hand]
Flyleaf, very faint pencil: p 173 [or 73]/ sensitive name [stage name?]
Some pp. uncut after p. 433, mostly in Circe.
P. 556 and back flyleaf: W B Yeats [GY's hand]

*1047. Jubainville, H[enri] D'Arbois de. LE CYCLE MYTHOLGIQUE IRLANDAIS ET LA MYTHOLOGIE CELTIQUE. Paris: Ernest Thorin, 1884. xii,411 pp.

Flyleaf, sketches of a sword and goblets.
Inserted, a horoscope, unidentified; birthdate is 22 Jan. 1897; "question Horn."

*1048. ———. INTRODUCTION À L'ÉTUDE DE LA LITTÉRATURE CELTIQUE. Paris: Ernest Thorin, 1883. [4], 412 pp.

Marginal marks, pp. 129, 153, 211, 246, 251, some reflecting a linguistic interest in old Irish.

*1049. Julian the Emperor. THE WORKS OF THE EMPEROR JULIAN. Translated by Wilmer Cave Wright. 3 vols. Loeb Classical Library. London: William Heinemann, 1913.

Vol. 1 only.
Marginal strokes, underscoring pp. 471 ("Hymn to the Mother of the Gods"), 473, 479, 489; especially refs. to Attis.

*1050. Jung, C[arl] G[ustav]. COLLECTED PAPERS ON ANALYTICAL PSYCHOLOGY. Translated by Constance E. Long. London: Baillière, Tindall and Cox, 1916. xviii,392 pp.

Five brief notes pp. 84, 129, 227, 237 defining terms such as "heuristic," "teleological," "cathartic," possibly WBY's or GY's.
Pencil strokes and underlining, pp. 89, 222, 223, 228, 231, 232, 234, 236.

*1051. Kabir. ONE HUNDRED POEMS OF KABIR. Translated by Rabindranath Tagore assisted by Evelyn Underhill. London: The India Society, 1914. xxvii,[1],67 pp.

Some pp. uncut.

1051A. Another ed. London: Macmillan, 1915. xlvi,105 pp.

Uncut.

1052. Kant, Immanuel. KANT'S CRITICAL PHILOSOPHY FOR ENGLISH READERS. 3rd ed. Vol. 2: THE PROLEGOMENA, translated by J.P. Mahaffy and J.H. Bernard. London: Macmillan, 1915. Bp: WBY

Pasted on flyleaf, 2146.
Half title p.: Antinomies - 103 [on p. 103 a stroke against passage dealing with antinomies].

*1053. ———. KANT'S CRITIQUE OF AESTHETIC JUDGEMENT. Translated by James Creed Meredith. Oxford: Clarendon Press, 1911. clxx,334 pp. Bp: WBY

Flyleaf: With the Author's Compliments.
Dedicated to WBY.

1054. Keats, John. THE COMPLETE WORKS. Edited by H. Buxton Forman. 5 vols. Glasgow: Gowars and Gray, 1901.

Vols. 4 and 5 only; LETTERS, 1814-1820.

*1055. ———. THE POEMS. Edited by Sidney Colvin. 2 vols. London: Chatto and Windus, 1920. Bps: WBY

*1056. ———. THE POETICAL WORKS. Edited by William T. Arnold. London: Kegan Paul, Trench, 1888. lvi,349 pp. Bp: WBY

Flyleaf: Easter Sunday 1902/ To the poet Yeats/ from Oliver Gogarty/ 'God's procreant waters flowing about your mind/ Have made you more than King or Queens'/ from 'Countess Cathleen'

1057. Keith, A[rthur] Berriedale. BUDDHIST PHILOSOPHY IN INDIA AND CEYLON. Oxford: Clarendon Press, 1923. 339 pp.

1058. ———. THE RELIGION AND PHILOSOPHY OF THE VEDA AND UPANISHADS. Harvard Oriental Series, vols. 31 & 32. Cambridge: Harvard Univ. Press, 1925.

Vol. 32, p. 503, corner turned back.

1059. Kelleher, D[aniel] L[awrence]. A POET PASSES. London: Ernest Benn, 1927. vi,30 pp.

1060. Kennedy, James. POEMS, Lyrical and Descriptive. Melbourne and Sydney: Lothian Publishing, 1936. 71 pp.

Flyleaf: With the compliments/ of the/ Author/ March 1937

1061. Khunrath, Henricus. AMPHITHEATRUM SAPIENTIAE aeternae solius verae, Christiano-Kabalisticum, divino-magicum .... [Edited by E. Wolfart]. Hanoviae: Guilielmus Antonius, 1609. 222,[1] pp. Sig.: Georgie Hyde Lees/ 1913

1062. King, Henry. THE POEMS OF BISHOP HENRY KING. Edited by John Sparrow. London: The Nonesuch Press, 1925. xxvii,197 pp. "out of series for review"/900

Some pp. uncut.

*1063. King, Richard Ashe. SWIFT IN IRELAND. The New Irish Library. London: T. Fisher Unwin, 1895. [8],204 pp.

*1064. Kingsford, Anna (Bonus). THE CREDO OF CHRISTENDOM and other addresses and essays on esoteric Christianity. And some letters by Edward Maitland. Edited by Samuel Hopgood Hart. London: John W. Watkins, 1916. viii, 256 pp.

Flyleaf: Yeats [Ezra Pound's hand]
Marks, underscorings, pp. 97, 100, 116, 117, 118, 119, 134, 135, 136 in same ink as on flyleaf; likely Pound's.
P. 135, at "In this aspect the Moon is the Initiatrix": ☽

1065. Kingston, William H[enry] G[iles]. ROGER WILLOUGHBY or The Times of Benbow. A Tale of the Sea and Land. London: James Nisbet, 1881. iv,[2],402 pp.

Flyleaf: To/ William Butler Yeats/ from/ his grand-mother/ E Pollexfen/ Decr. 25th 1880.
Dates are correct.

1066. [Kingsway Theatre (London) Program]. THE DYNASTS by Thomas Hardy. 25 November 1914.

Includes as a separate pamphlet "Notes on some of the lesser-known characters in the abridgment from "The Dynasts"...."
Inserted in 834.

1067. Kirby, William and William Spence. AN INTRODUCTION TO ENTOMOLOGY or Elements of the Natural History of Insects. People's ed. London: Longmans, Green, 1873. xxviii,607 pp. Sig.: WBY

Marginal strokes, underscoring, pp. 88, 89, 204, 221, 222, 224, 225, 272 (beehive as model city), 365 (bees as example of "Perfect Societies of Insects").

*1068. Kirk, Robert. THE SECRET COMMONWEALTH OF ELVES, FAUNS, AND FAIRIES. London: David Nutt, 1893. lxv,[3], 92 pp. Bp: WBY

Flyleaf: WBY./ from A[ugusta] G[regory].
Many pencil marks, a few brief notes pp. xxiv, lxiii, 7, 8, 9, 10, 11, 12, 13, 15, 17, 18, 19, 24, 25, 30, 33, 34, 35, 40, 41, 44, 50, 52, 54, 64, 65, 66, 69.
P. xxxvii, line 4: Theobold [not WBY's]
P. 19, first 4 lines: Penalty
P. 24, mid-page: treasure
P. 30 at passage dealing with a seer who has "the usuall artificiall Helps of optic Glasses": evidently the seer is learned, not mere 'folk' seer.
P. 37, last 4 lines: butter

1069. Ki Tsurayuki. THE TOSA DIARY. Translated by William N. Porter. London: Henry Frowde, 1912. 148 pp.

1070. Knight, G[eorge] Wilson. MYTH AND MIRACLE, An Essay on the Mystic Symbolism of Shakespeare. London: Edward J. Burrow, [1929]. 31,[1] pp.

KNORR VON ROSENROTH, See 1292.

1071. KOMUSASHINOKAMI MINAMOTO NO MORONAO. [biography of a Japanese court official]. No pub. info.

Includes colored prints of swordsmen, etc.

1072. Kosor, Josip. PEOPLE OF THE UNIVERSE. Four Serbo-Croatian Plays. London: Hendersons, 1917. 339 pp.

Includes THE WOMAN, PASSION'S FURNACE, RECONCILIATION, THE INVINCIBLE SHIP.

1073. Kramer, Henry and James Sprenger. MALLEUS MALEFICARUM. Translated by the Rev. Montague Sommers. [London]: John Rodker, 1928. xlvi,278 pp. 612/1275. Bp: WBY

Some pp. uncut.

*1074. Krans, Horatio Sheafe. WILLIAM BUTLER YEATS AND THE IRISH LITERARY REVIVAL. Contemporary Men of Letters Series. New York: McClure, Phillips, 1904. [4],ix, [3],196 pp.

Flyleaf: To William Butler Yeats/ with the compliments/ of the author/ April 15 1904

1075. Krishnamurti, M. LOVE SONNETS and other poems. Oxford: Shakespeare Head Press, 1937. [8],56 pp.

Flyleaf: With the Author's Compliments/ M. Krishnamurti/ Limbdi,/ Kathiawar (Qudia)

1076. Kurata, Hyakuzo. SHUNKAN. Translated by Kan-ichi Ando. Tokyo: Kenkyusha, 1925. iv,42 pp.

A play.

*1077. Lalor, James Fintan. THE WRITINGS OF JAMES FINTAN LALOR. Introduction by John O'Leary. The Shamrock Library. Dublin: T.G. O'Donoghue, 1895. xxiv,124 pp.

1078. Lamb, Charles. THE LAST ESSAYS OF ELIA. The Temple Classics. London: J.M. Dent, 1897. ix,258 pp. Bp: Elizabeth Corbet Yeats

Flyleaf: Lolly Yeats/ from W B Yeats,/ Xmas 1897

1079. ———. TALES FROM SHAKESPEARE. Designed for the use of young persons. 2 vols. 4th ed. London: M.J. Godwin, 1822. [5],261 pp. Bp: William Hay

Vol. 1 only.

1080. Landor, Walter Savage. IMAGINARY CONVERSATIONS. The Camelot Classics. London: Walter Scott, 1886. xxiv, 348 pp. Sig.: W B Yeats/ 1886

*1081. Another ed. Edited by Charles G. Crump. 6 vols. London: J.M. Dent, 1909. Bps: WBY

Light stroking and slips inserted all 6 vols. passim.

VOL. 1, in Contents, Dialogues 1, 2, and 14 checked.
Strokes, pp. 32, 43, 60, 61, 73, 79, 80, 90, 93, 94, 95, 97, 104.
P. 97, at note: Crump [unlikely WBY's]
Inside back cover: 32, 43, 60, 264, 279, 283, 290 W.S.L.
[page nos. correspond to marked passages in text]

VOL. 2, stroking passim.
Inside back cover: 292/ Gorgias/ 298/ Plato [not WBY's] Ireland - p. 257-8/ 261 [WBY's]

VOL. 3, inside back cover: 177, 178, 213, 220, 244, 270, 287 [possibly WBY's; passages marked on these pp.].
Pp. 277 and 281 marked by slip of newspaper, WW II period.

VOL. 4, inside back cover: 54/ 33 criticism/ 249 [passages marked on these pp.; possibly WBY's].

VOL. 5, inside back cover: 176, 359, 368, 369, 370, 391, 416 [passages marked in text, but symbols unlike WBY's]

VOL. 6, inside back cover: 30, 41, 47, 318, 320, 323, 324, 340 [passages marked in text; possibly WBY's].
P. 228 marked by newspaper slip, WW II era.

*1082. ———. THE LONGER PROSE WORKS. Edited by Charles G. Crump. 2 vols. London: J.M. Dent, 1911. Bps: WBY

VOL. 1, inside frt. cover: "Sudden thunder of wings" p. 161 [p. 161 is turned down at corner; text quotes line preceding from Swinburne's "Sappho"].
Flyleaf: 156, 320, 321 religion, 322, 341, 342, 352, 356 // 148, 153, 154, 1[??], 165, 173, 174, 184, 187, 203, 243, 257, 259, 260, 264, 269, 309.
Title p.: Index "Vol. X"
Pencil checks in "Pericles and Aspasia."

VOL. 2, pencil checks in "The Pentameron"
Inside back cover: 28, 38>, 43*, 43, 47, 52, 69, 72<, 77 W.B.Y., 97, 92, 95, 202, 204, 252,/ 103, 106, 110, 113 [passages on these pp. marked]
P. 77, two passages marked, "You and I were never passionately fond of the papacy, to which we trace in great measure the miseries of our Italy, its divisions and its corruptions, the substitution of cunning for fortitude, and of creed for conduct." Also, "May nations find out by degrees that the next evil to being conquered is to conquer, and that he who assists in making slaves gives over at last by becoming one!" (both in "The Pentameron").

*1083. ———. POEMS, DIALOGUES IN VERSE, AND EPIGRAMS. Edited by Charles G. Crump. 2 vols. London: J.M. Dent, 1909. Bps: WBY

VOL. 1, inside back cover: 202 [on that p. a stroke in margin against passage in "Giovanna of Naples"].
Appendix, at synposis of "COUNT JULIAN, a tragedy," four character names repeated in margin: Witiza // Theodofred - Roderick - Sisabert [? - canceled].

VOL. 2, p. 104, poem no. XLVI marked by pencil stroke.

*1084. ———. SELECTIONS FROM THE WRITINGS. Edited by Sidney Colvin. London: Macmillan, 1913. xxxvii,375 pp. Bp: WBY

Most pp. uncut.

*1085. Lang, Andrew. THE MAKING OF RELIGION. 2nd ed. London: Longmans, Green, 1900. xxii,[4],355 pp. Sig.: W B Yeats/ Nov./ 1900

Marginal strokes, pp. 31-33, 50, 54, 55, 57, 58, 61, 65, 71.
After p. 75, many pp. uncut.

*1086. Larminie, William. FAND AND OTHER POEMS. Dublin: Hodges, Figgis, 1892. [6],149 pp. Sig.: Jos. P. Quinn

1087. [Larsson, Carl]. CARL LARSSON [Swedish artist]. Sma Konstböcker, no. 4. Lund; Gleerupska Universitets-Bokhandeln, [1907?]. 64 pp.

1088. Laski, Harold J[oseph]. COMMUNISM. Home University Library. London: Williams and Norgate, 1927. ix,256 pp.

Pencil strokes pp. 56, 57, 58, 64, 83, 89.
Back flyleaf, pencil: For Hegel's relation to the materialistic interpretation of history see page 56.

1089. Last, Hugh. "Dr. H.R. Hall." Offprint from THE JOURNAL OF EGYPTIAN ARCHAEOLOGY. 17 (1931): 111-16.

1090. Lavery, Emmet. THE FIRST LEGION. A drama of the Society of Jesus. New York: Samuel French, 1934. 132 pp. Sig.: L. Robinson/ N.Y. 1935.

1091. Law, William. THE SPIRIT OF LOVE IN DIALOGUES. London: Griffith Farran, [1893]. 185 pp.

Inserted, holograph letter from Hugh Law to WBY, Stephen's Green Club, Dublin, 4 July 1926 presenting the book with the request that it eventually be forwarded to him at Marble Hill, Co. Donegal.

1092. Lawrence, Brother [Laurent, de la Resurrection]. THE PRACTICE OF THE PRESENCE OF GOD. The best rule of a holy life, being conversations and letters of Brother Lawrence. Authentic ed. London: Epworth Press, [1933]. 63 pp.

1093. Lawrence, D[avid] H[erbert]. THE COLLECTED POEMS. London: Martin Secker, 1933. vii,529 pp.

Flyleaf: The Wild Common 9/ Discord in Childhood 13/ Twilight 22/ Suburbs on a hazy day 41/ Sorrow 126/ In trouble and shame 168 [all excised in text, presumably for inclusion in OBMV, though first two do not appear there].

In Contents, "Hymn to Priapus" underscored and excised in text for OBMV.

1094. Lawrence, T[homas] E[dward]. SEVEN PILLARS OF WISDOM. London: Jonathan Cape, 672 pp.

Many pp. uncut.

*1095. Lawrence, W[illiam] J[ohn]. THE ELIZABETHAN PLAYHOUSE and other studies. Stratford: Shakespeare Head Press, 1912. ix,[7],265 pp. 466/760

*1096. ———. Second series. Stratford: Shakespeare Head Press, 1913. ix,[7],261 pp. 16/760

1097. Ledrede, Richard de, Bishop of Ossory. A CONTEMPORARY NARRATIVE OF THE PROCEEDINGS AGAINST DAME ALICE KYTELER. Edited by Thomas Wright. London: The Camden Society, 1843. xxxxii, [2],61,[3],36 pp.

Facing copyright p.: W.P. de Bathe, Feb. 1844/ 51 & 56, notes relating to my family.
P. xxi, corner turned back.
Narrative is in Latin.

*1098. Le Fanu, Joseph Sheridan. THE POEMS. Edited by Alfred Perceval Graves. London: Downey, 1896. xxviii,165 pp.

Stamped into title p.: With Downey and Co's Compliments.
Inside back cover: 13/17/96
Many pp. uncut.

1099. [Leinster, Edward Fitzgerald, 7th Duke of]. CATALOGUE OF IMPORTANT PICTURES BY OLD MASTERS sold by the order of the trustees of His Grace The Duke of Leinster.... Which will be sold by auction by Messrs. Christie, Manson, and Woods, at their Great Rooms 8 King Street, St. James Square, London, on Friday May 14, 1926. 27 pp., 8 plates

1100. THE LEISURE HOUR (London), part 448 (April 1889).

P. 233, a reproduction of a drawing by J.B. Yeats, "The Cavalier's Wife."

1101. Lempriere, J[ohn]. A CLASSICAL DICTIONARY. London: George Routledge, [1888]. xxxv,667 pp. Sig.: W B Yeats/ January 1898

1102. Lenin, V[ladimir] I[lich]. MATERIALISM AND EMPIRIO-CRITICISM. Translated by David Kvitko and Sidney Hook. London: Martin Lawrence, [1927]. xxiv,[2],342 pp. Sig.: WBY

*1103. [Leo, Alan]. A THOUSAND AND ONE NOTABLE NATIVITIES. Alan Leo's Astrological Manuals, no. 11. London: Modern Astrology Office, 1911. viii,124 pp. Bp: GY

In text, many names of famous personages underlined; some entries likely WBY's, e.g. Blake (58), Maud Gonne, (59). Inside back cover, various Russells have their moments of birth recorded, e.g. John, Charles, Janet, Archibald; not WBY's.

1104. ———. ASTROLOGY FOR ALL. Part 2. Calculations and Ephemeris. London: Modern Astrology, 1904. viii,208 pp. Bp: GY

Flyleaf: Dunsaney [sic]/ 24 July 1878 [pencil; WBY's]
In the sections giving "A Condensed Ephemeris of the Planets' Places for every seventh day, from 1850 to 1905 inclusive" and "The Moon's Place for every day during the same period" (pp. 93-182), penciled figures, many likely WBY's, appear frequently, as for the years 1864, 1865 (July 16, 23), 1871 and 1900.
P. 9, first par: 4 meridians = 1 degree [pencil; WBY's as are following]
P. 10 at (3): average mean time/ solar day
P. 13, top: gets earlier if you go West
P. 62, at "Log,": g m table?

1105. ———. HOW TO JUDGE A NATIVITY. London: Modern Astrology, 1912. xx,336 pp. Bp: GY

*1106. Leo, John. A GEOGRAPHICAL HISTORIE OF AFRICA. Translated and collected by John Pory. Londini: Impensis G. Bishop, 1600. 8,419,[1] pp. Bp: WBY

Some marginal notes in an old hand.

*1107. Lesage, Alain René. THE ADVENTURES OF GIL BLAS OF SANTILLANA. Translated by Henri van Laun. 4 vols. London: Gibbings, 1896.

Vol. 3, flyleaf, a sketch, perhaps for a stage set, of two persons before a window.

*1108. Levi, Eliphaz. THE MAGICAL RITUAL OF THE SANCTUM REGNUM INTERPRETED BY THE TAROT TRUMPS. Translated and edited by W. Wynn Wescott. London: George Redway, 1896. x,108 pp.

Title p.: The gift of SA; N.O.M./ to his friend Mrs. Bullock [SA, i.e. Sapere Aude, Order name of W. Wynn Wescott].

*1109. ———. TRANSCENDENTAL MAGIC. Its doctrine and ritual. Translated by Arthur Edward Waite. London: George Redway, 1896. xxiv,[2],406 pp. Bp: WBY

Flyleaf: Stone Cottage/ Colman Hatch/ Sussex [E. Pound's]

1110. Lewes, George Henry. THE LIFE OF GOETHE. 2nd ed. London: George Routledge, [1864]. xii,578 pp.

1111. Lewis, C[ecil] Day. COLLECTED POEMS, 1929-1933. Transitional Poem. From Feathers to Iron. The Magnetic Mountain. London: Hogarth Press, 1935. 156 pp.

1112. ———. FROM FEATHERS TO IRON. London: Hogarth Press, 1931. 58 pp.

1113. ———. A HOPE FOR POETRY. Oxford: Basil Blackwell, 1935. [2],78 pp.

Flyleaf: To/ W.B. Yeats/ from/ V.K. Narayana Menon./ Sep. 25, 1936.
P. 3, pencil strokes against passage referring to WBY, "Yeats, the last in the aristocratic tradition of poets, remains the most admired of living writers...."

1114. ———. A TIME TO DANCE AND OTHER POEMS. London: Hogarth Press, 1935. 64 pp.

Flyleaf: Page 53/ 54/ Page 15? [unlikely WBY's; "In Me Two Worlds" begins on p. 15].
Pp. 53-4, a section of "A Time to Dance" excised; appears as "I've heard them lilting at Loom and Belting" in OBMV.

1115. Lewis, M[atthew] G[regory]. THE MONK: A ROMANCE. 3 vols. 3rd ed. London: J. Bell, 1797. Bps: Edward Ricketts

1116. Lewis, Wyndham. THE APES OF GOD. London: Arthur Press, 1930. 625 pp.

Limitation p., instead of a limitation no. (750 signed and numbered copies): To William Butler Yeats/ from Wyndham Lewis./ June 1930.

1117. ———. THE ART OF BEING RULED. London: Chatto and Windus, 1926. xii,434,[1] pp.

1118. ———. THE CALIPH'S DESIGN. Architects! Where is your Vortex? London: The Egoist, 1919. 70,[1] pp.

1119. ———. THE CHILDERMASS. Section I. London: Chatto and Windus, 1928. [6],322 pp. Bp: WBY

Inserted, a short holograph letter of presentation from Lewis to WBY, from 33 Ossington St., Bayswater, W.2. London, 18 July 1928; Lewis says that he has heard that Yeats was interested in the ideas in a recent book of his (unnamed) and that he sends the present book because it incorporates the same ideas but in a different form.

1120. ———. COUNT YOUR DEAD: THEY ARE ALIVE! Or a new war in the making. London: Lovat Dickson, 1937. vii,358 pp.

1121. ———. THE DIABOLICAL PRINCIPLE and THE DITHYRAMBIC SPECTATOR. London: Chatto and Windus, 1931. xiv,242 pp.

1122. ———. HITLER. London: Chatto and Windus, 1931. ix,202 pp.

1123. ———. THE LION AND THE FOX. The Role of the Hero in the plays of Shakespeare. London: Grant Richards, 1927, 326 pp.

1124. ———. ONE-WAY SONG. A series of four poems. London: Faber and Faber, 1933. 132 pp.

Flyleaf: To W.B. Yeats/ with the greatest homage/ from his great admirer/ Wyndham Lewis.
Some pp. uncut.
Some slight textual corrections.

1125. ———. PALEFACE. The Philosophy of the 'Melting Pot.' London: Chatto and Windus, 1929. xi,304 pp.

1126. ———. TIME AND WESTERN MAN. London: Chatto and Windus, 1927. vi,487 pp. Sig.: WBY

P. 401, at "but still directly": St. John of the Cross; specter of communication with gods without the mediation of an angel as very rare. D. told us of certain spirits that so communicate - spirits who are perhaps god.

Pp. 409-67, marginal strokes and underlining in "The Object as King of Physical World" and "Space and Time."

P. 462, at "When Faust rejects": Buddhism says also "act"

P. 463, at "God must be a sexless image": S. Theresa

P. 463, bottom: We approach reality by personality - i.e. see the world as one and this personality only exists in the presence of the world of concrete imagination and action of art. Science "eliminates the personal factor."

P. 465, bottom, for the passage "Our consciousness of reality, he affirms is the consciousness that anything we apprehend belongs to Space-Time.": The theory of Graeco-Babylonian [?] astrology - all distances [are] measures of time, all characters are decided by their fate.

Pp. 468, 471, corners turned back.

Back flyleaf: Moriles Nector [?]/ R. Cruz. Conor [?]/ Cordoba [possibly WBY's].

1127. Lhote, André. GEORGES SEURAT. Rome: Éditions de Valori Plastici, 1922. 14 pp., 32 plates.

1128. LIFE AND LETTERS (London). 1 (Sept. 1928).

Includes "The Rare Books of Living Authors" by Oliver Brett, pp. 305-11.

P. 307, an "x' against "The writer has no copy of Mr. Yeats's first book, MUSADA [sic] (1886), worth some £ 80, but the same author's WHERE THERE IS NOTHING (1902) is almost as scarce."
P. 309, against "In the same way those who scour Paris for the pornographic incoherencies of ULYSSES": !

1129. ———. 10 (April 1934).

Includes a reference to WBY in "Cross Section," p. 108; also in a review of Eliot's AFTER STRANGE GODS, p. 112.

1130. ———. 11 (Nov. 1934).

Includes THE KING OF THE GREAT CLOCK TOWER.

1131. LIFE AND LETTERS TO-DAY. 13 (Winter Quarter, 1935-6).

Includes Yone Noguchi's "Three Scenes from Japanese Plays," pp. 32-40.

*1132. LIGHT: JOURNAL OF PSYCHICAL, OCCULT, AND MYSTICAL RESEARCH (London). 35 (30 Oct. 1915 - 25 Dec. 1915).

Bound vol.

*1133. ———. 36 (1 Jan. 1916 - 24 June 1916).

Bound vol.

1134. [Liljefors, Bruno]. BRUNO LILJEFORS [Swedish artist]. Sma Konstböcker, no. 5. Lund: Gleerupska Universitets-Bokhandeln, 1908. 64 pp.

1135. Limebeer, Ena. TO A PROUD PHANTOM. Poems. Richmond: Hogarth Press, 1923. 32 pp.

Inside frt. cover: H.V. Reade/ Ipsden Oxon. 5/5/24.
Flyleaf: H.V. Reade/ d.d. May 1924/ M.V.S.R. [?]

1136. Lindsay, Jack. HELEN COMES OF AGE. Three Plays. London: Fanfrolico Press, 1927. [8],221 pp. 109/500

Flyleaf: From Jack Lindsay/ to W.B. Yeats.
Only HELEN COMES OF AGE cut.
Verso, Contents p., a printed note, "Before each play I have placed a quotation from W.B. Yeats...."

1137. ———. MARINO FALIERO. A verse play. London: Fanfrolico Press, 1927. [1],104 pp. 215/450

Flyleaf: From Jack Lindsay/ to W.B. Yeats.

1138. Lindsay, Norman and Jack Lindsay. A HOMAGE TO SAPPHO. Poems. London: Fanfrolico Press, 1928. 64 pp. 50/70

Colophon p.: Jack Lindsay/ ποιητης / to William Butler Yeats.

1139. Lindsay, Vachel. GENERAL WILLIAM BOOTH ENTERS INTO HEAVEN and other poems. New York: Macmillan, 1921. [10],119 pp.

1140. Li-Po. THE WORKS OF LI-PO THE CHINESE POET. Translated by Shigeyoshi Obata. London and Toronto: J.M. Dent, 1923. xviii,236 pp.

1141. THE LISTENER (London). 16 (14 Oct. 1936).

First par. of Yeats's "Modern Poetry" has been deleted, "I have been asked to talk to you tonight about Modern Poetry, because the BBC people know that I have just finished making an anthology of it. And I am going to begin with a statement that may surprise you." Also many changes in accidentals, likely by GY for ESSAYS AND INTRODUCTIONS.

1141a. Another copy.

1142. Litchfield, Frederick. ILLUSTRATED HISTORY OF FURNITURE. From the earliest to the present time. 4th ed. London and New York: Truslove, Hanson, and Comba, 1899. xx, 272 pp.

Flyleaf: M F Tiddeman/ 175 Banbury Rd./ Oxford/ To my dear Wife/ Tetbury [?] 1901/ RHT
Inserted, 5 photographs of chests, carved panels, and tapestries, one with an identification by GY.

1143. THE LITTLE REVIEW (New York). 8 (Spring, 1922).

The Picabia Number

1144. Lomax, John A[very]. COWBOY SONGS and other frontier ballads. New York: Sturgis and Walton, 1916. xiii, 414 pp.

1145. Lombroso, Cesare. AFTER DEATH -- WHAT? Spiritistic phenomena and their interpretation. Translated by William Sloane Kennedy. London: T. Fisher Unwin, 1909. xii,[2],364 pp. Sig.: WBY

On cover, a label: Mudie's Select Library
Flyleaf: W B Yeats [ink] // B[orn?] 27/1/11 [pencil]
Half title p.: see pp. 349 [a passage on "mistakes" marked there] and 175 [verses marked].
Marginal strokes, pp. v, vi, vii, 3-11, 17, 21-3, 34, 36, 38, 62, 72, 75, 83, 98, 100, 102, 109, 227, 242, 243, 249, 250, 251, 279, 326, 330-4, 336, 338, 341, 346, 347, 349, 350.
P. 37, at "I'm so thirsty": compare with food left out
P. 176, at "haunted houses": see spirit movement in folk belief.
P. 280, at passage on Butler family: Ghost of the living
P. 325, at "Flournoy": medium

P. 345, at "When little children die....": Spirits grow older
Inside back cover, a list of page nos.: VI, 3, 4, 102, 109, 130, 154, 174, 6 [176?], 206, 249, 279, 305, 315, 318, 320, 1, 6.

LONDON MAGAZINE, See 976.

1146. THE LONDON MERCURY. 10 (Sept. 1924).

Contains "The Bounty of Sweden"

1147. ———. 16 (May 1927).

Contains "Two Songs from the Old Countryman" and "Four Songs from the Young Countryman"; all checked in text.

1148. ———. 16 (Aug. 1927)
Contains "Among School Children"

1149. ———. 30 (July 1934).

On cover: 1st Issue Yeats' article/ 1/6
Contains "Louis Lambert"

1150. ———. 31 (Dec. 1934).

Contains "Supernatural Songs"; titles checked in text.

1150a. Another copy.

1151. ———. 37 (April 1938).

Contains "The Wild Old Wicked Man," "An Acre of Grass," "Are You Content?," "Sweet Dancer."
Titles checked in text.

1151a. Another copy.

1152. ———. 38 (May 1938).

Contains "A Last Word on the Hugh Lane Affair" by D.S. MacColl, pp. 12-15.

1153. ———. 39 (March 1939).

Contains "The Statues," "News for the Delphic Oracle," "Long-Legged Fly," "A Bronze Head" (all checked in text) and various tributes to Yeats.

1153a-b. Two more copies.

1154. Londonderry, The Marchioness of. THE LAND OF THE LIVING HEART. Privately printed, 1936. 38 pp.

Flying travels.
Half-title p.: With homage and best/ wishes to Senator Yeats/ from E. Londonderry/ Christmas 1936.

1155. Long, Haniel. INTERLINEAR TO CABEZA DE VACA, his relation of the journey from Florida to the Pacific, 1528-1536. Sante Fe: Writers' Editions, 1936. 37, [1] pp.

Flyleaf: Lawrence/ with love from/ Sage/ Christmas/ 1937.

1156. Longford, The Earl of. YAHOO. A tragedy in three acts. Dublin: Hodges, Figgis, [1934]. [2],65 pp.

A play about Swift.

*1157. [Louvre]. LES CHEFS D'OEUVRE DU MUSÉE DU LOUVRE. Paris: Les Grand Magasins du Louvre, [1900?]. xiv, [2],120 pp.

LOWE, Robert W., See 48.

*1158. Lucas, St. John. THE OXFORD BOOK OF FRENCH VERSE. Xiii - Xix Centuries. New York: Oxford Univ. Press, [1907]. xxxiv,[1],492 pp. Bp: WBY

1159. Luce, A[rthur] A[ston], BERKELEY AND MALEBRANCHE. A study in the origins of Berkeley's thought. London: Oxford Univ. Press, 1934. x,[2],214 pp.

P. 113, corner turned back.

1160. ———. "Berkeley's COMMONPLACE BOOK -- Its Date, Purpose, Structure, and Marginal Signs." Offprint from HERMATHENA 22 (1932): 99 - 132.

1161. Lucian. TRUE HISTORY. Translated by Francis Hickes. Illustrated by Aubrey Beardsley and Others. London: A.H. Bullen, 1902. xxix,[1],117 pp.

Some pp. uncut.

1162. Lucretius, Carus (Titus). TITI LUCRETII CARI DE RERUM NATURA LIBRI SEX. Londini: Jacobi Tonson, 1712. Pagination very irregular.

Flyleaf: Oliver Gogarty/ e Coll. Vigone, Oxon./ 1904. Title p., top: "The shudder of holy awe thrills me when I listen to the austere chanting of that atheist who prayed." Month Nov. 09 p. 518 [Gogarty's]. Also: Archibald Bradford [old hand]

1162A. Another ed. Translated by H.A.J. Munro. 2 vols. 2nd ed. rev. Cambridge: Deighton Bell, 1866.

Vol. 2 only, TRANSLATION. Sig.: Oliver Gogarty/ E Coll. Vigone, Oxon./ 1904.

1163. Lutoslawski, W[incenty]. PRE-EXISTENCE AND REINCARNATION. London: George Allen, 1928. 157 pp. Bp: WBY

*1164. LYRICS FROM THE CHINESE. Adapted [from J. Legge's translation of the Shih Ching] by Helen Waddell. London: Constable, 1913. xiv,41 pp.

*1165. Lytton, Edward Bulwer, Lord. THE DRAMATIC WORKS. Comprising THE DUCHESS DE LA VALLIÈRE, RICHELIEU, THE LADY OF LYONS, MONEY, NOT SO BAD AS WE SEEM. New ed. London: George Routledge, [187?]. [7],496 pp. Sig.: Jessop Browne/ Xmas 1870

*1166. THE MABINOGION, from the Welsh of the Llyfr Coh O Hergest (The Red Book of Hergest) in the library of Jesus College, Oxford. Translated by Lady Charlotte Guest. London: Bernard Quaritch, 1877. xx,504 pp.

Half title p.: W.B. Yeats/ from the translator's daughter/ Enid Layard/ 1898.
P. 109, a book mark inserted in the Welsh text and a marginal stroke.
Slips inserted, pp. 268-9, 270-1, 284-5, 424-5 (on this: P. 217/ Ideas of Good and Evil/ [one word undecipherable]
Marginal strokes, pp. 306, 307
Corners turned back, pp. 273, 445.

1167. Macardle, Dorothy. THE IRISH REPUBLIC. A documented chronical of the Anglo-Irish conflict and the partitioning of Ireland, with a detailed account of the period 1916 - 1923. Preface by Eamon de Valera. London: Victor Gollancz, 1937. 1072 pp., map.

Reference to WBY, p. 62.
P. 693, marginal stroke at "A few days later."

1168. McCartan, Patrick. WITH DE VALERA IN AMERICA. New York: Brentano, 1932. xiv,[2],284 pp.

1169. McCarthy, Justin, ed.-in-chief. IRISH LITERATURE. 10 vols. Philadelphia: John D. Morris, 1904.

Vol. 3 missing.
WBY was a contributor; see WADE 261.
Vol. 8, p. 3071, pencil stroke.
Vol. 8, pp. 3244-46, "The Hymn Called Saint Patrick's Breast-Plate" translated by Whitley Stokes marked by pencil strokes.

1170. Mac Cathmhaoil, Seosamh (Joseph Campbell). THE RUSH-LIGHT. Poems. Dublin: Maunsel, 1906. [3],66,[1] pp.

On paper cover: W.B.Y. from AVM [book is dedicated to A.V.M.].

1171. McCrae, Hugh. SATYRS AND SUNLIGHT. Collected poetry. Illustrated and decorated by Norman Lindsay. London:

Fanfrolico Press, 1928. xix,[1],176 pp.

Limitation p., "550 copies"; instead of a limitation no.: William Butler Yeats/ from Jack Lindsay.

MCCURDY, Edward, See 181.

1172. M'Diarmid, Hugh. A DRUNK MAN LOOKS AT THE THISTLE. Edinburgh and London: William Blackwood, 1926. viii,108 pp.

1173. ———. SANGSCHAW. Edinburgh and London: William Blackwood, 1925. xii,58 pp.

1174. ———. SECOND HYMN TO LENIN and other poems. London: Stanley Nott, 1935. 77 pp.

1175. ———. SELECTED POEMS. London: Macmillan, 1934. 57,[2] pp.

Pp. 34-39, 45-6 excised for OBMV selections "Parley of Beasts," "O Wha's been here afore me, Lass," "Cattle Show."

1176. ———. STONY LIMITS and other poems. London: Victor Gollancz, 1934. 143 pp.

1177. ———. TO CIRCUMJACK CENCRASTUS or the curly snake. Edinburgh and London: William Blackwood, 1930. [8], 206 pp.

1178. [M'Diarmid, Hugh]. SPEAKING FOR SCOTLAND. TRIBUTES CONCERNING HUGH M'DIARMID. [No publisher, 1936]. 4 pp.

P. 2, under "Other Tributes," "You have done many lovely and passionate things. -- W. B. Yeats."

*1179. MacDonagh, Michael. BISHOP DOYLE, "J.K.L." A biographical and historical study. The New Irish Library. Edited by Sir Charles Gavan Duffy. London: T. Fisher Unwin, 1896. viii,[2],216 pp.

*1180. MacDonagh, Thomas. LITERATURE IN IRELAND. Studies Irish and Anglo-Irish. Dublin: Talbot Press, 1916. xiii,[1],248 pp. Bp: WBY

Many marginal strokes through p. 151, some for passages referring to WBY, e.g. pp. 67-8.
P. 130, next to lines from 9th cent. poem, "My riddled body must now part from thee a while, my soul to be tortured by the black demon...": agh!
Inside back cover, a list of p. nos. all with marginal stroking in text: 22, 47, 52-3, 55, 60, 61, 62, 65, 66, 68, 71, 73, 78, 82, 89, 92, 94, 112, 127, 129, 138, 141, 145, 149.

*1181. ———. LYRICAL POEMS. Dublin: Irish Review, 1913. Bp: WBY

Flyleaf: "5: vi: 1916/ To W.B. Yeats/ from Oliver Gogarty."

*1182. ———. THOMAS CAMPION AND THE ART OF ENGLISH POETRY. Dublin: Hodges, Figgis, 1913. ix,129 pp. By: WBY

Flyleaf: To/ W.B. Yeats,/ 12.ii 1913/ Thomas MacDonagh
Marginal strokes, mostly in "Music and Metre"
P. 39, two lines of verse added in pencil, not WBY's.
Inside back cover, a list of p. nos.; stroking on most of these pp.: 66-70, 73, 86 legato-staccato [a discussion of this subject on that p.].

*1183. Macdonald, J[ames]. NATIONAL DEFENCE, A study of militarism. London: George Allen and Unwin, 1917. 132 pp.

*1184. McDougall, William. BODY AND MIND. A history and a defense of animism. 2nd ed. London: Methuen, 1913. xx,384 pp.

Corners turned back, pp. 18, 143.

1185. ———. THE GROUP MIND. A sketch of the principles of collective psychology with some attempt to apply them to the interpretation of national life and character. Cambridge: Univ. Press, 1920. xvi,304 pp. Bp: WBY

Inserted, a business letter (about a broken candlestick) to Mrs. Yeates [sic], 14 April 1921, Oxford.

1186. ———. NATIONAL WELFARE AND NATIONAL DECAY. London: Methuen, 1921. vii,213, [1] pp. Sig.: GY

1187. M'Gee, Thomas D'Arcy. A MEMOIR OF THE LIFE AND CONQUESTS OF ART MACMURROUGH, King of Leinster, from A.D. 1377 to A.D. 1417. 2nd ed. Dublin: James Duffy, [1886]. xxiv,200 pp.

Inside frt. cover, possibly early WBY: "We're one at heart if you be Ireland's friend,/ Though leagues asunder our opinions tend./ There are but two great parties in the end.'/ Allingham [followed by a brief entry deleted].
Back flyleaf, recto: Hardiman's Irish Minstralsy [sic]/ Petrie's Irish Music/ Hayes [canceled]/ Transactions Royal Irish Academy [ink; possibly early WBY]
Back flyleaf, verso: O'Curry's Materials of I[rish?] H[istory?]/ Manners and Customs etc./ Standish O'Grady/ History of Ireland [ink; possibly early WBY]
Inside back cover: Ossianic Society/ Archaeological & Celtic Societies/ Hiberno [canceled] Celtic/
Irish Gaelic { Celtic
Children of Usnach

Atlantis { Children of Lir
Children of Tuirean
Sick Bed of Cuculain

Celtic & Archeological
- Feast of Dun na-Gedh
- Battle of Gabra
- Battle of Magh Rath (Moira)
- Battle of Moy Céana

Ossianic
- Diarmuid & Grainne
- Procession of Bards
- ?Battle of Ventry
- Ossianic lays (Land of Youth) [ink; possibly early WBY]

1188. McGreevy, Thomas. POEMS. London: William Heinemann, 1934. [8],60 pp.

Flyleaf: "Homage etc 30"/ Aodh 36" [both of these poems, "Homage to Jack Yeats" and "Aodh Ruadh O Donhaill" appear in OBMV and are excised; also excised the Note beginning p. 58 to supply note for "Aodh Ruadh" in OBMV].

1188a. Another copy.

1189. ———. RICHARD ALDINGTON, An Englishman. The Dolphin Books. London: Chatto and Windus, 1931. 73 pp.

1190. ———. THOMAS STEARNS ELIOT, a study. The Dolphin Books. London: Chatto and Windus, 1931. 71 pp.

Flyleaf: To George and W.B. Yeats/ from Thomas McGreevy / 22.1.31.

1191. Machiavelli. THE PRINCE. Translated by Luigi Ricci. The World's Classics, vol. 43. London: Grant Richards, 1903. viii,107 pp.

P. 14, some penciled nos., sums apparently, WBY's.

1192. Mackay, Eric. LOVE LETTERS OF A VIOLINIST and other poems. London: Walter Scott, 1886. xxix,201 pp. Sig.: W. B. Yeats/ Dublin/ 1887

*1193. Macleod, Fiona (William Sharp). FROM THE HILLS OF DREAM. Mountain songs and island runes. Edinburgh: Patrick Geddes, [1896]. cvi,149 pp.

*1193A. Another ed. Portland, Maine: Thomas B. Mosher, 1901. xiv,[2],148,[1] pp.

Flyleaf: To W.B. Yeats/ from/ Fiona Macleod.

*1194. ———. THE HOUSE OF USNA. A drama. Portland, Maine: Thomas B. Mosher, 1903. xxxii,75,[1] pp.

*1195. ———. THE IMMORTAL HOUR. A drama. Edinburgh and London: T.N. Foulis, 1908. xi,[3],53 pp.

Some pp. uncut.

*1196. ———. UNDER THE DARK STAR [and THE KINGDOM OF SILENCE and CHANT D'AMOUR]. Privately printed: n.d. 327,[1] pp.

Half title p., ink: Private Edition of Five Sets/ Set No. i/ Fiona Macleod.
P. 7, marginal stroke.

1197. Mac Mic Cuinn na M-Bocht, Moelmuiri. FLED BRICREND, THE FEAST OF BRICRIU. An early Gaelic saga, etc. Edited by George Henderson. Irish Texts Society, vol. 2. London: Published for the Irish Texts Society by David Nutt, 1899. lxvii,[2],217 pp.

1198. MacMillan, Dougald and Howard Mumford Jones, eds. PLAYS OF THE RESTORATION AND EIGHTEENTH CENTURY as they were acted at the Theatres-Royal.... London: George Allen and Unwin, 1931. ix,896 pp.

See NUC for complete listing of contents.

1199. MacNeice, Louis. POEMS. London: Faber and Faber, 1935. 66 pp.

Excised, "An Eclogue for Christmas," "Turf-stacks," and "Circe" for M's selection in OBMV. ("The Individualist Speaks," also in OBMV <u>not</u> excised.)
Inserted, an income tax statement from Methuen and Co. to WBY certifying that 2 copies of BIV were sold in U.K. in first six months of 1935.

1199a. Another copy.

In Contents, titles checked, "An Eclogue for Christmas," "Turk-stacks," "Spring Sunshine" (but check is canceled), "Circe," and "The Individualist Speaks." Some pp. uncut.

1199b. Another copy.

SEE ALSO 21.

1200. McTaggart, John McTaggart Ellis. A COMMENTARY ON HEGEL'S LOGIC. Cambridge: Univ. Press, 1910. xvi,311 pp.

1200a. Another copy.

1201. ———. HUMAN IMMORTALITY AND PRE-EXISTENCE. London: Edward Arnold, 1916. viii,119 pp.

Marginal strokes, pp. 28, 30, 33, 37-40.
P. 40, last 3 lines of note underlined.

1202. ———. THE NATURE OF EXISTENCE. 2 vols. Cambridge: Univ. Press, 1921. Bps: WBY

VOL. 1, flyleaf, impressed in paper but readable: O'Leary/ care Yeats/ returning Tuesday evening/ Yeats [WBY's; this has been transcribed above, in pencil, probably by G.Y.]

VOL. 1, many marks, notes, and comments; marginal strokes and underlining especially pp. 5, 44, 68, 114, 154, 227.

P. 41, at "Perception is the awareness of what Mr. Russell calls particulars" [to] "it is the awareness of substances as distinct from the awareness of characteristics": Are C[elestial] B[ody] and spirit universal but [??] not creative? But I must regard C.B. as a subtler alternative [?] and to confine word "perception" to sense data if the spirit and C.B. are mentally creative. May have to ask about this. I think the last correct for the Faculties which derive from Husk and P[assionate] B[ody] contain concepts etc. [3 words deleted]. Spirit is then less [?] known. [O]nly [?] spirits.

P. 71, at "nothing exists but spirits...": Hence [?] my teachers object to use of subject and object and prefer conceptions related to unity of being.

P. 112, in margin at pars 2-4: contingency

P. 113, at par. "No quality of a substance": contingency

P. 150, margin, at No. 137: A x O 3

P. 150, at "Possession by anything": Fact

Back flyleaf: Extrinsic determination: the determination of part by a whole which is a substance and therefore particular. My chair, implying by the term my chair in all its particular history, are described by its qualities - a leg broke, a torn seat or all legs quite new and a purple seat cover - or is my self and all my particular passing thought. Intrinsic determination is universal when one quality occurs, another follows. When a chair leg is broken the chair leg is unstable etc. This determination is one of cause when we are speaking of an actual chair (cause can only be between existants) and when it's between two qualities alone (broken and unstable). The relation of cause and effect is however one of time only; one proceeds the other.

VOL. 2, no markings.

1203. ———. STUDIES IN HEGELIAN COSMOLOGY. Cambridge: Univ. Press, 1918. xx,293 pp.

Marginal strokes, underscorings, brief notes on first 100 pp.

Marginal strokes, pp. 13, 14, 17, 18, 31, 33, 35, 50, 60, 61, 62, 64, 65, 68, 69, 70, 71, 76, 77, 78, 79, 80, 87, 95, 96, 98.

P. 19, at par. 1: Primary and antithetical

P. 66, at par. 4: Like two mirrors reflecting each other

P. 99, at par. 2: need for revelation

P. 99, at par. 3: a Christ would see further.

Inside back cover, pencil: Man who lost himself.

1204. ———. STUDIES IN THE HEGELIAN DIALECTIC. 2nd ed. Cambridge: Univ. Press, 1922. xvi,255 pp.

Some pp. uncut.

1205. Madeleva, Sister M[ary]. THE HAPPY CHRISTMAS WIND and other poems. Paterson, N.J.: St. Anthony Guild Press, 1936. v,20 pp.

1206. ———. PENELOPE and other poems. New York and London: D. Appleton, 1927. ix,59 pp.

1207. ———. A QUESTION OF LOVERS and other poems. Patterson, N.J.: St. Anthony Guild Press, 1936. vii,57 pp.

1208. Maeterlinck, Maurice. RUYSBROECK AND THE MYSTICS. With selections from Ruysbroeck. Translated by Jane T. Stoddart. London: Hodder and Stoughton, 1894. viii, 153 pp.

1209. Mahaffy, John Pentland. With the collaboration of Arthur Gilman. ALEXANDER'S EMPIRE. London: T. Fisher Unwin, 1920. xxii,323 pp.

1210. Mairet, Philippe. ARISTOCRACY AND THE MEANING OF CLASS RULE. An essay upon aristocracy past and future. London: C.W. Daniel, 1931. 101,[1] pp.

*1211. Maitland, Francis. POEMS. London: Elkin Mathews, 1917. 56 pp.

1212. Mallarmé, Stéphane. POEMS. Translated by Roger Fry. London: Chatto and Windus, 1936. xii,308 pp.

SEE ALSO 168.

1213. Malone, Andrew E. THE IRISH DRAMA. London: Constable, 1929. [1],351 pp.

1214. Malory, Sir Thomas. LE MORTE DARTHUR. Designs by Aubrey Beardsley. 2 vols. London: J.M. Dent, 1893.

Some pp. uncut.

1215. Mannin, Ethel. DRYAD, and other tales. London: Jarrolds, 1933. 313 pp.

Title p.: For W.B. Yeats/ from his friend/ Ethel Mannin/ With affection and admiration/ New Years Eve 1934-5.

*1216. Manning, Frederic. POEMS. London: John Murray, 1910. xii,96 pp.

1217. Manning-Sanders, Ruth. MARTHA WISH-YOU-ILL. London: Hogarth Press, 1926. 16 pp.

Poems.

*1218. Mantzius, Karl. A HISTORY OF THEATRICAL ART IN ANCIENT AND MODERN TIMES. Translated by Louise von Cossell [and C. Archer]. 6 vols. London: Duckworth, 1903-1921.

VOL. 1, Bp: WBY [above bp.:] Anne Yeats from WBY on her birthday/ Feb. 26 1937
Inserted, a short newspaper clipping, unidentified source, 1930's, describing WBY's visit to his son at St. Columba's school.

VOLS. 2-6, flyleaves: Anne from her father.

VOL. 3, inserted, 3 newspaper clippings, See 2136, 2138, 2142.

VOL. 6, inserted, a newspaper review, See 433.

1219. [Map]. BACON'S MOTORING AND CYCLING ROAD MAP. Stratford-on-Avon District. Stratford-on-Avon: A.J. Stanley, n.d.

1220. [Map]. BARTHOLOMEW'S QUARTER INCH MAP OF IRELAND. Killarney and Cork. Edinburgh and London: John Bartholomew, n.d.

1221. [Maps]. CAMBRIDGE MEDIEVAL HISTORY. MAPS. 8 vols. Cambridge: Cambridge Univ. Press, 1911-36.

Vols. 1-5 and 8 only.
Cover, vol. 5, pencil: See 52 p. [on p. 52, "Northern Italy in the Hohenstaufen Period," a light pencil mark near Parma and Reggio]

1222. [Map]. IRELAND, by Sidney Hall. London: Longman, Rees, Orme, Browne and Green, 1830.

1223. [Maps]. LONDON STREET GUIDE. With 4 maps. An entirely new ed. including L.C.C. changes of street names. London: Geographia, n.d.

*1224. [Maps]. MAPS OF OLD LONDON. Edited by G.E. Mitton. London: Adam and Charles Black, 1908.

1225. [Map]. NUOVA PIANTA DE VERONA. Firenze: Stabilimento Grafico Cartographico, n.d.

1226. [Map]. ORDNANCE SURVEY MAP OF KENMARE RIVER AND DISTRICT. Coloured ed. Sheets 191 and 198. Southampton: Ordnance Survey Office, n.d.

1227. Mardrus, Dr. J[oseph] C[arles]. THE QUEEN OF SHEBA. Translated by E. Powys Mather. London: Casanova Society, [1924]. 102,[1] pp.

*1228. Margaret [D'Angoulemne], Queen Consort of Henry II, King of Navarre. THE HEPTAMERON: TALES. [Translated by W.M. Thomson]. Unexpurgated ed. London: [Temple, 1896]. 362 pp.

*1229. Marillier, H[enry] C[urrie]. DANTE GABRIEL ROSSETTI. An illustrated memorial of his art and life. London: George Bell, 1899. xxiii,[1],270 pp. Bp: WBY

Flyleaf: W.B. Yeats from John Masefield/ "There is delight in singing though none hear/ Beside the singer, and there is delight/ In praising though the praiser sit alone/ And see the praised far off him - far alone."

*1230. THE MARIONETTE (Florence). 1 (Nov. 1918).

Contains a brief review of Pound's PAVANNES AND DIVISIONS by A.B.

1231. Maritain, Jacques. AN INTRODUCTION TO PHILOSOPHY. Translated by E.I. Watkin. London: Sheed and Ward, 1932. 272 pp.

*1232. ———. THREE REFORMERS. LUTHER - DESCARTES - ROUSSEAU. London: Sheed and Ward, 1928. viii,234 pp. Bp: WBY

1233. Marivaux [Carlet de Chamblain de Marivaux, Pierre]. THEATRE CHOISI DE MARIVAUX. [Edited by F. De Marescot and D. Jouaust?]. 2 vols. Paris: Librairie des bibliophiles, [1881].

Vol. 2 only; includes LE LEGS, LES FAUSSES CONFIDENCES, LES SINCERES, L'EPREUVE.

1234. Marlowe, Christopher. DOCTOR FAUSTUS. Edited by John Masefield. Decorated by Charles Ricketts. London: Ballantyne Press, 1903. li pp. Bp: WBY

Uncut.

1235. Marpicati, Arturo. THE ACHIEVEMENTS OF FASCISM. [N.p., 193?]. 51,[2] pp.

Apparently a translation of WERKE DES FASCHISMUS. [Rome?, 1934?].

1236. Marriott, Ernest. "Jack B. Yeats, Pictorial and Dramatic Artist." Reprint from the MANCHESTER QUARTERLY, no. 119. Manchester: For the Manchester Literary Club by Sherratt and Hughes, 1911. 14 pp.

Inserted, a reproduction of "The Wake House" by Jack B. Yeats; also a reproduction of a religious illustration with: Easter Greetings to/ Miss Yeats, with Love from/ Julia E. Ford.

1236a. Another copy.

Inserted as above, "The Wake House."
Uncut.

*1237. [Marsh, Edward Howard, ed.]. GEORGIAN POETRY, 1913-1915. London: Poetry Bookshop, 1915. [10],244 pp. Bp: WBY

In Contents, strokes against James Elroy Flecker's "Santorin" and Harold Monro's "Milk for the Cat" which has been excised in text. Both poems appear in OBMV.

*1238. Marston, John. THE WORKS OF JOHN MARSTON. Edited by A.H. Bullen. 3 vols. London: John C. Nimmo, 1887. 50/200

Vol. 1 uncut after p. 120.
Vol. 2 uncut after p. 57.
Vol. 3 uncut.

1239. Martyn, Oliver [H.O. White]. THE MAN THEY COULDN'T HANG. A Morrow Mystery. New York: William Morrow, 1933. ix,[3],301 pp. Sig.: WBY

Flyleaf: by H.O. White [Prof. of English, T.C.D.]/ Please leave at Abbey when read [canceled]/ Please Return [WBY's].

MARZIALS, Frant T., See 180.

*1240. Masefield, John. BALLADS. London: Elkin Mathews, 1903. 56 pp.

Flyleaf: To W.B. Yeats./ with John Masefield's/ best wishes./ Oct. 23, 1903.

1240A. 2nd ed., rev. and enlarged. 1910.

*1241. ———. BALLADS AND POEMS. London: Elkin Mathews, 1919. 100 pp.

Some pp. uncut.

1242. ———. THE COLLECTED POEMS. London: William Heinemann, 1935. x,[4],957 pp.

Marked in Contents and excised for OBMV, "Sea-Change," "Port of Many Ships," "A Valediction (Liverpool Docks)," "Trade Winds," "Cargoes," "Port of Holy Peter"; also marked in Contents and sometimes excised, "The Golden City of St. Mary," "A Wanderer's Song," "The Tarry Buccanneer," "Vagabond," "Personal," "Captain Stratton's Fancy," "And Old Song Re-sung," "St. Mary's Bells," "Posted."

1243. ———. THE DAFFODIL FIELDS. London: William Heinemann, 1918. 110 pp. Sig.: Katharine B. Scott

Marginal strokes, underscoring passim, same ink as sig. above.

1244. ———. THE DREAM. Illustrated by Judith Masefield. [Oxford]: Printed by Slatter and Rose, [1922?]. 13 pp.

Title p.: To Mr. and Mrs. Yeats./ from Judith Masefield/ Mar. 26, 1922
Variant of 1st ed.

*1245. ———. THE EVERLASTING MERCY. London: Sidgwick and Jackson, 1911. 89,[3] pp.

Inserted, p. 17, a card: Oxford Book of English Verse taken by W B Yeats Apr. 2 [WBY's]

*1246. ———. THE FAITHFUL. A tragedy in three acts. London: William Heinemann, 1915. vii,[3],131 pp.

1247. ———. GALLIPOLI. London: William Heinemann, 1917. viii,183 pp.

1248. ———. GOOD FRIDAY. A play in verse. London: William Heinemann, 1917. vii,[1],78,[1] pp.

1249. ———. THE HAWBUCKS. London: William Heinemann, 1929. 322 pp.

Flyleaf: For W.B. Yeats./ from John Masefield/ April, 1930.

1250. ———. LOLLINGDON DOWNS and other poems. London: William Heinemann, 1919. 92,[1] pp.

1251. ———. A MAINSAIL HAUL. Frontispiece by Jack Yeats. London: Elkin Mathews, 1905. 128 pp.

Flyleaf: W.B. Yeats./ from John Masefield. 27.5.1905

1252. ———. MIDSUMMER NIGHT and other tales in verse. London: William Heinemann, 1928. 207 pp.

Flyleaf: For W.B. Yeats./ from John Masefield. April, 1930.

1253. ———. ON THE SPANISH MAIN or some English forays on the isthmus of Darien, with a description of the buccaneers.... London: Methuen, 1906. xii,344 pp.

Dedicated to Jack Yeats.

*1254. ———. PHILIP THE KING and other poems. London: William Heinemann, 1914. vii,117,[2] pp.

1255. ———. REYNARD THE FOX or the ghost of Heath Run. London: William Heinemann, 1920. 123,[1] pp.

1256. ———. A TARPAULIN MUSTER. London: Grant Richards, 1907. 227,[1] pp.

Flyleaf: W.B. Yeats/ from John Masefield/ April 15, 1907.

*1257. ———. THE TRAGEDY OF NAN and other plays. London: Grant Richards, 1909. 114 pp.

Dedication to WBY.
Flyleaf: To that most reverend head to whom I owe/ All that I am in Arts, all that I know./ To my master,/ W.B. Yeats./ Sept. 7, 1909.

Half title p.: Yeats
Pasted in at end of book, a holograph letter of presentation, Masefield to WBY, Rectory House, Great Hampden, Great Minenden, Bucks., 7 Sept. 1909: It was you who taught me all that I know of drama, who first encouraged, helped, and corrected me.... It was in your room that I had my first success, and what was better, my first consciousness of progress; you helped me to production, and soothed the bitterness of failure....

*1258. ———. THE TRAGEDY OF POMPEY THE GREAT. London: Sidgwick and Jackson, 1910. 106,[1] pp.

Flyleaf: W.B. Yeats./ from John Masefield/ Apr. 5, 1910.

1259. ———. THE WANDERER OF LIVERPOOL. London: William Heinemann, 1930. viii,[2],119 pp. 7/20. Sig.: John Masefield

*1260. ———. THE WIDOW IN THE BYE STREET. London: Sidgwick and Jackson, 1912. 98 pp.

*1261. ———. WILLIAM SHAKESPEARE. New York: Henry Holt; London: Williams and Norgate, 1911. viii,256 pp.

Flyleaf: W B Yeats/ from John Masefield/ July 27, 1911.
Inserted, holograph letter of presentation from Masefield to WBY, 30 Maida Hill West, 27 July 1911: if there is anything good in it, it was probably suggested by you....

1261a. Another printing. [1925]

Back flyleaf: Geo. Taylor/ Lubben & Co./ Gaston Mayer [not WBY].

*1262. ———, ed. AN ENGLISH PROSE MISCELLANY. London: Methuen, 1907. xxi,292 pp.

Flyleaf: W.B. Yeats/ from John Masefield/ Nov. 5, 1907.

*1263. ———, ed. A SAILOR'S GARLAND. London: Methuen, 1906. xxx,328 pp.

Flyleaf: for W B Yeats./ from John Masefield./ Oct. 10, 1906.

*1264. ——— and Constance Masefield, eds. LYRISTS OF THE RESTORATION. From Sir Edward Sherburne to William Congreve. London: E. Grant Richards, 1905. xxiv,282 pp.

Flyleaf: W.B. Yeats/ with love from/ his sisters/ Xmas 1906.
Some pp. uncut.

*1265. THE MASK. A Quarterly Journal of the Art of the Theatre (Florence). 2 (Oct. 1909-Apr. 1910).

Bound vol.

*1266. ———. 3 (July 1910-Apr. 1911).

Bound vol.

*1267. ———. 3 (Oct. 1910).

Contains WBY's "The Tragic Theatre," pp. 77-81.

*1267a. Another copy.

*1268. ———. 4 (July 1911-Apr. 1912).

Bound vol.; April no. contains anonymous review of WBY's PLAYS FOR AN IRISH THEATRE.

*1269. ———. 5 (July 1912-Apr. 1913).

Bound vol.; July no. contains Allen Carric's "Captain Jack B. Yeats: A Pirate of the Old School" and Jack Yeats's "How Jack B. Yeats Produced his Plays for the Miniature Stage."
April no. contains Yeats's THE HOUR GLASS, pp. 327-346; only pp. 342-6 cut; p. 346, "on the instance he fulfilled" corrected (ink, WBY) to: on the instant be fulfilled.

*1270. ———. 6 (Oct. 1913-Apr. 1914).

Bound vol.

*1271. ———. 7 (May 1915).

Contains "From the Preface to PLAYS FOR AN IRISH THEATRE"; uncut.

1272. ———. 8 (May 1918).

Subject is William Blake.

1273. ———. 8 (Nov. 1918).

1274. ———. 8, no. 11 [1919?].

Inserted in 2342.

1275. ———. 11 (4 Oct. 1925).

P. 160, a one sentence contribution by Jack Yeats to "A Symposium On Design by San Gallo."

1276. ———. 12 (1 Jan. 1926).

1277. ———. 12 (3 July 1926).

1278. ———. 12 (4 Oct. 1926).

1279. ———. 12 (Oct.-Dec. 1927).

1280. ———. 14. (Apr.-June 1928.

1281. ———. 14 (July-Sept. 1928).

1282. ———. 14 (Oct.-Dec. 1928).

1283. ———. 15 (Apr.-June 1929).

1284. ———. 15 (July-Sept. 1929).

1285. ———. 15 (Oct.-Dec. 1929.

*1286. [Massinger, Philip]. PHILIP MASSINGER. Edited by Arthur Symons. 2 vols. The Mermaid Series. London: T. Fisher, Unwin, [1887-9].

Vol. 1 only; contains THE DUKE OF MILAN, A NEW WAY TO PAY OLD DEBTS, THE GREAT DUKE OF FLORENCE, THE MAID OF HONOUR, THE CITY MADAM.
Inside back cover: 13 Merrion Row/ Dublin Fencing Cl./ Hon. Sec./ D. Coffey Esq./ 5 Harcourt Ter./ Sat 5-7/ Monday. 5-7/ Wednesday [possibly WBY's; followed by a very crude diagram, possibly for stage business].

*1287. Masters, Edgar Lee. SPOON RIVER ANTHOLOGY. London: T. Werner Laurie, 1915. xvii,248 pp. Bp: WBY

Checked in text, "The Hill," "Hod Putt," "Cassius Hueffer," "Amanda Barker," "Chase Henry," "Frank Drummer."

1288. Mathers, E[dward] Powys. RED WISE. Waltham Saint Lawrence: Golden Cockerell Press, 1926. 99 pp. 170/500 Short fictional pieces.

1289. ———, trans. BLACK MARIGOLDS. Being a rendering into English of the "Panchasika of Chauras." Oxford: Basil Blackwell, [1919]. 22 pp.

Flyleaf: To Ezra Pound/ with gratitude for (I suspect)/ inspiring an invitation/ to the "Little Review", and/ with admiration, anyway/ from/ E. Powys Mathers./ 9.11.19.

*1290. ———, trans. COLOURED STARS. Versions of fifty Asiatic love poems. Oxford: Basil Blackwell, 1919. 62 pp.

Some pp. uncut.

1291. ———, trans. THE GARDEN OF BRIGHT WATERS. One hundred and twenty Asiatic love poems. Oxford: Basil Blackwell, 1920. 109 pp.

Uncut.

1292. Mathers, S. L[iddell] MacGregor, trans. THE KABBALAH UNVEILED (Kabbala Denudata). Containing the following books of the Zohar. 1. The Book of concealed mystery. 2. The Greater holy assembly. 3. The Lesser holy assembly. Translated from the Latin version of Knorr von Rosenroth, and collated with the original Chaldee and Hebrew text. London: George Redway, 1887. viii, 359 pp. Sig.: Georgie Hyde Lees./ February, 1914

Inside frt. cover: The Silent Witness/ Austin Freeman [GY's].
In margins, pp. 25, 26, 36, 49, 60, 61, 87, 91: Pico [this and the other light annotations likely GY's].
Inserted, a letter from Arland Ussher to GY, Dublin, 15 Dec. 1954 referring to Tarot pack and A VISION.

*1292a. Another copy. Bp: WBY

Some pp. uncut.

1293. ———, ed. THE KEY OF SOLOMON THE KING (Clavicula Salomonis). Now first translated and edited from Ancient MSS. in the British Museum. London: Kegan Paul, Trench, Trübner, 1909. ix,126 pp., plate.

Inserted, a slip with Hebrew characters and English equivalents, in pencil, not apparently WBY's.

1294. Maupassant, Guy de. BEL-AMI. Illustrations de Berdinand Bac. Gravures sur bois de G. Lemoine. Les Oeuvres Complètes Illustrées. Paris: Société d'editions littéraires et artistique, 1903. iv,444 pp.

1295. Maurois, Andre. VOLTAIRE. Translated by Hamish Miles. London: Thomas Nelson, 1938. 158 pp.

*1296. Mayne, Rutherford. THE TROTH. A play in one act. Dublin: Maunsel, 1909. 14,[1] pp.

*1297. Mazzini, Joseph. ESSAYS. Selected from the writings, literary, political, and religious. Edited by William Clarke. The Camelot Series. London: Walter Scott, 1887. xxviii,[4],332 pp. Sig.: W B Yeats./ Dublin/ December/ 1887

1298. Mead, G[eorge] R[obert] S[tow]. "The Spirit-Body: An Excursion into Alexandrian Psycho-physiology." Offprint from THE QUEST (London). [1 (Apr.1910)]: 472-88.

Marginal strokes, pp. 480-6.
P. 483, at par. 1: Blake's spirit hid in a cloud.

1299. ———. "The Augoeides or Radiant Body." Offprint from THE QUEST. [1 (July 1910)]: 705-24.

1300. [Medici Prints]. CATALOGUE OF THE MEDICI PRINTS AND OTHER COLOUR REPRODUCTIONS. London: The Medici Society, [1935]. 133 pp.

Inserted, p. 38, pencil drawing, unidentified.
Some reproductions excised, pp. 103-6.

*1301. THE MEDIUM AND DAYBREAK (London). A weekly journal devoted to the history, phenomena, philosophy, and teachings of spiritualism. 2 (13 Jan. 1871 - 29 Dec. 1871).

Bound vol.; some marks passim all vols.; unlikely WBY's.

*1302. ———. 3 (5 Jan. 1872 - 27 Dec. 1872).

Bound vol.

*1303. ———. 4 (3 Jan. 1873 - 26 Dec. 1873).

Bound vol.

1304. Meinhold, William. SIDONIA THE SORCERESS. The supposed destroyer of the whole reigning ducal House of Pomerania. 2 vols. London: Simms and M'Intyre, 1849.

Vol. 2 only.

1304A. ———. Another ed. Translated by Lady Wilde. 2 vols. London: Reeves and Turner, 1894. Bps: Anne Butler Yeats/ 1934

1305. Mercier, [Dēsirē Fēlicien] Cardinal. A MANUAL OF MODERN SCHOLASTIC PHILOSOPHY. Translated by T.L. Parker and S.A. Parker. 2nd ed. 2 vols. London: Kegan Paul, Trench, Trubner, 1921.

VOL. 1, p. 312, corner turned back.
VOL. 1, p. 314, par. marked off, "Plato and Descartes" to "anima rationalis est tota in toto corpore et tota in qualibert parte corporis."

VOL. 2, 2nd imp., 1919; corners turned back, pp. 225, 352, 357, 359.

1306. Meredith, George. CHILLIANWALLAH. Jamaica, Queensborough, New York: Printed at the Marion Press, 1909. unpag. 35/112

Includes "Note on George Meredith's Earliest Published Poem 'Chillianwallah,' Now Reprinted for the First Time" by William E. Comfort.

*1307. ———. EVAN HARRINGTON. A novel. London: Constable, 1909. vii,472 pp. Sig.: W B Yeats/ June 25/ 1910

Inside frt. cover: Cuala Library/ 82 Merrion Square

*1308. THE MERRY DEVIL OF EDMONTON. A comedy. Edited by Hugh Walker. Temple Dramatists. London: J.M. Dent, 1897. ix,79 pp.

Flyleaf, stamped: Dublin Drama League Library
Half-title p., stamp, as above and also stamped: Presented to the Library by [sig.] George Yeats.

1309. [Méryon, Charles]. OLD PARIS. Twenty etchings. With an essay on the etcher by Philip Gilbert Hamerton. Liverpool: Henry Young, 1914. 20 pp., 19 plates.

*1310. Meyer, Kuno, ed. THE VOYAGE OF BRAN SON OF FEBAL TO THE LAND OF THE LIVING. With an essay upon the Irish vision of the happy otherworld and the Celtic doctrine of rebirth by Alfred Nutt. With appendices the Transformations of Tuan Mac Cairill and the Dinnschenchas of Mag Slecht. 2 vols. London: David Nutt, 1895-7. Bps: Lady Gregory

VOL. 1, slight markings pp. 54, 57, 210, 214, 215, 216, 217, 227, 264.
VOL. 2, slight markings pp. 24, 169, 183, 188, 197, 199, 226.

1311. Meyerstein, E[dward] H[arry] W[illiam]. SELECTED POEMS. London: Macmillan, 1935. 44 pp.

Title p.: Was ever commerce 'twixt/ Nations, where Scorn was fixt,/ The Arbitress of each divine event?/ I know not; ask the Fates! I only know: To Yeats/ The anguish of a Saxon heart was sent./ Nov. 7, 1935.

*1312. Meynell, Everard. THE LIFE OF FRANCIS THOMPSON. London: Burns and Oates, 1913. xi,[1],360,[1] pp.

Half-title p.: W.B. Yeats/ in gratitude/ Everard Meynell/ June 1914.

1313. Michelangelo. THE SONNETS OF MICHAEL ANGELO BUONARROTI. Translated by John Addington Symonds. 3rd ed. London: John Murray, 1912. xx,102,[1] pp. Bp: Louise Alexander Billstein

Inside frt. cover, below bp: Florence, Sept. 22, 1921 [printed; hand unidentified].
Inserted, postcard, no message or address, of "Palazzo Ducalo - Il Cortile," Urbino.
Inserted, postcard, no addressee, from Omega Workshops, Artist Decorators, London [printed], 19 Dec. 1914: I discovered one more sound blue plate after you left yesterday, so the order is now complete [sig.] Alfred Pence [?].
Many pp. uncut, especially after p. 29.

1314. Milbanke, Ralph, Earl of Lovelace. ASTARTE. A fragment of truth concerning George Gordon Byron. London: Chiswick Press, 1905. xxxviii,337 pp., 8 facs. Bp: WBY

Flyleaf: To W. B. Yeats/ from S. C. Cockerell/ Jan. 17 1906.

1315. Millay, Edna St. Vincent. THE BUCK IN THE SNOW. And other poems. London: Harper, 1928. vi,69 pp.

In Contents, checked or underlined or both, "For Pao-Chin," "The Buck in the Snow," "To Those without Pity," Dirge without Music," "Winter Night."
P. 31, marginal stroke against last two lines of "The Anguish," "Happy are the toothless old and the toothless young,/ That cannot rend this meat."

1316. ———. FATAL INTERVIEW. Sonnets. London: Hamish Hamilton, [193?]. 64 pp.

1317. ———. POEMS. London: Martin Secker, 1931. 146 pp.

Checked in Contents, [Poem] I; [Poem] II; "Thursday," "To the Not Impossible Him," "She is Overheard Singing," "The Philosopher," "Elegy before Death," "Lament," "Memorial to D.C.," "Wild Swans."
Some of the above checked in text; also checked in text, "Chorus," p. 130.
In Contents, entered opposite "Unnamed Sonnets": (no. iii) [presumably to indicate sonnet III, p. 136, "Not with libations....].

1318. ———. WINE FROM THESE GRAPES. London: Hamish Hamilton, 1934. 78 pp.

Checked in Contents, "The Return," p. 13.

1319. Milton, John. EARLY POEMS. [edited by Charles Sturt?]. Decorations by Charles Ricketts. London: [Vale Press, 1896]. ciii,[2] pp. -/310

1320. ———. ON THE MORNING OF CHRIST'S NATIVITY. Illustrated by William Blake. Cambridge: Univ. Press, 1923. 32 pp.

1321. ———. PARADISE LOST. Illustrated by William Blake. Liverpool: Liverpool Booksellers, 1906. ix,[1],397 pp. Bp: WBY

1322. ———. PARADISE REGAINED. SAMPSON AGONISTES and other poems. Edited by W.H.D. Rouse. The Temple Classics. London: J.M. Dent, 1899. viii,372 pp.

P. 175, slight bracketing in "L'Allegro" of "Bosomed high in tufted trees/ Where perhaps some beauty lies,/ The cynosure of neighboring eyes."

1323. Mirsky, D[mitri] S[vyatopolk]. LENIN. Makers of the Modern Age. London: Holme Press, 1931. xii,225 pp.

Inside back cover, ink: Great men - see 210 [p. 210, stroked, "Great men are the embodiments of great social movements, and it is natural that the greater the movement the greater the 'great man' produced by it"].
Marginal strokes, same ink as note above, pp. 22-24, 66, 67, 69, 156, 169, 171, 172, 191, 193, 197, 209, 210.

1324. Mitchel, John. AN APOLOGY FOR THE BRITISH GOVERNMENT IN IRELAND. Dublin: O'Donoghue, 1905. vi,[2],90 pp.

1325. [Mitchell, Susan, ed.]. SECRET SPRINGS OF DUBLIN SONG. London: Fisher Unwin; Dublin: Talbot Press, 1918. xi,[1],51 pp. 43/500

1326. Mitsuru, Yamamiya, ed. and trans. BENISUZUME [an anthology of Modern poetry in English translated into Japanese]. [Kyoto: Naigai-shuppan, 1926]. 286 pp.

On back flyleaf, verso: To Mr. W.B. Yeats,/ with all good wishes/ Makoto Sangu./ Aug. 3, 1926.
Includes poems by Yeats.

1327. Moberly, C[harlotte] Anne E[lizabeth] and Eleanor F[rances] Jourdain. AN ADVENTURE. 4th ed. London: Faber and Faber, 1931. 104 pp., 4 maps.

Subject is apparitions from past.

1328. [Modern British Painters]. AN EXHIBITION OF PAINTINGS BY EIGHT MODERN BRITISH PAINTERS, July 2nd - July 26, 1930 (Catalog). Arthur Tooth, 155 New Bond Street, [London]. unpag.

Includes Augustus John, Innes, Sickert et al.

MOELLER VAN DEN BRUCK, Arthur. See 299.

*1329. Molière. THE DRAMATIC WORKS. Translated by Charles Heron Wall. 3 vols. London: George Bell, 1901.

Vol. 1 only; cut are THE JEALOUSY OF LE BARBOUILLÉ, THE AFFECTED LADIES, THE SCHOOL FOR WIVES CRITICISED.

1330. ———. THE KILTARTAN MOLIERE. Translated by Lady Gregory. Dublin: Maunsel, 1910. [6],231 pp.

Includes THE DOCTOR IN SPITE OF HIMSELF, THE MISER, and THE ROGUERIES OF SCAPIN.
Flyleaf: Abbey Theatre/ Dublin [unidentified hand]

1331. ———. OEUVRES COMPLÈTES DE MOLIÈRE. Avec des remarques nouvelles par Félix Lemaistre précédée de la vie de Molière par Voltaire. Nouvelle edition. 3 vols. Paris: Garnier Frères, [19??].

Cover of Vol. 3: George Yeats/ 42 Fitzwilliam Sq./ Dublin
Vols. 1 and 2, pp. uncut.

*1332. Molinos, Michael de. THE SPIRITUAL GUIDE, which disentangles the soul. Edited by Kathleen Lyttleton. 2nd ed. London: Methuen, 1911. xxii,203 pp. Sig.: W. B. Yeats/ Sept 1913

Some pp. uncut.

1332a. Another copy? Title p. and pp. through 48 lacking. [London]: Methuen, [1911?]. 202,[1 lacking?] pp. Sig.: Georgie Hyde Lees/ August, 1913

Flyleaf, verso: "The spirit of man is as the lamp of God wherewith he searcheth the inwardness of all secrets." Solomon [GY's]

Back flyleaf: "When the son came into the world to effect the salvation of mankind, he contrived a machine supporting 12 bowls, which being made to revolve by the motion of the spheres, attracts into itself the souls of the dying. There the great luminary takes and purifies with his rays, and then transfers them to the moon, and this is the way in which the disk of the moon is replenished." (Manes - Circa 70 AD) [GY]
"And will you harken to the Hebrew Rabbins? 'Your young men shall see visions, and your old men shall dream dreams.'" [GY]

1333. Molmenti, Pompeo. VENEZIA. Con 1 Tavola e 139 Illustrazioni. 3rd ed. Bergamo: Istituto Italiano d'Arti Grafiche, 1907. 133 pp.

1334. Monck, [Walter] Nugent. THE INTERLUDE OF HOLLY AND IVY made ... from fifteenth century sources. Norwich: Saint William Press, 1913. 11 pp. 20/150

1335. ———. NARCISSUS: A WATER FROLIC IN ONE ACT. Written and produced by Nugent Monck at Blickling Park. By the author, n.d. 32 pp.

1336. ——— and Martin Kinder. AUCASSIN AND NICOLETTE. Norwich: Saint William Press, 1913. 40 pp.

A play from the 12th century French song-story.

*1337. Monro, Harold. CHILDREN OF LOVE. London: Poetry Bookshop, 1919. 31 pp.

Checked in Contents, probably for OBMV, "Hearthstone," and "Milk for the Cat."

1338. ———. THE COLLECTED POEMS. Edited by Alida Monro. With a bio. sketch by F.S. Flint and a critical note by T.S. Eliot. London: Cobden-Sanderson, 1933. xx, 217 pp.

Flyleaf: Cat's Meat 131/ Hearthstone 158/ Milk for the Cat 162/ ?Midnight Lamentation [all excised for OBMV except "Milk for the Cat"]/ Mrs. Harold Monro/ 38 Great Russell Street/ London, W.C. 1.
Excised in text, "Bitter Sanctuary" and "From 'Natural History'" for OBMV.

1339. ———. REAL PROPERTY. London: Poetry Bookshop, 1922. 63 pp.

Flyleaf: W. B. Yeats/ from/ Harold Monro/ April 1922.

*1340. ———. STRANGE MEETINGS. London: Poetry Bookshop, 1917. 63 pp.

1341. ———. THE WINTER SOLSTICE. Drawings by David Jones. The Ariel Poems, no. 13. London: Faber and Gwyer, [1928?]. 3 pp.

1342. Montagu, Lady Mary Wortley. THE TRAVEL LETTERS. Edited by A.W. Lawrence. London: Jonathan Cape, 1930. 287 pp. Sig.: WBY

1343. Montaigne. ESSAYS OF MONTAIGNE. Edited by William Carew Hazlitt. Translated by Charles Cotton. New ed. London: Reeves and Turner, 1902. 4 vols.

Vol. 1, some pp. uncut.
Vol. 2, many pp. uncut.
Vol. 3, many pp. uncut; "Upon Some Verses of Virgil" wholly cut; pp. 295 and 351 turned back.
Vol. 4, almost wholly uncut.

1344. ———. LOVE AND MARRIAGE. Being Montaigne's Essay "Sur des Vers de Virgil." Translated by Constance Vera Norman. Woodcuts by Bruno Bramanti. Florence: Printed by the Tipografia Giuntina, [1930?]. 86 pp. 50/250

*1345. Montfaucon de Villars, Nicolas de. COMTE DE GABALIS. London: William Rider, [1913]. xxiv,[1],352 pp. Bp: WBY

Title p., stamped: Presentation Copy
In English, no translator given; subject is the Cabala.

1346. Moore, Francis. VOX STELLARUM. Or, a loyal Almanack for the year of human redemption 1835.... London: Printed for C. Baldwin by George Greenhill, [1834?]. 24 pp.

1347. ———. A further no. for 1921. London: Cassell, [1920?]. 128 pp.

1348. Moore, George. AVOWALS. London: William Heinemann, 1924. 297 pp.

Inside frt. cover: H.V. Reade/ Ipsden/ Oxon./ 28/11/24
Inserted, Reade's letter of presentation to GY, 5 Dec. 1924.
After p. 105, most pp. uncut.

*1349. ———. THE BENDING OF THE BOUGH. A comedy. London: T. Fisher Unwin, 1900. xx,145 pp.

P. 57, "was suddenly changed to wrong" revised [pencil, WBY] to: suddenly became wrong.

P. 132, the speech of dean partially deleted, pencil, from "Yes, I recognised" to "to free myself."

1350. ———. THE WORKS OF GEORGE MOORE. Vol. 11: THE BROOK KERITH. A Syrian story. London: William Heinemann, 1933.

Uncut after p. 213.
Inside back cover: 212 [probably to indicate where reading has stopped].

1351. ———. ELIZABETH COOPER. A Comedy. Dublin and London: Maunsel, 1913. 80 pp.

*1352. ———. EVELYN INNES. London: T. Fisher Unwin, 1898. [7],482 pp.

Half title p.: This is one of twelve copies/ revised by George Moore with a/ view to a third edition and privately/ printed./ W B Yeats
This is the "Trial Revised Edition" described by Edwin Gilcher in A BIBLIOGRAPHY OF GEORGE MOORE. DeKalb: NIU Press, 1970, pp. 53-4.
Dedicated to Symons and Yeats.
Pasted in on the following pp, slips with printed revisions, sometimes further revised in ink, 149-51, 184, 185-8, 239, 240, 242, 244, 263-4, 265 (inked rev.), 266-7, 293-300, 417-8.
Inked revs., pp. 194-5, 252.
Inside back cover, pasted in, an item cut from a newspaper, 1356.

1353. ———. HAIL AND FAREWELL! AVE. London: William Heinemann, 1911. [5],367 pp.

1354. ———. THE WORKS OF GEORGE MOORE. Vol. 9: HAIL AND FAREWELL! SALVE. London: William Heinemann, 1933.

1355. ———. THE WORKS OF GEORGE MOORE. Vol. 10: HAIL AND FAREWELL! VALE. London: William Heinemann, 1933.

1356. ———. "Morality in Literature." [WESTMINSTER GAZETTE, 24 June 1898].

Pasted in at back of 1352.

1357. ———, ed. PURE POETRY. An anthology. London: Nonesuch Press, 1924. ix,128 pp.

Flyleaf: For George Yeats,/ contritely/ Earńan O'Malley
Pp. 1-43 of intro. uncut.

*1358. Moore, T[homas] Sturge. ABSALOM. A chronicle play in three acts. London: Unicorn Press, 1903. [6],lxxxix pp.

*1359. ———. APHRODITE AGAINST ARTEMIS. A tragedy. London: Unicorn Press, 1901. [6],xxxvii pp.

1360. ———. ARMOUR FOR APHRODITE. London: Grant Richards and Humphrey Toulmin, 1929. xiv,208 pp.

*1361. ———. ART AND LIFE. London: Methuen, 1910. xi,314 pp.

*1362. ———. DANAE, AFORETIME, AND BLIND THAMYRIS. Poems. London: Grant Richards, 1920. 64 pp.

*1363. ———. HARK TO THESE THREE: TALK ABOUT STYLE. London: Elkin Mathews, 1915. 54 pp.

1364. ———. JUDAS. Poem. London: Grant Richards, 1923. 109 pp.

*1365. ———. THE LITTLE SCHOOL. London: Grant Richards, 1917. 61 pp.

Flyleaf: W.B. Yeats/ from his friend/ T. Sturge Moore.

*1366. ———. MARIAMNE. A play. London: Duckworth, 1911. lxxv pp.

*1367. ———. PAN'S PROPHECY. London: Duckworth, 1904. xxxi pp.

*1368. ———. POEMS. Collected in one volume. London: Duckworth, 1906. xxxiv, xxxiii, xxxi, xxx, xxxix, xxxv pp. Bp: WBY

1369. ———. THE POEMS. Collected ed. 4 vols. London: Macmillan, 1931.

VOL. 1, Bp: WBY

VOL. 2, Bp: WBY; some pp. uncut; slips inserted at pp. 186-7 (Two adaptations from Ronsard) and 196-7 ("Response to Rimbaud's Later Manner" and "Variation on Verlaine") presumably for OBMV, though not all appear there.

VOL. 3 missing.

VOL. 4, flyleaf: To W.B. Yeats/ from his old friend/ T. Sturge Moore/ Nov. 1933.
Slips inserted at pp. 52-3 ("The Event," "To Silence"); the first in OBMV; some pp. uncut.

*1370. ———. THE POWERS OF THE AIR. London: Grant Richards, 1920. 77 pp.

*1371. ———. THE SEA IS KIND. London: Grant Richards, 1914. 169 pp. Bp: WBY

1372. ———. SELECTED POEMS. London: Macmillan, 1934. x,207 pp.

Flyleaf: To Mr and Mrs W.B. Yeats/ from/ Tom and Marie Sturge Moore.

On Contents p., refs. to vol. nos. and p. nos. in Item 1369 for Moore's selection in OBMV: Response [to Rimbaud's Later Manner], [Vol.] II, [p.] 196; Variation [from Ronsard], [p.] 187; The Event, [Vol.] IV, [p.] 52. Checked in Contents and excised in text, "To Memory," "The Gazelles," "The Dying Swan" [all but the last appear in OBMV].

1373. ———. A SICILIAN IDYLL AND JUDITH. A Conflict. London: Duckworth, 1911, lxxii.

*1374. ———. THESEUS, MEDEA AND LYRICS. London: Duckworth, 1904. xxxvi pp.

*1375. ———. TRAGIC MOTHERS. Three verse plays: Medea, Niobe, Tyrfing. London: Grant Richards, 1920. 64 pp.

P. 6, a printed note giving WBY credit for suggesting the Noh form of these plays.

1376. ———. T. STURGE MOORE. Modern Woodcutters, no. 3. London: Little Art Rooms, 1921. unpag.; 14 plates.

1377. More, Dr. Henry. A COLLECTION OF SEVERAL PHILOSOPHICAL WRITINGS. An Antidote against Atheism. A Brief Discourse of the Nature, Causes, Kinds and Cure of Enthusiasm. Epistulae Quator ad Renatum Descartes. The Immortality of the Soul, Conjectura Cabalistica. Second ed. London: William Morden, 1662. xxvii,[7], 190,[12], 133,[1],234[12],184,[18] pp. Bp: WBY

In "Immortality of the Soul," corners turned back, pp. 34, 95, 107, 135, 150, 163, 178, 192, 193, 202. Marginal strokes, pp. 107, 115, 118-21, 190-3, 199, 200, 202, 203, 224.
P. 119, elemental symbols beside passages dealing with earth and air.
In "Conjectura Cabalistica," p. 101, a passage on "Golden thighed Pythagoras" underlined.
P. 162, an "x" beside passage "But by this shall every man know whether it be Complexion or Religion that reigns in him, if he love God with all his heart and all his soul, and his neighbour as himself...."

1378. ———. THE IMMORTALITY OF THE SOUL, so farre forth as it is demonstrable from the knowledge of nature and the light of reason. London: William Morden, 1659. [36],549,[31] pp. Bp: WBY

Flyleaf: E.D.
P. 16, corner turned back (beginning of Chapt. III).

1379. ———. PHILOSOPHICAL POEMS. Comprising Psychozoia and Minor Poems. Edited by Geoffrey Bullough. Manchester: Manchester Univ. Press, 1931. xc,250 pp. 78/450 Sig.: WBY

In Notes, some pp. uncut.

1380. ———. THE THEOLOGICAL WORKS. London: Joseph Downing. 1708. xiv,856 pp. Bp: WBY

Title p., next to "More, D.D.," the date 1597 entered. Marginal markings, pencil, passim, especially at passages explaining biblical symbols such as p. 128, trumpets, hail-stones, fire and p. 131, Temple. The no. "3" is entered frequently beside passages on pp. 143, 144, 281, 286-7, 319-21, etc., not likely WBY's.

1381. More, Sir Thomas. UTOPIA. Edited by Robert Steele. Translated by Ralph Robinson. London: Chatto and Windus, 1908. xvi,260 pp.

*1382. MORE ANCIENT CAROLS. The Shakespeare Head Press Booklets, no. 5. Stratford-on-Avon: Shakespeare Head Press, 1906. 30 pp.

1383. Morgan, A[rthur] E[ustace]. TENDENCIES OF MODERN ENGLISH DRAMA. London: Constable, 1924. [8],320 pp.

Some pp. uncut.
Chapt. XIII, "Synge," a card inserted.

*1384. Morley, Henry. THE LIFE OF HENRY CORNELIUS AGRIPPA VON NETTESHEIM. ... Commonly known as a magician. 2 vols. London: Chapman and Hall, 1856. Bps: WBY

VOL. 1, pp. 113-21 cut for discussion of Agrippa's first book of occult philosophy; otherwise almost wholly uncut.

VOL. 2, pp. 1-17, 56-65, 312 through index cut; otherwise almost wholly uncut.

1385. Morrell, Ottoline. A FAREWELL MESSAGE. [Memorial booklet]. Written in her journal on Feb. 1, 1936. No pub. info. 4 pp.

On cover, a note from Philip Morrell: To W.B.Y. in memory/ of a long and very precious friendship./ 15.12.38

*1386. Morris, H[erbert] N[ewall]. FLAXMAN, BLAKE, COLERIDGE and other men of genius influenced by Swedenborg. Together with Flaxman's allegory of the "Knight of the Blazing Cross." London: New-Church Press, 1915. viii, 166 pp.

Back flyleaf: at end of Sibly's Astrology is a letter from Arthur Bedford to the Bishop of Gloucester written in 1705 describing one who saw spirits./ P. 1121, 1124
Yeats's note would seem to be a ref. to 1912 though the page nos. do not correspond to that ed.

1387. Morris, William. ART AND THE BEAUTY OF THE EARTH. London: Chiswick Press, 1899. 31 pp.

1388. ———. ART AND ITS PRODUCERS AND THE ARTS AND CRAFTS OF TODAY. Two addresses delivered before the National Association for the Advancement of Art. London: Chiswick Press, 1901. 47 pp.

1389. ———. THE COLLECTED WORKS. 24 vols. London: Longmans, Green, 1910-15. 794/1500

Vol. 1, Bps. GY and WBY; above WBY's Bp.: Bought by George and William Yeats/ as a Christmas present for each other/ Thirty first of December nineteen nineteen
Both bps., vols. 5, 6, 7, 8, 14, 16, 22.
Some pp. uncut all vols.

1390. ———. THE DEFENCE OF GUENEVERE and other poems. Edited by Robert Steele. London: De La More Press, 1904. lvi,255 pp.

Some pp. uncut.

1391. ———. NEWS FROM NOWHERE. Large paper ed. London: Reeves and Turner, 1891. 238 pp. -/250

Flyleaf: W. B. Yeats from John Masefield./ 13th March, 1901.

1392. ———. SOME HINTS ON PATTERN DESIGNING. London: Chiswick Press, 1899. 45 pp.

Uncut.

1393. ———. USELESS WORK VERSUS USELESS TOIL. Socialist Platform, no. 2. London: Socialist League Office, 1886. 39 pp.

1394. ———. THE WELL AT THE WORLD'S END, a Tale. 2 vols. London: Longmans, Green, 1896.

Vol. 2, bp.: WBY.

SEE ALSO Items 166 and 2103.

1395. Morris, William and Eiríkr Magnússon, trans. THE SAGA LIBRARY. 6 vols. London: Bernard Quaritch, 1891-1905.

Pp. uncut throughout.

*1396. ———. VOLSUNGA SAGA: The Story of the Volsungs and Niblungs, with certain songs from the Elder Edda. Edited by H. Halliday Sparling. London: Walter Scott, 1888. xlv,276 pp. Sig.: W B Yeats/ September 6/ 1888/ London

Almost wholly uncut after p. 57.

1397. [Moses, William Stanton]. M.A., Oxon. SPIRIT-IDENTITY and HIGHER ASPECTS OF SPIRITUALISM. London: London Spiritualist Alliance, 1908. xii,107,[1],x,92 pp.

Marginal strokes pp. 78, 79, 82, 83.

1398. Muirhead, John H[enry]. COLERIDGE AS PHILOSOPHER. London: George Allen and Unwin, 1930. 287 pp.

Marginal strokes, underscoring, pp. 54n, 58, 67, 68.
P. 67, at "the substantiating power": exact description of imagination passage on fly leaf of my copy of my edition of Blake's "Poems" [See 209].
Back flyleaf: realism and the manifold 92 [on p. 92 first two lines are stroked; there follows a discussion of the "manifold"].

1399. ———, ed. CONTEMPORARY BRITISH PHILOSOPHY. Personal Statements. First Series. London: George Allen and Unwin, 1924. 432 pp.

Marginal strokes, notes, diagrams and a correction in J. Ellis McTaggart's "On Ontological Idealism," pp. 251-69.
P. 253, Yeats revises "either a quality of a relation, or having qualities" to: either a quality or a relation, or as having qualities.
P. 254, at first par.: exclusion a sufficient description
P. 254, at second par.: intrinsic determination
P. 255, bottom, a diagram illustrating the explanation of the last par.
P. 256, diagram illustrating last par.
P. 257, diagram illustrating first par.
P. 260, at first par.: self a simple quality

1400. ———. CONTEMPORARY BRITISH PHILOSOPHY. Personal Statements. Second Series. London: George Allen and Unwin, 1925. 365 pp.

Marks and comments in C.E.M. Joad's "A Realist Philosophy of Life," pp. 159-90 and in G.E. Moore's "A Defence of Common Sense," pp. 193-223.
P. 180, at "It was a meeting-place of objects": again no place for 'Ruskin's Cat' [a comment following is canceled, a ref. to a gyre and A VISION].
P. 182, at "A living creature":
P. 185, at "third stage" and "realization of something that is entirely new": B.V.
P. 188, bottom, referring to "For so long as we enjoy our vision of the end, the life force lets us alone": This *vision* of the *end* will destroy by its abstraction if there is no "resurrection of the body."
P. 193 (in Moore), at "I": (1) His certainties
P. 193, at "2": (2) resembles (1) in a certain reference and also certainties.
P. 194, at "my body": in what sense "my body"?
P. 194, at "in the familiar sense": in case of double image this may not be true
P. 194, at "surface of the earth": yes a flat and stationary earth unless his "I" excludes a great part of mankind and himself at many moments.

P. 200, at "the reality of material things, and the reality of Space": But in dreams and visions there is also "in a certain sense" a "reality of material things" and "a reality of space"
P. 201, at "least obviously": why not?
P. 203, at "knew to be true": "in the familiar sense"
P. 204, at "(1) are, in fact, true": (in a familiar sense)
P. 205, at "There have existed many human beings": Surely the correct statement is "if there have existed" etc., "none of this" etc.
P. 206, at "Yet all this seems to me to be no good reason for doubting....": Nietszche says "Am I a barrel [?] of memories that I should tell you my reasons."
P. 207, at "Common Sense view of the world <u>is</u>": seems
P. 207, at "if we know that they are features": His act of faith
P. 207, at "it follows that they <u>are</u>": seems
P. 207, at "But to speak with contempt": How does he select?
P. 208, at "logically dependent upon some mental fact ....": "familiar sense"
P. 208, at "That mantel piece is at present nearer...": not necessary if a double image comes in
P. 208, at "I mean of course, facts like them...": colour may change if we [two words illegible]
P. 214, end of par. 2: raises question of Ruskin's cat
P. 220, at "the sense-datum which he saw would sensibly appear to him to have qualities very different....," a comment largely undecipherable.

MUNTHE, Axel, See 178.

1401. Murasaki, Lady. BLUE TROUSERS, being the fourth part of the Tale of Genji. Translated by Arthur Waley. London: George Allen and Unwin, 1928. 333 pp.

1402. ———. THE SACRED TREE, being the second part of The Tale of Genji. Translated by Arthur Waley. London: George Allen and Unwin, 1926. 304 pp. Bp: GY

1403. ———. THE TALE OF GENJI. Translated by Arthur Waley. London: George Allen and Unwin, 1925. 300 pp. Bp: GY

1404. ———. A WREATH OF CLOUD, being the third part of The Tale of Genji. Translated by Arthur Waley. London: George Allen and Unwin, 1927. 312 pp. Bp: GY

*1405. Murdoch, Walter, ed. THE OXFORD BOOK OF AUSTRALASIAN VERSE. London: Oxford Univ. Press, 1918. viii,294 pp.

Flyleaf: To/ W.B. Yeats/ from/ Louis Esson [who is represented in the anthology.]

*1406. Murray, A[lexander] S[tuart]. A HISTORY OF GREEK SCULPTURE. From the earliest times down to the age of Pheidias. London: John Murray, 1880. xv,[1],295 pp.

1407. Murray, Margaret Alice. THE WITCH-CULT IN WESTERN EUROPE. A study in anthropology. Oxford: Clarendon Press, 1921. 303 pp. Bp: WBY

Flyleaf, pasted in, 1408.

1408. ———. Letter to the Editor of THE TIMES, 25 Jan. [1932, p. 13].

Subject is a refutation of a charge of Satanism directed against a picture of the Annunciation in the French Exhibition.
Inserted in 1407.

*1409. Murray, T[homas] C[ornelius]. SPRING and other plays. Dublin: Talbot Press, 1917. [4],43,[3],48,31 pp.

Flyleaf: To W.B. Yeats/ with the Author's/ compliments/ Jan 1918

*1410. Musset, Alfred de. COMEDIES. Translated by S.L. Gwynn. The Camelot Classics. London: Walter Scott, [1890]. xxii,199 pp.

Includes BARBERINE, FANTASIO, NO TRIFLING WITH LOVE.
Flyleaf, a signature unreadable; also: Bremna [WBY's?]

1410a. Another copy.

1411. Mussolini, Benito. THE POLITICAL AND SOCIAL DOCTRINE OF FASCISM. Translated by Jane Soames. London: Hogarth Press, 1933. 26 pp.

*1412. Mylne, Rev. R[obert] S[cott]. THE CATHEDRAL CHURCH OF BAYEUX and other historical relics in its neighbourhood. Bell's Handbook to Continental Churches. London: George Bell, 1904. xv,[1],80 pp., plates.

*1413. Naidu, Sarojini. THE BIRD OF TIME. Songs of Life, Death and the Spring. London: William Heinemann, 1912. xii,102,[1] pp.

Pasted on frt. flyleaf, an envelope containing a letter of presentation from the authoress to WBY, 26 October 1912.
Some pp. uncut.

*1414. ———. THE BROKEN WING. Songs of Love, Death and Destiny, 1915-1916. London: William Heinemann, 1917. xiv,107,[1] pp.

Flyleaf: W.B. Yeats from Sarojini Naidu/ Xmas 1919.

*1415. ———. THE GOLDEN THRESHOLD. Introduction by Arthur Symons. London: William Heinemann, 1905. 98 pp.

Almost wholly uncut.

1416. Nares, Robert. A GLOSSARY OF WORDS, PHRASES, NAMES AND ALLUSIONS IN THE WORKS OF ENGLISH AUTHORS, PARTICULARLY OF SHAKESPEARE AND HIS CONTEMPORARIES. New ed. with additions by J.O. Halliwell and Thomas Wright. London: George Routledge, 1905. ix,981 pp.

1417. Nandikesvara. THE MIRROR OF GESTURE, being the Abhinaya Darpana of Nandikesvara. Translated by Ananda Coomaraswamy and Gopala Kristnayya Duggirala. Cambridge: Harvard Univ. Press, 1917. vii,[1],52 pp., 15 plates. Sig.: WBY

Some pp. uncut.

1418. THE NATION (New York). 146 (12 March 1938).

Includes "The Old Stone Cross" and "To a Friend."

1418a-b. Two more copies.

1419. THE NATIONAL OBSERVER, 24 December 1892, pp. 12 (?), 33 only.

"The Twisting of the Rope" lightly revised; "There is a moment at gloaming" revised to: There is a moment at evening twilight
"that awakened the star" revised to: that awakened the stars

1420. ———, 27 May 1893, pp. 41-3 only.

"Out of the Rose" lightly revised and corrected; "look of mystery" revised to: leash of mystery
"Then his eyes closed, and fell apart" corrected to: Then his eyes closed, and his lips fell apart
Inserted, an untitled, unidentified illustration by J.B. Yeats of knights in armor, possibly for "Out of the Rose."

1421. [National Theatre Company program]. IRISH PLAYS, by the National Theatre Company, from the Abbey Theatre, Dublin. King's Theatre, Glasgow. 4 June [1906] for six nights.

Yeats's KATHLEEN NI HOULIHAN, A POT OF BROTH; Synge's IN THE SHADOW OF THE GLEN and RIDERS TO THE SEA; Lady Gregory's HYACINTH HALVEY, SPREADING THE NEWS; William Boyle's THE BUILDING FUND.

1421a-d. Four other copies.

1422. ———. IRISH PLAYS. Theatre Royal, Cardiff. Summer, 1906. Bp: Elizabeth Corbet Yeats

Same program as 1421.

1423. National Theatre Society. Rules of the National Theatre Society, Limited. Dublin: Cahill, [1903]. 19 pp.

Printed signatures of F.J. Fay, Augusta Gregory, W.B. Yeats, W.G. Fay, Vera Esposito, J.M. Synge, Sara Allgood, U. Wright.

1423a-b. Two more copies.

*1424. NERO AND OTHER PLAYS. Edited by Herbert P. Horne, Havelock Ellis, Arthur Symons, and A. Wilson Verity. The Mermaid Series. Unexpurgated large paper ed. London: Vizetelly, 1888. viii,488 pp.

Almost wholly uncut.
Includes also THE TWO ANGRY WOMEN OF ABINGTON, PARLIAMENT OF BEES, HUMOUR OUT OF BREATH, WOMAN IS A WEATHERCOCK, AMENDS FOR LADIES.

*1424A. Small paper ed. London: T. Fisher Unwin, [1904]. viii,488 pp.

1425. Nettleship, John T[rivett]. ROBERT BROWNING, ESSAYS AND THOUGHTS. London: Elkin Mathews, 1890. xii,454 pp. Sig.: J.T. Nettleship

1426. Nevinson, Henry W[ood]. THE PLEA OF PAN. London: John Murray, 1901. xix,[1],190 pp.

Flyleaf: To/ William B. Yeats/ from H.W.N. 1902.
Essays.

1427. Newman, John Henry, Cardinal. THE DREAM OF GERONTIUS. London: Burns Oates and Washbourne, [1911]. 53,[1] pp.

1428. Newson, Ranald. DUD PLANET. London: New Temple Press, 1934. 109,[1] pp.

Flyleaf: To W.B. Yeats/ from Ranald Newson
Verse dramas and poems.

1429. ———. NEW POEMS. London: New Temple Press, 1931. 23 pp.

Title p.: To Senator W.B. Yeats/ from Ranald Newson.

1430. ———. THIS ROUGH MAGIC. London: New Temple Press, 1934. 55 pp.

Inserted, letter from author, n.d., stating his great interest in meeting WBY.

1431. Newton, Sir Isaac. THE CHRONOLOGY OF ANCIENT KINGDOMS AMENDED. To which is Prefix'd, A Short Chronicle from the First Memory of Things in Europe, to the Conquest of Persia by Alexander the Great. London: Printed for J. Tonson, J. Osborn, and T. Longman, 1728. xvi,376 pp.

*1432. Nichols, Robert. ARDOURS AND ENDURANCES. Also a Faun's Holiday and Poems and Phantasies. London: Chatto and Windus, 1917. x,207 pp.

Flyleaf, list of p. nos. for poems in "Ardours and Endurances": 12 ["In the Grass: Halt by Roadside"], 13, 14 ["The Day's March"], 14 ["Nearer"], 18 ["Noon"], 42-3 ["The Last Morning"], 44 ["Fulfillment"], 60 ["Alone], 65 ["The Full Heart"], 67 ["Deliverance"]. Pp. for these poems excised; none appear in OBMV. Pp. uncut after section "Ardours and Endurances." Pasted in at back, a review of this vol. See 2147.

1433. ———. AURELIA and other poems. London: Chatto and Windus, 1920. vii,96,[1] pp.

Inside frt. cover: 1 D'Annunzio poem ["To D'Annunzio: Lines from the Sea"]/ 2 When the proud World p. 28/ 3 Though to your life p. 30/ 4 What [But] piteous things we are p. 41/ 5 Come, let us sigh p. 44/ 6 Aurelia p. 58/ 7 Before I woke p. 70/ 8 The Moon behind p. 73/ 9 Don Juan's Address to Sunset MS [poems numbered 2 to 8 above are excised; "Don Juan's Address to Sunset" is not in this vol.; WBY's notation suggests it was added from a mss.; the poems listed constitute Nichols's selection in the OBMV].

1434. ———. THE BUDDED BRANCH. Westminster: Beaumont Press, 1918. 41 pp. 170/200

Poems and a play.

*1435. ———. INVOCATIONS: War Poems and others. London: Elkin Mathews, 1915. 41 pp.

1436. ———. ROBERT NICHOLS. The Augustan Books of Poetry. London: Ernest Benn, [1932]. iv,30,[1] pp.

"To D'Annunzio: Lines from the Sea," pp. 27-30 excised for selection in OBMV.

*1437. Nietzsche, Friedrich. THE COMPLETE WORKS. Edited by Oscar Levy. Vol. 1: THE BIRTH OF TRAGEDY, or Hellenism and Pessimism. Translated by William A. Haussmann. Edinburgh and London: T.N. Foulis, 1909. 270/1000 [Vols. have been renumbered for collected ed.]

Some pp. uncut.

*1438. ———. Vol. 4: THOUGHTS OUT OF SEASON. David Strauss, the Confessor and the Writer. Richard Wagner in Bayreuth. Translated by Anthony M. Ludovici. Edinburgh and London: T.N. Foulis, 1909. 132/1000

Corners turned back, pp. 13, 26, 38, 45, 55, 145, 149.

*1439. ———. Vol. 5: THOUGHTS OUT OF SEASON. The Use and Abuse of History. Schopenhauer as Educator. Translated by Adrian Collins. Edinburgh and London: T.N. Foulis, 1909. 233/1000

Some pp. uncut.

*1440. ———. Vol. 14: THE WILL TO POWER. Translated by Anthony M. Ludovici. Edinburgh and London: T.N. Foulis, 1909. 569/1000

*1441. ———. Vol. 15: THE WILL TO POWER. [Part 2]. Translated by Anthony M. Ludovici. Edinburgh and London: T.N. Foulis, 1910. 142/1000

*1442. ———. NIETZSCHE IN OUTLINE AND APHORISM. Edited by A.R. Orage. Edinburgh and London: T.N. Foulis, 1907. viii,190 pp.

Brief notes, pp. 17, 33, not WBY's.
Corners turned back, pp. 41, 63.

*1443. ———. THE WORKS OF FRIEDRICH NIETZSCHE. Edited by Alexander Tille. Vol. 1: A GENEALOGY OF MORALS. POEMS. Translated by William A. Haussmann and John Gray. London: T. Fisher Unwin, 1899. Sig.: WBY

P. 185, corner turned back.

*1444. ———. Vol. 3: THE CASE OF WAGNER. NIETZSCHE CONTRA WAGNER. THE TWILIGHT OF THE IDOLS. Translated by Thomas Common. London: T. Fisher Unwin, 1899. Sig.: WBY

In Contents, marginal strokes against "Apopthegms and Darts" and "Roving Expeditions of an Inopportune Philosopher," both in "The Twilight of the Idols," and "The Antichrist."
At end of Contents: page 353 [on this p., passages stroked in margin from "the worm of sin for example ...."].
Marginal strokes, pp. 93, 113-5.

*1445. ———. Vol. 4: THE DAWN OF DAY. Translated by Johanna Volz. London: T. Fisher Unwin, 1903.

Half title p.: W B Yeats/ from A[ugusta] G[regory]
In Contents, a check next to section 541 of "The Dawn of Day" entitled "How we should turn to stone," p. 360. However, the check mark <u>may</u> refer to section 542, p. 360, "The philosopher and old age," a long passage relevant to A.G. and WBY's work.
P. 360, corner turned back.

1446. NIEUWE ROTTERDAMSCHE COURANT, 20 Aug. 1929

Pp. 1-2 only; on p. 2 "Yeats en Hildo Krop te Dublin." Inserted in 2240.

1447. NIPPON TOH (Japanese Sword]. Osaka: T. Nagahara for the Society for Distributing Gwassan's Sword, [1931]. 29,15 pp., plates

English text uncut.
The Japanese sword and its history.

1448. Noel, Roden. POEMS OF THE HON. RODEN NOEL. Edited by Robert Buchanan. London: Walter Scott, [1884?]. xxiv,368 pp.

With presentation from author to WBY; returned to library by Norman H. Mackenzie, 1972.
Uncut.

1449. NOGAKA-KOMEN SHŪ [Collection of Old Noh Masks]. Catalog. Published on occasion of the special exhibition at Onshi Kyōto Museum, Kyōto, 1933. Kyōto: Onshi Kyōto Hakubutsukan, 1933.

1450. Noguchi, Yone. HIROSHIGE. New York: Orientalia, 1921. [16],32,[12] pp., 19 plates.

Flyleaf: To W.B. Yeats/ from/ Yone Noguchi/ March 1921.

1451. ———. JAPANESE HOKKUS. Boston: Four Seas Company, 1920. 115 pp.

Flyleaf: To Yeats/ from Noguchi/ Nov 1920/ Nakano, near Tokyo, Japan

*1452. ———. THE PILGRIMAGE. New York: Mitchell Kennerley, 1912; London: Elkin Mathews, 1912. viii,142 pp.

Flyleaf: To Yeats/ from Yone Noguchi/ London Jun 1914 [followed by the first three lines of Noguchi's "Proem"].

Some pp. uncut.

1453. ———. SEEN AND UNSEEN or Monologues of a Homeless Snail. New ed. New York: Orientalia, 1920. unpag.

On a panel of the folded cover: To William Butler Yeats/ from Yone Noguchi [followed by an inscription in Japanese].

1454. ———. THE SPIRIT OF JAPANESE ART. London: John Murray, 1915. 114 pp.

Card inserted at p. 5: With compliments of/ Mr. Yone Noguchi/ Nakano, near Tokyo Japan

*1455. ———. THROUGH THE TORII. London: Elkin Mathews, 1914. [9],208 pp.

Flyleaf: To W.B. Yeats/ Yone Noguchi/ Christmas Night 1913.
Essays, mainly on Japanese topics but includes "A Japanese Note on Yeats," pp. 110-17.

1456. ———. THE UKIYOYE PRIMITIVES. Tokyo: By the author, 1933. xiii,[5],122 pp., 93 plates. 131/1000

Sig.: Yone Noguchi.
Half title p.: To Mr. W.B. Yeats/ from S. Oshima/ August 31, 1935.
Uncut.

1457. Norman, A.O. [Harry Felix?]. "George Russell," Offprint from YEAR BOOK OF AGRICULTURAL CO-OPERATION, [1936], pp. 11-27.

A eulogy; See Denson, PRINTED WRITINGS BY GEORGE W. RUSSELL, p. 196.

1458. [Norstedt, P.A. & Söner]. I ANLEDNING AV P.A. NORSTEDT & SÖNER 100-ARSJUBILEUM DEN 1 DECEMBER 1923. Stockholm: P.A. Norstedt, 1923. [4],105,[1] pp., 10 plates.

One hundred years of Swedish book design.

1459. Notzing, Baron von Schrenck. PHENOMENA OF MATERIALISATION. A contribution to the investigation of mediumistic teleplastics. Translated by E.E. Fournier d'Albe. London: Kegan Paul, Trench, Trubner, 1920. xii,340 pp., 225 illus. Bp: WBY

1460. Novalis [Friedrich von Hardenberg]. THE DISCIPLES AT SAÏS and other fragments. Translated by F.V.M.T. and U[na] C. B[irch]. London: Methuen, 1903. 176 pp.

Some pp. uncut.

*1461. Noyes, Alfred. THE LOOM OF YEARS. London: Grant Richards, 1902. 115 pp.

Poems.

*1462. Noyes, Ella. THE STORY OF FERRARA. Illustrated by Dora Noyes. London: J.M. Dent, 1904. xv,422 pp.

Inside frt. cover: Write up casts/ King - Vag [?] / Maeve - Chambru [?] [the rest of the short list undecipherable].
Flyleaf: Well of the Saints/ & Jackdaw/ Dervorgilla/ Shadow of Glen/ Golden Helmet [all cancelled]/ Golden Helmet/ Well of Saints/ Dervorgilla/ Shadow of Glen
This guidebook was apparently used by WBY on his tour of Italy (including Ferrara) with Lady Gregory and her son in April, 1907.
Pencil strokes in text, pp. 86, 93, 97, 103, 105, 106, 108, 111, 121, 124, 130, 132, 138, 141, 146, 156, 266, 267, 271, 272, 273, 274, 277-311; Chapter XIV, "Palaces, Churches and Streets" marked at beginning.
Key words and places inserted passim --
P. 132, lengthwise: Isabella, Gonzaga
P. 133: Mantua

P. 134: Urbino/ Milan
P. 151, at top: [one word undecipherable], Lucrezia Borgia, Ercole, Alfonso
P. 159: Piazza Nuova
P. 270: Banners [unlikely WBY's]
Some of the entries above may not be WBY's; if they are his, he uses here an uncharacteristically broad pencil.
Second flyleaf, end: May 30-31 V/w/ // June 3, 4, 5 Oxford/ & London 10 Tues. // Ariosto - hours/ Banners [one word in parenthesis undecipherable]/ Deomants/ University/ Saint Anne.
Back flyleaf, a list of characters for the revival (?) of THE KING'S THRESHOLD with possible (?) performers: [one word undecipherable] - W. Fay/ Old Servant - an Algood/ O'Rourke [??] - Cripple/ [Jack?] Keegan [?] - 2nd cripple/ Kearn[ey?] - 1st pupil/ ? Gorman [?] - Younger Pupil/ [Ernest?] Vaughan [?] - King/ [one word undecipherable] - Chamberlain/ [one word undecipherable] - Soldier/ Monk [canceled]. [there follows in heavier pencil]: They pace 31-39.
Inside back cover, play titles arranged in three columns: Well of Saints/ Rising of the Moon // King's Threshold/ Shadow of Glen/ Deirdre/ new comedy // Dervorgilla/ Golden [canceled] Helmet/ Spreading the News/ ? Deirdre
[below the lists of plays]: October & November

1463. NUOVO DIZIONARIO TASCABILE. Italiano-Inglese e Inglese-Italiano. Compilato da Prof. Jane Pulford. Milano: Bietti,[1939?]. xix,803,xxxv,582 pp.

1464. THE NUTBROWN MAID. The Shakespeare Head Press Booklets, no. 4. Stratford-on-Avon: Shakespeare Head Press, 1906. 32 pp.

1465. Nutt, Alfred. CELTIC AND MEDIAEVAL ROMANCE. Popular Studies in Mythology, Romance and Folklore, no. 1. London: David Nutt, 1899. 36 pp.

Mostly uncut.

1465a. Another copy, mostly uncut.

1466. ———. CUCHULAINN, THE IRISH ACHILLES. Popular Studies in Mythology, Romance and Folklore, no. 8. London: David Nutt, 1900. 52 pp.

P. 1, top: Brolly,/ 8 Burrell's Lane/ Glasgow/ St. Enoch, S Stuls Hotel [?] [possibly WBY's]

1466a. Another copy.

1467. ———. THE LEGENDS OF THE HOLY GRAIL. Popular Studies in Mythology, Romance and Folklore, no. 14. London: David Nutt, 1902. 80 pp.

*1468. O'Brien, R[ichard] Barry. THE LIFE OF CHARLES STEWART PARNELL, 1846-1891. 2 vols. London: Smith, Elder, 1898. Bp: Greene's Library Dublin, 1843 - 1912.

Vol. 2 only.
Marginal marks, pp. 120, 121, 135, 140; brief note p. 143, all unlikely WBY's.

THE OBSERVER (London), See 308.

1469. O'Byrne, Dermot. A DUBLIN BALLAD and other poems. Poetry Booklets, no. 2. Dublin: The Candle Press, 1918. -/425

Half-title p.: W.B. Yeats/ from Lennox Robinson/ June 23, '18.

1469a. Another copy.

1470. O'Casey, Sean. THE PLOUGH AND THE STARS. London: Macmillan, 1927. viii,136,[1] pp.

Flyleaf: To W.B. Yeats./ With Sean Ó Casey's/ great appreciation for the Poet/ & earnest admiration for the man./ Kensington. 1927.
Some pp. uncut.

1471. ———. THE SILVER TASSIE. London: Macmillan, 1928. viii,140 pp. Sig.: GY

1471a. Another copy. Sig.: J.W. Wilhem's [?]

1472. ———. TWO PLAYS. JUNO AND THE PAYCOCK. THE SHADOW OF A GUNMAN. London: Macmillan, 1925. v,[1],198,[1] pp.

Flyleaf: From Sean Ó Casey/ To W.B. Yeats - / a Remembrance of a merciless criticism/ of a bad play that provoked the/ Author to a passionate resolve to/ write a good one./ Sept. 1925.
Some pp. uncut in both plays.

1472a. Another copy. Sig.: GY/ 1925

1473. O'Connor, Frank. THE BIG FELLOW. A Life of Michael Collins. London: Thomas Nelson, 1937. xiv,298 pp.

1474. ———. GUESTS OF THE NATION. London: Macmillan, 1931. xi,[1],277,[1] pp.

1475. ———. THE SAINT AND MARY KATE. London: Macmillan, 1932. [8],301 pp.

Flyleaf: For W.B. Yeats,/ from/ 'Frank O'Connor.'

1476. ———. THREE OLD BROTHERS and other poems. London: Thomas Nelson, 1936. vii,[1],40 pp.

1476a-b. Two more copies, paper covers.

Some pp. uncut in both.

1477. O'Curry, Eugene. LECTURES ON THE MANUSCRIPT MATERIALS OF ANCIENT IRISH HISTORY. Delivered at the Catholic University of Ireland, during the sessions of 1855 and 1856. Dublin: William A. Hinch, 1872. xxviii,722 pp., 26 pl. Bp: WBY

Inserted on a slip of paper: The notes at the end of all O'Curry (4 vols.) are in Lady Gregory's writing. G.Y.
This vol. and the three in 1478 are in the possession of Senator Michael Yeats. He believes they were given to WBY by John O'Leary.

*1478. ———. ON THE MANNERS AND CUSTOMS OF THE ANCIENT IRISH. A series of lectures. Edited by W.K. Sullivan. 3 vols. London: Williams and Norgate, 1873. Bps: WBY

Back flyleaves, all 3 vols., notes and p. refs. by Lady Gregory. See insert and note for 1477.

1479. O'Donnell, F[rank?] Hugh. SOULS FOR GOLD! Pseudo-Celtic Drama in Dublin. London: By the author?, 1899. 14 pp.

Reprint of two letters to the editor of THE FREEMAN's JOURNAL protesting Yeats's THE COUNTESS CATHLEEN.
On paper cover: Lily Yeats/ April '99

1480. O'Donnell, Peadar. SALUD! An Irishman in Spain. London: Methuen, 1937. 256 pp. Sig.: George Yeats/ May 1937

1481. ———. WRACK. A play. London: Jonathan Cape, 1933. 95 pp. 53/1050

*1482. O'Donoghue, David J[ames]. THE LIFE OF WILLIAM CARLETON. Being his autobiography and letters and an account of his life and writings from the point at which the autobiography breaks off. 2 vols. London: Downey, 1896.

Vol. 1, p. 1, at a passage describing the hard life of a writer: The curse
Markings, pp. 4, 6, 7, 8, 9, 11, 26, 27, 34; mostly uncut after p. 113.
Vol. 2, some pp. uncut.

1483. ———. THE LIFE AND WRITINGS OF JAMES CLARENCE MANGAN. Edinburgh: Patrick Geddes, 1897. xxiv,[2],250 pp.

Flyleaf: W B Yeats/ from/ D J O Donoghue/ with regards/ March 14th '98
P. 66, query beside text of poem, "strew?" for "shew."

1484. ———. THE POETS OF IRELAND. A biographical dictionary with bibliographical particulars. 3 parts. London: By the author, 1892. Sig.: WBY

Part I only, A to F.

1485. O'Faoláin, Seán. "The Spurious Fenian Tale," offprint from FOLK-LORE, Transactions of the Folk-Lore Society, a Quarterly Review 41 (June 1930): 154-68.

P. 168, a ref. to WBY, "Mr. Yeats, perhaps, records the ultimate degradation of the hero and the heroic sagas when he records the tale wherein Fionn tumbles a rude fellow over a cock of hay while on his way, for some reason or other, to a police-court."

1486. Ó Faracháin, Roibeárd (Robert Farren). THRONGING FEET. London: Sheed and Ward, 1936. xiii,[1],95 pp.

Flyleaf: To/ W.B. Yeats/ with the respectful homage/ due a great artist/ Roibéard Ó Faracáin [sic].

Poems; some pp. uncut.

1487. O'Flaherty, Liam. THE INFORMER. London: Jonathan Cape, 1925. 272 pp. Sig.: GY

1488. ———. MR. GILHOOLEY. London: Jonathan Cape, 1926. 288 pp.

Flyleaf: To W. B. Yeats/ from/ Liam O'Flaherty/ Hazelbrook, Kimmage Road, 1927.

1489. ———. RED BARBARA and other stories. The Mountain Tavern, Prey, The Oar. New York: Crosby Gaige, 1928. [8],49,[1] pp -/600. Sig.: Liam O'Flaherty

*1490. O'Grady, Standish. THE COMING OF CUCULAIN. A romance of the heroic age of Ireland. London: Methuen, 1894. 160 pp.

*1491. ———. FINN AND HIS COMPANIONS. Illus. by J.B. Yeats. The Children's Library. London: T. Fisher Unwin, 1892. xvi,182 pp.

1492. ———. RED HUGH'S CAPTIVITY. A picture of Ireland, social and political, in the reign of Queen Elizabeth. London: Ward and Downey, 1889. viii,295 pp. Sig.: W B Yeats/ March 25th/ 1889

P. 233, two marginal strokes, one against ref. to Red Hugh's capture and escape, 1587 and 1590, the other against ref. to the failing strength of Red Hugh's mother in 1591.

1493. ———. THE STORY OF IRELAND. London: Methuen, 1894. viii,214 pp. Bp: Lily Yeats

Flyleaf: Lilly [sic] Yeats/ from W B Yeats/ Xmas, 93. P. 26, "Queen Meave" underlined in text; in pencil in margin: buried in a cavern on top of Knocknarae [sic] Sligo.

1494. O'Hegarty, P[atrick] S[arsfield]. SINN FEIN. An Illumination. Dublin and London: Maunsel, 1919. vi,[2], 56 pp.

1495. [Old Vic and Sadler's Wells]. ANNUAL REPORTS FOR SEASON 1935-36 OF THE OLD VIC AND SADLER'S WELLS with Balance Sheet and Accounts of Both Foundations. For the year ending 30th June, 1936. London: Williams and Strahan, [1936?]. 58 pp.

*1496. Oliphant, Laurence. SCIENTIFIC RELIGION or Higher Possibilities of Life and Practice through the Operation of Natural forces. Edinburgh and London: For the author by William Blackwood, 1888. xiii,[3],473 pp. Bp: Coventry Patmore

Flyleaf, verso: See C.P.'s important notes 327 [actually 326] and 339 [unlikely WBY's]
Numerous marginal marks uncharacteristic of WBY; some notes taking strong exception to Oliphant's understanding of Catholic doctrine, probably Patmore's.

1497. O'Malley, Ernie. ON ANOTHER MAN'S WOUND. Dublin: At the Sign of the Three Candles, 1936. 336 pp. Sig.: Ernie O Malley

1498. Omar Khayyam. FIFTY RUBAIYAT OF OMAR KHAYYAM paraphrased from literal translations by Richard Le Gallienne. Wausau, Wisc.: The Philosopher Press, 1901. unpag. 158/200. Sig.: Richard Le Gallienne [at limitation]

Title p.: To William Butler Yeats/ with Compliments of James Carleton Young/ Minneapolis, Minnesota/ August 22nd 1901.

*1499. ———. RUBÁIYÁT OF OMAR KHAYYÁM. Translated by Edward Fitzgerald. London: Macmillan, 1899. [4],112 pp.

1500. ———. LES RUBÁIYÁT D'OMAR KHAYYÁM. Traduits en vers français d'après la version anglaise d'Edward Fitzgerald. Extrait du CORRESPONDANT. Paris: Imprimerie Louis de Soye, 1932. 15 pp.

P. 3: To the great Celt/ William Butler Yeats/ his most humble and respectful admirer/ Yves-Gérard le Dantec.

1501. O'Neill, Eugene. DAYS WITHOUT END. New York: Random House, 1934. 157 pp. Bp: WBY. Sig.: WBY

1502. ———. THE GREAT GOD BROWN. THE FOUNTAIN. THE DREAMY KID. BEFORE BREAKFAST. London: Jonathan Cape, 1926. 6,112,118,33,16 pp.

Flyleaf: S J Waddeel/ Olney/ Foxrock/ Dublin

1503. ———. THE MOON OF THE CARIBBEES and six other plays of the sea. London: Jonathan Cape, 1923. 42 pp.

Inside frt. cover: George Yeats/ 1923/ (from James Stephens)

1504. ———. A PLAY, STRANGE INTERLUDE. New York: Boni and Liveright, 1928. 352 pp.

1505. O'Neill, Joseph. LAND UNDER ENGLAND. London: Victor Gollancz, 1935. 334 pp.

Foreword by A.E.; a novel.
On frt. cover: Proof [stamped]; Advance Uncorrected [crayon].
Inked corrections, revisions passim; not WBY's.

1506. O'Neill, Mary Devenport. PROMETHEUS and other poems. London: Jonathan Cape, 1929. 124 pp.

Flyleaf: To Dr W.B. Yeats/ from Mary Devenport O Neill/ Nov. 1929.

*1507. O'Neill, Moira. SONGS OF THE GLENS OF ANTRIM. Edinburgh and London: William Blackwood, 1900. x,61 pp.

Inserted, a printed slip, "With the Publishers' Compliments."

*1508. Orage, A[lfred] R[ichard]. THE DIONYSIAN SPIRIT OF THE AGE. London and Edinburgh: T.N. Foulis, 1906. 83 pp.

Stamped inside back cover: Shelley Bookshop Oxford

1509. O'Rahilly, Egan. THE POEMS. Edited by Rev. Patrick S. Dinneen. The Irish Texts Society, vol. 3. London: The Irish Texts Society, 1900. lxii,[2],304,[14] pp.

Many pp. uncut.

1510. ORION'S PROPHETIC GUIDE, WEATHER ALMANAC, AND EPHEMERIS FOR THE YEAR 1882. London: Simpkin, Marshall,[1881?].

1511. Another number, for 1887.

1512. O'Rourke, Horace T[ennyson] and the Dublin Civic Survey Committee. THE DUBLIN CIVIC SURVEY. Publications of the Civics Institute of Ireland, vol. 2. London: Hodder and Stoughton, 1925. xx,150 pp.

*1513. Osborne, Dorothy. LETTERS TO SIR WILLIAM TEMPLE, 1652-54. Edited by Edward Abbott Parry. London and Manchester: Sherratt and Hughes, 1903. [11],350 pp.

*1514. O'Sheel, Shaemas. THE BLOSSOMY BOUGH. New York: Franklin Press, 1911. 109 pp.

Uncut.

1515. Oshima, Shōtāro. SHISHŪ: HAKKON SOBI [The Twilight Rose: Poems]. Tokyo: Taibun Sha. B., [1928?].

Flyleaf: To W.B. Yeats. Esq.,/ with kind regards,/ S. Oshima./ Mizuhahi, Toyama-ken,/ June 5th, 1928.
Inserted, a calling card with the author's name and permanent address; also a slip with: The dedicatory epistle of this collection of my immature poems together with the translation of your five poems is addressed to you. The titles of the translation[s] of your poems are: - The Moods./ A Poet to his Belo[v]ed/ The Fisherman/ The Lake Isle of Innisfree/ He Wishes for the Cloths of Heaven.

1516. ———. "Some Notes on William Blake and Macpherson's 'Ossian.'" Reprint from THE STUDIES IN ENGLISH LITERATURE (Japan) 10 (October 1930). 15 pp.

On paper cover: To W.B. Yeats, Esq.,/ with the sincere regards of/ S. Oshima/ November 16, 1930.

1517. ———. UIRIAMU BATORA JEITSU KENKYU [W.B. Yeats: A Study]. Tokyo: Taibunsha, 1927. ix,v,402 pp.

Flyleaf: Nothing, nothing nothing!/ But a faint line of incense/ cloud out of my heart./ To W. B. Yeats Esq./ from his humble Srvt./ the Author, an/ ea[s]tern unknown/ poet/ June 18, 1927/ Tokyo. Japan./ special copy.

1518. ———. W.B. YEATS. Tokyo: Kenkyusha, 1934. [10],179, [2] pp.

Flyleaf: To William Butler Yeats, Esq.,/ from Shotaro Oshima./ July, 1936
Text in Japanese.

1519. Ossendowski, Ferdinand. BEASTS, MEN AND GODS. London: Edward Arnold, 1923. xii,325 pp.

P. 25, a slight correction, not WBY's.
Travels in Siberia and Mongolia.

1520. Osty, Eugene. SUPERNORMAL FACULTIES IN MAN. Translated by Stanley de Brath. London: Methuen, 1923. xii,245 pp.

Back flyleaf, verso: G.O. Sherrard/ 74 Pembroke Road/ Dublin [not WBY's]

*1521. O'Sullivan, Seumas. POEMS. Dublin: Maunsel, 1912. vii, [1],101 pp. Bp: WBY

Marked in Contents, some 35 poem titles, unlikely WBY's.

1522. O'Sullivan, Vincent. A DISSERTATION UPON SECOND FIDDLES. London: Grant Richards, 1902. [8],270 pp.

Half title p.: To W.B. Yeats,/ With the writer's compliments./ June: 1902.
A novel; mostly uncut.

1523. Otto, Rudolf. THE IDEA OF THE HOLY. Translated by John W. Harvey. 4th imp., rev., with additions. London: Oxford Univ. Press, 1926. xx,237 pp.

OTWAY, Thomas. See 608.

1524. Owlett, F[rederick] C[harles]. "The Eulogy of Marlow." Reprint from THE POETRY REVIEW (London) 26 (Jan.-Feb. 1935).

Essay.

OXFORD BOOK OF AUSTRALASIAN VERSE, See 1405.

OXFORD BOOK OF BALLADS, See 1652, 1652a.

OXFORD BOOK OF ENGLISH VERSE, See 1653, 1654.

OXFORD BOOK OF FRENCH VERSE, See 1158.

OXFORD BOOK OF MODERN VERSE, See 2454. 2454a-e.

OXFORD BOOK OF VICTORIAN VERSE, See 1655.

1525. Page, H.A. [Alexander Hay Japp]. THOREAU, HIS LIFE AND AIMS, A STUDY. London: Chatto and Windus, 1878. xi, 271 pp. Sig.: E. Blackburne/ 1878.

Inside frt. cover, a slight sketch, very faint.

1526. THE PAGEANT. Edited by C. Hazelwood Shannon and J.W. Gleeson White. London: Henry, 1896. [14],244,[1], vii. WADE 295.

Yeats contributed "Costello the Proud, Oona Macdermott, and the Bitter Tongue," pp. 2-13.
P. 3 (in "Costello"), "shall" revised to: will [twice]
P. 5, "Eoha" is circled and in margin: Costello De Angelo [unlikely WBY's]

1526a. Another copy.

Half title p.: Anne B. Yeats/ With love from/ Lily Yeats/ Oct. 1935.

1527. Palmer, Herbert Edward. THE COLLECTED POEMS. London: Ernest Benn, 1933. xiv,236,[1] pp.

1528. ———. TWO FISHERS and other poems. London: Elkin Mathews, 1918. 31 pp.

Flyleaf: To W.B. Yeats Eqre., March 10th 1919/ from Herbert E. Palmer.
Inserted, a letter of presentation dated 9 March 1919.

1529. ———. TWO FOEMEN and other poems. London: Elkin Mathews, 1920. 63 pp.

Half title p., verso: With kind regards/ to/ W.B. Yeats Esq./ from/ Herbert E. Palmer.
Half title p., Palmer has copied out lines from James Elroy Flecker's "Gates of Damascus," apparently to satirize it. See next item.

1530. ———. TWO MINSTRELS. THE WOLF KNIGHT: HIS BOOK. THE WOLF MINSTREL: CAEDOMON'S BOOK. London: Elkin Mathews, 1921. 31 pp.

Half title p., verso: With kind regards/ to W.B. Yeats Esqre./ from/ Herbert E. Palmer
Half title p., a holograph parody of Flecker's "Gates of Damascus."
On the paper cover and within the text various comic subtitles have been inserted which refer to a long letter, inserted, from Palmer to WBY, dated only "Whit Monday."

1531. ———. THE VAMPIRE AND OTHER POEMS AND RIMES OF A PILGRIM'S PROGRESS. London: J.M. Dent, 1936. ix,48 pp.

Flyleaf: For Senator W.B. Yeats/ with best wishes/ from/ Herbert Palmer: March 1936.

PALMER, Samuel. See 2202.

1532. PANCHATANTRA AND HITOPADESA STORIES. Translated by A.S. Panchapakesa Ayyar. Great Short Stories of India. Bombay: D.B. Taraporevala, 1931. viii,219 pp.

Flyleaf: With the best/ compliments of A S P Ayyar/ 20.12.32.
Sanskrit fables.

1533. Paracelsus. THE HERMETIC AND ALCHEMICAL WRITINGS OF AUREOLUS PHILIPPUS THEOPHRASTUS BOMBAST, of Hohenheim, called Paracelsus the Great. Translated and edited by Arthur Edward Waite. 2 vols. London: James Elliott, 1894. Bps.: WBY

VOL. 1, HERMETIC CHEMISTRY, p. 245, strokes and astrological symbols against a passage dealing with minerals and colors.
P. 247, a stroke against a passage dealing with Sulphur, Salt, and Mercury.

VOL. 2, HERMETIC MEDICINE AND HERMETIC PHILOSOPHY.

PARRY, Edward Abbott. See 48.

PARSONS, Thomas William. See 184.

1534. Partridge, John. MERLINUS LIBERATUS, being an Almanack for the year 1802. London: Company of Stationers, [1801?]. 48 pp.

1535. Patanjali, Bhagwān Shree. APHORISMS OF YOGA. Translated by Shree Purohit Swāmi. Introduction by WBY. London: Faber and Faber, 1938. Unpag. WADE 286

1535a-b. Two more copies.

1536. ———. THE YOGA-SYSTEM OF PATANJALI. Or the Ancient Hindu Doctrine of Concentration of Mind. Translated by James Haughton Woods. Harvard Oriental Series, vol. 17. Cambridge: Harvard Univ. Press, 1927. xli, [1],381 pp.

Inside back cover: P 75 TURIYA etc.
P. 72, at par. 35: supernatural senses on the tongue etc.
P. 75, a sketch added in margin to illustrate generally "the locus of the fourth turīya." Passage illustrated begins "In the middle of this [lotus] is the circle of the sun...."
P. 76, top margin, referring to pars. 1 and 38: the sense of personality from Tamas and from Rajas is Light.
Inserted, a sheet of paper with three sets of page and par. numbers: 19/6 [sources of valid ideas and misconceptions and predicate relations and sleep and memory] 80/42 ["Of these balanced states ..."] 96/50 ["The subliminal impression produced by this ... is hostile"].

1537. Pater, Walter. MARIUS THE EPICUREAN. 2 vols. London: Macmillan, 1902.

Inserted in Vol. 2 a small photograph of a medal or coin, apparently of "Harry Gibson."

1538. ———. PLATO AND PLATONISM. London: Macmillan, 1893. [8],259,[1].

Stamped on title p.: Presentation Copy
Through p. 68 many markings; thereafter none.
P. 6, at passage where Pater says one must follow Plato's thought "with strict indifference": It is part of his [the young scholar's] duty to love or hate what he reads, and form is all important to this. Pater's own solemn strain cannot be heard with indifference.
P. 16, at "lifeless background of an unprogressive world": No
P. 26: "Kanva"
P. 60-64, several refs. to Pater's "long" sentences.
P. 65, WBY revises a line Pater quotes from Vaughan's "The Retreat" from "In that state I came return" to "To that state, whence I came, return." There is no ref. to this alternative reading in L.C. Martin's ed. of Vaughan.

1539. ———. THE RENAISSANCE. Studies in Art and Poetry. London: Macmillan, 1935. xvi,222 pp.

Flyleaf: P. 116/ Anne Butler Yeats/ In memory of work/ done October 2, 1935! [GY's]
P. 116, the description of "La Gioconda," has been marked off in ink, and pencil strokes are added to indicate strophes; they do not entirely coincide with Yeats's arrangement of the passage at the beginning of the OBMV. Also added in ink over the passage: Mona Lisa [WBY's].

SEE ALSO 185.

*1540. Patmore, Coventry. POEMS. 2 vols. London: George Bell, 1906. Bps: WBY

Some pp. uncut.

*1541. ———. PRINCIPLE IN ART. Uniform ed. London: George Bell, 1907. viii,265 pp. Bp: WBY

Essays; some pp. uncut.

*1542. ———. RELIGIO POETAE. New ed. London: George Bell, 1898. viii,175 pp.

Essays.

*1543. [Patrick, Saint]. THE REMAINS OF ST. PATRICK, APOSTLE OF IRELAND. The Confession and Epistle to Coroticus. Translated by Sir Samuel Ferguson. Dublin: Sealy, Bryers and Walker, 1888. xxxi,[1],102 pp.

Flyleaf, a presentation to Miss Thompson from Marie Shea.

1544. Paul V, Pope. RITUALE ROMANUM PAULI V. 11th ed. Rome: Friderici Pustet, 1912. x,[2],271 pp.

1545. Pausanias. DESCRIPTION OF GREECE. Translated by W.H.S. Jones. 6 vols. Loeb Classical Library. London: William Heinemann, 1918.

Vol. 1 only.

1546. Pauw, Cornelius de. PHILOSOPHICAL DISSERTATIONS ON THE EGYPTIANS AND CHINESE. Translated by Capt. J. Thomson. 2 vols. London: T. Chapman, 1795.

Vol. 2 only.

1547. Peacock, T[homas] Love. NIGHTMARE ABBEY. Edited by Richard Garnett. London: J.M. Dent, 1891. 134 pp. Bp: Lady Gregory

Flyleaf: Lady Gregory/ Jan 3 93/ A.P.H.

SEE ALSO 899.

1548. Pearce, Alfred J[ohn]. THE TEXT-BOOK OF ASTROLOGY. Vol. 1: GENETHIALOGY. London: Cousins, [1879]. vi, 286,[2] pp. Bp: WBY

Entries in tables marked pp. 254, 255, 280, 281.
Index marked, p. 60, nativity of Prince Consort; p. 52, nativity of Princess Louisa.

*1549. Pearse, Padraic H[enry]. COLLECTED WORKS. Plays. Stories. Poems. Dublin and London: Maunsel, 1917. xix,[1],341,vi pp. Bp: WBY

Flyleaf, verso: I am Ireland/ as on written slip facing/ page 323/ The Wayfarer -- 341
P. 323, on a sheet of paper attached by paper clip, a revised version of Pearse's "I Am of Ireland" possibly considered for inclusion in OBMV:

I am Ireland
Older than the Hag of Beare.

Great my pride
I gave birth to brave Cuchulain.

Great my shame:
My own children sold their mother.

I am Ireland:
Lonelier than the Hag of Beare.
[ink; not WBY's]

1550. Pearse, Salem. THE COELESTIAL DIARY, OR AN EPHEMERIS FOR THE YEAR ... 1759. 41st impression. London: The Company of Stationers, [1758?].

Inside frt. cover: Wm. Lambeth b. Dec. 16 1765 2 a.m./ I.B. Johnston, printer. b. Oct 28 1777 [ink; not WBY's].
Flyleaf, two horoscopes have been cast, one for Wm. Lambeth's nativity; ink; not WBY's.
Flyleaf, verso, a list of numbers and dates in the 1700's, possibly WBY's.
Bound with this item are similar almanacs down to the year 1789; publishers vary.
Entered passim are birthdates and horoscopes, apparently in an 18th century hand.

1551. Pèguy, Charles. LE MYSTÈRE DE LA CHARITÉ DE JEANNE D'ARC. Sixième cahier, cahier pour le jour de Noël et pour le jour des rois de la onzième série. Paris: Cahiers de la quinzaine, [1910?]. 249,[1] pp.

1552. ———. OEUVRES COMPLÈTES, 1873-1914. 15 vols. Paris: Éditions de la Nouvelle Revue Française, [1916-34]. 422/1200

VOLS. 1, 4, 5, 8 only.
VOL. 1, LETTRE DU PROVINCIAL etc.; uncut after p. 145.
VOL. 4, NOTRE JEUNESSE etc.; mostly uncut.

VOL. 5, LE MYSTÈRE DE LA CHARITÉ DE JEANNE D'ARC etc.; mostly cut.
VOL. 8, CLIO, DIALOGUE DE L'HISTOIRE ET DE L'ÂME PAIENNE; uncut after p. 41.

*1553. Penny, A[nne] J[udith]. STUDIES IN JACOB BÖHME. London: John M. Watkins, 1912. xxviii,475 pp., plates. Bp:WBY

Mostly uncut, but "Communicating Spirits," pp. 104-142 cut.

1554. PEOPLE'S NATIONAL THEATRE MAGAZINE (London). 2 (Oct. 1935).

Reprints "Advice to Dramatists," a leaflet given to aspiring Abbey dramatists.

1555. Percival, Milton O[swin]. WILLIAM BLAKE'S CIRCLE OF DESTINY. New York: Columbia Univ. Press, 1938. viii, [4],334 pp.

Flyleaf: To William Butler Yeats/ with the compliments of the author.

*1556. Percy, Thomas, ed. RELIQUES OF ANCIENT ENGLISH POETRY. Re-edited by Henry B. Wheatley. 3 vols. London: Swan Sonnenschein, 1889. Bps: WBY

1557. PERSIAN ART. An illustrated souvenir of the exhibition of Persian Art at Burlington House, London, 1931. Second ed. [London]: Printed for the executive committee of the exhibition, [1931]. xix,[1] pp., 101 plates.

*1558. Petrarch. THE SONNETS, TRIUMPHS, AND OTHER POEMS OF PETRARCH. Translated by various hands. London: George Bell, 1904. cxl,416 pp.

1559. Petrie, W[illiam] M[athew]. THE REVOLUTIONS OF CIVILISATION. 3rd ed. London and New York: Harper, 1922. xii,135,[1] pp.

Slip of paper inserted, p. 126.

1559a. Another copy.

1560. Petronius. THE SATYRICON OF T. PETRONIUS ARBITER. Translated by Burnaby. The Abbey Classics. London: Simpkin, Marshall, Hamilton, Kent, [1923?]. xvi,226, [1] pp.

1561. ———. THE WORKS OF PETRONIUS ARBITER. Including his life and character by Monsieur St. Evremont; some other of the Roman poets, Catullus, Tibullus, and Propertius; translations from the Greek of Pindar, Anacreon, and Sappho. With a poem on Telemachus by the Duke of Devonshire and an essay on poetry by John Duke of Buckingham. Translated by various hands. 4th ed. London: Printed for Sam. Briscoe, 1713. x,360 pp.

*1562. Petrovitch, Woislav M[aximus]. HERO TALES AND LEGENDS OF THE SERBIANS. London: G. Harrap, 1914. xxiv, 394 pp. Bp: WBY

Some pp. uncut.

1563. Philalethes, Eugenius [Thomas Vaughan]. EUPHRATES OR THE WATERS OF THE EAST. 1655. With a commentary by S.S.D.D. [Florence Farr Emery]. Collectanea Hermetica. Edited by W. Wynn Westcott. Vol. 7. London: Theosophical Publishing Society, 1896. 91 pp.

P. 45, in "comments upon the Ninth Paragraph," underscored is "The sun and moon are allotted by Cornelius Agrippa to the eyes...."

1564. [Phillimore, Cecily]. PAUL: THE CHRISTIAN. London: Hodder and Stoughton, 1930. 336 pp.

Beginning on the flyleaf and continuing inside the frt. cover (since the book was turned upside down), a draft of the song beginning "Astrea's holy child" from THE RESURRECTION (COLLECTED PLAYS, pp. 368-9):

He could not see the Titans
That go [canceled]

He did not know the Titans
Had gathered round him
Day grew so dim;
The great [??] hands of those Titans
Tore him limb from limb.

Astrea's holy child
A rattle in a wood
Where a Titan [one word canceled, illegible] strode
His rattle drew the child
Into the solitude.

[continuing inside frt. cover:]

We wandering women
Wives for all that come
Tried to draw him home
Every wandering woman
Beat upon a drum.

[the above in pencil; extremely faint]

*1565. Philpotts, Eden. THE SECRET WOMAN. London: Duckworth, 1912. 90 pp.

1566. THE PHOENIX LIBRARIES. PROSPECTUS OF THE IRISH LIBRARY. [Dublin?]: Phoenix Publishing, n.d. 14 pp.

P. 3: Michael Hanlon/ 25 Parnell Sq. [not WBY's] Includes reproduction of a painting by JBY.

1567. Pico Della Mirandola, Giovanni. LE SETTE SPOSIZIONI. Intitolate Heptaplo, Sopra i sei Giorni del Genesi.

Tradotte in lingua Toscana da M. Antonio Buonagrazia. Pescia: Lorenzo Torrentino, 1555. 158 pp. Sig.: Georgie Hyde Lees./ 1914.

Marginal marks, pencil, pp. 13 – 15, 17, 20, 134. Brief pencil notes in English, p. 33, likely GY's.

1568. Piccoli, Raffaello. ITALIAN HUMANITIES. An inaugural lecture. Cambridge: Univ. Press, 1929. 38 pp.

1569. THE PICTURE OF DUBLIN; or, Stranger's Guide to the Irish Metropolis. With a brief description of the surrounding country and of its geology. New ed. Dublin: William Curry, 1843. [18],352 pp., plates, map.

1570. Pirandello, Luigi. ALL' USCITA, MISTERO PROFANO: Il dovere del medico, un atto; La Morsa; L'uomo dal fiore in bocca, dialogo. Firenze: F. Bemporad, 1926. 131 pp.

Pp. uncut.

1571. ———. L'AMICA DELLE MOGLI. Commedia in tre atti. Firenze: R. Bemporad, 1927. 158 pp.

Pp. uncut.

1572. ———. COME PRIMA MEGLIO DI PRIMA. Commedia in tre atti. Firenze: R. Bemporad, 1929. 182 pp.

Almost wholly uncut.

1573. ———. COME TU MI VUOI. Tre atti. Milano: Mondadori, 1930. 228 pp.

Stamped on title p.: Presented to the [Dublin Drama League] Library by [sig.:] George Yeats.

1574. ———. DIANA E LA TUDA. Tragedia in tre atti. 2nd ed. Firenze: R. Bemporad, 1926. 167 pp.

Pp. uncut.

1575. ———. IL GIUCO DELLE PARTI, in tre atti. Ma non è una cosa seria, commedia in tre atti. Milano: Fratelli Treves, 1919. 256 pp. Sig.: GY

1576. ———. L'IMBECILLE: Lumie di Sicilia; Cecè; La patente. Commedie in un atto. Firenze: R. Bemporad, 1926. 174 pp.

Almost wholly uncut.

1577. ———. NOVELLE PER UN ANNO. Vol. 6: In Silenzio. Firenze: R. Bemporad, 1923. vi,326 pp.

Mostly uncut.

1578. ———. TUTTO PER BENE. Commedia in tre atti. 2nd ed. Firenze: R. Bemporad, 1925. 140 pp.

Stamped on title p.: Dublin Drama League Library. Presented to the Library by [sig.:] George Yeats.

1579. ———. L'UOMO, LA BESTIA E LA VIRTÙ. Apologo in tre atti. Firenze: R. Bemporad, 1922. 151 pp.

1580. ———. Another printing, 1925.
This is an imperfect printing. The cover title is LA SIGNORA MORLI UNA E DUE. Commedia in tre atti. 2nd ed. Firenze: R. Bemporad, 1925. Pp. 17-170 comprise this play, but the title p. is for L'Uomo etc. as above and the first 16 pp. constitute the opening of this play.

1581. ———. VESTIRE GLI IGNUDI. Commedia in tre atti. 3rd ed. Firenze: R. Bemporad, 1927. 151 pp.

Uncut.
Inserted, 3 slips of paper pinned together, lists of possible essay topics?? First p.: 82 Pearce/ Swift - identified dates with Ireland??/ Typescript [two words illegible]/ 98 Celebration/ What has Ireland to do with Internationalism.

Second p.: Quinn letters/ Ballylee Castle July 23, 1918/ Lady G. Jan. 6, 1921/ Wm. S. March 22, 1923/ Per Amica.

Third p.: "The Irish" [??] (Countess Cathleen, George Moore letter)./ See article on Irish Fairies etc./ mss. cutting book. 1889 - 1891 [WBY's]

1582. ———. LA VITA CHE TI DIEDI. Tragedia in tre atti. Firenze: R. Bemporad, 1924. 110 pp.

Stamped on title p.: Presented to the Library by [sig.:] George Yeats.

*1583. Pitt, Ruth J. THE TRAGEDY OF THE NORSE GODS. London: T. Fisher Unwin, 1893. 256 pp.

Inside front cover: W.B. Yeats [and below this in pencil:] A.B. Yeats
Children's book.

1584. Pius X, Pope. ON SOCIAL REFORM. Catholic Social Guild Pamphlets, no. 4. London: Catholic Truth Society, 1910. 32 pp.

*1585. Plarr, Victor. ERNEST DOWSON, 1888-1897. Reminiscences, Unpublished Letters and Marginalia. Bibliography compiled by H. Guy Harrison. London: Elkin Mathews, 1914. 147 pp. Bp: WBY

1586. Plato. THE DIALOGUES. Translated by B. Jowett. 5 vols. 2nd ed. Oxford: Clarendon Press, 1875.

VOL. 1, Bp: WBY; markings and notes in PHAEDO, likely Stephen Gwynn's.

VOL. 2, Sig.: Stephen Gwynn
VOL. 3, notes, markings, transcriptions, list of initials presumably Stephen Gwynn's.
VOL. 4, a label indicating the vol. was a prize to Gwynn for composing Greek verse at St. Columba's. Markings, notes presumably by Gwynn.

*1587. ———. THE REPUBLIC. Translated by John Llewelyn Davies and David James Vaughan. New ed. London: Macmillan, 1885. xxxii,370 pp.

Flyleaf, verso: W.B. Yeats/ from/ Lionel Johnson./ 1893 [WBY's].
Half title p.: L.O. Johnson/ [an illegible place or month and day]/ 1885.
Inserted, a sheet of Cuala letterhead, 46 Palmerston Road, Dublin: Plato's 'Republic'/ given to WBY (inscribed)/ by Lionel Johnson 1893/ (Trans: John Llewelyn Davies/ and David James Vaughan/ Macmillan. 1885 [likely GY's].

1587A. ———. Another ed. Translated by Benjamin Jowett. 3rd ed. Oxford: Clarendon Press, 1908. 412 pp.

Flyleaf: G. H-L./ from/ H.V.R[eade?]./ Dec. 1913.

*1588. Plautus. FIVE OF HIS PLAYS. Translated by Sir Robert Allison. London: Arthur L. Humphreys, 1914. xxiii, 317 pp. Bp: WBY

Includes The Pot of Gold, The Captives, The Twin Brothers, The Tempest, Amphitryon.

1589. Plotinus. PLOTINUS. Translated by Stephen Mackenna. Vol. 1: THE ETHICAL TREATISES being the treatises of the first Ennead with Porphyry's life of Plotinus, and the Preller-Ritter extracts forming a conspectus of the Plotinian system. London: P.L. Warner for the Medici Society, 1917. Bp: GY

1590. ———. Vol. 2: PSYCHIC AND PHYSICAL TREATISES, comprising the second and third Enneads. London: P.L. Warner, 1921.

1591. ———. Vol. 3: ON THE NATURE OF THE SOUL, being the fourth Ennead. London: Medici Society, 1924.

1592. ———. Vol. 4: THE DIVINE MIND, being the treatises of the Fifth Ennead. London: P.L. Warner for the Medici Society, 1926.

P. 2, first par. of section 2 marked off, "Let every soul recall [to] is of eternal being."

1593. ———. Vol. 5: ON THE ONE AND THE GOOD, being the treatises of the sixth Ennead. Translated by S.M. and B.S. Page. London: P.L. Warner for the Medici Society, 1930.

*1594. ———. PLOTINUS ON THE BEAUTIFUL. Being the sixth treatise of the First Ennead. Translated by Stephen MacKenna. Stratford-on-Avon: Shakespeare Head Press, 1908. 26 pp. 74/300

1595. ———. SELECT WORKS OF PLOTINUS. With extracts from the Treatise of Synesius On Providence. With the substance of Porphyry's life of Plotinus. Translated by Thomas Taylor. London: By the author, 1817. lxxxiii, 590+ [pp. missing at end]. Sig.: Georgie Hyde Lees/ 1914

1595A. ———. Another ed. Edited by G.R.S. Mead. London: George Bell, 1895. lxxiv,353 pp. Sig.: Georgie Hyde Lees/ July, 1913

*1596. Plunket, Emmeline M[ary]. ANCIENT CALENDARS AND CONSTELLATIONS. London: John Murray, 1903. xvi,263 pp.

Corners turned back, pp. 17, 26, 57, 94.
Plate III (facing p. 40), "Relating to the Orientation of a Temple to Amon-Ra" has been annotated and corrected by WBY, apparently to reconcile it to his own system of Phases; e.g. at the graph line labeled "initial point/ Grecian Zodiac fixed by Hipparchus at equinox 150 B.C.": No - number/ understand that place of equinox/ 150 A.D. not initial point.
Other time lines in the graph have been given what appear to be Phase numbers, as the first line in Aries: P[hase] 15.

1597. Plutarch. THE LIVES OF THE NOBLE GRECIANS AND ROMANES [sic], compared together by that grave learned philosopher and historiographer, Plutarke of Chaeronea. Translated into French by James Amyot and into English by Thomas North. Stratford-upon-Avon: Basil Blackwell for the Shakespeare Head Press, 1928. 8 vols. 134/ 500

Vols. 1-5, Bps: WBY
Many pp. uncut in all vols.
Cut are "Alcibiades" (2); "Cato Utican" (5); "Cicero" (6); "Scipio African" (7); "Epaminondas" (8). Mostly cut "Plutarch" (8); "Seneca" (8).

*1598. ———. MORALS. [Vol. 1:] ETHICAL ESSAYS, translated by Arthur Richard Shilleto. Bohn's Classical Library. London: George Bell, 1908.

"Conjugal Precepts" wholly cut; "On Love" mostly cut; otherwise mostly uncut.

*1599. ———. [Vol. 2:] THEOSOPHICAL ESSAYS, translated by C.W. King. Bohn's Classical Library. London: George Bell, 1908.

Wholly cut.
P. 64, "On Isis and Osiris," the word "weasel" underlined.

1599a. Another copy.

Cut in part, "On the Apparent Face in the Orb of the Moon," pp. 197ff.; otherwise mostly uncut.

*1600. Poe, Edgar Allan. THE RAVEN. THE PIT AND THE PENDULUM. Illustrated by William Thomas Horton. London: Leonard Smithers, 1899. xxix,[3],37 pp.

Flyleaf: W.T. Horton/ to his friend/ W.B. Yeats/ with best wishes./ Saty. 22.7.99 [there follows Horton's quotation from Blake beginning "Underneath the net I stray"].

*1601. Poël, William. "Shakespeare's Jew and Marlowe's Christians." Reprint from THE WESTMINSTER REVIEW, [Jan. 1909]. 12 pp.

On cover: To W.B. Yeats Esq. ... April 1909.

1602. POEMS AND BALLADS OF YOUNG IRELAND. Dublin: M.H. Gill, 1888. viii,80 pp. Bp: Lily Yeats. WADE 289

Half title p.: Lilly Yeats/ from/ Katharine Tynan/ Dec./ 89.
Yeats contributed "The Stolen Child," "King Goll," "The Meditation of the Old Fisherman," and "Love Song."

1603. POETRY: A MAGAZINE OF VERSE (Chicago). 3 (Jan. 1914).

Includes "A Word from Mr. Yeats."

1604. ———. 37 (Feb. 1931).

1605. ———. 45 (Dec. 1934).

Includes "Supernatural Songs," and "Three Songs to the Same Tune" and a "Commentary on the Three Songs."

1605a-c. Three more copies.

1606. ———. 45 (March 1935).

Includes A FULL MOON IN MARCH.

1606a. Another copy.

1607. ———. 49 (Oct. 1936).

Includes under "Correspondence" a note by Ezra Pound.

1608. ———. 49 (Nov. 1936). Reprint, pp. 85-93 only, "Harriet Monroe, 1860-1936" by M.D.Z. Inserted in 1609.

1609. ———. 49 (Dec. 1936).

Includes Pound's "Vale" in "In Memory of Harriet Monroe." Inserted, 1608.

1610. ———. 49 (Jan. 1937).

"English Number" edited by W.H. Auden and Michael Roberts.
Includes a brief review of the OBMV, pp. 234-5.

*1611. Porphyry. PORPHYRY THE PHILOSOPHER TO HIS WIFE MARCELLA. Translated by Alice Zimmern. London: George Redway, 1896. 78,[1] pp.

Half title p.: With the Publishers Comps.

1612. Potocki, Geoffrey, Count de Montalk. SNOBBERY WITH VIOLENCE. A Poet in Gaol. The Here and Now Pamphlets, no. 10. London: Wishart, 1932. 53 pp.

P. 37, an anti-German passage marked and a comment taking exception to it, not WBY's.

*1613. Pound, Ezra. CANZONI. London: Elkin Mathews, 1911. viii,51,[1] pp.

*1614. ———. CATHAY. Translations ... for the most part from the Chinese of Rihaku from the notes of the late Ernest Fenollosa.... London: Elkin Mathews, 1915. 31,[1] pp.

P. 11, in "The River-Merchant's Wife: a Letter" WBY has altered line 7 from "At fourteen I married My Lord you" to: At fourteen we were married to one another.
Also, line 14, "Why should I climb the look out?" canceled.
P. 12, beneath "By Rihaku" WBY has written: 8th Century.
P. 16, the title "Lament of the Frontier Guard" checked.

1615. ———. DIALOGUES OF FONTENELLE. London: The Egoist, 1917. v,54 pp.

Some pp. uncut.

1616. ———. A DRAFT OF XVI CANTOS. Paris: Three Mountains Press, 1925. 65 pp. 21/70. Bp: GY

1617. ———. A DRAFT OF THE CANTOS 17-27. London: John Rodker, 1928. 56 pp. 6/15. Bp: GY

1618. ———. A DRAFT OF XXX CANTOS. London: Faber and Faber, 1933. 153,[1] pp.

Pp. 79-84 excised for Canto XVII which appears in OBMV.

*1619. ———. EXULTATIONS. London: Elkin Mathews, 1909. viii,51 pp.

Flyleaf: al summo poeta,/ from/ E.P. 1909.

*1619a. ———. Another copy. Sig.: George Hyde-Lees/ Xmas 09

Inserted at p. 9, "Guido invites you thus," a sheet with GY's transcription of Dante's "Guido, vorrei che tu e Lap ed io."

P. 45 GY has transcribed (pencil as above) the original Spanish text of Lope de Vega's "Song for the Virgin Mother."

1620. ———. GAUDIER-BRZESKA, A MEMOIR. London: John Lane, 1916. x,168 pp. Sig.: GY

1621. ———. HOMAGE TO SEXTUS PROPERTIUS. London: Faber and Faber, 1934. 35 pp.

1622. ———. INDISCRETIONS: or, Une revue de deux mondes. Paris: Three Mountains Press, 1923. 62 pp. 199/300. Sig.: GY

*1623. ———. INSTIGATIONS, together with an essay on the Chinese written character by Ernest Fenollosa. New York: Boni and Liveright, 1920. viii,388 pp.

Flyleaf: To/ Mrs. W.B. Yeats/ with the kind/ regards of/ John Quinn/ 58 Central Park West/ New York/ May 5, 1920.

*1624. ———. LUSTRA. [London: Elkin Mathews for the author, 1916]. 124 pp. 59/200. Bp: WBY

P. 81, corner turned back for "The River Merchant's Wife."
Pp. 106-7 uncut.

1624a. Another copy. 91/200

*1625. ———. LUSTRA, with earlier poems. New York: Alfred A. Knopf, 1917. 202 pp.

Flyleaf: To W.B. Yeats/ with the good/ wishes & kind/ regards of/ John Quinn/ New York/ November 1917.
Inserted a sheet folded quarto with a printed statement by John Quinn dated October 24, 1917, "Note on the two English editions and the two American editions of Ezra Pound's <u>LUSTRA</u>." At "Forty copies of the American trade edition were specially bound for me in blue cloth...." Quinn has written: One of these copies to you. JQ.

*1626. ———. PAVANNES AND DIVISIONS. New York: Alfred A. Knopf, 1918. 262 pp. Sig.: GY

*1627. ———. PERSONAE. London: Elkin Mathews, 1909. viii, 59 pp.

1628. ———. PERSONAE. The Collected Poems. Including Ripostes, Lustra, Homage to Sextus Propertius, H.S. Mauberley. New York: Boni and Liveright, 1926. [16], 231 pp. Bp: WBY

Flyleaf: "Li Po 117" [most of p. 117 has been excised but the "Li Po" remains].
Inside back cover a list of poem titles and page numbers, apparently a preliminary selection for the OBMV which

has, however, only 3 selections from Pound. Pages for all the following have been excised: Ripostes/ 1. Lake Isle 117/ The Return p. 74/ 3. Ité p. 95/ 4. Mauberley III p. 189/ 5. V [of Mauberley] p. 191/ 5a. Envoy [sic] p. 197/ 6. Yeux Glauques p. 192/ 7. Propertius VI p. 219/ 8. [Propertius] VIII p. 220/ 9. [Propertius] XI p. 223 [should be 225]/ From Cathay/ 10. The River Merchant p. 130/ 11. The Beautiful Toilet p. 128/ 12. South-Folk in Cold Country p. 139/ 13. A Ballad of the Mulberry Road p. 140.

1629. ———. A QUINZAINE FOR THIS YULE. Being selected from a Venetian sketch-book --- "San Trovaso." London: Elkin Mathews, 1908. 26,[1] pp.

Dedication p.: To Wm Butler Yeats, hoping that at/ some time -- still distant -- I/ may write something that will in/ part repay him for the pleasure/ his magic has brought me [followed by Pound's stylized initials].
Uncut, pp. 10-15, 18-23, 26-27.

1629a. Another copy.

Flyleaf: W B Yeats/ May 09/ E.P.
Poems checked in text, p. 8, "Night Litany"; p. 17, "Sandalphon."

*1630. ———. RIPOSTES. Whereto are appended the complete poetical works of T.E. Hulme. London: Stephen Swift, 1912. 63,[1] pp.

Flyleaf: Ezra Pound/ corrected copy.
P. 18, in "Portrait d'une Femme," line 9, "wonderful old work" revised to: stuff [Pound's?].
P. 18, line 13 of same poem, "new brighter stuff" revised to: ware.
Pp. 45, 48, 56, 57, revisions in accidentals.
Pp. of advertising at end excised.

1630a. Another copy.

Flyleaf: Georgie/ from O[livia] S[hakespear]/ Christmas 1912.
P. 53, "The Return" checked in text.
P. 53, bottom: Turn over [GY's].
P. 55, under title "Effects of Music upon a Company of People": Walter Rummel playing at Eva Fowler's [not WBY's].
Next to part II of "Effects," "From a Thing by Schumann": Phantasie F min [not WBY's].

1631. ———. SOCIAL CREDIT: AN IMPACT. London: Stanley Nott, 1935. 31 pp.

*1632. ———. THE SPIRIT OF ROMANCE. London: J.M. Dent, [1910]. x,251 pp.

Flyleaf: 10 Church Walk/ Kensington/ W. / cr. [care?] H.L. Pound/ U.S. Mint/ Philadelphia/ U.S.A. [Ezra Pound's].
Some pp. uncut.

1633. ———. TA HIO, The Great Learning. Seattle: Univ. of Washington Book Store, 1928. 35 pp.

Flyleaf: To Wm./ 'Appy Noo Year/ 1929/ wif' 'opes of enlightenment./ EP.

*1634. ———, ed. CATHOLIC ANTHOLOGY, 1914-1915. London: Elkin Mathews, 1915. vii,99 pp.

Contains WBY's "The Scholars."

1634a. Another copy.

*1635. ———, ed. DES IMAGISTES, an anthology. London: Poetry Bookshop, 1914; New York: Albert and Charles Boni, 1914. 63 pp.

Flyleaf: G.H.L./ from O[livia] S[hakespear]/ May 1914.

1636. ———, ed. PROFILE, an anthology collected in MCMXXXI. Milan: Privately printed for John Scheiwiller, 1932. 142 pp. 239/250

Contains WBY's "The Scholars."

SEE ALSO 356, 356a.

*1637. ——— and Ernest Fenollosa. <u>'NOH' OR ACCOMPLISHMENT.</u> A study of the classical stage of Japan. London: Macmillan, 1916. viii,267,[1] pp.

Inserted, 1015, 2143, 2144.

1638. Prescott, William H[ickling]. HISTORY OF THE REIGN OF PHILIP THE SECOND, KING OF SPAIN. London: George Routledge, [1872?]. xv,[1],255 pp. Bp: Eliz. C. Yeats

Vol. 3 only.
Inside frt. cover, a label from Godolphin Foundation School, Hammersmith indicating this is a prize in history for WBY.

1639. Pourtalès, Guy de. LOUIS II DE BAVIÈRE OU HAMLET-ROI. Paris: Gallimard, 1928. 253 pp.

1640. Prévost d'Exiles, Antoine François. MANON LESCAUT. Translated by D.C. Moylan. London: George Routledge, [1886?]. xii,319 pp.

1641. Prior, James. MEMOIR OF THE LIFE AND CHARACTER OF THE RIGHT HON. EDMUND BURKE. With specimens of his poetry and letters. London: Baldwin, Cradock, and Joy, 1824. xxiv,584 pp.

1642. Privat-Deschanel, Augustin. ELEMENTARY TREATISE ON NATURAL PHILOSOPHY. Translated by J.D. Everett. 4th ed. London: Blackie, 1878. xxviii,1069 pp.

1643. PROCEEDINGS OF THE SOCIETY FOR PSYCHICAL RESEARCH (Glasgow). 28 (Dec. 1915).

Contains Part 71 only, "A Contribution to the Study of Mrs. Piper's Trance Phenomena" by Mrs. Henry Sidgwick. In this article, markings pp. 24, 132, 455, 511, 513. Corners turned back, pp. 26, 35, 410.
P. 25, at "She would say, namely, that the sitter, when she first saw him, had looked to her very small and a long way off....": Mary Battle on faeries.
P. 337, last 3 lines: away.

1644. Prokosch, Frederic. THE ASSASSINS. London: Chatto and Windus, 1936. vii,46 pp.

Some pp. uncut.

1645. ———. THE BLACK HART. New Haven, Conn.: By the author, 1931. Unpag. 2/2. Sig.: Frederic Prokosch

Flyleaf: To/ William Butler Yeats/ "while that great Archer/ Who but awaits his hour to shoot, still hangs/ A cloudy quiver over Parc-na-Lee." Typescript carbon.

1646. ———. THREE DEATHS. New Haven, Conn.: By the author, 1932. 7,[2] pp. 21/40. Sig.: Frederic Prokosch

Flyleaf: For/ W.B.Y.

1647. ———. THE WOLVES. New Haven, Conn.: By the author, 1933. Unpag. -/3

Flyleaf: W.B.Y. from F.P. May 1933
Typescript carbon.

1648. Propertius and others. EROTICA. The Elegies of Propertius, the Satyricon of Petronius Arbiter, and the Kisses of Johannes Secundus/ the Love Epistles of Aristaenetus. Edited by Walter K. Kelly. Translated by R. Brinsley Sheridan and Mr. Halhed. Bohn's Classical Library. London: Henry G. Bohn, 1854. xi,500 pp.

Some pp. uncut.

1649. PROPHETIA ET ALIA. Venice: Bernardinum Benalium, 1516 LXXVIII. Sig.: Georgie Hyde Lees/ June 1915.

Lacks title p.; by Silvestrus Mencius??; in Latin.

1650. Ptolemy. THE TETRABIBLOS: or, Quadripartite of Ptolemy, being four books relative to the starry influences. Translated from the copy of Leo Allatius by James Wilson. London: William Hughes, [1828]. xxv,[1],iii,[1],224 pp. Sig.: Ralph Shirley

Marginal markings, pp. xvi, 42, 49, 150, 180, 186.

1651. [Puvis de Chavannes]. PUVIS DE CHAVANNES. Introduction by Arsène Alexandre. Newnes' Art Library. London: George Newnes, [1905]. xix,64 pp.

Reproductions.
Flyleaf: With love and best wishes/ from/ M.S. Dennett/ Stella/ Juliette/ Molly.

1652. Quiller-Couch, Arthur Thomas, ed. THE OXFORD BOOK OF BALLADS. Oxford: Clarendon Press, 1927. xxiii,[1], 871 pp.

Flyleaf, verso: W B Yeats/ from his friend/ Dorothy Wellesley/ 1936.

1652a. Another copy, 1920 printing.

*1653. ———. THE OXFORD BOOK OF ENGLISH VERSE, 1250-1900. Oxford: Clarendon Press, 1902. xii,1084 pp. Sig.: W B Yeats/ Nov. 3, 1903

Inside frt. cover: With Esther (Blunt) page 998/ Nightingales (Bridges) 1012/ Dead at Clonmacnois (Rolleston) 1025 [these poems appear in the OBMV, two with slightly altered titles].

1654. ———. THE OXFORD BOOK OF ENGLISH VERSE, 1250-1918. New ed. Oxford: Clarendon Press, 1939. xxviii,1172 pp. Sig.: George Yeats

Includes poems by WBY.

*1655. ———. THE OXFORD BOOK OF VICTORIAN VERSE. Oxford: Clarendon Press, 1912. xv,1023 pp. Bp: WBY

Some pp. uncut.

1656. "QUINN" CATALOGUE OF FIRST EDITIONS, no. 89, part 2. New York: Schulte's Book Store, 1926. 36 pp.

Lists works by WBY, JBY, and Jack Yeats.

1657. ———. Part 3. 34 pp.

Lists works by WBY and Jack Yeats.

1658. [Quinn, John]. "How German Agents Get Their Funds," Letter to the editor of THE NEW YORK TIMES, 6 Sept. 1917, p. 10

Contained in an envelope dated 8 Sept. 1917 with 1658a, 1659.

1658a. Reprint of 1658 but dated 5 Sept. 1917. 2 pp.

Text slightly augmented; in envelope as above.

1659. ———. "Remarks of Mr. John Quinn at the Lafayette Monument, Union Square, New York, Sept. 6, 1917." [1] p.

In envelope as above.

1659a. Another copy.

1660. [Quinn, John, ed.]. SOME CRITICAL APPRECIATIONS OF WILLIAM BUTLER YEATS AS POET, ORATOR AND DRAMATIST. N.p., [1903]. 23 pp.

SEE ALSO 650.

*1661. Rabelais, Francis. FIVE BOOKS OF THE LIVES, HEROIC DEEDS AND SAYINGS OF GARGANTUA AND HIS SON PANTAGRUEL. Translated by Sir Thomas Urquhart of Cromarty and Peter Antony Motteux. 3 vols. London: A.H. Bullen, 1904.

Some pp. uncut in Vol. 3.

1662. Racine, Jean. ATHALIE, tragedie. Edited by Henri Maugis. Paris: Larousse, [1933]. 108 pp.

1663. Radhakrishnan, S[arvepalli]. INDIAN PHILOSOPHY. 2 vols. London: George Allen & Unwin, 1923-1927.

Vol. 1, p. 165, annotation picks up terms from text: Manas/ Vijñāna/ Ānanda

P. 452 is underlined at "The shifting nature of the world conceals the stable reality": Marked by my wife who had opened the book at random to find what horse would win at Punchestown. W.B.Y.

Pp. 612-619, markings and brief notes, mostly in "II. The Vaibhāsikas."

P. 612 at "The Mahayana schools are the Yogacaras, who are idealists, and the Madhyamikas": Called transcendentalism in McGovern.

P. 613, at heading of chapter "The Vaibhāsikas": neo-realism.

P. 613, at note, "First the Madhyamika": transcendental

P. 613, at note, "second, they Yoga": deity

P. 613, at note, "The Sarvāstivādins": realist

P. 616, at "The Vaibhasikas maintain that the atom has six sides": compare geometric composite [?] in Plato (Tim[aeus]).

P. 617, at "Material things which offer resistance to sense-organs are collections of the fourfold substrata or rūpa, colour, smell, taste and touch": neo-realism

P. 619, at chapter heading "The Sautrantikas": critical realism.

Back flyleaf, recto: The six systems to be looked up in this book./ 1. Vedanta system. Chiefly Upanishads. (revival A.D. 800)/ 2. Samkhya system. Kapila -?. (K. may have been Buddha. P. 472./ 3. Patanjali Yoga

System. ?300 B.C. // Minor/ 4. Vaisheshutra [?] System. (Kanada). (older than 1)/ 5. Nyaya (Gotama). (last in date - early [?] B.C. System is logic)./ 6. Purva Mimamsa (Jainin). Salvation by the orthodox rule.

1664. Raphael [Robert C. Smith]. THE FAMILIAR ASTROLOGER. An Easy guide to fate, destiny, and foreknowledge, as well as to the secret and wonderful properties of nature. London: John Bennett, 1831. viii,362 pp.

1665. ———. RAPHAEL'S ASTRONOMICAL EPHEMERIS OF THE PLANETS. Places for 1852. 2nd ed. London: By the author, 1896.

Heavy marginal markings and underscorings passim.

1666. ———. For 1859. London, 1911.

Uncut.

1667. ———. 1860. London, 1911.

Uncut.

1668. ———. 1865. London, 1911.

June 13, WBY's birthday underscored.
Aug. 20, 68 days after WBY's birthday underscored and notation: 68.
Inserted, a slip of paper: Lennox Robinson, 4th Oct. 1886 about 10.30 p.m. at Cork [possibly WBY's].

1668a-b. Two more copies.

1669. ———. 1866. London, 1896.

1670. ———. 1867. London, 1896.

1671. ———. 1869. London, 1896.

1672. ———. 1870. London, 1896.

1673. ———. 1875. London, 1896.

1674. ———. 1876. London, 1896.

1675. ———. 1881. London, 188-?

1676. ———. Another ed. London, 1900.

1677. ———. 1884. London, 1900.

1678. ———. 1885. London, 1911.

Heavy markings.

1679. ———. 1886. London, 1911.

Heavy markings; e.g. 21 Nov. 1886: marriage

1679a-b. Two more copies. Another ed. London, 1925.

1680. ———. 1890. London, 1912.

1681. ———. 1891. London, 189?.

1681a. Another copy.

1682. ———. 1892. London, 1909.

GY's birthday, 10 Nov. 1892, marked in all copies. In this copy: married Oct. 1917 [WBY's?] Heavily marked throughout.

1682a. Another copy.

1682b-c. Two more copies. Another ed. London, 1927.

1683. ———. 1893. London, 1906.

Inserted, a slip of paper: Tuesday April 25, 1893/ 1:30 p.m. [not WBY's]

1683a. Another copy.

1684. ———. 1894. London, 1912.

1685. ———. 1896. London, 18??.

1686. ———. 1897. London, 189?.

1687. ———. 1898. London, 18??.

1688. ———. 1899. London, 1899.

1689. ———. 1900. London, 1900.

1690. ———. 1901. London, 1901.

1691. ———. 1902. London, 1902.

1692. ———. 1904. London, 1904.

1693. ———. 1906. London, 1906.

1694. ———. 1907. London, 1907.

1694a. Another copy.

1695. ———. 1909. London, 1909.

1696. ———. 1910. London, 1910.

1697. ———. 1911. London, 1911.

1698. ———. 1912. London, 1912.

1698a. Another copy.

1699. ———. 1913. London, 1913.

1699a. Another copy.

1700. ———. 1914. London, 1914.

At Aug. 4, 1914: E. war on/ G.

1700a. Another copy.

1701. ———. 1915. London, 1915.

1701a. Another copy.

1702. ———. 1916. London, 1916.

1703. ———. 1917. London, 1917.

1704. ———. 1918. London, 1918.

Heavy markings; inserted a slip: Sept. 28th 1854. Waterford.

1705. ———. 1919. London, 1919.

Moderate markings; at Feb. 26, 1919: Feb. 26 Anne Yeats 10 a.m.

1705a-c. Three more copies; unmarked.

1706. ———. 1920. London, 1920.

Heavily marked.

1706a. Another copy.

1707. ———. 1921. London, 1921.

Moderate markings.

1707a-b. Two more copies, one unmarked.

1708. ———. 1922. London, 1922.

1709. ———. 1923. London, 1923.

1709a. Another copy.

1710. ———. 1924. London, 1924.

1711. ———. 1925. London, 1925.

1712. ———. 1929. London, 1929.

Moderate markings.

1713. ———. 1930. London, 1930.

1714. ———. 1931. London, 1931.

1714a. Another copy.

1715. ———. 1932. London, 1932.

1716. ———. 1933. London, 1933.

1716a. Another copy.

1717. ———. 1934. London, 1934.

1717a. Another copy.

1718. ———. 1935. London, 1935.

1719. ———. 1937. London, 1937.

1719a. Another copy.

1720. ———. 1938. London, 1938.

1720a. Another copy.

1721. ———. Bound vol. 1861-70. London, 1896.

Moderate markings passim, including WBY's birth date.

1722. ———. Bound vol. 1871-80. London, 1882.

The numbers for 1872-4 are ZADKIEL'S ALMANAC. London: J.G. Berger.
Light markings.

1723. ———. RAPHAEL'S HORARY ASTROLOGY, by which every question relating to the future may be answered. London: Foulsham, 1906. xi,103 pp. Bp: GY

1724. ———. RAPHAEL'S PROPHETIC ALMANAC, or the prophetic messenger and weather guide for 1904. London: W. Foulsham, [1903?]. Unpag.

1725. ———. Another number for 1916. 126 pp.

1726. RAVENNA. Roma: Istitutio geografico visceglia, n.d. Sig.: GY

Guide to Ravenna with map; in Italian.
In Index a check against S. Vitale e Mauseleo de Galla Placidia.

1727. Raymond, Jean Paul [Charles Ricketts]. BEYOND THE THRESHOLD. Translated and illustrated by Charles Ricketts. Plaistow: Curwen Press, 1929. [10],48 pp.

Prose dialogues.
Flyleaf: To W B Yeats/ from/ his old friend/ The Author/ C R.

1728. Read, Herbert. POEMS, 1914-1934. London: Faber & Faber, 1935. 168 pp.

Partially uncut, including "The End of the War" which appears in OBMV.

1729. ———. POETRY AND ANARCHISM. London: Faber & Faber, 1938. 126 pp.

Some pp. uncut after p. 73.

1730. Reade, Winwood. THE MARTYRDOM OF MAN. London: Watts, 1924. xlvii,455 pp.

Inside frt. cover: George Yeats/ from/ Herbert V. Reade/ (nephew of the author)/ Aug. 1924.

*1731. Redesdale, Lord [Algernon B.F. Mitford]. TALES OF OLD JAPAN. With woodcuts by Japanese artists. London: Macmillan, 1908. xii,383 pp.

*1732. Redford, George. A MANUAL OF ANCIENT SCULPTURE. Egyptian, Assyrian, Greek, Roman. With a chronological list of ancient sculptors and their works. 2nd ed., enlarged. London: Sampson Low, Marston, Searle, & Rivington, 1886. xiii,[3],286 pp. Bp.: WBY

Some pp. in index uncut.

*1733. Reid, Forrest. W.B. YEATS, A CRITICAL STUDY. London: Martin Secker, 1915. 257,[1] pp. Bp: WBY

Flyleaf: W.B. Yeats/ from/ Forrest Reid/ Sept. 1915. Flyleaf, verso, affixed a review of this book, 2150.

*1734. Reinach, S[alomon]. APOLLO. An illustrated manual of the history of art throughout the ages. Translated by Florence Simmonds. New ed. London: William Heinemann, 1907. xvi,351 pp.

*1735. Renan, Ernest. THE POETRY OF THE CELTIC RACES. Translated by William G. Hutchison. London: Walter Scott, [1896]. xxxviii,[2],226 pp.

Marginal markings, underlinings, notes in "The Poetry of the Celtic Races" only, pp. 1-60.
Marginal markings, underlinings, pp. 5, 10, 21, 22, 31, 34, 37, 54-7 (underlined on p. 57 "the framework of the Divine Comedy owing to the Purgatory of St. Patrick").
P. 6, end of 1st par.: the blood bond
P. 7, at 1st par.: lost causes
P. 7, at 2nd par.: ruler and destiny
P. 7, at 3rd par.: sadness
P. 8, par. 1: Delicacy
P. 8, par. 2: a feminine race
P. 8, end of last par.: The Ideal of Woman
P. 9, beginning of 1st par.: Imagination

P. 35, at note on Lancelot: note player's card marks Lancelot [??].

1736. Renier, G[ustaaf] J[ohannes]. OSCAR WILDE. Short Biographies, no. 19. London: Thomas Nelson, 1938. [8], 164 pp.

1737. RESTORATION PLAYS FROM DRYDEN TO FARQUHAR. Introduction by Edmund Gosse. London and Toronto: J.M. Dent, 1925. xix,431 pp.

Includes Dryden's ALL FOR LOVE, Wycherley's THE COUNTRY WIFE, Congreve's THE WAY OF THE WORLD, Otway's VENICE PRESERVED, Farquhar's THE BEAUX STRATAGEM, Vanbrugh's THE PROVOKED WIFE.

1738. REVUE ANGLO-AMERICAINE (Paris). 1 (Oct. 1929).

Includes Thomas McGreevy's "Mr. W.B. Yeats as a Dramatist," pp. 19-36.

*1739. Reynolds, John Hamilton. THE FANCY. With a prefatory memoir by John Masefield and thirteen illustrations by Jack Yeats. London: Elkin Mathews, [1905]. 88 pp.

Flyleaf: W.B. Yeats/ from John Masefield/ Dec. 4, 1905. Some pp. uncut.

*1740. Rhys, Ernest. WELSH BALLADS. London: David Nutt, [1898]. x,[2],177 pp. Sig.: WBY

Flyleaf: Song of the Graves 86/ The Lament for Urien 92 [both excised in text to make R.'s selection for OBMV].

Contents p. (first): 10 translations from Welsh/ 1 translation from Irish/ 13 translations inspired by Welsh legends and history/ 18 translations inspired by Welsh scenery/ 1 theological.

Checked in Contents, "The Ballad of the Buried Sword," "The Ballad of Howel the Tall," "King Arthur's Sleep," "The Waking of King Arthur," "The Death of Merlin," "The Fairy Mass," "Two Little Ballads of Ievan's Wife--I. The Mead Brewing," II. "Ievan's Funeral," "The Poet of the Leaves," "The Ballad of the Green Book," "The Wedding of Pale Bronwen," "The Ballad of the Last Prince," "The House of Hendre," "Envoi--I'r Cymry ar Wasgar."

Marginal strokes and a slight textual correction appear in the Notes, pp. 170, 171, 173 (possibly WBY's).

*1741. Rhys, John. LECTURES ON THE ORIGIN AND GROWTH OF RELIGION AS ILLUSTRATED BY CELTIC HEATHENDOM. 2nd ed. The Hibbert Lectures. London: Williams and Norgate, 1892. xii,708 pp. Bp: WBY

*1742. Richardson, Samuel. THE HISTORY OF SIR CHARLES GRANDISON BART. 7 vols. London: Chapman & Hall, 1902. Bps.: Lady Gregory

Vol. 3 missing.
Many pp. uncut vols. 4-7.

1743. Richet, Charles. THIRTY YEARS OF PSYCHICAL RESEARCH. A treatise on metaphysics. Translated by Stanley De Brath. London: W. Collins, 1923. xvi,646 pp.

Some pp. uncut.

*1744. Richter, Helene. WILLIAM BLAKE. Mit 13 Tafeln in Lichtdruck und einem Dreifarbendruck. Strassburg: Heitz & Mundel, 1906. viii,[2],404,[4] pp., 13 plates.

Half title p.: W.B. Yeats Esq./ with the author's thanks & compliments./ Helene Richter/ Vienna Oct. 29th 1906.

1745. [Ricketts, Charles]. A BIBLIOGRAPHY OF THE BOOKS ISSUED BY HACON AND RICKETTS. London: Ballantyne Press, 1904. xli pp.

Mostly uncut; published at the demise of the Vale Press to illustrate the three founts of the press by listing the books published in each.

1746. ———. CHARLES RICKETTS R.A. Introduction by T. Sturge Moore. London: Cassell, 1933. unpag., 65 illus.

*1747. ———. PAGES ON ART. London: Constable, 1913. viii, 265,[1] pp. Bp: WBY

*1748. ———. TITIAN. London: Methuen, 1910. xvi,[2],195 pp., 181 plates.

Marked in List of Plates, CXLI, "Jupiter and Antiope" in the Louvre.

1749. ———. UNRECORDED HISTORIES. With six designs by the author. London: Martin Secker, 1933. 138,[1] pp. -/950

Short stories; some pp. uncut.

SEE ALSO 1727.

1750. Riding, Laura. COLLECTED POEMS. London: Cassell, 1938. xxviii,477 pp.

Proof copy?

1751. ———. POEMS. A joking word. London: Jonathan Cape, 1930. 171 pp.

Many pp. uncut.
P. 81, corner turned back for "Many Gentlemen."

1752. Robertson, Eric S[utherland]. THE CHILDREN OF THE POETS. An anthology. London: Walter Scott, 1886. xxxvi,[2], 273 pp.

Flyleaf: WB Yeats/ from K.R. Tynan/ 1886/ Dublin

Checked in Contents, 4 poems by R.L. Stevenson, "Young Night Thought," "The Land of Counterpane," "Escaped at Bedtime," "My Bed is a Boat;" also "Baby" by George Macdonald.
Back flyleaf, verso, slight sketches of two heads, possibly Jack Yeats's.

1753. Robertson, John M[ackinnon]. PAGAN CHRISTS. Studies in Comparative Hierology. 2nd ed., revised and expanded. London: Watts, 1911. xxvi,456 pp. Sig.: WBY

Title p.: Louis C. Purser/ 8 Waterloo Road/ Dublin

1754. Robinson, Edwin Arlington. NICODEMUS, a book of poems. New York: Macmillan, 1932. ix,90 pp.

1755. ———. SONNETS, 1889-1927. New York: Crosby Gaige, 1928. [10],91 pp. 547/561. Sig.: E.A. Robinson

1756. Robinson, Forbes. COPTIC APROCRYPHAL GOSPELS. Translations with some texts. Texts and Studies, Contributions to Biblical and Patristic Literature, vol. 4, no. 2. Cambridge: Univ. Press, 1896. xxxiv,264 pp.

Mostly uncut.

1757. Robinson, Lennox. THE BIG HOUSE. Four scenes in its life. London: Macmillan, 1928. vi,[2],112,[1] pp.

1758. ———. BRYAN COOPER. London: Constable, 1931. [12], 187 pp.

1759. ———. CRABBED YOUTH AND AGE. A little comedy. London and New York: G.P. Putnam's, 1924. 39 pp.

Half title p.: W.B. Yeats,/ from Lennox. 1924.

1760. ———. THE DREAMERS. A play. London and Dublin: Maunsel, 1915. [10],68,[1] pp.

1761. ———. EIGHT SHORT STORIES. Dublin: Talbot Press, [1920]; London: T. Fisher Unwin, [1920]. [6],114 pp.

Flyleaf: George Yeats/ from Lennox/ March 1923
Slight correction, not WBY's.

1761a. Another copy.

1762. ———. EVER THE TWAIN. A comedy. London: Macmillan, 1930. vii,157 pp.

Title p.: George:/ from Lennox/ Affectionately./ Nov. 1930.

1763. ———. THE FAR-OFF HILLS. A comedy. London: Chatto and Windus, 1931. 85 pp.

Title p.: George: from Lennox/ affectionately.

1764. ———. GIVE A DOG--. A play. London: Macmillan, 1928. v,[1],101,[1] pp.

1765. ———. MORE PLAYS. London: Macmillan, 1935. [6],165, [1] pp.

Flyleaf: W.B. Yeats/ fr Lennox/ Sept 1936
Mostly uncut.

1766. ———. PATRIOTS. A play. Dublin and London: Maunsel, 1912. 49,[2] pp.

Above epigraph: To Miss Yeats/ from Lennox Robinson./ April 1912.

1767. ———. PLAYS. The Round Table. Crabbed Youth and Age. Portrait. The White Blackbird. The Big House. Give A Dog--. London: Macmillan, 1928. viii,455 pp.

Half title p.: W.B. Yeats/ from Lennox Robinson/ June 11, 1928.
Cut are CRABBED YOUTH AND AGE and GIVE A DOG--.
Slight correction, p. 374, not WBY's.

1768. ———. THE ROUND TABLE. A comic tragedy. London and New York: G.P. Putnam's, 1924. 111 pp.

1769. ———. THE WHITE BLACKBIRD. PORTRAIT. Plays. Dublin and Cork: Talbot Press, [1926]. 120 pp.

Title p. for THE WHITE BLACKBIRD: George Yeats/ from Lennox.

1770. ———, ed. A GOLDEN TREASURY OF IRISH VERSE. London: Macmillan, 1925. xi,[1],346 pp.

Half title p.: W.B. Yeats./ from Lennox Robinson/ Affectionately -- March 1925.
Inside back cover: W.B. Yeats/ Riversdale/ Willbrook/ Rathfarnham/ Dublin/ Ireland
Includes 13 poems by WBY.

1770a. Another copy. Sig.: GY/ 1925

1771. Robinson, Stanford F[rederick] H[udson]. CELTIC ILLUMINATIVE ART IN THE GOSPEL BOOKS OF DURROW, LINDISFARNE, AND KELLS. Dublin: Hodges, Figgis, 1908. [30],li pp., 51 plates.

Flyleaf: Elizabeth C. Yeats/ [3 words in Gaelic, undecipherable]/ 1909.

1772. Robson, Vivian E[rwood]. THE FIXED STARS AND CONSTELLATIONS IN ASTROLOGY. London: Cecil Palmer, 1923. 264 pp.

Flyleaf: Cyril Fagan/ 7th January 1924.
Pp. 70-87, astrological symbols and numbers, possibly WBY's.

1773. ———. A STUDENT'S TEXT-BOOK OF ASTROLOGY. London: Cecil Palmer, 1922. viii,243 pp.

*1774. Rochas, Albert de. LES ÉTATS PROFONDS DE L'HYPNOSE. 5th ed. Paris: Bibliothèque Chacornac, 1904. 128 pp. [bound with this:] LES ÉTATS SUPERFICIELS DE L'HYPNOSE. 5th ed. Paris: Chamuel, 1897. viii,155 pp.

P. 12 of the second title is emphatically marked, "Deux polarités isonomes quelconques mises en contact (ou même simplement rapprochées, si leur energie est suffisante) produisent d'emblée une contracture ou une répulsion; deux polarités hétéronomes, dans les mêmes conditions, produisent decontracture ou attraction."

*1775. ———. L'EXTÉRIORISATION DE LA MOTRICITÉ. Recueil d'expériences et d'observations. 4th ed. Paris: Bibliothèque Chacornac, 1906. xi,[1],601,[1],pp.

Marginal markings, underscoring pp. 238, 239, 241, 242, 245, 248, 263, 354, 355, 359, 417, 521, 529, 586, 589, 590, 591, 592.
P. 552, next to a passage which describes persons enveloped in flames or sparks: See the Lay of Havelock the Dane where the flames are a sign of royal blood.
P. 590, next to a passage dealing with body and spirit (including the phrase "la matière brute"): "vitality/ odic force."

*1776. ———. L'EXTÉRIORISATION DE LA SENSIBILITÉ. Étude expérimentale et historique. 6th ed. Paris: Bibliothèque Chacornac, 1909. viii,212 pp., 4 plates.

Marginal checks, strokes and page references passim.
P. 16, the word "compass" appears in the margin as a translation of a French word from the text.

*1777. ———. LA SCIENCE DES PHILOSOPHES ET L'ART DES THAUMATURGES DANS L'ANTIQUITÉ. 2nd ed. Paris: Dorbon-Ainé, [1912]. iv,250,[2] pp.

Many pp. uncut after p. 75.

*1778. Rodker, John. POEMS. Whitechapel: By the author, [1914]. 31 pp. 34/50

Title p.: O'Raymond Dreg [?]/ With kind regards/ John Rodker/ Oct./ '14.
Inserted, a poem "The Wild Geese" by Dora Sigerson Shorter, clipped from a newspaper, unidentified.

1779. Rolfe, Fr. (Frederick Baron Corvo). HADRIAN THE SEVENTH. The Phoenix Library. London: Chatto and Windus, 1929. [8],413 pp.

*1780. Rolland, Romain. THE PEOPLE'S THEATER. Translated by Barrett H. Clark. New York: Henry Holt, 1918. viii, 146 pp.

1781. ———. PROPHETS OF THE NEW INDIA. Translated by E.F. Malcolm-Smith. London: Cassell, 1930. xxi,548 pp. Bp: WBY

Some pp. uncut.

1782. THE ROMAN MISSAL, in Latin and English for every day in the year. Edited by an Irish bishop. With supplements for Ireland and other English speaking countries. Dublin: M.H. Gill, [1938]. xv,1676 pp.

*1783. Ronsard, P[ierre] de. POESIES CHOISIES. Avec notes et index concernant la langue et la versification de Ronsard. Paris: Bibliothèque Charpentier, [1873]. xxxvi,396 pp. Bp: WBY

1784. Roosval, Johnny et al., eds. STOCKHOLMS STADSHUS vid dess invigning midsommar afton, 1923. 3 vols. Stockholm: Aktiebolaget Gunnar Tisells Tekniska Förlag, 1923.
Vol. 1, HISTORIA OCH BYGGNADSKONST.
Vol. 2, TEKNISK BESKRIVNING.
Vol. 3, SMYCKANDE KONST.

Some pp. uncut.

1785. Rose, William and G[ertrude] Craig Houston, eds. RAINER MARIA RILKE, ASPECTS OF HIS MIND AND POETRY. London: Sidgwick and Jackson, 1938. v,183 pp.

Flyleaf: To W.B. Yeats,/ With regards and admiration/ from/ William Rose/ June 1938.

1786. [Rosen, Georg Von]. G. VON ROSEN [Swedish artist]. Sma Konstböcker, no. 9. Lund: Gleerupska Universitets-Bokhandeln, [1910?]. 64 pp.

1787. Rosenberg, Adolf. A. VON WERNER. Mit 134 Ubbildungen nach Gemalden und Zeichnungen. Bielefeld und Leipzig: Velhagen & Klasing, 1900. [4],140 pp.

Flyleaf: Anne B. Yeats/ from her/ Aunt Lily Yeats/ March 1934/ Your grandfather's book/ L.Y.

*1788. Rossetti, Christina. POEMS. Edited by William M. Rossetti. London: Macmillan, 1905. xxvi,332 pp.

*1789. Rossetti, Dante Gabriel. THE COLLECTED WORKS. Edited by William M. Rossetti. 2 vols. London: Ellis and Elvey, 1897. Bps.: WBY

Some pp. uncut.

1790. ———. THE HOUSE OF LIFE. Sonnets and songs. Illustrated by Phoebe Anna Traquair. Edinburgh: William J. Hay, 1904. xiii pp., facsimiles. Bp: WBY

1791. ———. LETTERS OF DANTE GABRIEL ROSSETTI TO WILLIAM ALLINGHAM, 1854-1870. Edited by George Birkbeck Hill. London: T. Fisher Unwin, 1897. xxviii,307 pp.

Inside frt. cover: F.R.D. Needham, Oxford, 1920.
Flyleaf: Dear Mr Yeats. I think you said you were going through D.G.R.'s letters & had not seen these. Please keep this as long as you want. F.R.D.N.

SEE ALSO 164.

1792. Rossi, M[ario] M[anlio]. VIAGGIO IN IRLANDA. Milano: Doxa Editrice, 1932. 189,[2] pp. Sig.: Mario M. Rossi

"W.B. Yeats," pp. 140-144 cut; otherwise uncut.

1793. ——— and Joseph M[aunsell] Hone. SWIFT, OR THE EGOTIST. London: Victor Gollancz, 1934. 418 pp.

1794. Rowley, Richard. CITY SONGS and others. Dublin and London: Maunsel, 1918. [8],85 pp.

1795. Ruddock, Margot. THE LEMON TREE. [Edited by W.B. Yeats]. With an intro. by W.B. Yeats. London: J.M. Dent, 1937. xiv,29 pp. WADE 284

1796. Russell, Archibald G[eorge] B[lomefield]. THE ENGRAVINGS OF WILLIAM BLAKE. London: Grant Richards, 1912. 229 pp., 32 illus.

Flyleaf: W.B. Yeats/ from/ Archie Russell/ 29 Nov. 1912.

1797. Russell, Bertrand. THE ABC OF RELATIVITY. London: Kegan Paul, Trench, Trubner, 1925. vi,231 pp.

Corner turned back, p. 54.

1798. ———. AN OUTLINE OF PHILOSOPHY. London: George Allen & Unwin, 1927. vi,317,[1] pp.

Lightly marked to 84 (with exception of heavy underlining, p. 66), very heavily thereafter. Many annotations summarize key ideas, but many also take strong exception to Russell.
P. 84, at "This principle as the reader will remember ...": 'learned intuition.'
P. 86, at "Dr. Watson's infant": and by the deduction foretold Napoleon.
P. 88, at "When a child is being taught to read a given letter ...": but in signals by ships' flags, the colour not the form may be essential; <u>not</u> a form but a concept therefore.
P. 89, at "when we have learned to take A as a sign of B": "recurrence" and "sequence" perhaps.
P. 116, at "some make up the course of one light-wave": "recurrence" and "sequence."
P. 117, at "If a body can travel freely": Time and Space interchangeable.

P. 143, top margin, referring to third par.: Elsewhere he insists that mathematical truth is empirically observed (Berkeley) - by observation we know if a line is curved or straight - yet he tries to turn the truth into a law of "thing in itself."

P. 144, referring to "Physical space is neutral and public ... as I see it": He should say "in my mind." It is nonsense to say in effect that all space is in a small portion of itself - a star is [in?] my "head" [the note has been partially erased].

P. 146, top margin and continuing on top of p. 147: Elsewhere we know matters of this transit [?] but mathematics and these are empirically deduced from "percepts." A part of percept?

P. 146, at "what the physiologist sees is in his own "Brain": Why in his own brain? His own brain also is "physical space." In his mind or in "perceptible space" he says.

P. 149, referring to "mad dance of electrons and protons": How then can it explain "percept"? This confusion is through the whole book. He is pining for the "primary qualities" of 17th century materialists.

P. 155, referring to lines 5-6: Yet he has declared that mathematical form is itself empirically observed [on?] p. 260. He explains "percept" by "percept."

P. 156, the number "1" has been placed next to lines 19-23 and "2" next to lines 23-5. In the bottom margin: In 1 he states a psychologist's experience almost truly and at 2 begs the question. If mind is "a cause," it cannot be a cross-section of its own effect. If there is a matter to be [its own?] effect, we can know nothing of it for it is not a "percept."

P. 161, referring to "The events constituting lightwaves are only known through their effects upon our eyes, nerves, and brains": why call them "light waves"? He juggles to escape Kant and the Noumenon.

P. 162, referring to lines 5-8: When he says "region" he uses the language of "the percepts" from which space is deduced and of which it is a part.

P. 164, referring to "there are events": The Noumenon perhaps, yet it may be we ourselves who publish [?] all. Where is the story when I close the book?

P. 166, at end of Part II: In the first part of this chapter he seems to assume that whatever is common to individual percepts [?] is outside mind. He should, like Berkeley, stop [?] and assume there is a mind common to all minds or within all minds. "Outward" may be inward.
Russell's position - if logical - would be that of the "Commonplace Book." To go further we must accept "concepts." Berkeley's affirmation of the mind of God was an act of faith because he had this notion [?].

P. 169, last 4 lines: Berkeley's [??] outward which is inward and vice-versa.

P. 171, at "We ought to mean only that there are two successive thoughts": we cannot think without the concept of unity. The unity of unities is the self - God in one aspect.
P. 180-288, no markings.
Back flyleaf, WBY summarizes his reading of Russell: My mind follows abstraction with difficulty, but I think this is a fair summary. Events are ultimate reality, and from this time and space, spirit and matter are all emergent. What are to an "observer" side by side in space are to another one after-existences in time. But if this be so, surely we must go further and say what is present to one is mental to another (time equals sensitivity of mind). Mental and physical are as interchangeable as time and space.
The idea of this book and all books of the school is that thought, they say events, are "neutral" [?] between mind and matter. They think in terms of matter. Event, radiation, stuff, name all material being. In substituting "neutral stuff" for the union of subject and object, they are therefore by implication materialists.

1799. Russell, George (AE). THE CANDLE OF VISION. London: Macmillan, 1918. ix,[1],175 pp.

Flyleaf: For W B Yeats/ from his friend AE
Inserted, holograph letter from T. Sturge Moore, to WBY, from 20 St. James Square, Holland Park, W. [1912?]: Dear Yeats, I am returning O'Sullivan's Poems. I do not think he is as much an individuality or so competent a writer as either Clifford Bax or James Elroy Flecker and neither of these seem to me able to compete with Abercrombie either for beauty, imagination, or force. I see that you are right and "Mary and the Bramble" is 1910 not 1911./ However I have re-read St. Thomas and very strongly hold that nothing in these other books I have read or in Elsa Lorraine can compare with it in any way. They may seem to have more beauty of movement because they echo the movement of better poets (O'Sullivan is always paying you the tribute of the sincerest flattery), but Abercrombie's movement is a blank verse one much more difficult to command. It is his own, not imitative and though it has obvious faults and crudities, the passage beginning "O, but I would face all these Indian fears" on page 23 down to the end on p. 29 is almost entirely successful and I defy you or any one else to show a passage of equal length in Masefield or any of the others that can compete with it when read out loud or studied in detail. By either of these tests all the others will be found choked with redundancies, serving their metre instead of making it serve them./ I would be very grateful if you would read out the above remarks at the meeting on Monday to which I cannot come. I amused myself by

correcting one of O'Sullivan's poems and reduced his 95 words to 60, and I think improved both metre and sense in doing so. This is really the only test; as Durer says we ought to be able to prove what we mean with our hands. Yours very sincerely, T. Sturge Moore. [added as a postscript:] I have read Elsa Lorraine Mackail's young lady and do not think she can compete with any of the gentlemen mentioned.

*1800. ———. COLLECTED POEMS. London: Macmillan, 1913. xv,[1],275 pp. Bp: WBY

Flyleaf: W.B. Yeats/ with kind regards/ "A.E." 25, Sept. 1913
Flyleaf, verso: "A Memory of Earth"
Checked in Contents (some also queried as noted), "Reconciliation," "Immortality," "Desire," "The Great Breath," "The Symbol Seduces"?, "The Earth Breath," "Three Counsellors," "Sacrifice," "Freedom," "Refuge"?, "The Memory of Earth"?, "Sung on a By-way," "Janus," "Truth," "The Mountaineer"?, "The Pain of Earth," "Om."
Checked in text, "Dawn" and "Sacrifice."

1801. ———. COLLECTED POEMS. London: Macmillan, 1926. xviii,373 pp.

Flyleaf: W B Yeats/ from his friend/ AE/ 8:7:26.

*1802. ———. THE DIVINE VISION and other poems. London: Macmillan, 1904. xiii,[1],94,[1] pp.

Flyleaf: W.B. Yeats/ from his friend/ the writer/ 17. Jany. 1904.

*1803. ———. THE EARTH BREATH and other poems. New York and London: John Lane, the Bodley Head, 1897. 94,[1] pp. Sig.: WBY

Marks, underscorings throughout.
P. 52, at poem "The Man to the Angel": ? almost rhetoric

1804. ———. THE INNER AND OUTER IRELAND. Reprinted from Pearson's Magazine, U.S.A. Dublin: Talbot Press, 1921. 16 pp. Sig.: George Russell

1804A. Another ed. London: T. Fisher Unwin, 1921. 27 pp.

Uncut.

1805. ———. THE INTERPRETERS. London: Macmillan, 1922. viii,180 pp.

Mostly uncut.

1806. ———. IRELAND, PAST AND FUTURE. A paper read to the Sociological Society on 21st February, 1922. No publishing information. 20 pp.

*1807. ———. THE MASK OF APOLLO and other stories. Dublin: Whaley, [1904]. [5],53 pp.

Flyleaf: W B Yeats/ from his friend/ the writer/ 20.12. 04.
Mostly uncut.

*1808. ———. THE NATIONAL BEING. Some thoughts on an Irish Polity. Dublin and London: Maunsel, 1916. [6],176 pp. Bp: WBY

Flyleaf: W B Yeats/ from his friend/ the writer/ AE.

1809. ———. Review of REVERIES OVER CHILDHOOD AND YOUTH (1916) by WBY, [NEW IRELAND, 16 Dec. 1916, pp. 88-9].

Corrected, not WBY's
Inserted in 2414.

1810. ———. SALUTATION: A POEM ON THE IRISH REBELLION OF 1916. London: Privately printed by Clement Shorter, 1917. 12 pp. 21/25

1811. ———. SELECTED POEMS. London: Macmillan, 1935. xiii, [1],197,[1] pp.

Flyleaf: Dear Mr. Yeats/ You should have had this from father. I send it, as he would have wished me to./ Diarmuid Russell.

1812. ———. SONG AND ITS FOUNTAINS. London: Macmillan, 1932. v,[1],133 pp.

Marginal markings, pp. 17, 29, 120.
Slight correction in text, p. 26, possibly WBY's.

1813. ———. THOUGHTS FOR A CONVENTION. Memorandum on the State of Ireland. Dublin and London: Maunsel, 1917. 29,[2] pp.

On paper cover: Lily Yeats/ from her friend/ AE.

1814. ———. TO THE FELLOWS OF THE THEOSOPHICAL SOCIETY. March 20th, 1894. Dublin: Irish Theosophist Press, [1894]. 8 pp.

1815. ———. VALE and other poems. London: Macmillan, 1931. viii,[2],56 pp.

Pp. 3-6, 29-32, 43-4, 47-8 excised, apparently to make a selection for the OBMV; "New York," which appears in the anthology, is excised.

1816. ———. VERSES FOR FRIENDS. Dublin: By the author, 1932. [12] pp. -/25

On paper cover: W.B. Yeats from AE/ 17/12/32.

*1817. ———, ed. NEW SONGS. A lyric selection from poems by Padraic Colum, Eva Gore-Booth, Thomas Keohler, Alice

Milligan, Susan Mitchell, Seumas O'Sullivan, George Roberts, and Ella Young. Dublin: O'Donoghue, 1904. 56 pp.

Flyleaf: W.B. Yeats/ from his friend/ the Editor/ 7.3.04. Includes as frontispiece "The Plougher" by Jack B. Yeats.

1817A. Another ed. 2nd ed., 1904.

RUYSBROECK, See 1208.

*1818. Ryan, W[illiam] P[atrick]. THE IRISH LITERARY REVIVAL. Its history, pioneers and possibilities. London: Ward & Downey, [1894]. vi,[2],184 pp. Sig.: W B Yeats/ Coole 1899

Discussion of WBY with portrait, pp. 132-6.

1819. THE SAGA OF THE FAROE ISLANDERS. Translated by Muriel A.C. Press. London: J.M. Dent, 1934. xiii,113 pp.

1820. Sainte-Beuve, Charles Augustin. THE ESSAYS OF SAINT-BEUVE. Edited by William Sharp. 3 vols. London: Gibbings, 1901.

Many pp. uncut.

1821. Salkeld, Blanaid. THE ENGINE IS LEFT RUNNING. With cover and four pictures by Cecil ffrench Salkeld. Dublin: Gayfield Press, 1937. [8],71 pp. 13/250. Sig.: Blanaid Salkeld and Cecil ffrench Salkeld

1822. SAMHAIN. Edited by W.B. Yeats. No. 1 (Oct. 1901). WADE 227

Frt. cover: Lily Yeats/ Dublin/ Oct. 21st/ 1901.

1823. ———. No. 2 (Oct. 1902). WADE 228

Frt. cover: Lily Yeats/ Oct 29th/ 1902 Dublin

1824. ———. No. 3 (Oct. 1903). WADE 229

Frt. cover: Upper Castle Yard - O'My Council Chamber [possibly Lily Yeats's].
P. 35, the par. beginning "The next pleasure is for the eye" to the end has been underlined and bracketed.

1825. ———. No. 4 (Dec. 1904). WADE 230. Sig.: Lily Yeats

1826. ———. No. 6 (Dec. 1906). WADE 237

Pp. uncut.

1826a-b. Two more copies.

1826c. Another copy. The format of the cover is slightly different, "... and Thoughts upon the Work of the Abbey Theatre by the Editor, with list of plays produced by the National Theatre Society and its forerunners. The Sixth Number. Published by Maunsel & Co., Ltd., Dublin; and sold for sixpence net."

1827. ———. Bound vol., complete.

Flyleaf: George Yeats (bought August 1946).
Inserted, a 13 pp. typescript of "First Principles" for Samhain, 1908. The few corrections and additions (ink, WBY's) are incorporated in the printed version.

1828. Sanctis, Francesco de. HISTORY OF ITALIAN LITERATURE. Translated by Joan Redfern. 2 vols. London: Oxford Univ. Press, [1932]. Bp: WBY
Vol. 1 only.

1829. Sandars, Mary F[rances]. HONORÉ DE BALZAC. His life and writings. London: John Murray, 1904. xv,[1],396 pp.

Flyleaf: Charles Ruark [?]/ 5 Hans Mansions S.W./ Read 5 - 9 in 1906 [?] [not WBY's].

1830. Santayana, George. WINDS OF DOCTRINE. Studies in contemporary opinion. London: J.M. Dent, 1913; New York: Charles Scribner's Sons, 1913. vi,215 pp.

Some pp. uncut.

1831. Santesson, C[arl] G[ustaf]. LES PRIX NOBEL EN 1938. Stockholm: P.A. Norstedt, [1938?]. 97 pp., unpag. additions.

1832. Sa'di. GULISTAN OR FLOWER-GARDEN. Translated with an essay by James Ross. With a note on the translator by Charles Sayle. The Camelot Series. London: Walter Scott, [1890]. viii,311 pp.

Introductory material to p. 29 is cut; also Chapt. V. "On Love and Youth."

1833. AN SAORSTAT (The Free State). War Special, no. 8. 19 Aug. 1922.

Tribute to Arthur Griffith

1834. ———. 30 Aug. 1922.

Michael Collins Memorial Number

*1835. Sappho. MEMOIR. Text, selected renderings, and a literal translation by Henry Thornton Wharton. 3rd ed. London: John Lane, 1895. xx,217 pp.

*1836. ———. THE POEMS. An interpretive rendition by John Myers O'Hara. Chicago: By the author, 1907. 97 pp. 91/150. Sig.: John Myers O'Hara

1837. Sardou, V[ictorien], L. Illica and G. Giacosa. TOSCA [libretto]. Translated by W. Beatty-Kingston. London: G. Ricordi, 1900. 39 pp.

Inserted, a program. See 724.

1838. Sarolea, Charles. IMPRESSIONS OF SOVIET RUSSIA. London: Eveleigh Nash & Grayson, 1924. vi,276 pp. Sig.: GY, Nov. 1924

Markings, a few very brief annotations by GY, passim.

1839. ———. LETTERS ON POLISH AFFAIRS. With an intro. by G.K. Chesterton. Edinburgh: Oliver and Boyd, 1922. 140 pp.

1840. Sackville-West, V[ictoria]. COLLECTED POEMS. 2 vols. London: Hogarth Press, 1933. x,225 pp.

Vol. 1 only.
In Contents, a check against "Beechwoods at Knole," p. 42 and in text.
Excised for OBMV, "On the Lake," pp. 327-30 and a selection from "The Land" (called "The Greater Cats" in OBMV), pp. 105-8.

1841. Sassoon, Siegfried. THE HEART'S JOURNEY. London: William Heinemann, 1935. 45 pp.

The poems are numbered with Roman numerals. On flyleaf: XII 18 X/ Xvi 22 X/ XXIII 31 X/ XXV 33/ XXXI 39 X/ XXXII 40/ ? On reading war diary/ On Passing the New Menin Gate 30/ The Wisdom of the World 40 [last three titles refer apparently to another vol.].
Excised, apparently to make a preliminary selection for OBMV, pp. 18, 22, 31, 39, 40.

1842. ———. LINGUAL EXERCISES FOR ADVANCED VOCABULARIANS. Cambridge: Privately printed at the Univ. Press, 1925. 24 pp. -/99. Sig.: Siegfried Sassoon. Sig.: WBY

Inserted, a note from Sassoon, dated 31 March [1925?], London: Dear Mr. Yeats, I hope you will find a few lines in my little book which will give you pleasure. Yours sincerely, [sig.] Siegfried Sassoon.

1843. ———. MEMOIRS OF AN INFANTRY OFFICER. London: Faber & Faber, 1930. 334 pp.

Inside frt. cover: George Yeats/ from Lennox Robinson/ For her birthday, 1930, with/ love.

1844. ———. SATIRICAL POEMS. London: William Heinemann, 1933. 69 pp.

"On Reading the War Diary of a Defunct Ambassador" checked in text, p. 11.

1845. ———. TO MY MOTHER. Drawings by Stephen Tennant. The Ariel Poems, no. 14. London: Faber & Gwyer, [1928]. 3 pp.

1846. Saurat, Denis. BLAKE AND MODERN THOUGHT. London: Constable, 1929. xiv,[2],199,[1] pp.

Inside frt. cover: For Kathleen Raine/Christmas 1958/ George Yeats.
This item was returned to the library by Miss Raine some time after 1971.
Heavily annotated in pencil by WBY; his comments, often at the end of chapters frequently take exception to Saurat's comments on Blake.
P. 19, bottom, referring to "Without Contraries": Hegel's is Fichte's dialect in the rough. I think there was no such thought known in England in Blake's day. It is fundamental in Blake.
P. 25, referring to "Theotormon": not "generating love" or only that because we are in "the prison hour."
P. 26, referring to "Calling that Holy Love ...": compare next page.
P. 27, referring to "Sexual love is legitimate": Blake's definition [?], but not his thought. It would be more true to say he condemned sexual love because it could not go to all. The daughters of Beulah are states or rather spaces.
P. 31, bottom: One should read all Blake's moral theories in relation to a statement of his that we must keep the laws of "our prison hour." Blake is difficult and perhaps meant to be. Hayley was so clear.
P. 32, bottom, referring to "This culte de la sensibilité": The source of Blake's thought is not 'culte de la sensibilite' but 17th century theories about the sovereign powers of imagination as summarized in an anonymous writer in I think 1740. It alone "substantiates as it goes." [one word?] take place in it. It was considered perhaps the achievement of the world. The source may have been a passage attributed to Apolonius of Tyana (quoted by Croce). Blake's thought or style reverted to the 17th century.
P. 51, bottom, referring to "Noah" in first line: Blake considered Noah's flood to be the flood of time and space (I think Swedenborg did also). The three sons of Noah were painting, poetry, music, the only means of "conversing with eternity" left [after?] the flood. It is obvious that he could not have idealized [?] this flood though he could its symbol. The Druid Adam was not in time. I think the same problem arises with Swedenborg's "most ancient churches."
P. 63, bottom, referring to "Adam was a Druid. Consequently Blake calls him Albion": Compare the book of Mormon's staging an incarnation of Christ in ancient America and its American Indians [?] as a sacred people. Blake meant to assert the sacredness of

England as a part of the whole sacred earth as against the supposed special societies of Judea. He may have amused himself by theories of the historical significance of the Druids to balance that of the Jews but not as a serious part of his thought.

P. 64, referring to last par.: Blake is the opponent of Swedenborg. To Swedenborg etc. Jews are the symbolic race, their books alone inspired. Their flood is the flood of time and space. Blake substitutes England and its flood. It is a place for ordinary mankind.

P. 65, referring to "Adam was a Druid, and Noah also; Abraham was called to succeed the Druidical age": To be read in the light of Swedenborg and also of Kabbalistic Theories - a thousand symbolic years from Adam to Noah, a thousand from Noah to Abraham. Symbol not Jewish history [three words?]. Blake loved perplexing people. A thousand years are equal to a single day - pure symbol.

P. 67, referring to passage beginning "The heroes of this tradition were still living in the Welsh mountains.": The eternal world remains within that of time. Blake speaks of naked beings in the Welsh mountains and of hundreds as having seen them. He was never in Wales. Wales was a symbol. He saw them in his mind -- "in Eden."

P. 70, referring to passage "for his stolen bride": Blake had probably some mystic's interpretation of the fall of Troy.

P. 71, referring to "He alter'd the poles of the world": see Milton (quoted in "A Vision"); perhaps however a revolution of the Zoas.

P. 72, referring to "We must also admit that Blake could contradict himself occasionally": The imaginative world remains. There is no contradiction.

P. 72, bottom, referring to "Druids started from England": Blake tried to make England a symbol, as Judea was according to Swedenborg, as Egypt certainly was. The theory of the Druids as a source of ancient wisdom still lives. I think Alfred Nutt in "The Voyage of Bran" suggests a druid origin for the wisdom (or part of it) of Pythagoras.

P. 74, referring to "You have a tradition...": a recurrent idea perhaps suggested by the symbolical designs in Law's Boehme. I have not, however, seen those designs for 30 years.

P. 82, referring to "one of the most fundamental characteristics of the Anglo-Saxon race": Oh Saurat!

P. 82, bottom, referring to "The time has come. England awakes...": When England "awakes" she becomes the whole world because "the flood of time and space", has disappeared - you cannot localize or imperialize eternity.

P. 85, bottom: To sum[marize]. Blake did not think England the place of primitive humanity, or of the original wisdom because they were before the flood of time and space. The historical druids he thought degenerate man - "rocky druidom". He spoke of England and its past because he lived there. In the same way the folklore of the Echte hills in Galway says the last judgment will be among those hills. Blake seeks the near and the particular always. Saurat, like Blake's other critics, never recognises Blake's humour, his love of bewildering, his art student tricks.

P. 145, referring to "Auricular Nerves": annunciation by the word through the ear. See mosaics etc.

P. 146, at "porch" (underlined): ear

P. 150, middle margin: Albion is here Job. Note that Luvah gives boils.

P. 156, at last par.: light

P. 158, next to "Vortexes": X

1847. ———. MILTON, MAN AND THINKER. London: Jonathan Cape, [1925]. xvii,[3],363 pp.

Corners turned back, pp. 19, 75, 101, 139, 185, 205, 207, 254, 285, 303.

1848. THE SAVOY. 1 (Jan.-Aug. 1896). Bp: WBY

Bound vol. contains Nos. 1-4.
No. 1 contains WBY's "Two Love Poems - The Shadowy Horses: The Travail of Passion." Also "The Binding of the Hair. A Story."

No. 2 contains WBY's "Rosa Alchemica. A Story," "Two Poems concerning Peasant Visionaries: A Cradle Song: [and] The Valley of the Black Pig." Also "Verlaine in 1894" with slight verbal revisions which do not appear in the abbreviated version in AUTOBIOGRAPHIES.

No. 3 contains WBY's "William Blake and his Illustrations to The Divine Comedy: I. His Opinions upon Art" with penciled revisions pp. 41, 53 and 54, and deletions which have been incorporated in the version in E&I.
Also contains poem "O'Sullivan Rua to Mary Lavell." Lines 11 and 12 and "xed" and WIND AMONG THE REEDS (1899) (WADE 11) follows this deletion.

No. 4 contains "William Blake and his Illustrations to the Divine Comedy: II. His Opinions on Dante." Last two pars. deleted; E&I follows this.

1849. ———. 2 (Sept.-Dec. 1896). Bp: WBY

Bound vol. contains Nos. 5-8.

No. 5 contains "William Blake and his Illustrations to The Divine Comedy: III. The Illustrations of Dante."
P. 31, after "noisy and demagogic art" WBY deletes "an art heavy as with the rank breath of the mob."
P. 35, a revision to the phrase beginning "Clovio, working in the manner...."

P. 36, the last par. deleted and a phrase added to the new final sentence.
E&I follows these revisions.

Also contains poem "O'Sullivan Rua to the Secret Rose" in which lines 7-11 are numbered 7, 8, 9, 13, 15 apparently to indicate that 3 lines have been added in the next printing, WADE 10, THE SECRET ROSE (1897).

No. 7 contains two poems "Windlestraws. I. O'Sullivan Rua to the Curlew. II. Out of the Old Days." In "Out of the Old Days" which becomes "To his Heart, bidding it have no Fear" in WADE 11, THE WIND AMONG THE REEDS (1899) "wingèd multitude" revised (pencil) to:
wide-wingèd multitude [a unique variant which appears in no printing]
Also contains "The Tables of the Law. A Story."

1850. Sayler, Oliver M[artin], ed. MAX REINHARDT AND HIS THEATRE. Translated by Mariele S. Dudernatsch and others. New York: Brentano's, 1924. xxiii,381 pp. Sig.: GY

1851. Scherer, Valentin. DURER. Des Meisters Gemalde Kupferstiche Und Holzschnitte. Stuttgart: Deutsche Verlags-Anstalt, 1908. xxxiii,[3],424 pp.

Flyleaf: To G[eorgie] H[yde] L[ees] on her XVIIth Birthday/ with best wishes from H.T.T[ucker]

1852. Schmidt, Peter M.D. THE CONQUEST OF OLD AGE. Methods to effect rejuvenation and to increase functional activity. Translated by Eden and Cedar Paul. London: George Routledge, 1931. xviii,320 pp., plates.

Describes the Steinach operation, pp. 40ff.

1853. Schneider, Hermann. THE HISTORY OF WORLD CIVILIZATION. Translated by Margaret M. Green. 2 vols. London: George Routledge, 1931. Bp: WBY

Marginal strokes and comments in sections on Egyptian civilization.

Vol. 1, p. 41, at par. beginning "Egyptian history begins with Menes": 2800. First prime of 2nd culture.
P. 41, at "revolutionary period": Revolution
P. 41, at "Under their rule Egypt experienced the second prime of her earliest culture": Second Prime of 1st Culture.
P. 41, at "Then the empire was broken up": End of first culture.
P. 42, at first 8 lines: First Prime of Second Culture. 2100.
P. 42, end of 1st par.: End of second culture.
P. 42, last 4 lines: First Prime of Third Culture.
P. 44, top, at "barbarians": end of Third Culture.

Vol. 2, p. 390, a marginal stroke for par. beginning "If the Egyptians...."

1854. Schnitzler, Arthur. PROFESSOR BERNHARDI. A comedy. Translated by Hetty Landstone. London: Faber & Gwyer, 1927. 160 pp. Sig.: Lennox Robinson/ 1927

*1855. Schopenhauer, Arthur. THE ART OF CONTROVERSY. And other posthumous papers. Selected and translated by T. Bailey Saunders. London: Swan Sonnenschein, 1896; New York: Macmillan, 1896. viii,116 pp.

Many pp. uncut after p. 41.

*1856. ———. THE WISDOM OF LIFE. Being the first part of Aphorismen zur Lebensweisheit. Translated by T. Bailey Saunders. London: Swan Sonnenschein, 1891.

Considerable markings and annotations, not WBY's; possibly GY's.

*1857. Scot, Reginald. THE DISCOVERIE OF WITCHCRAFT. A reprint of the first ed. published in 1584. Edited by Brinsley Nicholson. London: Elliott Stock, 1886. ix,xlviii, xxxx,590 pp. Bp: WBY

P. 408, against a passage dealing with bewitching through malicious praise: overlooking [??]

1858. Scott, Geoffrey. A BOX OF PAINTS. With drawings by Albert Rutherston. London: At the Office of the Bookman's Journal, 1923. 36 pp. -/1000

1859. Scott, Sir Walter. IVANHOE. Edinburgh: Adam & Charles Black, 1871. [6],484 pp.

Half-title p.: To Willie/ from his Mama/ Xmas 1873.

1860. ———. LETTERS ON DEMONOLOGY AND WITCHCRAFT, addressed to J.G. Lockhart. London: John Murray, 1830. ix,[1], 402 pp. Bp: R.H. Robertson. Sig.: GHL, 1914

*1860A. Another ed. 4th ed. Morley's Universal Library. London: George Routledge, 1899. 320 pp.

1861. SCRIPTURE TOPOGRAPHY. Being some account of places mentioned in Holy Scripture. 4th ed. London: The Society for Promoting Christian Knowledge, 1852. xi,492 pp.

Bp. of SPCK designating this as a prize to Susan Pollexfen "For Superior Merit at an Examination" in St. John's Church Sligo, 31 Oct. 1855 by the Rev. Arthur Hyde.
Flyleaf: Given to Anne B. Yeats/ grand-daughter of/ Susan Pollexfen/ by her Aunt/ Susan M. Yeats (Lily)/ April 1935.

1862. Seignobos, Charles. HISTORY OF MEDIAEVAL CIVILIZATION. And of modern to the end of the seventeenth century. London: T. Fisher Unwin, 1908. xiii,433 pp.

1863. Sei Shonagon. THE PILLOW-BOOK OF SEI SHONAGON. Translated by Arthur Waley. London: George Allen & Unwin, 1928. 162 pp.

Marginal strokes and checks pp. 24, 27, 31, 41, 48, 103, 129.

*1864. Selden, John. DE DIS SYRIS, Syntagmata II. Editio altera. Lugduni: Ex Officina Bonaventurae & Abrahami Elsevir, 1629. xxxx,374 pp. Sig.: E Libris Comitis Guilford

Title p., faded writing in an older hand than sig. above.

1865. Sensier, Alfred. JEAN-FRANÇOIS MILLET. Peasant and Painter. Translated by Helena de Kay. London: Macmillan, 1881. xii,[6],230 pp. Bp: Lily Yeats; Bp: Anne Yeats. Sig.: Anne B. Yeats, 1934

Flyleaf, verso: J B Yeats
Title p.: Susan Mary Yeats (Lilly [sic]/ 1884-/ [there follows in a different ink:] Given to Anne Yeats/ by Her Aunt/ Lily Yeats/ Jan 26th 1934/ Dundrum/ Co. Dublin
Marginal markings passim.

1866. Sepharial [Walter Gorn Old]. DIRECTIONAL ASTROLOGY. To which is added a discussion of problematic points and a complete set of tables necessary for the calculation of arcs or direction. London: William Rider, 1915. ix,119,lxxii. Bp: GY

1867. ———. ECLIPSES, astronomically and astrologically considered and explained. London: W. Foulsham, [1915]. 112 pp. Bp: GY

1868. ———. PRIMARY DIRECTIONS MADE EASY. London: W. Foulsham, [1917]. viii,80 pp. Bp: GY

1869. ———. THE SCIENCE OF FOREKNOWLEDGE. London: W. Foulsham, 1918. vii,160 pp, illus.

Pasted on flyleaf, a one column newspaper clipping, unidentified, on the measurement of the diameters of the stars Betelgeuse and Antares.
Marginal strokes, underscorings, and brief annotations passim, not WBY's; possibly some GY's.

1870. SEPHER YETZIRAH. The Book of Formation, with the fifty gates of intelligence and the thirty-two paths of wisdom. Translated by W. Wynn Westcott. London: J.M. Watkins, 1911. 49,[1] pp. Sig.: Georgie Hyde Lees/ April 1914

Some marginal strokes and annotations, not WBY's; likely GY's.

*1871. Shakespear, Olivia. THE DEVOTEES. A novel. London: William Heinemann, 1904. 279 pp.

Flyleaf: W.B. Yeats/ June 1904/ O.S.

1872. ———. THE FALSE LAUREL. A novel. London: Osgood, McIlvaine, 1896. 271 pp.

Flyleaf: W.B. Yeats/ from the writer/ June 1896.

1873. ———. THE JOURNEY OF HIGH HONOUR. A novel. London: Osgood, McIlvaine, 1895. 195 pp.

Flyleaf: W.B. Yeats/ from/ O. Shakespear/ 1894.

1874. ———. LOVE ON A MORTAL LEASE. A novel. London: Osgood, McIlvaine, 1894. 355 pp.

Flyleaf: W.B. Yeats/ 1894/ from/ O. Shakespear.

SEE ALSO 663.

1875. Shakespeare, William. THE COMPLETE WORKS. Edited by W.J. Craig. London: Oxford Univ. Press, 1935. viii,1352 pp.

Inserted, a small slip with pp. numbers etc., not WBY's.

*1876. ———. A LOVER'S COMPLAINT AND THE PHOENIX AND TURTLE. The Shakespeare Head Press Booklets, no. 6. Stratford-on-Avon: Shakespeare Head Press, 1906. 31 pp.

1877. ———. OTHELLO THE MOORE OF VENICE. Edited by C.H. Hereford. The Warwick Shakespeare. London and Glasgow: Blackie, [1893?]. liv,[2],161 pp.

*1878. ———. SHAKESPEARE'S SONGS. The Shakespeare Head Press Booklets, no. 3. Stratford-on-Avon: Shakespeare Head Press, 1906. 30 pp.

1879. ———. THE SONNETS. Edited by Edward Dowden. The Parchment Library. London: C. Kegan Paul, 1881. lxii,251 pp.

Flyleaf: J.B. Yeats/ from/ Edward Dowden/ June 1881. Sketches on flyleaves, a brief comment at Sonnet 84, likely JBY's.

*1880. ———. THE WINTER'S TALE. An acting edition prepared with a preface by Granville Barker. With costume designs by Albert Rothenstein. London: William Heinemann, 1912. x,123 pp.

*1881. ———. THE WORKS. 10 vols. Stratford-on-Avon: Shakespeare Head Press, 1904-7. 218/1000. Bps: WBY

Cut or mostly cut are Two Gentlemen of Verona, Love's Labour's Lost, The Taming of the Shrew, Twelfth Night, Richard II, Henry the Fourth, I & II, Henry the Sixth, I, II, and III (through Act III), Troilus and Cressida, Titus Andronicus, Romeo and Juliet, Timon of Athens, Julius Caesar, Macbeth, Hamlet, King Lear, Othello, Antony and Cleopatra, Pericles, Lucrece, The Sonnets,

A Lover's Complaint, The Passionate Pilgrim, The Phoenix and the Turtle.
Coriolanus is cut through Act I; Venus and Adonis is about half cut.

1882. THE SHANACHIE. No. 1 (Spring 1906).

Includes WBY's "Against Witchcraft" and "The Praise of Deirdre."

1882a. Another copy.

1883. ———. 1 (Winter 1906).

Includes works by A.E., J.B.Y., and Jack Yeats.

1884. ———. 2 (March 1907).

Includes work by J.B.Y. and Synge.
Inside back cover, ink: 80 Rath [?]/ 31 Upper S. Columba's Rd./ Drumcondra [possibly WBY's]

1885. ———. 2 (Summer, 1907).

Includes an essay by J.B.Y.

1886. ———. 2 (Autumn 1907).

Includes WBY's "Discoveries."

*1887. Sharp, Elizabeth, ed. LYRA CELTICA. An anthology of representative Celtic poetry. With an intro. by William Sharp. The Celtic Library. Edinburgh: Patrick Geddes, 1896. li,[1],422 pp.

Includes 3 poems by WBY, "They Went Forth to Battle but They Always Fell," "The White Birds," and "The Lake of Innisfree" [sic].

*1888. Sharp, William. MADGE O' THE POOL. The Gypsy Christ and other tales. Westminster: Archibald Constable, 1896. [6],184 pp.

Flyleaf: To/ W.B. Yeats/ from his friend/ William Sharp.
Mostly uncut.

SEE ALSO MACLEOD, Fiona.

1889. Shaw, George Bernard. THE ADVENTURES OF THE BLACK GIRL IN HER SEARCH FOR GOD. London: Constable, 1932. 4, 74,[3] pp.

1889a. Another copy.

1890. ———. ANDROCLES AND THE LION. The Dramatic Works of Bernard Shaw, no. 23. London: Constable, 1927. cxiv, 51 pp.

Many pp. in Preface uncut.

1891. ———. CAESAR AND CLEOPATRA: A History. The Dramatic Works of Bernard Shaw, no. 9. London: Constable, 1923. [4],91-211 pp. Sig.: GY/ 1926

1892. ———. HEARTBREAK HOUSE, GREAT CATHERINE, and PLAYLETS OF THE WAR. London: Constable, 1926. xlix,[1],265 pp.

Some pp. uncut in Preface to HEARTBREAK HOUSE and in the plays following.

1893. ———. THE INTELLIGENT WOMAN'S GUIDE TO SOCIALISM AND CAPITALISM. London: Constable, 1928. xxxvi,494,[1] pp. Bp: GY

Back flyleaf: Margaret Solonns [?]/ Dublin, May 18, 1928/ 8.25 New time A.M. [WBY's]

1894. ———. THE IRRATIONAL KNOT. London: Constable, 1914. 335 pp.

1895. ———. OVERRULED, AND THE DARK LADY OF THE SONNETS. The Dramatic Works of Bernard Shaw, nos. 20 & 24. London: Constable, 1921. vi,53-147 pp.

Flyleaf: 6:30 Monday [not WBY's]
In OVERRULED, many marginal marks and one word comments possibly by someone interested in production; pp. 82-3 deletion of several speeches which might be considered indelicate; none of the preceding appears to be WBY's.

1896. ———. PYGMALION. The Dramatic Works of Bernard Shaw, no. 25. London: Constable, 1928. [4],97-205 pp.

1897. ———. SAINT JOAN. London: Constable, 1924. lxiv,114 pp.

Flyleaf: George/ From Lennox/ June, 1924.
Some pp. of the Preface and Epilogue uncut.

*1898. ———. THE SANITY OF ART: An exposure of the current nonsense about artists being degenerate. London: New Age Press, 1908. [4],104 pp.

1899. ———. TOO TRUE TO BE GOOD, VILLAGE WOOING, AND ON THE ROCKS. Three Plays. London: Constable, 1934. vi,273, [1] pp. Sig.: WBY

1900. ———. TRANSLATIONS AND TOMFOOLERIES. London: Constable, 1926. v,[1],246 pp.

A few pp. uncut.

1901. ———. WIDOWERS' HOUSES: A Play. The Dramatic Works of Bernard Shaw, no. 1. London: Constable, 1924. [2],70 pp.

1902. Shelley, Percy Bysshe. ESSAYS AND LETTERS. Edited by

Ernest Rhys. The Camelot Classics. London: Walter Scott, 1886. xxiv,392 pp. Sig.: WBY. Bp: Lily Yeats

In Contents WBY has entered dates of composition against "On Life," "Speculations on Metaphysics," "Speculations on Morals," and "The Assassins." For "On Life" he has entered two dates, 1815 and 1814, the first according to Rossetti, the second Dowden. These refs. appear again before the essay in the text.

1903. ———. THE LYRICAL POEMS AND TRANSLATIONS. Edited by C.H. Herford. London: Chatto & Windus, 1918. xxvi, 480 pp.

Flyleaf: George Yeats/ from/ Herbert V. Reade/ 1918.

1904. ———. THE LYRICS AND MINOR POEMS. With a prefatory notice by Joseph Skipsey. The Canterbury poets. London: Walter Scott, 1885. viii,288 pp. Sig.: WBY, 1886.

Flyleaves, front and back, sketches of women, one dated 1904; one fairly finished; all likely JBY's.

*1905. ———. THE POEMS OF PERCY BYSSHE SHELLEY. Edited by C.D. Locock. 2 vols. London: Methuen, 1911. Bps: WBY

Vol. 1, flyleaf: Pencil markings are by G.Y. not WBY [but there are no apparent pencil markings].
Back flyleaf, a horoscope, ink with note: Shelley's horoscope according to Allen Leo (see "How to Judge a Nativity" II.187 (First Edition) Should be verified [followed by a canceled entry, illegible, and:] notice♆☌MC♄☍MC/♃☌♂♆

[the horoscope and note WBY's]

1906. ———. THE POETICAL WORKS OF PERCY BYSSHE SHELLEY. [London: C. Daly, 1836? (1),v,572 pp.].

Copy lacking frt. cover, title pp.; pp. 1-572 only. 16 mo ed. BMC lists printings for 1836, '37 and '39.

1907. ———. THE POETICAL WORKS OF PERCY BYSSHE SHELLEY. Edited by Mrs. Shelley. 3 vols. London: Edward Moxon, 1847. Bps: Robert Corbet. Vols. 2 & 3, Bps: Lily Yeats

Sketches, some fairly crude, some rather finished, passim, all 3 vols.
In CENCI, annotations of a moralizing and descriptive nature, not WBY's.

*1908. ———. THE POETICAL WORKS OF PERCY BYSSHE SHELLEY. Edited by William B. Scott. Excelsior Series. London: George Routledge, [1880]. xxxi,603 pp.

Flyleaf: W.B. Yeats/ from his affectionate friend,/ Katharine Tynan./ January 24th 1888.

Some dates entered before poems; also occasional biographical comments as at p. 29, top: S[helley] in Switzerland for second time [ink].
"Adonais," pp. 387-97 has been heavily annotated by WBY, primarily to indicate classical sourses for the poem --
P. 387, the date 1821 entered before the poem.
P. 388, stanzas 7 & 8: Romeo & Juliet V.3
P. 390, stanza 17: Agamemnon (49-51)
P. 390, stanza 20: Lucretius II.990.1010
P. 390, stanza 21: adapted from Lucretius (II. 578-580)
P. 392, at "Wisdom the mirrored shield," stanza 27: 'scutum crystallinum of Pallas Athene' (C[lifton?] Collins).
P. 392, stanza 28, at "Who feed where desolation first has fed,/ And whose wings rain contagion": flow of matter/ Raven 'Doth shake contagion from his sable wings'.
P. 393, top, referring to "a light spear topped with a cypress cone," stanza 33: Cypress. Silvanus "teneram ab radice ferens, silvane cupressum" (Georgics I.20).
P. 393, stanza 33: Why is this emblem of the poet?/ Pansies = thoughts (Shakespeare [?]/ violets that wither/ violets = fidelity perhaps because Pliny called it one of the longest lived of flowers.
P. 394, stanza 39: fragment [??] Polyidus of Euripides
P. 394, stanza 42: Lucretius 990.1010.
P. 395, stanza 44: Dante. Inferno. Inf. 44/ St. 99.
P. 395, stanzas 45-46: Isaiah XIV. 9.-10.
P. 396, referring to "sustaining love" in stanza 54: 'The Artifices in the Timaeus' (C. Collins).

*1909. ———. PROMETHEUS UNBOUND. A lyrical drama in four acts. Edited by G. Lowes Dickinson. The Temple Dramatists Series. London: J.M. Dent, 1898. 20,132 pp.

Flyleaf: George Hyde Lees/ "Who would not have sacrificed/ a thousand Harriets for one Shelley"/ [sig.:] G.S. Streit
Flyleaf, verso, a horoscope cast in pencil. Above it: Per domandar il mio futuro/ 18 Jan 1924/ 8-10 p.m. GMT [not WBY's].
A few passages, especially in Act I, marked in pencil.

1910. ———. SHELLEY. 1914. Edited and printed by T.J. Cobden-Sanderson. [Hammersmith]: The Doves Press, [1914?]. 181 pp. Bp: WBY

1911. Sherard, Robert Harborough. ANDRÉ GIDE'S WICKED LIES ABOUT THE LATE MR. OSCAR WILDE IN ALGIERS IN JANUARY, 1895 AS TRANSLATED FROM THE FRENCH AND BROADCAST BY DR. G. J. RENIER. Calvi (Corsica), France: Vindex Publishing, 1933. 12 pp.

Pp. 2-3 uncut.

THE SHIH CHING. See 1164.

1912. Sibly, Ebenezer. A [COMPLETE] ILLUSTRATION OF [THE CELESTIAL SCIENCE OF] ASTROLOGY [or the art of foretelling future events and contingencies by the aspects positions, and influences of the heavenly bodies.] [London: Printed for Green & Co., 1784-88]. xii,[13],1126[4],11 pp]. Bp: John F. Cooper

Lacks title p.; this vol. or parts of it, have been disassembled and rebound with numerous blank leaves at beginning and end. Some of these leaves contain astrological entries in an old hand. The very mixed printed pagination has been struck through in ink and renumbered 1-276. Facts of publication are from running title and an illustration page as supplemented by BMC.

*1913. Sidgwick, Frank, ed. POPULAR BALLADS OF THE OLDEN TIME. First Series: Ballads of Romance and Chivalry. London: A.H. Bullen, 1903. liv,[2],212 pp.

*1914. ———. POPULAR BALLADS OF THE OLDEN TIME. Third Series: Ballads of Scottish Tradition and Romance. London: A.H. Bullen, 1906. xv,220 pp.

*1915. ———. POPULAR BALLADS OF THE OLDEN TIME. Fourth Series: Ballads of Robin Hood and other Outlaws. London: Sidgwick & Jackson, 1912. xxxii,229 pp.

1916. Sidney, Sir Philip. ASTROPHEL & STELLA. Edited by Mona Wilson. London: Nonesuch Press, 1931. xxxviii,193 pp. 189/1210

*1917. ———. THE POEMS. Edited by John Drinkwater. The Muses Library. London: George Routledge, [1910]. xvi,320 pp.

Back flyleaf and inside back cover, apparently two line refs. or drafts: Wherein I wrote etc./ [the second very difficult to decipher].

*1918. Sigerson, Dora (Mrs. Clement Shorter). BALLADS AND POEMS. London: James Bowden, 1899. viii,123 pp.

Checks, arrows and printer's marks, pp. 24, 30, 38, 39, 41, 56, 62.
In text of "The Fate of the Three Sons of Usneach," some lines "xed" as lines 36 & 37.

*1919. ———. THE FAIRY CHANGELING and other poems. London and New York: John Lane, 1898. viii,[1],100 pp.

Contains "Cean Duv Deelish" in a different version than in BIV.
Some pp. uncut.

*1920. ———. LOVE OF IRELAND. Poems and ballads. Dublin and London: Maunsel, 1916. 92,[1] pp.

SEE ALSO 1778.

*1921. Sigerson, George, trans. BARDS OF THE GAEL AND GALL. Examples of the poetic literature of Erinn. London: T. Fisher Unwin, 1897. xv,[1]435 pp. Sig.: WBY/ June, 1897

1922. Simmonite, W[illiam] J[oseph]. HORARY ASTROLOGY. The key to scientific prediction. New ed., with additions by John Story. London: W. Foulsham, [1896]. xx,240 pp. Bp: GY

1923. SINN FEIN REBELLION HANDBOOK. A complete and connected narrative of the Rising, with detailed accounts of the fighting at all points in Dublin and in the country. 2nd ed. Dublin: Compiled by the Weekly Irish Times, [1916]. xvi,243 pp. Sig.: Lily Yeats/ Dundrum

1924. Sitwell, Edith. ALEXANDER POPE. London: Faber & Faber, 1930. [13],316 pp.

Flyleaf: For/ W.B. Yeats/ with homage from/ Edith Sitwell.

1925. ———. ASPECTS OF MODERN POETRY. London: Duckworth, 1934. 264 pp.

Flyleaf: For/ W.B. Yeats/ with homage from/ Edith Sitwell.
Discussion of WBY, pp. 73-89.

1926. ———. THE COLLECTED POEMS. London: Duckworth, 1930. x,278 pp.

Flyleaf: For/ Mr. W.B. Yeats/ to whom all poets owe/ homage;/ and with deep personal gratitude/ from/ Edith Sitwell.
This was apparently WBY's working text for ES's selection in OBMV; in Contents 3 poems, "Metamorphosis," "Sylph's Song-Waltz," and "Gold Coast Customs" had long notes by WBY, now erased. Also marked in Contents, "The Lament of Edward Blastock," "Colonel Fantock," "Clown's Houses," "Trio for Two Cats," "Madame Mouse Trots," "Ass face," When the Sailor," "Thirty-eight Bucolic Comedies."
In text, some pp. checked in text and last stanza on p. 261 and first on 262: quote
Some slight corrections in text, possibly WBY's.

1927. ———. EPITHALAMIUM. Christmas 1931. London: Duckworth, [1931]. unpag. -/100

On limitation p., "No." canceled and: Presentation/ Edith Sitwell [also above this:] For/ our greatest poet/ with my hommage.

1928. ———. FIVE POEMS. London: Duckworth, 1928. 20,[1] pp. 255/275. Sig.: Edith Sitwell

Flyleaf: For/ Mr. W.B. Yeats/ with hommage from/ Edith Sitwell

1929. ———. FIVE VARIATIONS ON A THEME. London: Duckworth, 1933. 38 pp.

Flyleaf: For/ W.B. Yeats/ with my hommage/ Edith Sitwell.

1930. ———. GOLD COAST CUSTOMS. London: Duckworth, 1929. 63 pp. Bp: WBY

Flyleaf: For/ Mr. W.B. Yeats/ with homage from/ Edith Sitwell.

1931. ———. RUSTIC ELEGIES. London: Duckworth, 1927. 94 pp.

1932. ———, ed. THE PLEASURES OF POETRY. A critical anthology. First Series. Milton and the Augustan Age. London: Duckworth, 1930. viii,236 pp.

1933. ———, Osbert Sitwell, and Sacheverell Sitwell. POOR YOUNG PEOPLE. With drawings by Albert Rothenstein. London: Fleuron, 1925. [10],60 pp. 71/375

Poems.

1934. Sitwell, Osbert. WINTERS OF CONTENT. More discursions of travel, art, and life. London: Duckworth, 1932. 296 pp.

Flyleaf: For/ W.B. Yeats,/ with unfailing/ admiration,/ from/ Osbert Sitwell/ 13. October 1932.
P. 266, at beginning of Chapter VII, Names and Places, an "X".
P. 271, a stroke after the par. ending near the top of the page.

1935. ———, Edith Sitwell, and Sacheverell Sitwell. TRIO. Dissertations on some aspects of national genius. London: Macmillan, 1938. viii,248 pp. Sig.: GY

1936. Sitwell, Sacheverell. CANONS OF GIANT ART. Twenty Torsos in Heroic Landscapes. London: Faber & Faber, 1933. 225 pp.

Flyleaf: To/ W.B. Yeats/ 15.VIII.1933/ with homage/ to/ a great poet/ Sacheverell Sitwell.
"Agamemnon's Tomb" excised for OBMV.
Back flyleaf and continued inside back cover, a draft (pencil) very rough of "Beautiful Lofty Things":

speaker to ~~that~~
[one word illegible, canceled]
beautiful lofty things ~~sight,~~ O'Leary's noble head
Standish
O Grady standing drunk between the tables and speaking
-sensuous words
→Speaking to a drunken audience sweet high words
My father, the Abbey stage, before him a raging crowd
This land of saints and then as the applause died out
of plaster saints, his old beautiful [?]
mischievous [?] head thrown back

Certainly the grey hair [??; this line and the following very heavily canceled]
Augusta Gregory seated at her great ormolu table
Approaching her eightieth year [canceled]
Her eightieth year approaching; yesterday he threatened my life.
→But I [canceled] I told him that nightly from six to seven I wrote at the table
But I said that I wrote at this from six to seven [canceled]
nearly all night [canceled]
With the blinds pulled up. Maud Gonne waiting a train at Howth station
Pallas Athena in that straight back and arrogant head
All the Olympians, a sight no longer upon the eye [?]
I told him that nights from six to seven I wrote at the table
With the blinds pulled up. Maud Gonne at Howth station waiting a train
Maud Gonne awaiting a train at Howth [these last 3 lines inside frt. cover; to be inserted as indicated]

Inserted a ts. of 1-1/3 pp. of a satirical, apparently topical poem entitled "Rat Week." No indication of author or date.

1937. ———. COLLECTED POEMS. London: Duckworth, 1936. 593 pp.

1938. ———. DOCTOR DONNE AND GARGANTUA. The first six cantos. London: Duckworth, 1930. 79,[1] pp.

1939. ———. THE GOTHICK NORTH. A study of mediaeval life, art, and thought. 3 vols. London: Duckworth, 1929-30.

1940. ———. THE HUNDRED AND ONE HARLEQUINS. The New Readers Library. London: Duckworth, 1929. 128 pp.

1941. ———. THE PEOPLE'S PALACE. Oxford: B.H. Blackwell, 1918. 52,[1] pp.

1942. ———. THE THIRTEENTH CAESAR and other poems. London: Grant Richards, 1924. 112 pp. Sig.: Gwin [?] Russell

1942a. Another copy. London: Duckworth, 1927.

1943. ———. TWO POEMS, TEN SONGS. London: Duckworth, 1929. [8],32 pp. 146/275. Sig.: Sacheverell Sitwell

1944. ———. LA VIE PARISIENNE. A tribute to Offenbach. London: Faber & Faber, 1937. 108 pp.

*1945. Skeat, Walter. THE CHAUCER CANON. Oxford: Clarendon Press, 1900. xi,167 pp.

Mostly uncut.

*1946. Skipsey, Joseph. SONGS AND LYRICS. London: Walter Scott, 1892. viii,180 pp. 145/250. Sig.: J.S.

Flyleaf: To W.B. Yeats,/ With the Season's Greetings/ and the best regards of his sincere Admirer/ and friend,/ The Author/ New Year's Eve,/ 1895.

1947. Slater, Montagu. EASTER: 1916. A play. London: Lawrence and Wishart, 1936. 79 pp.

1948. Smart, John Semple. SHAKESPEARE, TRUTH AND TRADITION. London: Edward Arnold, 1929. 224 pp.

1949. Smith, G[rafton] Elliot. THE EVOLUTION OF THE DRAGON. Manchester: Univ. Press, 1919. xx,234 pp.

Comparative anthropology.

1950. Smith, Janet Adam, ed. POEMS OF TOMORROW. An anthology of contemporary verse, chosen from THE LISTENER. London: Chatto & Windus, 1935. [12],135 pp.

Flyleaf, apparently for OBMV: Spender/ Shapes of Death 115/ Charles Madge 63/ MacNeice 57/ Through 61.
Checked in Contents, MacNeice's "Snow" (but then crossed out), Madge's "The Times," "Loss," "Solar Creation," "At Watch," Spender's "The Shapes of Death."
Checked in text, MacNeice's "The Individualist Speaks" and "Snow."
Excised from text, pp. 63-4.

1951. Smith, William. A SMALLER DICTIONARY OF GREEK AND ROMAN ANTIQUITIES. 11th ed. London: John Murray, 1880. [4],474 pp. illus.

Front cover: Swaby [hand unidentified].

1952. Smith, W[alter] Whately. A THEORY OF THE MECHANISM OF SURVIVAL. The fourth dimension and its applications. London: Kegan Paul, Trench, Trubner, 1920. [12],195 pp.

Mathematics and psychic research.

1953. Smollett, Tobias. THE ADVENTURES OF FERDINAND COUNT FATHOM. London: Waverley Book Company, [189-]. xi,416 pp. Sig.: W. Sullivan

Some pp. uncut.

*1954. ———. THE ADVENTURES OF RODERICK RANDOM. London: George Routledge, [189-]. xvi,476 pp.

*1954a. Another printing. London: Waverley, [189-]. xvi,476 pp.

1955. ———. THE ADVENTURES OF SIR LAUNCELOT GREAVES and the history and adventures of an atom. London: Waverley, [189-]. vii,382 pp. Sig.: W. Sullivan

Some pp. uncut.

1956. ———. THE EXPEDITION OF HUMPHRY CLINKER. London: Waverley, [189-]. [6],372 pp. Sig.: W. Sullivan

1957. THE SOLDIERS' SONG BOOK. Stirring spirited songs of the soldiers who fought for the honour and the freedom of Ireland in every generation. Dublin: Irish Book Bureau, [1938]. 32 pp.

Contains "O'Donnell Abu," pp. 9-10.

1958. Solovyoff, Vladimir. THE JUSTIFICATION OF THE GOOD. An essay on moral philosophy. Translated by Nathalie A. Duddington. London: Constable, 1918. lxiv,475 pp.

1959. Sophocles. ANTIGONE. A new redaction in the American language by Shaemas O'Sheel. Brooklyn: By the author, 1931. xi,56,[1] pp. -/499

P. vii, "It all began when the Rev. William Norman Guthrie ... sponsored a reading, at his Church of St. Mark's-in-the-Bouwerie, New York, of the King Oedipus as done into prose and lyric verse by William Butler Yeats."

1960. ———. THE OEDIPUS AT COLONUS. Translated from the text of Jebb by Edward P. Coleridge. London: George Bell, 1892. xii,[1],75 pp.

1961. ———. OEDIPUS TYRANNUS. Literally translated by Roscoe Mongan. Kelly's Keys to the Classics, vol. 41. London: James Cornish, [1865]. 44 pp.

This is apparently the "translation published at a few pence for dishonest schoolboys" which WBY used in making his version of KING OEDIPUS. See LETTERS, p. 537n. and David R. Clark and James B. McGuire, "Yeats's Versions of Sophocles: Two Typescripts" in YEATS AND THE THEATRE. Edited by Robert O'Driscoll and Lorna Reynolds. [Toronto?]: Macmillan of Canada, 1975, pp. 216-7.

1962. ———. THE OEDIPUS TYRANNUS. As performed at Cambridge, Nov. 22-26, 1887. Translated in prose by R.C. Jebb with a translation of the Songs of the Chorus in verse adapted to the music of C. Villiers Stanford by A.W. Verall. Cambridge: Cambridge Univ. Press, 1887. xii, [4],138 pp.

This is the basic text, the point of departure, for WBY's version of KING OEDIPUS. This copy has been extensively edited by WBY, mostly to delete passages of archaic diction, but there are occasional very brief rewritings or additions as well. The deletions etc. are mostly followed in the Abbey ts. presented by Clark and McGuire, See 1961.

1963. ———. THE SEVEN PLAYS IN ENGLISH VERSE. Translated by Lewis Campbell. New ed., rev. World's Classics, vol. 116. London: Oxford Univ. Press, 1906. xxvii,316 pp.

In ANTIGONE WBY has blocked out scenes for performance, passim.
P. 11 he has condensed "Well, this prevailed, and the lot fell on me,/ Unlucky man! to be the ministrant/ Of this fair service. So I am present here" to: Well, this prevailed, and the lot fell on me,/ Unlucky man! & therefore I am present.

1964. ———. SOPHOCLE. Tome I. Ajax, Antigone, Oedipe-Roi, Electre. Traduit par Paul Masqueray. Paris: Société d'Édition "Les Belles Lettres," 1922. xxx,266 pp.

Parts of the introduction and introductory notices to each play uncut.
According to Norman Jeffares in W.B. YEATS: MAN AND POET, p. 246, WBY used Masqueray's text of OEDIPE-ROI in making his own version of KING OEDIPUS.

1965. ———. SOPHOCLE. Tome II. Les Trachiniennes, Philoctete, Oedipe à Colone, Les Limiers. Traduit par Paul Masqueray. Paris: Société d'Edition "Le Belles Lettres," 1924. 250 pp.

Uncut except for OEDIPE À COLONE, pp. 154-224.

1966. THE SOUTHERN REVIEW. 4 (Summer 1938).

On cover, WBY's: Cleanth Brooks Jr./ "Vision."
Includes Brooks's "The Vision of William Butler Yeats," pp. 116-42.

*1967. Sparling, H[enry] Halliday, ed. IRISH MINSTRELSY. Being a selection of Irish songs, lyrics, and ballads. London: Walter Scott, 1888. xxvii,516. WADE 290

Half title p.: W.B. Yeats/ from the compiler.
P. 379, in WBY's "The Priest of Coloony" ("The Ballad of Fr. O'Hart"), "There was no human keening" (line 29) revised to: Then was no human keening [ink; possibly WBY's, a unique variant]
Also line 31, "Knockasee" revised to: Knocknashee [followed in FFT, 1888].
In "Notes on Writers" death dates for a few authors inked or penciled in; that for Ellen O'Leary seems definitely WBY's.
Back flyleaf, a pencil sketch of a woman.

1968. THE SPECTATOR. 2 (2 June 1711 - 13 Sept. 1711).

Bound vol. published in Dublin: G. Grierson and G. and A. Ewing, 1753.
Facing title p.: Jane Taylor
Bp: Lily Yeats [and below this in ink:] Great Granddaughter of Jane Taylor/ who/ married John Yeats, rector/ of Drumcliffe Co. Sligo, Ireland,/ 1805.

1969. THE SPECTATOR (London). No. 5, 405 (Jan. 1932).

Contains WBY's "Ireland, 1921-1931."

1970. ———. No. 5,415 (9 April 1932).

Contains WBY's "My Friend's Book," a review of AE's SONG AND ITS FOUNTAINS.
Lightly edited (one correction), probably for ESSAYS 1931-1936.

1971. ———. No. 5,547 (19 Oct. 1934).

Contains WBY's "Two Poems, A Parnellite at Parnell's Funeral, Forty Years Later."

1972. ———. No. 5,656 (20 Nov. 1936).

Literary Supplement, p. 3 contains John Hayward's negative review of the OBMV.
Inserted, various reviews of the OBMV. See 517, 2141, 2149.

1973. Spender, Stephen. POEMS. London: Faber & Faber, 1933. 57 pp.

Flyleaf: An I can never 18 [excised in text for Spender's selection in OBMV].

1974. ———. VIENNA. London: Faber & Faber, 1934. 43 pp.

1975. Spengler, Oswald. THE DECLINE OF THE WEST. Form and actuality. Translated by Charles Francis Atkinson. 2 vols. London: George Allen & Unwin, [1926-9].

VOL. 1, marginal marks, underscoring, brief notes to p. 204 passim.
Marginal markings, underscorings pp. 36 (an "x" for Sect. XIII), 42, 57, 58, 66 ("That which cannot be drawn is not 'number'" is underscored), 94, 95, 98, 108-10, 112, 133, 168, 171, 172, 174, 200-203.
P. 22, end of sec. VII: Cambridge History
P. 66, at "secret doctrine of Pythagoreans": compare the astrological aspects.
P. 96, referring to "deep," mid-page: does he use "deep" to signify the amount of extension symbolized? Deep= extension. Form = symbol.
P. 97, at "In historical research, it appears as chronology ...": chronological number
P. 97, bottom margin, apparently referring to Section II which ends at top of p.: Classical man spatializes himself in Nature as human body (the near & small) ▷ Modern man spatializes himself in Nature as the abstract (the far and great) ◁ . Classical man takes [?] the infinite and contracts [it?].
P. 117, at "Destiny Idea": Antithesis [?] Primary
P. 117, at "The logic of understanding and of things understood": anti-primary [?]
P. 166, at "The child suddenly grasps the lifeless corpse for what it is": See page 167 [see first entry for that page].
P. 166, at "the higher thought originates as meditation

upon death": affirms immortality which is therefore the essential thought of man and causes all progress.
P. 167, at "every new culture is awakened in and with ... a sudden glimpse of death": child's first perception.
P. 167, at "the idea of the impending end of the world": prepares for final transcendence.
P. 169, at "ego fashions a formal unit": C[reative] M[ind]/ B[ody of] F[ate].
P. 175, at "Every individual symbol ...": Mask or Image
P. 177, at "swings mysterious": or flows or runs
P. 203, end of first par.: Chinese?

1975A. VOL. 2, Bp: WBY

Very lightly marked, pp. 181, 182, 433, 506.
P. 419, at "in China about 600, in the Classical about 45, for ourselves about 1700": Puts great period of great art and culture too late or ours too early. I put maximum at (say) 1450-1500, but the expression as power incited by attack later. Ignores literature and art. Swift was conscious of the decay of "the form."
P. 432 marked at passage "The Imperial Age, in every culture alike, signifies the end of the politics of mind and money."

1976. Spenser, Edmund. THE POEMS OF SPENSER. Edited by Roden Noel. London: Walter Scott, 1886. vi,344 pp. Sig.: WBY

1977. ———. POEMS OF SPENSER. Edited by W.B. Yeats. Edinburgh: T.C. & E.C. Jack, 1906. xlviii,292 pp. WADE 235

1978. ———. THE WORKS OF EDMUND SPENSER. Edited by J. Payne Collier. 5 vols. London: Bell and Daldy, 1862. Bps: WBY

VOL. 1, flyleaf: W.B. Yeats/ March, 1892/ A.G. [possibly Augusta Gregory, but this would be some four years before he is reported to have met her; but for a further suggestion that this set is from the Coole Park library, see insert described at end of entry.]
VOL. 1, in THE SHEPHERD'S CALENDAR, "February," "March," "October," "November," and "December" are checked (the final three appear in the Yeats-edited POEMS OF SPENSER (1906) and the annotations following were obviously made in preparing this ed.; all the selections in that ed. are marked or indicated -- with many additions. "June" is queried in the text.
P. 134, at the mention of "a Comet" in the introductory section to "December": See Shelley's Comet in Epipsychidion
P. 179, FAERIE QUEENE, Bk. I.1.11, "Amid the thickest woods. The Champion stout" marked by asterisk.
P. 187, the note at bottom glossing "edifyde" is marked.
Bk. I, Canto 4 "xed" at beginning.
At end of I.8: Canto II/ VI
P. 318 (end of Vol. 1): Canto II/ Canto VI/ ? Canto I, 2 quotations [i.e., possible selections from Bk. I]

1978A. VOL. 2 which includes the remainder of Bk. I and Bks. II and III (through Canto 8) very heavily marked.

End of Bk. I, Canto 9: give the whole of Despair episode from first meeting [?] with despairing knight
I.10.13, a symbol entered at description of Fidelia, apparently a cup and serpent.
I.10.14, at description of Speranza, symbol of anchor entered.
I.10.31 at "turtle doves" a drawing of doves entered.
I.10.37: house
I.10.38: fear
I.10.39: clothes
I.10.40: captives
I.10.41: sick
I.10.42: dead [?]
I.10.43: orphan
In II, Cantos 1 and 3, stanzas marked passim.
II.3.29-31: condense his description of his [one word?]
II.5.28-35, selection marked as in POEMS OF SPENSER.
II.6, stanzas marked passim
II.6.5: Shelley's boats
II.6.13-14: La Belle Dame Sans Merci
II.6.18, line 7 ("The slouthful wave") underlined, perhaps to indicate the textual crux noted by Collier.
P. 192, end of II.6: Quote whole of island episode down to the meeting of the knights
II.7, stanzas marked passim
II.7.46, symbols entered for each line descriptive of the "great gold chaine"
P. 215, end of II.7: possibly this whole canto
II.9, stanzas marked passim
II.9.19, symbols for sun and first quarter of moon entered at "borne of two faire Damsels"
P. 246, II.9.22, a diagram entered to illustrate the configuration of the House of Alma
P. 246, bottom, Collier's note on the "Diapase" describing its symbolism heavily marked.
II.9.24, line 3, "Marble far from Ireland brought": first sign of Irish influence
P. 253, bottom, at note to II.9.20, line 7: cuckoo/ child of Pan and Echo
P. 255, II.9.46-48, two drawings of Alma's castle entered.
II.9.57: memory not individual/ his castle [?] is an individual
II.10, some passages marked passim.
II.10.8: Dioclesian's 50 daughters
II.10.9: Brutus
II.10.13: Locrine
II.10.19: Sabrina
II.10.25: Huddibras
II.10.27: King Lear
II.10.29, line 5: Celtica/ Not Cellia [but text has Celtica]
II.10.41, line 8: Ireland
II.10.50, line 1: Cymbeline
II.10.53, line 7: Joseph of Aremethia

II.10.68, line 1: Uther/ Pendragon
II.10.68, end: End of History of England
II.10.70: Prometheus
II.10.71: Garden of Adonis
II.10.72: Cleopolis a city
II.10.73: Panthea a city
II.10.73, last line: bringer of thunder
II, end of 10: nothing here to quote but should speak of historical stanzas as [?] a poetical canon.
II.11 marked passim; some marks erased.
II, end of Canto 11: ? quote description of the attacking hosts and quote separately marked part of Arthur's fight with Maleger
Book II, Canto 12, stanzas and passages marked passim.
II.12.4: magnetic rock
II.12.11: wandering isles
II.12.24: sea monsters
P. 319, in note glossing "And eke the gate," the reference to Canto XVI, "Per l'entrata maggior" etc. of Tasso's GIERUSALEMME LIBERATA is underlined.
II.12.65, line 3, the female symbol entered.
P. 330, in the note glossing "And was arayd ..." the quotation in Italian from Tasso is marked.
Book II, end of Canto 12: quote all Canto 12/ it is most beautiful
Book III.2.49: flowers [canceled] herbs
III.2.50: spirits as a charm
P. 380, the gloss to III.2.50, "Th' uneven nomber for this busines is most fitt" is marked.
III.3.10: Merlin and the Lady of the Lake
III.3.14, line 8, "characters" underlined: the Irish accentuation
III.4, passages marked passim
III.4.2: quote in essay on mind of women
P. 425, end of III.4: quote episode of the Rock strand
III.5, first two stanzas marked.
III.5.32: herbs
P. 445, Book III, beginning of Canto 6: quote all this canto down to end of 51 or else [two words?] and garden from 30-42
III.6.2, at description of birth of Belphoebe, an astrological entry, reading in part, "Jupiter in Pisces or Saggitarius, probably in Saggitarius."
III.6.3: daughter of morning dew and of summer or rather of [astronomical sign for] the sun.
P. 446, the note glossing "Her berth was of the wombe of Morning dew" in 3.6.3 is emphatically marked.
III.6.6: see birth of 'Witch of Atlas'
III.6.8, at description of "Nilus inundation," symbols entered for fire, water, sun, and moon.
P. 449, the note suggesting Spenser's debt to Tasso for the story of Venus seeking her son is marked.
III.6.25, line 5 is queried.
III.6., end of 30: [symbol for] Venus rules vegetable life.

III.6.31 at description of the double nature of Old Genius: ? trine [?]
III.6.32: Spenser's pagan cosmogony - Venusia [?] [one word?] governs all life.
III.6.33: metempsychosis
III.6.34, at "eternall moisture": mystical water
III.6.35: all form is in the gardens of [symbol for] Venus [and an arrow leading to a further note at bottom of p.:] does not Spenser in one of the Muses [?] poems equate form and soul?
III.6.37: chaos = [symbol for] Venus form < body
III.6.38, at line 2: form = beauty
P. 459, the note referring to Claudian as a source for the gardens of Adonis is marked.
III, Canto 7, slight markings.
III.7.37, at "cords of wire": Blake has cords or nets of wire
P. 486, synopsis to III.8, at "The Witch creates a snowy Lady": figure of snow in Witch of Atlas
III.8.24: old man in Witch of Wondrous Isles

1978B. VOL. 3

III.11.28, at "a discolourd Snake": Blake's serpent
P. 77, end of Bk. III (after Canto 12.45): give all Canto 12 and if possible Canto 11 from stanza 21 probably leaving out stanzas from 30 to 46.
IV.10 marked almost entirely and at end: all this Canto perhaps.
IV.11 marked at beginning and end.
IV.12 marked entirely.
V. "Proem," pp. 305-9 marked entirely.
VI.2. 24 and 32, brief passages marked.

1978C. VOL. 4

VI.10.4, last 2 lines: (Moricent)
"The Ruins of Time" marked passim.
P. 312, note "C," the gloss on "Good Melibae, that hath a Poet got" in "Ruins" marked.
P. 315, stanza "I" of "Ruins" beginning "I saw an image, all of massy gold": Empire
P. 315, stanza "II" beginning "Next unto this a stately tower appeared,": art
P. 316, "III" of "Ruins" beginning "Then did I see a pleasant Paradize": pleasure
P. 316, "IV" of "Ruins" beginning "Soon after this a Giaunt": strength
P. 317, "V" of "Ruins" beginning "Then did I see a Bridge": beauty
P. 342ff. in "The Teares of the Muses" marked passim.
P. 344, in "Tears" at stanza beginning "Ne doo they care to have the auncestrie": See poetic history of England in Faerie Queene.
P. 358ff. in "Virgil's Gnat" passages marked passim.
P. 381, at "Prosopopoia": mastering of shapes

P. 411ff. in "Mother Hubbard's Tale" passages marked passim.
P. 436ff. in "The Ruins of Rome" passages marked passim.
P. 453, at "Muiopotmos": ([one word?] fate)
P. 463ff. in "Muiopotmos" passages marked passim.
P. 464 in "Muiopotmos," stanza beginning "And then again he turneth to his play": uses of flowers
P. 471 in "Muiopotmos" at stanza beginning "Not anie Damzell": delight in workmanship of all kinds mark of a still poetical polity
P. 474, end of "Muiopotmos": Is this poem allegorical? Is it Earth's talent (?) against desire, reason against instinct, calculation against genius or what? WBY.

1978D. VOL. 5

P. 39 ff. in "Colin Clout's Come Home Again," passages marked passim.
P. 55 in "Colin" at passage beginning "That as the trees do grow her name may grow": adulation
P. 62, line 861 of "Colin" "like giving" revised to: life giving
P. 76, the additional stanzas of "Astrophel" judged by Collier not to be Spenser's are marked: not by Spenser
P. 117ff. of "Amoretti," passages marked passim.
P. 123, at Sonnet xiv of "Amoretti": Compare Hymn to Beauty about true love not at first sight
P. 146, Sonnet lix of "Amoretti," male and female symbols entered.
P. 157, end of Sonnet lxxx of "Amoretti": insincerity of official poet
P. 186ff. in "An Hymne in Honour of Love" marked passim.
P. 187, line 73 at "her owne goodly ray" the female symbol entered.
P. 196, in "An Hymn in Honour of Beauty," third stanza: Compare Garden of Adonis.
P. 196ff., passages marked passim.
P. 197, stanza beginning "Thereof as every earthly thing partakes": Hence his ideal knight etc. His lack of puritanism. Note objections and then poems [?] liked [?] by certain ladies in E. Spenser's dedications.
P. 197, bottom: Beauty is the hidden Pattern but the light is from the star
P. 198, line 56 of "Hymn ... of Beauty," the symbol for the planet Venus entered at "Of thy bright starre."
P. 199, line 103 of "Hymn ... of Beauty" at "Unto her native planet" the symbol for the planet Venus entered.
P. 199, line 110ff.: [symbols for] Venus not sun [but erased].
P. 200, line 139 of "Hymn of Beauty," "For all that fair is, is by nature good": not puritan doctrine
P. 203, line 220 of "Hymn ... of Beauty": ? god or [symbols for] Venus or Sun. Surely Venus.
P. 206ff. in "An Hymne of Heavenly Love" passages marked passim.

P. 207, stanza 5 of "Hymne of ... Love," two circles entered to indicate Father and Son of Trinity.
P. 207, stanza 6, three circles entered to indicate 3 persons of Trinity
P. 208, stanza 8, three circles entered as above.
P. 208, stanza 8, at "Angels bright": angels
P. 210, in "Hymne of ... Love" at "Therefore of clay, base, vile": man
P. 212, line 170 of "Hymne of ... Love" at "glorious Morning-Starre," symbol for Venus entered.
P. 220 in "An Hymne of Heavenly Beautie" at stanza beginning "Faire is the heaven where happy soules have place" and continuing in the margin for the next two stanzas: 1. Souls 2. Ideas of Intelligence 3. Powers and Principalities [?] 4. Dominions 5. Cherubim 6. Seraphim 7. Angels/ Archangels
P. 223, line 183 of "An Hymne of Heavenly Beautie," the symbol for the sun and: Wisdom
P. 414 in "A View of the State of Ireland" the passage beginning "And those 4 garrisons issuing forth, at such convenient times as they shall have inteligence or espiall upon the enemy, will so drive him from one side to another" is marked, apparently by an exclamation point; and Eudoxus's passage beginning "Doe you then thinke the winter time fittest for the services of Ireland," is marked, apparently as the beginning of a selection that ends in the middle of p. 419 at Eudoxus's question "It is a wonder that you tell...."
P. 418, Irenaeus's description of "wretchednesse" in Munster after a siege of only a year and a half is marked.

Inserted in one of the vols. of Collier's Spenser on Coole Park stationery, no date, a note: Compare a stanza of Shelley's and perhaps one of Byron/ Why gentle Spenser? He is rather powerful than subtle/ Traditional themes and emotions - Ruins of Time/ vision on page 315 [refers to section I beginning "I saw an image, all of massy gold...." which is marked and annotated in text]/ The breaking of the old unity and classical knowledge had brought discontent - see Tears of Muses [and notes continuing on another leaf] Spenser on trees and flowers. Show how he knows and writes [?] of their uses and their legends - tradition and use - not contemplation, not a personal song merely - F[aerie] Q[ueene] and V[irgil's] Gnat. See also Vol. IV, P. 464 [a ref. to Muipotmos," lines 172-200, the passage beginning "Of every flowre and herbe there set in order...."; this passage is marked in text and annotated as noted earlier].

1979. Spoelberch de Lovenjoul, Charles. HISTOIRE DES OEUVRES DE BALZAC. 2nd ed. Paris: Calmann Lévy, 1886. ii,498 pp.

*1980. Squire, J[ohn] C[ollings]. THE BIRDS and other poems. London: Martin Secker, 1919. 30 pp.

Some pp. uncut.

*1981. ———. THE LILY OF MALUD and other poems. London: Martin Secker, 1917. 31 pp.

Some pp. uncut.

*1982. ———. TWELVE POEMS. Decorations by A. Spare. London: Morland Press, 1916. 28 pp.

Inserted, letter from Austin Spare to WBY, 17 Nov. 1916, on letterhead of FORM, A Quarterly Journal (which Spare edited) requesting a poem for the second number (none appeared). At end of letter: If you can manage to send us anything it had better in view of recent events, be a poem of which you have not given the American rights to Miss Harriet Monroe! [see WADE 114 for the copyright problems resulting from the delayed appearance of the first number of FORM].

1983. Stalin, Joseph. THE OCTOBER REVOLUTION. A collection of articles and speeches. New York: International Publishers, 1934. 168 pp.

Marking and underscoring pp. 40 & 42.

1984. THE STAR (London). 10 March 1794.

Newspaper; in pencil [not WBY's] at top of 1st p.: See back. [At back, p. 4 is marked an article headed "Dublin/ March 4" which gives a few short items of Dublin news. Names mentioned are Lord Thurles, Mr. Blair, Mr. Bushie, Mr. Alderman Sutton, Mr. Duguignan, Capt. Witherington.]

1985. Stead, William Force. FESTIVAL IN TUSCANY and other poems. London: Richard Cobden-Sanderson, 1927. 55 pp.

Flyleaf: To/ W.B. Yeats/ with the friendship/ and veneration of/ W.F.S./ Nov. 1927.
Checked in Contents, "How Infinite are thy Ways," which is also excised in text for OBMV. Checked also but not excised, "The Dream" and "Paestum."

1986. ———. THE HOUSE ON THE WOLD and other poems. London: Cobden-Sanderson, 1930. 62 pp.

Flyleaf: W.B. Yeats/ from W.F.S./ 1931.

1986a. Another copy.

Flyleaf: W.B. Yeats from W.F.S. 1931.

1987. ———. LYRICS. Oxford: By the author, 1922. 20 pp.

On papercover: W.B. Yeats/ from WFS/ Feb 4th 1923.

1988. ———. THE SWEET MIRACLE and other poems. London: Richard Cobden-Sanderson, 1922. 76 pp.

Flyleaf: To W.B. Yeats/ from his disciple and friend/ the author/ May 6th 1922.

1989. ———. URIEL, a hymn in praise of divine immanence. London: Cobden-Sanderson, 1933. xv,33 pp.

Flyleaf: W.B. Yeats/ from W.F.S./ Jan 1933
Mostly uncut.

1990. ———. VERD ANTIQUE. Poems. Oxford: Basil Blackwell, 1920. 61 pp.

Flyleaf: To W.B. Yeats/ A True Poet/ with the sincere/ admiration of/ W.F.S.

1991. ———. WAYFARING, songs and elegies. London: Richard Cobden-Sanderson, 1924. 75 pp.

Flyleaf: To/ W.B. Yeats/ from/ W.F.S./ June 1924.
In Contents, check against "Image" which is excised from text.
In text, checked are "Flitting," "Communion," "Ambition."

*1992. Stenbock, Count Stanislaus Eric. THE SHADOW OF DEATH. A collection of poems, songs, and sonnets. London: Leadenhall Press, 1893. 79 pp.

Slight corrections in text, not WBY's.

1993. Stendhal. THE ABBESS OF CASTRO and other tales. Translated by C.K. Moncrieff. London: Chatto and Windus, 1926. x,269 pp.

1994. ———. THE CHARTERHOUSE OF PARMA. Translated by C.K. Moncrieff. 2 vols. London: Chatto & Windus, 1926.

1995. ———. SCARLET AND BLACK. Translated by C.K. Moncrieff. 2 vols. London: Chatto & Windus, 1927.

1996. Stephen, Leslie. SWIFT. English Men of Letters. London: Macmillan, 1927. x,[2],215 pp. Sig.: WBY

1997. Stephens, James. COLLECTED POEMS. London: Macmillan, 1931. xxii,260 pp.

Marked in Contents, "The Rivals," "In the Night," "The Main-deep," "Deirdre," "A Glass of Beer" (also excised in text for OBMV); also marked "Anthony O Daly" and "On a Lonely Spray" (in text).

*1998. ———. THE CROCK OF GOLD. London: Macmillan, 1913. 31,[1] pp. Sig.: GHL/ May 1914

1999. ———. DEIRDRE. London: Macmillan, 1923. [6],285,[1] pp.

Flyleaf: Hommage/ from James Stephens/ to W.B. Yeats.

*2000. ———. THE DEMI-GODS. London: Macmillan, 1914. vii, [1],279,[1] pp.

2001. ———. ETCHED IN MOONLIGHT. London: Macmillan, 1928. v,[1],198,[1] pp.

Flyleaf: To W.B. Yeats:/ The only things in this worth/ reading are "Desire," "Etched in Moonlight," &, perhaps, "Hunger."/ James Stephens.

*2002. ———. THE HILL OF VISION. Dublin: Maunsel, 1912. viii,131 pp.

Many marks and a few brief notes in Contents and text. In Contents, at "A Prelude and a Song": 1st 5 verses In Contents, at "What the Devil Said": lines 6, 7, 8. Also marked, "In the Poppy Field," "The Sootherer," "The Spalpeen," "Peadar Og...," "Under the Bracken," "Treason," "The Fairy Boy," "The Tree," "Eve," "Psychometrist."

2003. ———. KINGS AND THE MOON. London: Macmillan, 1938. vi,83 pp. Sig.: GY/ 1938

*2004. ———. REINCARNATIONS. London: Macmillan, 1918. viii, 66 pp.

Back flyleaf and inside back cover, a list of topics for an essay or a chapter of AUTOBIOGRAPHIES??:
Fall of Parnell 1891/ start of secede [?]/ content with old/ Irish Celts [3 words undecipherable] - Red Hugh/ all in next Ten years/ rhetoric - analysis/ The Gaelic mind/ old Tower/ small halls. Our own Theatre/ [one word?]/ Daughter of Erin/ [two words?] Synge 98/ His Wanderings
[the following inside back cover:]
realists/ People's Theatre/ not wrote but lives [??]/ 1910 [1916??].

2004a. Another copy.

*2005. ———. SONGS FROM THE CLAY. London: Macmillan, 1915. vi,106 pp.

2006. ———. STRICT JOY. London: Macmillan, 1931. v,[1],57 pp.

Mostly uncut.

*2007. Sterne, Laurence. THE LIFE AND OPINIONS OF TRISTRAM SHANDY, GENTLEMAN, and A SENTIMENTAL JOURNEY THROUGH FRANCE AND ITALY. 2 vols. London: Macmillan, 1900.

Vol. 1, many pp. uncut.
Vol. 2, mostly uncut.

2008. Stevens, Wallace. OWL'S CLOVER. New York: Alcestis Press, [1936]. 65 pp. 36/105. Sig.: Wallace Stevens

Flyleaf: To William Butler Yeats/ with the admiration of/ the publisher, R.L.L. [J. Ronald Lane Latimer].

2009. Stokes, Margaret. HANDBOOK AND GUIDE TO IRISH ANTIQUITIES COLLECTION. EARLY CHRISTIAN ART IN IRELAND. National Museum of Science and Art, Dublin. Revised by G.N. Count Plunkett. Dublin: His Majesty's Stationery OFfice, 1911. x,[2],189 pp.

*2010. Stone, Walter George Boswell. SHAKESPEARE'S HOLINSHED THE CHRONICLE AND THE HISTORICAL PLAYS COMPARED. 2nd ed. London: Chatto & Windus, 1907. xxii,532 pp.

Some pp. uncut.

2011. Story, John, ed. THE DAILY GUIDE, with Simmonite's Prognostications on Revolutions or Solar Figures. Showing the daily events likely to occur throughout the natal year of any person's horoscope.... New ed. London: Foulsham, 1891. 56 pp.

2012. Strachey, Lytton. ELIZABETH AND ESSEX. London: Chatto & Windus, 1928. [1],244,[14] pp. 1039/1060. Sig.: Lytton Strachey

2013. ———. QUEEN VICTORIA. London: Chatto & Windus, 1921. [10],314 pp.

2014. Strong, Archibald. THREE STUDIES IN SHELLEY AND AN ESSAY ON NATURE IN WORDSWORTH AND MEREDITH. London: Oxford Univ. Press, 1921. 189 pp.

2015. Strong, Mrs. Arthur [Eugenie (Sellers)]. APOTHEOSIS AND AFTER LIFE. Three lectures on certain phases of art and religion in the Roman empire. London: Constable, 1915. xx,293 pp. Sig.: GHL/ 1916

2016. Strong, L[eonard] A[lfred] G[eorge]. AT GLENAN CROSS. A Sequence. Christmas 1928. Oxford: Basil Blackwell, 1928. 14 pp. 80/100

Flyleaf: With every good wish/ and remembrance/ L.A.G. Strong.

2017. ———. DIFFICULT LOVE. Oxford: Basil Blackwell, 1927. [10],64 pp.

Flyleaf: W.B. Yeats/ with every good wish/ L A G Strong/ Magistro discipulus.

2018. ———. DUBLIN DAYS. Oxford: Basil Blackwell, 1921. 31 pp.

2019. ———. A LETTER TO W.B. YEATS. Hogarth Letters, no. 6. London: Hogarth Press, 1932. 31 pp.

2020. ———. THE LOWERY ROAD. Adventures All, New Series, no. 1. Oxford: Basil Blackwell, 1923. xi,[1],55,[1] pp.

Flyleaf: W.B. Yeats/ with grateful memories of/ Monday nights at No 4 Broad Street/ from L A G Strong
Mostly uncut.

2021. ———. THE MINSTREL BOY. A PORTRAIT OF TOM MOORE. London: Hodder and Stoughton, 1937. xiii,[1],317 pp.

Flyleaf: W.B. Yeats/ in friendship and gratitude,/ from LAGS.

2022. ———. NORTHERN LIGHT. London: Victor Gollancz, 1930. 66 pp.

Flyleaf: W.B. Yeats/ with every good wish for/ his complete recovery/ from L.A.G. Strong.
Some pp. uncut.

2023. ———. SELECTED POEMS. London: Hamish Hamilton, 1931. viii,[4],103 pp.

Flyleaf: The Mad Man p. 4/ The Old Man etc. p. 5/ Ena - Meena etc. p. 22/ A Moment p. 37 [39]/ By the Road p. 57 [but canceled]/ The Gray Navvy p. 34/ The Knowledgeable Child p. 14. [All excised from text except "By the Road" and "The Gray Navvy"].
"Two Generations" also excised in text.
Strong's 3 poems in OBMV are "Two Generations," "The Old Man at the Crossing," and "The Knowledgeable Child."

2024. ———. SEVEN VERSES. Christmas, 1925. No publishing info.

Inside frt. cover: With best wishes to Mr. & Mrs. W.B. Yeats/ for Christmas and 1926/ from L A G Strong.

2025. ———. TWICE FOUR. Christmas, 1921. No publishing info. 8 pp.

Inside frt. cover: Mr and Mrs W.B. Yeats/ with best wishes for/ Christmas and the New Year/ from/ L.A.G. Strong.

2026. Strzygowski, Josef. ORIGIN OF CHRISTIAN CHURCH ART. New facts and principles of research. To which is added a chapter on Christian Art in Britain. Translated by O.M. Dalton and H.J. Braunholtz. Oxford: Clarendon Press, 1923. xvii,[1],267 pp. Bp: WBY

2027. ——— and others. THE INFLUENCES OF INDIAN ART. London: India Society, 1925. 151 pp.

2028. Stuart, H. [Francis]. WE HAVE KEPT THE FAITH. Poems. Dublin: Oak Leaf Press, 1923. 52 pp.

Flyleaf: To W.B. Yeats/ from/ Francis Stuart/ Xmas 1923.
Slight corrections, not WBY's.

2028a-c. Three more copies.

2029. Sturm, Frank Pearce. ETERNAL HELEN. Cover and decorations by T. Sturge Moore. Oxford: Basil Blackwell, 1921. vii,53 pp.

Opposite title p.: To W.B. Yeats/ from/ F.P. Sturm/ 29.x.21.
P. 9, the title "Rosa Aegyptiaca/ VIII. Still- heart" has been partially canceled to read simply "Still-heart." It appears under this title in OBMV.

2030. ———. UMBRAE SILENTES. London: Theosophical Publishing House, 1918. [6],98 pp.

Opposite title p.: To W.B. Yeats/ from/ F.P. Sturm/ 18.xi.18.
Inserted, holograph letter from Sturm to WBY, dated 5.VI.06, Aberdeen. After explaining that Yeats's letter to him had been accidentally diverted by a friend, he writes: With regard to the talismans, if the information is not too late to be of use to you, I have come to this: To make a talisman for an aspect arrange it so that the threatened planet is symbolically the stronger. In the case of your own horoscope I would make a silver pentagram set in a golden circle, that you might have solar energy to direct the lunar dreams, and in the middle of the pentagram I would place an inverted symbol of Mars, the evil influence, together with a symbol of Venus, his opposing influence. [Also refers to WBY's forthcoming COLLECTED POEMS.]

SUB SPE, SEE J.W. Brodie-Innes.

2031. Suckling, Sir John. THE POEMS. Edited by John Gray. Decorated by Charles Ricketts. London: Hacon & Ricketts, 1896. cxvii pp. Bp: WBY

2032. Sutherland, A[lexander] C[harles]. DRAMATIC ELOCUTION AND ACTION. With appendixes on the influence of mysticism on dramatic expression. London: W.H. & L. Collingridge, 1908. 381 pp.

2033. Suzuki, Daisetz Teitaro. ESSAYS IN ZEN BUDDHISM. First series. London: Luzac, 1927. x,[2],423 pp.

Marginal strokes, pp. 120-44.
P. 120, line 15 at "enlightenment": will/ Daimon/ pure act.

2034. ———. ZEN BUDDHISM AND ITS INFLUENCE ON JAPANESE CULTURE. The Ataka Buddhist Library, no. 9. Kyoto: Eastern Buddhist Society, 1938. xii,288 pp.

Marginal strokes, pp. 13, 15, 17, 21.
P. 43, referring to final 10 lines: Imperial house continued in prosperity not for long.

2035. Swami, Shri Purohit. AN INDIAN MONK. His life and adventures. Introduction by WBY. London: Macmillan, 1932. xxvi,203 pp. WADE 281

In WBY's Introduction, the titles "Christabel" and "Kubla Khan" (p. xxi) have been underlined. Also "Sing a Song of Sixpence" (p. xxiii).
P. xxvi, the corrections "paints" to "Saints"; "Sainful" to "painful" have been entered; at bottom of Intro. the date is canceled.

2035a. Another copy.
Corrections entered on p. xxvi as in 2035.

FOR APHORISMS OF YOGA, SEE 1535.

FOR THE GEETĀ, SEE 738.

FOR THE TEN PRINCIPAL UPANISHADS, SEE 2114.

2036. Swedenborg, Emanuel. ANGELIC WISDOM CONCERNING THE DIVINE LOVE AND CONCERNING THE DIVINE WISDOM. Translated by J.J. Garth Wilkinson and Rudolph L. Tafel. London: Swedenborg Society, 1883. xvi,214 pp.

Title p.: Edwin J. Ellis/ to W.B. Yeats/ with/ best wishes
Facing title p.: There is no good will. Will is always evil ...... (the rest rubbed out) [Ellis's].
Half-title p.: W B Yeats/ April 20th
Facing half-title p.: The annotations copied on the margins are transcribed from the annotations by William Blake in the British Museum copy of this book. WBY. The Museum copy was originally belonging to Tatham [in ink; below this in pencil:] Any markings made by me are in pencil. WBY.
Yeats's marginalia passim, pen, as described above.
Pencil markings, pp. 26-29, 32, 33, 37, 53, 54, 57, 73.
P. 28, at lines 2-3: head downwards falling
P. 31, at 1st line: In Genesis light is created before the Sun.
P. 36, at lines 5-10 of par. 103: above is within

2037. ———. ARCANA COELESTIA. The Heavenly Arcana contained in the Holy Scripture, or Word of the Lord Unfolded in an exposition of Genesis and Exodus. 13 vols. London: Swedenborg Society, 1891.

VOL. 1 only (translated by John Clowes).
P. 1, "The heavenly Canaan and Jerusalem" is underlined and a note in pencil: so called by Blake.
P. 1, last par.: Hence the correspondence of the robe of blood which makes a garment (or body) for Ololon in Milton with the Scriptures (see also Luvah robe of blood).
P. 5, top margin: comparison of this chapter with Boehme's shows how much more Blake was indebted to Boehme than to Swedenborg for his fundamentals. [also:] mysterium magnum

P. 5, par. 7: quote apropos of the 2nd [?] book of the Georgic [?] of the sun

P. 5, par. 8: compare second book of Los

P. 6: This whole chapter shows how little Swedenborg found where Boehme discovered the entire basis of modern metaphysics. Swedenborg is at his weakest when face to face with fundamentals. He is a moralist much more than a mystical philosopher. His "correspondences" are always much less suggestive than Boehme's "signatures."

P. 6, par. 16, last 4 lines: Los.

P. 11, at "for whatever is insinuated into the memory ...": memory

P. 15, last lines of par. 32: the seeress of Provost saw also the symbolic sun (see Kerner's life).

P. 16, lines 7-8: "spectres"

P. 16, at "The life of faith without life is like the light of the sun without heat": quote in general account.

P. 17, last three lines: quote apropos of night.

P. 18, par. 40: quote apropos of fish and of the drawing in America on page 13.

P. 19, par. 41 at "like a bony and black substance": The [one word?] skeleton symbol

P. 20, lines 5ff.: Whales are the generals of <u>scientific</u>.

P. 21, at "Beasts are of two kinds; the evil, so called because they are hurtful, and the good, which are harmless. Evils in man are signified by evil beasts, as by bears, wolves, and dogs; and the things which are good and gentle": quote

P. 22, at the note: The Zoas

P. 27, par. 2: Beulah

P. 28, "Waters issuing out of the sanctuary": quote apropos of the waters coming from Temple in Jerusalem.

P. 30, par. 66: the four styles of Biblical writing.

P. 31, end of chapter: 1st symbolic (Mon-archic Church)
2nd allegorical (Blakean term) (ancient church)
3rd Prophetic } Jewish Church
4th Psalms }

P. 34, par. 78: The rivers of Eden

P. 35, par. 81, middle: quote apropos of Blake's use of the word Death

P. 35, par. 3: for these classes Blake substitutes his three classes - Elect, Redeemed & Reprobate [?]

P. 38, par. 89, at "Jehovah ... of the spiritual man": compare "he who dwelt in flaming fire" and notice that he is called Jehovah. Jehovah is celestial and has to do with △ [fire].

P. 39, par. 91: "offspring of peace": vapour equals peace/ compare "peace the human dress [?]"

P. 40, par. 96: nostrils

P. 44, par. 109: compare the waters from the threshhold of the Temple in Jerusalem

P. 44, par. 110, Havilah

P. 48, across length of page: Egypt and Assyria/ Assyria must be Egypt in action
P. 50, across length of page: The tree of good and evil.
P. 55, first 2 lines: spiritual equals 🜁 [air]/ here is birds
P. 56, first par.: Names
P. 57, par. 149: skeleton of Urizen
P. 57, at "Man's proprium when viewed from heaven, appears altogether like something bony ...": quote
P. 58, par. 151: compare building of the moon of Ulro.
P. 59, par. 156: compare Milton putting red clay or Urizen.
P. 62, par. 1: children riding the serpent in Blake
P. 63, par. 172: two angels in various Blake drawings

The annotations and underlinings stop abruptly at Chapt. 3, though a few additional passages are marked as noted.
P. 72, pars. 194 and 204, dealing with the eating of the fruit in Eden as equated with scientific knowledge, heavily marked.
P. 145, par. 425: brass, gold, silver.

2038. ———. THE DELIGHTS OF WISDOM RELATING TO CONJUGIAL LOVE. After which follow the Pleasures of Insanity relating to Scortatory Love. Translated by A.H. Searle. London: Swedenborg Society, 1891. xxviii,544 pp.

2039. ———. THE PRINCIPIA or the First Principles of Natural Things. To which are added the Minor Principia and Summary of the Principia. Translated by James R. Rendell and Isaiah Tansley. 2 vols. London: Swedenborg Society, 1912.

VOL. 1, marginal strokes and "x's," pp. 69, 72, 75, 80, 114, 115, 228, 350, 354, 358, 363, 364, 366, 372-375, 380, 381, 384, Appendix, p. 544 stroked passim; pp. 473-504 uncut.

2039A. VOL. 2, marginal markings pp. 60, 166, 169, 299-302, 307, 561, 573, 593, 594, 596, 615, 616, 630, 631; pp. 65-120 largely uncut.

Last flyleaf, recto: ⌛ stet [?] see page 555 ⌛

[on that p. principles 19-21 describing the motions of cones (or gyres) are boldly marked by a line and a diagram of a spiraling gyre seen from the top]. Facing the flyleaf above, a draft (pencil) entitled "A Crowded Cross" [A Needle's Eye]:

A Crowded Cross

All the stream that's roaring by

Came out of a needle's eye

They [two words?] drive (goad) it on [line canceled]

What is un [line canceled]

Things unborn things that goa [line canceled]

All that's unborn, all that is gone

The needle's eye - still goad[s] it on.

[First published in final form in 1934].

*2040. ———. THE SPIRITUAL DIARY. Being the record during twenty years of his supernatural experience. Translated by George Bush and Rev. John H. Smithson. 5 vols. London: James Speirs, 1883-1902. Bps: WBY

VOL. 1, p. 16, end of par. 156: Egypt/ Assyria/ Israel
P. 24, at par. 178: Blake's wind and bread
P. 29, at passage beginning "I will, however, relate one fact worthy of being recorded, namely, that evil spirits ... continually desire to excite animosities one amongst the other": Marriage of Heaven & Hell
P. 117, par. 365 stroked.
P. 224, at par. 651: Blake's "Four fold union"
P. 237, end of par. 692 stroked.
P. 431, par. 1371: Feacla [?] sees the dead in a kind of cocoon.
Back flyleaf: Earthbound spirits 237 [see passage stroked above]

2040A. VOL. 2, p. 58, at "dark cloud": Blake
P. 58, at "scaly": Blake
P. 84, par. 1852: Believe they [Spirits] are the man they are with.
P. 86, top of page: 'Head / Heart / Loins' } Heat of this order of being
P. 86, at par. 1858: heat too interior/ felt as cold
P. 86, at par. 1859: left foot
P. 86, at par. 1861: left arm
P. 87, mid-page: occiput
P. 88, top: bloody fibre
P. 97, at par. 1906: Blake's River Storge
P. 145, par. 2087: Sphere of Tervation [?]
P. 178, par. 2203: shape changing [annotations now in pencil]
P. 178, par. 2205: transformation
P. 312, par. 2662: fighting
P. 313, par. 2665: thinks they are S[wedenborg's] body
P. 314, par. 2665: obsession
P. 339: Blake's spirits of vegetable life/ Blake's moment less than a heart beat.
Back flyleaf: (1) Below and left [?] from old Jerusalem. Those who produce delight of his body - dancing etc. (2) opened corner of right eye - paralyzed delight
Pp. uncut passim throughout this vol.

2040B. VOL. 3, verso of title p., a large five-pointed star with a crescent moon and the word "spirits" above it. Below the figure of the star: Feet. The under feet [?] // Under the ear below the buttocks are offspring of perverted man. Ancient churches.
P. 16, par. 3295: Is this Udan-Adan?
P. 19, par. 3308: "a sigh is the sound of an angel leaving"
P. 27, referring to par. 3332: Spirits only speak what [one word?] Christ. Anecdote of [one word?] quote
P. 37, at par. 3375: right side of head/ cupidity breast
P. 40, bottom: hair of genitals
p. 43, at par. 3392: body
P. 45, par. 3398: head and feet [figure of a five-pointed star] Inverted man.
P. 440, par. 4507: front to left
P. 441, par. 4515: left - death
Pp. uncut passim.

2040C. VOL. 4, mostly uncut.

2040D. VOL. 5, mostly uncut, but p. 169, last few lines: Compare Songs of Innocence.

2041. Swift, Jonathan. GULLIVER'S TRAVELS. The text of the first ed. edited by Harold Williams. London: First Edition Club, 1926. cii,490 pp.

Flyleaf: To/ W.B. Yeats/ with regard and esteem/ and in memory of an/ afternoon at Riversdale/ 21 May 1933/ from/ Harold Williams.
Some pp. uncut.

2042. ———. GULLIVER'S TRAVELS AND SELECTED WRITINGS IN PROSE AND VERSE. Edited by John Hayward. London: Nonesuch Press, 1934.

Flyleaf: For William Butler Yeats/ with deep admiration & respect:/ John Hayward/ London: November 13, 1934.
Inserted at p. 374, a slip of paper: Diaries/ Typescript P. 16 [possibly WBY's]

2043. ———. THE WORKS OF THE REV. DR. JONATHAN SWIFT, Dean of St. Patrick's, Dublin. Edited by Thomas Sheridan. New ed. 17 vols. London: Printed for W. Strahan, B. Collins and others, 1784. Bps: WBY

Vol. 10, p. 118, a note, not WBY's.

*2044. Swinburne, Algernon Charles. THE DUKE OF GANDIA. London: Chatto & Windus, 1908. 60 pp.

Flyleaf: W.B. Yeats. June/ 08./ A[nnie] E.F. H[orniman].

*2045. ———. POEMS AND BALLADS. London: John Camden Hotten, 1871. viii,344.

Half title p.: Georgie Hyde Lees./ January, 1912.

*2046. ———. Second series. 4th ed. London: Chatto & Windus, 1884. ix,240 pp. Sig.: Georgie Hyde Lees/ October 1910

*2047. ———. SONG OF ITALY. London: John Camden Hotten, 1867. 66 pp. Sig.: Georgie Hyde Lees/ October 5, 1910

*2048. ———. A STUDY OF VICTOR HUGO. London: Chatto & Windus, 1886. vi,148 pp. Sig.: H.T. Tucker/ August 1886

SEE ALSO Items 165, 183, 186.

*2049. Symonds, John Addington. BEN JONSON. English Worthies. London: Longmans, Green, 1888. 202 pp.

Many pp. uncut.

*2050. ———. A SHORT HISTORY OF THE RENAISSANCE IN ITALY. Edited by Alfred Pearson. London: Smith, Elder, 1893. vi,354 pp.

A few pp. uncut.

2051. Symons, A[lphonse] J[ames] A[lbert]. THE QUEST FOR CORVO. An experiment in biography. London: Cassell, 1934. [12],293 pp.

Flyleaf: To W. B. Yeats from/ James Joy./ Palma, 25.12. 1935.

*2052. Symons, Arthur. AMORIS VICTIMA. London: Leonard Smithers, 1897. x,71,[1] pp.

*2053. ———. A BOOK OF TWENTY SONGS. London: J.M. Dent, 1905. 34 pp.

Flyleaf: To W.B. Yeats/ from Arthur Symons.

*2054. ———. CITIES. London: J.M. Dent, 1903. xi,261 pp.

Some pp. uncut.

*2055. ———. THE FOOL OF THE WORLD and other poems. London: William Heinemann, 1906. vi,118 pp.

Many pp. uncut.

*2056. ———. IMAGES OF GOOD AND EVIL. London: William Heinemann, 1899. viii,179 pp.

Flyleaf: To/ W.B. Yeats/ from/ Arthur Symons/ May 8: 1900.

*2057. ———. KNAVE OF HEARTS. 1894-1908. London: William Heinemann, 1913. xi,163 pp.

In Contents checks against "Fantoches" and "Mandoline" which appear in OBMV.

*2058. ———. LONDON: A BOOK OF ASPECTS. London: Privately printed for Edmund D. Brooks, 1909. 78 pp.

Half title p.: W.B. Yeats/ from Arthur Symons/ June 29: 1909.
Inserted, part of an envelope with a holograph poem "Eros in the Moon" by Symons.

*2059. ———. LONDON NIGHTS. 2nd ed. London: Leonard Smithers, 1897. xv,106 pp.

Flyleaf: To/ W.B. Yeats/ from/ Arthur Symons

*2060. ———. PLAYS, ACTING, AND MUSIC. London: Duckworth, 1903. [11],196 pp.

*2061. ———. POEMS. 2 vols. London: William Heinemann, 1902.

Vol. 1, flyleaf: To W.B. Yeats/ from Arthur Symons/ Dec. 1902.
Checked in Contents "The Opium-Smoker," "Javanese Dancers," "After Love," "For a Picture of Watteau," "On the Doorstep," "Behind the Scenes," "La Melinite: Moulin Rouge," "At the Ambassadeurs," "From San Juan de la Cruz. I. The Obscure Night of the Soul" [appears in OBMV], "From Paul Verlaine."

*2062. ———. THE ROMANTIC MOVEMENT IN ENGLISH POETRY. London: Archibald Constable, 1909. xi,344 pp.

Half title p.: To Agnes Tobin with an immensity of thanks, Arthur Symons.

*2063. ———. SILHOUETTES. London: Elkin Mathews and John Lane, 1892. [8],95 pp. -/250

Flyleaf: Dora L. Todhunter/ Christmas 1892/ from J[ohn] T[odhunter].

*2064. ———. SILHOUETTES. 2nd ed. London: Leonard Smithers, 1896. xv,91 pp.

Flyleaf: W.B. Yeats/ from/ Arthur Symons.

*2065. ———. SPIRITUAL ADVENTURES. London: Archibald Constable, 1905. 314 pp.

Flyleaf: To W.B. Yeats/ from Arthur Symons
Tales; many pp. uncut.

2066. ———. STUDIES IN PROSE AND VERSE. London: J.M. Dent, [1904]. ix,291 pp.

Flyleaf: To W.B. Yeats/ from Arthur Symons/ Oct: 30: 1904.
Contains "Mr. W.B. Yeats," pp. 230-41.
P. 233, a marginal stroke against "This poet cannot see love [to] and beyond the end of time."

*2067. ———. STUDIES IN TWO LITERATURES. London: Leonard Smithers, 1897. xii,310 pp.

*2068. ———. THE SYMBOLIST MOVEMENT IN LITERATURE. London: William Heinemann, 1899. vi,197 pp.

Flyleaf: To W.B. Yeats/ from Arthur Symons/ March 5, 1900.
P. 90 in "Paul Verlaine" underlined "The ideal of lyric poetry, certainly, is to be this passive, flawless medium for the deeper consciousness of things, the mysterious voice of that mystery which lies about us, out of which we have come, and into which we shall return. It is not without reason that we cannot analyse a perfect lyric."

*2069. ———. THE TOY CART. A Play. Dublin and London: Maunsel, 1919. 114 pp.

*2070. ———. WILLIAM BLAKE. London: Archibald Constable, 1907. xviii,[2],433 pp.

Flyleaf: W.B. Yeats/ from Arthur Symons

SEE ALSO Item 169.

*2071. Synge, John M[illington]. THE ARAN ISLANDS. With drawings by Jack B. Yeats. Large paper ed. Dublin: Maunsel, 1907. xii,189 pp. 3/150. Sigs.: J.M. Synge, Jack B. Yeats

Half title p.: W.B. Yeats, June 23rd, 1907

2072. ———. THE ARAN ISLANDS. Small paper ed. Bp: Lily Yeats

Half title p.: J.B. Yeats/ Churchtown/ Dundrum
Also a fine sketch of a woman, perhaps Lily Yeats, by JBY.

*2073. ———. DEIRDRE OF THE SORROWS. Dublin: Maunsel, 1911. [6],98,2 pp.

Two speeches on aging marked in margins, Deirdre's, pp. 41-2 and Owen's pp. 46-7.
P. 64, Deirdre's, last of Act II, marked in margin.
P. 94, whole p. stroked in margin.
P. 95, all but the first few lines stroked in margin and a note: From Here [not WBY's].
Pp. 96 and 97 also stroked.

*2074. ———. THE PLAYBOY OF THE WESTERN WORLD. Dublin: Maunsel, 1907. vii,[1],86,[1] pp.

Mostly uncut.

2074a. Another copy, mostly uncut.

*2075. ———. THE WELL OF THE SAINTS. With an intro. by WBY.

Plays for an Irish Theatre, vol. 4. London: A.H. Bullen, 1905. xvii,[1],91,[1] pp. WADE 262

Almost wholly uncut, including the intro.

*2076. ———. THE WORKS OF JOHN M. SYNGE. 4 vols. Dublin: Maunsel, 1910. Bps: WBY

VOL. 1, IN THE SHADOW OF THE GLEN, pp. 10-11, 26-7 uncut.

VOL. 2, some pp. uncut in THE PLAYBOY; in DEIRDRE the same speeches on aging marked as in 2073.
Bottom half of p. 192 stroked in margin; also pp. 193 and 194 (all but last three lines).
In "Translations from Petrarch" checked are "He wishes he might die....," p. 233; "He understands the great cruelty of death," p. 238; "Laura waits for him in heaven," p. 242. (All are included in OBMV.) At one time corners of other pp. have been turned back in the translations.

VOL. 4, some pp. uncut.

2077. Tagore, Rabindranath. CREATIVE UNITY. London: Macmillan, 1922. vii,203 pp.

Essays, uncut.
Inserted on a printed slip, "With the compliments of Macmillan & Co."

*2078. ———. THE CRESCENT MOON. Translated by the author. London: Macmillan, 1913. xii,82 pp.

Inserted on a printed slip, "With the Author's Compliments."

2079. ———. THE CURSE AT FAREWELL. Translated by Edward Thompson. London: George G. Harrap, 1924. 63,[1] pp.

Inserted, a letter of presentation from Harrap & Co., 8 Sept. 1924: We are hoping that this new edition will arouse renewed interest in Tagore's work.

*2080. ———. THE CYCLE OF SPRING. London: Macmillan, 1917. vii,134 pp.

Uncut.

*2081. ———. FRUIT-GATHERING. London: Macmillan, 1916. 123 pp.

Uncut.

2082. ———. THE FUGITIVE. London: Macmillan, 1921. vii,200 pp.

Mostly uncut.

*2083. ———. THE GARDENER. Translated by the author. [Edited

by WBY and T. Sturge Moore.] London: Macmillan, 1913. 150 pp.

Some pp. uncut.

*2084. ———. GITANJALI (SONG OFFERINGS). Translated by the author. [Edited by WBY]. Introduction by WBY. London: India Society, 1912. xvi,64 pp. Bp: Lady Gregory. WADE 263

Almost wholly uncut.

2084a. Another copy.

2085. ———. GLIMPSES OF BENGAL. Selected from the letters, 1885 to 1895. London: Macmillan, 1921. vii,166 pp.

Almost wholly uncut.

2086. ———. GORA. A novel. London: Macmillan, 1925. vi, 408 pp.

Uncut after p. 9.

*2087. ———. THE HOME AND THE WORLD. Translated by Surendranath Tagore and revised by the author. London: Macmillan, 1919. viii,333 pp.

*2088. ———. THE KING OF THE DARK CHAMBER. Translated by the author. London: Macmillan, 1914. 200 pp. Sig.: GHY/ July, 1914

*2089. ———. LOVER'S GIFT AND CROSSING. London: Macmillan, 1918. 117 pp.

Inserted, a printed slip, "With the Compliments of Macmillan and Co."

*2090. ———. MASHI and other stories. Translated by various writers. London: Macmillan, 1918. 223 pp.

After p. 104, only partly cut.

*2091. ———. MY REMINISCENCES. London: Macmillan, 1917. xi, 272 pp.

Cut.

*2092. ———. NATIONALISM. London: Macmillan, 1917. v,135 pp.

Essays, uncut.

*2093. ———. THE PARROT'S TRAINING. Translated by the author. With eight drawings by Abanindra Nath Tagore. Calcutta and Simla: Thacker, Spink, 1918. [7] pp.

Inserted, a typed slip, "With Author's Compliments." Prose fable.

*2094. ———. PERSONALITY. Lectures delivered in America. London: Macmillan, 1917. 184 pp.

Mostly uncut.

2095. ———. "The Philosophy of our People." Reprint from THE MODERN REVIEW (Calcutta). No date. 8 pp. Presidential address at the Indian Philosophical Congress.

On cover: To W.B. Yeats/ from/ Rabindranath Tagore

2096. ———. PHALGUNI (The Cycle of Spring). A musical play. Performed in aid of the distressed at Bankura. Jan. 1916. No publishing info. 15 pp. Sig.: WBY

See 2080.

*2097. ———. THE POST OFFICE. Translated by Devabrata Mukerjea. Preface by WBY. London: Macmillan, 1914. vii, 88 pp. WADE 268

Uncut after Preface.

*2098. ———. SACRIFICE and other plays. London: Macmillan, 1917. 256 pp.

Cut for "Sanyasi, or the Ascetic" only.

*2099. ———. SADHANA. The Realisation of Life. London: Macmillan, 1913. xi,[1],164 pp. Bp: WBY

Philosophical prose; cut is "art. IV, "The Problem of Self."
Inserted, a holograph letter of presentation from Tagore to WBY, 21 Cromwell Road, South Kensington, London, 2 Sept. 1912: It has been such a great joy to me to think that things that I wrote in a tongue not known to you should at last fall in your hands and that you should accept them with so much enjoyment and love.... We intend to leave England in the beginning of November. I do hope I shall be able to see you before that, and, if possible to have a sight of my translations published with your introduction.

I hope you will kindly accept from me a copy of the English translation of my father's Autobiography [presumably Devendranath Tagore's AUTOBIOGRAPHY, Calcutta, 1909] which I left with Mr. Rothenstein to be sent to your address.

*2100. ———. STRAY BIRDS. New York: Macmillan, 1916. 91 pp.

2100A. Another ed. London: Macmillan, 1917. 84 pp.

Uncut.

2101. Taki, Sei-ichi and others. THE YEAR BOOK OF JAPANESE ART, 1929-30. Tokyo: National Committee on Intellectual Cooperation of the League of Nations Association of

Japan, 1930. xvi,176 pp. 98 plates.
Includes Blake's "Death of the Virgin Mary," Plate LII.

*2102. THE TALE OF GAMELYN. From the Harleian MS. No. 7334 collated with six other MSS. Edited by Walter W. Skeat. Oxford: Clarendon Press, 1884. xxxix,64 pp.

2103. THE TALE OF KING FLORUS AND THE FAIR JEHANE. Translated by William Morris. Portland, Maine: Thomas B. Mosher, 1898. 73 pp.

2104. Talmage, James. THE ARTICLES OF FAITH. A series of lectures on the principal doctrines of The Church of Jesus Christ of Latter-day Saints. 10th ed. Salt Lake City, Utah: The Deseret News, 1917. xi[1],485 pp.

*2105. TANTRA OF THE GREAT LIBERATION (Mahānirvāna Tantra). Translated with commentary by Arthur Avalon. London: Luzac, 1913. cxlvi,359 pp.

Mostly uncut after the Intro.

*2106. Tasso, Torquato. GODFREY OF BULLOIGNE, or the recovery of Jerusalem. Translated by Edward Fairfax. London: Printed for H. Herringman, 1687. 655 pp.

2107. Taylor, A[lfred] E[dward]. A COMMENTARY ON PLATO'S TIMAEUS. Oxford: Clarendon Press, 1928. xv,[1],700 pp.

Half title p.: New [Read??] Title 1929 etc.
Many pp. uncut.
Pp. 89-90, marginal strokes; subject is Aristotle and two kinds of matter and 19th century views of perception.
P. 93, at note, "Before we can be expected ... before our telescopes reveal it": Why not?
P. 216, at top: Perfect Number
P. 217, at top: Magnus Annus [below are strokes against passages dealing with the Great Year and a further note:] Proclus on M.G. [a mistake for M.A.?]
P. 219, at top: Magnus Annus.

2108. ———. PHILOSOPHICAL STUDIES. London: Macmillan, 1934. viii,423 pp.

P. 177, corner turned back in Chapt. IV, "The Philosophy of Proclus."

2109. ———. PLATO. The man and his work. London: Methuen, 1926. xi,[1],522 pp.

2110. ———. PLATONISM AND ITS INFLUENCE. London: George G. Harrap, [1925]. ix,[1],153 pp.

2111. Taylor, G[eorge] R[obert] Stirling. AN HISTORICAL GUIDE TO LONDON. Illus. with 56 photographs. London: J.M. Dent, 1911. xii,345 pp.

Some pp. uncut.

*2112. Taylor, J[ohn] F[rancis]. OWEN ROE O'NEILL. London: T. Fisher Unwin, 1896. vi,[2],249 pp.

*2112a. Another copy. Paper covers.

2113. DE TELEGRAAF (Amsterdam). 24 August 1929.

Pp. 9-10 only; an article on Hildo Krop with drawing. Inserted in 2239.

2114. THE TEN PRINCIPAL UPANISHADS. Translated by Shree Purohit Swami and W.B. Yeats. Preface by WBY. London: Faber & Faber, 1937. 160 pp. WADE 252

P. 7, "Preface" canceled in pencil.
P. 12, "W.B. Yeats" canceled and inserted: 1937
P. 17, "Let out reality" revised to: Let out truth
[but the original marked "stet"]
P. 60, "undecided knowledge" revised to: unbroken knowledge
P. 152, at last two words a revision to: think of another

2114a. Another copy.

2114A. Another ed. New York: Macmillan, 1937. WADE 253

2114Aa. Another copy.

2115. Tennyson, Alfred. THE WORKS OF ALFRED TENNYSON. Cabinet Edition. Vol. 3: LOCKSLEY HALL and other poems. London: Henry S. King, 1874.

Half title p.: F[rancis] A. Yeats./ Xmas. 1875.
Facing half title p., a draft of a poem of seven lines, pencil, lengthwise across page, WBY's, but from the evidence of the handwriting, not an early poem as the style and edition would indicate:

there is a glade well loved by sweet melodious pan
[line canceled]
there is a flowery sunny dotted ~~shade~~ glade
Well beloved by sweet melodious pan
[two words canceled]
is a beech ~~whose~~ with roots with mighty span-
Within whose cool green shade
the fat sleek satyres love to lie
in its branches are of Birds a small [one word?]
None others [utters?] sing [song?] like them for to
pour their [one word?]
their leaden [??]
all day long [this entire last line
lightly canceled]

Back flyleaf, brief biological notes with drawings of cells, same hand as draft above.

2116. Teresa of Jesus, St. THE BOOK OF THE FOUNDATIONS. With the visitation of nunneries, the rule and constitutions. Translated by David Lewis. New, rev. ed. London: Thomas Baker, 1913. lxxv,[1],489 pp.

2117. ———. THE INTERIOR CASTLE, OR THE MANSIONS. Translated by the Benedictines of Stanbrook. Revised and annotated by the Very Rev. Prior Zimmerman. 3rd ed. London: Thomas Baker, 1921. viii,307 pp.

2118. ———. THE LIFE OF ST. TERESA OF JESUS. Edited by Benedict Zimmerman. Translated by David Lewis. 5th ed. London: Thomas Baker, 1924. xxxx,516 pp.

Marginal marks and underscoring pp. 63, 67, 71.
P. 67 marked and underscored, "I was able to think of Christ only as a man." Also marked below, "This is why I was so fond of images."

2119. ———. THE LIFE, RELATIONS, MAXIMS, AND FOUNDATIONS. Also a history of St. Teresa's Journeys and Foundations. Edited by John J. Burke. New York: Columbus Press, 1911. lxxxiv,727 pp. Bp: WBY

2120. ———. MINOR WORKS. Conceptions of the love of God, Exclamations, Maxims and Poems. Translated by the Benedictines of Stanbrook. With a short account of the saint's death and canonisation by the translator. London: Thomas Baker, 1913. xl,278 pp.

2121. THE THEATRE OF THE GREEKS. [Edited by John William Donaldson]. 3rd ed. Cambridge: J. & J.J. Deighton etc., 1830. viii,[4],572 pp. Bp: The Right Honble W. H. Gregory, K.C.M.G./ Coole Park, Gort, Ireland

Includes "The More Important Parts of Aristotle's Poetics," translated by Twining; "From Bentley's Dissertation upon the Epistles of Phalaris"; "From Schlegel's Lectures on the Drama."
Inside back cover, notes, not WBY's.

2122. THE THIRTEEN PRINCIPAL UPANISHADS. Translated by Robert Ernest Hume. With an outline of the philosophy of the Upanishads. Revised with a list of recurrent and parallel passages by George C.O. Haas. London: Oxford Univ. Press, 1931. xvi,587,[1] pp.

Flyleaf, verso: Edmund Holmes/ from H.C.P./ Christmas 1931.
Heavily marked and annotated, pencil, very likely preparatory to making the translation of THE TEN PRINCIPAL UPANISHADS with Shri Purohit Swami.

P. 41, at "an illusory world": opposite poles.
P. 43, at "it could not become an object": but it is.
P. 44, at "Knowledge of the real nature of Brahma ...": But how is knowledge to be won? Buddha answered this question.

P. 50, at "only ignorance and persistence in the thought of a separate self keep one from actually being it": See below
P. 50, at "the loss of finite individuality in the real Self that is unlimited is the supreme achievement" [underlined]: How is then to be achieved? See below.
P. 50, at bottom of p.: Only the real self knows the Real Self. How am I to find my real self. By becoming it answers Buddha.
P. 51, at "individuality and self consciousness must be lost ere one reach that infinite Real": Yes, but not consciousness of the real self.
P. 54, end of last par.: as in Christianity and Islam.
P. 58, at "Sophists in Greece": not necessarily a substitute.
P. 66, at "metaphysical knowledge": ? real knowledge
Chapt. X, at first par., a note on self-transformation as Buddha saw it and taught it is impossible to decipher.
P. 72, a long note at end of chapter: Not a word is said in this essay about the relation of Buddha to the Upanishads. His teaching bridges the gap between the undivided self (the Ego) and the Real Self. He shows us how to become what we really are, i.e. by a true transformation of our being. For a true understanding of Buddhism we must get to the essence of the Upanishads; and vice versa.
P. 110, end of 13: Who then does the person become?
P. 118, at "the past and the present and the future": = was becoming, is becoming, will become.
P. 139, at "goes creaking": becomes.
P. 177, at "Thus has there been a discussion": becomes [the word "becomes" appears a number of times marginally after this].
P. 274, bottom: 12.1.32
P. 281, at "Practise virtue (dharma)": Walk according to dharma, i.e. conscience.
P. 377, at "He verily, who knows that supreme Brahma, becomes very Brahma": and vice versa/ ask [one word?] R.D.
Inside back cover: P. 164/ nay-forsooth/ Lo verily.

*2123. THIRTY SONGS FROM THE PANJAB AND KASHMIR. Recorded by Ratan Devi [Mrs. A.K. Coomaraswamy]. Translated by Ananda K. Coomaraswamy. With a foreword by Rabindranath Tagore. London: Old Bourne Press, 1913. vii,[1],76 pp.

2124. Thomas, Dylan. TWENTY-FIVE POEMS. London: J.M. Dent, 1936. vii,47 pp.

2125. Thomas, G. Bevan. THE BANSHEE. Holograph ms. [24] pp.

A play; no other info.

2126. Thomas, Edward. THE AUGUSTAN BOOK OF MODERN POETRY, EDWARD THOMAS. London: Ernest Benn, [1926]. 29,[1] pp.

*2127. Thompson, Francis. THE COLLECTED POETRY. Royal octavo ed. London: Hodder & Stoughton, 1913. xix,[1],413 pp. -/2500. Bp: WBY

*2128. ———. NEW POEMS. Westminster: Archibald Constable, 1897. vi,[2],223,[1] pp. Sig.: JBY

Faint marginal strokes and underscorings in "Contemplation," pp. 14-17.
Slight sketches, pp. 87 and 90, possibly JBY's.
A paper slip inserted at pp. 86-7.

2128a. Another copy.

*2129. ———. POEMS. London: Elkin Mathews and John Lane, 1894. viii,[1],81 pp.

2130. ———. THE POEMS. [Edited by Wilfrid Meynell]. London: Oxford Univ. Press, 1937. xi,367,[1] pp.

*2131. ———. SHELLEY. London: Burns and Oates, 1909. 91 pp.

*2132. ———. THE WORKS. 3 vols. London: Burns & Oates, 1913. Bps: WBY

VOL. 1, many pp. uncut; inserted, a letter from Hannah I. Gardner, Appleton, Wisconsin, 21 March 1920 referring to WBY's talk in Appleton March 5, and questioning his interpretation of Thompson's "Lilium Regis."
VOL. 2, some pp. uncut.
VOL. 3, prose, many pp. uncut.

2132a. Another copy, Vol. 1 only, pp. cut.

THOMSON, James. SEE 608.

2133. Thoreau, Henry David. WALDEN. With an introductory note by Will H. Dircks. London: Walter Scott, 1886. xxviii, 336 pp. Sig.: WBY/ April 2nd 1886

Flyleaf, pencil: Solomon-/ Art apart from morals not decorative [?]/ universal mind/ The Moods-/ Art the experience of mood/ symbol-association/ universal mood/ -egotism/ perfection.

2134. Thorndike, Lynn. A HISTORY OF MAGIC AND EXPERIMENTAL SCIENCE during the first thirteen centuries of our era. 2 vols. London: Macmillan, 1923.

*2135. THREE CHESTER WHITSUN PLAYS. With an intro. and notes by Joseph C. Bridge. Chester: Phillipson and Golder, 1906. xiv,49 pp.

Contains The Salutation and Nativity, The Play of the Shepherds, The Adoration of the Magi.

2136. THE TIMES (London). "Blackfriars Theatre," 21 Nov. 1921. p. 5.

Inserted in 1218.

2137. ———. "Changing Russia/ The Bourgeois Proletariat/ Capitalism Again," 2 Dec. 1921, p. [10].

Inserted in 2229A.

2138. ———. "The Globe Theatre," [28 Oct. 1921, p. 8].

Inserted in 1218; mistakenly labeled Nov. 28, 1921.

2139. ———. "Jewish World Plot/ An Exposure/ The Source of the Protocols," [16 Aug. 1921], p. 9.

Inserted in 2229A which has special reference to this topic.

2140. ———. "The Protocol Forgery/ Use in Russian Politics," [16 Aug. 1921], p. 9.

Inserted in 2229A which has special reference to this topic. Identified and dated by WBY.

2141. ———. Review of THE OXFORD BOOK OF MODERN VERSE edited by WBY, 20 Nov. 1936, p. 10.

Inserted in 1972.

2142. ———. "Shakespeare and Blackfriars," 17 Nov. 1921, p. 5.

Inserted in 1218.

2143. ———. "The Theatre in Japan: III. The Art of the Doll," [18 Dec. 1919], p. 10

Inserted in 1637.

2144. ———. "The Theatre in Japan: IV. The Tokyo Stage," [2 Jan. 1920], p. 8.

Inserted in 1637.
In margin, likely WBY's: Edwin Ellis, 11 June 1848/ Bath/ 11 November 1916 [Ellis's birth date should be 14 June 1848; elsewhere Yeats gives 1918 for Ellis's death, but 1916 is correct; see Ian Fletcher, "The Ellis-Yeats-Blake Manuscript Cluster," THE BOOK COLLECTOR 21 (1972): 80].

SEE ALSO 122, 193, 433, 1408.

2145. ———. LANDSCAPE AND LETTERS. A series of twenty pictures from THE TIMES. [London: Times Publishing, 1933]. 20 plates loose in a folder.

"The pictures in this folio were taken by staff photographers of THE TIMES in districts which have provided the setting for some of our greatest literature." Includes "In Yeats's Sligo: 'The Lake Isle of Innisfree.'"

2146. THE TIMES LITERARY SUPPLEMENT. "Recent Philosophy/ The School of Husserl," Recent German Literature Number, 18 Apr. [1929, pp. xv-xvi].

In an envelope inserted in 1052, labeled: Article on recent German philosophy from "Times Supplement" ("German Supplement") April 1929.

2147. ———. Review of ARDOURS AND ENDURANCES by Robert Nichols, 12 July 1917, p. 330.

Pasted into 1432.

2148. ———. Review of MOUNT EVEREST by Sven Hedin, [21 June 1923, p. 422].

Inserted in 867.

2149. ———. Review of THE OXFORD BOOK OF MODERN VERSE edited by WBY, 21 Nov. 1936, p. 957.

Inserted in 1972.

2150. ———. Review of W.B. YEATS, A CRITICAL STUDY by Forrest Reid, [30 Sept. 1915, p. 331].

Inserted in 1733.

2151. Titis, Placidus de. PRIMUM MOBILE, with theses to the theory, and canons for the practice; wherein is demonstrated, from astronomical and philosophical principles, the nature and extent of celestial influx upon the mental faculties and corporeal affections of man. Translated with notes by John Cooper. London: Davis and Dickson, [1814 or 1815]. xv,[1],462 pp.

Annotated, but not by WBY; back flyleaf, a long note on how to find the longitude of a star, an early hand.

2152. TO-DAY (London). 1 (June 1917).

Includes WBY's AT THE HAWK'S WELL.
On cover: Lily Yeats/ June 1917 [also] "At the Hawk's Well" WBY [pencil, WBY's]

2153. Todhunter, John. FOREST SONGS and other poems. London: Kegan Paul, Trench, 1881. ix,[1],103 pp. Bp: Lily Yeats

Half title p.: W.B. Yeats/ from/ J. Todhunter/ June 1882 [possibly 1881].
P. 1, inserted (pencil) after "raging beak": The 3 Birds/ Judas, Judas!/ Thy cursed dead [?] has made the 5 wounds of Christ to bleed [WBY's?]

2154. Toller, Ernst. MASSES AND MAN. A fragment of the social revolution of the twentieth century. Translated by Vera Mendel. London: Nonesuch Press, 1924. x,57,[1] pp.

Inside frt. cover: Dublin Drama League./ 82 Merrion Square.

On blank p. facing opening scene and p. 45 bottom, four sketches for staging the play. The name Gordon Craig appears prominently in all the diagrams, apparently to indicate portions of the set (probably screens) he was responsible for. Two separate hands, one possibly WBY's.

2155. [Toorop, Jan]. DE KRUISWEGSTATIES VAN JAN TOOROP IN DE ST. BERNULFUSKERK TO OOSTERBEEK. Hague: Koninklijke Kunstzaal Kleykamp, [1921?].

16 large sheets, loose in a folder; 14 reproductions of Toorop's Way of the Cross.
Inserted, a 3 p. translation of the Dutch introduction by Maria Viola, in bad English.

2156. Towner, R[utherford] H[amilton]. THE PHILOSOPHY OF CIVILIZATION. 2 vols. New York & London: G.P. Putnam's, 1923. Sigs.: Oliver St. J. Gogarty

Some markings, especially in Vol. 2, unlikely WBY's.

2157. Toynbee, Arnold J[oseph]. A STUDY OF HISTORY. 3 vols. 2nd ed. London: Oxford Univ. Press, 1935.

2158. [TRAITÉ SOMMAIRE D'ASTROLOGIE SCIENTIFIQUE]. [189?]. No publishing info. Imperfect copy, pp. 113-72 only. Includes "Représentation du ciel de nativité," "Interprétation du ciel de nativité," "Périodes d'Influences" and "Recueil d'exemples célèbres."

TRELAWNY, Edward John. SEE 899.

2159. Trent, A.G. [Richard Garnett]. THE SOUL AND THE STARS. Reprinted from THE UNIVERSITY MAGAZINE, March, 1880. Revised and extended by the author. Halifax, Yorkshire: Occult Book Co., 1893. 30 pp.

Notes and marks, not WBY's.

2159a-b. Two more copies, one bound.

TURMAIR, Johann. SEE Aventinus.

2160. Turner, W[alter] J[ames]. BLOW FOR BALLOONS, being the first hemisphere of the history of Henry Airbubble. London: J.M. Dent, 1935. 298 pp.

A novel.
Flyleaf: W.B. Yeats/ from/ W.J. Turner/ London, April 1936.

2161. ———. THE DARK FIRE. London: Sidgwick and Jackson, 1918. 70 pp.

Flyleaf: P. 36
In Contents, a check for "Epithalamium for a Modern Wedding," p. 36, and this poem excised from text for OBMV. Some pp. uncut.

2162. ———. THE DUCHESS OF POPOCATAPETL. London: J.M. Dent, 1939. 316 pp.

A novel.

2163. ———. HENRY AIRBUBBLE, or in search of a circumference to his breath, being the second hemisphere of the history of Henry Airbubble. London: J.M. Dent, 1936. 303 pp. Sig.: GY

2164. ———. IN TIME LIKE GLASS. London: Sidgwick and Jackson, 1921. 66 pp. Sig.: WBY

Flyleaf: First Four Poems
In Contents poems checked are "In Time Like Glass," p. 1; "The Navigators," p. 2; "Giraffe and Tree," p. 4 (but the choice is queried); "Man with Girl," p. 22; "A Love Song," p. 50; "The Dancer," p. 51
Excised, pp. 1-12, 49-52 for OBMV; "Giraffe and Tree," and "Man with Girl" do not appear there.

2165. ———. JACK AND JILL. London: J.M. Dent, 1934. 52 pp. Sig.: WBY

Flyleaf: The Fall/ 41 to 48 [and this poem excised; not in OBMV].

2166. ———. LANDSCAPE OF CYTHEREA, record of a journey into a strange country. London: Chatto & Windus, 1923. 50 pp.

Poems.

2167. ———. NEW POEMS. London: Chatto & Windus, 1928. viii, 52 pp.

Flyleaf: p 6/ p 15/ ?p 47
Poems indicated are "An October Birthday," "Cafe-Haunters," and "Song" ("Who shall remember thee"); none appear in OBMV.

2168. ———. PARIS AND HELEN. London: Sidgwick and Jackson, 1921. 46 pp.

A long poem; mostly uncut.

2169. ———. PURSUIT OF PSYCHE. London: Wishart, 1931. 47, [1] pp.

A long poem.
Flyleaf: p. 21/ p. 19 (with marks)/ p 26/27 (with marks)
On p. 19, the top stanza, beginning "Symbols of Unsatisfied Desire" is marked.
P. 21 excised.
Pp. 26-7, marked are four stanzas, "The beloved she is like a bridge [to] the mouth's living wound!"
None of the above appear in OBMV.

2170. ———. THE SEVEN DAYS OF THE SUN. A dramatic poem. London: Chatto & Windus, 1925. 55 pp.

P. 44, Section III of "Saturday" marked; not in OBMV. Pp. 25-9 excised.

2170a. Another copy.

Flyleaf: p. 12-13/ p. 22-25/ 27, 29, 30 (to mark)/ 32-3 (to mark). [pp. 21-34 excised; there are nine selections from this poem in OBMV].

2171. ———. SONGS AND INCANTATIONS. London: J.M. Dent, 1936. vi,74 pp.

"The Word made Flesh?" and "Hymn to Her Unknown" excised for OBMV.
P. 4, "The Flameless Moon" checked; not in OBMV.

2172. ———. W.J. TURNER. The Augustan Books of Poetry. London: Ernest Benn, [1926]. 31 pp.

*2173. Tylor, Edward B[urnett]. PRIMITIVE CULTURE: RESEARCHES INTO THE DEVELOPMENT OF MYTHOLOGY, PHILOSOPHY, RELIGION, LANGUAGE, ART AND CUSTOM. 2 vols. London: John Murray, 1873.

Vol. 2 only.
Corners turned back, pp. 136, 137, 139, 142, 149, but possibly accidental.

*2174. Tynan, Katharine. THE FLOWER OF PEACE. A collection of devotional poetry. London: Burns and Oates, 1914. vii,[1],101,[1] pp.

Flyleaf: To Willie Yeats/ from his old friend/ the Writer/ in affection & admiration/ Christmas 1915.
Some pp. uncut.

2175. ———. A LITTLE BOOK FOR JOHN O'MAHONY'S FRIENDS. Portland, Maine: Thomas B. Mosher, 1909. ix,[1],56 pp.

Uncut.

*2176. ———. POEMS. London: Lawrence and Bullen, 1901. xi,[1],277 pp.

Marked or queried in Contents, some 19 poems: ? The Wind in the Trees, ? In May, ? Adveniat Regnum Tuum, The Nurse, Mater Dei (perhaps omit a verse), Slow Spring (two verses), The Weeping Babe, The Birds' Bargain, Immortality, Alice (two verses), The Legend of St. Austin & the Child, St. Francis to the Birds, The Children of Lir, Sheep and Lambs, Of St. Francis and the Ass, In Iona, A Gardener-Sage, Lambs, The Foggy Dew [includes the four poems finally selected for BIV].

P. xi, last of Contents, a list of poem titles: Sheep and Lambs, Mater Dei, An Old Song Resung [canceled], The Lambs, An Old Song Resung, Immortality, The Weeping Babe [one title undecipherable], Michael, Adveniat Regnum tuum, The Only Child, The Nurse [?], St. Francis and the Birds, St. Francis and the Ass, The Children of Lir, Bird Bargain?, The Garden, The Garden's Life, Blessings, Doves, [two titles canceled, unreadable], Slow Spring, Foggy Dew, Alice, To a Beloved Dear.

P. 74, top, at beginning of "The Legend of St. Austin and the Child": might do -- if wanted to fill space - subject matter good, form poor.

Marks in text passim.

2177. ———. TWILIGHT SONGS. Oxford: Basil Blackwell, 1927. 63 pp.

Half title p.: To W.B. Yeats/ from his old friend & admirer/ Katharine Tynan/ Oct. 1st, 1927.

Uncut.

Inserted, holograph letter from Katharine Tynan Hinkson to WBY, London, 14 Aug. 1927. Refs. to an enclosed portion of a letter from her sister Nora.

2178. Tyrrell, G[eorge] N[ugent] M[erle]. SCIENCE AND PSYCHICAL PHENOMENA. London: Methuen, 1938. xv,[1],379 pp.

Flyleaf: Description of the S[ociety for] P[sychic] R[esearch] people. // They all belong to the English upper middle class, they all admire Gilbert Murray, they all have risen on stepping stones of their dead selves to higher things, they are all scholastic. 'What would they say, did their Catullus walk that way'. [pencil]

Marginal strokes, moderately heavy, passim.

P. 52, 2nd to last par.: reporter to H.P.B[lavatsky].

P. 259, at "specific name" (underlined): yes, with S P R mediums

P. 268, bottom: one must not make too much of the man's [mere??] sensuous nature, that which sensitive receives. So my using of arrow & star. There it is the sensuous symbol that is received.

P. 321, referring to the middle quotation: Bodin declared that "the devil was a body politic." Gave examples when he turned out to be some evil human ghost.

Inside back cover, five drafts of a single line: Having come this way before/ or/ You have come etc./ or/ So you have been etc./ or/ What ~~you~~ have come this way before/ So you have come the path before. [Appears in Purgatory, Act 1, line 12.]

2179. Uddgren, Gustaf. STRINDBERG THE MAN. Translated by Axel Johan Uppvall. Boston: Four Seas, 1920. 165 pp.

2180. UKIYO-E TAIKASHUSEI (Ukiyo-e Masters). 18 vols. Tokyo: Taihokaku, 1930-1. Vol. 7: BUNCHO IPPITSUSAI.

Japanese text.
Flyleaf: To W.B. Yeats Esq./ from S. Oshima/ at Christmas/ 1933, Toyama, Japan.
Inserted, four large sheets, holograph, which list the titles of the pictures in English. Sixty-nine titles listed on 4 sheets.

2181. ULAD: A LITERARY AND CRITICAL MAGAZINE (Belfast). 1 (Feb. 1905).

Includes "The Ulster Literary Theatre," pp. 4-8 with a mention of WBY; also AE's poem, "A Prayer"; and Colum's "Beauty Forsaken. A Donegal Ballad."

2181a. Another copy. Bp: E.C. Yeats

2182. Unamuno, Miguel de. THE TRAGIC SENSE OF LIFE IN MEN AND IN PEOPLES. Translated by J.E. Crawford Flitch. London: Macmillan, 1921. xxxv,[1],332 pp.

P. 320, at bottom, a check mark.

2183. Ure, P[ercy] N[eville]. THE GREEK RENAISSANCE. London: Methuen, 1921. viii,175 pp.

VALENTINE, Basil. SEE Basilius Valentinus.

2184. Valéry, Paul. CHARMES. Paris: Gallimard, 1926. 125 pp.

2185. ———. EUPALINOS OU L'ARCHITECTE, précédé de l'âme et la danse. Paris: Gallimard, 1924. 221 pp.

2186. ———. LE SERPENT. With an English translation by Mark Wardle. Intro. by T.S. Eliot. London: Published for the Criterion by R. Cobden-Sanderson, 1924. 51 pp.

2187. ———. VARIÉTÉ. Paris: Gallimard, 1924. 269 pp.

After p. 77, many pp. uncut.

2188. ———. VARIETY. Translated by Malcolm Cowley. New York: Harcourt, Brace, 1927. xviii,283 pp.

*2189. VanBrugh, John. SIR JOHN VANBRUGH. Edited by A.E.H. Swaen. The Mermaid Series. London: T. Fisher Unwin, [1896]. 501 pp.

Contains THE RELAPSE, THE PROVOK'D WIFE, THE CONFEDERACY, A JOURNEY TO LONDON.

2190. Vasari, Giorgio. LIVES OF SEVENTY OF THE MOST EMINENT PAINTERS, SCULPTORS AND ARCHITECTS. Edited and annotated by E.H. and E.W. Blashfield and A.A. Hopkins. 4 vols. London: George Bell, 1897. Sigs., vols. 2, 3, 4: E. Reginald Taylor/ May 19th 1902

Vols. 2 & 3, many pp. uncut.
Vol. 4, some pp. uncut.

2191. Vasiliev, A[leksandr] V[asil'evich]. SPACE TIME MOTION. An historical introduction to the General Theory of Relativity. Translated by H.M. Lucas and C.P. Sanger. Introduction by Bertrand Russell. London: Chatto & Windus, 1924. xxiv,232 pp. Bp: WBY

Flyleaf: For "Mechanical" philosophy/ see especially passage/ marked on page 202/ WBY.
On p. 202, passage marked from "Berkeley's arguments [to] mechanical view of the universe."
Corner turned back, p. 127.

*2192. Vaughan, Henry. THE WORKS. Edited by Leonard Cyril Martin. 2 vols. Oxford: Clarendon Press, 1914. Bps: WBY

Both vols. uncut.

2193. Vaughan, Robert Alfred. HOURS WITH THE MYSTICS. A contribution to the history of religious opinion. 2 vols. in one. 7th ed. London: Gibbings, 1895. xxxviiii,[1], 372,x,383 pp. Bp: WBY

*2194. Verhaeren, Emile. THE DAWN (Les Aubes). Translated by Arthur Symons. London: Duckworth, 1898. [4],110 pp.

Many pp. uncut.

2195. ———. THE PLAYS. The Dawn. The Cloister. Philip II. Helen of Sparta. Translated by Arthur Symons, Osman Edwards, F.S. Flint, and Jethro Bithell. London: Constable, 1916. v,325 pp.

2196. VERONA. LA CITTA DI GIULIETTA. Verona: ENTE Provinciale per il turismo, n.d.

Guidebook.

SEE ALSO 1225.

2197. Vesme, Caesar de. A HISTORY OF SPIRITUALISM. Vol. 1: Primitive Man. Translated by Stanley de Brath. London: Rider, 1931. li,[3],286 pp.

*2198. VIDYĀPATI: BANGĪYA PADĀBALI. Songs of the love of Rādhā and Krishna. With illustrations from Indian Paintings. Translated by Ananda Coomaraswamy and Arun Sen. London: Old Bourne Press, 1915, xi,[5],191,[1] pp.

Flyleaf: W.B. Yeats from Ananda Coomaraswamy.

*2199. Vielé-Griffin, Francis. SAPHO. [Play in three acts]. Paris: Bibliothèque de l'Occident, 1911. 67 pp.

Some pp. uncut.

2200. Villiers de L'Isle Adam, Comte. AXËL. Paris: Maison Quantin, 1890. v,300 pp.

2201. ———. AXEL. Translated by H.P.R. Finberg. Preface by WBY. Illustrated by T. Sturge Moore. London: Jarrolds, 1925. 296 pp. 104/500. Sig.: H.P.R. Finberg Bp: WBY. WADE 275

VILLON, François. SEE 165.

2202. Virgil. AN ENGLISH VERSION OF THE ECLOGUES OF VIRGIL. Translated by Samuel Palmer. Illustrated by Samuel Palmer. London: Seeley, 1883. xv,[1],102 pp.

2203. ———. THE WORKS. Literally translated into prose by C. Davidson. New ed., rev. with additional notes by Theodore Alois Buckley. Bohn's Classical Library. London: George Bell, 1875. ix,404 pp.

2204. VISVA-BHARATI QUARTERLY (Calcutta). New Series. 2 (Feb.-April 1937).

Inserted slip, "With the Editor's Compliments" [K.R. Kripalani].

2205. Volpe, Gioacchino. HISTORY OF THE FASCIST MOVEMENT. Roma: Soc. An. Poligrafica Italiana, [1934]. 169 pp.

Uncut.
Translation of STORIA DEL MOVIMENTO FASCISTA, originally published as an article in ENCICLOPEDIA ITALIANA (1932).

2206. Voltaire. LA HENRIADE, POËME. Londres: Whittaker, 1835. xii,142 pp.

Slight textual corrections passim, hand unidentifiable.

2207. ——— THE HISTORY OF CANDIDE. Abbey Classics, vol. 7. London: Chapman & Dodd, [1922]. xxii,233,[1] pp.

2208. ———. LE SIÈCLE DE LOUIS XIV. 2 vols. Paris: Garnier Frères, [1922?].

Flyleaf, vol. 1: George Yeats/ from Tom McGreevy/ October, 1924.

WADDELL, Helen. SEE 1164.

WADDELL, Samuel. SEE MAYNE, Rutherford.

*2209. Wagner, Richard. PROSE WORKS. Translated by William Ashton Ellis. Vol. 8: POSTHUMOUS etc. London: Kegan Paul, Trench, Trubner, 1899. xxii,440 pp.

Mostly uncut; the "Posthumous" section, pp. 249 ff. almost wholly uncut.

*2210. Waite, Arthur Edward. LIVES OF ALCHEMYSTICAL PHILOSOPHERS. With a biblio. of alchemy and hermetic philosophy. London: George Redway, [1888]. 315 pp. Bp: WBY

Many pp. uncut after p. 49.

*2211. ———. THE REAL HISTORY OF THE ROSICRUCIANS. Founded on their own manifestoes etc. London: George Redway, 1887. viii,446 pp. Bp: WBY

Flyleaf: The pencil marks in this book seem to be the work of some members of The Hermetic Students. They read as if made in early 90's. W B Yeats.

2212. ———, ed. ELFIN MUSIC: AN ANTHOLOGY OF ENGLISH FAIRY POETRY. London: Walter Scott, 1888. xxxv,[1],273 pp. Sig.: WBY/ August 4, 1888

2213. Waite, Herbert T. COMPENDIUM OF NATAL ASTROLOGY AND UNIVERSAL EPHEMERIS. London: Kegan Paul, Trench, Trubner, [1917]. 212 pp. Bp: GY

Underscorings and brief entries passim, not WBY's.

*2214. [Wakeman, William Fredrick]. WAKEMAN'S HANDBOOK OF IRISH ANTIQUITIES. Edited by John Cooke. 3rd ed. Dublin: Hodges, Figgis, 1903. xvi,414 pp.

2215. Waley, Arthur. AN INTRODUCTION TO THE STUDY OF CHINESE PAINTING. London: Ernest Benn, 1923. xii,261,[1] pp., 49 plates. Bp: WBY

Inserted at Plate XLIII ("Rain" After Hsia Kuei), a bookmark from Yamanaka and Co., London with Chinese Epochs on verso.
Corner turned back, plate XXXI, "Lohan, Attributed to Kuan-Hsiu."

2216. ———. A HUNDRED AND SEVENTY CHINESE POEMS. London: Constable, 1920. xii,168 pp.

Many pp. uncut.

2217. ———. THE NÒ PLAYS OF JAPAN. With letters by Oswald Sickert. London: George Allen & Unwin, 1921. 319 pp. Bp: WBY

2218. ———, trans. THE TEMPLE AND OTHER POEMS. With an intro. essay on early Chinese poetry, and an appendix on the development of different metrical forms. London: George Allen & Unwin, 1925. 150,[1] pp. Bp: WBY

Some pp. uncut.

2219. [Walker, Sir Emery]. SIR EMERY WALKER [memorial]. Born 2nd April 1851/ Died 22nd July/ 1933. [London]: Privately printed, [1933]. [18 pp.].

Collects newspaper obituaries and letters of 1933.

2220. Wallace, William. PROLEGOMENA TO THE STUDY OF HEGEL'S PHILOSOPHY and especially of his logic. 2nd ed., rev. and augmented. Oxford: Clarendon Press, 1894. xvi, 366 pp.

Corners turned back, pp. 178, 186, 193.

2221. Walpole, Horace. THE LETTERS. Edited by Peter Cunningham. 9 vols. London: Bickers, 1877. Sig.: GY

Vol. 3 almost wholly uncut; vols. 4, 5, 7, 8, 9 mostly uncut.

2222. Walton, Izaak. THE LIVES OF DR. JOHN DONNE, SIR HENRY WOTTON, MR. RICHARD HOOKER, MR. GEORGE HERBERT, AND DR. ROBERT SANDERSON. New ed. London: Henry Washbourne, 1840. Bp: WBY. Sig.: C. Bowles.

A few marginal strokes in the life of Donne, possibly by earlier owner.

2223. ——— and Charles Cotton. THE COMPLEAT ANGLER. Edited by Richard Le Gallienne. Illus. by Edmund H. New. London and New York: John Lane, 1897. lxxxiv,427,[15 pp.

Flyleaf: W.B. Yeats/ from/ John Masefield.
Some pp. uncut.

2224. Ward, Adolphus William. SIR HENRY WOTTON. A biographical sketch. Westminster: Archibald Constable, 1898. iii, [1],171,[1] pp. Bp: WBY

A few initial and final pp. cut only.

2225. ———, G.W. Prothero and Stanley Leathes. THE CAMBRIDGE MODERN HISTORY ATLAS. 2nd ed. Cambridge: Univ. Press, 1924. xix,229 pp.

Some pp. uncut.

*2226. Ward, Richard. THE LIFE OF THE LEARNED AND PIOUS DR. HENRY MORE. With divers philosophical poems and hymns. Edited by M.F. Howard. London: Theosophical Publishing Society, 1911. xiv,310 pp.

Some pp. uncut.

2227. Warren, Samuel. A COMPENDIUM OF THE THEOLOGICAL WRITINGS OF EMANUEL SWEDENBORG. London: Swedenborg Society, 1909. xxxxii,776 pp.

Markings, pp. xxxviii, xxxix (Blake's year of birth marked), 2, 4, 6, 7, 8, 603, 604, 611, 612, 614, 615, 617-24, 626, 629, 630, 638, 643, 646-53, 662, 663, 691, 692, 697.
P. 619, midpage: personation/ unconscious.
P. 624, at first 2 pars.: All images in an intermediate state 'representative' symbolic.
P. 628, midpage: compare with change of seasons.
P. 642, last 3 lines: Compare revival of season in folk lore of Ireland.

P. 645: 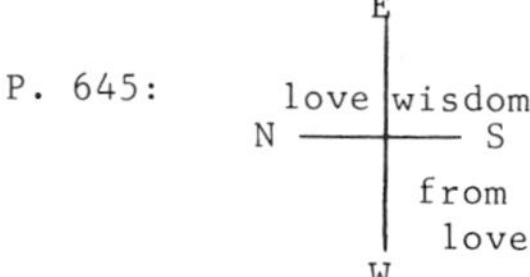

P. 653, midpage: Gold & Silver
P. 660, at "simulation": ?have they deceit
P. 661, first par.: Balzac tried 1) love of God 2) love of neighbour 3) love of self
P. 661, lower margin: see my own MS experiences [?] 1899 etc.
P. 684, at first 12 lines: They move to their spring?
P. 700, at "coverings": Term used in E R's script.
P. 700, at "dark forests ... wild beasts": Blake's Tiger.

WATSON, Rosamund Marriott. SEE 174.

2228. Webster, John and Cyril Tourneur. WEBSTER AND TOURNEUR. The Mermaid Series. [Edited by John Addington Symons.] Unexpurgated ed. London: Vizetelly, 1888. xxiii,432 pp. Sig.: WBY/ Oct. 9, 1888

Contains The White Devil, The Duchess of Malfi, The Atheist's Tragedy, The Revenger's Tragedy

*2229. Webster, Nesta H[elen]. THE FRENCH REVOLUTION. A study in democracy. London: Constable, 1919. xv,519 pp. Bp: WBY

Some pp. uncut.

2229A. ———. WORLD REVOLUTION. The plot against civilization. London: Constable, 1921. xi,327 pp.

Inserted, 2139, 2140.

2230. WEBSTER'S NEW INTERNATIONAL DICTIONARY OF THE ENGLISH LANGUAGE. Completely rev. General ed. London: G. Bell, 1924. cxii,2620 pp.

*2231. Weekes, Charles. REFLECTIONS AND REFRACTIONS. London: T. Fisher Unwin, 1893. viii,114 pp.

Flyleaf: To W.B. Yeats/ from the Author/ May 1893.

2232. WEEKLY SUN LITERARY SUPPLEMENT (London), 1 Dec. 1895.

Includes W.P. Ryan's "Poetry in 1895" with a one column discussion of WBY, with sketch.

2233. Weichardt, C[arl]. LE PALAIS DE TIBÈRE et autre édifices romains de Capri. Traduit par J.A. Simon. Paris: Schleicher Frères, [1902?]. vi,123,[2] pp.

2234. WEIRD TALES. SCOTTISH. London and Edinburgh: William Paterson, [1888]. 256 pp. Sig.: WBY/ Jan. 16, 1889

Includes stories by Sir Thomas Dick Lauder, Sir Walter Scott, John Wilson, Hugh Miller, Allan Cunningham, John Mackay Wilson and two anonymous stories.

2235. Wellesley, Dorothy. POEMS OF TEN YEARS, 1924-1934. London: Macmillan, 1934. xi,323,[1] pp.

Flyleaf: Copy for general anthology. [not WBY's; but there follows a list, WBY's, of poem titles, page numbers and page allotments, which partially corresponds to D.W.'s selection in OBMV:] Fire/ Horses p. 47/ The Arid Desert, 108/ Fishing, 177/ The Lost Forest, 109-216/ Tryst, 241-242/ The Buried Child, p. 249/ Cousin/ The Judas Tree // 8/ 6½/ 6

Some poems canceled in text, others excised; revised in pencil by WBY are "Lenin," "Cousin, I," and "Tryst, a Dream." For a discussion of this vol. and its relationship to the other copies of POEMS OF TEN YEARS and of the revisions as they appear in OBMV and D.W.'s SELECTIONS (edited by WBY), see Edward O'Shea, "Yeats as Editor: Dorothy Wellesley's SELECTIONS," ENGLISH LANGUAGE NOTES 11 (December 1973): 112-18.

Back flyleaf: D.W./ 30 July. Midnight/ Surrey [there follows a computation starting with the year of D.W's birth, 1889, apparently to determine that she was 46 years old in 1935].

2235a. Another copy.

On cover: W B Yeats (Notes)
Inside frt. cover: Hogarth Living Poets/ No 17/ A Broadcast Anthology [D.W. the author of these] // E. Sitwell/ Daphne/ The Sleeping Beauty [and much lower on page:] ?Dixon

Flyleaf: W B Yeats [there follows a list, WBY's, with p. allotments, which partially corresponds to his selection for D.W.'s SELECTIONS:] Portrait, 2½/ Horses, 2¼/ Asian Desert, 1½/ Fishing 2½/ Deserted Houses, 29/ The Buried Child, 1/ Crete, 1/ England,

1/ Sheep, 1/ Granmama, 1/ Arabia, 17/ Fire, 7/ ? The Old Mill, 3½ as cut/ ? The Sled Pond [canceled]/ [?] so pale, top, p. 13 ½/ The Poet and the Sower as cut/ Snakes, 2/ Lenin (as cut) [there follows a column of figures which added up yields (incorrectly) the figure 63, apparently an estimate of page allotments.

In text, deletions, revisions, and excisions of a number of poems; most but not all the revised poems appear in D.W.'s SELECTIONS. See note to 2235.

Inside back cover, a list of poems by Kipling, two of which appear in OBMV: The Coastwise Lights/ A Dedication [from Barrack-Room Ballads (?) or "To Soldier's Three"(?)]/ We are Dreamer's Dreaming Greatly (The Faery Alms) [? Kipling?]/ The Looking Glass/ St. Hellena Lullaby/ Danny Deever [and below this list another:] 'The Coastwise Light'/ 'The Looking Glass' / Danny Deever

2235b. Another copy.

Flyleaf: SELECTIONS (With Introduction by WBY) [there follows a list of poems as they appear in D.W.'s SELECTIONS, though "Cousin" has been altered to "The Thorn Tree" and "The Morning After" to "The Judas Tree." Hand not WBY's; likely GY's].
In text, the revisions made in 2235 and 2235a have been carefully copied in the same hand as above, though some new ones have been introduced. For an explanation of the place of this copy in the making of SELECTIONS, see the citation in 2235.

2235c. Another copy.

Flyleaf: To my friend/ W.B. Yeats/ from/ Dorothy Wellesley/ Aug 1935.
Many pp. uncut.

2236. ———. SELECTIONS FROM THE POEMS OF DOROTHY WELLESLEY. [Edited by W.B. Yeats]. With an intro. by WBY and a drawing by Sir William Rothenstein. London: Macmillan, 1936. xviii,126 pp. WADE 283

Flyleaf: W.B. Yeats/ from/ Dorothy Wellesley/ June 1936/ Penns in the Rocks
Some pp. uncut.

2236a. Another copy.

In Introduction, first par. has been canceled; also canceled WBY's printed signature at end of Intro.
Also an asterisk at Coleridge quotation at end of Intro. and a citation: Ode to Georgiana, Duchess of Devonshire, on the twenty-fourth stanza in her "Passage over Mount Gothard." [likely GY's; it appears this intro. was being prepared for a collection.]
Many pp. uncut.

2236b. Another copy.

Some pp. uncut.

2237. ———. SIR GEORGE GOLDIE, FOUNDER OF NIGERIA. A memoir. London: Macmillan, 1934. xiii,195,[1] pp.

Flyleaf: W.B. Yeats/ from/ Dorothy Wellesley.

2238. Wells, Warre B[radley]. AN IRISH APOLOGIA. Some thoughts on Anglo-Irish relations and the war. Dublin and London: Maunsel, 1917. 82 pp. Sig.: Lily Yeats

Reference to WBY, pp. 72-3.

2239. WINDINGEN (Antwerp). No. 1 (1927).
Contains photographs of works by Hildo Krop who produced the masks for THE ONLY JEALOUSY OF EMER.

Inserted, a photograph of a head or mask by Hildo Krop. On reverse, ink: Bronze [?] from the Mask for "Genesius."
Inserted, 2113.

2240. ———. No. 1 (1929)

Plates uncut.
Inserted, 1446.

*2241. Wentz, Walter Yeeling Evans. THE FAIRY-FAITH IN CELTIC COUNTRIES. Its psychical origin and nature. Ph.D. dissertation, Université de Rennes, 1909. xxii,314 pp.

Flyleaf: With the author's compliments/ to his Celtic friend,/ William B. Yeats, Esq./ Oxford, Aug. 17, 1909.

2242. ———. London: Oxford Univ. Press, 1911. xxviii, 524 pp. Bp: WBY

Flyleaf: With the author's/ best wishes to his/ friend and helper,/ William Butler Yeats, Esq./ Oxford, Nov. 24, 1911.
Some pp. uncut.
P. 57, at "voices like children's heard round Ben Bulbin [sic]": note - G[eorge] P[ollexfen] heard children-like voices at Rosses
P. 57, at "He looked into my face, and then let me go": In Swedenborg spirits commune with us by looking you in the face.
P. 58, at "wonderful music of Sidhe heard at Rosses Point": Yes, I have heard it - like cathedral bells. L[ucy?] M[iddleton?], G[eorge] P[ollexfen?] and I heard it.
P. 271, at mention of church ritual for exorcism of sick animals: Church Ritual
P. 281, corner turned back.

2243. ———. THE TIBETAN BOOK OF THE DEAD, or the after-death experiences on the Bardo Plane, according to Lama

Kazi-Samdup's English rendering. London: Oxford Univ. Press, 1927. xliv,248 pp.

Flyleaf: To my friend A.E./ with all good wishes,/ W.Y. Evans-Wentz./ Jesus College, Oxford, 13 August 1927.
Marginal strokes in brown crayon, pp. 8, 9, 11, 13, 15-17, 29-35, 44, 121, 157-60.
Page corners turned back passim.

*2244. Weston, Jessie L[aidlay]. KING ARTHUR AND HIS KNIGHTS. A survey of Arthurian romance. Popular studies in mythology, romance & folklore, no. 4. London: David Nutt, 1899. 40 pp.

*2245. ———. THE ROMANCE CYCLE OF CHARLEMAGNE. Popular studies in mythology, romance & folklore, no. 10. London: David Nutt, 1901. 46 pp.

*2246. WHEELS: AN ANTHOLOGY OF VERSE. [Edited by Edith Sitwell]. Oxford: Basil Blackwell, 1916. viii,84 pp.

2247. [Whistler, James Abbott McNeill]. OILS, WATER COLORS, PASTELS, & DRAWINGS. An exhibition at the galleries of M. Knoedler, 556 Fifth Ave., commencing April 2nd, 1914. [28 pp.]

Includes an introductory notice, "Whistler," by JBY.

2248. Whistler, Laurence. THE EMPEROR HEART. Decorated by Rex Whistler. London: William Heinemann, 1936. 54 pp.

Poems.

2249. ———. FOUR WALLS. London: William Heinemann, 1934. [6],51 pp.

Poems.

2250. White, Robert. THE COELESTIAL ATLAS, or a new ephemeris for the year of our Lord 1795. 46th imp. London: Printed for the Company of Stationers, [1795?].

Inked entries passim, as below, not WBY's.

2251. ———. London, 1797.

2252. ———. London, 1798.

2253. ———. London, 1799.

2254. ———. London, 1800.

2255. ———. London, 1830.

2256. ———. London, 1800-1811. Bound vol.

Inside frt. cover: A. Beresford

Flyleaf: Samuel Wilberforce. Sept. 7, 1805/ d. July 19, 1873 (afternoon). [not WBY's]

2257. ———. London: 1812-1824. Bound vol.

Inside frt. cover: A. Beresford
Inked entries, passim, not WBY's.

2258. Whitehead, Alfred North. SCIENCE AND THE MODERN WORLD. Lowell Lectures, 1925. Cambridge: Univ. Press, 1926. xi,[1],296 pp. Sig.: WBY

Very heavily marked and annotated throughout.
P. 105, at lines 6-12: Intellectually Completed Primary
P. 111, on a slip of paper inserted: P. 111 Whitehead// "The concrete enduring entities are organisms etc."/ This may scientifically explain what worried Dr. MacDonald (REMINISCENCES OF A MAYNOOTH PROFESSOR), p. 401 obsessed [?] with the necessity of reconciling Catholic Theology with a thoroughly scientific mechanism - the doctrine, formulated by the Council of Vienna, with anathema attached, that the soul is substantial form of the body
P. 114, top margin: The dry rib (Pope) becomes Eve/ (Nature) with Wordsworth.
P. 114, bottom margin: basic [one word?] focus [?]
P. 124, at line 7: Moore and Russell
P. 124, at "for as there is dependence ...": Compare Gentile whose form is itself activity
P. 126, top margin: In thought we transcend the mind, in action the will.
P. 126, at "our personal experience": What lies beyond men = B[ody of] F[ate]/ Self-transcendence = Mask
P. 127, at "self of his solitariness": self is not isolated - we share mental as much as physical images.
P. 129, top: "event which is the bodily life" = daimon
P. 150, refers to line 11: opposite to [?] rule of antithesis here, I think [?] is "almost possible."
P. 153, at line 17, "the external environment": Without
P. 153, at line 21, "various temporal sections": Within
P. 153, at lines 30-5: Daimon
P. 169, top margin: an event = a pattern of patterns endures through successive parts of event even in life history of pattern.
P. 170, at "the whole body": Unity of being.
P. 172, in margin, referring to "the two sets": an object may be contemporaneous with event, not contemporaneous with each other.
P. 175, top margin: substance = activity
P. 185, across right hand margin: See the poem of Blake where every particle of light shows itself as a minute human being.
P. 190, right hand margin: spatialisation = arresting
P. 191, top, referring to "quanta of time which are the successive vibratory periods of the primate":

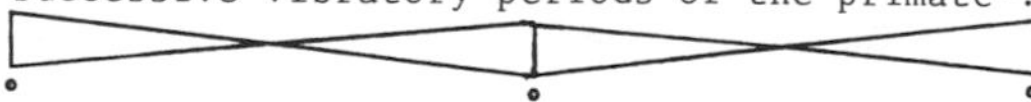

[The chapter "Science and Philosophy" is unmarked until p. 209.]

P. 209, at "private psychological field ...": C[reative] M[ind].

P. 210, referring to "are aspects of other events": B[ody of] F[ate].

P. 212, bottom margin: Pattern, activity, process as [is?] taken in relation to time may be substance. The pattern is not universal as are the sounds [one word?] etc., but event [??] is made by itself [?] within reason [??], to be unique in space for all time?

P. 217, bottom margin: Whitehead evidently feels and I think rightly that B[erkeley] intended no external Deus ex Machina but an internal urge of thought. There is a B[erkeley] letter bearing on this or a letter to him while he was at Rhode Island.

P. 222, at "among possibilities": Hence non-moral nature of Daimon.

P. 223, in text a "1" has been entered at "determinateness" and a "2" at indeterminateness": in (1) rainbow on (2) palette.

P. 224, top: determinateness of a = quality of the man implying daimonic passivity // determinateness of A = quality of daimon implying passivity of man.

P. 224, at "relationship between A & a" and "truth and falsehood": dual life of man in system. This is deep peace [??] after death.

P. 225, at last four lines: historic cones v. cones

P. 226, top margin: Daimon = the individual spatio-temporal continuum as distinct from particular individual occasions.

P. 232, top margin: method of realization of relationship is expressed by place of A in space-time scheme.

P. 236, top: Vertex

P. 236, in margin at lines 22-6, "This grade forms the base of hierarchy":

Vertex

proximate grade

P. 242, at lines 10-18: Does the predominance of "truth" survive p[hase] 22? Can it be present in p[hase] 23?

P. 247, bottom, referring to last 5 lines: Yet the individual activity must be individually eternal. The cause of the unique must itself be unique.

P. 249, at par. 3, line 5, "of actual occasions": world as illusion.

P. 276, at par. 2: p[hase] 16 to p[hase] 22.

P. 277, at "Wisdom is the fruit of balanced development": Goethe's idea of culture

P. 282, bottom, referring to lines 22-25: event here = Gentile's "becoming."

P. 284, along left margin: Blake saw the same thing.

Inside back cover: "events" = "souls"/ Aspects of other "events" = visible world/ Aspects are seen in patterns, which can be analysed with "eternal objects" (scents, colours etc.) and "enduring" objects (mountains etc.)/ The "eternal objects" are not localised in space./ What is the relation between "an event" & the aspect it shows of another event? What is its relation to the colour "seen" etc. which it shows as? Swedenborg makes spiritual beings define themselves by "colours" etc. to which they are related by correspondence - Whitehead's thought is hardly the same, but what is it? Do we not get very close to Berkeley if as Whitehead advises we accept "naive experience"? Do we not get a visible world which is the least common denominator of the imagined worlds of all individuals? Mohini Chatterjee thought this from which I assume it Brahmanism.

*2259. Whitman, Walt. THE BOOK OF HEAVENLY DEATH. Compiled from LEAVES OF GRASS by Horace Traubel. Portland, Maine: Thomas B. Mosher, 1905. xxi,[1],102,[1] pp.

Flyleaf: New York/ May 1906 [not WBY's]

2260. ———. POEMS. Edited by William Michael Rossetti. London: John Camden Hotten, 1868. xii,403 pp. Sig.: JB Yeats, Novr. 1869

Half title p.: J B Yeats/ 23 Fitzroy Road/ Regents Park
Sketches on flyleaves, likely JBY's.
Some marginal markings and underscoring.

2261. ———. SPECIMEN DAYS IN AMERICA. Rev. by the author. Camelot Series. London: Walter Scott, 1887. x,312 pp. Sig.: WBY/ 3 Blenheim Road/ Bedford Park

*2262. Wicksteed, Joseph H[artley]. BLAKE'S VISION OF THE BOOK OF JOB. With repros. of the illus. London: J.M. Dent, 1910. 168 pp.

*2263. Wiel, Alethea. THE STORY OF VERONA. Illus. by Nelly Erichsen and Helen M. James. London: J.M. Dent, 1904. xvi,314 pp., map.

2264. Wijdeveld, H[enricus] Th[eodorus]. AN INTERNATIONAL GUILD. A project. Santpoort, Holland: C.A. Mees, 1931. 17, [1] pp., 16 plates.

Flyleaf: To W. Butler Yeats/ respectfully/ H. Th. Wijdeveld/ July/ 1931 Amsterdam

2265. Wilde, Jane Francesca Speranza, Lady. ANCIENT CURES, CHARMS, AND USAGES OF IRELAND. Contributions to Irish Lore. London: Ward and Downey, 1890. xi,[1],256 pp.

Inserted, a slip of paper with note by GY: Marked by WBY.
Marginal markings, heavy, passim.
P. 64, at first par.: Friday [and the astronomical symbol for that day]

P. 65, the astronomical symbols for the days of the week have been added to the popular rhyme.
P. 91, at first par.: no they died.
P. 117, at "The number two is esteemed the most unlucky of all numbers.": Because symbolizes the first fall from Unity-Deity.
P. 118, line 5: Black sheep have to do with the fairies.
P. 121, at "no alteration in size is permitted of the death garments": quote [one word?] Sigerson story.
Many check marks against proverbs at the end of the book.

*2266. ———. ANCIENT LEGENDS, MYSTIC CHARMS, AND SUPERSTITIONS OF IRELAND. With a chapter on "The Ancient Race of Ireland" by Sir William Wilde. 2 vols. London: Ward and Downey, 1887-1888.

Vol. 1, half title p.: W B Yeats/ 3 Blenheim Road/ Bedford Park/ Chiswick/ London.
Some pp. uncut.
Vol. 2 (1887), title p.: T W Rolleston/ Jan. '87.
A few annotations, not WBY's.

2267. Wilde, Oscar. DE PROFUNDIS. London: Methuen, 1905. ix,[1],151 pp.

2268. ———. INTENTIONS. Leipzig: Heinemann and Balestier. 1891. [6],212 pp.

Slight note p. 212, not WBY's.

2269. ———. RESURGAM. Unpublished letters. London: Privately printed by Clement Shorter for distribution among his friends, 1917. 12 pp. 19/25. Sig.: Clement Shorter

2270. ———. THE RISE OF HISTORICAL CRITICISM. Hartford, Conn.: Privately printed by Sherwood Press, 1905. 45 pp. 42/225

Reprint of an early essay.
Uncut.

2271. ———. SALOME. London: John Lane, 1906. [6],65,[1] pp.

Title p. (red ink): W.B. Yeats./ Feb. 07/ The parts marked in red ink are those cut in the play as set/ to music by Richard Strauss. [WBY's ??]
In the text of the play, many deletions as consistent with the initial inscription; also numerous substantive revisions, in red ink, but the hand is <u>not</u> WBY's.

2272. ———. SEBASTIAN MELMOTH. London: Arthur L. Humphreys, 1904. [4],222 pp.

Uncut.

SEE ALSO 175,179.

2273. ——— and J.A. McNeill Whistler. WILDE V. WHISTLER. Being an acrimonious correspondence on art. London: Privately printed, 1906. 20 pp.

2274. Wilenski, R[eginald] H[oward]. A MINIATURE HISTORY OF EUROPEAN ART. London: Oxford Univ. Press, 1930. xvi, 80 pp., 24 plates. Sig.: WBY

2275. ———. THE MODERN MOVEMENT IN ART. London: Faber & Gwyer, 1927. xxii,237 pp. Bp: WBY

2276. Wilhelm, Theodor and Gerhard Graefe. GERMAN EDUCATION TODAY. 2nd ed. Berlin: Terramare Office, 1937. 44, [1] pp.

P. 45, annotations to the list of credits for the illustrations, one in German, not WBY's.

2277. [Wilhelmson, Carl]. CARL WILHELMSON [Swedish artist]. Sma Konstböcker, no. 19. Lund: Gleerupska Universitets-Bokhandeln, [1915?]. 64 pp.

2278. W[ilkinson], J[ames] J[ohn] G[arth]. IMPROVISATIONS FROM THE SPIRIT. London: W. White, 1857. viii,408 pp. Sig.: WBY, Oct. 1916

Mostly uncut.

2279. WILLIAM BUTLER YEATS, AETAT. 70. Reprint from THE IRISH TIMES, 13 June 1935. 16 pp.

Appreciations by Francis Hackett, Sean O'Faolain, F.R. Higgins, Denis Johnston, Aodh de Blacam, Andrew E. Malone.

2279a-d. Four more copies.

2280. Williams, Harold. DEAN SWIFT'S LIBRARY. With a facsimile of the original sale catalogue and some account of two manuscript lists of his books. Cambridge: Univ. Press, 1932. viii,93,16 pp.

*2281. Williams, Rose Sickler and others. CHINESE, COREAN AND JAPANESE POTTERIES. Descriptive catalog of a loan exhibition at M. Knoedler Galleries, New York, 2-21 March 1914. New York: Japan Society, 1914. x,[2],129 pp. 107/1500. Bp: WBY

2282. Wilson, Andrew. LEAVES FROM A NATURALIST'S NOTEBOOK. London: Chatto & Windus, 1882. [8],255 pp. Sig.: WBY

2283. Wilson, Harriette. HARRIETTE WILSON'S MEMOIRS OF HERSELF AND OTHERS. London: Peter Davies, 1929. xiv,671 pp.

Title p.: GY/ D[orothy] T. S[hakespear?] 6-11-29.

2284. Wilson, James. A COMPLETE DICTIONARY OF ASTROLOGY. London: William Hughes, 1819. xxii,410,[1] pp., 3 plates.

Flyleaf, an inscription partially torn away: [Poll?]exfen Esq. from John Varley - 1895.
Marginal markings, brief notes passim, not WBY's.

2285. Wilson, Mona. THE LIFE OF WILLIAM BLAKE. London: Nonesuch Press, 1927. xv,[1],397 pp.

Many pp. uncut.
Paper slips inserted, pp. 172, 300.
Inserted, two colored reproductions of Blake watercolors, "The River of Life" and "Jacob's Ladder."

2286. Wilson, R[obert] N[oble] D[enison]. THE HOLY WELLS OF ORRIS and other poems. London: John Lane, 1927. viii, 53,[1] pp.

Flyleaf: W.B. Yeats/ In homage/ from/ R.N.D. Wilson./ 19. Nov. '27.
Some pp. uncut.

WITHER, George. SEE 272.

2287. Wolfe, Humbert. HUMBERT WOLFE. The Augustan Books of Modern Poetry, first series. London: Ernest Benn, [1926]. iii,31 pp.

2288. ———. TROY. Drawings by Charles Ricketts. The Ariel Poems, no. 12. London: Faber & Gwyer, [1928]. [4] pp.

2289. Wollstonecraft, Mary. LETTERS TO IMLAY. London: C. Kegan Paul, 1879. lxiii,207 pp.

Title p.: To J B Yeats/ from Henrietta Paget
Some marginal strokes.

2290. Wood, Charles Erskine Scott. CIRCE. A drama with a prologue. Portland, Oregon: By the author, 1919. 94 pp.

On paper cover: Loaned to my friend Kathleen O'Brennan with full leave to lend freely but in the trust that it will eventually be returned to me at 1601 Taylor St. San Francisco./ Charles Erskine Scott Wood/ Aug 14- 1919-/ Marginal criticisms invited [but none here].

WOODS, Margaret L. SEE 182.

*2291. Worcester, John. PHYSIOLOGICAL CORRESPONDENCES. Boston: Massachusetts New-Church Union, 1895. iv,432 pp. Bp: WBY

*2292. Wordsworth, William. THE POETICAL WORKS. Edited by Edward Dowden. Aldine Edition of the British Poets. 7 vols. London: George Bell, 1892. Bps: WBY (all vols.)

VOL. 1, many pp. uncut; Dowden's "Memoir" cut.
P. 184, last page of "We are Seven": Impossible poem.

W.W. tries in vain to discover the words of the real child amid the sentimentality.
P. 189, stanza 4 bracketed.
P. 190, last page of "Anecdote for Fathers": As charming as "We are Seven" is abominable.
VOL. 2, check and stroke marks on pp. 88 ("A Night-Piece"), 98 ("Reverie of Poor Susan") and 307.
VOL. 3, some pp. uncut.
VOL. 4, some pp. uncut; p. 13, lines 265-280 of "The White Doe of Rylstone: Shape Changers" are marked.
VOL. 5 about half cut.
VOL. 6, p. 212, lines 806-13 in "Church-Yard Among the Mountains: Psychometry [? ; lines 829-31 marked].
Corners turned back passim.
VOL. 7, many marginal strokes and underscorings, and some comments in "The Prelude."
P. 46 (III.117-53 of "Prelude"): Compare Tagore writer of mystic happiness in nature.
P. 69 (IV.247), "Jupiter, my own beloved star!" underlined and a comment: Sound astrology. He must have been a [Zodiacal sign for Jupiter] man.
P. 152 (VIII.151-72): Note. Wordsworth leaves unused almost all this material. He has no folk life or very little, or uses folk thought in a way alien to it.
P. 157 (VIII.312-39): He is full of passages like this. True meditation gives no final form - prose and not always very good prose.
P. 160 (VIII.443-47): He really does this all through his life.
P. 215 (XI.300-05): The cause of his change. He does not seem to have been made afraid as is generally said by French revolutionary crimes or Napoleon but by a subjective concern.
P. 248 (XIV.158-60): Must have come upon him after 1808 or 9 for his powers then declined unless cause was purely aesthetic.
P. 250 (XIV.194-6), at textual reference to "cavern": Shelley's symbol.
In "Chronological Table," 329-31 marks against various titles, "Margaret, or the Ruined Cottage," "The Reverie of Poor Susan," "We are Seven," "Anecdote for Fathers," "A Whirlblast from behind the Hill," "The Thorn," "Goody Blake and Harry Gill," "Her eyes are Wild," "Simon Lee," "Peter Bell," "Tintern Abbey," "There was a Boy," "Three years she grew in sun and shower," "The Danish Boy," "The Prelude," "Nutting," "Hart-Leap Well," "The Waterfall and the Eglantine."

*2293. ———. THE PRELUDE OR GROWTH OF A POET'S MIND. [Edited by G.C. Moore Smith]. The Temple Classics. London: J.M. Dent, 1896. viii,264 pp. Sig.: WBY/ May 1897

Some pp. uncut.

*2294. ———. WORDSWORTH'S GUIDE TO THE LAKES. Edited by Ernest De Selincourt. 5th ed. London: Henry Frowde, 1906. xxxii,203 pp. Bp: WBY

2295. THE WREN BOYS. Dublin: Cuala Press, [1920]. 8 pp.

"Words and music taken down from groups of boys singing this traditional rhyme, from house to house, on St. Stephen's day."

2296. Wright, Thomas. THE LIFE OF DANIEL DEFOE. London: Cassell, 1894. xxix,432 pp.

2297. ———. THE LIFE OF WILLIAM BLAKE. 2 vols. Olney, Bucks.: Thomas Wright, 1929. Bps: WBY

*2298. Wycherley, William. WILLIAM WYCHERLEY. Edited by W.C. Ward. The Mermaid Series. London: T. Fisher Unwin, [190?]. xlviii,508 pp.

Includes Love in a Word, The Gentleman Dancing Master, The Country Wife, The Plain Dealer.

*2298a. Another copy.

2299. Wylie, Elinor. BLACK ARMOUR. Poems. London: Martin Secker, 1927. viii,[2],77 pp.

Checked in Contents, "Prophecy," "Drowned Woman," "Preference," "Let No Charitable Hope," "This Hand," "Parting Gift."
Checked in text, pp. 15, 17, 32, 68.
Excised probably for an initial selection for OBMV that was never used, pp. 19-20, 35-8.

2300. ———. NETS TO CATCH THE WIND. London: Alfred A. Knopf, 1928. vi,41 pp.

Checked in Contents and text, "The Eagle and the Mole."
Checked in text, "The Lion and the Lamb."

2301. ———. TRIVIAL BREATH. New York and London: Alfred A. Knopf, 1928. vii,80 pp.

Inside frt. cover: L[ennox] R[obinson]/ 1929.
Checked in Contents and text, "Confessions of Faith."

2302. Wynne, Frances. WHISPER! London: Kegan Paul, Trench, Trubner, 1890. 61 pp.

Half title p.: W.B. Yeats,/ from his affectionate friend/ K[atharine] T[ynan]/ Dec. 1890.
In Contents, titles checked, pp. 24, 28, 30, 32, 40.
P. 52, underlining in "This Life's Pleasant Days."
Excised, pp. 23-34, 39-42, presumably for titles marked in Contents.

2303. THE YALE REVIEW. 27 (Spring, 1938). Sig.: GY

Includes Archibald MacLeish's "Public Speech and Private Speech in Poetry," pp. 536-47 with a ref. to WBY, p. 544.

P. 538, marginal stroke against last 3 lines.

2304. Yashiro, Yukio. SANDRO BOTTICELLI. 3 vols. London and Boston: The Medici Society, 1925. 327/630

Inside frt. cover: W.B. Yeats/ from George Yeats/ February 4, 1926.
Vol. 1, Bp: WBY; some pp. uncut.

2305. Yeats, Jack B[utler]. THE AMARANTHERS. London: William Heinemann, 1936. [4],273 pp.

Flyleaf: W B Yeats/ With the love and good wishes of/ Dublin Jack/ August 17th, 1936.
A novel.

2306. ———. APPARITIONS. Three Plays. Apparitions. The Old Sea Road. Rattle. Illus. from drawings by the author. London: Jonathan Cape, 1933. 157 pp.

*2307. ———. LIFE IN THE WEST OF IRELAND. Drawn and painted by the author. Dublin and London: Maunsel, 1912. [10],111 pp.

2308. ———. SAILING SAILING SWIFTLY. London: Putnam, 1933. [6],169,[1] pp.

A novel.

2309. ———. SLIGO. London: Wishart, 1930. 158 pp.

Flyleaf: Miss Grigsby from W B Yeats, July 21, 1930.

2309a. Another copy.

Flyleaf: For W. B. Yeats/ from Jack B. Yeats/ June 4th, 1930/ good health now.

2310. ———. THE TREASURE OF THE GARDEN. Coloured by the author. London: Elkin Mathews, [1902]. Unpag.

Half title p.: To Lilly with Jack's/ love. Oct. 30th, 1902.
Includes a small sketch of an actor on a set.

2311. Yeats, John Butler. ESSAYS IRISH AND AMERICAN. Dublin: Talbot Press, 1918. 95 pp. Bp: Lily Yeats

Flyleaf: Lily Yeats/ June 28th 1918./ Dundrum, Dublin

2312. ———. "On the Stones," in THE MANCHESTER GUARDIAN, 28 Jan. 1905, p. 7.

A story.

SEE ALSO 704-8, 912.

2313. [Yeats, Susan Mary]. THE ORDER FOR THE BURIAL OF THE DEAD. London: For W.G. Barratt, n.d. 16 pp.

P. 2, In Memorian/ Susan Mary Yeats,/ Died 3rd January, 1900,/ Aged 58 years./ Interred in Acton Cemetery,/ 6th January.

2314. Yeats, W[illiam] B[utler]. [AT] THE HAWK'S WELL [Program]. Concert in aid of the Social Institute's Union, at 8 Chesterfield Gardens, W. By kind permission of Lord and Lady Islington. Under the patronage of Her Majesty Queen Alexandra. [4 April 1916].

Item 5 on the program which included music conducted by Sir Thomas Beecham.
On back of program, pencil: You must stop as the Queen has a bad throat & can't stay long [Queen Alexandra in fact attended the program and was forced to leave early because of hoarseness].

2315. ———. THE AUGUSTAN BOOKS OF ENGLISH POETRY. Second Series. Number Four. London: Ernest Benn, 1927. iv, [32] pp.

In Contents, numbers are entered before the first nine poems: 5, 6, 11, 12, 20, 22, 24, 27, 28 [likely GY's; possibly to indicate positions in a collected ed.]
Also in Contents, a note referring to poems from "The Hosting of the Sidhe" to end: All collated twice [GY's]
In Contents, right margin: accept this [GY's]
Pp. 8, 10 and on a slip of paper inserted at p. 24, the number "203" entered, possibly a galley number.
In text, the lines of "The Shadowy Waters" are numbered.

2315a. Another copy.

Bound in floral decorated boards; label affixed to frt. cover: Poems/ By/ W.B. Yeats
In Contents, many of the poems have been dated in the left margin, likely by GY:
"The Indian Upon God,": 1886
"The Indian to his Love": 1889
"Down by the Salley Gardens": 1888
"The Rose of Battle": 1888
"The Lake Isle of Innisfree": 1890
"The Fiddler of Dooney": March 1892
"Dedication to 'The Shadowy Waters'": Sept. 1900
"No Second Troy": 1908
"Fallen Majesty": 1913
"Men Improve with the Years": 1916
"The Collar-Bone of a Hare": 1916
"A Song": 1916
"To a Young Girl": 1915
Poems also dated in text, apparently at different times, for some are in ink, some pencil, again likely GY's.
In texts of these poems, many changes in accidentals, presumably also GY's; in most cases these first appear

in COLLECTED POEMS, 1933. Dates are given following only if they differ from those given above.
"The Indian Upon God": Oct. 1886
"The Indian to His Love": 1886
"To an Isle in the Water": 1886
"Down by the Salley Gardens": 1889
"The Rose of the World": Oct. 1891 (parts Jan. 2, 1892) [this must mean published, for it was first published in THE NATIONAL OBSERVER on 2 Jan. 1892]
"The Lake Isle of Innisfree": Oct. 13, 1890
"When You are Old": Oct. 20, 1891
"The Hosting of the Sidhe": 1893 [and in text "Caolte" corrected to:] Caoilte
"The Moods": 1893
"The Lover Tells of the Rose in His Heart": Nov. 12, 1892
Title "The Fisherman" changed to: The Fish [first in COLLECTED POEMS, 1933]
In "He Remembers Forgotten Beauty" "gods'" changed to: Gods' [first in COLLECTED POEMS, 1933]
"A Poet to his Beloved": 1895
"He Tells of the Perfect Beauty": Dec. 1895
"The Fiddler of Dooney": Nov. 1892
"In the Seven Woods": August 1902
"No Second Troy": Oct. 1908
"Fallen Majesty": Colville, 1913
"Men Improve with the Years": July 1916
"The Collar-Bone of a Hare": July 1916
"To a Young Girl": 1915
"Lines Written in Dejection": 1915

2315b. Another copy.

All the titles in the Augustan Books series are checked in margins.

2315c. Another copy.

In Contents, many poem titles are numbered from 5 to 204 (see 2315 for similar numbering) possibly to indicate placement in a collected ed.; also poem titles are bracketed and the section titles entered as in COLLECTED POEMS, from "Crossways" to "Michael Robartes and the Dancer." Likely GY's.

2315d-e. Two more copies.

2316. ———. AUTOBIOGRAPHIES. London: Macmillan, 1926. viii, 480 pp. WADE 151

Inside frt. cover: Corrected copy./ April 14, 1939/ G. Yeats
Flyleaf: Corrected/ see page/ 352
Second flyleaf: corrected/ see page 352/ 385, 152 [GY's]
Corrections and some identifications by GY on pp. 41, 96, 130, 152, 160, 161, 180, 181, 203, 217, 222, 262, 265, 266, 272, 278, 279, 352, 385, 387, 399, 411, 429, 450,

456, 457, 460, 461, 467. The corrections, some substantive, have not been incorporated in subsequent eds.
P. 130, section xxxii, at "when I heard that my grandmother was dead": 1892 [GY's as all following]
P. 217, section xviii of "Four Years," at "I brought a very able Dublin woman to see her": Sarah Purser
P. 411, end of section xvi: see 1930 Diary
P. 460, at "There was a London coroner in those days learned in the cabbala": Wynn Wescott

2316a. Another copy.

Flyleaf: George's own copy/ must not be taken by me/ W.B.Y. Oct. 7, 1926.
P. 359, after section III in "The Tragic Generation": Mss. p. 73 [GY's as are following]
P. 433, after "The Stirring of the Bones": Mss p. 39
P. 147, section iv of "Four Years": Mss IIIa
[These notations seem to be cross references only; no additional material has been added from mss. sources in subsequent eds.]

2317. ———. THE AUTOBIOGRAPHY. New York: Macmillan, 1938. viii,480 pp. WADE 198

2318. ———. CATHLEEN NI HOULIHAN. London: A.H. Bullen, 1906. 16 pp. WADE 62

2319. ———. CATHLEEN NI HOULIHAN. London: Bullen, 1909. 14, [2] pp. WADE 63

2319a-b. Two more copies.

2320. ———. THE CELTIC TWILIGHT. London: Lawrence Bullen, 1893. xii,212 pp. WADE 8

This copy was apparently presented to Lionel Johnson by WBY then returned to Yeats by Archie Russell some years later.
Flyleaf: Lionel Johnson/ from his friend/ W B Yeats/ Dec/ 93
Below this the bp of Archibald Russell and above: W.B. Yeats/ from his friend/ Archie Russell/ 24 May 1909.
Inside frt. cover: Sancte Joannes de Cruce

Ora pro amica meo
  Galielmo Yeats
Ut in Corpus Christi
  Mysticum
Ne pereat, intret.

Lionel Johnson

[and below this:]

Better than book of mine could be
Is this, where all enchantment blew
This book of Celtic phantasy
Made by the faeries and my friend.

Here will the charmed heart joy find.
The sounds of the ancient seas:
The wailings of the mistful winds
This all fair, strange things like to hear.

The fire and dew of Irish dreams
Shine here within a Twilight frail
This is the magic twilight gleam
The secret soul of Inisfail.

Lionel Johnson.

Pp. 88-9, "Gate of Horn" and "Ivory Gate" are transposed, possibly WBY's.
Added to printed list of Yeats's books at end are BLAKE'S POEMS and BLAKE'S WORKS, not WBY's.
Back flyleaf: [one word?] deep, occult philosopher
As learned as the Wild Irish sea
Havilias [not WBY's]
No nation in the world is more addicted to this occult philosophy than the wild Irish, as appears by the whole practice of their lives, of which see Camden in his description of Ireland.
Butler [not WBY's]

2320a. Another copy. Sig.: WBY

Some pp. uncut.

2320b. Another copy. Sig.: WBY, 5 May 1925

2320c. Another copy. Bp: Lily Yeats

Flyleaf: J B Yeats from Lily Yeats

2321. ———. THE CELTIC TWILIGHT. Dublin: Maunsel, 1905. [2],x,236 pp. WADE 37

2322. ———. THE CELTIC TWILIGHT. London: A.H. Bullen, 1912. [2],xii,224 pp. WADE 38. Bp: GY. Sig.: GY, Oct. 1913

In text, some comments in pencil, not WBY's.
Inside back cover: your young men shall see visions; your old men shall dream dreams [GY's]

2323. ———. THE COLLECTED POEMS. London: Macmillan, 1933. xvi,476 pp. WADE 172

Inside frt. cover: When WBY was correcting the proofs of this book he said "I have spent my life saying the same things in many different ways. I denounced old age before I was twenty, and the Swordsman throughout repudiates the Saint - though with vacillation". [GY's]
Flyleaf: George Yeats/ From W.B.Y./ November 1933
[below this]: The poems that have been dated in pencil in this book are dated by authority of <u>MSS</u>. [GY's]

Throughout this copy GY has methodically entered dates of composition and short quotations from WBY from mss. sources as well as some places of publication, alternate readings, and possible alterations and revisions.

In text, "The Song of the Happy Shepherd" retitled "Song of the Last Arcadia[n]"; also lines numbered through 13; "Xes" inserted before lines 13, 16, 17, 18, 20, 21, 42, 47, 48, 49, 52 as numbered in VARIORUM; after line 13 an earlier version has been inserted: Where are now the old kings hoary/ They were of no words moody.
After the poem: 1885 D.U.R.
Beside title "The Sad Shepherd," an earlier title inserted: Miserrimus
After the poem: D.U.R. Oct. 1886/ See letter from Robert Bridges
"Anashyya and Vijaya": title - "Jealousy" 1899. "Xes" inserted before a number of lines.
"The Indian Upon God": "Kanva, the Indian on God/ 1899/ (On the Nature of God. 1886. D.U.R.)
"The Indian to his Love": "An Indian Song" 1886
Many lines "Xed."
After the poem: D.U.R. 12/ 1886
In "Ephemera" some lines "Xed"; after the poem: 1884 Mss.
"The Madness of King Goll": 1st publication 9/1887
For "The Stolen Child" some earlier line versions are inserted.
"To an Isle in the Water": 1st publication Oct. 1886/ unchanged since 1899.
"Down by the Salley Gardens": "An Old Song Resung"/ unchanged since 1899 except for title
"The Meditation of the Old Fisherman": June 1886/ MSS. See changes
"The Ballad of Moll Magee": 1889 version.
Some earlier line versions inserted; at end: 1889
"The Ballad of the Foxhunter": MSS. undated
"Fergus and the Druid": Pub. NAT. OBSERVER, May 21, 1892.
"A Cradle Song": SCOTS OBSERVER, April 19, 1890.
"The Sorrow of Love": Mss. October 1891.
"When You are Old": Mss. Oct 21, 1891.
"The White Birds": NATIONAL OBSERVER, May 4, 1892
"A Dream of Death": Mss early version
"Who Goes with Fergus?": re-written Oct. 27, 1927
"The Man Who Dreamed of Faeryland": NATIONAL OBSERVER, Feb. 7, 1891.
"The Dedication To a Book of Stories Selected from the Irish Novelists": re-written at Coole. "I think that removes the last sentimentality." Letter to L.G.
"The Lamentation of the Old Pensioner": SCOTS OBSERVER, Nov. 15, 1890.
"The Ballad of Fr. Gilligan": SCOTS OBSERVER, July 5, 1890.
"The Two Trees": MSS.
"The Moods": First published Bookman, 8/1893.
"Into the Twilight": Mss "June 31" (1893?).
"He Mourns for the Change": 1895

"He Bids His Beloved Be at Peace": 1895
"The Cap and the Bells": NATIONAL OBSERVER, 17/3/94.
In "The Lover Speaks to the Hearers" in line 6, "the Attorney for Lost Souls" is underlined.
"He Thinks of his Past Greatness": re-written for 1922 ed.
"The Fiddler of Dooney": THE BOOKMAN. Dec. 1892. Written Nov. 1892.
In "The Arrow" at "Tall and noble but with face and bosom/ Delicate in colour as apple blossom": re-written Oct. 7, 1909. MSS Book XYZ
"The Ragged Wood": MSS Book XYZ Jan. 7, 1910.
"His Dream": MSS. Sept. 1909. Notebook XYZ/ "corrected version to poem written a year ago."
"A Woman Homer Sung": April 18, 1910. MSS Book XYZ.
"No Second Troy": December 1908. MSS Book XYZ.
"Reconciliation": Feb. 1909/ MSS Book XYZ. "Written about five [?] months ago."
"King and No King": December 7, 1909. MSS. XYZ.
"Against Unworthy Praise": MSS Book XYZ. May 11, 1910.
"The Fascination of What's Difficult": Sept. 1910. MSS. Book XYZ.
"A Drinking Song": Mirandolina [play by Lady Gregory]. See letter to Lady G. Feb. 17, 1910.
"The Coming of Wisdom with Time": March 1910. MSS. XYZ. [also a note too faint to read].
"On Hearing that the Students...": April 3, 1912. MSS. Book XYZ.
"To a Poet, Who would Have Me...": April 1909. MSS. Book XYZ
"The Mask": MSS. Book XYZ. 1911.
"Upon a House...": August 7, 1909. MSS Book XYZ with <u>note</u>.
"At the Abbey Theatre": Aug. 1911. MSS. Book XYZ. "Written in Paris, May."
"These are the Clouds": MSS Book XYZ. 1911
"At Galway Races': (early version Oct. 21, 1908/ Stella Campbell's album [?])
"A Friend's Illness": written a few days after hearing of Lady G's serious illness. See Vellum book XYZ/ note 50-2/ Feb. 1909?
"Pardon, Old Fathers": MSS signed "Dec. 1913. W. B. Yeats"/ "Jan. 1914"
"The Grey Rock": MSS 1913
"To a Wealthy Man": Dec. 24, 1912. MSS.
"To a Friend Whose Work ... ": See letter to Lady G. asking for IRISH TIMES report of the meeting of Dublin Corporation "as I may get a poem out of it."
"Paudeen": MSS./ Sept. 16, 1913/ Written at "The Prelude"/ Coleman's Hatch/ Sussex
"To a Shade": Parnell [and after the date as printed] Coole
"When Helen Lived": 1913/ MSS. undated
"On Those that Hated ... ": April 1910/ MSS Book XYZ/ 1909 (Wade).

Apparently referring to "The Three Beggars": Sept. 1913 MSS [and after this poem] 1913.
"The Three Hermits": March 5 ?, 1913/ see letter to Lady G.
At first line of "Beggar to Beggar Cried": "Time to be old and take in sail." Emerson? [and after the poem] MSS. "March 5?, 1913"
"Running to Paradise": Coole, Sept. 20, 1913.
"The Hour Before Dawn": MSS. Oct. 19, 1913.
"The Realists": MSS
"The Witch": May 25, 1912. MSS XYZ/ 1913 Nov. 16
"The Peacock": "This poem is companion to 'Toil and grow rich' which you know [two words undecipherable] WB Yeats" / Written to O[livia] S[hakespear]. In [?] letter except the poem was torn off. G.Y. [at end of poem]: see letter (torn) to O.S.
"The Mountain Tomb": MSS. Colleville 1912
"To a Child Dancing in the Wind": MSS. "Colleville" (1912)
"Two Years Later": December 3. MSS [followed by an erasure]
"Fallen Majesty": Colleville. MSS. 1912.
"Friends": January 1911. MSS.
"The Magi": Sept. 1913.
"The Dolls": "Xmas 1912" & 1913.
"A Coat": 1912 MSS.
"While, I from that reed-throated ... ": 1914
"In Memory of Major Robert Gregory": 1918-19
"An Irish Airman Foresees His Death": 1918. MSS. undated.
"Men Improve with the Years": July 19, 1916. MSS.
"The Collar-Bone of a Hare": "July 5" 1916 MSS.
"Under the Round Tower": Glendalough. 1918.
"Solomon to Sheba": 1918. Glendalough.
"The Living Beauty": MSS. 1917. First published 1918 Oct.
"A Song": 1915.
"To a Young Beauty": Iseult Gonne
"To a Young Girl": 1918/ Iseult Gonne [and after the poem] 1913-15.
"The Scholars": 1914/ "April 1915"
"Tom O'Roughley": re-written 1929 [and after] 1918.
"Shepherd and Goatherd": "I am trying a poem in manner like the one Spenser wrote for Sir Philip Sydney" Feb. 22, 1918 to Lady G. [and after] "a pastoral modelled on what Virgil wrote for some friend of his." March 19, 1918 to Lady G. [at end of poem]: Glendalough. March 1918.
"Lines Written in Dejection": 1915
"The Dawn": Sept. 1916
"On Woman": May 25, 1914
"The Fisherman": June 4, 1914/ Brown leather MSS
Book "from Maud Gonne. Xmas 1916"
"The Hawk," before last stanza: MSS to here
"Memory": MSS. undated
"Her Praise": MSS Jan. 27, 1915
"The People": Jan. 10, 1915. MSS.

"His Phoenix," after line 16: Sept. 1915
"His Phoenix," next to line 17: See WBY MSS note to typescript.
"His Phoenix," after the poem: Mss. "Jan 1915" "W.B. Yeats"
"A Thought from Propertius": MSS. undated. "Coole Park Paper"
"Broken Dreams": 1st 2 stanzas Oct. 24, 1915.
"A Deep-Sworn Vow": Oct. 17, 1915
"Presences": November 1915. (1 MSS. undated)
"The Balloon of the Mind": MSS. undated.
"To a Squirrel at Kyle-Na-No": MSS. Sept. 1912.
"On Being Asked for a War Poem": Feb. 6, 1915.
"In Memory of Alfred Pollexfen": MSS. "WBY August 1916" See letter to Lady G. Jan. 24, 1917.
"Upon a Dying Lady"
I. Her Courtesy: MSS. Jan. 1913.
II. Certain Artists bring her Dolls and Drawings: Jan. 1912.
IV. The End of Day: MSS
"Ego Dominus Tuus," at "The struggle of the fly in the marmalade": Coleridge [and below] Landor's phrase? At end of poem: "Oct. 5, 1915" first published Nov. 1917.
"A Prayer on Going into My House": 1918 (MSS. undated)
"The Phases of the Moon": MSS. undated.
"The Cat and the Moon": Colleville 1917 (MSS undated)
"Two Songs of a Fool": 1918 Ballinamantane
"Michael Robartes and the Dancer," 1st 8 lines: St. George with Dragon. Paris Bordone [?]. National Gallery, Dublin. [and at end] 1918. 96 Stephen's Green
"Solomon and the Witch": 1918 Glendalough
"An Image from a Past Life": Summer 1919. Ballylee.
"Sixteen Dead Men," stanza 2: see letter from Lady G. 1914-5. [and at end] "Oct. 17, 1917 (?) 1916" See MSS. Also letter to Lady G. Oct. 17, 1917.
"The Rose Tree": April 7, 1917.
"On a Political Prisoner": Jan. 10, Jan. 29, 1919 at Lucan. See letter to Lady G. Jan. 29, 1919.
"The Leaders of the Crowd": 1918-19.
"Towards Break of Day": Enniskerry Dec. 1918. A dream. See MSS in early version script book. Dec. 1918.
"Demon and Beast," at "old Luke Wadding's portrait": National Portrait Gallery, Dublin.
"Demon and Beast," at "Beside the little lake": Stephen's Green, Dublin.
"Demon and Beast," at "exultant Anthony": Thebaid
"Demon and Beast," at end: Nov. 23, 1918. MSS.
"The Second Coming": 1919 (1st published 1920)
"A Prayer for My Daughter": 1st drafted April 1919
"A Meditation in Time of War": Nov. 1914
"To be Carved on a Stone at Thoor Ballylee": 1918
"Sailing to Byzantium": 1st draft. See rather Augustan Variorum ed. [and at end] MSS. Sept. 26, 1926.

"The Tower": October 7, 1925
"Meditations in Time of Civil War"
I. Ancestral Houses, at "O what if gardens where the peacock strays": Garsington
"Nineteen Hundred and Nineteen": 1919-1922
"The Wheel": Sept. 1921. Euston Station on way to Dublin.
"The New Faces": MSS. December 1912. MSS Book XYZ and note.
"A Prayer for my Son": (1921? [and at end] 1922 Oct.
"Two Songs from a Play": Resurrection. See letter from Coole
"Fragments": See letter
"Leda and the Swan": September 1923. MSS Book XYZ.
"Among School Children," section VI: See letter to O.S. Sept. 24, 1926. [and at end] June 14, 1926.
"Owen Aherne and his Dancers": October 24, 29, 1917.
"A Man Young and Old," section I: Letter to O.S. Oct. 7, 1926/ May 25
"A Man Young and Old," section IV: MSS. Jan. 31, 1926
"A Man Young and Old," section XI: First version in letter to O.S. March 13, 1927. [also] 1926-7.
"In Memory of Eva Gore-Booth and Con Markiewicz": Seville. November.
"Death": (Kevin O'Higgins) Sept. 13, 1927.
"A Dialogue of Self and Soul": July-December 1927
"Blood and the Moon": MSS. dated August 1927
"Oil and Blood," first stanza: St. Theresa
"Oil and Blood," at end: 1928-9.
"Veronica's Napkin": Suggested by a conversation with Iseult [and at end] Portofino 1929. "Oct. 1930"
"Symbols": See letter to O.S. Oct. 2, 1927 [and at end] Oct. 1927
"Spilt Milk": November 8, 1930 in letter to G.Y. of that date.
"The Nineteenth Century and After": 1929 March 2. See first version at end of volume
"Statistics": 1931 (Passive) [?]
"Three Movements": (Goethe to end of Romanticism) [at end] January 26, 1932.
"The Seven Sages": January 30, 1931
"The Crazed Moon": "a lyric written in 1923 and lost. Just found in August 1930" (Rapallo MSS. book. 1928-30).
"Coole Park, 1929": See letter to G.Y., 1931. [and at phrase "the mounting swan"] See letter to G.Y., Feb. 3, 1931. [and at end of poem] Written at Coole - 1930. Final version on February 13, 1932.
"For Anne Gregory": Sept. 1930 (at Coole)
"Swift's Epitaph": Written at Coole 1929? Sept.-1930.
"At Algeciras - A Meditation upon Death": Algeciras-Hotel Reina Justine [?] "Feb. 4, 1929"
"Mohini Chatterjee": "Feb. 9, 1929" MSS Book
"Byzantium": September 1930
"The Mother of God," after 1st stanza: Sept. 3, 1931 [and at end of poem] re-written September 12, 1931

"Vacillation," after title: Coole. 1931 [and at "A tree there is"] Mabinogion, page 49 [?] [and referring to the rest of the stanza] See alphabetical book of notes used for "Vision" under "Planets." [and at "Attis' image hangs"] Julian - Hymn to the Mother of the Gods.
Before section VI: See letter to G.Y. Jan. 1, 1931 "notes to a Chinese book." [and at "Let all things pass away."] "Homer was wrong in saying 'would that strife might perish from gods and men.' He did not see that he was praying for the destruction of the universe; for, if his prayers were heard, all things would pass away." Heraclitus. [and at end] Jan.-March 5, 1931 at Coole.
At section VII: See letter to O.S. Jan 3, 1932.
At section VIII: January 3, 1932 [also in margin] Seville. See letter to G.Y. 1931.
"Quarrel in Old Age": Nov. 1931
"The Results of Thought": August 18 and 28th, 1931
"Remorse for Intemperate Speech": MSS. Written at Francis and Iseult Stuart's house.
"Crazy Jane and the Bishop": See letter to O.S. March 2, 1929. [and at end] 1929
"Crazy Jane Reproved": March 27, 1929
"Crazy Jane and Jack the Journeyman": November 1931. MSS. undated.
"Crazy Jane on God": July 18, 1931. MSS. undated.
"Crazy Jane Talks with the Bishop": November 1931. Coole.
"Girl's Song": March 29, 1929.
"Young Man's Song": 1929.
"Her Anxiety": 1929.
"His Confidence": 1929
"Love's Loneliness": April 17, 1929
"Her Dream": 1929
"His Bargain": 1929
"Three Things": March 1929
"Lullaby": March 1929
"After Long Silence": See letter to O.S. Oct. 16, 1929. [and at end of poem] December 1929. (Nov. in Rapallo 1928-29 MSS. book).
"Mad as the Mist and Snow": Feb. 12, 1929.
"Those Dancing Days Are Gone": March 8, 1929.
"The Dancer at Cruachan and Cro-Patrick": See No. XXIV. [and at end] August 1931
"Tom the Lunatic": June 29, 1929 (at Coole). July 27, 1931.
"Tom at Cruachan": July 29, 1931.
"Old Tom Again": See letter to G.Y. 13 Oct. 1931 "a reply to the dancer's song." Also 2nd letter "Saturday." [and at end] Coole. Oct. 1931.
"The Delphic Oracle Upon Plotinus": See letter to G.Y. Aug. 1931 [and at end] MSS.
"Father and Child": See letter to O.S. July 2, 1926 [and at end] Anne Yeats??/ Fergus Fitzgerald.
"Her Triumph": Nov. 1929

"Consolation": See letter to O.S. June 1927. [and at end] June 1927.
"Parting": Aug. 1926.
"Her Vision in the Wood": 1926.
"A Last Confession": "WBY. June 1926"
"Meeting": August 1926/ "July 23 or 24"
"From the 'Antigone'": 1926-7 (WBY)/ (1927-8 E.P.)/ Corrected by Ezra Pound. Rapallo. 1927 or 8. See typescript.

2323a. ———. Another copy. Blue leather binding in slipcase.

2323b. ———. Another copy. 1937 printing.

Occasional notes, likely GY's, with one exception as indicated.
P. 52, next to "The Lamentation of the Old Pensioner": For interesting account of the Oisin of this poem see DUBLIN MAGAZINE, article by A.E. 1935?. This version very different from the earlier one [and a further note after this in red] Note is by Joseph Hone.
P. 244, next to "Among School Children," section V: used in Hawk's Well.
P. 247, next to "Owen Aherne and His Dancers": 1917
P. 299, next to no. XIII of "Words for Music Perhaps," "Her Dream," at "Berenice's burning hair": x Veronica?
P. 422, line 183 in "The Two Kings," "whirling dance" revised to : wandering dance
Inserted at end, a fragment of a review of Louis MacNeice's THE POETRY OF W.B. YEATS (1941).
Also inserted, a slip of paper with WBY's note in pencil: "pottery"/ C.P. London/ p. 228/ (My Table. line 18)/ corrected in CP. USA. 1933 ed. [reference is to section III of "Meditations in Time of Civil War"; VAR. shows no variant reading].

2323c. ———. Another copy. 1950 printing.

Flyleaf: corrections, p. 331
P. 331, in "He and She" "sacred moon" corrected to: scared moon [likely GY's].

2323A. ———. Another ed. New York: Macmillan, 1933. xviii, 478 pp. WADE 171

2324. ———. THE COLLECTED PLAYS. London: Macmillan, 1934. vi,618 pp. WADE 177

2324A. ———. Another ed. New York: Macmillan, 1935. x,618 pp. WADE 178. Sig.: GY

2325. ———. COLLECTED WORKS IN VERSE AND PROSE. Vol. 1: POEMS LYRICAL AND NARRATIVE. Stratford: Shakespeare Head Press, 1908. 2,x,248 pp. WADE 75. Sig.: GY

In Contents, most of the titles in THE WIND AMONG THE REEDS have been checked.

P. ix in Contents, THE WANDERINGS OF OISIN with Notes have been canceled and marked: omit

P. ix, below, a draft, ink, WBY's of "The New Faces," first printed in SEVEN POEMS AND A FRAGMENT, 1922 (with revisions):

If you that have grown old were the first dead,
Neither catalpa tree nor scented lime
Should hear my living feet, nor would I tread
Where we wrought that shall break the teeth of time.
Let the new faces play what trick they will
In the old rooms; for all they do or say.
Our shades will walk the garden gravel still
The living seem more shadowy than they.
Dec 1912.

Also inserted, two unsigned drafts of a letter to T. Fisher Unwin dated Oct. 14th [190?] possibly in regard to the fourth English ed. of POEMS published by Unwin in 1904. Unwin had sought to publish an unnamed play by Yeats, but WBY says that he had already promised it to Elkin Mathews. As for a reprint of other poems (not specified), he is willing to let Unwin publish them, but only under the condition that the copyright would revert to him after an unspecified period so that he could bring them out with a good Irish publisher if one should appear. Yeats in the second draft shows he is sensitive about having had most of his work published in England: "I believe that an Irish public will emerge in the course of years, and I know this exclusive English publication is something of a reproach."

P. xi, WIND AMONG THE REEDS dated: 1892 - 1899

P. 41, "The Old Age of Queen Maeve" dated: 1903

P. 50, "Baile and Aillinn" dated: 1902

P. 63, IN THE SEVEN WOODS dated: 1899-1903

P. 66, line 5 of "The Arrow" revised from "Blossom pale, she pulled down the pale blossom" to: Her complexion of the apple-blossom

P. 66, line 6, revised from "At the moth hour and hid it in her bosom" to: The untroubled blossoming of her bosom
[These variants appear in no printed ed.]

P. 68, line 1 of "Old Memory" revised from "I thought to fly to her when the end of day" to: O Thought fly to her when the end of day [rev. first appears in POEMS: SECOND SERIES, London, 1909]

P. 78, on a piece of paper pasted over the printed poem, another version (ink, WBY's) of "The Ragged Wood":

Ragged
The ~~Hollow~~ Wood

O Hurry where by water among trees
The delicate-stepping stag & his lady sigh,
When they have but looked upon their images,-
O that none ever loved but you & I!

[break]

Or have you heard that sliding silver-shoed
Pale silver-proud queen woman of the sky,
When the sun looked out of his golden hood;
O that none other loved but you and I!

[break]

O hurry to the ragged wood, for there
I have
~~I'll~~ halloo all those lovers out and cry-
O my share of the world, O yellow hair!
No one has ever loved but you and I.
[This version, including title change, largely followed in Tauchnitz ed., WADE 103].

P. 85, after "Early Poems/ I/ Ballads and Lyrics" the date inserted: 1889.
P. 135, after "Early Poems, II/ The Rose" the date inserted: 1889 - 1899.
P. 169, "Early Poems" etc. canceled and marked: omit Pp. canceled through p. 175.
Books II and III of WANDERINGS OF OISIN canceled.

2326. ———. Vol. 2: THE KING'S THRESHOLD, ON BAILE'S STRAND, DEIRDRE, SHADOWY WATERS. Stratford: Shakespeare Head Press, 1908. viii,260 pp. WADE 76

Inserted at half title p., apparently a piece of proof paper, approx. 4"x5" with the printed text of a poem entitled "The Watch-Fire":

THE WATCH-FIRE

This song unto all who would gather together and hold
Brother by brother;
A watch and a ward by the watch-fire of Eri, our old
And long-weeping mother.

[break]

This song unto all who would stand by the fire of her hope,
And droop not nor slumber;
But keep up the high and the mirthful proud courage to cope
With wrongs beyond number.

[break]

This song unto all who would gather and help yet once more
Eri, our mother;
And do nought that would anger the famous and great gone before
Brother by brother.

W. B. Yeats

[For a discussion of this unpublished Yeats poem and its history, see POETRY 135 (Jan. 1980): 223-6.]
P. 38, line 456 in THE KING'S THRESHOLD revised from "I do believe you would, but I won't help you" to: Do what you please but do it without my help. [no printed version follows]

P. 88, lines 258-259 of ON BAILE'S STRAND revised from "You rail at them/ Because you have no children of your own" to: You rail at them/ Because the war and changes of land and sea/ Have left you with no children of your own. [no printed version follows]

Also inserted at this p., another version, ink, on a slip of lined paper: You rail at them/ Because changes of storms & war & travel/ Have left you with no children of your own. [no printed version follows]

P. 129, in the initial stage directions in DEIRDRE "and a wine flagon and a loaf of bread" is deleted.

P. 139, line 149 of DEIRDRE "You are welcome lady" to end of p. canceled and a note: (see appendix) [this and subsequent refs. to appendices apparently refer to the alternative versions in the 3 appendices to this vol.]

P. 140 and first 3 lines on p. 141 deleted.

P. 144, lines 217-8 of DEIRDRE revised from "Before you came/ I had to threaten these that would have weighed" to: I had to threaten these/ Before you came because they would have.... [not followed exactly in any printing].

P. 151, after Deirdre's lines at beginning: (see appendix)

P. 155, beginning with line 389 of DEIRDRE, has been extensively revised:

Naisi: Tell Conchubar to meet me in some place
Where none can come between us but our swords.
For I have found no truth on any tongue
That's not of iron.
Messenger: I am Conchubar's man;
And take no message but he bids me to it.
Naisi: I bid you. I will have you swear to take it.
Fergus: Some enemy has paid him well for this. I know...

[These revisions first appear in WADE 86.]

P. 167, line 585 of DEIRDRE revised from "You will be/ praised/ By Everybody" to: And there is no one/ That will not praise you

P. 172, line 676 revised from "For I'll go with you and do all your will" to: I shall do all you bid me but not yet/ Because I have to do what's customary

P. 174, line 174 revised from "No; but I will trust/ the Strength you have spoken of" to: No; but I will trust/ The strength that you have praised....

Pp. 181-229 in THE SHADOWY WATERS, no verbal revisions, but many lines have been numbered and "Xed."

P. 221, line 519 (as numbered here in pencil): collated to 519 twice.

2326A. THE KING'S THRESHOLD AND STORIES OF RED HANRAHAN, comprising pp. 1-68 of WADE 76, Vol. II of THE COLLECTED WORKS and pp. 195-262 of WADE 79, Vol. V of the COLLECTED WORKS, bound as one vol., blue covers, quarter cloth, lettered on spine, ink, WBY's: Kings Threshold Apparently a unique copy.

2327. ———. Vol. 3: THE COUNTESS CATHLEEN, THE LAND OF HEART'S DESIRE, THE UNICORN FROM THE STARS. Stratford: Shakespeare Head Press, 1908. viii,240 pp. Bp: WBY. WADE 77

P. 220, line 24, "know" corrected to: no
P. 222 in Notes, the "Music for Use in the Performance of these Plays" has deletions and revisions.
P. 224, after above, a long holograph note beginning "Since I wrote these words, I did test in performance Miss Farr's Deirdre music" and continuing as on p. 443 of WADE 136, PLAYS IN PROSE AND VERSE, 1922 with one deletion indicated: who could chant or sing modern poetry (and Miss Allgood is too full of folk music to succeed with music like Miss Farr's.) [material in brackets deleted]
Before p. 231, a holograph setting of music for THE POT OF BROTH pasted in, not WBY's.
P. 233, the music for CATHLEEN NI HOULIHAN marked: "Irish Traditional Air"
P. 234, "Music for Lyrics" deleted and inserted: IV Poems for the Psaltery [also a note in margin:] Insert after "Speaking to the Psaltery" "Ideas of Good and Evil" page 20
P. 235, at "a fine scholar in poetry": Mr. A.H. Bullen [and the section dated] 1907
P. 235, "Note by Florence Farr" numbered "V" and date inserted at end: 1907.
Some deletions and editing marks passim, apparently to provide copy for ESSAYS, 1924, WADE 141.

2328. ———. Vol. 4: THE HOUR-GLASS, CATHLEEN NI HOULIHAN, THE GOLDEN HELMET, THE IRISH DRAMATIC MOVEMENT. Stratford: Shakespeare Head Press, 1908. viii,248 pp. WADE 78

P. 18, line 268 of HOUR-GLASS, "If there is one amongst you that believes" revised to: If there is one amongst you that has not changed [first in WADE 92, PLAYS FOR AN IRISH THEATRE]
P. 20, lines 302ff. of HOUR-GLASS beginning with "Out, out from my sight ..." revised to: Out, out from my sight! I want someone who has not changed. That is the grain the Angel spoke of. I must find it before I die. I tell you I must find it. The sands are running [canceled] falling there and you answer me with arguments. [first in WADE 92]
P. 143, "prepared" revised or corrected to: produced [?]
P. 168, first par. marked in margin
P. 176, "their own day" corrected to: our own day
P. 183, a line inserted after "as a true fine art."
P. 192, "under the conventional idealisms" revised to: overpowered by the conventional
Pp. 212, 214, minor verbal corrections.

2329. ———. Vol. 5: THE CELTIC TWILIGHT AND STORIES OF RED HANRAHAN. Stratford: Shakespeare Head Press, 1908. xvi,264 pp. WADE 79

Pp. 257-61 have been bound in twice.

2330. ———. Vol. 6: IDEAS OF GOOD AND EVIL. Stratford: Shakespeare Head Press, 1908. viii,268 pp. WADE 80

P. 16, slight verbal corrections.
P. 155, "little" revised to: literal reverence
Inserted, a holograph letter from Robert Bridges to WBY dated 15 June [18]97, Yattendon. This is the original of the letter printed from transcriptions in THE CORRESPONDENCE OF ROBERT BRIDGES AND W.B. YEATS. Edited by Richard J. Finneran. London: Macmillan, 1977, pp. 13-16. The text follows this printed version with three amplifications:

> I was at Oxford on Friday and Saturday, and on Sunday had two visitors here from London. One was Binyon.....
> ....
> The accounts of the gleeman are splendid - and the humour all through is of the best.
> ....
> I expect that while we agree absolutely about the necessity for mysticism, we do not take quite the same view of the value of the phenomena in themselves....

2331. ———. Vol. 7: THE SECRET ROSE. ROSA ALCHEMICA. THE TABLES OF THE LAW. THE ADORATION OF THE MAGI. JOHN SHERMAN AND DHOYA. Stratford: Shakespeare Head Press, 1908. viii,304 pp. WADE 81

Pp. uncut passim.

2332. ———. Vol. 8: DISCOVERIES. EDMUND SPENSER. POETRY AND TRADITION. AND OTHER ESSAYS. Stratford: Shakespeare Head Press, 1908. 2,vi,288 pp. WADE 82

Pp. 18-136, slight corrections, some substantive.
P. 137, "Cuchulain of Muirthemne" deleted and a new title inserted in pencil: Irish heroic age./ Cuchulain & his cycle.
P. 137, top: Copy from here
P. 149 retitled: Fion and his cycle
P. 168, before IX: end here

2333. ———. THE COUNTESS CATHLEEN. N.p. N.d. 96 pp.
Cover missing. This is very likely the copy described at WADE 17 as belonging to Mr. O'Hegarty and perhaps used as a rehearsal copy for the first production of the Irish Literary Theatre.
Stage directions (some WBY's) very full and explicit.
Some revisions by WBY.
Wade states accurately that the type of this copy seems to be that of the main entry for WADE 17, POEMS, 1899. But the evidence of the VAR. suggests that the text here

is not WADE 17 but WADE 15, POEMS, 1895 and the revisions in this copy were followed in WADE 18, POEMS, 1901.

2334. ———. THE COUNTESS CATHLEEN. London: T. Fisher Unwin, 1912. 128 pp. WADE 95

Frt. cover, ink: Corrected/ Dec. 1912
Within, pp. 21, 22, 33, 63, 64, 71, 75, 78, 79, 84, 85, revisions have been made on neatly typed slips pasted in some cases over inked revisions. Some additional revisions in ink on the typed slips. This revised copy apparently provided the copytext for WADE 100, POEMS, London, 1913.
P. 115, ink: Do not pay attention to alteration in 'notes'. They are a mistake of typist. WBY.
Notes have been canceled to p. 122, "The Countess Cathleen was acted...."
Back flyleaf, verso: Abbey Theatre/ Dublin 2 [not WBY's]

2334a. Another copy. Sig.: LY

2334b. Another copy.

2334c. Another printing. "Ninth ed.," 1916.

2334d. Another printing. "Thirteenth ed.," 1922.

Parchment covers, lettered in green inside rules as described in Wade.

2335. ———. THE COUNTESS CATHLEEN [and THE LAND OF HEART'S DESIRE.] London: T. Fisher Unwin, 1924. WADE 95

This is the vol. described by Wade in dark red ribbed cloth lettered in gold on spine etc.

2335a. Another printing, 1925. This is the "Cabinet Library Edition" described by Wade in green ribbed cloth.

2335b. Another printing, 1929. "Benn's Essex Library, No. 12." Issued in white and blue decorated wrapper.

Frt. flyleaf: 'An aimless job is a pure job'/ WB Yeats/ July 28/ 1932

2336. ———. THE CUTTING OF AN AGATE. New York: Macmillan, 1912. x,262 pp. Bp: WBY. WADE 102

Title p., pencil: see page 208 [on that p. a mark before the line beginning "copying hawk ..."].
In Contents "Thoughts on Lady Gregory's Translations" is canceled; there is a check mark before Preface to the 1st ed. of THE WELL OF THE SAINTS.
In "Discoveries" there are check marks before most of the poems to p. 103, "The Tresses of the Hair."
"Poetry and Tradition" and all titles to end checked.
P. 252, note on bottom is checked.

2337. ———. THE CUTTING OF AN AGATE. London: Macmillan, 1919. viii,224 pp. WADE 126

Stamped on title p.: Presentation copy.

2337a. Another copy. Some pp. uncut.

2338. ———. DEIRDRE. London: A.H. Bullen, 1907. viii,48 pp. WADE 69

Frt. flyleaf, two sketches, one likely WBY's.
List of books by same writer, verso: 1473 60th [?] St. Borough Park.
Inside back cover and last flyleaf, recto and verso, sketches of a woman.
Moderate revisions in pencil and ink in this item and the following apparently to provide copytext for WADE 86, DEIRDRE, 1911.
Inserted is 2339, "Alterations in 'Deirdre'"

2339. ———. ALTERATIONS IN 'DEIRDRE.' [1908]. 4 pp. WADE 70

Inserted in 2338. Revised, as above, apparently to provide copytext for WADE 86.

2340. ———. DEIRDRE. Stratford: Shakespeare Head Press, 1911. 32 pp. WADE 86

Frt. cover, ink: <u>Marked Copy</u>
Title p., (above title), pencil: play should be put on again before America
Title p., (below title): Suggestion - 1 musician to keep to L. of stage til just before Deirdre's entrance--no changes of light except darker before torches are lit. - green light on side. Musician to have hands covered. Small tin of lime and hot ashes on brazier to make smoke. Fergus & Naisi to talk over chessboard more naturally; 'to chat' as it were. Concubar [sic] to look at Deirdre during long speech about 'no blood in their veins' [line 577].
[signed] WBY - June - 1911
Title p., verso: Deirdre enters and faces to L before she speaks.
Pp. 14, 18, slight corrections.
P. 20, lines 444-6, from "I have loved truly" to "at the cage's door" are deleted but a query (?) in margin and no printing follows deletion.
P. 24, lines 528 to 534, beginning "Women, if I die": should be played with some suggestion of wandering in sudden changes of thought [pencil].
P. 24, lines 531-2 stroked in margin.
P. 32, at end of play, pencil: Naisi & Concubar to be quicker up at end/ general quickening of lines.

2340a. Another copy.

2340b. Another copy.

2341. ———. DRAMATIS PERSONAE. ESTRANGEMENT. THE DEATH OF SYNGE. THE BOUNTY OF SWEDEN. New York: Macmillan, 1936. viii,200 pp. WADE 186

In dust jacket.

2341a. Another copy. In dust jacket.

2342. ———. DRAMATIS PERSONAE etc. London: Macmillan, 1936. viii,192 pp. WADE 187

Inserted loose, bookplate with design by T. Sturge Moore of Helen emerging from egg; with inked inscription: "Animate the trivial days and rain them with the sun" WB Yeats.
Also inserted, a copy of THE MASK, 1274.

2342a. Another copy. In dust jacket.

2343. ———. EARLY POEMS AND STORIES. London: Macmillan, 1925. 2,x,532 pp. WADE 147

Mostly uncut.

2344. ———. EARLY POEMS AND STORIES. New York: Macmillan, 1925. WADE 148

On cover, a small white label pasted on: C
Flyleaf: Franklin Price from WB Yeats/ Nov 12, 1925 [canceled]
P. 101, top of p., at "Fergus and the Druid," a note but completely canceled and illegible.
P. 118, line 6 of "When You are Old" "will" corrected (?) to: with
P. 527, first 3 lines of "Notes" marked delete.
P. 528, beginning "I have left out a few passages in 'The Celtic Twilight'" to end marked delete.
End of notes, after "W.B.Y.": 1925

2344a. Another copy. Limited ed. in brown paper boards. 191/250. Sig.: WBY

In "Wanderings of Usheen" lines have been numbered in the text and some "Xed," as lines 9, 18, 54, 56, 64, 96, 138, 145; if these are deletions, no printing follows.

2345. ———. EIGHT POEMS. Transcribed by Edward Pay. London: Published by "Form" at the Morland Press, 1916. Unpag. WADE 114

Title p., verso, ink: This pamphlet was brought out by a magazine called "Form" to save my copyright as the poems were being published in America and the magazine was delayed. WB Yeats.
Misprints in four of the poems corrected in pencil, not WBY's; one annotation, not WBY's.

2345a. Another copy. Sig.: LY, June 1916

2345b. Another copy.

2345c. Another copy.

2346. ———. ENHÖRNINGEN FRÅN STJÄRNORNA DROTTNINGEN [THE UNICORN FROM THE STARS. THE PLAYER QUEEN]. Stockholm: P.A. Norstedt, 1924. 152 pp. WADE, p. 373

2347. ———. ESSAYS. London: Macmillan, 1924. viii,540 pp. WADE 141

Flyleaf: George Yeats. Her copy/ not to be taken by me/ WB Yeats
P. v, dedication p., canceled and a note above: delete for Scribner [GY's?]
Slips of paper inserted passim to mark corrections or slight verbal revisions; many are WBY's, though some, especially of typographical errors, seem GY's. These corrections and revisions have been followed in ESSAYS AND INTRODUCTIONS.

2348. ———. ESSAYS. New York: Macmillan, 1924. WADE 142

Flyleaf: George Yeats/ Corrected Copy [last two words lightly canceled]
GY's corrections and identifications appear passim to p. 227, with few thereafter; the Blake essays are heavily corrected; in "William Blake and His Illustrations to the Divine Comedy" the corrections or revisions in substantives (not accidentals) have been followed in ESSAYS AND INTRODUCTIONS.

2349. ———. FOUR PLAYS FOR DANCERS. London: Macmillan, 1921. xii,140 pp. WADE 129

Pp. 91ff., in Dulac's music for AT THE HAWK'S WELL some pencil annotations passim, apparently for a performance or recording; not WBY's.

2350. ———. FOUR PLAYS FOR DANCERS. New York: Macmillan, 1921. 2,xii,142 pp. WADE 130

Title p., referring to AT THE HAWK'S WELL: 1st published March 1917 "Harper's Bazaar" N.Y. USA [GY's]
P. 6, the Second Musician's line "I am afraid of this place" is deleted; no printing follows.
P. 19 "and if you drink the first" is underlined and in margin: music refrain [WBY's]
P. 25, title p. for THE ONLY JEALOUSY OF EMER: Oxford, 1917-8 [GY's]
P. 51, title p. of THE DREAMING OF THE BONES: August 1917/ re-written 1918 summer [GY's]
P. 93, in music for AT THE HAWK'S WELL, after "He has made a little heap of leaves": empty well [GY's]
P. 93, after music for "Better grow old and sleep," some verbal revisions, GY's.
P. 138, notes for CALVARY are dated: Summer 1929 [GY's]

2351. ———. A FULL MOON IN MARCH. London: Macmillan, 1935. viii,72 pp. WADE 182

Dustjacket: Copy corrected by WBY [GY]s
Pp. 48-53, "Three Songs to the Same Tune" are heavily revised in ink. They are retitled "Three Revolutionary Songs" and constitute a unique unpublished intermediate draft between the FULL MOON IN MARCH version and "Three Marching Songs" first appearing in WADE 200. An asterisk above the revised title refers to a note at the bottom of the p.: I published a first confused version of these songs some years ago. I hope they are now clear & singable.
The revised version follows:

I.

[lines 1-6 as in WADE 182]

7. Robbers had taken his old guitar [canceled] tambourine
8. But he took down the moon
9. And rattled out a tune
10. Robbers had taken his old guitar [canceled] tambourine

[lines 11-16 as in WADE 182]

17. Robbers had taken his old guitar [canceled] tambourine
18. But he took down the moon
19. And rattled out a tune
20. Robbers had taken his old guitar [canceled] tambourine

[lines 21-6 as in WADE 182]
27. Robbers had taken his old guitar [canceled] tambourine
28. But he took down the moon
29. And rattled out a tune
30. Robbers had taken his old guitar [canceled] tambourine

II.

1. Remember all those renowned generations
[lines 2-6 as in WADE 182]

7. Go ask the curlew if night is finished [canceled] is gone
8. Or if the gangling mind
9. Bears and begets its kind
10. Go ask the curlew if night is finished [canceled] is gone

11. Remember all those renowned generations
12. Remember all that have sunk in their blood,
13. Remember all that have died on the scaffold,
14. Remember all that have fled, that have stood,
[lines 15-6 as in WADE 182]

17. Go ask the curlew if night is finished [canceled] has gone
18. Or if the animated [canceled] gangling mind
19. Still bears and begets its kind;
20. Go ask the curlew if night is finished [canceled] has gone

21. Fail, and [canceled but marked "stet"; the rest as in WADE 182]

[lines 22-6 as in WADE 182]

27. Go ask the curlew if it is finished [3 words canceled]
night has gone.
28. Or if the gangling mind
29. Still bears and begets its kind;
30. Go ask the curlew if it is finished [3 words canceled]
night has gone.

III.

[lines 1-6 as in WADE 182]
7. Remember the saints when the night is finished [canceled] has gone.
8. Night now and much to do.
9. Night now and a reckless crew;
10. Remember the saints when the night is finished [canceled] has gone.

[lines 11-13 as in WADE 182]
14. [last phrase revised but marked "stet"]
15. Dogs can bark and slaves can sigh
16. Fools mark us marching by
[lines 15-6 further revised at bottom]
15. Dogs bark, slaves drop a tear
16. Old fools cock up an ear.

17. Remember the saints when the night is finished [canceled] has gone
18. Night now and much to do,
19. Night now and a reckless crew;
20. Remember the saints when the night is finished [canceled] has gone

[lines 21-2 as in WADE 182]
23. What tears down a tree that has nothing within it?
24. A blast of the wind O a marching wind
25. Blast, blast, Blast of the wind [canceled]
25. March wind, How does it run -
26. O any old words to a tune.

27. Remember the saints when the night is finished [canceled] has gone
28. Night now and much to do,
29. Night now and a reckless crew;
30. Remember the saints when the [canceled] night is finished [canceled] has gone.

P. 63 ff., the "Supernatural Songs" have been dated and annotated by GY:

II. "Ribh denounces Patrick": July 1934
III. "Ribh in Ecstasy": 1934
IV. "There": 1934
V. "Ribh considers Christian Love insufficient": WBY "the point of the poem is that we beget because of the incompleteness of our love."

VI. "He and She": August 1934
VII. "What Magic Drum?": 1933-4
VIII. "Whence Had They Come?": 1933-34
IX. "The Four Ages of Man," the symbols for the alchemical elements of earth, water, air, and fire respectively entered beside the four couplets. Also, the date: 1934 August
X. "Conjunctions": see Letter to OS. August 23, 1934. [also] 1934.
XII. "Meru": 1934

2352. ———. THE GOLDEN HELMET. New York: John Quinn, 1908. 36 pp. 15/50. WADE 74

Flyleaf, at limitation notice: To W.B. Yeats/ with the Publisher's/ Compliments/ New York/ John Quinn/ 1908

2352a. Another copy. 22/50

Some stage directions are verbal revisions entered; in some cases these are similar to the first verse version, but some verbal revisions are not followed in any printing; not WBY's.

2352b. Another copy. 24/50

2353. ———. GRAFIN CATHLEEN [THE COUNTESS CATHLEEN]. Hellebrau: Jakob Hegner, 1925. 100 pp. WADE, p. 374

Almost wholly uncut.

2354. ———. THE GREEN HELMET. Stratford: Shakespeare Head Press, 1911. 16 pp. WADE 89

Galley copy.
Title p. canceled and entered in crayon: 4
Title p., verso, canceled.
P. 3, a number stamped at top: # 12219
Text is marked from "gal 8" to "gal 19," not WBY's.
P. 16, "The End" is canceled.

2354a. Another copy. Partially cut.

2354b. Another copy. Uncut.

2354c. Another copy. Uncut.

2355. ———. THE GREEN HELMET AND OTHER POEMS. New York and London: Macmillan, 1912. viii,92 pp. WADE 101

Half title p. and title p. canceled.
Half title p., verso, after "From 'The Green Helmet' and other Poems": 1909 - 1912 [ink traced over pencil; possibly WBY's] [and below this] on separate page [but canceled]
P. 1, above "His Dream": From "The Green Helmet and other Poems, 1909-1912" [thoroughly canceled]

A number of poems have been canceled in text, others checked.
P. 27, the title "A Lyric from an Unpublished Play" canceled and substituted: The Mask [first in WADE 106]
P. 33, "At Galway Races" line 1 revised from "Out yonder, where the race course is" TO: There where the race course is [not followed exactly in any printed version]
P. 33, line 3 of "Galway Races," "Riders upon the swift horses" TO: The Riders upon the galloping horses [first in WADE 103]
P. 33, line 4 of "Galway Races," "The field that closes in behind" TO: The crowd that closes [first in WADE 103]
P. 37, after "The Young Man's Song": Book ends here [and from here to end, pp. all torn out]

2355a. Another copy.

2355b. Another copy.

2356. ———. GREVINNAN CATHLEEN [THE COUNTESS CATHLEEN]. Translated by Teresia Euren. Stockholm: Thure Wahledows, 1923. 88 pp. WADE, p. 371

Cover, ink: To Mr. W.B. Yeats/ in token of respectful admiration from Teresia Euren

2357. ———. THE HERNE'S EGG. London: Macmillan, 1938. vi,74 pp. WADE 195

Flyleaf: WB Yeats/ not to be given or lent/
Corrected copy.
Moderately revised in ink and pencil; the revisions first appear in WADE 211D, COLLECTED PLAYS, 1952.
P. 15, revision follows Scene II, lines 117-9 as in VAR.
P. 16, lines added as in II. 131-4 in VAR.
P. 40, three drafts of IV. 94-6; two canceled, the third as in VAR.
P. 50, a draft of V. 39-41 as in VAR.
P. 56, bottom, pencil, a draft of lines 96-7, scene 5: Because I am married to a god/ All I would have one man among the [but this is canceled and below in ink the version in VAR.]
P. 59, bottom, two drafts of line 28 of scene VI: Stop that. That tune is lucky [this in pencil but canceled; another draft, ink over pencil:] Hush, for that is an unlucky tune [VAR. follows closely]
P. 72, a draft of line 166 of scene VI, ink over pencil, as in VAR.

2358. ———. THE HERNE'S EGG AND OTHER PLAYS. New York: Macmillan, 1938. viii,136 pp. WADE 196

In dustjacket.

2358a. Another copy. In dustjacket.

2358b. Another copy. In dustjacket.

2359. ———. THE HOUR-GLASS. London: William Heinemann, 1903. 16 pp. WADE 51

Bound in blue covers; lettered in gold on spine.

2360. ———. THE HOUR-GLASS. New York: Macmillan, 1904. viii,116 pp. WADE 52

P. 32, line 332 revised from "pig is fattening well" to: linen is bleaching a while.
P. 37, line 392, "There is no heaven; there is no hell" is canceled, and added to next line is: There is nothing we cannot see, there is nothing we cannot touch.
Revisions above are followed in WADE 53, the London ed. of 1904 which Wade indicates was published three months later than the American ed.
Also includes CATHLEEN NI HOULIHAN revised throughout. These revisions were apparently copied from WADE 40, the 1902 London ed. of CATHLEEN to make this vol. the convenient copytext for WADE 53.
Also includes A POT OF BROTH with revisions, followed in WADE 53; but on p. 88, line 56, before "Looks at the stone," inserted: She's as hard-hearted as this stone [not followed in any printing]

2360a. Another copy. 1906 printing. Bp: Eliz. C. Yeats

Does not incorporate the revisions above, and thus a simple reprinting.
Back flyleaf, a prose note of six lines, WBY's, difficult to decipher, apparently a plot summary mentioning an Englishman, an American, and "an interlude in an eventful life."

2361. ———. THE HOUR-GLASS. London: A.H. Bullen, 1907. 16 pp. WADE 67

This copy and the three that follow are heavily revised in ink from p. 9 to end. The revisions, with the exception of a word or two, are identical in each copy, as if they were transcribed from one to another, presumably to be used as acting copies.
P. 10, line 302 has been revised to: I want somebody who has not changed. That is the grain the angel spoke of - I must find it before I die. The Sands are falling through, and you answer me with arguments. Out of my sight, out of my sight. [No printed version follows exactly, but WADE 92 follows most closely.]
P. 11, lines 339-43 are added as first in WADE 73, THE UNICORN FROM THE STARS etc., New York, 1908. But in one copy: They have answered as I have done.
P. 15, line 457 m, revised to: that they may be given a sign and carry their souls out of this dying world [first in WADE 73].
These and other revisions seem to indicate that this stage of revisions provided a copytext for WADE 73--in addition to its use as acting text.

2361a. Another copy. Revised as above.

2361b. Another copy. Revised as above.

2361c. Another copy. Revised as above.

2361d. Another copy. Unrevised.

2361e. Another copy. Unrevised.

2361f. Another copy. Unrevised.

2362. ———. THE HOUR-GLASS. CATHLEEN NI HOULIHAN. THE POT OF BROTH. London: A.H. Bullen, 1904. viii,84 pp. WADE 53

Flyleaf, stamped: The National Theatre Society/ Abbey Theatre/ Dublin
Inserted, a single sheet, WBY's, giving the location, date and cast for the first production of THE HOUR-GLASS, as in Robinson, IRELAND'S ABBEY THEATRE, p. 33. Additions to CATHLEEN NI HOULIHAN, mostly stage directions, which seems consistent with the Abbey stamp. THE HOUR-GLASS has been heavily revised and some stage directions added which appear in no printed version. Most revisions are followed in WADE 73, THE UNICORN FROM THE STARS etc., New York, 1908, but others (see following) are not incorporated in any printing. It seems clear that the revisions were made for an acting version and subsequently incorporated in the printed text.
P. 18, lines 247-8 revised to: Is there any one amongst you who believes that there is something in us that can never pass away.
P. 24, lines 353-5 revised to: Oh, run out, Bridget, and see if they have found somebody that believes that he can never die.
P. 26, lines 397-401 revised to: You are just as bad as the others, just as bad as the others! Do not run away. Come back. I will teach you better.
Immediately following THE HOUR-GLASS, p. 32, is a fair hand copy, WBY's, of the untitled poem "I was going the road one day" (VAR. POEMS, 778). It first appears in printed form in WADE 78 and is intended as an optional song for the Pupils in THE HOUR-GLASS on making their first or second entrance. Yeats identifies the poem as a translation of "three of the many verses of a Gaelic ballad." Pasted on the half title p. of THE HOUR-GLASS is the text, in Irish and set to music, of a ballad "The Gruagach Uasal" ("The Noble Enchanter") preceded by a printed note by Lady Gregory explaining the poem. This is presumably the "Gaelic ballad" Yeats refers to.

2362a. Another copy. Bp: Lily Yeats

Flyleaf: George Russell/ from his friend/ the writer, March, 1904. [this canceled and a note added in pencil, apparently by Lily Yeats:] JB Yeats/ This book went to G. Russell/ years [?] later.

2362b. Another copy. Uncut.

2363. ———. THE HOUR-GLASS. CATHLEEN NI HOULIHAN. THE POT OF BROTH. Dublin: Maunsel, 1905. ii,84 pp. WADE 54

CATHLEEN NI HOULIHAN and THE POT OF BROTH are altogether uncut, but THE HOUR-GLASS is heavily revised from pp. 18-32. A few revisions duplicate those in 2362, but many (see following) are unique, not incorporated in any printing--

P. 18, line 256 revised to: The heart remains unchanged. It only pretends to listen. It knows all the time.
P. 18, line 260 revised to: If you tell me I have not been able to change you I shall be glad and not angry.
P. 19, line 268ff. revised to: If there is one amongst you who has said to himself - 'let him say what he pleases. I know' - if there is one who has said that he will be my best friend.
P. 20, line 282 revised to: It is hard to understand. If you will be patient I will explain it all. [this canceled and another version stands:] It is my belief that we become undying - that was what the angel said. It is by belief that we come to understanding. It is hard but if you are patient ....
P. 22, line 315 revised to: Why did I not speak to her first. She is lost if I can't save her, but no, I am sure she believes as she always did. My pupils have nothing in their minds but what I put there, but when I speak she sits thinking of something else, smiling, as if she listens - but only pretending to listen. Besides women always believe.
P. 23, line 328, the phrase "about the things you used to believe in" revised to: about angels, about the soul.
P. 25, line 376 revised to: There is no hope. She is lost. My child as my pupils & myself.
P. 25, line 381 ff. revised to: But she spoke of my child. I must call my child. My child will believe .... Bridget, Bridget, send me my child.
P. 26, line 388 ff. revised to: Speak quickly. There is very little time and do not be afraid. You believe that there is something eternal - no you will not understand that. When children laugh in their sleep we say that they can see the angels. Do you ever see the angels child? Do you believe that they are always about us, that there is a world we cannot see?
P. 26, line 390 deleted.
P. 26, line 391 revised to: Child. O no, father. All that is imagination and fancy.
Pp. 26,27, lines 397-402 deleted and the following substituted: Wise Man (taking child by the hand). Come to your mother (going to door). Bridget teach this

child all that you believed once about angels - teach him that belief is the mother of truth, not its child. Run to your mother. She will teach you - but no Bridget will not listen. She is baking a cake & she could not understand. Help them, O God!
P. 28, lines 425-6 revised to: You believe in the soul and in heaven.
P. 30, lines 457a-c canceled and substituted: Once I was alone on the hills and an angel came by and said 'Teig if your body was to wither as your wits are withered, your soul would shake on the little fistful of dust. If the world were broken like an egg your soul would not be broken but go shouting and laughing through the country of the summer's stars,' and that wise man is why I am always happily cracking my nuts.
Two items inserted in uncut pages, the first an advertisement by Maunsel of Synge's new book on the Arran [sic] Islands. Large paper ed. with drawings by Jack Yeats.
Also, a holograph letter from A.H. Bullen of Shakespeare Head Press to WBY, 29/10/1907:

My Dear Yeats,

I have written to A.P. Watt that I am going to town next week and that I will make an appointment to see him. If he can't turn up I must see one of the sons, though I should greatly prefer to discuss with the father. How goes on the Unicorn? In regard to the John Sherman volume: I take it that the order is to be John Sherman, Dhoya / Secret Rose (dedication to A.E.), The Binding of the Hair [but it does not appear in WADE 81, the subject of this letter], Wisdom of the Kings, Where there is Nothing, Crucifixion of the Outcast/ Out of the Rose, Curse of the Fires and of the Shadows, Heart of the Spring, Costello the Proud etc./ (The Book of the Great Dhoul not to be included, though it's far better than some of the others), The old Men of the Twilight, Rosa Alchemica, Tables of the Law, The Three Magi. Is this right? And will you kindly let me have the corrected copy as quickly as you possibly can? You said some time ago that it was quite ready for press. Of course I should have preferred to go straight on with the Unicorn after Land of Heart's Desire, and finish off that volume before beginning another; but I suspect that you will want to give further revision to the Unicorn. At the end of the last volume there can be a bibliographical appendix giving the dates of publication of the various pieces. I would be glad to get a reduced photograph of Mancini's pastel and an early proof of Augustus John's etching.

Yours, A.H. Bullen

2364. ———. HRABĚNKA CATHLEENOVÁ [THE COUNTESS CATHLEEN]. Vprazle: Nova Biblioteka, 1929. 88 pp. WADE, p. 375

Uncut.

2365. ———. IDEAS OF GOOD AND EVIL. London: A.H. Bullen, 1903. viii,344 pp. WADE 46

2365a. Another copy. 2nd ed. Sig.: WBY

A few initial pp. uncut.

2365b. Another copy. 2nd ed.

2366. ———. IDEAS OF GOOD AND EVIL. New York: Macmillan, 1903. WADE 47. Bp: Elizabeth Corbet Yeats. Sig.: Mrs. Whidden Grahame

Flyleaf, verso: - the land of faery
Where nobody gets old and godly and grave,
Where nobody gets old and crafty and wise,
Where nobody gets old and bitter of tongue
[not WBY's]

Back flyleaf, a pencil drawing, simply executed, of a torso, possibly a sketch for a costume.

2367. ———. IDEAS OF GOOD AND EVIL. Dublin: Maunsel, 1905. WADE 48

Marked "Second Edition" but according to Wade actually sheets of the 2nd English ed. sold only in Ireland. Some pp. uncut.

2368. ———. IN THE SEVEN WOODS. New York: Macmillan, 1903. vi,90 pp. WADE 50

Many poems are checked in pencil in the text; lines of longer poems are numbered in pencil.
P. 77, a slip inserted: all poems could be checked.

2368a. Another copy.

2369. ———. THE IRISH NATIONAL THEATRE. Roma: Reale Accademia D'Italia, 1935. 16 pp. WADE 181

Mostly uncut, as also the following copies.

2369a. Another copy.

2369b. Another copy.

2369c. Another copy.

2369d. Another copy.

2369e. Another copy, but format not described in Wade: Reale Accademia D'Italia/ Classe Delle Lettere [long rule]/ IV Convegno "Volta"- Tema: Il Teatro/ Roma 8-14 Ottobre 1934 - XII [short rule]/ Relazioni [short rule] William Butler Yeats/ THE IRISH NATIONAL THEATRE/ Roma/ Reale Accademia. 14 pp.

2370. ———. IS THE ORDER OF R.R. AND A.C. TO REMAIN A MAGICAL ORDER? N.p., 1901. 32 pp. WADE 33

On cover: see page 23 [possibly WBY's]
P. 23, a correction of "whose" to: its [WBY's?]

2370a. Another copy. Pp. uncut.

2370b. Another copy. Pp. uncut.

2371. ———. JOHN SHERMAN AND DHOYA. 2nd ed. London: T. Fisher Unwin, 1891. iv,196 pp. Bp: Eliz. C. Yeats. WADE 4

No. 10 of the Pseudonym Library.
Flyleaf: Jany./ 1900/ WB

2372. ———. THE KING OF THE GREAT CLOCK TOWER. New York: Macmillan, 1935. x,46 pp. WADE 179A

In dust jacket.
Inserted, a slip of paper with: (237)
Next to first stanza of No. 3 of "Supernatural Songs," "Ribh Considers Christian Love Insufficient": See Notebook "PROSE" [WBY's?]

2373. ———. THE KING'S THRESHOLD. Stratford: Shakespeare Head Press, 1911. 40 pp. WADE 90

Pp. uncut.

2374. ———. THE KING'S THRESHOLD. London: Macmillan, 1937. 52 pp. WADE 189

2374a. Another copy.

2374b. Another copy.

2374c. Another copy.

2374d. Another copy.

2374e. Another copy.

2375. ———. THE LAKE ISLE OF INNISFREE. San Francisco: John Henry Nash, 1924. 8 pp. WADE 143

2375a. Another copy.

2375b. Another copy.

2375c. Another copy.

2375d. Another copy.

2375e. Another copy.

2376. ———. THE LAND OF HEART'S DESIRE. Chicago: Stone and Kimball, 1894. iv,48 pp. WADE 11

2377. ———. THE LAND OF HEART'S DESIRE. Portland, Maine: Thomas Mosher, 1903. vi,36 pp. WADE 13

Grey paper boards.

2377a. Another copy. In grey slipcase. Pp. uncut.

2377b. Another copy. In grey slipcase. Pp. uncut.

2377c. Another copy. 10th ed. March 1912.

SEE ALSO 172-172f.

2378. ———. THE LAND OF HEART'S DESIRE. London: T. Fisher Unwin, 1904. 48 pp. WADE 10

This is apparently the copy described in WADE and conjectured there to have been WBY's own copy. It is lacking the three fleurons on the cover after the word "Desire." No printed slip.

2379. ———. THE LAND OF HEART'S DESIRE. New York: Dodd, Mead, 1909. 56 pp. WADE 14. Sig.: WB Yeats/ May 5/ 1925

2380. ———. THE LAND OF HEART'S DESIRE. 7th ed. London: T. Fisher Unwin, 1912. 48 pp. WADE 94

2380a. Another copy.

2380b. Another copy. 10th impression, 1916.

On cover, ink: <u>THEATRE</u>. Prompt. [likely WBY's]
Pp. 8-9, a plan for the stage set; below a list of locations for characters, e.g.: Bridget sitting alone fire [sic]
Throughout, diagrams, apparently WBY's, in ink and pencil, for placing the characters on the stage.
Also, numerous cuts; these generally follow the cuts WBY suggests to amateurs. Cf. VAR, p. 182. No verbal revisions.

2380c. Another copy. 11th impression, 1919.

2380d. Another copy. 23rd impression, 1925. Parchment covers; green ruled.

2381. ———. LAST POEMS. London: Macmillan, 1940. viii, 128 pp. WADE 203

On dustjacket: Dated Copy [GY's as all following]
Flyleaf: Dated Copy
In Contents, poems have been numbered consecutively, except that "The Great Day," "Parnell," and "What Was Lost" are bracketed and numbered: 23.

In Contents, "News from the Delphic Oracle" has been corrected to: News for ...

In text GY has dated most of the poems, in some cases noted the place of composition or made other identifications.

"The Gyres": 1937
"Lapis Lazuli": July 1936
"Imitated from the Japanese": Dec. 30, 1937
"Sweet Dancer": Margot Collis at Barcelona. March 1936/ Jan. 1937
"The Three Bushes": Sept. 1936
"The Lady's First Song": 1936
"The Lady's Second Song": July 1936
"The Lady's Third Song": July 1936
"The Lover's Song": Nov. 1936
"The Chambermaid's First Song": Nov. 1936
"The Chambermaid's Second Song": Nov. 1936
"An Acre of Grass": Riversdale 1932-1939/ 1935.
"What Then": Cf. "dawn of day" ?Nietzsche. "or else my ___, or else?" Look up [Nietzsche's] letters to Peter Fast - 1879./ Jan. 1937.
"Beautiful Lofty Things": 1936
"A Crazed Girl": Margot Collis at Barcelona in May 1936
"To Dorothy Wellesley": Aug. 1936
"The Curse of Cromwell": Jan. 1937
"Roger Casement": Nov.-Dec. 1936
"The Ghost of Roger Casement": Dec. 1936
"The O'Rahilly": Jan. 1937
"Come Gather Round Me, Parnellites": Sept. 1936
"The Wild Old Wicked Man": June 1936
"The Great Day": Jan. 1937
"Parnell": Jan. 1937
"What Was Lost": Jan. 1937
"The Spur": Dec. 7, 1936
"A Drunken Man's Praise ...": 1937
"The Pilgrim": Feb. 1937
"Colonel Martin": See various typescripts with F.R. Higgins alterations/ / Aug. 1937
"A Model for the Laureate": July 1937
"The Old Stone Cross": MSS. April-May 1937 Steyning. Chantry House, Sussex, Home of Edith Shackleton Heald and sister.
"The Spirit Medium": 1937
"Those Images": Aug. 13, 1937
"The Municipal Gallery Revisited": Aug.-Sept. 1936
"Are You Content?": srette soddisfatto? (Shelley's ghost)
"In Tara's Halls": Riversdale. June 1938.
"News for the Delphic Oracle": 1938. Cf. 'Cleft in the Rock.' Denforny [?], p. 8.
"Three Marching Songs": Dec. (?) 1938
"Long-Legged Fly": Apr. 1938
"A Bronze Head": 1937-8
"John Kinsella's Lament ...": 29 July 1938
"Hound Voice": June-Aug. 1938

"High Talk": Aug. 1938
"The Apparitions": March-April 1938
"A Nativity": Aug. 1936
"Why Should Not Old Men Be Mad": Jan. 1936
"The Statesman's Holiday": Monte Carlo. Winter 1936.
"Crazy Jane on the Mountain": July 1938
"The Circus Animals' Desertion": July-Oct. 1938
"Politics": May 1938
"The Man and the Echo": July 1938
"Cuchulain Comforted": a dream on the night of January 7th dictated in its prose form at 3 a.m.
PURGATORY: 1938
THE DEATH OF CUCHULAIN: Dec. 1938 - Jan. 1939

2381a. Another copy. Bp: GY

Poems numbered consecutively in Contents by GY.
Many poems dated etc. in text by GY; an entry follows only if the date differs from that in 2381.
"Imitated from the Japanese": Jan. 1937
"The Three Bushes": Summer 1936
"The Lady's First Song": Nov. 1936
"The Ghost of Roger Casement": Jan. 1937
"The O'Rahilly": Oct. 1936
"Come Gather Round Me, Parnellites": Sept.-Oct. 1936
"The Old Stone Cross": June 1937 (at Steyning)
"Three Songs to the One Burden": Aug.-Oct. 1938
"The Statues": Re-written June 1938
"Long-Legged Fly": "London. Nov. 1937" Re-written Apr. 1938
"A Bronze Head": Mentone. Feb. 20, [1938]
"The Statesman's Holiday": Apr. 1938
"The Man and the Echo": July-Oct. 1938
PURGATORY: Apr. 1938
P. 22, in "The Curse of Cromwell," at "Because it proves that things both can and cannot be": X see p. 90 "Essays"
P. 48ff, "The Municipal Gallery Revisited" revised in accidentals; many of these changes first appear in WADE 211, COLLECTED POEMS, 1950.
P. 59, title "News For the Delphic Oracle" corrected to: News From ...
P. 73, in "High Talk" "Daddy-long-legs" revised to: Daddy longlegs [no printing follows]
P. 98, in PURGATORY, a box around "I saw it fifty years ago" and a line leading to a note at top: interpolated as proof of 'Boiler' by WBY. Dec. 1938 correspondence.
In PURGATORY, many changes in accidentals, but they do not appear in any printing.

2381b. Another copy.

Flyleaf: George Yeats/ To be returned
P. 99, line 40 in PURGATORY revised to: The dream must end; if upon themselves [GY's; first in WADE 211D]
P. 107, line 205 of PURGATORY revised to: because had he grown up [GY's; first in WADE 211D]

2381c. Another copy. Bp: GY

Markings by GY.
P. 11, after "The Lady's First Song": Nov. 1936?
P. 76, in "Why Should Not Old Men be Mad?" the comma is canceled after line 7 and: note to T. March. This comma was interpolated - did not exist in copy for 'Boiler.' [VAR. confirms this]
P. 98, a box around line 11 of "The Statesman's Holiday" and a note: interpolated in Oct. 1938 proof of 'Boiler' [one word undecipherable].
In text, many queries about accidentals.
After PURGATORY: April 1930
After THE DEATH OF CUCHULAIN: Dec. 1938 - Dec. 1939
Back flyleaf, a note for PURGATORY: Check hyphenation in [word or words canceled] i.e. p. 123 "fighting-man"/ p. 102 "knife-wound"/ etc./ p. 103 "whiskey-bottle"/ p. 101 "eighteenth-century" [the note continues:] P. 97. "And that's" should be "And that" _______/ P. 98. "Upon themselves" should be "If upon themselves"

2381d. Another copy. Bp: Lily Yeats

Flyleaf: Lily from George/ February 18, 1940.
Pasted inside back cover, a review of this vol. from IRISH TIMES, 1940.
Inserted, an envelope postmarked Dec. 29, [18]96, no enclosure, French stamp, addressed to: W.B. Yeats Esq./ 203 Boulevard Raspain/ Paris

2382. ———. LATER POEMS. London: Macmillan, 1922. xiv, 368 pp. WADE 134

Flyleaf: corrected copy. not to be given away/ WB Yeats/ June 1923.
Table of contents has been excised.
Revisions following are in green crayon.
P. 64, line 94 of "Baile and Aillinn" revised to: Our hearts can hear the voices chide. [first in LATER POEMS, London, 1924]
P. 177, line 16 of "The Grey Rock" revised to: They sang a drowsy song [first in LATER POEMS, London, 1924]
P. 177, line 18 revised to: The smoky torches ... [as above]
P. 226, line 9 of "Friends" revised to: Mind and delighted mind [first in LATER POEMS, London, 1924]
P. 251, lines 1-3 of "The Living Beauty" revised to: I bade, because the wick is trimed [sic] and the oil spent/ And frozen all the channels of the blood,/ My discontented heart draw content [followed approximately in WADE 172].
P. 253, in "To a Young Beauty" "Beaujolet" corrected to: Beauvarlet [first in LATER POEMS, London, 1926]
P. 255 in "The Scholars" lines 7-10 and line 12 revised as in VAR. [first in WADE 172)

P. 287, line 2 of "On being asked for a War Poem" revised as in VAR. (first in LATER POEMS, London, 1926)
P. 318, line 39 of "The Double Vision of Michael Robartes" revised as in VAR. (first in LATER POEMS, London, 1926)
P. 327, a very elaborate revision of "Solomon and the Witch" in pencil, green crayon, and ink. The revisions flow over onto p. 326.
P. 327, top, a draft in pencil canceled in crayon for lines 6-7, "And he that knew/ All sounds by bird or angel sung": All things by bird or angel sung
or what the cats and tiger call.
Answered - a crested cockerel crew
A hundred years before the Fall
Upon a blossoming etc.
P. 327, bottom, a further draft of the same lines as above:
Who understood
All that is thought or said or sung
All that is brayed, or cried, or crowed
Thereon explained "A cockerel
P. 326, bottom, a further draft of the lines above:
who understood
whatever has been said or sung
or miawed, howled brayed
brayed cried sighed
aired
Thereon explained: "a cockerel
[This last draft canceled as the following which appears immediately above:]
crew
cried out
meyowd
Or howled, mewed, yelled bellowed brayed cried
crowed
P. 326, lengthwise in margin, another draft:
who understood
what ever has been said, sighed sung
howled miewed [Xed] miau-d [Xed, but] barked brayed
[restored]
[above]
belled, yelled, cried crowed
Thereon explained "a cockerel
[This last draft approximates the version in LATER POEMS, London, 1924.]
Pp. 355-64, the notes, have been excised.

2382a. Another copy.

P. 297, lines 35-7 in "Ego Dominus Tuus": Paradiso xviii/57
P. 297, lines 38ff.: Tu proverai si como sudi sale/
Il pane d'altrui, e com e duro calle/
Lo scendere e i salire poe l'atrui scale.
[Likely GY's as above]

2382b. Another copy. Dec. 1922 reprinting.

On bp, Helen emerging from egg by T.S. Moore: Not to be given away. Dates written in by George. WBY.
P. 3, "Hosting of the Sidhe": unaltered [GY's as all following]
P. 6, "The Lover Tells of the Rose in His Heart": title altered for 1908 Ed. Bullen ed.
P. 9, "The Fisherman": originally "Breasal the Fisherman" [no indication of this in VAR.]
Continuing to p. 46, GY has entered earlier variant titles.
P. 242, lines 57-64 in "In Memory of Major Robert Gregory": interpolated after the poem was finished at Mrs. Robert Gregory's request.
P. 244, after "In Memory of Major Robert Gregory": Ballinamontane & Ballylee/ Summer 1918.
P. 245, after "An Irish Airman Foresees his Death": 1918
P. 249, "Under the Round Tower": Glendalough - March 1918.
P. 253, after "To a Young Beauty": Stephens Green - Winter 1918-19
P. 279, after "His Phoenix": Stone Cottage. Coleman Hatch, Winter 1914
P. 300, after "A Prayer on Going into My House": Ballylee, Summer 1918.
P. 309, after "Phases of the Moon": Ballylee 1919 Summer
P. 314, after "Two Songs of a Fool": Ballinamontane, Summer 1918, Gort.
P. 315, after "Another Song of a Fool": Ballinamontane, Summer 1918
P. 319, after "The Double Vision of Michael Robartes": Glenmalure 1918
P. 326, after "Michael Robartes and the Dancer": 96 Stephens Green. Winter 1918-19.
P. 331, after "Image from a Past Life": Ballylee - Summer 1919
P. 333, after "Under Saturn": Oxford
P. 340, after "On a Political Prisoner": Stephens Green/ Winter 1918-19
P. 343, after "Towards Break of Day": Enniskerry/ Winter 1918-19
P. 345, after "Demon and Beast": Stephens Green. Winter 1918-19
Inserted is a notice from Greystones Parish Church dated 1965.

2382c. Another copy. 1922 printing.

In Contents, many poems checked.
P. 309, in line 2 of "The Realists" "can" revised to: could [WBY's?; no printing follows]
P. 253, "Beaujolet" canceled.
P. 360, slight changes in the note to Prefatory Poem.
Back flyleaf and inside back cover, brief notes on poetry and specifically Yeats's poetry, possibly GY's.

Inserted, a sheet of blue notepaper with apparently a transcribed (?) critique of THE PLAYER QUEEN, authorship unknown.

2382d. Another copy. March 1926 reprinting; in dustjacket.

The numbers 1 to 8 have been inserted from pp. 1-152, as galley numbers?

2383. ———. LATER POEMS. New York: Macmillan, 1924. xvi, 368 pp. WADE 135

Lines are numbered in "The Secret Rose," "Old Age of Queen Maeve," and "Baile and Aillinn."
In "The Shadowy Waters" and "The Harp of Aengus" some lines are "xed."
P. 175, apparently a fair hand revision of lines 5, 7, 9-12, 13, 16 in "Pardon, old Fathers." The inserted revisions as in VAR. main text; they first appear in SELECTED POEMS, London, 1929.
Lines in "The Grey Rock," "The Two Kings," and "The Three Beggars" are numbered in pencil.
P. 212, line 4 of "The Hour Before Dawn" is "xed."
P. 240, inserted, a note in ink on the flap of an envelope: Do you make out that Butler has changed his allegiance in the last version of the poem on Anastor. It is not quite clear. [not WBY's]
P. 253, in "To a Young Beauty" Beaujolet revised to: Beauvarlet
P. 255, lines 7-10 and 12 heavily revised in ink, in 3 drafts. Below the printed text:

All shuffle there, cough in the ink
Wear out the carpet with their shoes
Think what other people think,
Know the man their neighbour knows. [canceled]
[and another draft below]
Cough ink or their pot of ink,
All wear the carpet etc.
    wear out etc. [canceled]
[and at top, the final draft]
All shuffle there, all cough in ink,
All wear the carpet with their shoes,
All think what other people think,
All know the man their neighbor knows,
[First in SELECTED POEMS, London, 1929, except accidentals]

Line 12, "Should" revised to: Did [first in SELECTED POEMS]
On a slip inserted at p. 278: (179) [this slip on reverse has holograph text of a letter (?) or poem (?) but too fragmentary to be decipherable.]

2383a. Another copy. 10/250 Sig.: WBY

Limited ed. in brown paper boards.
Most pp. uncut.

2384. ———. LETTERS TO THE NEW ISLAND. Cambridge: Harvard Univ. Press, 1934. xvi,224 pp. WADE 173

Flyleaf: For W.B. Yeats, this copy/ of his own book./ with the homage of the editor [Horace Reynolds].
P. 104, next to the passage "I have never heard verse better spoken than by the lady who takes the part of the shepherdess heroine, Amaryllis": Florence Farr.
P. 117, next to "Mrs. Edward Emery": Florence Farr
P. 118, next to "war correspondent who prefers to remain hidden under the name of Mr. Smith": Heron-Allen

2385. ———. MODERN POETRY. The Eighteenth of the Broadcast National Lectures. London: BBC, 1936. 28 pp. WADE 188

2386. ———. NINE ONE-ACT PLAYS. London: Macmillan, 1937. vi,218 pp. WADE 190

In dustjacket.

2387. ———. NINE POEMS. [New York:] Privately printed for John Quinn and his friends, 1914. 36 pp. WADE 109

Copy described by Wade with no label on frt. cover. The copy described by Wade with the label printed in red with WBY's name on cover is not in the library.

2388. ———. NINE POEMS. London: Privately printed by Clement Shorter, 1918. ii,18 pp. WADE 122

2389. ———. ON BAILE'S STRAND. Dublin, Maunsel, 1905. ii,120 pp. Bp: Eliz. C. Yeats. WADE 58

Pp. uncut, but inserted a small slip: [seal]/ Godolphin Foundation School/ Hammersmith/ Chemistry 1 prize/ WB Yeats
Also inserted, a review of Yeats's and Moore's DIARMUID AND GRANIA, 709.

2390. ———. ON BAILE'S STRAND. London: A.H. Bullen, 1907. 36 pp. WADE 68. Sig.: WBY

2390a-f. Six more copies.

2391. ———. ON THE BOILER. Dublin: Cuala Press, 1939. 48 pp. WADE 202

2391a-c. Three more copies.

2392. ———. PER AMICA SILENTIA LUNAE. London: Macmillan, 1918. 2,vi,96 pp. WADE 120

P. 9, "... and how should I keep my head among images of good and evil, crude allegories" revised in ink to: and how should I keep my head amid wooden allegories painted in black and gold and vermillion.
P. 17, "to slake it with" revised to: to appease it with

P. 24, "for that only which comes easily can never be a portion of our being, 'soon got, soon gone,' as the proverb says" revised to: for that only which comes easily stays not in our being but as the proverb puts it 'ill got, soon gone.'
P. 24, after "ripened by the sun" a space is indicated.
P. 72, in "The Moods": And the mountains and the [canceled] woods. [a correction]
P. 75, "Caesarea" corrected to: Caesarion

2392a. Another copy.

Corrections on pp. 72, 75 as above.

2392b. Another copy.

On a slip of paper inserted: (157) could be checked [followed by six page numbers in the 300's; obviously not in this volume]

2392c-d. Two other copies.

Pp. uncut.

2393. ———. PER AMICA SILENTIA LUNAE. New York: Macmillan, 1918. 98 pp. WADE 121

2393a-c. Three more copies.

2394. ———. THE PLAYER QUEEN. London: Macmillan, 1922. iv,64 pp. WADE 138

2394a. Another copy.

2395. ———. PLAYS AND CONTROVERSIES. London: Macmillan, 1923. 2,x,464 pp. WADE 139

Flyleaf: Edith Ellen Tucker/ At Kenyon Cottage/ Sidmouth

2396. ———. PLAYS AND CONTROVERSIES. New York: Macmillan, 1924. WADE 140

On cover, a label pasted with: "B"
P. 85, "Witcherly" corrected to: Wycherly
P. 103, "pictures her" revised to: picture it
P. 147, "under that of" revised to: overpowered by
Pp. 171-2, slight corrections.
P. 198: Insert here essay from Samhain/ Nov. 1908.
Pp. 301-2, the Preface to THE LAND OF HEART'S DESIRE has been canceled.
Pp. 421-4, the music for AT THE HAWK'S WELL is torn out.

2396a. Another copy.

Pp. torn out through half title p.
Frontispiece, verso, sig.: GY

2397. ———. PLAYS FOR AN IRISH THEATRE. London and Stratford: A.H. Bullen, 1911. 6,xvi,230 pp. WADE 136

Flyleaf, verso: seance 2 [o'clock?]
2nd flyleaf: George's copy. I am not to take it whatever the need/ WBY
Many pp. uncut.
Pasted on back cover, recto, a white label, ruled: Plays for an Irish Theatre etc.

2397a. Another printing, 1913.

On cover, a label pasted with: A
On title p., the title is canceled.
Pp. iv-xiv, the Preface excised.
P. xv, Contents, canceled.
P. 1, title p. for DEIRDRE, a galley notation ?: 19/T.G.
P. 5, next to first scene description: o & i
Pp. 12-21, lines 165-71, 206-10, 309-18, 336-40, 351-9, 370-4, 389-402 of DEIRDRE have been heavily revised in ink. On pp. 19, 20, 21, slips have been pasted over the text with WBY's inked revisions. The revisions are fair hand, as if copied from another source, apparently to provide copytext for WADE 136, PLAYS IN PROSE AND VERSE, London, 1922; the revisions are followed there exactly. For an earlier version of some of the same revised lines, see 2326.
Printer's marks (?), pp. 29, 34 etc.
P. 36, at the list of characters in THE GREEN HELMET a notation to move the list to the verso of the half title p.
THE GREEN HELMET is marked passim.
Pp. 91-158, THE KING'S THRESHOLD wholly excised.
P. 161, below THE HOUR-GLASS: (In Prose)
Pp. 177 and 178, typed slips have been pasted over the text beginning with "Fool. Ah now that is different" to end. Again these revisions are followed exactly in WADE 136.
CATHLEEN NI HOULIHAN marked passim.
P. 195, the description of the set of THE SHADOWY WATERS has been slightly revised in pencil; again the revision has been followed in WADE 136.

2397b. Another copy, 1913 printing. Sig.: GHY, 1914

Preface, pp. iv-xiv, excised.

2398. ———. PLAYS IN PROSE AND VERSE. London: Macmillan, 1922. 2,x,452 pp. WADE 136

Flyleaf: George Yeats (not to be taken by me. WBY)
P. 144, lines 547-53, revised, ink, WBY's: It was woven/ By women of the Country-under-Wave/ Out of the fleeces of the sea. [all canceled] Say that I heard a raven croak and was afraid./ Conchubar. Witchcraft has troubled his mind. [no printing follows]
Many pp. uncut.

2398a. Another copy.

Flyleaf: George Yeats her book not to/ be taken by me. WB Yeats.

2398b. Another copy. Dec. 1922 printing.

Many pp. uncut; in dustjacket.

2399 ———. PLAYS IN PROSE AND VERSE. New York: Macmillan, 1924. x,460 pp. WADE 137

"Published March, 1924"
Pp. 425 to end, notes and music torn out.

2399A. Another, limited ed. 167/250. Sig.: WBY

Most pp. uncut.

2400. ———. POEMS, 1899-1905. London: A.H. Bullen, 1906. xvi,280 pp. Bp: Lily Yeats. WADE 64

Flyleaf: To my father. WB Yeats
P. 105, line 435 of ON BAILE'S STRAND revised from "one of those" to: were of those [followed in WADE 68]
P. 105, line 437 revised from "though you held" to: thought you held [no printing follows]

2401. ———. POEMS: SECOND SERIES. London: A.H. Bullen, 1909. viii,164 pp. WADE 83

This volume has been rebound in grey boards, apparently as printer's copy; all pp. (including title p.) between flyleaf and half title p. have been excised. The white label with black printing described by Wade has been pasted on the front. Also on cover, a white label with: A
The misprint "host of the hair" described by Wade is in this copy.
Throughout are directions to the printer as "caps" etc.; also, apparently, galley notations as "H.7." Dates have been entered after some of the poems as after THE WIND AMONG THE REEDS: 1892 - 1899.
P. 64, lines 126-7 in "Baile and Aillinn" added in ink as they first appear in WADE 134, LATER POEMS, London, 1922.
P. 72, lines 5-6 of "The Arrow" canceled and substituted in ink the version which first appears in WADE 134.
P. 73, lines 5-7 of "The Folly of Being Comforted" revised, ink, as first in WADE 134.
P. 78, lines 14-18 revised in ink:

And thereupon
That beautiful mild woman for whose sake
There's many a one shall find out all heartache
On finding that her voice is sweet and low
Chimed for an answer all we women know

[This is a working revision rather than a fair hand insertion as the entries above; lines 15 and 17 first appear in WADE 134, but line 18 appears in no printed version.]

P. 84, lines 17-18 of "Under the Moon" revised, ink, as first in WADE 134.
P. 85, lines 1, 2, 4, 9, and 10 revised in "The Hollow Wood" which is retitled "The Ragged Wood." The revisions in the title and in lines 1, 2 and 9 have apparently been copied from WADE 103, the Tauchnitz ed. and a further revision in line 4 added to make the copytext for WADE 134 except for line 10 which shows a slight variation from the Tauchnitz and a further revision in WADE 134:
I'll hello all those lovers out, and cry- [not followed exactly in any printing]
P. 93, "The Musician's Songs from Deirdre" marked delete.
P. 95-8, the three songs marked delete.
THE SHADOWY WATERS has been heavily revised to p. 110, lightly thereafter. Again, these revisions are first followed in WADE 134, LATER POEMS, London, 1922.
Pp. 145-60, the notes, have been ripped from this copy.

2402. ———. POEMS. London: T. Fisher Unwin, 1912. xvi,324 pp. WADE 99

In Contents, checks against "The Lake Isle of Innisfree" and "The Ballad of Father Gilligan."
Pp. uncut to 41.
Pp. 142-54, lines in many poems marked with "x."
In "The Wanderings of Oisin," pp. 249ff., lines are numbered passim; in some cases an "x" precedes the line number, as x9, x54, x56, x63, x64, x96 etc. There are no revisions in the text, but apparently this notation indicates that a line is to be revised, probably to remove archaic diction. Many revisions in the marked lines first appear in WADE 165, SELECTED POEMS, London, 1929, as for example in line 9 where "maidens dancing" becomes "merry couples."
P. 276 in Book II of "The Wanderings of Oisin" marked by a paper slip with: (32E)
On this p. a note in pencil after line 112: could [?] be to here
Book III of "Oisin" is unmarked.

2402a. Another copy.

Has T.S. Moore's bp. of Helen emerging from egg with: 'An aimless joy is a pure joy' WB Yeats.
This copy has the slip bound in before the frontispiece as described by Wade.

2403. ———. POEMS. London: T. Fisher Unwin, 1922. xvi,316 pp. WADE 100. Sig.: M Davies Webster

A later printing of the 1913 ed. The title p. is slightly different from the copy described in Wade: T. Fisher Unwin Ltd. [red]/ London: Adelphi Terrace.
Frt. cover is stamped blind.

2403a. Another printing, 1923.

At epigraph and on Contents pp. numbers inserted, as printer's marks?

On half title p., pencil: insert/ "The Countess Cathleen/ from book A pages/ 219 to 284 inclusive [this canceled as is the title "The Countess Cathleen." But following, another note, ink:] Insert "The Countess Cathleen from Book B pages 219 to 284 inclusive, or [if] not completely resetting this book correct by this version. There are over a few corrections. [The ref. to "Book B" is uncertain. Though 2396 is so designated and contains the play, it dates from 1924.]

Pp. xviii-103 canceled in pencil.

P. 111 canceled and a note above, ink: insert here 'Fergus and the Druid' from Book C pages 101 to 103 or correct this version.

P. 114, ink: insert instead of the poem "Cuchulain's Fight with the sea" from Book C pages 104 to 112 inclusive. ["The Death of Cuchulain" on this p. is canceled, but some lines are numbered and some marked x3, x4 etc.]

P. 125, "A Cradle Song Canceled," and above a note, ink: insert here instead of this poem "A Cradle Song" from Book C page 115.

P. 127, "The Sorrow of Love" canceled and a note: insert here instead of this poem "The Sorrow of Love" from Book C page 117.

P. 128, in "When You are Old" the revision in line 6 from "will" to: with [first in WADE 171]

P. 131, line 3 of "A Dream of Death," "face" is circled.

P. 136, line 42 of "The Man who Dreamed of Faeryland" revised to: proclaiming with a low and reedy cry [first in WADE 165]

P. 137, "The Dedication to a Book of Stories ..." canceled and a note: Insert instead of this/ poem of same name in book C page 126 & 127.

P. 139, "The Lamentation of the Old Pensioner" canceled and a note: Insert instead of this the poem of same name in Book C page 128.

P. 145, "To Ireland in the Coming Times" canceled and a note: insert instead of this/ poem of same name from Book C pages 134-135.

P. 149, the title p. for THE LAND OF HEART'S DESIRE canceled and a note: "Land of Heart's Desire." Insert here from Book B pages 297 to 327 inclusive [But this too has been canceled and the original marked "stet"].

Pp. canceled to 191.

P. 197, lines are numbered in "The Song of the Happy Shepherd."

P. 235, title p. for THE WANDERINGS OF USHEEN, a note: Instead of the poem insert "Wanderings of Usheen" from Book C pages 1 to 57 or if not completely resetting correct by this version. There are only a few alterations.

In Books I and II of WANDERINGS many lines are "xed" as x9, x54, x56, x63, x64, x96 etc. See note for 2402.

P. 257, a slip of paper inserted with: (32K)
P. 299, the last two entries marked delete.
P. 312, first five entries deleted.
P. 313, after "like an epilogue": W.B.Y. 1912 [and a line leading to a note at the top:] when revised last spring the passages between brackets were left out. WBY.
P. 314, after text: WBY. 1912 [and a note:] Insert here note from Book C pages 527 and 528.

2404. ———. POEMS. London: Ernest Benn, [1929]. xii,324 pp. WADE 154

On flyleaf, the long note by WBY as recorded in Wade.
Before "The Countess Cathleen in Paradise" and again before "Who Goes with Fergus": 32

2405. ———. POEMS WRITTEN IN DISCOURAGEMENT, 1912-1913. Dundrum: Cuala Press, 1913. 8 pp. WADE 107

2406. ———. THE POETICAL WORKS OF WILLIAM B. YEATS. Vol. 1: LYRICAL POEMS. London: Macmillan, 1906. 2,xiv,340 pp. WADE 65. Bp: Lily Yeats

Flyleaf: To Miss Lily Yeats/ with the kind/ regards of/ John Quinn/ Dec 9, 1907.

2407. ———. Vol. 2: DRAMATICAL POEMS. New York: Macmillan, 1907. x,530 pp. WADE 71. Bp: Lily Yeats. Sig.: Lily Yeats

Inside frt. cover, pasted, two photographs of WBY, one clipped from a newspaper.
Inserted 4 loose pp. advertising novels by various authors.
Folded in at end of book, an Abbey Theatre Program, SEE 5.

2407a. Another copy. Bp: Lily Yeats. Sig.: Lily Yeats

2408. ———. THE POETICAL WORKS OF WILLIAM B. YEATS. Rev. ed. Vol. 2: DRAMATIC POEMS. New York: Macmillan, 1914. x,534 pp. WADE 98. Bp: WBY

2409. ———. THE POT OF BROTH. London: A.H. Bullen, 1905. 16 pp. WADE 60

2410. ———. THE POT OF BROTH. 2nd theatre ed. London: A.H. Bullen, 1911. 16 pp. WADE 61

2410a-f. Six more copies. Uncut.

2411. ———. LES PRIX NOBEL EN 1923. THE IRISH DRAMATIC MOVEMENT. Stockholm: P.A. Norstedt, 1924. 12 pp. WADE 144

2411a-c. Three more copies.

2412. ———. RESPONSIBILITIES AND OTHER POEMS. London: Macmillan, 1916. xii,188 pp. WADE 115. Bp: WBY

On cover, a square of paper pasted on with: A
Revisions and corrections in this copy were apparently made to provide a partial copytext for WADE 134, LATER POEMS, London, 1922.
P. 40, title changed to: On those that hated 'The Playboy of the Western World,' 1907 [first in WADE 134]
P. 66, Poem II of "To A Child Dancing in the Wind" is given a separate title: Two Years Later [first in WADE 134].
P. 76, line 9 of "An Appointment" is restored from the first printing: Nor heavy knitting of the brow
P. 78, in "The Dolls" "balls" corrected to: bawls [first in WADE 134].
P. 80, in line 6 of "A Coat" "eye" revised to: eyes [first in WADE 134].
P. 90, in line 6 of "The Fascination of What's Difficult" "an Olympus" to: Olympus [first in WADE 134].
P. 104, a slip inserted with: (149)
P. 104, line 4 of "To a Poet, who would have me Praise ..." revised to: But was there ever a dog that praised his fleas? [WADE 134 follows except for "ever"].
P. 137, in THE HOUR-GLASS, "who" revised to: whom I spoke to.
P. 162, line 440 revised to: Said that my soul was lost unless I found [first in WADE 136, PLAYS IN PROSE AND VERSE, London, 1922].
Pp. 183-4 torn out.
P. 185-6, the notes to "These controversies" marked delete.

2412a. Another copy.

On slip on cover, ink: B. Put first the section called "From the Green Helmet & Other Poems" (page 85)
The revisions here seem to provide additional copytext for WADE 134; apparently this vol. was meant to be used in conjunction with 2412.
On half title p. [the title p. has been torn out]: 1912-1914 [and] insert before the section called "The Green Helmet & Other Poems." See page 85 [but the number 83 in pencil below this; the title p. for "The Green Helmet" begins on p. 83].
P. xi, the epigraph p., "Responsibilities" canceled.
P. 4, line 17 of "The Grey Rock" "meal" revised to: meat [first in WADE 134].
P. 4, line 19 of "The Grey Rock" revised to: On metal Goban had hammered at [first in WADE 134, but lacking "had"].
P. 4, lines 20-6 revised as in VAR. (First in WADE 134).
P. 28, line 217 of "The Two Kings" revised to: For he had heard a noise on the horizon [no printing follows].
P. 37, line 17 of "To a Shade" revised through similar versions to: Your enemy, an old foul mouth, had set [first in WADE 134].

P. 40, lines 3-5 of "On those that hated 'The Playboy'..." revised as in VAR. (First in WADE 134).
P. 43, lines 44-53 revised as in VAR. (First in WADE 134).
P. 49, "The Well and the Tree" canceled.
P. 53, line 30 of "The Hour before Dawn" revised to: sleep sound: no phantom by his look. [No printing follows]
P. 53, line 32a, "Young Red-head" etc. deleted.
P. 54, on a piece of paper pasted over the text, a fair hand insertion, ink, of a revision of lines 33-64 of "The Hour before Dawn." The revised text is identical to VAR. with the following exceptions which represent unique variants, with one exception as noted.

line 37 to: Tired of his grave and wakened me?
line 42 to: Stay what you please but from day-break
line 54 to: Merely for stumbling on this whole
line 57 to: I will sleep until the winters gone [follows WADE 115]
line 63: 'I had no better plan. At first

P. 55, lines 53-64 canceled as required above.
P. 55, line 65 revised as in VAR (First in WADE 134).
P. 56, line 91 to: 'You cry aloud O would t'were spring [WADE 134 follows except for accidentals].
P. 83, "From the Green Helmet and Other Poems" dated: 1904-1912.
P. 103, title revised to: On Hearing that the Students of our New University have joined the Agitation against Immoral Literature [first in WADE 134].
P. 117 to end, THE HOUR-GLASS and notes torn out.

2412b. Another copy.

Inside frt. cover: Cover design [not WBY's]

2412c. Another copy. 1917 printing.

Poems marked in Contents; strokes in text passim.
Pp. 119-31, 133-48, 153-81 (to notes) torn out.
P. 150 in THE HOUR-GLASS lines 334a-334e canceled and in margin: Late- [?] A [although there is no revision here, a new version of these lines first appears in WADE 136].
P. 150, line 345 canceled but marked: Stet
P. 151 in THE HOUR-GLASS, lines 345a-345e canceled and a note: Late B [substitution first in WADE 136]
P. 151, lines 345f-g canceled but marked: stet [but they are in fact revised in WADE 136]
P. 152, a complex and incomplete revision of lines 358-61. Line 358 has been put into Latin (WBY's) as in VAR., but there it is the First Pupil's. Line 361 has been revised a number of times. One version reads: We are convinced by all that you have taught. [But all of this has been canceled including the letter "C" which appears in the margin.]

2412d. Another copy. 1917 printing.

Likely GY's copy.
In Contents, the poems in "Responsibilities" are dated from Mss. by GY; many poem titles are marked "Mss. undated"; those dated follow.

"Introductory Rhymes": Dec. 1913-Jan. 1914
"The Two Kings": Mss. Oct. 1912
"To a Wealthy Man": Mss. Oct. 25, 1912 [but in the left margin] Dec. 24, 1912
"Paudeen": Mss. Sept. 1913
"To a Shade": Sept. 29, 1913
"The Hour Before Dawn": Mss. Oct. 19, 1913
"The Mountain Tomb": Mss. undated "Colville"
"Fallen Majesty": Mss. "Colville"
"Friends": Mss. Jan. 1911

Apparently referring to "The Dolls": Broleatus [?] Mss.
Apparently referring to "A Coat": BM [as above?] Xmas [?] 1912 [?]
Inserted at back, a holograph letter from Sean O'Casey to WBY dated 25 Feb. 1935/ 49 Overstrand Mansions. This is the "missing letter" referred to in <u>The Letters of Sean O'Casey</u>. Edited by David Krause. Vol. 1: 1910-1941. Macmillan, 1975, p. 546. O'Casey expresses his sympathy for Yeats's recent illness with the hope that he will recover and continue to write.
Also inserted at end, a draft of a poem in ink on letterhead 18 Woburn Buildings, n.d.:

The red blood and our laden heavy heart[s]
have shut us in
We are bored [bound?] by flowers and [one word?] by the grass
All then is deceit in the singing [?] of the breast [?]
Mountain & cloud & wave delude us
It is time that we left it all
The stars & the planets succour [?] us
The sun calls the moon in a prayer, far [?]
& yonder [?] is the cold & silent [canceled]
cold & silent night [last word canceled]
& cleansing night.
May the dawn come by the golden day
in our open [?]

Also inserted, holograph copies, GY's apparently, of "Ephemera"/ "1899 Version," "The Meditation of the Old Fisherman"/ "1899 Version," and "A Song of the Rosy-Cross" from THE BOOKMAN. Oct. 1895.

2413. ———. RESPONSIBILITIES AND OTHER POEMS. New York: Macmillan, 1916. xii,196 pp. WADE 116

P. 28, "The Two Kings" numbered in pencil in text.
P. 52ff, in "The Hour Before Dawn" lines numbered in text and some "xed" as x32, x33, x36, x40, x46; in some cases this seems to indicate lines to be deleted or revised for WADE 134, but no revisions are made here.
P. 76, in "An Appointment," for line 8, "Nor the tame will, nor timid brain" has been substituted: No heavy

knitting of the brow [an insertion from the original ENGLISH REVIEW printing].
P. 78, the correction or revision in line 2 of "The Dolls," for "balls": bawls.
P. 80, in line 6 of "A Coat" the revision from "eye" to: eyes.
Inserted, a page from a constellation chart showing common constellations with the figures drawn in, as Cygnus the Swan, Scorpio etc.

2413a. Another copy.

Pp. uncut.

2414. ———. REVERIES OVER CHILDHOOD AND YOUTH. New York: Macmillan, 1916. viii,136 pp. WADE 112

In slipcase, title pasted on bottom.
Flyleaf: Lily Yeats/ May 1916 from/ John Quinn
A note inserted, GY's: Annotated by Lily/ Left to G.Y.
The annotations consist of identifications of characters, dates of death, birth etc. appearing anonymously in WBY's memoirs.
P. 2, at "It is Fitzroy Road": 23 Fitzroy Rd. Regent's Park
P. 2, at "William Middleton": Grandmama Pollexfen's brother
P. 3, at "The house was so big ...": Merville. Sligo. Now a convent. Nazareth House.
P. 4, at "William Pollexfen": W.P. son of Anthony Pollexfen. B. 1811 in The Forts, Barry Head Tipperary. Married his cousin Elizabeth Middleton. Sligo 1837. Died Sligo 1892.
P. 8, at "an uncle called me out of bed": F.H. Pollexfen
P. 8, at "awoke my cousin": Middleton
P. 10, at "His father had been in the Army ...": Anthony Pollexfen. Died 1833. Buried in Brisham [?], Devon.
P. 10, at "some old family place": Kitley Manor
P. 10, at "His mother had been a Wexford woman": Mary Stevens
P. 12, at "The youngest of my uncles was stout": Uncle Alfred Pollexfen. Died 1916.
P. 12, at "He was a clever man": Uncle William Pollexfen. Died 1913.
P. 12, at "George Pollexfen": Born 1839. Died 1910.
P. 13, at "that younger uncle": F.H. P[ollexfen]
P. 22, at "to see another little boy": our cousin George Middleton went to Florida. Died there some years ago. L.Y. 1935
P. 23, at "my sister": Lily Yeats
P. 24, at "had designed a steamer": The Janet designed by Uncle John Middleton. Merchant in Glasgow. Died 1892.
P. 29, at "Two-storied house": Leview [?]. Great Aunt Mary Yeats['s] house. Born Drumcliffe 1821. Died 1891 in Dublin.
P. 30, at "the oldest-looking cat": Pussyharris [?]

P. 31, at "my great-great-grandfather": Benjamin Yeats
P. 31, at "a widow": Great Aunt Ellen Yeats. Né Terry.
P. 32, at "my great-uncle Mat Yeats and his big family of boys": Fort Louis at Rathbroughan near Sligo. House by a ruined mill with a stream flowing in front of it.
P. 32, at "a King's County Soldier": General John Armstrong. Died 1742. F.R.S. quarterly ordnance. Buried in Tower of London. Portrait of him in the Marlborough at Blenheim.
P. 32, at "when his nephew came to dine": Colonel Young of Labraid [?] Co. Cavan, our great-great-grandbrother's brother.
P. 33, at "another ancestor": one of the Butlers
P. 34, at "grandfather had been Robert Emmett's friend": Rev. John Yeats of Drumcliffe.
P. 34, at "A great-uncle had been Governor of Penang": Major Patrick Corbet. Born 1841 at Madras in Royale house.
P. 34, at "an uncle of a still older generation": Alexander Armstrong. Great-grandmother Corbet's brother.
P. 34, at "An old man who had entertained many famous people": Great Uncle Robert Corbet. Born 1795, lost from mail boat 1870 or 71.
P. 34, at "battlement and tower": Sandymount Castle-Dublin
P. 34, at "illegitimate son": Armstrong I think.
P. 36, at "Mat Yeats": great uncle
P. 36, at "great-great-grandfather": "Patrick Corbet" Prattle run [?] Dublin. Died 1791.
P. 37, at "a Yeats": J.B.Y.
P. 37, at "my great-grandmother Corbet": Grace. Daughter of Capt. Robert Armstrong. Hackwood [?] Co. Cavan. Married 1791 William Corbet, son of P[atrick] C[orbet].
P. 37, at "He was the friend of Goldsmith": must have been his father that was G's friend.
P. 41, at "my eldest sister": Lily
P. 41, at "where an old gentlewoman taught us spelling": Miss Armstrong had been bridesmaid to Mama so she can't have been old.
P. 42, at "I read this encyclopaedia a great deal": Bought in London by Great grandfather Middleton in his wedding trip about 1817 or 1818.
P. 45, at "my younger brother Robert": Born London 1870. Died 1873.
P. 50, at "Burne Jones's house": 14 Eustace Villas
P. 50, at "Bedford Park": 8 Woodstock Rd.
P. 52, at "Sometimes my sister came with me": Lily
P. 60, at "my grandfather, William Yeats": Rev. WB Yeats. Born 1806. Died 1861?
P. 64, at "my friend the athlete": Cyril Veasey went to India.
P. 76, at "He is a cousin": Alexander Middleton
P. 79, at "a well-known pre-Raphaelite painter": Thomas Rooke.

P. 81, at "a pretty model": Nelly Whelan. Mother Italian. Father Irish. She sent telegram to W.B.Y. on his 70th birthday.
P. 92, at "The captain": Captain Keebler afterwards Harbour Master at Sligo.
P. 96, at "the pilot": Michael Gillen
P. 97, at "His father, the County Down Rector": Rev. W.B. Yeats
P. 99, at "a brawling squireen": John Robert Greenah [?]
P. 102, at "a long thatched house": Balscadden Cottage
P. 103, at "an old tenant": John Doran [?]
P. 104, at "the head-master": Wilkens
P. 110, at "My London school-fellow": Cyril Veasey
P. 113, at "Our house for the first year": only one winter I think. L.Y.
P. 113, at "a house overlooking the harbour": "Island View" facing Howth Harbour. A horrible little house.
P. 126, at "George Pollexfen": Born Sligo 1839. Died Sligo 1910.
P. 126, at "a tall, bare house": now the girl's high school, Sligo.
P. 132, at "he had once ridden steeplechases": rode under the name Paul Hamilton. Colours primrose & violet. L.Y.
P. 138, at "I called upon a cousin": Charles Middleton.
P. 143, at "A pretty girl": Laura Armstrong.
P. 145, at "cousins at Avena house": Middletons
P. 145, at "My girl cousin": Lucy Middleton
P. 150, at "we had moved from Howth to Rathgar": 10 Ashfield Terrace now 418 Harold's Cross Road.
P. 175, at " his father was a notorious Orange leader": W. Johnston of Bally Kittby [?]
P. 173, at "My friend, now in his last year at school": Charles Johnson went into the Indian C.S. but gave it up and went to New York where he died.
P. 200, at "I made with pastels upon the ceiling of my study a map of Sligo": small room with balcony at back of 3 Blenheim Road, my bedroom for years. L.Y.
P. 211, at "My grandfather" etc.: our grandparents died in Rathedmond, Sligo in Oct. or Nov. 1892.
Pasted in at end, two reviews of this book, one an unidentified review by Robert Lynd. For the other see 1809.

2415. ———. REVERIES OVER CHILDHOOD AND YOUTH. London: Macmillan, 1916. 2,x,216 pp. WADE 113. Bp: WBY

Flyleaf, pencil: Revs. 33, 36 [possibly WBY's]
P. 33, the passage "the notorious Major Sirr who betrayed the brothers Shears, taking their children upon his knees to question them, if the tale does not lie" canceled and revised to: arrested Lord Edward Fitzgerald and gave him the bullet which he died of in jail. [AUTOBIOGRAPHIES follows]
P. 36, "and how when the agent" revised to: of a speech of his when the agent [AUTOBIOGRAPHIES follows].

2415a. Another copy. Second printing, 1917.
In dustjacket; mostly uncut.

2416. ———. THE SECRET ROSE. London: Lawrence and Bullen, 1897. xii,268 pp. WADE 21. Bp: Lily Yeats. Sig.: Lily Yeats/ May 25/ '97

Inside back cover, pasted in, an unidentified photograph of WBY from a newspaper; apparently taken in the 1890's.

2417. ———. SELECTED POEMS. New York: Macmillan, 1921. viii,310 pp. WADE 128

Flyleaf: Not to be lent or given as it contains corrections/ W.B. Yeats/ 4 Broad St./ Oxford.
In Contents, numbers next to the poems, possibly galley notations.
P. 137, line 121, "terror strucken" to: terror- stricken [first in COLLECTED POEMS, WADE 171].
P. 145, line 126ff. of "Baile and Aillinn" revised to: Then seeing that he scarce had spoke/ Before her love-worn heart he broke/ Then ran and laughed until he came [No printing follows exactly, but WADE 134 is close].
P. 157, line 17 of "Under the Moon," an incomplete revision to: Because of something that I heard under the horn of the Hunter's moon
or
Because of something [one word?] under it
famished horn
of the hunter's moon [for WADE 134?]
P. 158, lines 14-17 revised as in VAR., but line 18: Chimed in an answer "all we women know [no printing follows].
P. 261, line 17 of "To a Shade" revised to: One that had slandered you, an old foul mouth, had set [No printing follows].
P. 269, line 22 of "The Wild Swans at Coole" the correction to: have not grown old
P. 289, line 10 of VI of "Upon a Dying Lady" the correction (?): into the face of Death.
P. 296, a deletion of "W.B. Yeats" in the second note.

2417a. Another copy.

On flyleaf, a list of poems in this vol. with page numbers interspersed with comments and subjects. Possibly a notation for a poetry reading with transitional comments interspersed; some of the late BBC programs broadcast by WBY include a number of these poems: Sligo Allingham Thoreau
1. Innisfree.5/ 2. Fiddler of D.9/ Mary Battle/ 3. Hosting of the S. 107/ 4. Father Gilligan.18/ Old man-nothing that he has observed/ cats - hedgehogs - spirit/ 5. Wandering Aengus.112/ 6. Happy Townland.162/ 7. Running to P. 264/ 8. Red Hanrahan.160/ 9. Irish Airman.275/ old poetic of love poetry/ 10. [He wishes for the] Cloths of Heaven.129/ 11. Never give all the Heart.153/ 12. The Cap and Bells.120/ (why do you write in this way)

In Contents, all the above poems are marked; also "The Cap and Bells," "He Wishes for the Cloths of Heaven," and "Never Give All the Heart" are labeled: Love Poems
Pp. 5 and 6 excised.
Pp. 301-4, bottom third, excised for notes for COUNTESS CATHLEEN etc.
First flyleaf at end, verso, notes continue in pencil: People Theater/ origin/ gaelic movement/ [one word?] village [?]
Second flyleaf at end, verso: Drunken Poet/ Hyde/ Much grown [?] - not [one word?]/ English/ People Theater
Inside back cover: Drunken sailor poet/ Hyde/ not creator - he was [one word?]/ English - Dialect - Synge. Lady G. & myself/ [one line canceled]/ Songs/ Mary Hynes/ Dramatic Movement/ Daughter of Erin [one word?]/ Two Fays/ My work [?]/ Truth and beauty/ Emigrants/ Rising of the Moon.

2417b. Another copy.

As in 2417a, flyleaf, the same poems are marked in contents from 1-12.
Pp. 306-8, bottom, notes canceled.

2417c. Another copy.

Flyleaf: 'only the wasteful virtues earn the sun'/ WB Yeats/ Jan 1925
In grey paper boards. (The previous three copies are in grey-green cloth.)
In Contents, some titles canceled.

2418. ———. SELECTED POEMS, LYRICAL AND NARRATIVE. London: Macmillan, 1929. 2,x,204 pp. WADE 165.

In Contents, "The Wanderings of Usheen (1889)" has been canceled; also checked in Contents "Down by the Salley Gardens," "He Wishes for the Cloths of Heaven." "The Grey Rock" is underlined.
Poems checked in text are "Sixteen Dead Men," "The Rose Tree," "On a Political Prisoner," "Demon and Beast," "Sailing to Byzantium"; in "Meditations in Time of Civil War" checked are "My Descendants" and "The Road at my Door."
After "Demon and Beast": SECOND COMING
After "A Prayer for My Daughter": Towards Break of Day/ Meditation Nov. 1914
After "Sailing to Byzantium": Whole Tower
In "Meditations" "The Stare's Nest by my Window" has been correctly numbered "VI."

2419. ———. A SELECTION FROM THE POETRY OF W.B. YEATS. Leipzig: Bernhard Tauchnitz, 1913. 272 pp. WADE 103. Bp: WBY

Preface uncut.
In Contents, a note at top, ink: include all that is not

marked 'omit'/ WB Yeats [Marked "omit" are "The Rose of the World," "The Rose of Peace," "The White Birds," "The Wanderings of Oisin." Added to the Contents is:] The Land of Hearts Desire (1893-1912) [and a note follows from this:] also notes for "Dramatic Works" [and a further note:] Add these from "poems": When you are old, The Ballad of Father Gilligan, The Indian upon god

P. numbers of all poems to the end are canceled; but at end a note: add poems marked in "Responsibilities" and "Wild Swans" beginning with those in "Responsibilities" WB Yeats

Pp. 246 and 247, checked in text are "A Woman Homer Sung," "That the Night Come," and "Friends."

P. 253, in line 4 of "At Galway Races," "field" corrected to: crowd

P. 17 of notes, "Pronunciation of the Irish Words" canceled and marked: omit

It appears that with the deletions and additions noted above, this vol. was intended as the copytext for WADE 128, SELECTED POEMS, New York, 1921.

2420. ———. THE SHADOWY WATERS. London: Hodder and Stoughton, 1900. 60 pp. WADE 30

Flyleaf: Miss Horniman/ from her friend/ W B Yeats/ Dec. 19, 1900.

P. 25, after "wings": M.S.S. ends [possibly WBY's as also the following]

P. 26, at "Two hover": MSS begins again

P. 27, after "bulwark": [MSS] ends

P. 44, the passage from "Edaine" to the end of the p. is circled with the comment: The Harp of Aengus

2420a. Another copy.

Flyleaf: To Mabel Dearmer/ with profound respect./ Jan. 21st 1901 [not WBY's]

2420b. Another, incomplete copy.

Copy ends at p. 8; the rest is made up of blank pp. Possibly a trial proof because the arrangement of the title p. differs slightly from WADE 30, above, and the typeface is more ornamental: THE SHADOWY WATERS/ By/ W. B. YEATS/ LONDON/ HODDER AND STOUGHTON/ 17 PATERNOSTER ROW/ MCM

Lacks the dedication to Lady Gregory. "In the Seven Woods" here, as much as appears, follows WADE 30.

2421. ———. THE SHADOWY WATERS. London: A.H. Bullen, 1907. 28 pp. WADE 66

Extensively revised in ink. The revisions are first incorporated in WADE 92, PLAYS FOR AN IRISH THEATRE, London, 1911, except lines 125-6 revised to: It may be that the dead have lit upon it/ Or those that never die - no mortal can [no printing follows exactly]

2421a-i. Nine more copies; some with pp. uncut.

2422. ———. THE SINGING HEAD AND THE LADY. Bryn Mawr: Privately printed by Frederic Prokosch, 1934. Unpag. WADE 180

Copy "A" on rice paper.

2422a-b. Copies "d" and "e" on rice paper.

2422c-d. Copies "III" and "IV" on Dresden.

2422e-g. Copies "2," "3," and "6" on Oland.

2423. ———. SOPHOCLES' KING OEDIPUS. London: Macmillan, 1928. viii,62 pp. WADE 160

On cover: George Yeats [WBY's]
P. 42, "Oedipus seemed blessed" revised in ink to: He seemed a blessed man [WBY's; not followed in any printing]

2423a. Another copy. Bp: Lily Yeats

Half title p., on a paper label pasted on: WB Yeats

2423b. Another copy.

Flyleaf: George Yeats copy./ W.B.Y.

2423c-e. Three more copies.

2424. ———. A SPEECH AND TWO POEMS. Dublin: For the Author at the Three Candles, 1937. 12 pp. WADE 193. 1/70

Flyleaf: Patrick Mai [the rest illegible; not WBY's]

2424a. Another copy. 65/70

Flyleaf: for Reginald Addyes-Scott/ from George Yeats/ February 12, 1945

2424b. Another copy. 70/70

Flyleaf: Toma S. Beppa/ from/ George Yeats
Inserted is a loose bp., TSM's Helen emerging from egg, signed by WBY.

2424c. Another copy. Unnumbered.

Includes the same bp. above pasted in with GY's inscription that runs off the bp onto the title p.: To Hon. James A. Farley with most deep gratitude and the [one word?] for his generous [?] appreciation and practical help which made possible the ending of life as tranquilly as I believe WBY himself wanted/ George Yeats. April 1939.

2425. ———. STORIES OF RED HANRAHAN. THE SECRET ROSE. ROSA ALCHEMICA. London: A.H. Bullen, 1913. viii,232. WADE 104

Largely uncut.

2426. ———. STORIES OF RED HANRAHAN. THE SECRET ROSE. ROSA ALCHEMICA. New York: Macmillan, 1914. vi,242 pp. WADE 105. Bp: WBY

P. 154, "Where there is Nothing, There is God" marked delete.
Pp. 77-8, the long dedication to A.E. has been marked delete and on the title p. facing, in ink: put a page after this with the words upon it/ To A.E.
P. 108, the passage beginning "Already, the Voice told him, the wayward light of the heart was shining" revised, ink, to: Already, the Voice told him that light was shining less brightly, and as it paled, corruption touched the stars and the hills and the grass and the trees, and none of those who had seen clearly the truth...
P. 109, the passage "and so they must prove their anger against the Powers of Corruption by dying in the service of the Rose of God" revised to: ... by finding death in the service of the Rose.

2426a. Another copy.

Inserted as bookmark, an American ad. for bookplates.

2426b. Another copy.

Inserted at p. 100, a small slip with: (142)

2427. ———. STORIES OF RED HANRAHAN AND THE SECRET ROSE. London: Macmillan, 1927. viii,184 pp. WADE 157

In paper wrapper.

2427a. Another copy. In paper wrapper.

2428. ———. THE TABLES OF THE LAW. THE ADORATION OF THE MAGI. London: Privately Printed, 1897. 48 pp. WADE 24 68/110. Bp: Lily Yeats

Flyleaf: Lily Yeats/ from/ WB Yeats/ Dec 29th/ 97
Back flyleaf, pencil: James Joyce in 1904 [possibly WBY's]

2429. ———. THREE THINGS. No. 18 of The Ariel Poems. London: Faber and Faber, 1929. Unpag. WADE 166

2429a-e. Five more copies.

2430. ———. THE TOWER. London: Macmillan, 1928. 2,vi,110,2 pp. WADE 158

P. 90ff., in "The Gift of Harun Al-Rashid" lines are numbered in pencil, likely WBY's.

2430a. Another copy.

Inserted at back, an early photograph of Thoor Ballylee; the wall is missing to the left of the bridge as one approaches the tower etc. Verso: Thoor Ballylee [WBY's] Return to Mrs. Yeats [GY's; and stamped:] Cuala Industries Ltd. 133, Lower Baggot St./ Dublin, Eire. Also inserted, a piece of notepaper headed "Riversdale, Willbrook, Rathfarnham, Dublin" with a list of poems for a radio broadcast entitled "In the Poet's Garden." Some of these poems were read in other broadcasts, but they do not seem to have been used all on the same program, nor is there a program with this title in WADE: 1. ah dancer song/ 2. Come dance with me. sung and spoken/ 3. Hokku. Spoken - two voices/ 4. Sankorin [Santorin?]. Spoken - two voices/ 5. King of China's daughter, song or Thur [?] Thin. (two voices, one sing)/ 6. Friar John of the crown [?]. one voice spoken/ 7. The morning after. one voice spoken/ 8. The mother of god. one voice spoken

2430b. Another copy.

Most pp. uncut.

2430c. Another copy. March 1928 printing.

Flyleaf: To Sato/ from his friend/ WB Yeats
In dustjacket.
In "Meditations" line 2 of "The Road at my Door" "Falstaffan" corrected (?) to: Falstaffian
In "Nineteen Hundred and Nineteen," line 58 "of gong" revised to: of a gong. [first in WADE 171]
In "Among School Children" in line 28 "mass of shadows" revised to: mess of shadows

2430d. Another copy. March 1928 printing.

Checked in Contents are "The Tower, "On a Picture of a Black Centaur," "The Three Monuments," "All Soul's Night."
In "Meditations in Time of Civil War" stress marks, apparently, have been added above some words.
Pp. 70ff. in "A Man Young and Old" "First Love" is marked "1x," "Human Dignity" "2x," etc. perhaps to indicate that the subtitles are to be dropped.

2430e. Another copy. March 1928 printing.

Flyleaf: George Yeats' copy/ not to be given away/ or taken to cut up/ or for any other purpose/ by me/ WBY.
In "Nineteen Hundred and Nineteen" and "Among School Children" the revisions as in 2430c, likely GY's.

2430f. Another copy. March 1928 printing.

Flyleaf: George/ from WBY Sept. 1913
Checked are "The Tower," "Meditations in Time of Civil War," "Nineteen Hundred and Nineteen," "The Wheel," "A

Prayer for my Son," "Wisdom," "On a Picture of a Black Centaur," "The Hero, the Girl, and the Fool," "The Three Monuments," "From 'Oedipus at Colonus,'" "All Souls' Night."
P. 48, Number II of "Two Songs from a Play," lines 7-8 revised to: Made all Atic tolerance vain/ Vain all Doric discipline. [GY's; no printing follows]
Inserted at end, a slip of paper with: eternity is Passion [not WBY's]

2431. ———. TRAGEDIE IRLANDESI. Milano: Studio Editoriale Lombardo, 1914. xlviii,140 pp. WADE, p. 369

Uncut; in dustjacket.

2431a-b. Two more copies. Uncut.

2432. ———. THE TREMBLING OF THE VEIL. London: Privately Printed, 1922. 2,viii,248 pp. WADE 133. 214/1000

Half title p.: Mrs. Tucker [GY's mother]/ From WB Yeats, Oct. 21/ 1922

2432a. Another copy. 561/1000

P. viii, Contents, is canceled.
Heavily corrected and revised in pencil by WBY, and there are a number of ts. insertions when the revisions get long. The revised and corrected text here is followed with very few exceptions in WADE 151, AUTOBIOGRAPHIES, London, 1926.
Revisions, deletions and corrections, pp. 4, 5, 29, 39, 40, 46, 56-7, 63-5, 68-73, 86-7, 100, 104, 108, 125, 135, 147, 157, 211-3.
Ts. insertions, pp. 70, 149, 212.
P. 242, inserted as copytext are p. 315ff of the July 1923 number of THE CRITERION entitled "A Biographical Fragment"; this text is also revised.
P. 135, an asterisk at "Hodos Chameliontos" indicating a note: Hodos Camelionis was the word used by the Hermetic Society, a mixture of Greek and Latin typical of sixteenth and seventeenth century magical writings.
P. 157, for first production of A DOLL'S HOUSE in England corrected from Royalty Theatre to: Novelty Theatre [but WADE 151 does not follow].

2433. ———. A VISION. London: Privately Printed, 1925. xxiv, ii,256,2 pp. WADE 149. 83/600. Sig.: WBY

In dustjacket.

2433a. Another copy. 366/600. Bp: GY

On dustjacket, ink: Copy for Printer, July 26, 1937
Below bp.: To Dobbs [GY] in memory of all tribulation when we were making this work/ W.B. Yeats
Below frontispiece, "from the Speculum Angelorum et Homenorum" marked delete.

P. xiv, the diagram of the Great Wheel has been altered (GY's?).
P. 13, the diagram has been slightly amended at the symbols for Loins and Heart.
P. 20, Section V changed to: VII
P. 22, VI to: VIII
P. 23, VII to: IX
P. 23, VIII to: X
P. 24, IX to: XII
P. 26, X to: XIII
P. 26, XI to: X
P. 38, "The Twenty-Eight Embodiments" revised to: The Twenty-Eight Incarnations [GY's]
P. 59, "one divines some quarrel, not recorded in his biography" to: one divines a quarrel, with the thought of his fathers... [GY's]
P. 93, "At Phase 8 there is a similar interchange, but it does not display its significance" revised to: At Phase 8 there may or may not be a similar interchange; nothing is clear...
P. 184, "by some dominant belief (Phase 25)" revised to: by belief in what intellect cannot analyse (phase 25).
P. 202, "great traditional faith" revised to: Greek traditional faith [GY's]
P. 206, "1650" revised to: 1680
For the import of these and the following revisions in the making of the 1937 A VISION, see Richard Finneran's "On Editing Yeats: The Text of A VISION (1937)," TSLL 19 (1977): 119-34.

2433b. Another copy. 385/600

Inside frt. cover, the bp of GY., but her name has been canceled at top; also a note, possibly an inscription that had been made at the top, with date, is largely torn out.
On frontispiece, "Homenorum" corrected to: Hominum
P. 36, WBY has indicated that the two columns "Earth, Water, Air, Fire" and "First quarter, Second quarter" etc. be transposed.
P. 36, also the final scheme has been revised and annotated by WBY: Where the Four Faculties predominate.
First quarter...creative mind
Second quarter...Mask
Third quarter...Will
Fourth quarter...body of fate
P. 202, "great traditional faith" corrected to: Greek traditional faith
P. 206, "1650" revised to: 1680

2433c. Another copy. 498/600

Covered in brown oilcloth.
On cover: Keep clean. W.B. Yeats/ "A Vision"/ Book A [GY's]
Flyleaf: This copy must not be given to any body on any excuse however plausible/ WB Yeats/ George Yeats [WBY's]

On verso of the list of privately printed books:
Extracts for new Vision to be taken from this book & as corrected here/ W.B.Y.

As noted in Finneran (above), this revised and corrected copy provided the copytext for WADE 191, A VISION (1937).

On frontispiece, "homenorum" corrected to: hominum

P. xiv, in the diagram of The Great Wheel the two symbols on the innermost ring for phases 2 and 4 have been corrected by pasting small cutouts over the original versions; thus corrected it appears in WADE 191.

P. xvii, following from "Speculum Angelorum et Hominorum" a line leading to a note: ? in the ungrammatical dog Latin of the time

P. 8, "I. The Wheel and the Phases of the Moon" shortened to: The Phases of the Moon

P. 14, note, "creative genius" capitalized.

P. 16, "II. The Place of the Four Faculties on the Wheel" canceled.

P. 17, first 9 lines canceled.

P. 17, "Between Phase 12 and Phase 13, and between Phase 4 and Phase 5" revised to: At Phase 11 and Phase 12 in diagram 1 occurs... [this whole passage transposed to the very end of this section (III) and the last three lines canceled, from "The geometrical reasons" TO "are discussed in Book II." But in margin:] Stet.

P. 17, "IV" revised to: VI

P. 18, line 1 revised to: an inherited scenario

P. 18, from "and for that reason the Masks" TO "Convito" is canceled.

P. 20, "The being may return up to four times before it can pass on" revised to: the being may return several times before it can pass on

P. 20, "By being is understood that which divides into Four Faculties" to: The automatic script defines being as

P. 20, "V" revised to: VII

P. 21, next to "the Body of Fate is inimical to antithetical natures," a printer's name apparently, and perhaps a galley number: J Henethy [?] 38 [doubtful WBY's]

Such notations appear passim.

P. 22, "VI revised to: VIII [and the renumbering continues from here]

P. 25, "<u>deception</u> is used as a technical term": deception is a technical term of my teachers and may be substituted for "desire."

P. 26ff., section XI canceled to p. 30.

P. 30, section "XII" revised to: XIII

P. 30, next to table of "Will, Mask" etc.: Bred [?] Centaur

P. 34, a revision to notes: At first my instructors divided the great year also into ten divisions....

P. 37, at bottom, the revision in WADE 191, p. 104 from "Enforced and Free Faculties" TO: Body of Fate discords [but the revision here lacks "The Two Directions"]

P. 38, "The Twenty-Eight Embodiments" revised to: The Twenty-eight Incarnations

P. 38, added to the passage at the end of Phase One is: None of those phases where the tinctures are closed, except phase 27, produce characteristics of sufficient distinctiveness to become historical [WADE 191 follows with slight variation]

P. 38ff., section numbers revised, I to XIX, II to XX etc.

P. 59, the first three lines of "The Opening of the Tincture" canceled and below: Just before the place on the phase for the splitting or opening of each [but this also canceled]

P. 60, at the end of the first paragraph, "the Creative Mind as reason, The Body of Fate as desire": (This I do not understand). [but canceled]

P. 65, last paragraph revised to: From now, if not from Phase 12, and until Phase 17 or Phase 18 has passed, happy love...

P. 84, "reverse" corrected to: reveres

P. 112, "and we shall discover" TO "hypnogogic vision" deleted and also the note following from this.

P. 125, "wondering vegetative dream" corrected to: wandering

P. 132, "Birkett" to: Burnet

Pp. 135-6, the reference letter "A" changed to: C

Pp. 135-6, the revised passage reads: between C which is the energy, and D which is its <u>Destiny</u> or beauty, and that between A, which is mind, and B which is its <u>Fate</u> or Truth. [and a note in margin:] cones are reversal [?] shadow cone is [the rest undecipherable].

P. 136, line 8 revised to: That is to way when B is three quarter antithetical and one quarter primary...

P. 141, first par. revised to: We may represent the two qualities of life by two circles one within the other which move in opposite directions, the Lunar from West to East according to the Moon's phasal movements, the Solar from East to West according to the Sun's apparent daily movement, or we may call the first the moon's zodiacal movement and the second that of the precessional sun.

P. 143, a revision or correction of the diagram, apparently the notation for "South."

P. 159, bottom, a note: I think there is an error or rather clumsy statement in this chapter. The Four Principles are I now think better placed [?] in one whole cone whereas the Faculties on a half cone. See MSS notebook (vellum)

P. 177, next to "The Historical Cones": Centaur

P. 177, the date "May 1925" entered in ink in the phrase "to the present moment May 1925."

P. 180, "2. The Great Wheel and History" revised to: Book V. Dove or Swan

P. 183, the par. from "Each age unwinds" TO "living each other's death" is canceled but also marked: stet [and it remains in WADE 191]

Pp. 194 and 195, "at the South" revised to: Full Moon

P. 196, "When the tide changed and God no longer suffices" revised to: Faith no longer sufficed
P. 196, the note at bottom canceled and revised: My instructors distinguish...
P. 196, "The stream of recurrence" to: the stream
P. 202, the correction "Greek traditional faith"
P. 207, "Lady Bessborough's rises before me" marked delete.
P. 210, after "the possibility of science" a printer's note: do not set past this point. R. Young.
P. 210, after "There is always civil war" a line to a note at bottom of p.: written at Capri, February 1925. [also two printer's notations]
P. 214, "Second Fountain" revised to: new revelation
P. 221, "Daimon's Body" revised to: Daimon's Creative Mind
P. 253, a note after "All Soul's Night": As in latest text COLLECTED POEMS [not WBY's]
P. 253, line 21 of "All Soul's Night" "Horton's" revised, ink over pencil to: Horton is [unlikely WBY's and no printing follows]
It seems that the revisions of the accidentals in "All Soul's Night" have been copied from WADE 171, COLLECTED POEMS, 1933, but the revision of line 61 ("I call MacGregor Mathers from his grave") first appears in WADE 191, A VISION (1937). Although ink traced over pencil, the hand does not appear to be WBY's.
Line 90 of "All Soul's Night" revised to: Should laugh and weep an hour upon the clock. [not WBY's]

2434. ———. A VISION. London: Macmillan, 1937. viii,308 pp. WADE 191

In dustjacket.
Flyleaf: George Yeats' own copy/ not to be taken by me/ WB Yeats, December, 1937
[also] Partially/ corrected copy/ July 1939 [GY's]
[also] Pages 260 | 245 | 79 — WBY
Inserted, two slips of paper, the first on letterhead: 4, Winton Road, Dublin
p. 250/ Not Solely of Immortality/ Great years/ MORTALITIES/ J H [see below for the correction in Francis Thompson's poem; not apparently WBY's]
On the second slip, ink, apparently WBY's: 260/245/79 [these refer to the three corrections by WBY in the text; the others are GY's; for the chronology of these corrections, see the article cited in 2433a].
P. 79, "Phase 1 and Phase 28" corrected to: Phase 1 and Phase 15
P. 245, the comma removed in "the day before, the fifteenth day of the solar March."
P. 260, "Shru Purhoit Swami" corrected to: Shree Purohit Swami

The corrections etc. that follow are GY's.
P. 12, "Cabalistic" to: Cabbalistic
P. 12, "Cabala" to: Cabbala
Pp. 18 and 19, "phases" to: Phases
P. 27, "Sea-shanties" to: sea-shanties
P. 28, the full stop after "his own eyes" is queried.
P. 59, line 6 of "The Phases of the Moon" "late risen" to: late-risen [followed in later printings]
P. 62, line 81 of "The Phases" "perfected, completed" to: separate, perfect [this restores an earlier reading]
P. 88, "The whole" to: The Whole
P. 91, "Sec. XII" to: Section XII
P. 97, in phase 12 in the chart, "Enforced law" to: enforced lure [written in twice, in ink and pencil]
P. 99, in chart, at phase 24, "Enforced success in action" to: of action
P. 104, "Phase 29 is Spiritual Objectivity" to: Phase 28
P. 104, "Phase 22 is Well" corrected to: Will
P. 124, "cut table" to: cut Tables
P. 124, at Phase 11 the direction: See table
P. 129, at Phase 13 the direction: See table
P. 153, "Thomas Luke Harris" corrected to: Lake
Pp. 154, 5, 6, "Self-adaption" to: Self-adaptation
P. 157, the "breaking of strength" to: Temptation through strength
Pp. 219 and 220: "Cimetière Marine" to: Marin
P. 222, "Mandooka Upanishad" to: Mandookya
P. 232, "Aeneids" to: Enneads
P. 233, in note at bottom, "that is not him who sleeps" to: and it is not he
P. 250, in Francis Thompson's poem, "Immortalities" to: mortalities
P. 260, "Shru Purhoit" corrected to: Shree Purohit
Most, but not all, of these corrections and revisions were followed in A VISION, London, 1962.

2435. ———. A VISION. New York: Macmillan, 1938. 2,viii, 310 pp. WADE 192. Sig.: GY

GY has entered some of the same corrections and revisions as appear in 2434 and has lightly annotated the text as follows.
P. 24, "pulsaters" revised to: pulsations
P. 44, at "malachite things": Masefield's gift to WBY.
P. 243, after "Virgil sang his song": IVth Eclogue.
P. 261, after "When the automatic script began, neither I nor my wife knew, or knew that we knew, that any man had tried to explain history philosophically": Untrue. GY had read Hegel's philosophy of history.
P. 273, the passage "Seeking images, I see her anoint her bare limbs according to a medical prescription of that time..." is marked and a comment: Diary 1930.
P. 278, at "The founder of his school was Ammonius Sacca, an Alexandrine porter. His thought and that of Origen, which I skimmed in my youth" [underlining added]: and re-read in Sept. 1913 at the Prelude, Coleman's Hatch/ G Y.

P. 280, "Ravenne" corrected to: Ravenna
P. 288, at "The mosaic pictures grown transparent fill the windows...": Justinian and Theodora.

2436. ———. THE WANDERINGS OF OISIN AND OTHER POEMS. London: Kegan Paul, 1889. 2,vi,156 pp. WADE 2

Title p.: WB Yeats/ marked for Mrs. M. Hunt/ March 23, 1935.
In parts I, II, and III of "The Wanderings of Oisin" lines are numbered consecutively, stanzas indicated by letters.
P. 31, bridging first two stanzas: cf. the lyrical scene in Schiller
P. 31, after "thunder": Maria Stuart
P. 68, referring to title "Kanva on Himself": Originally called "Kanvi hymn to his spirit" [not WBY's]
P. 134, referring to "Quatrains and Aphorisms": Originally called "The Keystone of Truth" [not WBY's]

2437. ———. WHEELS AND BUTTERFLIES. London: Macmillan, 1934. 2,x,184 pp. WADE 175

Flyleaf: To Junzo Sato with apologies/ for dedicating to him 'Resurrection'/ without remembering to ask leave/ WB Yeats.
In dustjacket.

2437a. Another copy.

Flyleaf: To Hildo van Krop/ with apologies/ for dedicating to him/ 'Fighting the Waves'/ without remembering to ask his leave/ WB Yeats [Hildo Krop designed and made the masks for the play.]
In dustjacket.

2437b. Another copy.

2438. ———. WHEELS AND BUTTERFLIES. New York: Macmillan, 1935. x,166 pp. WADE 176

A paper marker inserted with: (236)

2439. ———. WHERE THERE IS NOTHING. New York: John Lane, 1902. viii,100 pp. WADE 42

On cover: Corrected Copy/ 1st proof/ Please indicate any further changes or corrections on this copy [not WBY's]
The text is heavily revised, mostly for accidentals but also for some substantives in a hand not WBY's apparently to provide the copytext for WADE 43 and subsequent printings.
Back flyleaf: Morley Roberts, Author's Club, 3 Whitehall Court, LW. [doubtful WBY's]

2440. ———. WHERE THERE IS NOTHING. [New York]: Privately printed for John Quinn, 1902. 2,viii,102 pp. WADE 43. 11/30. Sig.: WBY

Pp. uncut.

2441. ———. WHERE THERE IS NOTHING. London: A.H. Bullen, 1903. xii,132 pp. WADE 44. Bp: Lily Yeats

2441a. Another copy.

Some pp. uncut.

2442. ———. WHERE THERE IS NOTHING. New York: Macmillan, 1903. 216 pp. WADE 45. Bp: Elizabeth C. Yeats

Half title p.: "To J.B. Yeats/ with kind regards/ of John Quinn./ May 23, 1903."

2442a. Another copy. Large paper ed. No limitation notice.

Wholly uncut.

2443. ———. WHERE THERE IS NOTHING. [Theatre Program]. The Stage Society. The Fifth Production (Fifth Season) at the Royal Court Theatre, Sloane Square. 26 June 1904.

2444. ———. THE WILD SWANS AT COOLE. London: Macmillan, 1919. 2,x,116 pp. WADE 124

Flyleaf: this copy not to leave the house/ WBY
P. 13, line 9 of "An Irish Airman Foresees His Death" revised to: No law, no duty bade me fight, [no printing follows].
P. 13, line 10 revised to: Nor the emotion of great crowds, [no printing follows].
P. 13, line 11 revised but queried and canceled: The lone impulse of my delight [no printing follows].
P. 34 in "The Sad Shepherd" ["Shepherd and Goatherd"] a transposition of line 70 ("To his shape in the lengthening shadows,") to make it follow line 71. No printing follows.
P. 34, line 71 revised to: Where sheep are thrown in the pool, [no printing follows].
P. 39, in "Lines Written in Dejection" line 6ff. revised:
Their angry tears, are gone;
The holy centaurs of the hills are banished,
That white in the white moon beam shone
That in the unconquered moonlight shone [can.]
Banished my Mother moon and vanished
For now that I have come... [but the original reading of this line restored]
[THE WILD SWANS AT COOLE, London, 1920, follows approximately the revision in line 9 only.]
P. 76, line 4 of "Upon a Dying Lady, VI" revised to: Amid that first astonishment... [first in SELECTED POEMS, New York, 1921]

2444a. Another copy.

A square of paper pasted on cover with: C
On half title p., dates entered: (1914-1919)

Pp. v-vi, the Preface is marked delete.
Contents pp. torn out.
P. 54, "His Phoenix" marked: C3
P. 56, lines 25-6 revised to:
There'll be that crowd that barberous crowd, through all the centuries,
And who can say but some young girl may walk to make men wild
[line 25 followed in LATER POEMS, London, 1922, but no printing follows line 26 exactly]
P. 72 marked: C5
P. 94 marked: C5
P. 115, the note, excised.

2444b. Another copy.

All poems checked in Contents.
P. 49, "Her Praise" dated: Jan. 27. 1915 [doubtful WBY's as the following]
P. 53, "The People" dated: Jan. 10, 1915
P. 57, "His Phoenix" dated: Jan. 1915.
P. 67, "To a Squirrel at Kyle-na-no" dated: Sept. 1912
P. 71, "In Memory of Alfred Pollexfen" dated: August 1916
P. 83, next to "The struggle of the fly in marmalade": Landor

2444c. Another copy.

Some pp. uncut.

2445. ———. THE WIND AMONG THE REEDS. London: Elkin Mathews, 1899. 2,viii,108 pp. WADE 27. Bp: Lily Yeats

Below bp: Given to Anne B. Yeats/ grand daughter of/ J.B.Y. Nov. 1937/ Dundrum/ Lily Yeats
Flyleaf: JB Yeats/ from/ WB Yeats
In Contents, 10 poem titles are checked.
Line 9 of "Aedh Hears the Cry of the Sedge" corrected to: Your breast will not lie by the breast [WBY's]
P. 101, bottom, a faint pencil note, not WBY's, about "a bottle of nine goddesses" as "seen by a young man who died."

2445a. Another copy. Second ed. No errata slip.

Flyleaf: Bought by George Yeats. 1939. [GY's]
Second flyleaf: [erasure] from Katharine/ April 1899
In Contents, "Mongan laments the Change that has come upon Him and His Beloved" is checked; "Hanrahan laments because of his Wanderings" is queried.
In text, lines are numbered in "The Secret Rose."
Following "Hanrahan laments": omitted in 1922 ed. [not WBY's - followed by a query in another hand:] of what?
P. 73, "Irish form of Hugh" is underlined and queried.
P. 96, "son" is circled.

2446. ———. THE WIND AMONG THE REEDS. 3rd ed. London: Elkin Mathews, 1900. x,viii,108 pp. WADE 29

Flyleaf: Edith Hyde Lees/ Feb. 1901
But I being poor, have only my dreams;
I have spread my dreams under your feet.
Tread softly because you tread on my dreams. [not WBY's]
Inserted, a slip, not WBY's, with a list of 4 p. numbers and titles followed by queries.

2446a. Another copy. Rebound. No advertising at end.

Flyleaf: Corrected edition [not WBY's; the 3rd ed. had corrected the errors of the 1st and 2nd eds.]

2446b. Another copy. 4th ed., 1903. Bp: WBY

Gold design in white calf unrecorded in Wade.
Most titles are checked in Contents and in text.

2446c. Another copy. 6th ed., 1911. Sig.: GHL/ May 1913

In Contents, the Savoy publication dates in 1896 are entered for seven poems; not WBY's.
In text, the original Savoy titles for the seven poems are entered; not WBY's.
Pp. 54-5, a list of p. numbers.

2447. ———. THE WINDING STAIR. New York: The Fountain Press, 1929. xii,28 pp. WADE 164. 343/642. Sig.: WBY

Flyleaf: Inscribed for my friend/ Shotaro Oshima/ WB Yeats/ 'Wisdom is a butterfly/ And not a gloomy bird of prey'

2447a. Another copy. 432/642

2448. ———. THE WINDING STAIR. London: Macmillan, 1933. 2,x,104 pp. WADE 169. Bp: WBY

P. 90, at line 10 of "A Woman Young and Old, IV," "Saint George or else a pagan Perseus": Bardoni [Bordoni?]

2448a. Another copy.

Flyleaf: To George/ WB Yeats/ Sept. 1933
Inserted at end, a holograph letter from Augustus John to WBY dated 28 Feb. 1931. On the reverse is the letterhead "Fryer Court/ Nr. Fordingbridge Salisbury."

Dear W.B. Yeats,
I received your letter after some delay having been abroad. I have instructed Trench & Sons [?] to send you a photograph of the portrait.
I hope you keep fit. Please give my affectionate regards to Lady Gregory. [Sig.] Augustus John

2448b. Another copy.

Flyleaf: Never send a book to an author to be autographed (1) because he has [no] sealing wax (2) because he has no string (3) because he does not know how to tie up a parcel (4) because you will probably not get the book back. Thomas Hardy once showed me a corner cupboard full of such books. He gave them to his friends on their birthdays./ WB Yeats.

2448c. Another copy.

Flyleaf torn out; in dustjacket.

2448d. Another copy.

Pp. uncut; in dustjacket.

2449. ———. THE WINDING STAIR. New York: Macmillan, 1933. x,102 pp. WADE 170

Inserted at p. 10, a slip of paper with: (227)

2449a. Another copy.

In dustjacket; pp. cut.

2449b-c. Two other copies.

In dustjackets; pp. uncut.

2450. Yeats, W.B., ed. A BOOK OF IRISH VERSE. 2nd rev. ed. London: Methuen, 1900. xxxii,260 pp. WADE 225

In Contents, WBY's notes to himself apparently for a new ed. that was never made; although there were further "editions" (as recorded following), they were in fact simple reprintings of the 1900 ed. and do not follow the changes suggested here.

P. vii of Contents, a note at bottom: Add some verses by Swift and by Mrs. [?] O'Rourke [?] 'noble [one word?] must never to forget' [?] and look [up?] this Moore [one word?]

P. viii, a possible addition to Mangan's selection is indicated: ? Babylon

P. viii, Walsh's "From the Cold Sod that's o'er you" is bracketed.

P. ix of Contents, Dowden's one inclusion, "Lady Margaret's Song" is canceled and queried.

P. ix, after "Song" by Arthur O'Shaughnessy, a line to a note at bottom: Music Makers

P. x of Contents, an indication of additions to D. Hyde's selection: Some verses from a play and his curse.

P. x, Rose Kavanagh's "Lough Bray" has been canceled and queried.

P. x, a note from Katharine Tynan's "St. Francis to the Birds": ending this section

P. x, "Names" by John Eglinton and "That" by Charles Weekes are canceled and queried.

P. xi of Contents, a note indicating that material is to

be added to the authored selections (i.e., before the anonymous section):
give poems of Synge/ Add some prose translations from the Irish by Lady Gregory and Hyde's curse on England. Boyd's little poem about a dead [?] friend ["Ballyvourney"?]. A verse or two of Colum, Stephens etc. or else must not limit to a date [??]. ?translations from Irish in a special section [but canceled]. Also add 'God Save Ireland.' Add some verse [?] from Moira O'Neil and Dr. [?] Sigerson's 'Great love swift and soon' [??].
P. xv, at end of Preface a pencil note, faint, very difficult to read indicating that a "P.S." is to be added to the Preface. At end of the pencil note: Set [?] that introduction in a form as given in collected edition with that PS given thus.
Inserted, a brief note from GY to Allan Wade.

2450a. Another copy. 3rd ed., Sept. 1911.

Inside frt. cover: Cuala Library/ 82 Merrion Square
A reprinting of the 2nd rev. ed.
Inserted, a review of the 1895 ed. See 62.

2451. ———. FAIRY AND FOLK TALES OF THE IRISH PEASANTRY. London: Walter Scott, 1888. xx,326 pp. WADE 212.
Sig.: WB Yeats/ November/ 1891

Red leather with gold lettering.
In Contents, all major section headings ("The Trooping Fairies" etc.) except "The Devil" and "Kings, Queens" etc. are checked.
Also added as first section and checked: Introd.
Also in Contents some selections, especially in "The Trooping Fairies" are checked.
Also entered in Contents are headings and p. numbers for Yeats's intros. to the Pooka and the Banshee.
In Contents the selection "Bewitched Butter" is queried: By whom?
Pp. 59-60, some lines in "The Stolen Child" are "xed."

2451a. Another copy. Bp: Lily Yeats
Flyleaf: George Pollexfen/ from his affectionate/ nephew the compiler.
Red cloth.

2451b. Another copy. Scott Library; smooth dark red cloth.

2452. ———. IRISH FAIRY TALES. London: T. Fisher Unwin, 1892. viii,236 pp. WADE 216

Title p.: 'only the wasteful virtues earn the sun'/ WB Yeats, Feb. 27, 1931
First impression.

2452a. Another copy. Second impression.

Spine is detached and inserted.

2452b. Another copy. Second impression.

A label or bp. has been removed from inside frt. cover. On half title p. the stamped seal of the Corporation of Dublin Public Libraries, Charleville Mall.

2453. ———. IRISH FAIRY TALES [i.e. FAIRY AND FOLK TALES OF THE IRISH PEASANTRY]. Illus. by James Torrance. London and Felling-on-Tyne: Walter Scott. New York: n.p., n.d. xviii,326,[2] pp. WADE 223?

In red cloth covers with design and lettering stamped blind; lettered in gold on spine.
While the title p. lists 7 illustrations, there is in fact only the frontispiece.
Flyleaf: Angela Liston. 23 Lindsay Rd. Glasnevin. Dublin/ 21st January 1920.
Inserted in a scrap from a newspaper dated 24 Feb. 1923.

2454. ———. THE OXFORD BOOK OF MODERN VERSE. Oxford: Clarendon Press, 1936. 2,xlviii,452 pp. WADE 250. Sig.: WBY

Corrections entered in Acknowledgements, Index of Authors, and Index of First Lines; most of these corrections were made in subsequent reprintings, though not immediately (see 2454b).
P. 38, in Wilde's "The Ballad of Reading Gaol" deletion of the passage from "I never saw a man" to "So wistfully at the day" (but not followed in reprintings).
P. 218 in "Santorin" pencil marks to indicate a change in spacing or a deletion; also last two lines are canceled.
Pp. 292ff. publishers inserted after W.J. Turner's poem titles to indicate that they have not been acknowledged.
P. 317, in F.R. Higgins's "Song for the Clatter Bones" "though her bones lack a back" revised to: though her ghost lacks a back.
P. 429, two Auden lyrics have been printed as one; a line is entered before "Before this loved one" to indicate that this is a separate selection, and it is numbered: 369

2454a. Another copy.

2454b. Another copy. Dec. 1936 reprinting.

P. v, "Introduction" is canceled.
P. xlii, last par. of Intro. canceled.
Some but not all the corrections made in 2454 are followed in this reprinting. But Auden's two lyrics are still printed as one.

2454c. Another copy. Dec. 1936 reprinting.

From half title p. to Acknowledgements, including Intro. torn out.

2454d-e. Two more copies. Dec. 1936 reprinting.

2455. ———. REPRESENTATIVE IRISH TALES. 2 vols. New York and London: G.P. Putnam's, [1891]. WADE 215

Decorated paper boards.
Vol. 1 (only vol. here), sig.: WB Yeats/ 1891

SEE ALSO 208-10, 220, 1977.

2456. [Yonge, Charlotte Mary]. THE PRINCE AND THE PAGE. A story of the last crusade. New ed. London: Macmillan, 1873. vi,256 pp. Sig.: WB Yeats/ 14 Eustace Villas

2457. [Yoshida, Kenko]. THE MISCELLANY OF A JAPANESE PRIEST (Tsure-Zure Gusa). Translated by William N. Porter. London: Humphrey Milford, 1914. 216 pp.

2458. Zachrisson, Valdemar, ed. BOKTRYCKERI-KALENDAR 1902-1903 [Printing-office Almanac]. 9th and 10th year. Goteborg, Sweden: V. Zachrissons Boktryckeri, n.d. [4],iii,192 pp.

Includes discussions of T.J. Cobden-Sanderson, Morris, Blake, Walter Crane as book illustrators.

2459. ZADKIEL'S ASTRONOMICAL EPHEMERIS. Places for 1840. London: J.G. Berger, n.d. [Publishers vary ff.]

2460. ———. 1841.

2461. ———. 1842.

2462. ———. 1843.

2463. ———. 1844.

2464. ———. 1845.

2465. ———. 1846.

2466. ———. 1847.

2467. ———. 1848.

2468. ———. 1849.

2469. ———. 1850.

2470. ———. 1851.

2471. ———. 1852.

2472. ———. 1853.

2473. ———. 1854.

2474. ———. 1855.

2475. ———. 1856.

2476. ———. 1858.

2477. ———. 1879.

2478. ———. 1883.

2479. ———. 1884.

2480. ———. 1890.

2481. ———. 1891.

2482. ———. 1895.

2483. ———. 1896.

2484. ———. 1914.

2485. ———. 1915.

2486. ———. 1916.
Marked.

2487. ———. 1917.
Marked for Oct. 17, Oct. 20, "12:15 pm.," June 13.

2487a. Another copy.

2488. ———. 1922.
Marked for June 14, July 7 & 20th.

2489. ———. 1923.
Marked.

2490. ———. Bound vol. 1881-1890. London: Cousins, n.d.
1886 is RAPHAEL'S ASTRONOMICAL EPHEMERIS.
1888 is ORION'S PROPHETIC ALMANAC, WEATHER GUIDE, AND EPHEMERIS. London: Simpkin, Marshall, n.d.
1889 and 1890 are RAPHAEL'S.
Some markings passim, as underscoring for Nov. 21, 1886.

2491. Zola, Emile. THE DREYFUS CASE. Four Letters to France. London and New York: John Lane, 1898. xiii,[1],45,[1] pp.
A few pp. uncut.

2492. Zoroaster, the Magician. THE CHALDAEAN ORACLES OF ZOROASTER. Edited by Sapere Aude [W. Wynn Wescott]. Collectanea Hermetica, vol. 6. London: Theosophical Publishing Society, 1895. 54 pp.

SUBJECT INDEX

INDEX OF AUTOGRAPHS

(Including Owners, Presenters, and Annotators, but not WBY)